The *Essay Connection*

READINGS FOR WRITERS

Fifth Edition

Lynn Z. Bloom
The University of Connecticut

Houghton Mifflin Company
Boston   New York

Senior Sponsoring Editor: Dean Johnson
Editorial Assistant: Mary Furlong Healey
Project Editor: Elena Di Cesare
Editorial Assistant: Angela Schoenherr
Senior Production/Design Coordinator: Carol Merrigan
Senior Manufacturing Coordinator: Sally Culler
Senior Marketing Manager: Nancy Lyman

Cover design by Harold Burch, Harold Burch Design, New York City
Cover photography: Robert Nease Photography

Text Credits appear on pages 726–731, which constitute a continuation
of the copyright page.

Printed in the U.S.A.

Library of Congress Catalog Card Number: 97-72444

ISBN: 0-395-87107-7

56789-CW-01 00

Contents

Part I   On Writing   1

❀ *Student writings.*

Part IV   Arguing Directly and Indirectly   563

Topical Table of Contents

❀ *Student writings.*

2 People and Portraits

3 Families

4 The Natural World

5 Places

6 Science

9 Society and Community

10 Turning Points/Watershed Experiences

11 Literature and the Arts

12 Humor and Satire

Preface

Like the symbolic bridge on the cover of this book, *The Essay Connection* attempts to span the distance between reading and writing and bring the two activities closer together. To read, to write is to be human, to be empowered. "Writing," observes Toni Morrison, "is discovery; it's talking deep within myself." In *The Essay Connection* the voices in this conversation are many and varied—professionals and students side by side. Their good writing is good reading in itself, provocative, elegant, engaging. This writing is also a stimulus to critical thinking, ethical reflection, social and literary analysis, and humorous commentary—among the many possibilities when students write essays of their own.

What's Familiar, What's New

The fifth edition of *The Essay Connection* incorporates a number of new features and new essays into the format and essays retained from the fourth edition.

Readings. This edition includes seventy-eight readings, lively, varied, timely, provocative—and of high literary quality. New to this edition are two short stories of distinction, Bobbie Ann Mason's "Shiloh" and Raymond Carver's "What We Talk About When We Talk About Love." This edition also includes two multi-faceted short pieces by Margaret Atwood, "The Page" and "Fiction: Happy Endings," that combine commentaries on the nature of writing, the nature of storytelling, and the nature of human nature. Indeed, all of the fictive works included here are intended to resonate throughout the book, as commentaries on many of the other essays, and on one another. Forty-nine favorite essays have been retained from the previous edition, by such authors as Eudora Welty, E. B. White, Elie Wiesel, Frederick Douglass, Joan Didion, Peter Elbow, Maxine Hong Kingston, Martin Luther King, Jr., Richard Rodriguez, and Mark Twain. Stephen Dunn's poem, "The Sacred," and Margaret Atwood's "The Page" serve as epigraphs to this edition of *The Essay Connection*. Cathy N. Davidson's "Laughing in English" opens the essay readings; Atwood's "Fiction: Happy Endings" concludes the book. Although these and humorous works by James Thurber and Judy Brady signal the book's up-beat tone, they do not diminish the seriousness of its essential concerns or its underlying ethical stance.

New Authors. Among the authors new to *The Essay Connection* are Stephen Dunn, Roger Angell, Patricia J. Williams, Tom and Ray Magliozzi ("Click and Clack"), Bobbie Ann Mason, Kathleen Norris, Shirley Geok-lin Lim, Deborah Tannen, Bailey White, Raymond Carver, Lani Guinier, Alan Dershowitz, John Kenneth Galbraith, Robert Reich, and Terry Tempest Williams. The representations of women, cultures, and writers who address issues of class and race have again increased in this edition, as in its predecessor.

Student Authors. Sixteen essays are by students, although a total of twenty-nine pieces of student work appear because thirteen excerpts from student notebooks are combined in one selection. Student writings include an entry from Sylvia Plath's diary written when she was seventeen. Although all the student works were written when the students were enrolled in American universities, these students have come from many parts of the United States and Canada, ranging from Montreal to Colorado and Hawaii, and from Korea and the People's Republic of China. These distinguished student writings not only discuss compelling subjects (coming to terms with oneself, one's parents, or one's ethnic background; understanding endangered species—from African animals to family farms) but provide models of excellent writing that other students may reasonably be expected to emulate.

Whole Essays. In order to maintain the integrity of the authors' style and structure as well as their arguments, most of these essays are printed in their entirety, averaging three to six pages; a number are chapters or self-contained sections of books. Footnotes are the authors' own.

Varied Subjects, Varied Disciplines. The essays in this edition are drawn from many sources, mostly engaging and distinguished contemporary writing on varied subjects, as indicated in the Topical Table of Contents, with a leavening of classics by such authors as Swift, Lincoln, and Darwin. In addition to professional writers, the authors include scientists, ecologists, naturalists, social analysts, a physician, a president, and critics.

The Writing Process. The book's first section concentrates on the writing process, from its start in "Laughing, Speaking, and Reading" (Chapter 1), to "Reasons for Writing" (Chapter 2), to "Getting Started" (Chapter 3), to "Writing: Re-Vision and Revision" (Chapter 4). Works by professional writers of distinction (Amy Tan, Eudora Welty, Elie Wiesel) are joined by equally memorable student writing. Thus the writer's notebook of Mark Twain joins an excerpt from seventeen-year-old Sylvia Plath's diary and notebook entries from eleven other students of diverse ages, ethnic backgrounds, life experience, and sexual preference. The section concludes with ten drafts of student Mary Ruffin's work, culminating in the stunning essay, "Mama's Smoke."

Critical Thinking, Reading, and Writing. Many readings are clustered to encourage dialogue and debate among authors, and among student readers and writers. This thematic arrangement is far more extensive in this edition than in the earlier editions. For example, Chapter 5, "Narration," emphasizes the significance of family and ancestry, race and class. Chapter 6, "Process Analysis," clusters essays on science and mechanics. Chapter 7, "Cause and

Effect," focuses on education as it pertains to both margin and mainstream and on our understanding of how social policies affect individuals and families; Chapter 9, "Division and Classification," extends the subject to totalitarian, democratic, and post-colonial societies. Chapter 8, "Description," concentrates on places, natural and unnatural, and the values and folkways of people who live in these diverse habitats. Chapter 11, "Definition," deals with the nature, meaning, and interpretations of symbols—including those of *wife* and *cripple*—and with our more literal understanding of natural phenomena—natural selection and acid rain. In Chapter 12, "Comparison and Contrast," essays by Stephen Jay Gould, on evolution, and Vicki Hearne, on animal rights, refract with Darwin's "Understanding Natural Selection" in Chapter 11. Chapter 13, "Appealing to Reason," debates civil rights and civil disobedience; and issues of social class and poverty, domestic and world-wide. Chapter 14, "Appealing to Emotion and Ethics," features essays on power and oppression, life and death—of individuals, nations, farms, and families; while Chapter 15, "Critical Argument," provides various perspectives on critical textual analysis, with essay clusters on "The Gettysburg Address" and on "Cinderella."

Conceptual Context of the Book. *The Essay Connection* is informed conceptually by extensive classroom testing of the essays and writing assignments included here. The book is likewise informed by contemporary scholarship in the dynamic fields of composition, literary and rhetorical theory, autobiography, and the teaching of writing. The language of *The Essay Connection* intentionally remains clear and reader-friendly.

Blended Types. In difficulty the essays range from the easily accessible to the more complicated. They have been chosen to represent the common essay types indicated by the chapter divisions, from narration and definition through argumentation and critical analysis. Nevertheless, because these are real essays by real writers, who use whatever writing techniques suit their purpose, there are very few "pure" types. An essay of definition, such as Nancy Mairs's "On Being a Cripple," for instance, includes illustrations and examples, comparisons and contrasts, narrative, description. The entire essay, like many others in this book, could in fact be considered an argument for the author's point of view. Consequently, although the introduction to each essay and the study questions following it often encourage the reader to view the work through the lens of its designated category in the Table of Contents, the reader should be aware that the category represents only one segment of a broad spectrum of possible readings.

Apparatus. The essays are placed in a context of materials designed to encourage reading, critical thinking, and good writing. The following materials reinforce *The Essay Connection's* pervasive emphasis on the process(es) of writing.

- **Tables of Contents.** The main Table of Contents reflects the book's organization, by types of writing. The Topical Table of Contents offers an alternative organization by subject ("Science," "Society and Community," "Human and Civil Rights," "Turning Points/Watershed Experiences," etc.). This arrangement provides many alternative possibilities for discussion and writing.
- **Chapter introductions.** These have two purposes. They define the particular type of writing in the chapter and identify its purposes (descriptions, process analysis, etc.), uses, and typical forms. They also discuss the rhetorical strategies authors typically use in that type of writing (for instance, how to structure an argument to engage a hostile audience), illustrated with reference to essays in the chapter. For quick reference, these strategies are summarized in a checklist at the end of the introduction.
- **Biographical introductions to each author.** These capsule biographies are intended to transform the writers from names into real people. They focus on how and why the authors write (in general, and in particular) and how and for what audience they wrote the work that appears in *The Essay Connection.*
- **Study questions.** These follow most of the essays, and are intended to encourage thoughtful discussion and writing about Content, rhetorical Strategies/Structures, Language, and larger concerns.

- **Suggestions for Writing.** Each set of study questions ends with suggestions For Writing pertinent to a given work. Many chapters end with a longer list of Additional Topics for Writing that encourage dialogue and debate about essays related in theme, technique, or mode. Often these incorporate strategic suggestions, derived from extensive classroom testing, for writing particular papers and for avoiding potential pitfalls.
- **Glossary.** The Glossary (pp. 709–725) defines terms useful in discussing writing (analogy, argument, voice) with illustrations from the essays.

Acknowledgments

The Essay Connection has, in some ways, been in the making for the past thirty-eight years, and I am particularly indebted to the candid commentaries of multitudes of writing students over the years whose preferences and perplexities have so significantly influenced both the shape and emphasis of this volume, and the process-oriented style of teaching that it reflects. I am likewise grateful for the thoughtful suggestions of writing teachers throughout the country who have commented on earlier editions of *The Essay Connection:* Susan Ahern, Chris Anderson, Lois Avery, Lynn Dianne Beene, Judith L. Bleicher, Ruth Brown, Larry Carver, Roberta Clipper-Sethi, Pat Coldwell, Sara G. Cutting, Daryl Dance, Charla Dawson, Charles R. Duke, Janet E. Eber, Mark Edelstein, David Fleming, J. Vail Foy, Tahita Fulkerson, Donald Gadow, Edgar Glenn, Howard Hamrick, Sandra Hanson, Joanne M. Haynes, Nan Johnson, Daniel Kasowitz, Robert Keane, Walter Klarner, Geraldine Lash, Kay Litten, Arline March, Jay K. Maurer, John M. McCluskey, Alvin W. Past, Linda H. Peterson, Edna H. Shaw, Charles Smith, Louise Z. Smith, William E. Smith, Jeffrey Smitten, Bill Stiffler, Barbara Stout, Frank Thornton, Arthur Wagner, Tom Waldrep, Cheryl L. Ware, Rosemary Winslow, Margarett Ann Wolfe, Marie Woolf, Pauline Wheeler, and Richard Yarborough.

I am also indebted to the reviewers who contributed to the development of the fifth edition of *The Essay Connection:* Kathleen

Danker, South Dakota State University; Arline B. March, Granby Memorial High School, Connecticut; Charles C. Nash, Cottey College, Missouri; Elaine J. Roberts, Judson College, Illinois; Karen Sylte, Southwest State University, Minnesota; Barbara Turnwall, Northwestern College, Iowa; and Rosemary Winslow, The Catholic University of America, District of Columbia.

To Donald M. Murray, University of New Hampshire, who contributed an original text on revising, and Margaret Whitt, University of Denver, who contributed student essays, I am particularly grateful. I also owe special thanks to the students who contributed to this volume not only their essays but comments on how they wrote them: Genevieve Brassard, Rosalind Bradley Coles, Janna Cunningham, Ann Upperco Dolman, Art Greenwood, Amy Jo Keifer, Kristin King, Richard Loftus, Leslie S. Moore, Andrew Nakamura, Mary Ruffin, Stephen E. Ryan, Barbara Schofield, Kelly Shea, Craig Swanson, Seung Hee Suh, Betty J. Walker, Cheryl Watanabe, Tammy Weast, Jill Woolley, Susan Yoritomo, and Ning Yu.

Laird Bloom (yes, he is my son), a recent graduate of Massachusetts Institute of Technology, read much of the manuscript with uncommonly good critical sense and the parodist's intolerance of the banal and the sentimental—a perspective supplemented by the critical scrutiny of Stephen Albrecht, a graduate student at the University of Connecticut. Bard Bloom (yes, he too is my son), also an MIT grad, provided computer expertise. Ning Yu served with intelligence and good cheer as a research assistant on the third edition when he was a doctoral student at the University of Connecticut. He far exceeded the expectations of, as he says, "an old China hand." He translated the version of "Cinderella" (pp. 688–691) that he reads in Chinese to his young son. Combining his knowledge of ancient and contemporary Chinese history and literature with his graduate studies in English, he wrote an incisive critical essay on the two Chinese "Cinderellas" (pp. 692–700). His reading of American essays through the texts and subtexts of another culture, another literature, refined the study questions and sharpened their answers. Valerie Smith Matteson, doctoral student at the University of Connecticut and research assistant on the fifth edition, like her predecessor Sarah Aguiar, in the manner of James Boswell willingly "ran half over

London" to locate obscure information and double-check the facts. Her ever-increasing knowledge as a critic and teacher made her an ideal contributor to the *Instructor's Guide*. Lori Corsini-Nelson of the University of Connecticut managed the paper flow with grace and efficiency.

For the first four editions, D. C. Heath was *The Essay Connection*'s publisher and the editorial process was conducted with thoughtful care by Paul Smith, Linda Bieze, and Rosemary Jaffe. At Houghton Mifflin, Dean Johnson and Elena Di Cesare have assumed equivalent responsibilities with comparable good will, good humor, and good sense. Craig Mertens's painstaking attention to permissions deserves special thanks.

When the first edition of *The Essay Connection* was in process, my sons were in high school. Over the intervening fifteen years they've earned doctorates (in biology and computer science), have married inspiring women, Sara (a U.S. attorney) and Vicki (a food scientist), and parented joyous children, Paul and Elizabeth Anna. An ever-active participant in the protracted process of making *The Essay Connection* more friendly to readers has been my writer-friendly husband, Martin Bloom, social psychologist, professor, and fellow author. He has provided a retentive memory for titles and key words that I've called out from an adjacent lane during our early morning lap swims, homemade apple pies at bedtime, and all the comforts in between. My whole family keeps me cheerful; every day is a gift.

Lynn Z. Bloom

The *Essay*
Connection

Part I

On Writing

1 *Writers in Process— Laughing, Speaking, and Reading*

You will encounter essays in this book that, as E. B. White remarked, philosophize, scold, jest, tell stories, argue, or plead, among the many things they can do. You'll be able to read essays more easily and understand them better if you bear in mind as you read some of the following questions concerning the essay's author, intended audience, type, purposes, and rhetorical strategies, as well as your own responses as a reader.

Who Is the Author?

a. When did the author live? Where? Is the author's ethnic origin, gender, or regional background relevant to understanding this essay?

b. What is the author's educational background? Job experience? Do these or other significant life experiences make him or her an authority on the subject of the essay?

c. Does the author have political, religious, economic, cultural or other biases that affect the essay's treatment of the subject? The author's credibility? The author's choice of language?

What Are the Context and Audience of the Essay?

a. When was the essay first published? Is it dated, or still relevant?

b. Where (in what magazine, professional journal, or book, if at all) was the essay first published?

c. For what audience was the essay originally intended? How much did the author expect the original readers to know about the subject? To what extent did the author expect the original readers to share his point of view? To resist that view?

d. Why would the original audience have read this essay?

e. What similarities and differences exist between the essay's original audience and the student audience now reading it?

f. What am I as a student reader expected to bring to my reading of this essay? My own or others' beliefs, values, past history, personal experience? Other reading? My own writing, previous or in an essay I will write in response to the essay(s) I am reading?

What Are the Purposes of the Essay?

a. Why did the author write the essay? To inform, describe, define, explain, argue, or for some other reason or combination of reasons?

b. Is the purpose explicitly stated anywhere in the essay? If so, where? Is this the thesis of the essay? Or is the thesis different?

c. If the purpose is not stated explicitly, how can I tell what the purpose is? Through examples? Emphasis? Tone? Other means?

d. Does the form of the essay suit the purpose? Would other forms have been more appropriate?

What Are the Strategies of the Essay?

a. What does the author do to make the essay interesting? Is he or she successful?

b. What organizational pattern (and subpatterns, if any) does the author use? How do these patterns fit the subject? The author's purpose?

c. What emphasis do the organization and proportioning provide to reinforce the author's purpose?

d. What evidence, arguments, and illustrations does the author employ to illustrate or demonstrate the thesis?

e. On what level of language (formal, informal, slangy) and in what tone (serious, satiric, sincere, etc.) does the author write?

f. Have I enjoyed the essay, or found it stimulating or otherwise provocative? Why or why not?

g. If I disagree with the author's thesis, or am not convinced by or attached to the author's evidence, illustrations, or use of language, am I nevertheless impelled to continue reading? If so, why? If not, why not?

The ways we read and write, and how we think about the ways we read and write, have been dramatically altered in the past quarter century. The New Critics, whose views dominated the teaching of reading and writing during early and mid-century, promoted a sense of the text as a static, often enigmatic entity, whose sleeping secrets awaited a master critic or brilliant teacher to arrive, like Prince Charming on a white horse, and awaken their meaning. The numerous courses and textbooks encouraging students to read for experience, information, ideas, understanding, and appreciation, reflect that view.

Yet contemporary literary theory encourages the sense of collaboration between author, text, and readers to make meaning. How we interpret any written material, whether a recipe, computer manual, love letter, or Martin Luther King, Jr.'s "Letter from Birmingham Jail" (pp. 569–586) depends, in part, on our prior knowledge of the subject, our opinion of the author, our experience with other works of the genre under consideration (what other recipes, or love letters, have we known)?, and the context in which we're reading. We read Dr. King's "Letter" differently today than when he wrote it, jailed in Birmingham in 1963 for civil rights protests; liberals read it differently than conservatives; African Americans may read it differently than whites, Southern or Northern. Where readers encounter a piece of writing greatly influences their interpretation, as well. Readers might read Dr. King's "Letter" as a document of news, history, social protest, argument, literary style—or some combination of these—depending on whether they encounter it in a newspaper of the time, in a history of the United States or of the civil rights movement, or in *The Essay Connection.*

A variety of critical theories reinforce the view that a work invites multiple readings, claiming that strong readers indeed bring powerful meanings to the texts they read. The two selections in *The Essay Connection* by Margaret Atwood, "The Page" (pp. 7–9) and "Fiction: Happy Endings" (pp. 704–707) open up a world of possibilities in interpreting not only what's on the waiting page, "pretending to be blank," but also what is *"beneath the page."* What's there for the writer, as for the reader, is not just another story but an assemblage of stories, "everything that has ever happened" in one's life and thought, waiting to bleed through and into the paper on which these stories, in all their variations, will be told. Readers and writers alike are always in process, always in flux, no matter what their sources of inspiration or places to think—for the students in Stephen Dunn's "The Sacred" (pp. 6–7), in their cars lies the power, "in having a key/and putting it in, and going."

As we experience and learn more, our understanding changes. Eudora Welty and Richard Wright, who grew up concurrently in Jackson, Mississippi, wrote years afterward to explain the phenomenon of learning to read from dramatically different perspectives. Welty's "In Love with Books" (pp. 29–34) explains part of her own background, showing how very young children can learn to love both reading and being read to. Wright's "The Power of Books" (pp. 409–418) offers yet a different focus on the relations between writers and readers, showing how an awakened social or racial consciousness can radically affect the reader. When several (or more) readers share a background, common values, and a common language, they may be considered a *discourse community.* In "Mother Tongue" (pp. 21–28), Amy Tan explores how her writing reflects her Chinese-American discourse community. She understands, and uses, "all the Englishes I grew up with" (p. 22)—one for formal writing, another for intimate conversation with Chinese family members, and a combination of public and private languages for storytelling. All the languages we speak, all the languages we understand (including the nonverbal communication of body language and social conventions), invariably influence how we write, for ourselves and those strangers who become friends—or antagonists—as they read our writing.

STEPHEN DUNN

Dunn, born in New York in 1939, graduated from Hofstra in 1962, and played semiprofessional basketball with the Williamsport (Pennsylvania) Billies for a season before a five-year stint as a copywriter and editor with Ziff-Davis publishers. Since 1974 he has been a professor of creative writing and poet-in-residence at Stockton State College, Pomona, New Jersey. He has published a dozen volumes of poetry and essays, the most recent being *Between Angels* (1989), *Walking Light: Essays and Memoirs* (1993), *New and Selected Poems* (1994), and *Venice in Watercolours* (1994). Of his poetry, widely praised and honored with prizes, Dunn himself says, "My poetry must speak for itself; I have no comments about it."

Like the students in the poem that follows, readers may have a "sacred place," whose "bright altar" can transport them from the everyday, ordinary world to a site where one has "the key" and is in control—but of what? Such a place becomes "sacred" because it allows the imagination to roam free. Thus it becomes a good place to write.

The Sacred

After the teacher asked if anyone had
    a sacred place
and the students fidgeted and shrank

in their chairs, the most serious of them all
5   said it was his car,
being in it alone, his tape deck playing

things he'd chosen, and others knew the truth
    had been spoken
and begin speaking about their rooms,

10   their hiding places, but the car kept coming up,
    the car in motion,
music filling it; and sometimes one other person

who understood the bright altar of the dashboard
    and how far away
a car could take him from the need
to speak, or to answer, the key
    in having a key
and putting it in, and going.

MARGARET ATWOOD

Atwood, novelist and poet of international distinction, was born
in Ottawa in 1939. During her teen years, determined to become a
writer, she scrawled "inky poems, about snow, despair, and the
Hungarian Revolution." And she typed, "finger-by-finger on an
ancient machine," short stories about "girls who'd had to get
married, and dispirited, mousy-haired high-school English
teachers—to end up as either was . . . my vision of Hell." She
published her first book of poetry, *Double Persephone*, in 1961,
the year she graduated from the University of Toronto; she
earned an M.A. from Radcliffe in 1962. She has since published
some twenty volumes of poetry and eleven novels, as well as
short stories, essays, and children's books.

In the process Atwood has become to Canadian literature
what Gordon Lightfoot is to Canadian music, as much institution
as individual. Her novels, enormously popular with critics and
readers on both sides of the border, include *The Edible Woman*
(1969), *Surfacing* (1972), *Cat's Eye* (1989), and the chilling, dys-
topian *Handmaid's Tale* (1985). In this feminist *Brave New World,*
women subvert the repressive male-dominated religious state
which holds them captive, their secret motto, "Don't let the
bastards get you down," an appropriate epigraph also for *The
Robber Bride* (1993).

In "Nine Beginnings" (in Janet Sternburg's *The Writer on Her
Work*, 1991), Atwood offers nine increasingly complex answers to
the question, "Why do you write?" After some deliberate diver-
sionary replies—"Because I want to discover the patterns in the
chaos of time. Because I must. Because someone has to bear
witness"—she finally concludes, "There's the blank page, and

the thing that obsesses you. There's the story that wants to take you over and there's your resistance to it. . . . There's the laborious revision. . . . Next day there's the blank page. You give yourself up to it like a sleepwalker."

The Page

1   1. The page waits, pretending to be blank. Is that its appeal, its blankness? What else is this smooth and white, this terrifyingly innocent? A snowfall, a glacier? It's a desert, totally arid, without life. But people venture into such places. Why? To see how much they can endure, how much dry light?

2   2. I've said the page is white, and it is: white as wedding dresses, rare whales, seagulls, angels, ice and death. Some say that like sunlight it contains all colours; others, that it's white because it's hot, it will burn out your optic nerves; that those who stare at the page too long go blind.

3   3. The page itself has no dimensions and no directions. There's no up or down except what you yourself mark, there's no thickness and weight but those you put there, north and south do not exist unless you're certain of them. The page is without vistas and without sounds, without centres or edges. Because of this you can become lost in it forever. Have you never seen the look of gratitude, the look of joy, on the faces of those who have managed to return from the page? Despite their faintness, their loss of blood, they fall on their knees, they push their hands into the earth, they clasp the bodies of those they love, or, in a pinch, any bodies they can get, with an urgency unknown to those who have never experienced the full horror of a journey into the page.

4   4. If you decide to enter the page, take a knife and some matches, and something that will float. Take something you can hold onto, and a prism to split the light and a talisman that works, which should be hung on a chain around your neck: that's for getting back. It doesn't matter what kind of shoes, but your hands should be bare. You should never go into the page with gloves on. Such decisions, needless to say, should not be made lightly.

There are those, of course, who enter the page without 5 deciding, without meaning to. Some of these have charmed lives and no difficulty, but most never make it out at all. For them the page appears as a well, a lovely pool in which they catch sight of a face, their own but better. These unfortunates do not jump: rather they fall, and the page closes over their heads without a sound, without a seam, and is immediately as whole and empty, as glassy, as enticing as before.

5. The question about the page is: what is beneath it? It seems 6 to have only two dimensions, you can pick it up and turn it over and the back is the same as the front. Nothing, you say, disappointed.

But you were looking in the wrong place, you were 7 looking *on the back* instead of *beneath*. *Beneath the page* is another story. Beneath the page is a story. Beneath the page is everything that has ever happened, most of which you would rather not hear about.

The page is not a pool but a skin, a skin is there to hold 8 in and it can feel you touching it. Did you really think it would just lie there and do nothing?

Touch the page at your peril: it is you who are blank 9 and innocent, not the page. Nevertheless you want to know, nothing will stop you. You touch the page, it's as if you've drawn a knife across it, the page has been hurt now, a sinuous wound opens, a thin incision. Darkness wells through.

CATHY N. DAVIDSON

Davidson, born in 1949, grew up in Chicago, earned a B.A. from Elmhurst College (1970), and a Ph.D. in English at the State University of New York at Binghamton (1974). Before becoming professor of English at Duke University in 1989, where she is the editor of *American Literature,* Davidson taught English at Michigan State. She has published books on *Mothers and Daughters in Literature* (1980), Ambrose Bierce (1984), American novels (1986), and *Writers and Their Love Letters* (1992).

"Laughing in English" is from *36 Views of Mount Fuji* (1993), Davidson's autobiographical account of "finding myself in

Japan" as a teacher of English at Kansai Women's University in Osaka in the 1980s. The book is titled after the series of Hokusai woodblocks depicting Mount Fuji, "the soul of Japan," in the context of multiple glimpses of "different, even contradictory, aspects of Japanese life." Like the Hokusai prints, Davidson's book uses "individual encounters, intimate moments, and small revelations" not only to "make sense of Japan," but to explain the ongoing process of attaining a better understanding of herself. She says, "what I learned almost immediately after I arrived in Japan for the first time, in 1980, was that I was destined to failure. My Japanese language skills were minimal, and I faced a culture that operated on assumptions completely different from my own. But I also learned that the Japanese were willing to tolerate my mistakes so long as I *acknowledged* them as mistakes, rather than as 'the right way' (read: The American Way) to do things. Most of my Japanese friends were willing to meet me more than halfway, also acknowledging those features of their culture that were specifically 'Japanese.' Over and over, I learned that a little laughter goes a long way towards smoothing over the places where cultures clash. I laughed a lot in Japan, and incorporated laughing into my classroom teaching as a way of easing cultural tensions and creating a comfortable environment where my students would feel less self-conscious about speaking English."

"Sometimes it is the person passing through . . . who has the clearest view," she adds. "I was in Japan to see, to experience, to learn, to understand. I wanted to be a good tourist, receptive to new experiences, new sights and sounds. It never occurred to me . . . that I would *become* one of the sights—examined, not just the examiner." In several senses, "Laughing in English" is about how two cultures, American and Japanese, learn to "read" each other and themselves.

Laughing in English

1   There was only one course in which Professor Sano, my depart- ment head, thought I might have trouble. I was assigned to teach Oral English for Non-English Majors, the B class, and Professor Sano made a point of warning me that these students would be very different from my English majors. Few, if any,

would have had any contact with English except through the traditional Japanese educational system. Intelligent young women, they still would have learned English the way my young friend Kenji had—lots of "who" and "whom," virtually nothing resembling practical conversational English. Most never would have heard a native speaker of English, except in Hollywood movies. The "English" taught in their Japanese schoolrooms was actually *katakana*, the Japanese syllabary for foreign words, a way of transliterating all foreign sounds into the forty-six basic Japanese sound patterns: *r* becomes *l*, *v* becomes *b*, each consonant (except *n*) must be followed by a vowel. *Rocket* is *rokketo* (pronounced "locketo"), *ventilator* is *benchireta,* and, the classic example, *blacklist* is the six-syllable *burakku-risuto.*

Perhaps because I was struggling so hard to learn even the ² most rudimentary Japanese, I was eager to teach these students English. My dislike of the traditional Japanese way of teaching English also made me feel almost a missionary zeal upon entering my Oral English course at KWU. I'd never taken any courses in the field of TOESL, Teaching of English as a Second Language, but I certainly knew from colleagues that the way English is taught in the Japanese schools is exactly the *wrong* way to encourage people to really communicate in a new language.

I tried a different tack, beginning with the conscious demoli- ³ tion of *sensei* ["teacher"]. Unlike many language teachers who refuse to speak anything but the language being taught, I delighted in speaking to the students in my execrable Japanese. Partly this was selfish; I practiced more Japanese in beginner's Oral English class than anywhere else. But it was also pedagogical. I figured if they realized that *sensei* wasn't ashamed to make mistakes, they certainly didn't have a right to be—a way of using the Japanese proclivity for authoritarianism and punctiliousness against itself. To show what I expected on the first formal presentation, a requirement in all of the Oral English sections, I initially prepared the same assignments—in Japanese. At first I thought I'd intentionally throw in a few mistakes, but quickly realized my Japanese was quite bad enough on its own without my having to invent errors.

I came up with a whopper. It is the kind of mistake often ⁴ made by native English-speakers, who have a hard time differentiating between repeated consonants. Mine, I found out later, was already a famous mistake; it happened when an American introduced the oldest and most revered woman in the Japanese parliament on national television. The American meant to say that this legislator was not only "very distinguished" but also "very feminine" (*onna-rashii*). She ended up saying the legislator was both distinguished and *onara shi* (which means, roughly, to cut a fart).

5   "That double *n* is hard for foreigners," I said when one of my students started to giggle. "We can't really hear the difference between *onna ra* and *onara*."

6   The students were now all laughing, but in polite Japanese-girl fashion, a hand covering the mouth.

7   "Wait!" I shouted in my sternest voice. "This is Oral English class!"

8   The laughter stopped. They looked ashamed.

9   "No, no. In this class, you must *laugh* in English. Think about it. You've all seen American movies. How do you laugh in English?"

10   I could see a gleam in Miss Shimura's eye, and I called on her: "Would an American woman ever put her hand over her mouth when she laughed, Miss Shimura?"

11   "No, *sensei*—I mean, teacher."

12   "Show me. Laugh like an American movie star."

13   Miss Shimura kept her hands plastered at her side. She threw back her head. She opened her mouth as far as it would go. She made a deep, staccato sound at the back of her throat. *Hanh. Hanh. Hanh.*

14   We all laughed hysterically.

15   "Hands down!" I shouted again. "This is Oral English!"

16   They put their hands at their sides and imitated Miss Shimura's American head-back, open mouth plosive laugh.

17   "What about the body?" I asked.

18   I parodied a Japanese laugh, pulling my arms in to my sides, bowing my head and shoulders forward, putting a hand coyly to my mouth.

19   Again they laughed. This time it was American-style.

20   "Oral English is about bodies too, not just words," I smiled.

21   Miss Kato raised her hand.

22   "Hai?" (Yes?)

"Americans also laugh like this." She put her head back, 23
opened her mouth, and rocked her upper body from side to side,
her shoulders heaving and dodging, like Santa Claus.

There were gleeful shouts of "Yes! Yes!" and again a room- 24
ful of American-style laughter. It would start to die down, then
someone would catch her friend doing the funny American
laugh, and she'd break into hysterics again, the hand going to her
mouth, me pointing, her correcting herself with the Santa Claus
laughter. I continued to laugh Japanese-style, which made them
laugh even louder, bouncier. We were off and running, laughing
in each other's languages.

I'm convinced shame kills language learning faster than anything, 25
even more so in Japan, where shame lurks so close to the surface
of every social interaction. The laughing routine was childish
exercise, but then all language learning is childish, inherently in-
fantilizing, a giving up and a giving in, a loss of control. Learning
a language means returning to a state of near-idiocy.

And honesty. Language learning is so consuming, there's no 26
energy left over for invention. Ask someone to tell you their
height and weight in a beginning foreign language class, and
you'll likely get a much more reliable answer than the one on her
driver's license.

This quickly became the case in beginners' Oral English, 27
where I learned aspects of Japanese life that the sophisticated,
cosmopolitan students in the advanced classes at KWU would
not have revealed, under normal circumstances, to a *gaijin*. My
beginners talked in English the way they might talk in Japanese,
among friends. They didn't know enough about Western culture
to anticipate what we might consider strange or exotic, controversial or even reprehensible. Consequently, they spoke without
excessive censoring, something I never experienced later on,
when I taught an Advanced Oral English class.

My advanced students often dodged my questions with 28
polite evasions. "The Japanese myth of racial homogeneity is as
erroneous as the American myth of the melting pot," offered a
student who has spent several years in the States. I had thought
my opening question, "What is racism?", would provoke a heated

debate that would lead us around, by the end of the class period, to addressing each country's particular brand of racism. Typically, Japanese are happy to discuss American racism but blind to the equivalent prejudice in their own country. The student's pointed answer effectively short-circuited the lesson I had hoped to make that day by anticipating what my own point of view might be. The rest of the class period was filled with platitudes and bored and knowing nods. The students in the advanced class knew exactly where to fudge.

29   After summer break, I require students in beginning Oral English for Non-Majors to give a brief presentation on what they've done over the vacation. It's designed to be simple, to ease them back into the term. They've been in Oral English since April, the beginning of the Japanese school year. They have had six weeks off for the summer, and now must return to classes for three more weeks before the grueling end-of-semester exams in late September.

30   I call on the first student.

31   "I was constipated most of the way to Nikko," a lovely young woman in a Kenzo flower-print jumper begins her talk.

32   I set my face like a Japanese mask, careful to express no emotion, and steal glances around the room. No one seems even remotely surprised at this beginning except me, and I know that it is absolutely mandatory that I act as if this is the most ordinary opening in the world.

33   "I was with the tennis club, and my *sensei* made sure I ate *konnyaku* for my constipation."

34   At this point she gets flustered. She is obviously embarrassed.

35   "It's okay," I jumped in hastily, searching for my most soothing and encouraging Japanese. "You're doing very well. Please go on."

36   "It's just," she stammers, also in Japanese, "I don't know the English for *konnyaku*. Do you know?"

37   I assure her that there's no American equivalent. *Konnyaku* is a glutinous substance, made from the root of a plant that seems to grow only in Japan. In America, I tell her, most people eat bran to cure constipation or we take over-the-counter medicines such as Ex-Lax.

"Ecks Racks," she repeats solemnly, then breaks into giggles   38
(American-style). So does everyone.

The word sounds so funny. It becomes the class joke for the   39
next few weeks. If anyone forgets a word in English, someone else
inevitably whispers to a friend, loud enough for the rest of us to
hear, "Ecks Racks!"

Three or four other speeches that morning give blow-by-   40
blow reports of near gastro-intestinal crises and how they were
averted, usually by the wise intervention of some *sensei*.

What surprises me most about the morning is how embarrassed   41
I am, although I think I've concealed it pretty well. These students
would wilt with shame if they had any inkling that this is not
something we would talk about in America, and I find myself in
a quandary. They trust me to tell them about Western culture, but
I know that if I tell them it's not considered polite to talk about
one's bowel movements in Western society, it will destroy the
easy camaraderie I've worked so hard to foster this year. But if I
don't tell them, I'm violating a trust.

I decide to resolve this by keeping a list of things they bring   42
up that wouldn't be acceptable in the West. All semester I've been
working to correct certain Japanese misconceptions and stereotypes, especially their idea that English is a completely logical and
direct language, and that Americans always say exactly what they
mean, regardless of social status or power relationships. Often my
students say things that sound very rude because they've been
taught that English lacks the politeness levels of Japanese. These
are topics we discuss all the time, so it will work just fine to devote
the last week of the semester to lecturing, in my comical Japanese,
about misconceptions and cultural differences that I've discovered
during my year in Japan. I can tell them about how surprised I
was the first time I used a public restroom that turned out to be
coed or about bathing Japanese-style with a group of women I
barely knew or having a male colleague slip around a corner on
the way home from a party. I started to follow, then realized he
was taking a quick pee. I know I can act out my own surprise,
making my Westerner's prudishness about bodily functions seem
funny but also relevant. This is as close as I can come to having my
pedagogical cake and eating it too.

43   From my beginning non-English majors in Oral English, I
learn a great deal about Japan, including the rituals and superstitions that have not been effaced by the rampant capitalism of
modern, urban Japanese life. They tell of phone numbers one can
call for horoscopes, fortunes, curses, cures. Rituals for marriages,
pregnancies, births, divorces. A kind of Japanese voodoo that takes
place in the forest on a certain kind of night. Number symbolism.
Lucky and unlucky days, lucky and unlucky years, lucky and unlucky directions ("Never sleep with your head to the North, the
way the dead are buried"). Blood-type match-making. Tengu, the
wicked long-nosed trickster goblin. Kappa, the amphibious river
imp. Tanuki, the raccoonlike creature with the money bag and
enormous testicles, a symbol of plenty. Dragons, supernatural
foxes, thunder gods, long-life noodles, boiled eels for stamina on
hot summer days, chewy *mochi* rice cakes for strength and endurance on the New Year, the ashes of a burnt *imori* (salamander)
served to someone you want to fall in love with you. They talk
seriously about prejudice and injustice toward the *burakumin*
(Japan's untouchable caste) the Ainu (the indigenous people, now
almost extinct), and Koreans (who must take Japanese names
before being allowed citizenship or who are denied citizenship
even two or three generations after their family immigrated to
Japan and who must carry alien registration papers with their
thumbprint, like foreigners). They talk of burial customs, going to
the crematorium with the long chopsticks to pick out the vertebra
that goes into the urn in the family altar at home.

44   When they talk of *omiai* and arranged marriage, one woman
starts to cry. Her friends comfort her. It's the only time I've ever
seen someone express personal sorrow in a Japanese classroom.
Several students insist that they will never marry an eldest son,
because they do not want to be responsible for taking care of his
aged parents. Two say they will never have children because they
do not want their children to hate them the way they hated their
mothers all through school. One young woman says if she
marries, it will be to a foreigner because she knows from the
movies that foreign husbands help around the house. Another
protests that she wouldn't want to marry a *gaijin*, because she
doesn't want a *gokiburi teishu* (a cockroach husband), some man

scurrying around underfoot in her kitchen. Funny or serious, they talk with candor. And, mostly, they talk. In English.

"There was so much laughing going on in the next room this semester, I checked the schedule," sniffs one of the part-time teachers. "It's your Oral English class. My students are getting jealous. All we hear from your room is laughter. Is anyone learning anything at all in there?"   45

I've had conversations before with this woman, none of them pleasant. She teaches at one of the more conventional Japanese universities and come to Kansai Women's University only one day a week. I've heard her say more than once that she's been here so long that now "she's more Japanese than the Japanese."   46

We're sitting and talking together over our *bento* boxes, eating our lunch in the faculty room. I tell her, proudly, that my students are learning to speak English very well, and, maybe more importantly, they are learning to speak freely and confidently.   47

"And you think that's a good thing?" she asks rhetorically. "They graduate and get to be OLs [office ladies] for a while. Then they're married off to some jerk of a *sarariiman*. But it's okay, you've taught them how to 'speak freely.'"   48

I am not liking this woman. I am not liking the insinuation in her voice or the smirk on her face. But I can't ignore her comment. I've thought about it myself, many times, especially on the train to and from the university, as I watch the faces of older Japanese women and think about where and how my students will fit in.   49

Most of these KWU students will graduate and they will, indeed, work as OLs for a few years before marriage, smiling politely and serving tea for busy male executives in Japanese firms. The closest they will come to real "business" might be working the Xerox machine or the paper shredder. Since only about a quarter of the population at four-year colleges in Japan is female (compared to well over half in the United States), there are lots of women available to work after the completion of secondary schools. OLs are perpetually replenishable, an eternally young group of women. Most quit—or are fired—once they are married or after they become pregnant.   50

51   The KWU women are the *crème de la crème* of Japanese female students. Some might advance further in corporate life than the OLs. A few might even achieve their dreams. One of my students wants to be a composer. Another wants to be an international news correspondent. Still others want to be doctors, lawyers. The odds are stacked against them, but the very fact that they are here shows that they are good at overcoming odds. "My dream is be a housewife and a mother," one of my Oral English students said in class one day. "But when I am a mother, I will give my children a *choice* of whether or not they want to go to *juku*. I will help to improve Japanese society by allowing my children to be free."

52   *To be free.* It's a phrase I've heard a lot this year, and I suspect some of this is just student grandstanding to please the *gaijin* teacher. Some of it is probably wishful thinking. Many of these smart, polished young women will become thoroughly conventional upper-middle-class housewives and mothers. It's hard for me to understand the point of all their study, all their years of deprivation, all those hours in *juku* cramming for "examination hell," just so one day they, too, can become "education moms," sending their young sons and daughters off under the falling cherry blossoms, the whole cycle beginning again with a new generation.

53   "We are told Japanese workers are better than American," one of my students says in an assignment about the work ethic. "We are told this so that we keep working—hard, harder, and hardest. Even as children, we're told to work hard. We Japanese work ourselves to death."

54   She is as startled as the rest of us by the burning quality of her speech. Her accent isn't perfect and her vocabulary has its limits but her eloquence is unmistakable. We have heard her. She returns to her seat, flushed with attention.

55   When I take the train home to my apartment in Nigawa that afternoon, I can't help noticing that the only men on the train are elderly, retired. The train is filled with mothers coming home from shopping and with schoolchildren in uniform, finished with one more day of regular school and now on their way to *juku*.

56   I find myself asking the big question, the dangerous question. What am I really doing here? My students are having fun, they're

learning English, but what is my role here? I have learned a lot teaching at Kansai Women's University, and I know my students have learned things too. I don't think it's romanticizing to say we've touched one another, shown each other glimpses of one another's culture. Is that enough?

I can tell sometimes, as I look out over the classroom, that   57
something like love is happening in there. It scares me. My students are convinced I look like a Western movie star. If I wear my shoulder-length hair up in a twist on a hot day, I can predict that at least a dozen of them will have their hair in a twist the next week. If I roll my jacket sleeves, they will roll theirs. My Oral English class has fun imitating my American slang, especially my habit of saying "Oh wow!" They have fun telling me their culture's secrets. They have fun making jokes and laughing and speaking English, hair in a twist, jacket sleeves rolled.

Maybe that's my function. Not very consequential but   58
perhaps necessary. "Visiting Foreign Teacher" is the official title on my visa. The students call me *"sensei,"* but I'm not like other *sensei* in the Japanese scheme of things. I am exotic and I am temporary. My embittered colleague might be right. In the sum total of their existence, it doesn't matter greatly that their English has improved. At my most cynical, I think of myself as a diversion, a respite from frenetic Japanese life, the pedagogical equivalent of the *sarariiman's* whiskey.

But I don't think you can be a teacher unless you believe in   59
the possibility of change. When I'm feeling optimistic, I like to think I give my Japanese students the same thing I try to give my American students back home: a space in which to speak and be heard.

Sometimes I look at middle-aged women in Japan and I'm   60
filled with awe. Often they *look* middle-aged—not engaged in the frantic and self-defeating American quest to look forever young—and often they look happy. Their children grown, many become adventurous. For some, it's ballroom dancing or traditional Japanese *koto,* hobbies given up during the busy child-rearing years. For others, it's running for local government or working for school reform or in the peace or environmental movements. KWU recently started accepting "returning women"—older women, including mothers whose children are grown—into its graduate

program, and the success rate, both in school and for subsequent employment, has been impressive.

61   That's what I think about when I teach the brilliant young women of Kansai Women's University. I think about their future, and hope that someday, soon or late, they will stop and hear the sound of their voices and remember their young fire.

Content

1. What does Davidson teach her students—explicitly and implicitly—when she teaches them to "laugh in English"?

2. How do we learn what's polite in our own culture and what's not? (In other words, how do we learn to "read" that particular aspect of the culture?) How can a person tell someone else—politely—that they're not being polite (see ¶s 31–42)?

3. "I don't think you can be a teacher unless you believe in the possibility of change," says Davidson (¶ 59). What changes occurred in Davidson's Japanese students during the time she taught them? What changes occurred in her? On what grounds is the rival teacher critical of Davidson's teaching (¶s 45–50)? Is the criticism justified, or is the other teacher simply jealous?

Strategies/Structures

1. Very early in the essay Davidson admits—to her students and her readers—the "whopper" and other mistakes she made in learning Japanese (¶s 3–5). What is the effect of such an admission on her students? On the character she presents to her readers?

2. What is the effect of Davidson's admission "I can tell sometimes, as I look out over the classroom, that something like love is happening in there. It scares me. My students are convinced I look like a Western movie star" [and they imitate me] (¶ 57)?

3. Assuming that Davidson is writing for an American audience, why is it important that her confession of the mistakes she makes as a teacher begin the essay that ends with an acknowledgement of the "love that is happening" in the classroom?

Language

Why is laughter, though nonverbal, a type of "language"? What do Davidson and her students immediately communicate through laughter?

In what ways does this laughter resonate throughout the remainder of the class sessions? Throughout this essay?

For Writing

1. Can—and should–learning be fun? Write an argument for, or against, laughing in any language as a way of learning to "read" or understand the culture it represents.

2. Write an essay to convince people wanting to learn another language that "to understand a language it is necessary to understand the culture of its native speakers." To illustrate your point, use examples from "Laughing in English" and your own experiences (or the experiences of others you know well) in learning another language and in trying to understand another culture, including making mistakes!

3. Identify a common means of nonverbal communication, such as laughing, smiling, frowning, looking someone straight in the eye, standing, sitting, walking, gesturing. Identify several typical expressions of your chosen means of communication (such as a broad smile, a faint smile, a come-hither smile) in particular contexts, and show how their meaning changes depending on the nature of the occasion, the place, the communicator's intent and skill, and the needs and understanding of the receiver of the message. Since the communication is nonverbal, and often (though not always) subtle, how can the communicator make sure the audience gets the point?

AMY TAN

Tan has always been fascinated with language, as revealed in the essay that follows, and on the relation of speaking to writing and reading. Born in Oakland, California, in 1952, Tan earned a B.A. in English at San Jose State University (1973), from which she also obtained an M.A. in linguistics in 1974. After working as a language development specialist for developmentally disabled children, she made a major career switch at age thirty, becoming a freelance business writer the week after her former boss told her "that writing was my worst skill." So successful was she at writing speeches for executives that she was soon working ninety hours a week. To relieve her workaholism and find her own voice she switched careers again, writing the first of the stories that ultimately comprised *The Joy Luck Club,* whose publication in 1989 brought her immediate fame, fortune, and critical esteem.

Tan followed this book with the equally successful *The Kitchen God's Wife* (1991), a novel modeled on her mother's traumatic life in China before she emigrated to the United States after World War II, and *The Hundred Secret Senses* (1995). Indeed, as Tan explains in the essay, "Mother Tongue," originally published in *Threepenny Review* in 1990, her ideal reader became her mother, "because these were stories about mothers." Tan wrote "in all the Englishes I grew up with"—the "simple" English "I spoke to my mother," the "broken" English "she used with me," my "'watered down' translation of her Chinese," and her "internal language"—"her intent, her passion, her imagery, the rhythms of her speech and the nature of her thoughts." Her mother paid the book the ultimate compliment. "'So easy to read.'" Hearing these multiple languages by reading the essay aloud weds the words and the music.

Mother Tongue

1   I am not a scholar of English or literature. I cannot give you much more than personal opinions on the English language and its variations in this country or others.

2   I am a writer. And by that definition, I am someone who has always loved language. I am fascinated by language in daily life. I spend a great deal of my time thinking about the power of language—the way it can evoke an emotion, a visual image, a complex idea, or a simple truth. Language is the tool of my trade. And I use them all—all the Englishes I grew up with.

3   Recently, I was made keenly aware of the different Englishes I do use. I was giving a talk to a large group of people, the same talk I had already given to half a dozen other groups. The nature of the talk was about my writing, my life, and my book, *The Joy Luck Club.* The talk was going along well enough, until I remembered one major difference that made the whole talk sound wrong. My mother was in the room. And it was perhaps the first

time she had heard me give a lengthy speech, using the kind of English I have never used with her. I was saying things like, "The intersection of memory upon imagination" and "There is an aspect of my fiction that relates to thus-and-thus"—a speech filled with carefully wrought grammatical phrases, burdened, it suddenly seemed to me, with nominalized forms, past perfect tenses, conditional phrases, all the forms of standard English that I had learned in school and through books, the forms of English I did not use at home with my mother.

Just last week, I was walking down the street with my 4 mother, and I again found myself conscious of the English I was using, the English I do use with her. We were talking about the price of new and used furniture and I heard myself saying this: "Not waste money that way." My husband was with us as well, and he didn't notice any switch in my English. And then I realized why. It's because over the twenty years we've been together I've often used that same kind of English with him, and sometimes he even uses it with me. It has become our language of intimacy, a different sort of English that relates to family talk, the language I grew up with.

So you'll have some idea of what this family talk I heard 5 sounds like, I'll quote what my mother said during a recent conversation which I videotaped and then transcribed. During this conversation, my mother was talking about a political gangster in Shanghai who had the same last name as her family's, Du, and how the gangster in his early years wanted to be adopted by her family, which was rich by comparison. Later, the gangster became more powerful, far richer than my mother's family, and one day showed up at my mother's wedding to pay his respects. Here's what she said in part:

"Du Yusong having business like fruit stand. Like off the 6 street kind. He is Du like Du Zong—but not Tsung-ming Island people. The local people call putong, the river east side, he belong to that side local people. That man want to ask Du Zong father take him in like become own family. Du Zong father wasn't look down on him, but didn't take seriously, until that man big like become a mafia. Now important person, very hard to inviting him. Chinese way, came only to show respect, don't stay for dinner. Respect for making big celebration, he shows up. Mean give lots of respect. Chinese custom. Chinese social life that way. If too important won't have to stay too long. He come to my wedding. I didn't see, I heard it. I gone to boy's side, they have YMCA dinner. Chinese age I was nineteen."

7   You should know that my mother's expressive command of English belies how much she actually understands. She reads the *Forbes* report, listens to *Wall Street Week,* converses daily with her stockbroker, reads all of Shirley MacLaine's books with ease—all kinds of things I can't begin to understand. Yet some of my friends tell me they understand 50 percent of what my mother says. Some say they understand 80 to 90 percent. Some say they understand none of it, as if she were speaking pure Chinese. But to me, my mother's English is perfectly clear, perfectly natural. It's my mother tongue. Her language, as I hear it, is vivid, direct, full of observation and imagery. That was the language that helped shape the way I saw things, expressed things, made sense of the world.

8   Lately, I've been giving more thought to the kind of English my mother speaks. Like others, I have described it to people as "broken" or "fractured" English. But I wince when I say that. It has always bothered me that I can think of no way to describe it other than "broken," as if it were damaged and needed to be fixed, as if it lacked a certain wholeness and soundness. I've heard other terms used, "limited English," for example. But they seem just as bad, as if everything is limited, including people's perceptions of the limited English speaker.

9   I know this for a fact, because when I was growing up, my mother's "limited" English limited *my* perception of her. I was ashamed of her English. I believed that her English reflected the quality of what she had to say. That is, because she expressed them imperfectly her thoughts were imperfect. And I had plenty of empirical evidence to support me: the fact that people in department stores, at banks, and at restaurants did not take her seriously, did not give her good service, pretended not to understand her, or even acted as if they did not hear her.

10   My mother has long realized the limitations of her English as well. When I was fifteen, she used to have me call people on the phone to pretend I was she. In this guise, I was forced to ask for information or even to complain and yell at people who had

been rude to her. One time it was a call to her stockbroker in New York. She had cashed out her small portfolio and it just happened we were going to go to New York the next week, our very first trip outside California. I had to get on the phone and say in an adolescent voice that was not very convincing, "This is Mrs. Tan."

And my mother was standing in the back whispering loudly, "Why he don't send me check, already two weeks late. So mad he lie to me, losing me money." 11

And then I said in perfect English, "Yes, I'm getting rather concerned. You had agreed to send the check two weeks ago, but it hasn't arrived." 12

Then she began to talk more loudly. "What he want, I come to New York tell him front of his boss, you cheating me?" And I was trying to calm her down, make her be quiet, while telling the stockbroker, "I can't tolerate any more excuses. If I don't receive the check immediately, I am going to have to speak to your manager when I'm in New York next week." And sure enough, the following week there we were in front of this astonished stockbroker, and I was sitting there red-faced and quiet, and my mother, the real Mrs. Tan, was shouting at his boss in her impeccable broken English. 13

We used a similar routine just five days ago, for a situation that was far less humorous. My mother had gone to the hospital for an appointment, to find out about a benign brain tumor a CAT scan had revealed a month ago. She said she had spoken very good English, her best English, no mistakes. Still, she said, the hospital did not apologize when they said they had lost the CAT scan and she had come for nothing. She said they did not seem to have any sympathy when she told them she was anxious to know the exact diagnosis, since her husband and son had both died of brain tumors. She said they would not give her any more information until the next time and she would have to make another appointment for that. So she said she would not leave until the doctor called her daughter. She wouldn't budge. And when the doctor finally called her daughter, me, who spoke in perfect English—lo and behold—we had assurances the CAT scan would be found, promises that a conference call on Monday would be held, and apologies for any suffering my mother had gone through for a most regrettable mistake. 14

15   I think my mother's English almost had an effect on limiting my possibilities in life as well. Sociologists and linguists probably will tell you that a person's developing language skills are more influenced by peers. But I do think that the language spoken in the family, especially in immigrant families which are more insular, plays a large role in shaping the language of the child. And I believe that it affected my results on achievement tests, IQ tests, and the SAT. While my English skills were never judged as poor, compared to math, English could not be considered my strong suit. In grade school I did moderately well, getting perhaps B's, sometimes B-pluses, in English and scoring perhaps in the sixtieth or seventieth percentile on achievement tests. But those scores were not good enough to override the opinion that my true abilities lay in math and science, because in those areas I achieved A's and scored in the ninetieth percentile or higher.

16   This was understandable. Math is precise; there is only one correct answer. Whereas, for me at least, the answers on English tests were always a judgment call, a matter of opinion and personal experience. Those tests were constructed around items like fill-in-the-blank sentence completion, such as, "Even though Tom was _____, Mary thought he was _____." And the correct answer always seemed to be the most bland combinations of thoughts, for example "Even though Tom was shy, Mary thought he was charming," with the grammatical structure "even though" limiting the correct answer to some sort of semantic opposites, so you wouldn't get answers like, "Even though Tom was foolish, Mary thought he was ridiculous." Well, according to my mother, there were very few limitations as to what Tom could have been and what Mary might have thought of him. So I never did well on tests like that.

17   The same was true with word analogies, pairs of words in which you were supposed to find some sort of logical, semantic relationship—for example, "*Sunset* is to *nightfall* as _____ is to _____." And here you would be presented with a list of four possible pairs, one of which showed the same kind of relationship: *red* is to *spotlight, bus* is to *arrival, chills* is to *fever, yawn* is to *boring.* Well, I could never think that way. I knew what the tests were asking, but I could not block out of my mind the images

already created by the first pair, *"sunset* is to *nightfall"*—and I would see a burst of colors against a darkening sky, the moon rising, the lowering of a curtain of stars. And all the other pairs of words—red, bus, spotlight, boring—just threw up a mass of confusing images, making it impossible for me to sort out something as logical as saying: "A sunset precedes nightfall" is the same as "a chill precedes a fever." The only way I would have gotten that answer right would have been to imagine an associative situation, for example, my being disobedient and staying out past sunset, catching a chill at night, which turns into feverish pneumonia as punishment, which indeed did happen to me.

I have been thinking about all this lately, about my mother's   18
English, about achievement tests. Because lately I've been asked as a writer, why there are not more Asian Americans represented in American literature. Why are there few Asian Americans enrolled in creative writing programs? Why do so many Chinese students go into engineering? Well, these are broad sociological questions I can't begin to answer. But I have noticed in surveys— in fact, just last week—that Asian students, as a whole, always do significantly better on math achievement tests than in English. And this makes me think that there are other Asian-American students whose English spoken in the home might also be described as "broken" or "limited." And perhaps they also have teachers who are steering them away from writing and into math and science, which is what happened to me.

Fortunately, I happen to be rebellious in nature and enjoy the   19
challenge of disproving assumptions made about me. I became an English major my first year in college, after being enrolled as premed. I started writing nonfiction as a freelancer the week after I was told by my former boss that writing was my worst skill and I should hone my talents toward account management.

But it wasn't until 1985 that I finally began to write fiction.   20
And at first I wrote using what I thought to be wittily crafted sentences, sentences that would finally prove I had mastery over the English language. Here's an example from the fist draft of a story that later made its way into *The Joy Luck Club,* but without this line: "That was my mental quandary in its nascent state." A terrible line, which I can barely pronounce.

21   Fortunately, for reasons I won't get into today, I later decided I should envision a reader for the stories I would write. And the reader I decided upon was my mother, because these were stories about mothers. So with this reader in mind—and in fact she did read my early drafts—I began to write stories using all the Englishes I grew up with: the English I spoke to my mother, which for lack of a better term might be described as "simple"; the English she used with me, which for lack of a better term might be described as "broken"; my translation of her Chinese, which could certainly be described as "watered down"; and what I imagined to be her translation of her Chinese if she could speak in perfect English, her internal language, and for that I sought to preserve the essence, but neither an English nor a Chinese structure. I wanted to capture what language ability tests can never reveal: her intent, her passion, her imagery, the rhythms of her speech and the nature of her thoughts.

22   Apart from what any critic had to say about my writing, I knew I had succeeded where it counted when my mother finished reading my book and gave me her verdict: "So easy to read."

Content

1. What connections does Tan make throughout the essay between speaking and writing? Why is it necessary for the writer to be "keenly aware of the different Englishes" she uses?
2. What is Tan's relationship with her mother? How can you tell?
3. What problems does Mrs. Tan experience as a result of not speaking standard English? Are her problems typical of other speakers of "limited" English?
4. Do you agree with Tan that "math is precise," but that English is "always a judgment call, a matter of opinion and personal experience" (¶ 16)? Why or why not? If English is so subjective, how is it possible to write anything that is clear, "so easy to read" (¶ 22)?

Strategies/Structures

Tan uses illustrative examples: a story told in her mother's speech (¶ 6), her mother's altercation with the stockbroker (¶s 10–13), her mother's encounter with rude and indifferent hospital workers who lost her CAT scan (¶ 14). What is the point of each example? Does Tan have to explain them? Why or why not?

story with "Cuckoo," and at night when I'd got in my own bed. I must have given her no peace. Sometimes she read to me in the kitchen while she sat churning, and the churning sobbed along with *any* story. It was my ambition to have her read to me while *I* churned; once she granted my wish, but she read off my story before I brought her butter. She was an expressive reader. When she was reading "Puss in Boots," for instance, it was impossible not to know that she distrusted *all* cats.

2   It had been startling and disappointing to me to find out that story books had been written by *people,* that books were not natural wonders, coming up of themselves like grass. Yet regardless of where they came from, I cannot remember a time when I was not in love with them—with the books themselves, cover and binding and the paper they were printed on, with their smell and their weight and with their possession in my arms, captured and carried off to myself. Still illiterate, I was ready for them, committed to all the reading I could give them.

3   Neither of my parents had come from homes that could afford to buy many books, but though it must have been something of a strain on his salary, as the youngest officer in a young insurance company, my father was all the while carefully selecting and ordering away for what he and Mother thought we children should grow up with. They bought first for the future.

4   Besides the bookcase in the livingroom, which was always called "the library," there were the encyclopedia tables and dictionary stand under windows in our diningroom. Here to help us grow up arguing around the diningroom table were the Unabridged Webster, the Columbia Encyclopedia, Compton's Pictured Encyclopedia, the Lincoln Library of Information, and later the Book of Knowledge. And the year we moved into our new house, there was room to celebrate it with the new 1925 edition of the Britannica, which my father, his face always deliberately turned toward the future, was of course disposed to think better than any previous edition.

5   In "the library," inside the mission-style bookcase with its three diamond-latticed glass doors, with my father's Morris chair and the glass-shaded lamp on its table beside it, were books I could soon begin on—and I did, reading them all alike and as they came, straight down their rows, top shelf to bottom. There

was the set of Stoddard's lectures, in all its late nineteenth-century vocabulary and vignettes of peasant life and quaint beliefs and customs, with matching halftone illustrations: Vesuvius erupting, Venice by moonlight, gypsies glimpsed by their campfires. I didn't know then the clue they were to my father's longing to see the rest of the world. I read straight through his other love-from-afar: the Victrola Book of the Opera, with opera after opera in synopsis, with portraits in costume of Melba, Caruso, Galli-Curci, and Geraldine Farrar, some of whose voices we could listen to on our Red Seal records.

6   My mother read secondarily for information; she sank as a hedonist into novels. She read Dickens in the spirit in which she would have eloped with him. The novels of her girlhood that had stayed on in her imagination, besides those of Dickens and Scott and Robert Louis Stevenson, were *Jane Eyre, Trilby, The Woman in White, Green Mansions, King Solomon's Mines.* Marie Corelli's name would crop up but I understood she had gone out of favor with my mother, who had only kept *Ardath* out of loyalty. In time she absorbed herself in Galsworthy, Edith Wharton, above all in Thomas Mann of the *Joseph* volumes.

7   *St. Elmo* was not in our house; I saw it often in other houses. This wildly popular Southern novel is where all the Edna Earles in our population started coming from. They're all named for the heroine, who succeeded in bringing a dissolute, sinning roué and atheist of a lover (St. Elmo) to his knees. My mother was able to forgo it. But she remembered the classic advice given to rose growers on how to water their bushes long enough: "Take a chair and *St. Elmo.*"

8   To both my parents I owe my early acquaintance with a beloved Mark Twain. There was a full set of Mark Twain and a short set of Ring Lardner in our bookcase, and those were the volumes that in time united us all, parents and children.

9   Reading everything that stood before me was how I came upon a worn old book without a back that had belonged to my father as a child. It was called *Sanford and Merton.* Is there anyone left who recognizes it, I wonder? It is the famous moral tale written by Thomas Day in the 1780s, but of him no mention is made on the title page of this book; here it is *Sanford and Merton in Words of One Syllable* by Mary Godolphin. Here are the rich boy and the

poor boy and Mr. Barlow, their teacher and interlocutor, in long discourses alternating with dramatic scenes—danger and rescue allotted to the rich and the poor respectively. It may have only words of one syllable, but one of them is "quoth." It ends with not one but two morals, both engraved on rings: "Do what you ought, come what may," and "If we would be great, we must first learn to be good."

This book was lacking its front cover, the back held on by 10 strips of pasted paper, now turned golden, in several layers, and the pages stained, flecked, and tattered around the edges; its garish illustrations had come unattached but were preserved, laid in. I had the feeling even in my heedless childhood that this was the only book my father as a little boy had had of his own. He had held onto it, and might have gone to sleep on its coverless face: he had lost his mother when he was seven. My father had never made any mention to his own children of the book, but he had brought it along with him from Ohio to our house and shelved it in our bookcase.

My mother had brought from West Virginia that set of 11 Dickens; those books looked sad, too—they had been through fire and water before I was born, she told me, and there they were, lined up—as I later realized, waiting for *me.*

I was presented, from as early as I can remember, with books 12 of my own, which appeared on my birthday and Christmas morning. Indeed, my parents could not give me books enough. They must have sacrificed to give me on my sixth or seventh birthday— it was after I became a reader for myself—the ten-volume set of Our Wonder World. These were beautifully made, heavy books I would lie down with on the floor in front of the diningroom hearth, and more often than the rest volume 5, *Every Child's Story Book,* was under my eyes. There were the fairy tales—Grimm, Andersen, the English, the French, "Ali Baba and the Forty Thieves"; and there was Aesop and Reynard the Fox; there were the myths and legends, Robin Hood, King Arthur, and St. George and the Dragon, even the history of Joan of Arc; a whack of *Pilgrim's Progress* and a long piece of *Gulliver.* They all carried their classic illustrations. I located myself in these pages and could go straight to the stories and pictures I loved; very often "The Yellow Dwarf" was first choice, with Walter Crane's Yellow Dwarf in full color making his terrifying appearance flanked by turkeys. Now that volume is as worn and backless and hanging apart as my father's poor *Sanford and Merton*. The precious page with Edward Lear's "Jumblies" on it has been in danger of slipping out for all these years. One measure of my love for Our Wonder World was that for a long time I wondered if I would go through fire and water for it as my mother had done for Charles Dickens; and the only comfort was to think I could ask my mother to do it for me.

13   I believe I'm the only child I know of who grew up with this treasure in the house. I used to ask others, "Did you have Our Wonder World?" I'd have to tell them the Book of Knowledge could not hold a candle to it.

14   I live in gratitude to my parents for initiating me—and as early as I begged for it, without keeping me waiting—into knowledge of the word, into reading and spelling, by way of the alphabet. They taught it to me at home in time for me to begin to read before starting to school. I believe the alphabet is no longer considered an essential piece of equipment for traveling through life. In my day it was the keystone to knowledge. You learned the alphabet as you learned to count to ten, as you learned "Now I lay me" and the Lord's Prayer and your father's and mother's name and address and telephone number, all in case you were lost.

15   My love for the alphabet, which endures, grew out of reciting it but, before that, out of seeing the letters on the page. In my own story books, before I could read them for myself, I fell in love with various winding, enchanted-looking initials drawn by Walter Crane at the heads of fairy tales. In "Once up a time," an "O" had a rabbit running it as a treadmill, his feet upon flowers. When the day came, years later, for me to see the Book of Kells, all the wizardry of letter, initial, and word swept over me a thousand times over, and the illumination, the gold, seemed a part of the world's beauty and holiness that had been there from the start.

Content

1. Most professional writers of quality have been in love with books since childhood. Why?
2. How can parents encourage their children to become avid readers? What are the benefits of this process?

3. What else does Welty's adoration of books as a child reveal about her as a person? What does her discussion of how she came to know and love books reveal about her parents?

Strategies/Structures

1. Throughout the essay Welty describes the context in which she encountered the books she loved; why are these contexts important?

2. Welty refers to several books that people don't read anymore, such as *St. Elmo* and *Sanford and Merton*—perhaps even *Pilgrim's Progress*. How can her readers understand what's she's talking about if they haven't read the books?

Language

Comment on Welty's rich, embellished language in the last paragraph. How does it fit the subject?

For Writing

1. If you love to read, write an essay for an audience of television viewers explaining the joys of reading, either in general or with reference to particular kinds of books or other materials. See also Wright, "The Power of Books" (pp. 409–418).

2. Describe your ideal collection of books, general or specialized, either as a child or as an adult. Let your readers see, as Welty does, why your favorites are so treasured.

3. See the suggestion for writing in connection with Kozol's essay, "The Human Cost of an Illiterate Society" (pp. 264–273).

2 | The Essay, a Vision: Definition and Reasons for Writing

There are two sorts of essays in this book, essays of literary non-fiction (sometimes called *literature of fact,* or *creative nonfiction,* or *belletristic essays*) and articles. In essays of literary nonfiction, the writer's artistry is paramount, illuminated by, as Elizabeth Hardwick says, an "individual intelligence and sparkle. We consent to watch a mind at work, without agreement often, but only for pleasure." Essays of literary nonfiction, which some people claim are the only true essays, are short prose pieces that use many of the same techniques that fiction does. They can present characters in action, in dialogue (even in interior monologue), in context, and in costume. They can play with time, with language, with points of view, and with narrative persona. As professional essayist E. B. White claims in "The Essayist and the Essay" (pp. 39–41), an essayist "can pull on any sort of shirt, be any sort of person, according to his mood or his subject matter—philosopher, scold, jester, raconteur, confidant, pundit, devil's advocate, enthusiast."

According to this view, the essay, says Annie Dillard, "can do everything a poem can do, and everything a short story can do—everything but fake it. The elements in any nonfiction should be true not only artistically, the connections must hold at base and must be veracious," for essayists claim and readers believe that what they're reading is the truth. As Dillard says, "there's a lot of truth out there to work with. The real world arguably exerts a greater fascination on people than any fictional one. . . . The essayist thinks about actual things. He can make sense of them analytically or artistically."

The Essay Connection includes many types of essays of literary nonfiction: *memoir* and *partial autobiography,* such as Scott Russell Sanders's "Under the Influence" (pp. 420–433); *character sketches,* among them student Leslie S. Moore's "Framing My Father" (pp. 282–287); *descriptions of a place,* as in Mark Twain's "Uncle John's Farm" (pp. 312–318), or of *an experience,* such as the excerpts from Zitkala-Sa's *The School Days of an Indian Girl* (pp. 254–262); *narratives of events,* including Frederick Douglass's account of how he stood up to his cruel overseer ("You have seen how a man was made a slave; you shall see how a slave was made a man.") (pp. 150–156); *interpretive reviews* that comment at length on a work or a performance, as in Gilbert Highet's "The Gettysburg Address" (pp. 674–681); and *social commentary,* such as Jonathan Kozol's "The Human Cost of an Illiterate Society" (pp. 264–273) and Mike Rose's " 'I Just Wanna Be Average' " (pp. 243–252).

Articles, in contrast, claims critic William Gass, are more concerned with substance than with style, for charm and elegance "will interfere with the impression of seriousness" they wish to maintain. An article, Gass continues, "must appear complete and straightforward and footnoted and useful and certain," for the article "pretends that everything is clear, that its argument is unassailable, that there are no soggy patches, no illicit interferences." Articles, he says, are written by professionals whose personality is unobtrusive in academic prose that "sounds like writing written down" rather than spoken aloud.

Although Gass clearly prefers essays to articles, he is also exaggerating the case to make his point. Indeed, much of your writing in college will be articles in the language and conventions of the particular subjects you study—critical interpretations of literature, position papers in philosophy or political science, interpretive presentations of information in history, case histories in psychology or business or law—or auto mechanics. For instance, Thomas S. Kuhn's "The Route to Normal Science" (pp. 197–208) explains and interprets the complex process of how scientists do their work, while in the course of explaining what's "Inside the Engine" (pp. 209–215), master mechanics Tom and Ray Magliozzi tell readers how and why motor oil keeps the engine humming smoothly. Dr. Martin Luther King, Jr., in "Letter from Birmingham Jail" (pp. 569–586) uses evidence from world religions, his own life experience and that of numerous other African-Americans, theology, history and the law to make the case for civil disobedience. And Stephanie Coontz interprets American public policy as it affects numerous aspects of everyday life from home mortgages to education subsidies to show how such policy makes the vast American middle class "A Nation of Welfare Families" (pp. 275–280).

Gass's preference for essays notwithstanding, articles such as these do not have to be dry, dull, and devoid of a point of view. For instance, the science writings of Isaac Asimov (pp. 184–195), Vicki Hearne (pp. 524–534), and Jane Brody (pp. 216–227) are known for their reader-friendly clarity as well as their absolute accuracy. And we can always count on them to have a point of view—Brody invariably favors what is moderate and healthful.

Why a person writes often determines his or her point of view on a particular subject. George Orwell claims that people write for four main reasons, "sheer egoism," "esthetic enthusiasm," "historical impulse," and—his primary motive—"political purpose, the desire to push the world in a certain direction." Joan Didion, echoing Orwell, believes that writers are always pushing and nagging and tugging at their readers, saying *"listen to me, see it my way, change your mind."* In "Why I Write: Making No Become Yes" (pp. 51–57), Elie Wiesel interprets *"see it my way,"* as the role of the writer as witness. The survivor of imprisonment in several Nazi concentration camps, Wiesel explains, "I was duty-bound to give meaning to my survival, to justify each moment of my life. . . . Not to transmit an experience is to betray it." In this eloquent essay Wiesel, winner of the 1986 Nobel Peace Prize, demonstrates his continuing commitment to make survivors, the entire world, continually remember the meaning of the Holocaust: "Why do I write? To wrench those victims from oblivion. To help the dead vanquish death."

If you wish, you can use the definitions of *essay* and *article* provided here. Or for simplicity's sake you can consider all the writings in this book to be *essays.* No matter what you call them, we hope you'll find them engaging, provocative, stimulating examples of minds at work, ideas at play, artistry in action.

E. B. WHITE

Born in peaceful Mount Vernon, New York, in 1899, White was
editor of the Cornell *Daily Sun* during his senior year in college
1920–1921. In 1927, he joined the staff of the year-old *New Yorker,*
writing "Talk of the Town" and "Notes and Comments" columns.
Over the next thirty years he also wrote an estimated thirty
thousand witty rejoinders to "newsbreaks," mangled sentences
and misprints that filled out *New Yorker* columns and appeared
under headings that White invented, such as "Letters We Never
Finished Reading." In 1957 the Whites moved permanently to
Allen Cove, Maine, where White wrote until his death in 1985.
His distinguished works include the essays collected in *One Man's
Meat* (1944), *The Second Tree from the Corner* (1954), and *The Points of
My Compass* (1962); landmark advice on how to write clear, plain
prose, *The Elements of Style* (rev. 1973), with his Cornell professor,
William Strunk; and three classic children's books, *Stuart Little*
(1945), *Charlotte's Web* (1952), and *The Trumpet of the Swan* (1970).

In this essay White amplifies upon Samuel Johnson's definition of the familiar, personal essay as "an irregular, undigested
piece" of writing. He underestimates the skill of essayists, including himself, in considering them self-consigned to "second-class
citizenship" in comparison with novelists, poets, and playwrights.
In fact, the essays in this book are skillful works of thought and art,
carefully controlled in structure, substance, language, and tone. In
many essays the writer appears as a character or persona in his or
her own work, speaking in a distinctive voice and interpreting the
subject from an equally individualist—some would say idiosyncratic—point of view, as White does here and in all of his essays.

The Essayist and the Essay[1]

The essayist is a self-liberated man, sustained by the childish
belief that everything he thinks about, everything that happens to him, is of general interest. He is a fellow who thoroughly

1

---

[1] Title supplied.

enjoys his work, just as people who take bird walks enjoy theirs. Each new excursion of the essayist, each new "attempt," differs from the last and takes him into new country. This delights him. Only a person who is congenitally self-centered has the effrontery and the stamina to write essays.

2   There are as many kinds of essays as there are human attitudes or poses, as many essay flavors as there are Howard Johnson ice creams. The essayist arises in the morning and, if he has work to do, selects his garb from an unusually extensive wardrobe: he can pull on any sort of shirt, be any sort of person, according to his mood or his subject matter—philosopher, scold, jester, raconteur, confidant, pundit, devil's advocate, enthusiast. I like the essay, have always liked it, and even as a child was at work, attempting to inflict my young thoughts and experiences on others by putting them on paper. I early broke into print in the pages of *St. Nicholas.* I tend still to fall back on the essay form (or lack of form) when an idea strikes me, but I am not fooled about the place of the essay in twentieth-century American letters— it stands a short distance down the line. The essayist, unlike the novelist, the poet, and the playwright, must be content in his self-imposed role of second-class citizen. A writer who has his sights trained on the Nobel Prize or other earthly triumphs had best write a novel, a poem, or a play and leave the essayist to ramble about, content with living a free life and enjoying the satisfactions of a somewhat undisciplined existence. (Dr. Johnson called the essay "an irregular, undigested piece"; this happy practitioner has no wish to quarrel with the good doctor's characterization.)

3   There is one thing the essayist cannot do, though—he cannot indulge himself in deceit or in concealment, for he will be found out in no time. Desmond MacCarthy, in his introductory remarks to the 1928 E. P. Dutton & Company edition of Montaigne, observes that Montaigne "had the gift of natural candour. . . ." It is the basic ingredient. And even the essayist's escape from discipline is only a partial escape: the essay, although a relaxed form, imposes its own disciplines, raises its own problems, and these disciplines and problems soon become apparent and (we all hope) act as a deterrent to anyone wielding a pen merely

because he entertains random thoughts or is in a happy or wandering mood.

I think some people find the essay the last resort of the egoist, a much too self-conscious and self-serving form for their taste; they feel that it is presumptuous of a writer to assume that his little excursions or his small observations will interest the reader. There is some justice in their complaint. I have always been aware that I am by nature self-absorbed and egoistical; to write of myself to the extent I have done indicates a too great attention to my own life, not enough to the lives of others. I have worn many shirts, and not all of them have been a good fit. But when I am discouraged or downcast I need only fling open the door of my closet, and there, hidden behind everything else, hangs the mantle of Michel de Montaigne, smelling slightly of camphor.

Content

1. How can the writer avoid the deceit or concealment that White says is impossible for an essayist, and nevertheless engage in any sort of pose he wants, as White claims in paragraph 2?
2. If you are familiar with some of the essays in this book, refer to them in commenting on White's assertion that essayists are "by nature self-absorbed and egoistical" (¶ 4).

Strategies/Structures

What kind of a person does White appear to be in this essay? Does he in fact seem to be "self-absorbed and egoistical"? Does he seem to be the sort of person who would write essays, as he defines them?

Language

1. White refers to essayists as self-imposed second-class citizens (¶ 2). Explain why you agree or disagree.
2. Is the essay "an irregular, undigested piece," as Dr. Samuel Johnson remarked, or expressive of "a ramble" through "a free life . . . of a somewhat undisciplined existence"?

For Writing

1. Like love, the essay may be a form that everyone recognizes but that is hard to define; like love, the essay may have as many definitions as there are practitioners. For readers and writers of essays, write a definition of the essay that is broad enough to encompass some of its characteristic types.

2. Explain how an essay is a work of revelation, concealment, and shaping (or manipulation) of facts. Use a specific essay, preferably one from *The Essay Connection*, to illustrate your analysis.

PAULE MARSHALL

Marshall was born in Brooklyn in 1929, the daughter of immigrants from Barbados; this bicultural focus permeates much of her fiction. With degrees from Brooklyn College (1953) and Hunter College (1955), Marshall became a staff writer for *Our World* while writing her first novel after hours, *Browngirl, Brownstones* (1959, reissued 1981). Since then, aided by awards from the Guggenheim, Ford, and MacArthur Foundations and the National Endowment for the Arts, Marshall has written *Soul, Clap Hands and Sing* (1961), *The Chosen Place, The Timeless People* (1969), *Praisesong for the Widow* (1983), and *Daughters* (1991). A participant in various literary symposia in Nigeria, Barbados, Mexico, China, and elsewhere, she is a professor emerita of English at Virginia Commonwealth University.

In her own writing Marshall tries to convey the "variety of voices" that is her heritage—West Indian dialect and black American English, as well as the standard English of educated Americans. "I'm always being urged to write a novel that's set exclusively in the States," but, she says, she can't do this "because my way of seeing the world has been so profoundly shaped by my dual experience, those two communities, West Indian and African-American. Those two great traditions—they nurtured me, they inspired me, they formed me. I am fascinated by the interaction of the two cultures, which is really, as I see it, one tradition, one culture." As she analyzes the speech of these "poets in the kitchen," Marshall conveys their sense of personal and racial pride and their imaginative use of language to achieve the solidarity, visibility, and power denied to them in the alien white world.

The Making of a Writer[1]

S ome years ago, when I was teaching a graduate seminar in 1
fiction at Columbia University, a well known male novelist
visited my class to speak on his development as a writer. In discussing his formative years, he didn't realize it but he seriously
endangered his life by remarking that women writers are luckier
than those of his sex because they usually spend so much time
as children around their mothers and their mothers' friends in
the kitchen.

What did he say that for? The women students immediately 2
forgot about being in awe of him and began readying their attack
for the question and answer period later on. Even I bristled. There
again was that awful image of women locked away from the
world in the kitchen with only each other to talk to, and their
daughters locked in with them.

But my guest wasn't really being sexist or trying to be pro- 3
vocative or even spoiling for a fight. What he meant—when he got
around to explaining himself more fully—was that, given the way
children are (or were) raised in our society, with little girls kept
closer to home and their mothers, the woman writer stands a better
chance of being exposed, while growing up, to the kind of talk that
goes on among women, more often than not in the kitchen; and
that this experience gives her an edge over her male counterpart
by instilling in her an appreciation for ordinary speech.

It was clear that my guest lecturer attached great importance 4
to this, which is understandable. Common speech and the plain,
workaday words that make it up are, after all, the stock in trade of
some of the best fiction writers. They are the principal means by
which characters in a novel or story reveal themselves and give
voice sometimes to profound feelings and complex ideas about
themselves and the world. Perhaps the proper measure of a
writer's talent is skill in rendering everyday speech—when it is
appropriate to the story—as well as the ability to tap, to exploit,
the beauty, poetry and wisdom it often contains.

---

[1] Title supplied.

5   "If you say what's on your mind in the language that comes to you from your parents and your street and friends you'll probably say something beautiful." Grace Paley tells this, she says, to her students at the beginning of every writing course.

6   It's all a matter of exposure and a training of the ear for the would-be writer in those early years of apprenticeship. And, according to my guest lecturer, this training, the best of it, often takes place in as unglamorous a setting as the kitchen.

7   He didn't know it, but he was essentially describing my experience as a little girl. I grew up among poets. Now they didn't look like poets—whatever that breed is supposed to look like. Nothing about them suggested that poetry was their calling. They were just a group of ordinary housewives and mothers, my mother included, who dressed in a way (shapeless housedresses, dowdy felt hats and long, dark, solemn coats) that made it impossible for me to imagine they had ever been young.

8   Nor did they do what poets were supposed to do—spend their days in an attic room writing verses. They never put pen to paper except to write occasionally to their relatives in Barbados. "I take my pen in hand hoping these few lines will find you in health as they leave me fair for the time being," was the way their letter invariably began. Rather, their day was spent "scrubbing floor," as they described the work they did.

9   Several mornings a week these unknown bards would put an apron and a pair of old house shoes in a shopping bag and take the train or streetcar from our section of Brooklyn out to Flatbush. There, those who didn't have steady jobs would wait on certain designated corners for the white housewives in the neighborhood to come along and bargain with them over pay for a day's work cleaning their houses. This was the ritual even in the winter.

10   Later, armed with the few dollars they had earned, which in their vocabulary became "a few raw-mouth pennies," they made their way back to our neighborhood, where they would sometimes stop off to have a cup of tea or cocoa together before going home to cook dinner for their husbands and children.

11   The basement kitchen of the brownstone house where my family lived was the usual gathering place. Once inside the warm safety of its walls the women threw off the drab coats and hats,

seated themselves at the large center table, drank their cups of tea or cocoa, and talked. While my sister and I sat at a smaller table over in a corner doing our homework, they talked—endlessly, passionately, poetically, and with impressive range. No subject was beyond them. True, they would indulge in the usual gossip: whose husband was running with whom, whose daughter looked slightly "in the way" (pregnant) under her bridal gown as she walked down the aisle. That sort of thing. But they also tackled the great issues of the time. They were always, for example, discussing the state of the economy. It was the mid and late 30's then, and the aftershock of the Depression, with its soup lines and suicides on Wall Street, was still being felt.

Some people, they declared, didn't know how to deal with adversity. They didn't know that you had to "tie up your belly" (hold in the pain, that is) when things got rough and go on with life. They took their image from the bellyband that is tied around the stomach of a newborn baby to keep the navel pressed in. 12

They talked politics. Roosevelt was their hero. He had come along and rescued the country with relief and jobs, and in gratitude they christened their sons Franklin and Delano and hoped they would live up to the names. 13

If F.D.R. was their hero, Marcus Garvey was their God. The name of the fiery, Jamaican-born black nationalist of the 20's was constantly invoked around the table. For he had been their leader when they first came to the United States from the West Indies shortly after World War I. They had contributed to his organizations, the United Negro Improvement Association (UNIA), out of their meager salaries, bought shares in his ill-fated Black Star Shipping Line, and at the height of the movement they had marched as members of his "nurses' brigade" in their white uniforms up Seventh Avenue in Harlem during the great Garvey Day parades. Garvey: He lived on through the power of their memories. 14

And their talk was of war and rumors of wars. They raged against World War II when it broke out in Europe, blaming it on the politicians. "It's these politicians. They're the ones always starting up all this lot of war. But what they care? It's the poor people got to suffer and mothers with their sons." If it was *their* 15 sons, they swore they would keep them out of the Army by giving them soap to eat each day to make their hearts sound defective. Hitler? He was for them "the devil incarnate."

16   Then there was home. They reminisced often and at length about home. The old country. Barbados—or Bimshire, as they affectionately called it. The little Caribbean island in the sun they loved but had to leave. "Poor—poor but sweet" was the way they remembered it.

17   And naturally they discussed their adopted home. America came in for both good and bad marks. They lashed out at it for the racism they encountered. They took to task some of the people they worked for, especially those who gave them only a hard-boiled egg and a few spoonfuls of cottage cheese for lunch. "As if anybody can scrub floor on an egg and some cheese that don't have no taste to it!"

18   Yet although they caught H in "this man country," as they called America, it was nonetheless a place where "you could at least see your way to make a dollar." That much they acknowledged. They might even one day accumulate enough dollars, with both them and their husbands working, to buy the brownstone houses which, like my family, they were only leasing at that period. This was their consuming ambition: to "buy house" and to see the children through.

19   There was no way for me to understand it at the time, but the talk that filled the kitchen those afternoons was highly functional. It served as therapy, the cheapest kind available to my mother and her friends. Not only did it help them recover from the long wait on the corner that morning and the bargaining over their labor, it restored them to a sense of themselves and reaffirmed their self-worth. Through language they were able to overcome the humiliations of the work-day.

20   But more than therapy, that freewheeling, wide-ranging, exuberant talk functioned as an outlet for the tremendous creative energy they possessed. They were women in whom the need for self-expression was strong, and since language was the only vehicle readily available to them they made of it an art form that—in keeping with the African tradition in which art and life are one—was an integral part of their lives.

And their talk was a refuge. They never really ceased being 21 baffled and overwhelmed by America—its vastness, complexity and power. Its strange customs and laws. At a level beyond words they remained fearful and in awe. Their uneasiness and fear were even reflected in their attitude toward the children they had given birth to in this country. They referred to those like myself, the little Brooklyn-born Bajans (Barbadians), as "these New York children" and complained that they couldn't discipline us properly because of the laws here. "You can't beat these children as you would like, you know, because the authorities in this place will dash you in jail for them. After all, these is New York children." Not only were we different, American, we had, as they saw it, escaped their ultimate authority.

Confronted therefore by a world they could not encompass, 22 which even limited their rights as parents, and at the same time finding themselves permanently separated from the world they had known, they took refuge in language. "Language is the only homeland," Czeslaw Milosz, the emigré Polish writer and Nobel Laureate, has said. This is what it became for the women at the kitchen table.

It served another purpose also, I suspect. My mother and 23 her friends were after all the female counterpart of Ralph Ellison's invisible man. Indeed, you might say they suffered a triple invisibility, being black, female and foreigners. They really didn't count in American society except as a source of cheap labor. But given the kind of women they were, they couldn't tolerate the fact of their invisibility, their powerlessness. And they fought back, using the only weapon at their command: the spoken word.

Those later afternoon conversations on a wide range of topics 24 were a way for them to feel they exercised some measure of control over their lives and the events that shaped them. "Soully-gal, talk yuh talk!" they were always exhorting each other. "In this man world you got to take yuh mouth and make a gun!" They were in control, if only verbally and if only for the two hours or so that they remained in our house.

For me, sitting over in the corner, being seen but not heard, 25 which was the rule for children in those days, it wasn't only what the women talked about—the content—but the way they put things—their style. The insight, irony, wit and humor they brought to their stories and discussions and their poet's inventiveness and daring with language—which of course I could only sense but not define back then.

26   They had taken the standard English taught them in the primary schools of Barbados and transformed it into an idiom, an instrument that more adequately described them—changing around the syntax and imposing their own rhythm and accent so that the sentences were more pleasing to their ears. They added the few African sounds and words that had survived, such as the derisive suck-teeth sound and the word "yam," meaning to eat. And to make it more vivid, more in keeping with their expressive quality, they brought to bear a raft of metaphors, parables, biblical quotations, sayings and the like:

27   "The sea ain' got no back door," they would say, meaning that it wasn't like a house where if there was a fire you could run out the back. Meaning that it was not to be trifled with. And meaning perhaps in a larger sense that man should treat all of nature with caution and respect.

28   "I has read hell by heart and called every generation blessed!" They sometimes went in for hyperbole.

29   A woman expecting a baby was never said to be pregnant. They never used that word. Rather, she was "in the way" or, better yet, "tumbling big." "Guess who I butt up on in the market the other day tumbling big again!"

30   And a woman with a reputation of being too free with her sexual favors was known in their book as a "thoroughfare"—the sense of men like a steady stream of cars moving up and down the road of her life. Or she might be dubbed "a free-bee," which was my favorite of the two. I liked the image it conjured up of a woman scandalous perhaps but independent, who flitted from one flower to another in a garden of male beauties, sampling their nectar, taking her pleasure at will, the roles reversed.

31   And nothing, no matter how beautiful, was ever described as simply beautiful. It was always "beautiful-ugly": the beautiful-ugly dress, the beautiful-ugly house, the beautiful-ugly car. Why the word "ugly," I used to wonder, when the thing they were referring to was beautiful, and they knew it. Why the antonym, the

contradiction, the linking of opposites? It used to puzzle me greatly as a child.

There is the theory in linguistics which states that the idiom of a people, the way they use language, reflects not only the most fundamental views they hold of themselves and the world but their very conception of reality. Perhaps in using the term "beautiful-ugly" to describe nearly everything, my mother and her friends were expressing what they believed to be a fundamental dualism in life: the idea that a thing is at the same time its opposite, and that these opposites, these contradictions make up the whole. But theirs was not a Manichaean brand of dualism that sees matter, flesh, the body, as inherently evil because they constantly addressed each other as "soully-gal"—soul: spirit; gal: the body, flesh, the visible self. And it was clear from their tone that they gave one as much weight and importance as the other. They had never heard of the mind/body split.   32

As for God, they summed up His essential attitude in a phrase. "God," they would say, "don't love ugly and He ain' stuck on pretty."   33

Using everyday speech, the simple commonplace words— but always with imagination and skill—they gave voice to the most complex ideas. Flannery O'Connor would have approved of how they made ordinary language work, as she put it, "double-time," stretching, shading, deepening its meaning. Like Joseph Conrad they were always trying to infuse new life in the "old old words worn thin . . . by . . . careless usage." And the goals of their oral art were the same as his: "To make you hear, to make you feel . . . to make you *see*." This was their guiding esthetic.   34

Content

1. How is Marshall justified in calling "ordinary" housewives and mothers "poets"—if they seldom "put pen to paper" (¶ 8), let alone write poetry? Why does Marshall so carefully compare and contrast these "poets in the kitchen" with the conventional appearance and activities of other poets (¶ 7–*passim*)?

2. What are some of the functions of the poets' talk in the kitchen (¶s 19–25)? Are these the same for the speakers as they are for Marshall in

her role as eavesdropping daughter? What particularly memorable types of expressions do they use? Why does Marshall consider these important?

3. What does Marshall mean by referring to her mother and her mother's friends as "the female counterpart of Ralph Ellison's invisible man" (¶ 23)—indeed, they suffered a triple invisibility, being black, female and foreigners" (¶ 23)?

Strategies/Structures

1. This essay is divided into four parts. Show where each begins and ends and how they relate to one another. What part gets the most space and emphasis? Why?

2. Marshall published this work in 1959, some thirty to forty years after the historical events of the Barbadian immigration and the Depression took place. What information does she include here to make sure her readers understand these events (¶s 11–18)?

Language

1. Does Marshall's essay demonstrate the truth of Grace Paley's assertion, "If you say what's on your mind in the language that comes to you from your parents and your street and friends you'll probably say something beautiful" (¶ 5)? If so, how does the essay do this? If not, why not?

2. How is it possible for Marshall and Welty (pp. 29–34), as accomplished adult writers, to write about themselves as little girls without sounding juvenile?

3. Does giving a label, such as "poets in the kitchen," "the Chicago Seven," "the post-Impressionists," "Hell's Angels," identify it, explain it, or restrict its meaning to stereotypes? Does such labeling function differently for different groups?

For Writing

1. Marshall shows that she was concurrently an insider and an outsider in the group on which she was eavesdropping. Write a brief essay in which you demonstrate your dual status as an insider/outsider in a group, and show the effects of this dual status.

2. Pick ten colorful, evocative words or phrases that you and other members of a group (your family, friends, fellow students, coworkers, or others) use. Write these up as dictionary entries: define the terms and explain their use in context (i.e., with one or two examples). If possible, offer an etymology (historical explanation) of how each one originated.

ELIE WIESEL

Wiesel, a survivor of the Holocaust, explains, "For me, literature abolishes the gap between [childhood and death]. . . . Auschwitz marks the decisive, ultimate turning point . . . of the human adventure. Nothing will ever again be as it was. Thousands and thousands of deaths weigh upon every word. How speak of redemption after Treblinka? and how speak of anything else?" As a survivor, he became a writer in order to become a witness: "I believed that, having survived by chance, I was duty-bound to give meaning to my survival, to justify each moment of my life. I knew the story had to be told. Not to transmit an experience is to betray it." Wiesel has developed a literary style that reflects the distilled experience of concentration camps, in which "a sentence is worth a page, a word is worth a sentence. The unspoken weighs heavier than the spoken. . . . Say only the essential—say only what no other would say . . . a style sharp, hard, strong, in a word, pared. Suppress the imagination. And feeling, and philosophy. Speak as a witness on the stand speaks. With no indulgence to others or oneself."

In May 1944, when he was fifteen, Wiesel was forcibly removed from his native town of Sighet, Hungary ("which no longer exists," he says, "except in the memory of those it expelled"), to the first of several concentration camps. Although six million Jews died in the camps, including members of his family, Wiesel was liberated from Buchenwald in April 1945 and sent to Paris, where he studied philosophy. For twenty years "of exploration and apprenticeship" he worked as a journalist for Jewish newspapers, but the turning point in his career as a writer came in 1954 when he met novelist François Mauriac, who urged him to speak on behalf of the children in concentration camps. This encouraged Wiesel (who has lived in New York since 1956) to write some twenty-five books of fiction, nonfiction, poetry, and drama, starting in 1958 with *Night*, which opens, "In the beginning was faith, confidence, illusion." In 1985 Wiesel, who protested President Reagan's visit to the cemetery in Bitburg, Germany, where Nazi SS soldiers are buried, was awarded the Congressional Gold Medal. In 1986 this "messenger to mankind" received the Nobel Peace Prize for his efforts epitomized in "Why I Write: Making No Become Yes," originally published in the *New York Times Book Review*, April 14, 1985.

Why I Write:
Making No Become Yes

1   Why do I write?

2   Perhaps in order not to go mad. Or, on the contrary, to touch the bottom of madness. Like Samuel Beckett, the survivor expresses himself "en désepoir de cause"—out of desperation.

3   Speaking of the solitude of the survivor, the great Yiddish and Hebrew poet and thinker Aaron Zeitlin addresses those—his father, his brother, his friends—who have died and left him: "You have abandoned me," he says to them. "You are together, without me. I am here. Alone. And I make words."

4   So do I, just like him. I also say words, write words, reluctantly.

5   There are easier occupations, far more pleasant ones. But for the survivor, writing is not a profession, but an occupation, a duty. Camus calls it "an honor." As he puts it: "I entered literature through worship." Other writers have said they did so through anger, through love. Speaking for myself, I would say—through silence.

6   It was by seeking, by probing silence that I began to discover the perils and power of the word. I never intended to be a philosopher, or a theologian. The only role I sought was that of witness. I believed that, having survived by chance, I was duty-bound to give meaning to my survival, to justify each moment of my life. I knew the story had to be told. Not to transmit an experience is to betray it. This is what Jewish tradition teaches us. But how to do this? "When Israel is in exile, so is the word," says the Zohar. The word has deserted the meaning it was intended to convey—impossible to make them coincide. The displacement, the shift, is irrevocable.

7   This was never more true than right after the upheaval. We all knew that we could never, never say what had to be said, that we could never express in words, coherent, intelligible words, our experience of madness on an absolute scale. The walk through flaming night, the silence before and after the selection, the monotonous praying of the condemned, the Kaddish of the dying,

the fear and hunger of the sick, the shame and suffering, the haunted eyes, the demented stares. I thought that I would never be able to speak of them. All words seemed inadequate, worn, foolish, lifeless, whereas I wanted them to be searing.

Where was I to discover a fresh vocabulary, a primeval language? The language of night was not human, it was primitive, almost animal—hoarse shouting, screams, muffled moaning, savage howling, the sound of beating. A brute strikes out wildly, a body falls. An officer raises his arm and a whole community walks toward a common grave. A soldier shrugs his shoulders, and a thousand families are torn apart, to be reunited only by death. This was the concentration camp language. It negated all other language and took its place. Rather than a link, it became a wall. Could it be surmounted? Could the reader be brought to the other side? I knew the answer was negative, and yet I knew that "no" had to become "yes." It was the last wish of the dead.

The fear of forgetting remains the main obsession of all those who have passed through the universe of the damned. The enemy counted on people's incredulity and forgetfulness. How could one foil this plot? And if memory grew hollow, empty of substance, what would happen to all we had accumulated along the way? Remember, said the father to his son, and the son to his friend. Gather the names, the faces, the tears. We had all taken an oath: "If, by some miracle, I emerge alive, I will devote my life to testifying on behalf of those whose shadow will fall on mine forever and ever."

That is why I write certain things rather than others—to remain faithful.

Of course, there are times of doubt for the survivor, times when one gives in to weakness, or longs for comfort. I hear a voice within me telling me to stop mourning the past. I too want to sing of love and of its magic. I too want to celebrate the sun, and the dawn that heralds the sun. I would like to shout, and shout loudly: "Listen, listen well! I too am capable of victory, do you hear? I too am open to laughter and joy! I want to stride, head high, my face unguarded, without having to point to the ashes over there on the horizon, without having to tamper with facts to hide their tragic ugliness. For a man born blind, God himself is blind, but look, I see, I am not blind." One feels like shouting this, but the shout changes to a murmur. One must make a choice; one must remain faithful. A big word, I know. Nevertheless, I use it, it suits me. Having written the things I have written, I feel I can afford no longer to play with words. If I say that the writer in me wants to remain loyal, it is because it is true. This sentiment moves all survivors; they owe nothing to anyone, but everything to the dead.

12   I owe them my roots and my memory. I am duty-bound to serve as their emissary, transmitting the history of their disappearance, even if it disturbs, even if it brings pain. Not to do so would be to betray them, and thus myself. And since I am incapable of communicating their cry by shouting, I simply look at them. I see them and I write.

13   While writing, I question them as I question myself. I believe I have said it before, elsewhere. I write to understand as much as to be understood. Will I succeed one day? Wherever one starts, one reaches darkness. God? He remains the God of darkness. Man? The source of darkness. The killers' derision, their victims' tears, the onlookers' indifference, their complicity and complacency—the divine role in all that I do not understand. A million children massacred—I shall never understand.

14   Jewish children—they haunt my writings. I see them again and again. I shall always see them. Hounded, humiliated, bent like the old men who surround them as though to protect them, unable to do so. They are thirsty, the children, and there is no one to give them water. They are hungry, but there is no one to give them a crust of bread. They are afraid, and there is no one to reassure them.

15   They walk in the middle of the road, like vagabonds. They are on the way to the station, and they will never return. In sealed cars, without air or food, they travel toward another world. They guess where they are going, they know it, and they keep silent. Tense, thoughtful, they listen to the wind, the call of death in the distance.

16   All these children, these old people, I see them. I never stop seeing them. I belong to them.

17   But they, to whom do they belong?

18   People tend to think that a murderer weakens when facing a child. The child reawakens the killer's lost humanity. The killer can no longer kill the child before him, the child inside him.

But with us it happened differently. Our Jewish children had   19
no effect upon the killers. Nor upon the world. Nor upon God.

I think of them, I think of their childhood. Their childhood   20
is a small Jewish town, and this town is no more. They frighten
me; they reflect an image of myself, one that I pursue and run
from at the same time—the image of a Jewish adolescent who
knew no fear, except the fear of God, whose faith was whole,
comforting, and not marked by anxiety.

No, I do not understand. And if I write, it is to warn the   21
reader that he will not understand either. "You will not understand, you will never understand," were the words heard everywhere during the reign of night. I can only echo them. You, who
never lived under a sky of blood, will never know what it was
like. Even if you read all the books ever written, even if you listen
to all the testimonies ever given, you will remain on this side of
the wall, you will view the agony and death of a people from afar,
through the screen of a memory that is not your own.

An admission of impotence and guilt? I do not know. All I   22
know is that Treblinka and Auschwitz cannot be told. And yet I
have tried. God knows I have tried.

Have I attempted too much or not enough? Among some   23
twenty-five volumes, only three or four penetrate the phantas-
magoric realm of the dead. In my other books, through my other
books, I have tried to follow other roads. For it is dangerous to
linger among the dead, they hold on to you and you run the risk
of speaking only to them. And so I have forced myself to turn
away from them and study other periods, explore other destinies
and teach other tales—the Bible and the Talmud, Hasidism and
its fervor, the shtetl and its songs, Jerusalem and its echoes, the
Russian Jews and their anguish, their awakening, their courage.
At times, it has seemed to me that I was speaking of other things
with the sole purpose of keeping the essential—the personal experience—unspoken. At times I have wondered: And what if I
was wrong? Perhaps I should not have heeded my own advice
and stayed in my own world with the dead.

But then, I have not forgotten the dead. They have their right-   24
ful place even in the works about the Hasidic capitals Ruzhany
and Korets, and Jerusalem. Even in my biblical and Midrashic
tales, I pursue their presence, mute and motionless. The presence

of the dead then beckons in such tangible ways that it affects even the most removed characters. Thus they appear on Mount Moriah, where Abraham is about to sacrifice his son, a burnt offering to their common God. They appear on Mount Nebo, where Moses enters solitude and death. They appear in Hasidic and Talmudic legends in which victims forever need defending against forces that would crush them. Technically, so to speak, they are of course elsewhere, in time and space, but on a deeper, truer plane, the dead are part of every story, of every scene.

25   "But what is the connection?" you will ask. Believe me, there is one. After Auschwitz everything brings us back to Auschwitz. When I speak of Abraham, Isaac and Jacob, when I invoke Rabbi Yohanan ben Zakkai and Rabbi Akiba, it is the better to understand them in the light of Auschwitz. As for the Maggid of Mezeritch and his disciples, it is in order to encounter the followers of their followers that I reconstruct their spellbound, spellbinding universe. I like to imagine them alive, exuberant, celebrating life and hope. Their happiness is as necessary to me as it was once to themselves.

26   And yet—how did they manage to keep their faith intact? How did they manage to sing as they went to meet the Angel of Death? I know Hasidim who never vacillated—I respect their strength. I know others who chose rebellion, protest, rage—I respect their courage. For there comes a time when only those who do not believe in God will not cry out to him in wrath and anguish.

27   Do not judge either group. Even the heroes perished as martyrs, even the martyrs died as heroes. Who would dare oppose knives to prayers? The faith of some matters as much as the strength of others. It is not ours to judge, it is only ours to tell the tale.

28   But where is one to begin? Whom is one to include? One meets a Hasid in all my novels. And a child. And an old man. And a beggar. And a madman. They are all part of my inner landscape. The reason why? Pursued and persecuted by the killers, I offer them shelter. The enemy wanted to create a society purged of their presence, and I have brought some of them back. The world denied them, repudiated them, so I let them live at least within the feverish dreams of my characters.

29   It is for them that I write, and yet the survivor may experience remorse. He has tried to bear witness; it was all in vain.

After the liberation, we had illusions. We were convinced ₃₀
that a new world would be built upon the ruins of Europe. A new
civilization would see the light. No more wars, no more hate, no
more intolerance, no fanaticism. And all this because the witnesses would speak. And speak they did, to no avail.

They will continue, for they cannot do otherwise. When ₃₁
man, in his grief, falls silent, Goethe says, then God gives him the
strength to sing his sorrows. From that moment on, he may no
longer choose not to sing, whether his song is heard or not. What
matters is to struggle against silence with words, or through another form of silence. What matters is to gather a smile here and
there, a tear here and there, a word here and there, and thus justify the faith placed in you, a long time ago, by so many victims.

Why do I write? To wrench those victims from oblivion. To ₃₂
help the dead vanquish death.

(Translated from the French by Rosette C. Lamont)

Content

1. Wiesel says, "The only role I sought [as a writer] was that of witness" (¶ 6). What does he mean by "witness"? Find examples of this role
throughout the essay.
2. What does Wiesel mean by "not to transmit an experience is to betray it" (¶ 6)? What experience does his writing transmit? Why is this
important to Wiesel? To humanity?
3. Does "Why I Write" fulfill Wiesel's commitment to "make no become yes" (¶ 8)? Explain.

Strategies/Structures

1. Identify some of Wiesel's major ethical appeals in this essay. Does he
want to move his readers to action as well as to thought?
2. Why would Wiesel use paradoxes in an effort to explain and clarify?
Explain the meaning of the following paradoxes:
    a. "No, I do not understand. And if I write, it is to warn the reader
        that he will not understand either" (¶ 21).
    b. I write "to help the dead vanquish death" (¶ 32).
3. For what audience does Wiesel want to explain "Why I Write"?
What understanding of Judaism does Wiesel expect his readers to have?
Of World War II? Of the operation of concentration camps? Why does he

expect his reasons to matter to these readers, whether or not they have extensive knowledge of any of them?

Language

1. Does Wiesel's style here fulfill his goals of a style that is "sharp, hard, strong, pared"? Why is such a style appropriate to the subject?
2. Explain the meaning of "concentration camp language" (¶ 8). Why did it negate all other language and take its place (¶ 8)?

For Writing

1. Write an essay for someone who doesn't like to write comparing Elie Wiesel's and Amy Tan's reasons for writing as expressed in their essays "Why I Write" (pp. 51–57) and "Mother Tongue" (pp. 21–28).
2. Write an essay exploring for yourself how you know when you get ideas that are interesting or otherwise compelling enough to write about. If you're devoid of ideas, what are some ways you might go about getting some? In addition to the essays by White and Wiesel, consider the essay by Marshall in Chapter 2, the essays by Elbow and Least Heat-Moon in Chapter 3, and the Writers' Notebooks (pp. 90–100).

3 | *Getting Started*

To expect some people to learn to write by showing them a published essay or book is like expecting novice bakers to learn to make a wedding cake from looking at the completed confection, resplendent with icing and decorations. Indeed, the completed product in each case offers a model of what the finished work of art should look like—in concept, organization, shape, and style. Careful examination of the text exposes the intricacies of the finished sentences, paragraphs, logic, illustrative examples, and nuances of style. The text likewise provides cues about the context (intellectual, political, aesthetic . . .) in which it originated, its purpose, and its intended audience. But no matter how hard you look, it's almost impossible to detect in a completed, professionally polished work much about the process by which it was composed— the numerous visions and revisions of ideas and expression; the effort, frustration, even exhilaration. Blood, sweat, and tears don't belong on the printed page any more than they belong in the gymnast's flawless public performance on the balance beam. The audience doesn't want to agonize over the production but to enjoy the result.

Becoming a Writer

You've been training to become a writer all your life. Whether you want to become a professional writer or merely to write well enough to survive in college or on the job, your senses (particularly of sight and hearing) were functioning—even before you could interpret and understand in words the stimuli they conveyed. Indeed, the three sections of Eudora Welty's *One Writer's*

Beginnings focus on the topics "Listening" (excerpted on pp. 29–34), "Learning to See," and "Finding a Voice." Paule Marshall's "The Making of a Writer" (pp. 42–49) reinforces Welty's emphasis on how important listening is to a writer's development, not just to the words but to the music, literal and figurative. The precise and colorful language of Marshall's mother and her friends, in such expressions as "'God don' love ugly and He ain' stuck on pretty,'" gave these working-class, immigrant black women visibility, control over their lives, and the chance to think and to be creative.

Getting started for many people is the most difficult part of writing. It's hard to begin if you don't know what to write about. Starting to write may be especially difficult if you put it off until the last minute, when you're tired or under pressure to produce something good in a hurry. Writing freely, explains Peter Elbow in "Freewriting" (pp. 69–73), can help writers to find something to say and the "voice"—a natural sound, texture, and rhythm—in which to say it. Making "A List of Nothing in Particular" (pp. 74–78), as William Least Heat-Moon did when he drove his van through the "barren waste" of west Texas on a circuit of the country, can enable one to extract some meaning, some significance even out of a territory where "'there's nothing out there.'" His list ranges from "mockingbird" to "jackrabbit (chewed on cactus)" to "wind (always)." Talking with others, making an "idea tree," brainstorming, reading, thinking—even dreaming or daydreaming—all of these can provide you with something to write about, if you remain receptive to the possibilities.

Writers' Notebooks

Keeping a writer's diary or notebook, whether you do it with pencil, pen, typewriter, or word processor, can be a good way to get started—and even to keep going. Writing regularly—and better yet, at a regular time of the day or week—in a notebook or its equivalent, as Mark Twain did throughout the fifty-five years of his adult life, beginning long before he became a professional writer, can give you a lot to think about while you're writing, and a lot to expand on later. You could keep an account of what you do every day (6:30–7:30, swimming laps, shower; 7:30–8:15, break-

fast—toasted English muffin, orange juice, raspberry yogurt. . .),
but if your life is routine that might get monotonous.

The notebook entries included in this section were written in
a variety of circumstances. Twain made the entries "Aboard a
Mississippi River Steamboat" (pp. 80–87) during the nostalgic trip
he took in 1882 in preparation for expanding the seven in-
stallments of *Old Times on the Mississippi* into *Life on the Mississippi*
(1883). "Selections from Student Writers' Notebooks" (pp. 90–100)
met not only course requirements but were also obviously outlets
for many types of expressions and explorations ranging from the
meaning of education, race, and sexuality to the importance of
family, music, an ordered environment, and writing. "Sylvia Plath
at Seventeen" (pp. 88–90) revealed to herself what she could not
tell the world.

A provocative and potentially useful writer's notebook might
contain any or all of the following types of writing, and more:

- Reactions to one's reading: "I should pick up *Mansfield Park*
  again. Reading Austen or anyone that good reminds me of
  what I could be saying, and of the work that has to be put
  into it" (Loftus, p. 91).
- Provocative quotations—invented, read, or overheard; appealing figures of speech; dialogue, dialect: " 'They have
  Irish whiskey [in Ireland]. . . . But I don't use much mesilf
  [sic]. I am not a hard drinker, sir. Give an Irishman lager
  beer for one month and he's a dead man. An Irishman is
  lined inside with copper and the lager beer corrodes it"
  (Twain, pp. 82–83).
- Lists—including sights, sounds, scents: "On one wall [of
  the living room] was a dart board with no darts and the
  wall behind pocked with holes. The lining had been torn
  from the bottom of a yellow Chippendale sofa and stuffing
  poked through. . . On the carpet . . . was a bowl of milk with
  Cheerios floating" (King, p. 96).
- Memorable details—of clothing, animals, objects, settings,
  phenomena, processes: "The camp seems loudest at night. A
  huge, dulled murmur flows up from the valleys with hacking, rattling coughs, unending moaning like mantras, mules
  braying, wails, and shrieks like a child stepped on a nail.

Clank tap-tapping, metal pots clanking and wood chopping sounds but no sounds of laughter" (Ryan, p. 99).

- Personal aspirations, fears, joy, anger: "I am afraid of getting older. I am afraid of getting married. Spare me . . . from the relentless cage of routine and rote. I want to be free" (Plath, p. 89).
- Sketches of people, either intrinsically interesting or engaged in intriguing activities, whether novel or familiar: "One of the 3 mates on this boat is of the ancient tribe. He is one of the old-fashioned, God-damn-your-soul kind. Very affable and sociable. . . . (This man talks like the machine Barnum had around with his circus for a while. Has that same guttural indistinct, jumbling, rasping way of talking. But this mate can out-swear the machine)" (Twain, p. 84).
- Analyses of friendships, family relationships: "My parents are getting divorced. . . . We did not put up a [Christmas] tree. . . . This year [since dad was gone] mom said we could eat when we wanted. But we never did. I ate a beans n franks dinner [by myself]. My brother went to drink his gift certificate" (Weast, pp. 95–96).
- Commentary on notable events, current or past, national or more immediate: "In California thongs are still Nipper Flippers or Jap Slaps. . . . December seventh is the Ides of March. I'm asked how I can see, is my field of vision narrowed?" (Watanabe, p. 99).
- Possibilities for adventure, exploration, conflict: "Today in class Dudley said he's 'tired of racial issues in class.' Well— if he's tired of them, how does he think I feel? For years I have been the only Black (or at most one of two or three) in class and I have had to deal with white negativism towards Blacks" (Coles, p. 97).
- Jokes, anecdotes, and humorous situations, characters, comic mannerisms, punch lines, provocative settings: "Stopped at Arkansas City April 24. This is a Hell of a place. One or two streets full of mud; 19 different stenches at the same time. A thriving place nevertheless" (Twain, p. 87).

You'll need to put enough explanatory details in your notebook to remind yourself three weeks—or three years—later what something meant when you wrote it down, as the notebook keepers here have done. As all of these notebook entries reveal, those of "Sylvia Plath at Seventeen" (pp. 88–90) and other student writers in particular, in a writer's notebook you can be most candid, most off guard, for there you're writing primarily for yourself. You're also writing for yourself when you're freewriting—writing rapidly, with or without a particular subject, without editing, while you're in the process of generating ideas. As you freewrite you can free-associate, thinking of connections among like and unlike things or ideas, exploring their implications. Anything goes into the notebook, but not everything stays in later drafts if you decide to turn some of your most focused discussion into an essay. If you get into the habit of writing regularly on paper, you may find that you're also hearing the "voices in your head" that professional writers often experience. As James Thurber explained to an interviewer, "I never quite know when I'm not writing. Sometimes my wife comes up to me at a party and says, 'Dammit, Thurber, stop writing.' Or my daughter will look up from the dinner table and ask, 'Is he sick?' 'No,' my wife says, 'he's writing something.'"

Playing around with words and ideas in a notebook or in your head can also lead to an entire essay: a narrative, character sketch, reminiscence, discussion of how to do it, an argument, review, or some other form suitable for an extended piece of writing. After several drafts (pp. 121–128), Mary Ruffin's evocative portrait of her mother, who died when Mary was thirteen, emerged from fragments in her writer's notebook to become the polished "Mama's Smoke" (pp. 128–132), sophisticated in concept and techniques.

No matter what you write about, rereading a notebook entry or a freewriting can provide some material to start with. Ask yourself, "What do I want to write about?" "What makes me particularly happy—or angry?" (Don't write about something that seems bland, like a cookie without sugar. If it doesn't appeal to you, it won't attract your readers either.) As you write you will almost automatically be using description, narration, comparison and contrast, and other rhetorical techniques to express yourself, even if you don't attach labels to them. Enjoy.

LINDA HOGAN

Hogan is a Chickasaw born in Denver in 1947. She earned an M.A. at the University of Colorado, Boulder, in 1978 and was a professor of American and American Indian studies at the University of Minnesota before joining the faculty of the University of Colorado. Her reputation as a poet is based on six volumes, the most recent of which is *Book of Medicines* (1993). Hogan's fourth poetry collection, *Seeing Through the Sun* (1985), received an American Book Award. She has also published short stories and two novels, *Mean Spirit* (1990) and *Solar Storms* (1995).

Hogan says of her work, "My writing comes from and goes back to . . . both the human and the global community. I am interested in the deepest questions, those of spirit, of shelter, of growth and movement toward peace and liberation, inner and outer." That Hogan is also an ardent conservationist is clear from "Hearing Voices," which amplifies these views. Here she emphasizes how important it is to listen, as Indians do, to the literal "language of this continent," the stories of this earth, "the stones giving guidance, the trees singing, the corn telling of inner earth, the dragonfly offering up a tongue."

Hearing Voices

1   When Barbara McClintock was awarded a Nobel Prize for her work on gene transposition in corn plants, the most striking thing about her was that she made her discoveries by listening to what the corn spoke to her, by respecting the life of the corn and "letting it come."

2   McClintock says she learned "the stories" of the plants. She "heard" them. She watched the daily green journeys of growth from earth toward sky and sun. She knew her plants in the way a healer or mystic would have known them, from the inside, the inner voices of corn and woman speaking to one another.

3   As an Indian woman, I come from a long history of people who have listened to the language of this continent, people who have known that corn grows with the songs and prayers of the

people, that it has a story to tell, that the world is alive. Both in oral traditions and in mythology—the true language of inner life—account after account tells of the stones giving guidance, the trees singing, the corn telling of inner earth, the dragonfly offering up a tongue. This is true in the European traditions as well: Psyche received direction from the reeds and the ants, Orpheus knew the languages of earth, animals, and birds.

This intuitive and common language is what I seek for my   4
writing, work in touch with the mystery and force of life, work that speaks a few of the many voices around us, and it is important to me that McClintock listened to the voices of corn. It is important to the continuance of life that she told the truth of her method and that it reminded us all of where our strength, our knowing, and our sustenance come from.

It is also poetry, this science, and I note how often scientific   5
theories lead to the world of poetry and vision, theories telling us how atoms that were stars have been transformed into our living, breathing bodies. And in these theories, or maybe they should be called stories, we begin to understand how we are each many people, including the stars we once were, and how we are in essence the earth and the universe, how what we do travels clear around the earth and returns. In a single moment of our living, there is our ancestral and personal history, our future, even our deaths planted in us and already growing toward their fulfillment. The corn plants are there, and like all the rest we are forever merging our borders with theirs in the world collective.

Our very lives might depend on this listening. In the Cher-   6
nobyl nuclear accident, the wind told the story that was being suppressed by the people. It gave away the truth. It carried the story of danger to other countries. It was a poet, a prophet, a scientist.

Sometimes, like the wind, poetry has its own laws speaking   7
for the life of the planet. It is a language that wants to bring back together what the other words have torn apart. It is the language of life speaking through us about the sacredness of life.

This life speaking life is what I find so compelling about the   8
work of poets such as Ernesto Cardenal, who is also a priest and was the Nicaraguan Minister of Culture. He writes: "The armadilloes are very happy with this government. . . . Not only humans desired liberation/the whole ecology wanted it." Cardenal has

also written "The Parrots," a poem about caged birds who were being sent to the United States as pets for the wealthy, how the cages were opened, the parrots allowed back into the mountains and jungles, freed like the people, "and sent back to the land we were pulled from."

9   How we have been pulled from the land! And how poetry has worked hard to set us free, uncage us, keep us from split tongues that mimic the voices of our captors. It returns us to our land. Poetry is a string of words that parades without a permit. It is a lockbox of words to put an ear to as we try to crack the safe of language, listening for the right combination, the treasure inside. It is life resonating. It is sometimes called Prayer, Soothsaying, Complaint, Invocation, Proclamation, Testimony, Witness. Writing is and does all these things. And like that parade, it is illegitimately insistent on going its own way, on being part of the miracle of life, telling the story about what happened when we were cosmic dust, what it means to be stars listening to our human atoms.

10   But don't misunderstand me. I am not just a dreamer. I am also the practical type. A friend's father, watching the United States stage another revolution in another Third World country, said, "Why doesn't the government just feed people and then let the political chips fall where they may?" He was right. It was easy, obvious, even financially more reasonable to do that, to let democracy be chosen because it feeds hunger. I want my writing to be that simple, that clear and direct. Likewise, I feel it is not enough for me just to write, but I need to live it, to be informed by it. I have found over the years that my work has more courage than I do. It has more wisdom. It teaches me, leads me places I never knew I was heading. And it is about a new way of living, of being in the world.

11   I was on a panel recently where the question was raised whether we thought literature could save lives. The audience, book people, smiled expectantly with the thought. I wanted to say, Yes, it saves lives. But I couldn't speak those words. It saves spirits maybe, hearts. It changes minds, but for me writing is an incredible privilege. When I sit down at the desk, there are other women who are hungry, homeless. I don't want to forget that, that the world of matter is still there to be reckoned with. This writing

is a form of freedom most other people do not have. So, when I write, I feel a responsibility, a commitment to other humans and to the animal and plant communities as well.

Still, writing has changed me. And there is the powerful need we all have to tell a story, each of us with a piece of the whole pattern to complete. As Alice Walker says, We are all telling part of the same story, and as Sharon Olds has said, Every writer is a cell on the body politic of America.

Another Nobel Prize laureate is Betty William, a Northern Ireland co-winner of the 1977 Peace Prize. I heard her speak about how, after witnessing the death of children, she stepped outside in the middle of the night and began knocking on doors and yelling, behaviors that would have earned her a diagnosis of hysteria in our own medical circles. She knocked on doors that might have opened with weapons pointing in her face, and she cried out, "What kind of people have we become that we would allow children to be killed on our streets?" Within four hours the city was awake, and there were sixteen thousand names on petitions for peace. Now, that woman's work is a lesson to those of us who deal with language, and to those of us who are dealt into silence. She used language to begin the process of peace. This is the living, breathing power of the word. It is poetry. So are the names of those who signed the petitions. Maybe it is this kind of language that saves lives.

Writing begins for me with survival, with life and with freeing life, saving life, speaking life. It is work that speaks what can't be easily said. It originates from a compelling desire to live and be alive. For me, it is sometimes the need to speak for other forms of life, to take the side of human life, even our sometimes frivolous living, and our grief-filled living, our joyous living, our violent living, busy living, our peaceful living. It is about possibility. It is based in the world of matter. I am interested in how something small turns into an image that is large and strong with resonance, where the ordinary becomes beautiful. I believe the divine, the magic, is here in the weeds at our feet, unacknowledged. What a world this is. Where else could water rise up to the sky, turn into snow crystals, magnificently brought together, fall from the sky all around us, pile up billions deep, and catch the small sparks of sunlight as they return again to water?

15   These acts of magic happen all the time; in Chaco Canyon, my sister has seen a kiva, a ceremonial room in the earth, that is in the center of the canyon. This place has been uninhabited for what seems like forever. It has been without water. In fact, there are theories that the ancient people disappeared when they journeyed after water. In the center of it a corn plant was growing. It was all alone and it had been there since the ancient ones, the old ones who came before us all, those people who wove dog hair into belts, who witnessed the painting of flute players on the seeping canyon walls, who knew the stories of corn. And there was one corn plant growing out of the holy place. It planted itself yearly. With no water, no person to care for it, no overturning of the soil, this corn plant rises up to tell its story, and that's what this poetry is.

Content

1. What does Hogan mean by "the language of this continent" (¶ 3)? Even if we listen intently, respectfully, how can we be sure that what we're hearing is "the true language of inner life" (¶ 3)? How can we understand—and interpret—what we hear?

2. How can a person's writing "have more wisdom" than the writer? Hogan says her writing "teaches me, leads me places I never knew I was heading" (¶ 10)? How does this process work for Hogan? How might it work for you?

3. "We are all telling part of the same story," says Hogan, quoting Alice Walker with approval (¶ 12). What is that story?

4. Why does Hogan associate writing with "survival, with life and with freeing life, saving life" (¶ 14)?

Strategies/Structures

1. Why does Hogan begin with the illustration of Barbara McClintock, who made her Nobel prize–winning discoveries "by listening to what the corn spoke to her" (¶ 1)? Where else does Hogan use the corn plant in this essay? Why does she conclude with the image of the solitary corn plant, "growing out of the holy place," without water or cultivation (¶ 15)?

2. How do these concrete illustrations help to explain the intuitive process of writing poetry (see especially ¶ 15)?

Language

1. What does Hogan mean by the metaphors she uses to define poetry, as "a string of words that parades without a permit," "a lockbox of words to put an ear to as we try to crack the safe of language," "life resonating" (¶ 9)?

2. Hogan says she seeks "intuitive and common language" (¶ 4) that is "simple," "clear," "direct" (¶ 10). How does she define these terms? Do your definitions agree with hers? Has she written "Hearing Voices" in the language she values?

For Writing

1. Select an object or an experience that symbolizes the meaning of something very important to you, such as life, freedom, writing, truth, or justice. Describe the object or explain the experience, interpreting it to make clear the connection between its concrete and symbolic meanings.

2. Have you ever heard a life-saving story, told either through words or through indirect means, such as the wind that spread the story of the Chernobyl nuclear disaster (¶ 6)? If so, tell that story, either orally or in writing, to a group of your peers—who will, in turn, share their stories with you. Or, tell the story out loud first, get feedback and answer questions from your audience; then write the story in a way that accommodates both your initial and more recent understanding of its significance.

PETER ELBOW

Elbow was born in New York in 1935 and educated at Williams College, Oxford, Harvard, and Brandeis. Known for his innovative methods of teaching writing, Elbow has taught and directed writing programs at the Massachusetts Institute of Technology, Evergreen State College, SUNY–Stony Brook, and the University of Massachusetts–Amherst. Elbow's philosophy of writing is explained in two well-regarded books, *Writing without Teachers* (1973) and *Writing with Power* (1981), intended to help people teach themselves how to write with ease, control, and confidence. He consistently advocates clear, unpretentious writing that pleases not only readers, but the writers themselves.

In "Freewriting," from *Writing without Teachers,* Elbow explains to his intended readers, writing students and their teachers, that a writer's "only source of power" is his or her "voice"— a natural sound, texture, and rhythm "that will make a reader listen." Writing freely, without editing prematurely, can help the writer find that voice. Try it.

Freewriting[1]

1   The most effective way I know to improve your writing is to do freewriting exercises regularly. At least three times a week. They are sometimes called "automatic writing," "babbling," or "jabbering" exercises. The idea is simply to write for ten minutes (later on, perhaps fifteen or twenty). Don't stop for anything. Go quickly without rushing. Never stop to look back, to cross something out, to wonder how to spell something, to wonder what word or thought to use, or to think about what you are doing. If you can't think of a word or a spelling, just use a squiggle or else write, "I can't think of it." Just put down something. The easiest thing is just to put down whatever is in your mind. If you get stuck it's fine to write "I can't think what to say, I can't think what to say" as many times as you want; or to repeat the last word you wrote over and over again; or anything else. The only requirement is that you *never* stop.

2   What happens to a freewriting exercise is important. It must be a piece of writing which, even if someone reads it, doesn't send any ripples back to you. It is like writing something and putting it in a bottle in the sea. The teacherless class helps your writing by providing maximum feedback. Freewritings help you by providing no feedback at all. When I assign one, I invite the writer to let me read it. But I also tell him to keep it if he prefers. I read it quickly and make no comments at all and I do not speak with him about it. The main thing is that a freewriting must never be evaluated in any way; in fact there must be no discussion or comment at all.

---

[1] Title supplied.

Here is an example of a fairly coherent exercise (sometimes 3
they are very incoherent, which is fine):

> I think I'll write what's on my mind, but the only thing on
> my mind right now is what to write for ten minutes. I've
> never done this before and I'm not prepared in any way—
> the sky is cloudy today, how's that? now I'm afraid I won't
> be able to think of what to write when I get to the end of
> the sentence—well, here I am at the end of the sentence—
> here I am again, again, again, at least I'm still writing—
> Now I ask is there some reason to be happy that I'm still
> writing—ah yes! Here comes the question again—What am
> I getting out of this? What point is there in it? It's almost
> obscene to always ask it but I seem to question everything
> that way and I was gonna say something else pertaining
> to that but I got so busy writing down the first part that I
> forgot what I was leading into. This is kind of fun oh don't
> stop writing—cars and trucks speeding by somewhere out
> the window, pens clittering across peoples' papers. The sky
> is still cloudy—is it symbolic that I should be mentioning
> it? Huh? I dunno. Maybe I should try colors, blue, red,
> dirty words—wait a minute—no can't do that, orange,
> yellow, arm tired, green pink violet magenta lavender red
> brown black green—now that I can't think of any more
> colors—just about done—relief? maybe.

Freewriting may seem crazy but actually it makes simple 4
sense. Think of the difference between speaking and writing.
Writing has the advantage of permitting more editing. But that's
its downfall too. Almost everybody interposes a massive and
complicated series of editings between the time words start to be
born into consciousness and when they finally come off the end
of the pencil or typewriter onto the page. This is partly because
schooling makes us obsessed with the "mistakes" we make in
writing. Many people are constantly thinking about spelling and
grammar as they try to write. I am always thinking about the
awkwardness, wordiness, and general mushiness of my natural
verbal product as I try to write down words.

But it's not just "mistakes" or "bad writing" we edit as we 5
write. We also edit unacceptable thoughts and feelings, as we do

in speaking. In writing there is more time to do it so the editing is heavier: when speaking, there's someone right there waiting for a reply and he'll get bored or think we're crazy if we don't come out with *something*. Most of the time in speaking, we settle for the catch-as-catch-can way in which the words tumble out. In writing, however, there's a chance to try to get them right. But the opportunity to get them right is a terrible burden: you can work for two hours trying to get a paragraph "right" and discover it's not right at all. And then give up.

6   Editing, *in itself,* is not the problem. Editing is usually necessary if we want to end up with something satisfactory. The problem is that editing goes on *at the same time* as producing. The editor is, as it were, constantly looking over the shoulder of the producer and constantly fiddling with what he's doing while he's in the middle of trying to do it. No wonder the producer gets nervous, jumpy, inhibited, and finally can't be coherent. It's an unnecessary burden to try to think of words and also worry at the same time whether they're the right words.

7   The main thing about freewriting is that it is *nonediting*. It is an exercise in bringing together the process of producing words and putting them down on the page. Practiced regularly, it undoes the ingrained habit of editing at the same time you are trying to produce. It will make writing less blocked because words will come more easily. You will use up more paper, but chew up fewer pencils.

8   Next time you write, notice how often you stop yourself from writing down something you were going to write down. Or else cross it out after it's written. "Naturally," you say, "it wasn't any good." But think for a moment about the occasions when you spoke well. Seldom was it because you first got the beginning just right. Usually it was a matter of a halting or even garbled beginning, but you kept going and your speech finally became coherent and even powerful. There is a lesson here for writing: trying to get the beginning just right is a formula for failure—and probably a secret tactic to make yourself give up writing. Make some words, whatever they are, and then grab hold of that line and reel in as hard as you can. Afterwards you can throw away lousy beginnings and make new ones. This is the quickest way to get into good writing.

The habit of compulsive, premature editing doesn't just 9 make writing hard. It also makes writing dead. Your voice is damped out by all the interruptions, changes, and hesitations between the consciousness and the page. In your natural way of producing words there is a sound, a texture, a rhythm—a voice—which is the main source of power in your writing. I don't know how it works, but this voice is the force that will make a reader listen to you, the energy that drives the meanings through his thick skull. Maybe you don't *like* your voice; maybe people have made fun of it. But it's the only voice you've got. It's your only source of power. You better get back into it, no matter what you think of it. If you keep writing in it, it may change into something you like better. But if you abandon it, you'll likely never have a voice and never be heard.

Freewritings are vacuums. Gradually you will begin to 10 carry over into your regular writing some of the voice, force, and connectedness that creep into those vacuums.

Content

1. What is freewriting (¶ 1)? What does Elbow recommend if the writer gets stuck or can't think of anything to write about?
2. What differences does Elbow find between the process of speaking and the process of writing (¶s 4, 5)?
3. Elbow identifies "compulsive, premature editing" as the main inhibitor of good writing (¶ 9). What does he mean by this? Do you think he's right? What other factors might inhibit you or others from writing well?
4. What does Elbow mean by "voice" (¶ 9)? How can you identify your natural voice in writing?
5. What advice does Elbow give for writing good introductory sentences and paragraphs (¶ 8)?

Strategies/Structures

1. Does Elbow's example of freewriting (¶ 3) make his point clearly? Does it resemble any freewriting you might have tried?
2. For what audience is "Freewriting" intended? Identify some words or phrases that Elbow uses to give confidence to his readers.
3. Why does Elbow use the simile that freewriting "is like writing something and putting it in a bottle in the sea" (¶ 2)?

Language

1. What is the tone of Elbow's "Freewriting"? How does this reinforce the relationship he is trying to establish with his readers?
2. Why doesn't Elbow define "editing" (¶ 6)? Is Elbow's meaning apparent in context? When you edit your writing, what do you do?

For Writing

Try freewriting for ten or fifteen minutes every day for a week, following Elbow's guidelines. Experiment by writing at different times of the day or evening and in different settings (such as your room, or the library) to determine under what circumstances it's easiest for you to write. Does the writing become easier as the week goes on? Does it become more focused? More interesting? Could any of your daily writings be expanded into essays, stories, or poetry? How can freewriting help you with the types of writing that you usually do? Is it more useful for some types than for others?

WILLIAM LEAST HEAT-MOON

William Least Heat-Moon, as William Trogdon renamed himself to acknowledge his Osage Indian ancestry, was born in 1939 in Kansas City, Missouri. He earned four degrees from the University of Missouri–Columbia, including a B.A. in photojournalism (1978), and a Ph.D. in literature (1973). His most recent book is *PrairyErth* (1991). On one cold day in February, 1979, "a day of canceled expectations," Least Heat-Moon lost both his wife ("the Cherokee") and his part-time job teaching English at a Missouri college.

True to the American tradition, to escape he took to the road, the "blue highways"—back roads on the old road maps—in the van that would be home as he circled the United States clockwise "in search of places where change did not mean ruin and where time and men and deeds connected." His account of his trip, *Blue Highways* (1982), is an intimate exploration of America's small towns, "Remote, Oregon; Simplicity, Virginia; New Freedom,

Pennsylvania; New Hope, Tennessee; Why, Arizona; Whynot, Mississippi; Igo, California (just down the road from Ono). . . ." Though he tried to lose himself as a stranger in a strange land, as he came to know and appreciate the country through its back roads and small towns, Least Heat-Moon came inevitably to know and come to terms with himself. "The mere listing of details meaningless in themselves, at once provides them with significance which one denies in vain," says novelist Steven Millhauser. "The beauty of irrelevance fades away, accident darkens into design." Consequently, traveling—moving along a linear route—lends itself to list making, a good way to impose design on happenstance, to remember where you're going, where you've been, whom you've met, what you've seen or done.

A List of Nothing in Particular

S traight as a chief's countenance, the road lay ahead, curves so   1
long and gradual as to be imperceptible except on the map. For nearly a hundred miles due west of Eldorado, not a single town. It was the Texas some people see as barren waste when they cross it, the part they later describe at the motel bar as "nothing." They say, "There's nothing out there."

Driving through the miles of nothing, I decided to test the   2
hypothesis and stopped somewhere in western Crockett County on the top of a broad mesa, just off Texas 29. At a distance, the land looked so rocky and dry, a religious man could believe that the First Hand never got around to the creation in here. Still, somebody had decided to string barbed wire around it.

No plant grew higher than my head. For a while, I heard   3
only miles of wind against the Ghost; but after the ringing in my ears stopped, I heard myself breathing, then a bird note, an answering call, another kind of birdsong, and another: mocking-bird, mourning dove, an enigma. I heard the high zizz of flies the color of gray flannel and the deep buzz of a blue bumblebee. I made a list of nothing in particular:

 1. mockingbird
 2. mourning dove
 3. enigma bird (heard not saw)
 4. gray flies
 5. blue bumblebee
 6. two circling buzzards (not yet, boys)
 7. orange ants
 8. black ants
 9. orange-black ants (what's been going on?)
10. three species of spiders
11. opossum skull
12. jackrabbit (chewed on cactus)
13. deer (left scat)
14. coyote (left tracks)
15. small rodent (den full of seed hulls under rock)
16. snake (skin hooked on cactus spine)
17. prickly pear cactus (yellow blossoms)
18. hedgehog cactus (orange blossoms)
19. barrel cactus (red blossoms)
20. devil's pin cushion (no blossoms)
21. catclaw (no better name)
22. two species of grass (neither green, both alive)
23. yellow flowers (blossoms smaller than peppercorns)
24. sage (indicates alkali-free soil)
25. mesquite (three-foot plants with eighty-foot roots to reach water that fell as rain two thousand years ago)
26. greasewood (oh, yes)
27. joint fir (steeped stems make Brigham Young tea)
28. earth
29. sky
30. wind (always)

That was all the nothing I could identify then, but had I waited until dark when the desert really comes to life, I could have done better. To say nothing is out here is incorrect; to say the desert is stingy with everything except space and light, stone and earth is closer to the truth.

I drove on. The low sun turned the mesa rimrock to silhouettes, angular and weird and unearthly; had someone said the far side of Saturn looked just like this, I would have believed him.

The road dropped to the Pecos River, now dammed to such docility I couldn't imagine it formerly demarking the western edge of a rudimentary white civilization. Even the old wagonmen felt the unease of isolation when they crossed the Pecos, a small but once serious river that has had many names: Rio de las Vacas (River of Cows—perhaps a reference to bison), Rio Salado (Salty River), Rio Puerco (Dirty River).

West of the Pecos, a strangely truncated cone rose from the valley. In the oblique evening light, its silhouette looked like a Mayan temple, so perfect was its symmetry. I stopped again, started climbing, stirring a panic of lizards on the way up. From the top, the rubbled land below—veined with the highway and arroyos, topographical relief absorbed in the dusk—looked like a roadmap.

The desert, more than any other terrain, shows its age, shows time because so little vegetation covers the ancient erosion of wind and storm. What appears is tawny grit once stone and stone crumbling to grit. Everywhere rock, earth's oldest thing. Even desert creatures come from a time older than the woodland animals, and they, in answer to the arduousness, have retained prehistoric coverings of chitin and lapped scale and primitive defenses of spine and stinger, fang and poison, shell and claw.

The night, taking up the shadows and details, wiped the face of the desert into a simple, uncluttered blackness until there were only three things: land, wind, stars. I was there too, but my presence I felt more than saw. It was as if I had been reduced to mind, to an edge of consciousness. Men, ascetics, in all eras have gone into deserts to lose themselves—Jesus, Saint Anthony, Saint Basil, and numberless medicine men—maybe because such a losing happens almost as a matter of course here if you avail yourself. The Sioux once chanted, "All over the sky a sacred voice is calling."

Back to the highway, on with the headlamps, down Six Shooter Draw. In the darkness, deer, just shadows in the lights, began moving toward the desert willows in the wet bottoms. Stephen Vincent Benét:

> *When Daniel Boone goes by, at night,*
> *The phantom deer arise*
> *And all lost, wild America*
> *Is burning in their eyes.*

9   From the top of another high mesa: twelve miles west in the flat valley floor, the lights of Fort Stockton blinked white, blue, red, and yellow in the heat like a mirage. How is it that desert towns look so fine and big at night? It must be that little is hidden. The glistening ahead could have been a golden city of Cibola. But the reality of Fort Stockton was plywood and concrete block and the plastic signs of Holiday Inn and Mobil Oil.

10   The desert had given me an appetite that would have made carrion crow stuffed with saltbush taste good. I found a Mexican cafe of adobe, with a whitewashed log ceiling, creekstone fireplace, and jukebox pumping out mariachi music. It was like a bunkhouse. I ate burritos, chile rellenos, and pinto beans, all ladled over with a fine, incendiary sauce the color of sludge from an old steel drum. At the next table sat three big, round men: an Indian wearing a silver headband, a Chicano in a droopy Pancho Villa mustache, and a Negro in faded overalls. I thought what a litany of grievances that table could recite. But the more I looked, the more I believed they were someone's vision of the West, maybe someone making ads for Levy's bread, the ads that used to begin "You don't have to be Jewish."

Content

1. What details of the desert landscape does Least Heat-Moon use to describe it? How clearly can you visualize this place? Although this desert can be precisely located on a highway map, do you need to know its exact location in order to imagine it? What does it have in common with other deserts? Does it have any unique features?

2. Travel writer Paul Theroux says, "The journey, not the arrival, matters." Is that true for Least Heat-Moon? Explain your answer.

Strategies/Structures

1. Least Heat-Moon structures this chapter from *Blue Highways* according to time (daylight to night) and distance. How does the structure relate to the subject matter?

2. What is the effect of ending this trip through the desert with the image of "three big, round men"—an Indian, a Chicano, and a black

(¶ 10)? Does the reference to Levy's Jewish rye bread in the last sentence trivialize this example?

3. What kind of character does Least Heat-Moon play in his own narrative? Is this character identical to the author who is writing the essay?

Language

1. Least Heat-Moon includes many place names. With what effect? Do you need to read the essay with a map in hand?

2. Why are the parentheses in the list? Why do they appear beside some items and not others?

For Writing

1. Make a list of "nothing in particular" that you observe in a place so familiar that you take its distinguishing features for granted: your yard, your refrigerator, your clothes closet, your desk, a supermarket or other store, a library, or any other ordinary place. Write down as many specific details as you can, in whatever order you see them. (Use parenthetical remarks, too, if you wish.) Then, organize them according to some logical or psychologically relevant pattern (such as closet to farthest away, most to least dominant impression, largest to smallest, whatever) and put them into a larger context. For instance, how does the closet or the refrigerator relate to the rest of your house? Does organizing the list stimulate you to include even more details? What can you do to keep your essay from sounding like a collection of miscellaneous trivia?

2. Write an essay about some portion of a trip you have taken, where you have been a stranger in a strange land. Characterize yourself as a traveler, possibly an outsider, with a particular relationship to the place you're in (enjoyment, curiosity, boredom, loneliness, fear, fatigue, a desire to move on, or any combination of emotions you want to acknowledge.)

Writers' Notebooks

There are no study questions for the notebook entries of either professional or student writers because these were not intended to be finished, unified artistic works. You can read these entries for diversity of content, tone, modes of expression, point of view, self-characterization, and persona. You can also consider how each entry might be a springboard for a full-blown essay.

MARK TWAIN

Mark Twain (a riverman's term for "two fathoms deep," the pen name of Samuel Clemens) celebrated in his writing a life-long love affair with the Mississippi River, which he regarded as "the great Mississippi, the majestic, the magnificent Mississippi, rolling its mile-wide tide along, shining in the sun." In *The Adventures of Tom Sawyer* (1876) and *The Adventures of Huckleberry Finn* (1885) he immortalized the riverfront town of Hannibal, Missouri, where he was born (1835) and whose folkways he absorbed. In 1875 he published *Old Times on the Mississippi,* a zestful account of his apprenticeship and experiences as a steam-boat pilot, when he fulfilled a "permanent childhood ambition." He returned with great pleasure to the Mississippi in 1882 for the nostalgic trip downriver, recorded in the notebook entries reprinted here, partly to collect the material he used to expand *Old Times* into *Life on the Mississippi* (1883).

Even before he became a professional writer, Twain kept writer's notebooks, beginning in 1855, when he was twenty, and composing forty-nine volumes between 1855 and his death in 1910. (They have been published in a scholarly edition as *Mark Twain's Notebooks and Journals.*) Many of the entries are fragmentary—memorable names (some with comic possibilities) of people and places, epigrams or quotations provocative either for their dialect or their substance ("Paris papers small & dirty are dated a day ahead & contain last week's news"), ideas for later expansion ("My dream—talk with the Devil"). Longer entries record conversations, jokes, incidents, or other material that often emerged in Twain's published writing. The entries that follow exhibit these characteristics and epitomize a trip that was particularly happy when Twain was allowed to pilot the boat. He recalled, "When we got down below Cairo, and there was a big, full river—for it was high-water season and there was no danger of the boat hitting anything. . . I had her most of the time on [Lem Gray's] watch. He would . . . leave me there to dream that the years had not slipped away; that there had been no [Civil] war, no mining days, no literary adventures; that I was still a pilot, happy and care-free as I had been twenty years before."

Aboard a Mississippi River Steamboat[1]

New York to St. Louis
Apl. 18, 1882

T he grace and picturesqueness of female dress seem to dis-   1
appear as one travels west away from N. York. . . .

Scene near Greenville, O.
Tendency to the esthetic:—A rather plain, white-painted wooden   2
house[;][2] facing the R.R. In the yard two composition Dogs guarding the walk; both with glass eyes—one with a fire-red head &
ears; nearer the door two [lions] Lions couchant, regarding [pas]
our train and other passing events with a ferocious smile/rigid
ferocity; aspect of the dogs more benignant;—half a dozen [a]
urns and vases;—near the center a cast-iron swan, not dying but
evidently pretty sick. All these and other adornments in a door
yard barely 50 feet square!

April 19th—
This morning struck into the region of full "goatees"—sometimes   3
in company with moustaches, but usually not.

All the R.R. station loafers west of Pittsburgh carry *both* hands in   4
their pockets. Further east one hand is sometimes out of doors.
Here never. This is an important fact in Geography. . . .

Apl. 20th A.M.
The companionway was less than 2 inches deep in dirt, showing   5
that she had n't been washed down for perhaps a couple of days.

---

[1] Title supplied.
[2] Bracketed material denotes cancellations in Twain's original notebook. Footnotes are those of the Twain editors unless indicated by LZB.

The saloon round about the stove was guttered up and splintered, showing that she had n't been repaired as to floors since I was in St. Louis last.

6   Four iron spittoons around the stove—not particularly clean, but clean enough to show that there hadn't been any passengers aboard this year. Green, wooden chairs, can seated, all more or less venerable; a venerable colored chambermaid;—everything venerable. No decoration except a painted, pale-green diamond over the state room doors. This boat built by Fulton; has not been repaired since.

7   Mem:—Comparative scarcity of steam boats now. In old days the boats lay simply with their *noses* against the wharf, wedged in, stern out in the river[.], side by side like sardines in a box. Now the boats lie end to end.—The "Anchor Line" appears to [line] monopolise.

8   Boarded the "Gold Dust" 5 p.m. Apl. 20th.

9   Encountered on the deck before starting a vendor of books and papers. His name is Sullivan—of pure Irish extraction. He says he came into the world on the 23[d] Sept 1800. Has lived here 34 years and never crossed the Miss. Says if you meet an Irishman *prove* he is an Irishmn. Not an Irishmn because he is born in Ireland no more than a man is a horse because he's born in a stable. Thousands born in Ireland who are not Irishmen. His ancestors came to Ireland 300 years after the flood and he gave their names. Referring to his business of vending literature, he says:—"I read quite a little in my youthful days. Some say a person has no right to read fiction but I tell ye that all the great men of the day read fiction. I niver met a great man who didnt rade fiction. When you rade the Greek and Latin languages you're rading fiction. Go to-night and rade the firmament; the stars, [are] ivery [o] wan of 'em tells of fiction. Indade, its necessary for a man to rade fiction to be a scholar."

10   (By Johnson)[3] "Do they have Scotch whiskey in Ireland?"

11   "They have *Irish* whiskey sir. They have the best kind. ["] But I don't use much mesilf. I am not a hard drinker, sir. Give an

---

[3] Mark Twain was trying out fictional names for his traveling companions.

Irishman lager beer for one month and he's a dead man. An Irishman is lined inside with copper and the lager beer corrodes it."

(By Sampson) "I suppose the whiskey, on the other hand, tends to polish off the copper."   12

"Bedad that's the truth of it, sir." . . .   13

April 21—
Landed at 6 o'clock this morning at a God forsaken rocky point where there was an old stone warehouse, gradually crumbling to ruin; two or three decayed dwelling houses, and nothing else suggestive of human life visible. X[4] Nobody put in an appearance except a tallow-faced [man o(f)] beardless man of about 30 carrying one cubic foot of baggage tied up in a red handkchf. As he came aboard his eye caught our Mr. Johnson seated on the forward deck. Something in the stern aspect of Johnson convinced this passenger that he was actually gazing upon the Captain of the Boat. [and a] A self-deprecatory look immediately overspread his features and he quickly crept in out of range of Johnson's eagle glances. X   14

We put ashore a gentleman and a lady, well-dressed[,] with good Russia leather bags; also two very nicely dressed lady like young girls. There was no carriage awaiting and they marched off down the road to go God knows where. It seemed a strange place for civilized folks to land. But the mystery was explained when we got under way again for these people were evidently bound for a large town which lay in behind a towhead two miles below the landing. I couldn't remember that town; couldn't place it; couldnt call its name; couldn't remember ever to have seen it before; couldn't imagine what the damned place might be. I guessed that it might be St. Genevieve—and that proved to be correct. The town is completely fenced in. Even at this [stage] excellent stage of the water a boat can't land within two miles of it. It is one of the oldest towns in Mo. Built on high ground, handsomely situated; once had good river privileges, but [is] it is no longer a river town. It is town out in the country. . . .   15

---

[4] Twain's marks. [LZB]

16   Went up to the pilothouse when we were approaching Chester (where the big Illinois penitentiary is located). Found everything familiar in the pilothouse except that they blow the whistle with a foot-treadle and have a bell-pull that I wasn't acquainted with to call for the electric light, and a big speaking tube under the breast board, whose use I don't know.

17   Something which suggests short packet lines and quick trips is the absence of spars.

18   Another brand new thing is the suspending of the "stages" from derricks, letting them swing in the air projecting forward. Admirable contrivance both for quickness and convenience in handling. There is no nighthawk on the jack staff. There is an electric light where it used to be, and that is used in place of the ancient torchbasket. There is an electric headlight over the companionway which can be turned in any direction by the Capt. from his position on deck—so that the landing of a steamboat at night is as easy work as in the day time. They couldnt use the nighthawk lamp to land by because it would blind the pilot.

19   The officers of this line will go into uniform on the 1st of May. They are quiet and dignified according to the ancient custom. Also the mates; whereas it used to be required of the mate to rip and curse by way of emphasizing orders. One of the 3 mates on this boat is of the ancient tribe. He is one of the old-fashioned, God-damn-your-soul kind. Very affable and sociable. Pointed out a country residence saying, "There, that's a God damned fine place. That place was built out of the profits of the flesh brokerage business in St. Louis. The old bitch that owns that place has the biggest [h] whore house in St. Louis. She don't know how much she's worth. Brings the girls down here into the country to freshen them up for work. A man told me he had seen 47 "shimmies" hanging on one line there. She's got a husband and if he don't go straight she licks him. She makes him do as she God damn pleases.

20   This other place down here is owned by old what's-his-name He's got an income of $100,000. a month. *He* don't give a God-damn. He Don't know how much he's worth."

21   (This man talks like the machine Barnum had around with his circus for a while. Has that same guttural indistinct, jumbling, rasping way of talking. But this mate can out-swear the machine.)

Our passenger from Nebraska thinks the dinner on the boat 22 was the best he ever "sot" down to. Soup & fish & two kinds of meat and several kinds of *Pie!*

He said to Phelps to-day, "Say, that friend of yours is up in 23 the pilot house. I jest heard him talking & he's an old pilot himself. Now, he's been giving me taffy, representing that he didnt know much about this river. Judging by his conversation I think he knows *all* about it."

Friday Eve'g Apl 21ˢᵗ.

Visited the pilot house this morning to get warm, and was be- 24 trayed by one of the boys—the pilot on watch. He said, "I have seen somebody sometime or other who resembled you very strongly and a great many years ago I heard a man use your voice. He is sometimes called Mark Twain—or Sam Clemens."

I said, "Then don't give me away" and made no further ef- 25 fort to keep up the shallow swindle. The pilot said he recognized me partly by my voice and face and this was confirmed by my habit of running my hands up thro my hair.

The river is so thoroughly changed that I can't bring it back 26 to mind even when the changes have been pointed out to me. It is like a man pointing out to me a place in the sky where a cloud has been. I can't reproduce the cloud. Yet as unfamiliar as all the aspects have been to-day I have felt as much at home and as much as in my proper place in the pilot house as if I had never been out of the pilot house. I have felt as if I might be informed any moment it was my watch to take a trick at the wheel.

To-night when some idiot approaching Cairo didn't answer 27 our whistle but rounded to across our bows and came near get- ting himself split in two I felt an old-time hunger to be at the wheel and cut him in two,—knowing I had fulfilled the law and it would be his fault. By shipping up and backing we saved him, to my considerable regret—for it would have made good practi- cal literature if we had got him.

Found Cairo looking very natural by the light of the gas and 28 our own electric light from the pilot house, and concluded to wait till morning and go ashore and examine it.

Found government lights everywhere all down the river. 29 This is too much. It takes away [all the] a great deal of the agony of piloting and must make it even more enjoyable than it used to be,—and it was always enjoyable enough. . . . Birds Point looked as it always looked, except that the river has moved Mr. Bird's house ¾ mile nearer to the front than it used to be.

30   Mem: The only thing that remains to me now of the technical education which I got on the river is the faculty of remembering numbers, streets and addresses,—which I trace to the automatic remembering of the depths of water by the lead. . . .

Napoleon, Ark. Apl. 24.

31 The town (2000 inhab.) used to be where the river now is. Washed entirely away by a cut-off and not a vestige of it remains—except one little house and the chimney of another which were out in the suburbs once.

The Captain's[5] Story.

32 Senator Bogy of Mo.[6] had a son a pompous sort of fellow. His name was Joe. Joe was fond of being known as the son of Senator Bogy, and liked to be introduced at parties and gatherings as "Mr. Bogy son of Senator Bogy."

33   That ancient mariner went up thro the [shoot] chute down the river up thro the [shoot] chute and down again all thro' his watch. Supposed was going down the river all the time. A darkey saw the boat so often and said, "Clar to gracious! I reckon dar must be a whole line o' dem ar Skylarks."

34 The "Eclipse" was [th] noted as being the fastest boat.[7] She had just passed an old darkey on shore who happened not to recognize her name. Presently some one asked him, "Any boat gone up?" "Yes sah." "Was she going fast?" "Oh, so-so, loafing along." "Now, do you know what boat that was?"

35   "No, sah."

36   "Well, that was the Eclipse."

---

5 John T. McCord entertained Clemens with the three anecdotes which follow.
6 Lewis Vital Bogy, a Saint Louis attorney and businessman, had served as United States senator from 1872 until his death in 1877.
7 In 1852 and 1853 the Eclipse made record runs from New Orleans to Natchez, Cairo, and other upstream ports. Mark Twain described her exploits in "Old Times on the Mississippi" (*Atlantic Monthly*, August 1875) in a section published as chapter 16 of *Life on the Mississippi*.

"Oh, well, she just went by here a sparkling!"   37

The pilot thinking I was a greenhorn put up a great deal of re-   38
markable river information on me.

The Capt. said that if this boat were to sink right here (Ark. sec-   39
tion) in less than one hour there would be a hundred pirates out
here in skiffs after plunder.

Down here we are in the region of boots again. They don't wear   40
shoes.

Fence-rail quarrel.

During the high water one man's fence rails washed down on an-   41
other mans ground and the latter's rails around on to former's
ground. Kind of exchange of rails. In the eddy they got mixed
somehow. One said to the other "[let]Let it remain so; I will use
your rails & you mine." But the other wouldn't have it so. One
day the first man came down on the other's place to get his rails.
The other said "I'll kill you, you son of a bitch," and went for him
with a revolver. The other said "I'm not armed" and the assailant
threw down his revolver and came at him with a knife, cut his
throat all around but not severing the jugular vein or arteries.
Struggling around the man whose throat was cut got hold of the
other's revolver on the ground and shot him dead[.], but survived his own injuries.

Another.

Two shop-keepers in adjoining stores had a quarrel. One of them   42
put his hand back in his hip pocket to get some documents. The
other thought he was going for a weapon, drew his pistol and
began firing. The first called out "Im not armed; don't kill an
unarmed man." But the other kept on firing and killed him. Was
acquitted by the jury. . . .

     Neither this country nor any other can ever prosper until   43
the votes of the two parties are nearly equal

Stopped at Arkansas City April 24. This is a Hell of a place. One   44
or two streets full of mud; 19 different stenches at the same time.
A thriving place nevertheless. A R.R. here—the Little Rock, Miss.
river & Texas R.R.

SYLVIA PLATH

> Sylvia Plath's diary entry for November 13, 1949, written when
> she was a high-achieving high school senior preparing to enter
> Smith College (B.A., 1955), reflects the conflict between her two
> consuming goals, to attain perfection as a writer and as a beauti-
> ful woman. Women who came of age in the 1950s were expected
> to marry early and have children—a deterrent to creativity, Plath
> believed. Yet Plath fulfilled all these expectations, marrying
> English poet Ted Hughes in 1956 and having two children by
> the early 1960s, while establishing her reputation as a poet with
> *The Colossus* (1960). She explored her inability to resolve this con-
> flict in the comic, semi-autobiographical novel *The Bell Jar* (1963),
> and in much of her best poetry, angry and sardonic, published
> posthumously in *Ariel* (1963). Her suicide in 1963 contributed to
> the myth into which critics claim she increasingly transformed
> her life, using not only her poetry but her *Letters Home* (1975)
> and *Journals* (1982) to focus on the tragic "fall from childhood
> innocence to adult experience, from grace to loss."

❄ *Sylvia Plath at Seventeen*[1]

November 13, 1949

1   As of today I have decided to keep a diary again—just a place where I can write my thoughts and opinions when I have a moment. Somehow I have to keep and hold the rapture of being seventeen. Every day is so precious I feel infinitely sad at the thought of all this time melting farther and farther away from me as I grow older. *Now, now* is the perfect time of my life.

2   In reflecting back upon these last sixteen years, I can see tragedies and happiness, all relative—all unimportant now—fit only to smile upon a bit mistily.

---

[1] Title supplied.

I still do not know myself. Perhaps I never will. But I feel 3
free—unbound by responsibility, I still can come up to my own
private room, with my drawings hanging on the walls . . . and
pictures pinned up over my bureau. It is a room suited to me—
tailored, uncluttered and peaceful. . . . I love the quiet lines of the
furniture, the two bookcases filled with poetry books and fairy
tales saved from childhood.

At the present moment I am very happy, sitting at my desk, 4
looking out at the bare trees around the house across the
street. . . . Always I want to be an observer. I want to be affected
by life deeply, but never so blinded that I cannot see my share
of existence in a wry, humorous light and mock myself as I mock
others.

I am afraid of getting older. I am afraid of getting married. 5
Spare me from cooking three meals a day—spare me from the
relentless cage of routine and rote. I want to be free—free to know
people and their backgrounds—free to move to different parts of
the world, so I may learn that there are other morals and standards besides my own. I want, I think, to be omniscient. . . . I think
I would like to call myself "The girl who wanted to be God." Yet
if I were not in this body, where *would* I be? Perhaps I am *destined*
to be classified and qualified. But oh, I cry out against it. I am I—
I am powerful—but to what extent? I am I.

Sometimes I try to put myself in another's place, and I am 6
frightened when I find I am almost succeeding. How awful to be
anyone but I. I have a terrible egotism. I love my flesh, my face,
my limbs, with overwhelming devotion. I know that I am "too
tall" and have a fat nose, and yet I pose and prink before the mirror, seeing more and more how lively I am. . . . I have erected in
my mind an image of myself—idealistic and beautiful. Is not that
image, free from blemish, the true self—the true perfection? Am I
wrong when this image insinuates itself between me and the mer-
ciless mirror? (Oh, even now I glance back on what I have just
written—how foolish it sounds, how overdramatic.)

Never, never, never will I reach the perfection I long for with 7
all my soul—my paintings, my poems, my stories—all poor, poor
reflections . . . for I have been too thoroughly conditioned to the
conventional surroundings of this community . . . my vanity desires luxuries which I can never have. . . .

8   I am continually more aware of the power which change
plays in my life. . . . There will come a time when I must face myself at last. Even now I dread the big choices which loom up in my
life—what college? what career? I am afraid. I feel uncertain.
What is best for me? What do I want? I do not know. I love freedom. I deplore constrictions and limitations. . . . I am not as wise
as I have thought. I can see, as from a valley, the roads lying open
for me, but I cannot see the end—the consequences. . . .

9   Oh, I love *now*, with all my fears and forebodings, for now
I still am not completely molded. My life is still just beginning. I
am strong. I long for a cause to devote my energies to. . . .

❄ *Selections from Student Writers' Notebooks*

RICHARD LOFTUS, JILL WOOLLEY, ART GREENWOOD,
BARBARA SCHOFIELD, SUSAN YORITOMO,
BETTY J. WALKER, TAMMY WEAST, KRISTIN KING,
ROSALIND BRADLEY COLES, CHERYL WATANABE,
STEPHEN E. RYAN

> The students who kept these writers' notebooks in courses at the
> University of Connecticut, Virginia Commonwealth University,
> and the College of William and Mary in recent years majored in
> a variety of subjects: King, Loftus, Ryan, and Watanabe, English;
> Woolley, archaeology; Greenwood, general studies; Schofield,
> education; Yoritomo, filmmaking; Walker, human resource man-
> agement; Weast, mass communications; Coles, biology and
> creative writing. All share a love of the sounds as well as the
> sense of words, all like to play around with the language; some
> read omnivorously while others focus on visual images. All bring
> creativity to their work, which ranges from assisting on archaeo-
> logical digs to personnel administration to pharmacological
> laboratory research to editing publications for a hospital and
> for the Wolf Trap music foundation.

The selections from their notebooks reflect a range of interests and moods as varied as the writers. Reactions to keeping a notebook ("It's better to do it than to talk about it"), a satiric recipe ("Oh, Mom, was there ever a worse cook than you?"), self-analysis ("I could get by, looking good"), an attempt at self-improvement ("I've been trying to put cigarettes down for six years now"), explorations of sound ("HE'LL BANG EM AND HIS CYMBALS CRASH AND HISS"), analysis of an apartment style that mirrors the writer's personal style ("My apartment is stark. I'm stark"), a humorous tirade against housework ("I hate it"), the devastating impact of a divorce on a family's Christmas ("I ate a beans n franks dinner later. My brother went to drink his gift certificate"), reactions to being black in a white world (Coles), homosexual in a straight world (Loftus), Asian in America (Watanabe). And a joyous reaction to the writer's first publication—"and not in the Letters to the Editor column, either."

These entries offer just a hint of the infinite potential of writers' notebooks.

Richard Loftus

I read something in some book from some new author in some   1
bookshop somewhere to the effect that writer's block is "reading old fat novels instead of making new skinny ones." My secret is out.

•   •   •

I don't feel like writing now. I should pick up *Mansfield Park*   2
again. Reading Austen or anyone that good reminds me of what I could be saying, and of the work that has to be put into it. How often have I begun a journal and stopped because two days later it didn't seem so good? I suppose I saved myself from some self-flagellation, but also from a record of growth. There are some people in the class who write often, and though their perceptions are no more acute or their difficulties in writing no less than my own, I feel that they're ahead. I must remember what Susan said to me, that "It's better to do it than talk about it." This is doing it, huh? This is getting it down on paper. Knowing that I have to keep this record is the best part.

• • •

Green Bean Surprise Casserole

1 can green beans, drained
1 can cream of mushroom soup
1 box cheez-bits

Layer ingredients—beans, then soup and cheez-bits—in greased casserole. Place casserole in preheated 350° oven. Bake forty-five minutes. Serve.

3   I'm telling you something I've never told anyone. Never, through the long years of dinners made possible by the invention of the electric can opener and the publication of Peg Bracken's *The I Hate to Cook Cookbook*. Never, though the mention of meatloaf still conjures images of a dark, brick-like thing, ketchup glazed and gurgling angrily in a sea of orangish drippings in a pyrex baking dish. Never, even when her mantra spun in my brain like an old forty-five: "Some people live to eat, Richard (my name spoken with accusative gravity), *I* eat to live." Oh, Mom, was there ever a worse cook than you?

Jill Woolley

4   I don't want to be a scholar. I run on intuition. My pleasure is in creating. . . . I hate collecting information and acting like I have something new and exciting to say about any of it. I'm not an organizer. Maybe I'm not a synthesizer. I'm all talent and no discipline. I can get away with some sweat and inspiration. I can get by with bullshit because my bull is better than 85% of everybody else's hard work. But I know what's coming off the top of my head. I know I'm a phony. At least that's how I feel. No substance. I've disconnected my soul. I've sold myself out because I could get by, looking good.

• • •

5   I meant to throw these boots away. I had them in a box for the Salvation Army pick-up. Somehow they worked their way back on to my feet. It's the same with so many things—boots, men,

cigarettes—you try to get them out of your life and they keep coming out on top.

I've been trying to put cigarettes down for six years now, on and off. Still, day after day, I pay my money for a pack of poison. Why is it easier to smoke than to not smoke? It certainly isn't easier to exercise than to not exercise. It isn't easier to work hard than to not work hard. So why is it easier to smoke? 6

I try all kinds of tricks. I count how many cigarettes I've smoked in a day. I wait until dark to light up. I brush my teeth after every cigarette. But these gimmicks soon fall away and again I'm chain smoking from the time I get up until I retire. 7

I guess I'll keep trying though. Tomorrow, the boots go back on the pile for the Salvation Army. It's a start. 8

Art Greenwood

I live in an apartment with two musicians. Stan is a black man with a deep voice and a mild relaxed demeanor, who plays the drums. Meloni is his complement, fair-skinned and youthful , she sings and she plays the guitar. The are both rock musicians, per- haps, but their types of music are very different. STANLEY—HE PLAYS HIS DRUMS, SOMETIMES, AND HE BANGS EM, HE BANGS EM AND HE BANGS EM, HE'LL ROLL EM, BACK AND FORTH AND BACK REAL QUICK WITH A BASE THUMP, AND HE'LL BANG EM AND HE'LL BANG EM AND HIS CYMBALS CRASH AND HISS WHILE HE BANGS EM AND THE BASE THUMPS. And when he does this it's loud, and the place gets filled, and it feels good, as if you were in your own heart while it was beating. Meloni's music, though, is as different from his as she is, physically, from him. The deep rhythm of his drums doesn't surface in the trickling stream of her singsong. He puts you in your heart, but she leads you through your head. When you listen to her it's like the breeze in the trees or butter- flies in springtime: light, airy, and hopeful. 9

Barbara Schofield

Sitting in class I realized that I would never be more naked than when I shared my writing. It is painful; it is frightening, because you open your very soul to acceptance or rejection by your peers. 10

All this attempt to communicate with others is complicated by each individual's understanding of language; we try to present ourselves to others with as much clarity and understanding as is possible for another human being to comprehend of another.

11   In my mind's eye, I see all my physical, and thus symbolically, mental scars and deformities, and I wonder. Do my classmates see the moles on my neck? Do they see the puffy rolls of my flesh, my stretch-marked belly reminiscent of three pregnancies? Do they see the eight inch long scars down the sides of each thigh that resemble railroad tracks? What about the broken blood vessel at the back of my left knee that came with the stress of the second hip surgery? Do they see the peculiar scar on the first digit of my right hand, a constant reminder of the day I sliced a piece of me off with the salami onto the deli scale? If they do, do they recognize these things for what they are, representations of someone's life? Do they accept all this? Do they reject it? And if they do, does it really matter? Have they not come naked to this class also, and aren't their scars just as visible? Of course they are, or so I tell myself, but it barely soothes me enough to honestly write about who I am, and how I came to be the way I am, today.

Susan Yoritomo

12   I want to be safe, so I'll hide in my apartment. I'm always hiding in my apartment. I love my apartment. I can see the sunset from one window and sunrise from another. And it's not really hiding, there's no one after me. It's isolation. It's windows and doors and walls and floors and ceilings, the physical barriers I cherish. I have plants. I wonder and worry and care for them, but it's very technical. There's no love. I like them because they soften the sterile interior of my apartment. As a friend said, they are the "bare minimum" in the way of plants. I have to agree. They are the pointy, blade-like plants which are called tropical but are reminiscent of the desert. Stark. My apartment is stark. I'm stark. I strive for starkness. I hate those irresponsible, indulgent feminine traits that are me, the real me. I want my masculine, minimal, logical, problem-solving self to dominate. I want that hard, durable exterior that is not unlike a wall. A cool marble wall that endures.

Betty J. Walker

HOUSEWORK—Housework—I hate it. I have tried for the past   13
20 years to learn to like but to no avail. It is so boring. It is repetitive and stagnates the mind. Anyone can do it; it requires no
real talent except the willingness to do the same thing over and
over again.

Now take dusting . . . an exercise in sheer futility. You take   14
a cloth and spray some type of polish on it. You move it around
on the surface of the table or chair or whatever and pick up the
dust on the rag. You move around the room dusting whatever
level surface there is available that does not move. You move
on from room to room. After a lapsed period of perhaps 20 minutes, you return to the room you dusted first. What do you find
there . . . dust!

How about dishwashing and cooking. Those two things will   15
drive you crazy. The cooking goes on forever and you no sooner
get one meal completed then it is time to begin another. . . . Over
the years I have developed a standard menu of things I can prepare that I don't burn or cause people to be poisoned. My family
has learned that if it's Tuesday, it must be hamburgers. Or, if
it's Friday, it must mean that we'll eat out. You see, I don't cook
on Fridays. . . .

Lest you form the opinion that I am lazy, let me reassure   16
you—I am. I will work all day at something I enjoy doing. Writing or sewing or creating something keeps me interested and
busy and I am never bored. But the repetitive things drive me up
the walls. The trouble with housework is that once you have it all
done and the house is all clean and shining, six months later you
have to do it all over again.

Tammy Weast

What makes Christmas Christmas? It is not the carols, the deco-   17
rations, nor the cold weather. It is not even Santa Claus or turkey
advertisements on TV. It must be something in the mind. That's
it. Christmas is a state of mind.

My parents are getting divorced. This was the first Christ-   18
mas my mom, brother, and I have spent without my dad. We did
not put up a tree. I got the decorations out of the attic though. The

first box I opened contained dad's stocking. Mom cried so I put it all away.

19   December 25th was weird. I did not get up until 11 A.M. The whole world had opened their presents while I slept. My brother gave me a leather briefcase. I gave him a $50. gift certificate from Darryl's restaurant. He goes there and drinks a lot lately.

20   Dinnertime has always been around 3 P.M. on holidays. That was because my dad liked to watch the football games. This year mom said we could eat when we wanted. But we never did. I ate a beans n franks dinner later. My brother went to drink his gift certificate.

21   I worked the day after Christmas. All the secretaries in my office had new gold necklaces from men. They all cooed about what a wonderful holiday they had had. I got nauseous because everyone was asking me, "How was your holiday, Tammy?" or "What did Santa bring you?" or "How long will you be eating turkey leftovers?"

22   I went home early. Mom and my brother were all early too. We each seemed to have upset stomachs. It must have been something we didn't eat. Or maybe it was just our state of mind.

Kristin King

23   They lived in a three-hundred-thousand-dollar house that looked like a sty. I remember walking into the living room once and seeing the abuse. On one wall was a dart board with no darts and the wall behind pocked with holes. The lining had been torn from the bottom of a yellow Chippendale sofa and stuffing poked through where the buttons had been ripped off. In front of the sofa was a cherry table with a half-finished model spread out and a tube of glue dripping. There were several high-backed chairs in the room, one windsor without an arm, another with a torn velvet cover. On the carpet in front of the chair was a bowl of milk with Cheerios floating. An empty pop bottle lay on the brick hearth. Someone had tossed a crumpled McDonald's bag on the ashes of last winter's fires. A Steinway stretched underneath a broad picture window. Water rings spoiled the finish and a Tinker Toy was wedged between two keys. The piano bench, loaded with *Sports Illustrated,* was pushed against the wall. A china bureau, filled

with Wedgwood and Lenox, stood in the corner next to the door. A lacrosse stick was propped against one of its broken panes. A black woman in a blue housecoat was attempting to compensate for the absence of a cat's litter box by pushing a vacuum back and forth over the stained carpet.

Rosalind Bradley Coles

Today in class Dudley said he's "tired of racial issues in class." 24 Well—if he's tired of them, how does he think I feel? For years I have been the only Black (or at most one of two or three) in class and I have had to deal with white negativism towards Blacks. . . . Every time I've taken writing classes I've had to deal with some white person who had to put a Black person in their story— unfortunately the Black person is never a professional or middle class person, but illiterate, poor, kitchen workers or country hicks or rapists. Even Dudley in his first essay continuously used the word nigger derogatorily (although that's the only way whites can use it). . . . In the same week Grace had a sentence in her essay about a rural man who "knew the difference between a nigger and a colored man." Buffy is writing a story about two Blacks (with college degrees) who interact with a white lawyer. She is trying to adopt a Black dialect for her characters that has rhythm. What she has produced are illiterate Blacks.

Sometimes I wonder if these stories are written simply be- 25 cause it was what the author wanted to tell, or if it is a personal attack against me (which really isn't fair to assume, but it has happened so often). It's easy for Dudley to be tired of racial issues when he's white and surrounded mostly by whites. But what about me? Dudley's tired of racial issues. Well, I'm tired of having to see only the negative side of my people portrayed by my peers.

Richard Loftus, again

Should I write about sex? Not to be sensational. That's purpose- 26 less. I don't think it would be wrong to write about sex, because sex is so personal a subject that to use it is akin to plowing up earth. In the wake of the plow you find things you would not have expected to find, fragments of bone, earthworms, snakes, an old boot, strange rocks, an old wristwatch. Talking about sex digs down and throws up old lies, new lies, guilt, excess, happy memories, all manner of self perceptions ranging from the most superficial to most basic. So sex becomes the catalyst towards some reaction.

27   I think I see my own sexuality—my homosexuality—as the thing that made me a better listener. Because it was at thirteen something unpleasant to own up to. Can you imagine having to admit to yourself that you're black? Almost amusing, because I can remember little of my self-consciousness of that particular time, but it was definitely the experience of being the outsider, living through my friends' heterosexual fumblings, being the uninvolved sexless sage. Later, having come out, an experience that has now been appropriated by ostomites, alcoholics, barren parents and anorexics, I was learning the joys of rhetoric. Gay politics is nothing if not rich in rhetoric. The difference between homosexual and gay? Homosexual is what the *New York Times* calls you; gay is what you earn the right to call yourself.

28   It was always surprising to listen to others, if somehow they were aware of my sexuality, if, somehow, the subject came up. Listening to them as they revealed their positions, feigned acceptance, gushed too readily their acceptance, or guarded their words, or condemned—it seemed always to be an exercise in measuring and dissecting. They say this, they mean that. It made me even more careful to choose words that expressed my own individual sense and that told the truth. It also made me aware of how to lie, without *really* lying (hah!). Through listening, nuance is learned.

Cheryl Watanabe

29 After the homes were lost, the businesses destroyed, after the furniture was sold or stolen, after the fathers were taken away and the rights of the land-born children erased you come—to offer money and recognition. Deeds not willing to be forgotten haunt you: Utah or California, horse stalls for hotels, manure for freshener, the death of our sons in Italy whose parents, buried deep in the desert, watered the brush with tears. But your offer comes too

late. The children have grown, the night classes paid for, the businesses reestablished, and prominence regained. We have wealth
enough to forgive with charity. Just put it in the textbooks, you
never put it in the textbooks.

In California thongs are still Nipper Flippers or Jap Slaps.   30
People imitate Japanese (or is it Chinese?) when I walk by. December seventh is the Ides of March. I'm asked how I can see, is
my field of vision narrowed? Would I like to go to Japan? Only
after I've seen Europe and Israel. Do I speak Japanese? No. How
come? Do you, being fourth generation French, Polish, Greek,
speak French, Polish, or Greek? "I was hoping you'd be Buddhist."
"Say some Japanese for me." "Play for me, dance for me, sing for
me, cook for me—I love rice." Prejudice is the spear of Ignorance.
"You write English very well. Where are you going for vacation?"
Back to California. "Have you ever been there?" Yes, I was born in
San Mateo and raised in San Jose.

Stephen E. Ryan

Refugee Camp 2
Turk/Iraqi Border
Company A, 2nd Battalion, 10th Special Forces Group (Airborne)
April, 1991
Day 6

The camp seems loudest at night. A huge, dulled murmur flows   31
up from the valleys with hacking, rattling coughs, unending
moaning like mantras, mules braying, wails and shrieks like a
child stepped on a nail. Clank tap-tapping, metal pots clanking
and wood chopping sounds but no sounds of laughter. The footsteps and shifting of thousands make a pressure on the ear just
below the level of a sound. And no strong wind whistles close distractions or carries the sound away. Rising to the hill in the middle
of 85,000 Kurdish refugees, the sounds articulate our mission.

In the morning, A–10 jets fly across in a low, slow demon-   32
stration. The screaming whine of their turbofans demands acknowledgement of their habitual, matin visits. The men look up
out of makeshift tents with squinted eyes in a fearful reflex drawn
from the sound. They have been down south where the wells still

burn. Former conscripts twice fleeing, they fled Coalition destruction and then fled Saddam's genocide. But they and we and
the Iraqi division beneath the border know the jet's other sound;
the harsh, ripping bellow of the main gun, the tank killer. Welcome, sweet, fearsome companion.

33   Under the wide, banking circles, the women walk the morning road carrying clutched bundles pressed close. The bundles are
soft-wrapped like cocoons, the folds unlike the sharp creases in
the strained faces of the mothers' dry silent anguish carrying children to graves. Behind them, men carry angular, longer, wrapped
burdens as the dust rises.

34   Above, a rhythmic, tympanic beat from the north begins the
helos' arrivals. They approach the small landing pad at full
power remonstrating loudly at their heavy loads in the thin, high
altitude air. They settle in ungraceful bobs and tilts as wheels un-
evenly touch down and sag with rotor blade slowing, drooping,
giving back their cargo's weight to the ground. Today's arrival of
rations, medicine and plastic-bottled water is too late for some,
desperate hope for many.

Betty J. Walker, again

35   GOOD NEWS. . . . When it first happened, I was so excited I
wanted to just jump up and down and hug the world. I felt like a
balloon being blown up and up and up until I was about ready to
explode—a feeling of excitement and satisfaction, a pleased-with-
myself feeling. I wanted to tell everyone, but at the same time I
wanted to keep it as a delicious secret. . . . I am going to have
something that I have written published in the newspaper, and
not in the Letters to the Editor column, either.

4 Writing: Re-Vision and Revision

The pun is intentional. *Re-vision* and *revision* both mean, literally, "to see again." The introduction to this book's first part, "On Writing," briefly identified some of the dramatic changes in the ways we currently think about reading and writing, our own and others' works (1–4).

The examples of revision by Donald Murray and student Mary Ruffin reveal the passionate commitment writers make to their work. Because they are fully invested in their writing, mind, heart, and spirit, they care enough about it to be willing to rewrite again and again and again until they get it right—in subject and substance, structure and style.

Of course, these examples are meant to inspire you, as well, to be willing "to see again." When you take a second, careful look at what you wrote as a freewriting or a first draft, chances are you'll decide to change it. If and when you do, you're approaching the process that most professional writers use—and your own work will be one step closer to professional. As playwright Neil Simon says, "Rewriting is when writing really gets to be fun. . . . In baseball you only get three swings and you're out. In rewriting, you get almost as many swings as you want and you know, sooner or later, you'll hit the ball."

Many people think that revision means correcting the spelling and punctuation of a first—and only—draft. Writers who care about their work know that such changes, though necessary, are editorial matters remote from the heart of real revising. For to revise is to rewrite. And rewrite. Novelist Toni Morrison affirms,

"The best part of all, the absolutely most delicious part, is finishing it and then doing it over. . . . I rewrite a lot, over and over again, so that it looks like I never did. I try to make it look like I never touched it, and that takes a lot of time and a lot of sweat."

When you rewrite, you're doing what computer language identifies as *add, delete, move* (reorganize), and *edit.* The concept of "draft" may have become elusive for people writing on a computer; one part of a given document may have been revised extensively, other parts may be in various stages of development, while others have yet to be written. For simplicity's sake, I'll use the term *draft* throughout *The Essay Connection* to refer to one particular version of a given essay (whether the writer considers it finished or not), as opposed to other versions of that same document. Even if you're only making a grocery list, you might add and subtract material, or change the organization. If your original list identified the items in the order they occurred to you, as lists often do, you could regroup them by categories of similar items, easier to shop for: produce, staples, meat, dairy products. You might provide specially detailed emphasis on the essentials, "a pound of Milagro super-hot green chilies," and "a half gallon of double chocolate extra fudge swirl ice cream."

Some writers compose essentially in their minds.* They work through their first drafts in their heads, over and over, before putting much—if anything—down on paper. As Joyce Carol Oates says, "If you are a writer, you locate yourself behind a wall of silence and no matter what you are doing, driving a car or walking or doing housework . . . you can still be writing." There's a lot of revising going on, but it's mostly mental. What appears on the paper the first time is what stays on the paper, with occasional minor changes. This writing process appears to work best with short pieces that can easily be held in the mind—a poem, a writing with a fixed and conventional format (such as a lab report), a short essay with a single central point, a narrative in which each point in the sequence reminds the writer of what comes next, logically, chronologically, psychologically. If you write that way,

---

* *Note:* Some material on pp. 102–103 is adapted from Lynn Z. Bloom, *Fact and Artifact: Writing Nonfiction,* 2nd ed. (Englewood Cliffs, N.J.: Blair Press [Prentice Hall], 1994), 51–53.

then what we say about revising on paper should apply to your mental revising, as well.

Other writers use a first draft, and sometimes a second, and a third, and more, to enable themselves to think on paper. Novelist E. M. Forster observed, "How do I know what I think until I see what I say?" How you wrote the first draft may provide cues about what will need special attention when you revise. If you use a first draft to generate ideas, in revising you'll want to prune and shape to arrive at a precise subject and focus and an organization that reinforces your emphasis, as Mary Ruffin did between the ninth draft and final version of "Mama's Smoke" (pp. 121–132). Or your first draft may be a sketch, little more than an outline in paragraph form, just to get down the basic ideas. In revising you'd aim to flesh out this bare-bones discussion by elaborating on these essential points, supplying illustrations, or consulting references that you didn't want to look up the first time around. On the other hand, you may typically write a great deal more than you need, just to be sure of capturing random and stray ideas that may prove useful. Your revising of such an ample draft might consist in part of deleting irrelevant ideas and redundant illustrations.

In *Write to Learn* (New York: Holt, 1984), Donald Murray suggests a three-stage revising process that you might find helpful in general, whether or not you've settled on your own particular style of revising:

1. A quick first reading "to make sure that there is a single dominant meaning" and enough information to support that meaning.
2. A second quick reading, only slightly slower than the first, to focus on the overall structure and pace.
3. A third reading, "slow, careful, line-by-line editing of the text . . . here the reader cuts, adds, and reorders, paragraph by paragraph, sentence by sentence, word by word" (167).

First you look at the forest, then at the shape and pattern of the individual trees, then close up, at the branches and leaves. Although this may sound slow and cumbersome, if you try it, you'll find that it's actually faster and easier than trying to catch everything in one laborious reading, alternating between panoramic views and close-ups.

John Trimble, in *Writing with Style* (Englewood Cliffs, N.J.: Prentice Hall, 1975), offers a number of suggestions for writing in a very readable style that work equally well for first drafts as well as for revision. Trimble's cardinal principles are these: (1) Write as if your reader is a "companionable friend" who appreciates straightforwardness and has a sense of humor. (2) Write as if you were "talking to that friend," but had enough time to express your thoughts in a concise and interesting manner. He also suggests that if you've written three long sentences in a row, make the fourth sentence short. Even very short. Use contractions. Reinforce abstract discussions with "graphic illustrations, analogies, apt quotations, and concrete details." To achieve continuity, he advises, make sure each sentence is connected with those preceding and following it. And, most important, "Read your prose aloud. *Always* read your prose aloud. If it sounds as if it's come out of a machine or a social scientist's report . . . spare your reader and rewrite it" (p. 82).

use example / illustrations

If your language sounds familiar, as if you've heard it before, you probably have—maybe many times, as is apparent in Roger Angell's parody, "Return of the Cliché Expert" (pp. 117–120). Such familiar language is likely to be full of clichés that will need to be weeded out, uprooted entirely to keep the writing fresh.

Ernest Hemingway has said that he "rewrote the ending of *A Farewell to Arms,* the last page of it, thirty-nine times before I was satisfied"—which means a great deal of rewriting, even if you don't think he kept exact count.

"Was there some technical problem?" asked an interviewer. "What had you stumped?"

"Getting the words right," said Hemingway.

That is the essence of revision.

STRATEGIES FOR REVISING

1. Does my draft have a *thesis,* a focal point? Does the thesis cover the entire essay, and convey my attitude toward the subject?
2. Does my draft contain sufficient *information, evidence* to support that meaning? Is the writing developed sufficiently, or do I need to provide additional information, steps in an argument, illustrations, or analysis of what I've already said?

3. Who is my intended *audience*? Will they understand what I've said? Do I need to supply any background information? Will I meet my readers as friends, antagonists, or on neutral ground? How will this relationship determine what I say, the order in which I say it, and the language I use?

4. Do the *form* and *structure* of my writing suit the subject? (For instance, would a commentary on fast-food restaurants be more effective in an essay or description, comparison and contrast, analysis, some combination of the three—or as a narrative or satire?) Does the *proportioning* reinforce my emphasis (in other words, do the most important points get the most space)? Or do I need to expand some aspects and condense others?

5. Is the writing recognizably mine in *style, voice,* and *point of view*? Is the body of my prose like that of an experienced runner: tight and taut, vigorous, self-contained, and supple? Do I like what I've said? If not, am I willing to change it?

DONALD M. MURRAY

Murray was a successful writer long before he began teaching others to write. Born in Boston in 1924, he was educated at the University of New Hampshire (B.A., 1948) and Boston University. He wrote editorials for the *Boston Herald*, 1948–1954, for which he won a Pulitzer Prize in 1954; in retirement, he now writes a weekly column for the *Boston Globe*. During his quarter-century of teaching at the University of New Hampshire, Murray wrote numerous essays, volumes of short stories, poetry, and a novel, *The Man Who Had Everything* (1964). *A Writer Teaches Writing* (1964, rev. 1985), an explanation of how people really write (as opposed to how the rule books say they should), has been highly influential in persuading writing teachers to encourage their students to focus on the process of writing, rather than on the finished product.

Revision, in Murray's view, is central to the writing process: "Good writing is essentially rewriting." Murray offers a straight-forward account of just how writers move through the process of revising, by making changes—in content, in form and in proportion, and finally in voice and word choice—that will substantially improve their work, even though "the words on a page are never finished." The history of this essay illustrates his points. Murray completely rewrote the essay twice before it was first published in *The Writer* in 1973. Then, for an anthology, Murray "re-edited, re-revised, re-read, re-re-edited" it again. A draft of the first twelve paragraphs of the "re-edited, revised" version, with numerous changes is reprinted below. As you examine both versions, note that many changes appear in the final ("re-re-edited") version that are not in the "revised" draft.

THE MAKER'S EYE: REVISING YOUR OWN
MANUSCRIPTS* by DONALD M. MURRAY

1. When ~~the beginning writer~~ *students* complete~~s~~ ~~his~~ *a* first draft, ~~he~~ *they* ~~usually reads it through to correct typographical errors and~~ consider~~s~~ the job of writing done *-- and their teachers too often agree.* ~~When the~~ professional writer~~s~~ complete~~s~~ ~~his~~ *the* first draft, ~~he~~ *they* usually feel~~s~~ ~~he is~~ *they are* at the start of the writing process. ~~Now that he has~~ *when* a draft *(is completed, the job of* ~~he can begin~~ writing *can begin.*

2. That difference in attitude is the difference between amateur and professional, inexperience and experience, journeyman and craftsman. Peter F. Dru~~g~~*c*ker, the prolific business writer, for example, calls his first draft "the zero draft"--after that he can start cou~~r~~*n*ting. Most ~~productive~~ writers share the feeling ~~that~~ the first draft^ and ~~most of those~~ *all* which follow~~is an~~ *are* opportunit~~y~~*ies* to discover what they have to say and how they can best say it.

~~Detachment and caring~~

3. To produce a progression of drafts, each of which says more and says it better, the writer has to develop a special *kind of* ^reading skill. In school we are taught to ~~read~~ *decode* what ~~is~~ *appears* on the page*, as finished writing.* ~~We try to comprehend what the author has said, what he meant and what are the implications of his words.~~

4. *Writers, however, face a different category of possibility and responsibility. To them, the words are never finished on the page. Each can be changed, rearranged, set off a chain reaction of confusion or clarified meaning. This is a different kind of reading, possibly more difficult and certainly more exciting.*

---

* A different version of this article was published in *The Writer,* October 1973.

5   ~~The~~ writer~~s of such drafts~~ must [learn to] be ~~his~~ [their] own best enemy. [Writers] ~~He~~ must accept the criticism of others, and be suspicious of it; ~~he~~ [they] must accept the praise of others, [-- especially teachers --] and be even more suspicious of it. [Writers] ~~He~~ cannot depend on others. [They] ~~He~~ must detach ~~himself~~ [themselves] from ~~his~~ [their] own page[s] so that ~~he~~ [they] can apply both ~~his~~ [their] caring and ~~his~~ [their] craft to ~~his~~ [their] own work.

6   Detachment is not easy. Science fiction writer Ray Bradbury supposedly puts each manuscript away for a year and then rereads it as a stranger. Not many writers can afford the time to do this. We must read when our judgment may be at its worst, when we are close to the euphoric moment of creation. The writer "should be critical of everything that seems to him most delightful in his style," advises novelist Nancy Hale. "He should excise what he most admires, because he wouldn't thus admire it if he weren't . . . in a sense protecting it from criticism."

7   ~~The writer must learn to protect himself from his own ego, when it takes the form of uncritical pride or uncritical self-destruction.~~ As poet John Ciardi points out, ". . . the last act of the writing must be to become one's own reader. It is, I suppose, a schizophrenic process, to begin passionately and to end critically, to begin hot and to end cold; and, more important, to be passion-hot and critic-cold at the same time."
    ~~Just as~~ [unproductive] ~~dangerous as the protective writer is the despairing one, who thinks everything he does is terrible, dreadful, awful. If he is to publish, he must save what is effective on his page while he cuts away what doesn't work. The writer must hear and respect his own voice.~~

Remember ~~how each~~ [how the] craftsman you have seen--the carpenter [looking at the lie] ~~eyeing the level~~ of a shelf, the mechanic listening to the motor--takes the instinctive step back. This is what ~~the~~ writer[s] [have to] ~~has to~~ do when ~~he~~ [they] read[s] ~~his~~ [their] own work. "The writer must survey his work critically, coolly, and as though he were a stranger to it," says children's book writer Eleanor Estes. "He must be willing to prune, expertly and hard-heartedly. At the end of each revision, a manuscript may look like a battered old hive, worked over, torn apart, pinned together, added to, deleted from, words changed and words changed back. Yet the book must maintain its original freshness and spontaneity."   **9**

¶ We are aware of ~~the~~ writers who think everything they have written is literature but a more ~~serious~~ frequent and serious problem ~~is the~~ are writers ~~is~~ who are ~~overly~~ overly critical of each page, tears up each page and never completes a draft. The ~~cut~~ writer must cut what is bad to ~~save~~ reveal what is good.   **8**

~~It is far easier for most beginning writers to understand the need for rereading and rewriting than it is to understand how to go about it. The publishing writer doesn't necessarily break down the various stages of rewriting and editing, he just goes ahead and does it.~~ ¶ ~~One of our most~~ [in the English-speaking world,] prolific ~~fiction~~ writer[s], (Anthony Burgess,) says, "I might revise a page twenty times." Short story and children's writer Roald Dahl states, "By the time I'm nearing the end of a story, the first part will have been reread and altered and corrected at least 150 times. . . . Good writing is essentially rewriting. I am positive of this."   **10**

11   There is nothing ~~virtuous in~~ ~~itself about~~ the rewriting process. [isn't virtuous] It is simply an essential condition of life for most writers. There are [a few] writers who do very little rewriting, mostly because they have the capacity and experience to create and review a large number of invisible drafts in their minds before they get to the page. And ~~many~~ [some] writers ~~perform~~ [who slowly produce finished pages, performing] all ~~of~~ the tasks of revision simultaneously, page by page, rather than draft by draft. But it is still possible to break down the process of rereading one's own work into the sequence most published writers follow [most of the time.] ~~as he studies his own page.~~

~~Seven elements~~

12   Many writers ~~at first just~~ scan their manuscript, reading as quickly as possible ~~for~~ [to catch the larger] problems of subject and form. [They take the] ~~In this craftsman's step back~~ ~~way, they stand back~~ from the more ~~technical~~ [superficial] details of language [the larger problems in writing.] so they can spot ~~any weaknesses in content or in organization.~~ [Then as they reread — and reread and ~~the reader~~ reread — they] ~~when the writer reads his manuscript, he is usually looking~~ [move in closer in a logical] sequence which usually ~~must~~ [involves,] ~~for~~ [seven elements.]

13   The first is subject. [As a writer] ~~Do you have anything to say? If~~ [Sometimes writers are lucky, they] [Writers look first to discover if they have] ~~you are lucky, you will find~~ ~~that~~ indeed ~~you do~~ have something to [that they] [anything to say] [said] say, perhaps a little more than you expected. ~~If the subject~~ [anything] [writers know they can't write] [nothing,] is not clear, or if it is not yet limited or defined enough for you to handle, don't go on. ~~What you have to say is~~ [SAVE] ~~always more important than how you say it.~~

[Novelist Elizabeth Janeway says, "I think there's a nice cooking word ~~which~~ that explains a little of what happens while (the manuscript is) standing. It clarifies, like a consommé perhaps."]

The Maker's Eye: Revising Your Own Manuscripts

When students complete a first draft, they consider the job of writing done—and their teachers too often agree. When professional writers complete the first draft, they usually feel they are at the start of the writing process. When a draft is completed, the job of writing can begin.

That difference in attitude is the difference between amateur and professional, inexperience and experience, journeyman and craftsman. Peter F. Drucker, the prolific business writer, calls his first draft "the zero draft"—after that he can start counting. Most writers share the feeling the first draft, and all which follow, are opportunities to discover what they have to say and how they can best say it.

To produce a progression of drafts, each of which says more and says it more clearly, the writer has to develop a special kind of reading skill. In school we are taught to decode what appears on the page as finished writing. Writers, however, face a different category of possibility and responsibility when they read their own drafts. To them the words on the page are never finished. Each can be changed and rearranged, can set off a chain reaction of confusion or clarified meaning. This is a different kind of reading which is possibly more difficult and certainly more exciting.

Writers must learn to be their own best enemy. They must accept the criticism of others and be suspicious of it; they must accept the praise of others and be even more suspicious of it. Writers cannot depend on others. They must detach themselves from their own pages so that they can apply both their caring and their craft to their own work.

Such detachment is not easy. Science fiction writer Ray Bradbury supposedly puts each manuscript away for a year to the day and then rereads it as a stranger. Not many writers have the discipline or the time to do this. We must read when our judgment may be at its worst, when we are close to the euphoric moment of creation.

6   Then the writer, counsels novelist Nancy Hale, "should be critical of everything that seems to him most delightful in his style. He should excise what he most admires, because he wouldn't thus admire it if he weren't . . . in a sense protecting it from criticism." John Ciardi, the poet, adds, "The last act of the writing must be to become one's own reader. It is, I suppose, a schizophrenic process, to begin passionately and to end critically, to begin hot and to end cold; and, more important, to be passion-hot and critic-cold at the same time."

7   Most people think that the principal problem is that writers are too proud of what they have written. Actually, a greater problem for most professional writers is one shared by the majority of students. They are overly critical, think everything is dreadful, tear up page after page, never complete a draft, see the task as hopeless.

8   The writer must learn to read critically but constructively, to cut what is bad, to reveal what is good. Eleanor Estes, the children's book author, explains: "The writer must survey his work critically, coolly, as though he were a stranger to it. He must be willing to prune, expertly and hard-heartedly. At the end of each revision, a manuscript may look . . . worked over, torn apart, pinned together, added to, deleted from, words changed and words changed back. Yet the book must maintain its original freshness and spontaneity."

9   Most readers underestimate the amount of rewriting it usually takes to produce spontaneous reading. This is a great disadvantage to the student writer, who sees only a finished product and never watches the craftsman who takes the necessary step back, studies the work carefully, returns to the task, steps back, returns, steps back, again and again. Anthony Burgess, one of the most prolific writers in the English-speaking world, admits, "I might revise a page twenty times." Roald Dahl, the popular children's writer, states, "By the time I'm nearing the end of a story, the first part will have been reread and altered and corrected at least 150 times. . . . Good writing is essentially rewriting. I am positive of this."

10   Rewriting isn't virtuous. It isn't something that ought to be done. It is simply something that most writers find they have to do to discover what they have to say and how to say it. It is a condition of the writer's life.

There are, however, a few writers who do little formal rewriting, primarily because they have the capacity and experience to create and review a large number of invisible drafts in their minds before they approach the page. And some writers slowly produce finished pages, performing all the tasks of revision simultaneously, page by page, rather than draft by draft. But it is still possible to see the sequence followed by most writers most of the time in rereading their own work. 11

Most writers scan their drafts first, reading as quickly as possible to catch the larger problems of subject and form, then move in closer and closer as they read and write, reread and rewrite. 12

The first thing writers look for in their drafts is *information*. They know that a good piece of writing is built from specific, accurate, and interesting information. The writer must have an abundance of information from which to construct a readable piece of writing. 13

Next writers look for *meaning* in the information. The specifics must build to a pattern of significance. Each piece of specific information must carry the reader toward meaning. 14

Writers reading their own drafts are aware of *audience*. They put themselves in the reader's situation and make sure that they deliver information which a reader wants to know or needs to know in a manner which is easily digested. Writers try to be sure that they anticipate and answer the questions a critical reader will ask when reading the piece of writing. 15

Writers make sure that the *form* is appropriate to the subject and the audience. Form, or genre, is the vehicle which carries meaning to the reader, but form cannot be selected until the writer has adequate information to discover its significance and an audience which needs or wants that meaning. 16

Once writers are sure the form is appropriate, they must then look at the *structure*, the order of what they have written. Good writing is built on a solid framework of logic, argument, narrative, or motivation which runs through the entire piece of writing and holds it together. This is the time when many writers find it most effective to outline as a way of visualizing the hidden spine by which the piece of writing is supported. 17

The element on which writers may spend a majority of their time is *development*. Each section of a piece of writing must be 18 adequately developed. It must give readers enough information so that they are satisfied. How much information is enough? That's as difficult as asking how much garlic belongs in a salad. It must be done to taste, but most beginning writers underdevelop, underestimating the reader's hunger for information.

19   As writers solve development problems, they often have to consider questions of *dimension.* There must be a pleasing and effective proportion among all the parts of the piece of writing. There is a continual process of subtracting and adding to keep the piece of writing in balance.

20   Finally, writers have to listen to their own voices. *Voice* is the force which drives a piece of writing forward. It is an expression of the writer's authority and concern. It is what is between the words on the page, what glues the piece of writing together. A good piece of writing is always marked by a consistent, individual voice.

21   As writers read and reread, write and rewrite, they move closer and closer to the page until they are doing line-by-line editing. Writers read their own pages with infinite care. Each sentence, each line, each clause, each phrase, each word, each mark of punctuation, each section of white space between the type has to contribute to the clarification of meaning.

22   Slowly the writer moves from word to word, looking through language to see the subject. As a word is changed, cut, or added, as a construction is rearranged, all the words used before that moment and all those that follow that moment must be considered and reconsidered.

23   Writers often read aloud at this stage of the editing process, muttering or whispering to themselves, calling on the ear's experience with language. Does this sound right—or that? Writers edit, shifting back and forth from eye to page to ear to page. I find I must do this careful editing in short runs, no more than fifteen to twenty minutes at a stretch, or I become too kind with myself. I begin to see what I hope is on the page, not what actually is on the page.

24   This sounds tedious if you haven't done it, but actually it is fun. Making something right is immensely satisfying, for writers begin to learn what they are writing about by writing. Language leads them to meaning, and there is the joy of discovery, of

understanding, of making meaning clear as the writer employs the technical skills of language.

Words have double meanings, even triple and quadruple   25
meanings. Each word has its own potential for connotation and denotation. And when writers rub one word against the other, they are often rewarded with a sudden insight, an unexpected clarification.

The maker's eye moves back and forth from word to phrase   26
to sentence to paragraph to sentence to phrase to word. The maker's eye sees the need for variety and balance, for a firmer structure, for a more appropriate form. It peers into the interior of the paragraph, looking for coherence, unity, and emphasis, which make meaning clear.

I learned something about this process when my first bifo-   27
cals were prescribed. I had ordered a larger section of the reading portion of the glass because of my work, but even so, I could not contain my eyes with this new limit of vision. And I still find myself taking off my glasses and bending my nose towards the page, for my eyes unconsciously flick back and forth across the page, back to another page, forward to still another, as I try to see each evolving line in relation to every other line.

When does this process end? Most writers agree with the   28
great Russian writer Tolstoy, who said, "I scarcely ever reread my published writings, if by chance I come across a page, it always strikes me: all this must be rewritten; this is how I should have written it."

The maker's eye is never satisfied, for each word has the   29
potential to ignite the new meaning. This article has been twice written all the way through the writing process, and it was published four years ago. Now it is to be republished in a book. The editors made a few small suggestions, and then I read it with my maker's eye. Now it has been re-edited, re-revised, re-read, re-re-edited, for each piece of writing to the writer is full of potential and alternatives.

A piece of writing is never finished. It is delivered to a dead-   30
line, torn out of the typewriter on demand, sent off with a sense of accomplishment and shame and pride and frustration. If only there were a couple more days, time for just another run at it, perhaps then. . . .

Content

1. Why does Murray say that when a first "draft is completed, the job of writing can begin" (¶ 1)? If you thought before you read the essay that one draft was enough, has Murray's essay convinced you otherwise?

2. How does Murray explain John Ciardi's analysis of the "schizophrenic process" of becoming one's own reader, "to be passion-hot and critic-cold at the same time" (¶ 6)? Why does he consider it so important for writers to be both?

3. What are writers looking for when they revise? How can writers be sure that their "maker's eye" has in revision an accurate perception of the "need for variety and balance, for a firmer structure, for a more appropriate form. . . . for coherence, unity, and emphasis" (¶ 26)? How do you, as a writer, know whether your writing is good or not?

Strategies/Structures

1. Many of Murray's revisions are for greater conciseness. For example, the first sentence of paragraph 11 initially read, "There is nothing virtuous in the rewriting process." Murray then revised it to "The rewriting process isn't virtuous." The published version says, "Rewriting isn't virtuous." What are the effects of these successive changes? And of other comparable changes?

2. Compare and contrast the deleted paragraph 8 of the original version and the rewritten paragraphs 8 and 9 of the typescript with paragraphs 7 and 8 in the printed version. Why did Murray delete the original paragraph 8? Which ideas did he salvage? Why did he delete the first two sentences of the original paragraph 9? Are the longer paragraphs of the printed version preferable to the shorter paragraphs of the original?

Language

1. In many places in the revision typescript (see ¶s 1, 5) Murray has changed masculine pronouns (he, his) to the plural (they, their). What is the effect of these changes? What occurred in America between 1973, when the essay was first written, and 1980, when it was again revised, to affect this usage?

2. In the typescript Murray has added references to students and teachers which were not in the original published version. For whom was the original version intended? What do the additions reveal about the intended readers of the revision?

For Writing

Prepare a checklist of the points Murray says that writers look for in revising a manuscript: information, meaning, audience, form, structure, development dimension, voice (¶s 13–20). Add others appropriate to your writing, and use the checklist as a guide in revising your own papers.

ROGER ANGELL

Angell was born in New York in 1920 into a milieu devoted to the ethics and meticulous craftsmanship of distinguished writing. His mother, Katherine Sergeant Angell, was for years the fiction editor of the *New Yorker;* his stepfather, whom his mother married when Roger was nine, was E. B. White, who took young Roger "Once More to the Lake" (pp. 142–148). As a Harvard student (B.A., 1942) he "did some reading and general [editorial] work" for his parents; the strongest influence on his style was White, whom Angell says "suffered [when he was] writing but made it look easy."

His mother, described by White as a "baseball nut and devoted parent," reinforced her son's enthusiasm for "the summer game." Angell's elegant writing about baseball transforms the sport into an art form, as the game and its analysis are played out first in the *New Yorker* and then collected in books, including *The Summer Game* (1972), *Late Innings* (1982), *Season Ticket* (1988), and *Once More around the Park* (1991). Indeed, Angell responds to "the game's great narrative powers," as one commentator has observed, as if "an Aesop, a Dickens, a Stephen King is out there somewhere, biting his quill and staring at the ceiling and then diving back into his manuscript."

Master stylists, ever alert to the nuances of good writing, are intolerant of the banal and the bad, as Angell's satire on clichés indicates. Angell uses the format of Frank Sullivan's earlier dialogues in the *New Yorker,* in which an invented character, Mr. Arbuthnot, spoke with unquestionable authority on every cliché under the sun known to man.

Return of the Cliché Expert

1   Q: Good morning, Mr. Arbuthnot. It's a pleasure to see you again, and to hear further testimony from you on the subject of clichés.

2   A: Wrong man. You're thinking of my uncle, Dr. Magnus Arbuthnot, who is no longer with us. Bought the farm, checked out, fumed out, popped off, slipped his cable, went over the pass, hit the throughway. I mean, he's gone-zo. I'm Chip Arbuthnot, his heir. His *spiritual* heir.

3   Q: But you are here to give us your views on current and established clichés, are you not?

4   A: No way.

5   Q: You're not?

6   A: I'm here to share my views.

7   Q: I see. And you are an expert in the field, are you not?

8   A: Arguably.

9   Q: You wish to argue with the court?

10   A: No, I'm arguably an expert. The adverb allows me to say something and then partly take it back.

11   Q: I think I understand.

12   A: Don't worry about it. This stuff isn't written in stone.

13   Q: You're very kind.

14   A: There's a reason for that.

15   Q: I can almost guess what it is. It's on the tip of my tongue.

16   A: I'm a people person.

17   Q: I knew it! Now, Mr. Arbuthnot, may I ask a strange question? What's that on your head?

18   A: This is my other hat.

19   Q: Your *other* hat?

20   A: This is the hat I wear when I'm being the cliché expert. When I'm doing something else, I wear a different other hat, not this one.

21   Q: Hmm. Are you telling us that being a cliché expert is not a full-time occupation?

22   A: As if. Get a grip.

23   Q: You must be a busy man, holding so many demanding jobs.

A: None of this is rocket science. But, yes, my plate is full.   24

Q: And you must have to maintain a constant schedule of   25 travels to different parts of the country, if not the world, to keep up with regional as well as occupational clichés, is that not the case?

A: Been there, done that.   26

Q: Tell me, do most people know when they're speaking in   27 clichés? Or is that a dumb question?

A: I'm not comfortable with it. If I said it was a no-brainer,   28 I'd be sending the wrong message. Let's say that some folks who think they're pushing the envelope conversationwise ain't.

Q: Mr. Arbuthnot, are there specific occupations that pro-   29 duce a greater preponderance of clichés in daily human inter-course than others do?

A: "Daily human intercourse" is very fine. Congratulations.   30

Q: Shall I repeat the question?   31

A: No, because I'm going to pass. This is a slippery slope.   32

Q: What about the sexes? Are women more likely than men   33 to—

A: Whoa. Back off, Mister. Don't go there. It's a no-win   34 situation.

Q: Oh, I'm sorry.   35

A: You're putting me between a rock and a hard place.   36

Q: I didn't mean to upset you. I apologize.   37

A: You mean you empathize.   38

Q: That's what I meant to say.   39

A: You feel my pain.   40

Q: Yes, I do, I do!   41

A: Historically, you have concerns.   42

Q: That's right!   43

A: Unless I miss my guess, you're also pro-active.   44

Q: Yup.   45

A: At the same time, you're a very private person.   46

Q: Absolutely. How did you know?   47

A: Trust me, it's easy. All you have to do is listen to your   48 inner child.

Q: So any of us can become a cliché expert—is that what   49 you're saying?

50   A: How did we end up here? Hello?

51   Q: Oop, I'm going too fast again, aren't I? Just *using* clichés doesn't do the trick—is that right?

52   A: No. You have to talk the talk and walk the walk.

53   Q: But of course. I wish we could go on with this and perhaps find out how you got to ask all the questions, instead of the court. But our time is up. I hope you've enjoyed our little meeting.

54   A: You've made my day.

55   Q: You have enlightened us all.

56   A: It doesn't get any better than this.

57   Q: Thank you, Mr Arbuthnot.

58   A: No problema.

Content

1. What's the point of writing a dialogue such as this? What's the point of reading such a dialogue?

Strategies/Structures

1. In what ways does the question and answer format suit the subject? Who is doing the questioning? For what apparent purpose? Is this the real purpose?

2. What other form or forms could Angell have used to make his point? Would any other forms have worked as effectively? Explain.

3. Describe the character of Mr. Arbuthnot, the Cliché Expert. Even though Mr. Arbuthnot is humorous, should readers take his point seriously?

Language

1. Angell uses an abundance of clichés to criticize speech (or writing) that employs them. At what point in your reading do you recognize what he's doing? Does the reader need to understand all or most of the clichés in order to understand this selection?

2. If one or two clichés are a drug on the market, why is writing so chockablock full of them such a gas, a hoot?

3. Does the excessive use of clichés necessarily make a piece of writing comic? What other characteristics make "Return of the Cliché Expert" humorous?

4. Is it ever appropriate to use clichés—even one or two—in one's writing?

For Writing

1. Write a humorous dialogue in the manner of "Return of the Cliché Expert" in which you ridicule the subject of the dialogue. To make your point, create a character, modeled on Mr. Arbuthnot, who purports to have all the answers.

2. Write a serious dialogue in which you discuss a meaningful subject. If you use Plato's Socratic dialogues as models, remember that one character always subtly or not-so-subtly guides the dialogue toward the views that reinforce the author's point.

MARY RUFFIN

Ruffin was born in Richmond, Virginia, in 1964. She earned a B.A. in English and philosophy from Virginia Commonwealth University in 1984 and an M.A. in 1986. Her mother, an artist and aspiring writer, died when Ruffin was thirteen. As a college student, Ruffin attempted for several years in her writing to come to terms with the meaning of her mother's life and death. The nine notebook entries that follow show the genesis and evolution of "Mama's Smoke" over a two-month period. They include one freewriting (#1), three drafts of a poem (#2, 3, 7), a playful free association of words (#6), and the completed poem (#8)—with which she was "never happy." In retrospect, she found the poem's first draft "far better than [its] final draft . . . because the VOICE IS REAL! I killed it."

The three preliminary prose versions (#4, 5, 9) developed from the original freewriting. The ninth and tenth (final) versions both included the same topics and most of the same language. However, at her classmates' suggestions during group discussion, Ruffin decided to revise the paper so that the opening paragraphs reinforced the theme of the title and the ultimate message of the essay. Note that Ruffin tried dramatically different modes of writing—poetry, free association, and prose—in the process of discovering the version that best suited her and her subject.

"Mama's Smoke," the resulting combination of epitaph, eulogy, and portrait, is a tribute to the continuing complexity of their relationship. Ruffin's characterization of her mother epitomizes her own complicated narrative technique and illustrates the poetic aspects of her prose: "She is something like a sequel to herself, elliptical and confusing, out of context. She speaks in fragments, interrupting in the middle of my own sentences, giving to others the illusion that I have spoken her words. But the others don't know her, don't know her words from mine. The illusion is mine." As the smoke through which Ruffin imagines her mother swirls and eddies, the image of her mother merges with precision, the different aspects of her activities and of her relationship with her daughter coalescing through the catalyst of love.

❄ Writer's Notebook Entries: The Evolution of "Mama's Smoke"

2/23   #1
Freewriting

A freewrite is all I can do again because the page is glaring more ominous even than its traditional blank stare.

The poetry won't come. I've killed it with the spearhead of desire to be Outstanding English Major.

The prose won't come because it can't break out of the stillborn poetry.

The academics won't come because they're forced into the name-dropping realm of pretension. . . . Plus, I hate traditional white male southern writers. With those accents that sound like my mother but aren't my mother at all. . . .

There must be a starting point somewhere—a thread to grasp.

Can't do it all. Must at least reach out to the part that reaches back.

Mama.

2/24 #2
Writer's Notebook, first poem draft

Mama had fierce green eyes and black hair
I know from the black and white pictures
forty years old and more
and the salt and pepper I remember
and the tired hazel that I ~~be~~ inherited
for she could have been my grandma.

Jet black hair so thick the sheen
Matched the fierceness of green eyes
That were my Mama I know cause I've
heard tell and seen the faded black and
white pictures stuffed in the cookie tin
she had for twenty some odd years
and I've kept for ten, and the memory
of the permed salt and pepper I played
in dangling my feet in mid air hung
over the chair back and the tired
hazel nestled in the hooded lids,
I inherited her eyes but without
the green snap

2/25   #3
Writer's Notebook, second poem draft

Rites

~~when~~
Back
~~Back~~ When
It was cool to smoke, she did, and was
I imagine, of course not able to remember,
the picture of glamourousness. It was
In the days before that surgeon general
Determined the hazardousness
that ~~immediately~~ ~~co rings in my ears in unison~~ is now as immediate as
with "once upon a time", ~~steeped in~~ possessing
The familiarity of ~~what raised~~ that with which
                                    reared.
Unfiltered   we were ~~raised~~. Or ~~reared,~~   ~~She was never without~~
Camels in   An ivory holder I've heard tell
and seen the legendary
~~the~~ flash of her ^fierce green eyes
~~in the wrinkled~~   rusted   ~~yellowed~~
yellowing and wrinkled in the ^cookie tin of ^black and
                    snapshots
white ~~photos~~ she hung onto for
twenty some odd years, and I now
for ten.   difficult
The lid is ~~not easy~~ to pry open.
~~She passed on a spark to me, hazel~~
~~eyes~~   miraculously
The spark ~~somehow~~ passed on,
          barely discernible in my hazel,
miscellaneous   by chromosomes
          ~~mediated by brown~~ and the bloodshot
~~irritant~~   of Menthol Virginia Slim^ully Lights
itches ~~smolders and goes cold.~~ incessant.
Itches ~~a dry itch, beyond my years.~~

2/27   #4
Writer's Notebook, first prose draft

She was a smoker, but that began in the days when it was cool to
smoke. Long before that surgeon general determined the hazardousness of the habit, and the behaviorists blasted it as an in-

fantile fixation, she was glamorous. It was unfiltered Camels in the beginning, though by the time I was around she had gone to Merits, clunky with thick filters wrapped in blotchy brown.

My mother was an artist. She used to paint, in a turquoise studio smock, portraits of everyone she knew. Though I don't remember her ever painting herself—that is except for the red polish on her toenails. Her fingernails stayed natural yellow, she said because of the turpentine, but I think nicotine contributed to the hue. I've heard that when she was young she was never without her ivory cigarette holder. She readily admitted to her vanity.

later, 2/27
Writer's Notebook, first prose draft, second installment (excerpt)

She comes to me in the middle of the night, or rather I come to her, chase her even, through strange landscapes and insidescapes. Sometimes she is an old crone, witch-like, her black hair full of salt and her green eyes bloodshot knifeslits. . . .

3/3/85   #5
Writer's Notebook, second prose draft

She can surface without warning, anytime, anyplace. Sometimes she comes and goes so quickly that I hardly notice her presence. The other day, for instance, I stood in the kitchen staring at the can of Crisco and a tattered, encrusted cookbook page. Spoon in hand, I wondered blankly for a moment how to measure solid shortening. When the idea of displacement struck me and I filled the cup half full with water, I thought it was the ghost of a physics text. By the time I realized that it had been her, she was long gone and I had to shake my head. That's the way it happens frequently.

She never answers to her name—she almost seems to run away when she comes to mind. She is called Peggy, the only nickname for Margaret she could ever tolerate. She told me once that was why I had such a simple name, something virtually unalterable, to have forever. I resemble Peggy slightly, but just like the futility of calling her, when I look for the resemblance in the mirror it isn't there—It's those other times, catching an unexpected glimpse of my reflection out of the corner of my eye, that she suddenly appears.

3/10   #6
Writer's Notebook, "playing" (free association)

Dragons

Cookie tin—shining armor—rusty knight
Desert—fire—camels—dragons
Green dragons
Slain dragons & fair maidens
Dark fair maidens—unfair damsels
Once upon atime hazardousness—dragon
Dragon—take a "drag on" a cigarette
Smoke—cool smoke—hot smoke—smoke breath
Dragon's lair—womb—cave
cookies & stories—yellowing green
eyes & hazel bloodshot
Grendel's mother
Damsel in distress
Legend—spark of the divine
Glamourousness—amourousness—clamourousness
Reptiles—evolution—snake—fake—fang
Red nails—red lips—glamour is dark—beauty light
Medieval—Middle Ages—
Middle age—
The Tale—the monomyth—hero's journey
Separation—Initiation—Return
Smoke—illusion
Birthrite—legacy—heir—air—smoke
Glamour as aloof passion—cool hotness—
artifice—surface image—imagination
hard—glamour = armor—defense mechanism
Smoking as oral fixation
Smoking as magic
Fairy tales—scales—fear in fairy tails—wicked
stepmother—poison

3/17   #7
Writer's Notebook, third poem draft (excerpt)

Rites

Back when it was cool to smoke, she did, and was
I imagine, of course not able to remember, the picture
of glamourousness. It was in the days before the surgeon
general determined the dreadful gnawing
hazardousness that is now as immediate as
once-upon-a-time, possessing the familiarity
of that with which we were reared. . . .

3/28/85   #8
Writer's Notebook, final poem

Once Upon a Time

Back when it was cool to smoke, she did, and was
I imagine, of course not able to remember, the picture
of glamourousness.
Chains of unfiltered Camels, never without the ivory
holder between blood-red nails, I've heard tell
and seen the legendary flash of her fierce green
eyes yellowing and wrinkled in the rusted
cookie tin filled to brimming with brittle
undated black and white snapshots she hung onto
for twenty-some-odd years, and I still keep.

It is difficult to pry open the lid.

Once I caught her in the mirror, her tears
a simple bewilderment to me then,
turning more complex. Now
I catch her only on the edges
of my own reflection. Her spark in my hazel,
barely discernable, bloodshot
itches, runs, waters, burns
incessant.

4/2   #9
Writer's Notebook, third prose draft
(excerpt of entire essay)

Mama's Smoke

"Not 'plain'! Pure and ageless, incorruptible! That's what your name is. I always hated mine with a passion! When people called me 'Margaret' I felt squeamish. And 'Maggie'—ugh—a literal punch in the stomach! But it's awkward to go through life with a nickname. It makes you feel always like you're not quite ever really yourself. I didn't want that for you."

Peggy wanted only the best for me, the best being an abstraction she pondered incessantly. When I was little, I would sit on the ancient wobbly wooden stool in the corner of the kitchen, rocking and squeaking, listening to her. I liked that spot because it was right over the heat duct in the winter, and caught the breeze from the screen door in the utility room in the summer. Evenings, I asked her all kinds of questions—never afraid to broach any subject—and her answers usually took off miraculously, soaring.

Sometimes I just listened to the rhythm of her plastic-soled slippers. . . .

4/23   Mama's Smoke #10
final prose version (whole essay, revised and completed)

Mama's Smoke

1   I never thought I would smoke. With her it was different— she started way back when it was cool to smoke—had been the very picture of glamour. But that was before the surgeon general determined the hazardousness that is as immediate in the origins of my consciousness as once-upon-a-time.

2   Myths are absorbing. I've been told of the chains of unfiltered Camels she used to smoke, never without the legendary ivory holder between fingers with blood-red nails. By the time I was around she had switched to Merits.

Peggy thrived on craving. She wanted only the best for me, the best being an abstraction she pondered incessantly. When I was little I would sit on the ancient wobbly wooden stool in the corner of the kitchen, rocking and squeaking, listening to her. I liked the spot because it was right over the heat duct in the winter, and caught the breeze through the screen door in the utility room in the summer. Evenings, I asked her all kinds of questions—never afraid to broach any subject—and her answers usually took off miraculously, soaring. 3

"Not 'plain'! Pure and ageless, incorruptible! That's what your name is. That's why I gave it to you. I always hated mine with a passion! When people called me 'Margaret' I felt squeamish. And 'Maggie'—ugh—a literal punch in the stomach! But it's awkward to go through life with a nickname. It makes you feel always like you're not quite ever really yourself. I didn't want that for you." 4

If I didn't understand the songs she sang, I knew the syllables by heart. Sometimes I would just listen to the rhythm of her plastic-soled slippers. I creaked my stool in time as her slippers slid on the red and white tiles, moving from one end of the long counter to the other and back, to the sink, ice box, sink again, stove, counter. There was a regularity to the irregularity that soothed me. 5

As I draw deeply on my menthol Virginia Slims Light, looking through the yellowing black and white snapshots in the rusty old cookie tin she held onto for twenty-some-odd years, I wonder what happened to make me start smoking. The lid is difficult to open. Inside there are faces, one face altered over and over, with fierce green eyes flashing, despite the brittle fadedness of the images. My hazel eyes have the spark, but only enough of a spark to torment me, to always make me seem not quite all me. Peggy stays away when I look at the pictures of her—maybe she doesn't identify with them anymore herself. She certainly used to. 6

But she also used to answer me when I called, and she no longer does that either. Often deep in my sleep I glimpse her and chase her through strange insidescapes, but she always refuses to recognize me. Once recently she consented to meet me in an abandoned ice rink. When I skated in late, she simply stared down my apologies. Suddenly busying herself with an old movie 7 projector, her back to me, she became a flailing chaos of limbs in the darkness of the rink. I gave in to the oppression of futility and seated myself behind her. At first the picture jumped and lurched on the screen, out of focus, broke once, and then smoothed out. Peggy danced a vaudeville set in our old kitchen, twirling whisks and spatulas to the soundtrack of "Clementine." When the lights came on she had disappeared, and I was alone shivering, with the distorted tune ringing in my ears.

8   Usually she surfaces so briefly and unobtrusively that I'm not sure she has been there until after she's gone. Sometimes she appears an old haggard crone, the salt in her hair so thick that the pepper looks like dirt streaks washing away. Other times she is vital, younger than I am, the sheen of her black hair almost blinding. In the buttered daylight of my kitchen, as I stand blankly staring at the can of Crisco and the Pyrex measuring cup, I guess it is the sudden memory of a physics lesson that makes me think of using water to measure the solid substance. Displacement. Only later, as I gently knead the biscuit dough, careful not to bruise it, I realize that she has been there. Her smirk of disgust at the soybean powder in the open cabinet gave her away—she couldn't resist a mild "eee-gad" under her breath.

9   · Peggy is steeped in colloquialism, figures of speech that barely escape the shallows of cliché. She wrote a novel once, some kind of sequel to *Gone with the Wind* and now she comes to me at the typewriter sometimes, though rarely at the notebook stage, and whispers more criticism than commentary. She burned it, burned it in a fit of rage. Justified, for they wouldn't make her known. One attempt, one refusal. The only grace is to make a clean break.

10   She is something like a sequel to herself, elliptical and confusing, out of context. She speaks in fragments, interrupting in the middle of my own sentences, giving to others the illusion that I have spoken her words. But that's not exactly accurate either. The others don't know her, don't know her words from mine. The illusion is mine.

11   The hiss of the word "fixatif" on a spray can evokes a frustrated whimper of reminiscence. The bite of turpentine and linseed oil draws her. She is a painter of portraits and has rendered a likeness of almost everyone she is close to at one time or another, I

believe, with the exception of herself. When I pick up a piece of charcoal she jumps in and jerks my hand, refusing to let me catch an image clearly. I have forsaken our art and she will not let me be forgiven so easily. But when I settle back and contemplate my own regrets, she relents. I feel her take her dry brush in hand and trace my features, a delicious tickle I revered as a child.

The legacy of paint stains on her pale turquoise smock, like the rhythm of the shuffle of her slippers on the floor, is her highest art. She denies it, of course, as obstinately as she refuses to appear when I look for her in the mirror. But she proves it as she shows up at those moments when I catch my reflection unexpectedly out of the corner of my eye.   12

The conversations we have now in black coffee cups and clouds of smoke are the closest we come to shared sustenance. They are always late, the times when it's most conspicuous to be awake. We plan the colors for the drapes and the throw pillows to furnish some future studio. The studio gradually takes shape, perfect, and then shatters in a coughing fit. I hear her in another room, hacking, fading, and then she's gone.   13

Just as she never stays, she never stays away for long. She was beautiful in her day and she still preens, still believes underneath in the ultimate importance of surfaces.   14

At parties, her old acquaintances appear as her friends. They ask me if I'm in art school and the flinching negative reply is overridden by their awe at my study of "philosophy."   15

"So like her! Right down to the hair and eyes, though not quite so dark, not quite so green. But underneath, Peggy *was* a philosopher, she was, so wise. . . ."   16

And Peggy surfaces and "eee-gads" so loudly in my ear that the friends' politenesses go under and my own return politenesses are just-not-quite-right. I sip my wine and kick Peggy in the shin. The acquaintances wander off whispering, "Almost the spitting image, except not nearly so . . . *genuine*. . . . This new generation. . . ."   17

Later, Peggy and I have pillow fights. The pillows are wet. The stains in the morning are on my face in the angry mirror. My eyes are hazel, murky. Peggy's eyes are clear, stinging green. When the lids began to droop, right before they closed for good, she cried bitterly in the mirror. Then I felt simple bewilderment,   18 turning more complex. She still will not understand that her spattered smock is finer than the portraits. We light up. We cough out our truce.

For Writing

These various drafts of notebook, poetry, freewriting, and prose demonstrate the evolution of Mary Ruffin's "Mama's Smoke." You can compare and analyze these for evidence of development of character, style, narrative persona, changes in organization, incorporation of poetic language into the prose versions, and control over tone and relationship between the mother and daughter. You might also want to try to write a poem as a preliminary draft of a prose paper. Just play around with words, ideas, images, and sounds until they coalesce.

• • •

The three pieces of fiction that conclude Parts I, II, and III of *The Essay Connection* are "On Discovery" (pp. 132–135), from Maxine Hong Kingston's *China Men*, and the short stories "Shiloh" (pp. 289–304), by Bobbie Ann Mason, and "What We Talk About When We Talk About Love" (pp. 547–560), by Raymond Carver. Because these pieces have resonance with topics, issues, and techniques used in other selections throughout the book, they are not followed by study questions. They are intended to provide focus for far-ranging discussions as determined by the individual instructor and class.

MAXINE HONG KINGSTON

Kingston's autobiographical writings are haunted by questions of gender and identity and belonging: what relation has she and the others she writes about to China, to other family members, to America, how much to herself alone? And what belongs to her? Kingston was born in Stockton, California, in 1940, the eldest American-born child of recent Chinese immigrants. At home she learned Chinese, her only language until she started first grade (which caused her to score "zero" on her first I.Q. test, in English), and Chinese customs from stories exchanged in her parents' laundry. She graduated from the University of California at Berkeley in 1962, married actor Earll Kingston, had a son, and lived in Hawaii before returning to Berkeley. She publishes poetry, stories, and essays in national magazines, but is best known for her autobiography, *The Woman Warrior: Memoirs of a Girlhood Among Ghosts* (1975), winner of the National Book Critics Circle Award for nonfiction, and *China Men* (1980), winner of the American Book Award. Her most recent book is a novel, *Tripmaster Monkey* (1989).

    China Men focuses primarily on the meaning of immigration, cultural displacement, and cultural assimilation for Chinese men who emigrated to America, the "Gold Mountain" of Chinese legend. Its opening section, "On Discovery," is a parable in which a traditional Chinese man arrives by accident in the Land of Women, where he is forced into looking and behaving like a woman through the painful processes of having his ears pierced, his foot bones broken and bound, his eyebrows plucked and face made up—much to his embarrassment and shame. This metaphorical definition of a Chinese woman implies an equation: Chinese women are to Chinese men as Chinese men are to Americans. And this equation defines China men (note the connotation of fragility) in America. Metaphors and parables are useful devices for making meaning—explaining, discovering, or inventing new significance.

On Discovery

O nce upon a time, a man, named Tang Ao, looking for the   1
Gold Mountain, crossed an ocean, and came upon the Land of Women. The women immediately captured him, not on guard against ladies. When they asked Tang Ao to come along, he followed; if he had had male companions, he would've winked over his shoulder.

    "We have to prepare you to meet the queen," the women   2
said. They locked him in a canopied apartment equipped with pots of makeup, mirrors, and a woman's clothes. "Let us help you off with your armor and boots," said the women. They slipped

his coat off his shoulders, pulled it down his arms, and shackled his wrists behind him. The women who kneeled to take off his shoes chained his ankles together.

3   A door opened, and he expected to meet his match, but it was only two old women with sewing boxes in their hands. "The less you struggle, the less it'll hurt," one said, squinting a bright eye as she threaded her needle. Two captors sat on him while another held his head. He felt an old woman's dry fingers trace his ear; the long nail on her little finger scraped his neck. "What are you doing?" he asked. "Sewing your lips together," she joked, blackening needles in a candle flame. The ones who sat on him bounced with laughter. But the old women did not sew his lips together. They pulled his earlobes taut and jabbed a needle through each of them. They had to poke and probe before puncturing the layers of skin correctly, the hole in the front of the lobe in line with the one in back, the layers of skin sliding about so. They worked the needle through—a last jerk for the needle's wide eye ("needle's nose" in Chinese). They strung his raw flesh with silk threads; he could feel the fibers.

4   The women who sat on him turned to direct their attention to his feet. They bent his toes so far backward that his arched foot cracked. The old ladies squeezed each foot and broke many tiny bones along the sides. They gathered his toes, toes over and under one another like a knot of ginger root. Tang Ao wept with pain. As they wound the bandages tight and tighter around his feet, the women sang footbinding songs to distract him: "Use aloe for binding feet and not for scholars."

5   During the months of a season, they fed him on women's food: the tea was thick with white chrysanthemums and stirred the cool female winds inside his body; chicken wings made his hair shine; vinegar soup improved his womb. They drew the loops of thread through the scabs that grew daily over the holes in his earlobes. One day they inserted gold hoops. Every night they unbound his feet, but his veins had shrunk, and the blood pumping through them hurt so much, he begged to have his feet re-wrapped tight. They forced him to wash his used bandages, which were embroidered with flowers and smelled of rot and cheese. He hung the bandages up to dry, streamers that dropped

and draped wall to wall. He felt embarrassed; the wrappings were like underwear, and they were his.

One day his attendants changed his gold hoops to jade 6 studs and strapped his feet to shoes that curved like bridges. They plucked out each hair on his face, powdered him white, painted his eyebrows like a moth's wings, painted his cheeks and lips red. He served a meal at the queen's court. His hips swayed and his shoulders swiveled because of his shaped feet. "She's pretty, don't you agree?" the diners said, smacking their lips at his dainty feet as he bent to put dishes before them.

In the Women's Land there are no taxes and no wars. Some 7 scholars say that the country was discovered during the reign of Empress Wu (A.D. 694–705), and some earlier than that, A.D. 441, and it was in North America.

Part II

Determining Ideas in a Sequence

$$\boxed{5}\ Narration$$

Narration, telling a story, is a particularly attractive mode of writing. Ours is a storytelling culture. It is as old as Indian legends, Br'er Rabbit, Grimm's fairy tales, and the stories of Edgar Allan Poe. It is as new as speakers' warm-up jokes ("A funny thing happened on my way to . . .") and anecdotal leads to otherwise impersonal news stories. Thus *Newsweek* begins a lead article, "The Agony of Pan Am Flight 73," with a dramatic vignette that starts

> It was hot inside the cabin and the lights were growing
> dim. Four jittery gunmen had herded 374 passengers and
> 15 crew members into the center of the Boeing 747. Then
> at 9:55 p.m. the lights went out for good. The terrorists
> opened fire. Two grenades exploded. Shouting "Jihad!
> Jihad!" the gunmen randomly fired their automatic
> weapons into the panic-stricken pack of innocents.

This paragraph contains the major elements of a narrative: *characters* (in this case, the bad guys, "four jittery gunmen," and the good guys, "374 passengers and 15 crew members"); the *conflict* (evil versus good); the *motives* (hijacking versus safety/survival); the *plot* (which side will win or prevail? how?); the *setting* (the hot interior of a Boeing 747 at 9:55 P.M.; *point of view* (the third-person account of a nonparticipant—in this case, not even an eyewitness); even a bit of *dialogue* ("Jihad! Jihad!"). All these features make the above incident or any vivid narrative a particularly easy form of writing for readers to remember. As this narration reveals, a narrative does *not* necessarily have to be a personal essay.

Narratives can be whole novels, stories, essays, or segments of other types of writings. They can be as long and complicated as Charles Dickens's novels or an account of the Watergate break-in, trial, and aftermath. Or they can be as short and to the point as the following narrative by student Myrna Greenfield, complete in a single paragraph:

> now every dream i'd ever dreamed about college room-mates said they are your best friends and the two of you fall in love with two men who are best friends and you get married after college to the best friends and you move to minneapolis or new rochelle and live next door and you have kids who grow up to be best friends with your best friend's kids. but kim was coolish and i was warmish and kim loved beethoven and i loved beatles and kim was neat and i was sloppy and kim was quiet and i was noisy as all hell broke loose. so much for the dream.

Myrna, as an author writing in the first person, has efficiently (although with unconventional punctuation) narrated two stories. The first, structured by a unified chronological progression, relates the myth of a college woman's stereotyped life history. The second, emphasizing variations on the theme of incompatibility, tells the story of the actual relationship between the author and her roommate. There are two main characters in the first story: Myrna's idealized version of herself and Kim. The two characters in the second story are the actual roommates. Each story has a setting: college and the suburbs in the first; college in the second. Each story covers a period of time—the entire life span in the first; the recent past in the second. The second sentence negates the first and leads to the short, punchy emotional climax, "so much for the dream."

A narrative need not be fictional, as the above examples and the essays in this section indicate. When you're writing a narrative based on real people, actual incidents, you shape the material to emphasize the *point of view, sequence of action* (a chase, an exploration), a *theme* (greed, pleasure), a *particular relationship between characters* (love, antagonism), or the *personalities of the people involved* (vigorous, passive). This shaping—supplying information or other specific details where necessary, deleting trivial or irrelevant material—is essential in transforming skeletal diary entries (see Twain in Chapter 3) into three-dimensional configurations.

A narrative can *exist for its own sake.* As sixteenth-century poet and courtier Sir Philip Sidney observed, such writing can attract "children from play and old men from the chimney corner." Though Ann Upperco Dolman's comic tale of "Learning to Drive" (pp. 174–177) typifies the experiences of thousands of new teenage drivers, it won't improve anyone's learning curve—but everyone who has ever survived driving lessons will enjoy it. Through a narrative you can also *illustrate or explore a personality or an idea.* In the classic "Once More to the Lake" (pp. 142–148), E. B. White uses his own experiences on a timeless summer vacation to explore the continuity of generations of parents and children, embedding short narrative vignettes into the overarching narrative structure. In "The Death of the Profane" (pp. 165–172), Patricia Williams narrates a single narrative incident—the refusal of a clerk to admit her to a Benetton store where she wanted to shop. Interpreting this experience explicitly from three different perspectives (though more are implicit), Williams extends her understanding of a profound personal problem to encompass race relations in the United States.

If you wish to write a personal narrative you can *present a whole or partial biography or autobiography,* as does Frederick Douglass in "Resurrection,"(pp. 150–156). This excerpt from Douglass's *Life and Times* recounts his defiance of a Simon Legree–like overseer. This was "the turning-point in my career as a slave. . . . It recalled the departed self-confidence, and inspired me again with a determination to be free."

Through narration you can *impart information* or *an account of historical events,* either from an impartial or—more likely—an engaged eyewitness point of view, as Zitkala-Sa does in excerpts from *The School Days of an Indian Girl* (pp. 254–262). Through narration you can, as Zitkala-Sa also does, *present a powerful argument, overt or implicit.* Lynda Barry's "The Sanctuary of School" (pp. 647–651) also uses the example of herself (and her brother—"children with the sound turned off") to present the implied argument that for neglected youngsters public schools are a lifeline and should be funded at a level that reflects their vital importance. Fables, parables, and other *morality* or *cautionary tales* are as old as Aesop, as familiar as the Old and New Testaments, as contemporary as Judith Ortiz Cofer's narrative about storytelling itself, "*Casa:* A Partial Remembrance of a Puerto Rican Childhood" (pp. 157–163). Here, the process of telling and interpreting a story with a moral reinforces the close female community of tellers and listeners.

To write a narrative you can ask, What do I want to demonstrate? Through what characters, performing what actions or thinking what thoughts? In what setting and time frame? From what point of view do I want to tell the tale? Do I want to use a first-person involved narrator who may also be a character in the story, as are the narrators of all the essays in this section? Or a third-person narrator, either on the scene or depending on the reports of other people, as in the *Newsweek* account quoted on page 137? An easy way to remember these questions is to ask yourself

1. *Who* participated?
2. *What* happened?
3. *Why* did this event/these phenomena happen?
4. *When* did it (or they) happen?
5. *Where* did it (or they) happen?
6. *How* did it (or they) happen? Under what circumstances?

Narratives have as many purposes, as many plots, as many characters as there are people to write them. You have but to examine your life, your thoughts, your experiences, to find an unwritten library of narratives yet to tell. Therein lie a thousand tales. Or a thousand and one. . . .

STRATEGIES FOR WRITING— NARRATION

1. You'll need to consider, "What is the purpose of my narrative?" Am I telling the tale for its own sake, or using it to make a larger point?
2. For what audience am I writing this? What will they have experienced or be able to understand, and what will I need to explain? How do I want my audience to react?
3. What is the focus, the conflict of my narrative? How will it begin? Gain momentum and develop to a climax? End? What emphasis will I give each part, or separate scenes or incidents within each part?
4. Will I write from a first- or third-person point of view? Will I be a major character in my narrative? As a participant or as an observer? Or both, if my present self is observing my past self?
5. What is my attitude toward my material? What tone do I want to use? Will it be consistent throughout, or will it change during the course of events?

E. B. WHITE

> "Once More to the Lake," a narrative of father and son, timeless
> generations in the eternal Maine countryside, conveys significant
> intangibles (love—parental and filial; the importance of nature;
> the inevitability of growth, change, and death) through memo-
> rably specific details. White leads us to the lake itself ("cool and
> motionless"), down the path to yesteryear, where the continuity
> of generations intermingles past, present, and future until they
> become almost indistinguishable: "The years were a mirage
> and there had been no years. . . ." Everywhere White's son,
> thoroughly identified with his father, does the same things White
> had done at the same lake as a boy—putting about in the same
> boat, catching the same bass, drinking the same soda pop,
> enjoying the same ritualistic swim after the same summer thunder-
> storm (see also Scott Russell Sanders's "The Inheritance of Tools"
> [pp. 319–328]). The mood of "peace and goodness and jollity" that
> White recreates indelibly shifts, however, as the cosmic chill of
> the last sentence reminds us of the inevitable passing of genera-
> tions. (For a biographical sketch of E. B. White, see page 39.)

Once More to the Lake

1   One summer, along about 1904, my father rented a camp on a
lake in Maine and took us all there for the month of August.
We all got ringworm from some kittens and had to rub Pond's Extract on our arms and legs night and morning, and my father
rolled over in a canoe with all his clothes on; but outside of that
the vacation was a success and from then on none of us ever
thought there was any place in the world like that lake in Maine.
We returned summer after summer—always on August 1st for
one month. I have since become a salt-water man, but sometimes
in summer there are days when the restlessness of the tides and
the fearful cold of the sea water and the incessant wind which
blows across the afternoon and into the evening make me wish
for the placidity of a lake in the woods. A few weeks ago this feeling got so strong I bought myself a couple of bass hooks and a

spinner and returned to the lake where we used to go, for a week's fishing and to revisit old haunts.

I took along my son, who had never had any fresh water up 2 his nose and who had seen lily pads only from train windows. On the journey over to the lake I began to wonder what it would be like. I wondered how time would have marred this unique, this holy spot—the coves and streams, the hills that the sun set behind, the camps and the paths behind the camps. I was sure the tarred road would have found it out and I wondered in what other ways it would be desolated. It is strange how much you can remember about places like that once you allow your mind to return into the grooves which lead back. You remember one thing, and that suddenly reminds you of another thing. I guess I remembered clearest of all the early mornings, when the lake was cool and motionless, remembered how the bedroom smelled of the lumber it was made of and of the wet woods whose scent entered through the screen. The partitions in the camp were thin and did not extend clear to the top of the rooms, and as I was always the first up I would dress softly so as not to wake the others, and sneak out into the sweet outdoors and start out in the canoe, keeping close along the shore in the long shadows of the pines. I remembered being very careful never to rub my paddle against the gunwale for fear of disturbing the stillness of the cathedral.

The lake had never been what you would call a wild lake. 3 There were cottages sprinkled around the shores, and it was in farming country although the shores of the lake were quite heavily wooded. Some of the cottages were owned by nearby farmers, and you would live at the shore and eat your meals at the farmhouse. That's what our family did. But although it wasn't wild, it was a fairly large and undisturbed lake and there were places in it which, to a child at least, seemed infinitely remote and primeval.

I was right about the tar: it led to within half a mile of the 4 shore. But when I got back there, with my boy, and we settled into a camp near a farmhouse and into the kind of summertime I had known, I could tell that it was going to be pretty much the same as it had been before—I knew it, lying in bed the first morning, smelling the bedroom, and hearing the boy sneak quietly out and go off along the shore in a boat. I began to sustain the illusion that he was I, and therefore by simple transposition, that I was my father. This sensation persisted, kept cropping up all the time we were there. It was not an entirely new feeling but in this setting it grew much stronger. I seemed to be living a dual existence. I would be in the middle of some simple act, I would be picking up a bait box or laying down a table fork, or I would be saying something, and suddenly it would be not I but my father who was saying the words or making the gesture. It gave me a creepy sensation.

5   We went fishing the first morning. I felt the same damp moss covering the worms in the bait can, and saw the dragonfly alight on the tip of my rod as it hovered a few inches from the surface of the water. It was the arrival of this fly that convinced me beyond any doubt that everything was as it always had been, that the years were a mirage and there had been no years. The small waves were the same, chucking the rowboat under the chin as we fished at anchor, and the boat was the same boat, the same color green and the ribs broken in the same places, and under the floorboards the same fresh-water leavings and debris—the dead helgramite, the wisps of moss, the rusty discarded fishhook, the dried blood from yesterday's catch. We stared silently at the tips of our rods, at the dragonflies that came and went. I lowered the tip of mine into the water, tentatively, pensively dislodging the fly, which darted two feet away, poised, darted two feet back, and came to a rest again a little farther up the rod. There had been no years between the ducking of this dragonfly and the other one— the one that was part of memory. I looked at the boy, who was silently watching his fly, and it was my hands that held his rod, my eyes watching. I felt dizzy and didn't know which rod I was at the end of.

6   We caught two bass, hauling them in briskly as though they were mackerel, pulling them over the side of the boat in a businesslike manner without any landing net, and stunning them with a blow on the back of the head. When we got back for a swim before lunch, the lake was exactly where we had left it, the same number of inches from the dock, and there was only the merest suggestion of a breeze. This seemed an utterly enchanted sea, this lake you could leave to its own devices for a few hours and come back to, and find that it had not stirred, this constant

and trustworthy body of water. In the shallows, the dark, water-soaked sticks and twigs, smooth and old, were undulating in clusters on the bottom against the clean ribbed sand, and the track of the mussel was plain. A school of minnows swam by, each minnow with its small individual shadow, doubling the attendance, so clear and sharp in the sunlight. Some of the other campers were in swimming, along the shore, one of them with a cake of soap, and the water felt thin and clear and unsubstantial. Over the years there had been this person with the cake of soap, this cultist, and here he was. There had been no years.

Up to the farmhouse to dinner through the teeming, dusty   7
field, the road under our sneakers was only a two-track road. The middle track was missing, the one with the marks of the hooves and the splotches of dried, flaky manure. There had always been three tracks to choose from in choosing which track to walk in; now the choice was narrowed down to two. For a moment I missed terribly the middle alternative. But the way led past the tennis court, and something about the way it lay there in the sun reassured me; the tape had loosened along the backline, the alleys were green with plantains and other weeds, and the net (installed in June and removed in September) sagged in the dry noon, and the whole place steamed with midday heat and hunger and emptiness. There was a choice of pie for dessert, and one was blueberry and one was apple, and the waitresses were the same country girls, there having been no passage of time, only the illusion of it as in a dropped curtain—the waitresses were still fifteen; their hair had been washed, that was the only difference—they had been to the movies and seen the pretty girls with the clean hair.

Summertime, oh summertime, pattern of life indelible, the   8
fade-proof lake, the wood unshatterable, the pasture with the sweet fern and the juniper forever and ever, summer without end; this was the background, and the life along the shore was the design, the cottages with their innocent and tranquil design, their tiny docks with the flagpole and the American flag floating against the white clouds in the blue sky, the little paths over the roots of the trees leading from camp to camp and the paths leading back to the outhouses and the can of lime for sprinkling, and at the souvenir counters at the store the miniature birchbark

canoes and the post cards that showed things looking a little better than they looked. This was the American family at play,
escaping the city heat, wondering whether the newcomers in the
camp at the head of the cove were "common" or "nice," wondering whether it was true that the people who drove up for Sunday
dinner at the farmhouse were turned away because there wasn't
enough chicken.

9   It seemed to me, as I kept remembering all this, that those
times and those summers had been infinitely precious and worth
saving. There had been jollity and peace and goodness. The
arriving (at the beginning of August) had been so big a business
in itself, at the railway station the farm wagon drawn up, the first
smell of the pine-laden air, the first glimpse of the smiling farmer,
and the great importance of the trunks and your father's enormous authority in such matters, and the feel of the wagon under
you for the long ten-mile haul, and at the top of the last long hill
catching the first view of the lake after eleven months of not seeing this cherished body of water. The shouts and cries of the other
campers when they saw you, and the trunks to be unpacked, to
give up their rich burden. (Arriving was less exciting nowadays,
when you sneaked up in your car and parked it under a tree near
the camp and took out the bags and in five minutes it was all over,
no fuss, no loud wonderful fuss about trunks.)

10   Peace and goodness and jollity. The only thing that was
wrong now, really, was the sound of the place, an unfamiliar nervous sound of the outboard motors. This was the note that jarred,
the one thing that would sometimes break the illusion and set the
years moving. In those other summertimes all motors were in-
board; and when they were at a little distance, the noise they
made was a sedative, an ingredient of summer sleep. They were
one-cylinder and two-cylinder engines, and some were make-
and-break and some were jump-spark, but they all made a sleepy
sound across the lake. The one-lungers throbbed and fluttered,
and the twin-cylinder ones purred and purred, and that was a
quiet sound too. But now the campers all had outboards. In the
daytime, in the hot mornings, these motors made a petulant, irri-
table sound; at night, in the still evening when the afterglow lit
the water, they whined about one's ears like mosquitoes. My boy
loved our rented outboard, and his great desire was to achieve

singlehanded mastery over it, and authority, and he soon learned the trick of choking it a little (but not too much), and the adjustment of the needle valve. Watching him I would remember the things you could do with the old one-cylinder engine with the heavy flywheel, how you could have it eating out of your hand if you got really close to it spiritually. Motor boats in those days didn't have clutches, and you would make a landing by shutting off the motor at the proper time and coasting in with a dead rudder. But there was a way of reversing them, if you learned the trick, by cutting the switch and putting it on again exactly on the final dying revolution of the flywheel, so that it would kick back against compression and begin reversing. Approaching a dock in a strong following breeze, it was difficult to slow up sufficiently by the ordinary coasting method, and if a boy felt he had complete mastery over his motor, he was tempted to keep it running beyond its time and then reverse it a few feet from the dock. It took a cool nerve, because if you threw the switch a twentieth of a second too soon you would catch the flywheel when it still had speed enough to go up past center, and the boat would leap ahead, charging bull-fashion at the dock.

We had a good week at the camp. The bass were biting well and the sun shone endlessly, day after day. We would be tired at night and lie down in the accumulated heat of the little bedrooms after the long hot day and the breeze would stir almost imperceptibly outside and the smell of the swamp drift in through the rusty screens. Sleep would come easily and in the morning the red squirrel would be on the roof, tapping out his gay routine. I kept remembering everything, lying in bed in the mornings—the small steamboat that had a long rounded stern like the lip of a Ubangi, and how quietly she ran on the moonlight sails, when the older boys played their mandolins and the girls sang and we ate doughnuts dipped in sugar, and how sweet the music was on the water in the shining night, and what it had felt like to think about girls then. After breakfast we would go up to the store and the things were in the same place—the minnows in a bottle, the plugs and spinners, disarranged and pawed over by the youngsters from the boys' camp, the Fig Newtons and the Beeman's gum. Outside, the road was tarred and cars stood in front of the store. Inside, all was just as it had always been, except there was more

Coca-Cola and not so much Moxie and root beer and birch beer and sarsaparilla. We would walk out with a bottle of pop apiece and sometimes the pop would backfire up our noses and hurt. We explored the streams, quietly, where the turtles slid off the sunny logs and dug their way into the soft bottom; and we lay on the town wharf and fed worms to the tame bass. Everywhere we went I had trouble making out which was I, the one walking at my side, the one walking in my pants.

12   One afternoon while we were there at that lake a thunder-storm came up. It was like the revival of an old melodrama that I had seen long ago with childish awe. The second-act climax of the drama of the electrical disturbance over a lake in America had not changed in any important respect. This was the big scene, still the big scene. The whole thing was so familiar, the first feeling of oppression and heat and a general air around camp of not want-ing to go very far away. In midafternoon (it was all the same) a curious darkening of the sky, and a lull in everything that had made life tick; and then the way the boats suddenly swung the other way at their moorings with the coming of a breeze out of the new quarter, and the premonitory rumble. Then the kettle drum, then the snare, then the bass drum and cymbals, then crackling light against the dark, and the gods grinning and lick-ing their chops in the hills. Afterward the calm, the rain steadily rustling in the calm lake, the return of light and hope and spirits, and the campers running out in joy and relief to go swimming in the rain, their bright cries perpetuating the deathless joke about how they were getting simply drenched, and the children scream-ing with delight at the new sensation of bathing in the rain, and the joke about getting drenched linking the generations in a strong indestructible chain. And the comedian who waded in carrying an umbrella.

13   When the others went swimming my son said he was going in too. He pulled his dripping trunks from the line where they had hung all through the shower, and wrung them out. Lan-guidly, and with no thought of going in, I watching him, his hard little body, skinny and bare, saw him wince slightly as he pulled up around his vitals the small, soggy, icy garment. As he buckled the swollen belt suddenly my groin felt the chill of death.

Content

1. Characterize White's son. Why is he referred to as "my son" and "the boy" but never by name?
2. How do the ways in which the boy and his father relate to the lake environment emphasize their personal relationship? In which ways are these similar to the relationship between the narrator and his father, the boy's grandfather? Are there any significant differences, stated or implied?
3. White emphasizes the "peace and goodness and jollity" of the summers at the lake. What incidents and details reinforce this emphasis? Why, then, does White end with "As he buckled the swollen belt suddenly my groin felt the chill of death" (¶ 13)?

Strategies/Structures

1. Many narratives proceed chronologically from the beginning to the end of the time period they cover, relating the events of that period in the sequence in which they occurred. Instead, White organizes this narrative topically. What are the major topics? Why do they come in the order they do, concluding with the thunderstorm and its aftermath?
2. What are the effects of White's frequent repetition of phrases ("there had been no years") and words ("same")? What details or incidents does he use to illustrate the cycle of time?

Language

1. What language contributes to the relaxed mood of this essay? In what ways does the mood fit the subject?
2. Beginning writers are often advised when writing description to be sparing of adjectives and adverbs—to put the weight on nouns and verbs instead. Does White do this? Consistently? Pick a paragraph and analyze it to illustrate your answer.

For Writing

1. Tell the story of your experiences in a particular place—school building, restaurant, vacation spot, hometown, place visited—that emphasizes the influence of the place on your experiences and on your understanding of them. Identify what makes it memorable, but do not describe it in the picture-pretty manner of a travel brochure.

2. Write a narrative in which you focus on a significant relationship between yourself at a particular age and another member of your family of a different generation, either older or younger. If you emphasize its specific features you will probably capture some of its common or universal elements as well.

FREDERICK DOUGLASS

Douglass (1817–1895) was born a slave in Talbot County, Maryland. Unlike many slaves, he learned to read, and the power of this accomplishment coupled with an iron physique and the will to match, enabled him to escape to New York in 1838. For the next twenty-five years he toured the country as a powerful spokesperson for the abolitionist movement, serving as an adviser to Harriet Beecher Stowe, author of *Uncle Tom's Cabin*, and to President Lincoln, among others. After the war he campaigned for civil rights for African-Americans and women. In 1890 his political significance was acknowledged in his appointment as minister to Haiti.

Slave narratives, written or dictated by the hundreds in the nineteenth century, provided memorable accounts of the physical, geographical, and psychological movement from captivity to freedom, from dependence to independence. Douglass's autobiography, an abolitionist document like many other slave narratives, is exceptional in its forthright language and absence of stereotyping of either whites or blacks; his people are multidimensional. Crisis points, and the insights and opportunities they provide, are natural topics for personal narratives (see also Patricia Williams's "The Death of the Profane" [pp. 165–172], Richard Rodriguez's "None of This Is Fair" [pp. 375–380], and Richard Wright's "The Power of Books" [pp. 409–418]). This episode, taken from the first version (of four) of *The Narrative of the Life of Frederick Douglass, an American Slave* (1845), explains the incident that was "the turning point in my career as a slave," for it enabled him to make the transformation from slave to human being.

Resurrection

I have already intimated that my condition was much worse, during the first six months of my stay at Mr. Covey's, than in the last six. The circumstances leading to the change in Mr. Covey's course toward me form an epoch in my humble history. You have seen how a man was made a slave; you shall see how a slave was made a man. On one of the hottest days of the month of August, 1833, Bill Smith, William Hughes, a slave named Eli, and myself, were engaged in fanning wheat. Hughes was clearing the fanned wheat from before the fan. Eli was turning, Smith was feeding, and I was carrying wheat to the fan. The work was simple, requiring strength rather than intellect; yet, to one entirely unused to such work, it came very hard. About three o'clock of that day, I broke down; my strength failed me; I was seized with a violent aching of the head, attended with extreme dizziness; I trembled in every limb. Finding what was coming, I nerved myself up, feeling it would never do to stop work. I stood as long as I could stagger to the hopper with grain. When I could stand no longer, I fell, and felt as if held down by an immense weight. The fan of course stopped; every one had his own work to do; and no one could do the work of the other, and have his own go on at the same time.

Mr. Covey was at the house, about one hundred yards from the treading-yard where we were fanning. On hearing the fan stop, he left immediately, and came to the spot where we were. He hastily inquired what the matter was. Bill answered that I was sick, and there was no one to bring wheat to the fan. I had by this time crawled away under the side of the post and rail-fence by which the yard was enclosed, hoping to find relief by getting out of the sun. He then asked where I was. He was told by one of the hands. He came to the spot, and, after looking at me awhile, asked me what was the matter. I told him as well as I could, for I scarce had strength to speak. He then gave me a savage kick in the side, and told me to get up. I tried to do so, but fell back in the attempt. He gave me another kick, and again told me to rise. I again tried, and succeeded in gaining my feet; but, stooping to get the tub with which I was feeding the fan, I again staggered and fell. While down in this situation, Mr. Covey took up the hickory slat with which Hughes had been striking off the half-bushel measure, and with it gave me a heavy blow upon the head, making a large wound, and the blood ran freely; and with this again told me to get up. I made no effort to comply, having now made up my mind to let him do his worst. In a short time after receiving this blow, my head grew better. Mr. Covey had now left me to my fate. At this moment I resolved, for the first time, to go to my master, enter a complaint, and ask his protection. In order to do this, I must that afternoon walk seven miles; and this, under the circumstances, was truly a severe undertaking. I was exceedingly feeble; made so as much by the kicks and blows which I received, as by the severe fit of sickness to which I had been subjected. I, however, watched my chance, while Covey was looking in an opposite direction, and started for St. Michael's: I succeeded in getting a considerable distance on my way to the woods, when Covey discovered me, and called after me to come back, threatening what he would do if I did not come. I disregarded both his calls and his threats, and made my way to the woods as fast as my feeble state would allow and thinking I might be overhauled by him if I kept to the road, I walked through the woods, keeping far enough from the road to avoid detection, and near enough to prevent losing my way. I had not gone far before my little strength again failed me. I could go no farther. I fell down, and lay for a considerable time. The blood was yet oozing from the wound on my head. For a time I thought I should bleed to death; and think now that I should have done so, but that the blood so matted my hair as to stop the wound. After lying there about three quarters of an hour, I nerved myself up again, and started on my way, through bogs and briers, bare-footed and bareheaded, tearing my feet sometimes at nearly every step; and after a journey of about seven miles, occupying some five hours to perform it, I arrived at master's store. I then presented an appearance enough to affect any but a heart of iron. From the crown of my head to my feet, I was covered with blood. My hair was all clotted with dust and blood; my shirt was stiff with blood. My legs and feet were torn in sundry places with briers and thorns, and were also covered in blood. I suppose I looked like a man who had escaped a den of wild beasts, and barely escaped them. In this state I appeared before my master, humbly entreating him to interpose his authority for my protection. I told him all the circumstances as well as I could, and it seemed, as I spoke, at times to affect him. He would then walk the floor, and seek to justify Covey by saying he expected I deserved it. He asked me what I wanted. I told him, to let me get a new home; that as sure as I lived with Mr. Covey again, I should live with but to die with him; that Covey would surely kill me; he was in a fair way for it. Master Thomas ridiculed the idea that there was any danger of Mr. Covey's killing me, and said that he knew Mr. Covey, that he was a good man, and that he could not think of taking me from him; that, should he do so, he would lose the whole year's wages; that I belonged to Mr. Covey for one year, and that I must go back to him, come what might; and that I must not trouble him with any more stories, or that he would himself *get hold of me.* After threatening me thus, he gave me a very large dose of salts, telling me that I might remain in St. Michael's that night, (it being quite late,) but that I must be off back to Mr. Covey's early in the morning; and that if I did not, he would *get hold of me,* which meant that he would whip me. I remained all night, and, according to his orders, I started off to Covey's in the morning, (Saturday morning,) wearied in body and broken in spirit. I got no supper that night, or breakfast that morning. I reached Covey's about nine o'clock; and just as I was getting over the fence that divided Mrs. Kemp's fields from ours, out ran Covey with his cowskin, to give me another whipping. Before he could reach me, I succeeded in getting to the cornfield; and as the corn was very high, it afforded me the means of hiding. He seemed very angry, and searched for me a long time. My behavior was altogether unaccountable. He finally gave up the chase, thinking, I suppose, that I must come home for something to eat; he would give himself no further trouble in looking for me. I spent that day mostly in the woods, having the alternative before me—to go home and be whipped to death, or stay in the woods and be starved to death. That night, I fell in with Sandy Jenkins, a slave with whom I was somewhat acquainted. Sandy had a free wife who lived about four miles from Mr. Covey's; and it being Saturday, he was on his way to see her. I told him my circumstances, and he very kindly invited me to go home with him. I went home with him, and talked this whole matter over, and got his advice as to what course it was best for me to pursue. I found Sandy an old adviser. He told me, with great solemnity, I must go back to Covey; but that before I went, I must go with him into another part of the woods, where there was a certain *root*, which, if I would take some of it with me, carrying it *always on my right side*, would render it impossible for Mr. Covey, or any other white man, to whip me. He said he had carried it for years; and since he had done so, he had never received a blow, and never expected to while he carried it. I at first rejected the idea, that the simple carrying of a root in my pocket would have any such effect as he had said, and was not disposed to take it; but Sandy impressed the necessity with much earnestness, telling me it could do no harm, if it did no good. To please him, I at length took the root, and, according to his direction, carried it upon my right side. This was Sunday morning. I immediately started for home; and upon entering the yard gate, out came Mr. Covey on his way to meeting. He spoke to me very kindly, bade me drive the pigs from a lot near by, and passed on towards the church. Now, this singular conduct of Mr. Covey really made me begin to think that there was something in the *root* which Sandy had given me; and had it been on any other day than Sunday, I could have attributed the conduct to no other cause than the influence of that root; and as it was, I was half inclined to think the *root* to be something more than I at first had taken it to be. All went well till Monday morning. On this morning, the virtue of the *root* was fully tested. Long before daylight, I was called to go and rub, curry, and feed, the horses. I obeyed, and was glad to obey. But whilst thus engaged, whilst in the act of throwing down some blades from the loft, Mr. Covey entered the stable with a long rope; and just as I was half out of the loft, he caught hold of my legs, and was about tying me. As soon as I found what he was up to, I gave a sudden spring, and as I did so, he holding to my legs, I was brought sprawling on the stable floor. Mr. Covey seemed now to think he had me, and could do what he pleased; but at this moment—from whence came the spirit I don't know—I resolved to fight; and, suiting my action to the resolution, I seized Covey hard by the throat; and as I did so, I rose. He held on to me, and I to him. My resistance was so entirely unexpected, that Covey seemed taken all aback. He trembled like a leaf. This gave me assurance, and I held him uneasy, causing the blood to run where I touched him with the ends of my fingers. Mr. Covey soon called out to Hughes for help. Hughes came, and while Covey held me, attempted to tie my right hand. While he was in the act of doing so, I watched my chance, and gave him a heavy kick close under the ribs. This kick fairly sickened Hughes, so that he left me in the hands of Mr. Covey. This kick had the effect of not only weakening Hughes, but Covey also. When he saw Hughes bending over with pain, his courage quailed. He asked me if I meant to persist in my resistance. I told him I did, come what might; that he had used me like a brute for six months, and that I was determined to be used so no longer. With that, he strove to drag me to a stick that was lying just out of the stable door. He meant to knock me down. But just as he was leaning over to get the stick, I seized him with both hands by his collar, and brought him by a sudden snatch to the ground. By this time, Bill came. Covey called upon him for assistance. Bill wanted to know what he could do. Covey said, "Take hold of him, take hold of him!" Bill said his master hired him out to work, and not to help whip me; so he left Covey and myself to fight our own battle out. We were at it for nearly two hours. Covey at length let me go, puffing and blowing at a great rate, saying that if I had not resisted, he would not have whipped me half so much. The truth was, that he had not whipped me at all. I considered him as getting entirely the worst end of the bargain; for he had drawn no blood from me, but I had from him. The whole six months afterwards, that I spent with Mr. Covey, he never laid the weight of his finger upon me in anger. He would occasionally say, he didn't want to get hold of me again. "No," thought I, "you need not; for you will come off worse than you did before."

This battle with Mr. Covey was the turning-point in my career as a slave. It rekindled the few expiring embers of freedom, and revived within me a sense of my own manhood. It recalled the departed self-confidence, and inspired me again with a determination to be free. The gratification afforded by the triumph was a full compensation for whatever else might follow, even death itself. He only can understand the deep satisfaction which I experienced, who has himself repelled by force the bloody arm of slavery. I felt as I never felt before. It was glorious resurrection, from the tomb of slavery, to the heaven of freedom. My long-crushed spirit rose, cowardice departed, bold defiance took its place; and I now resolved that, however long I might remain a slave in form, the day had passed forever when I could be a slave in fact. I did not hesitate to let it be known of me, that the white man who expected to succeed in whipping, must also succeed in killing me.

Content

1. Twelve years after he successfully defied Mr. Covey, Douglass identified this incident as "the turning-point in my career as a slave" (¶ 3). Why? Would Douglass have been able to recognize its significance at the time or only in retrospect?
2. What, if anything, does Douglass expect his audience to do about slavery, as a consequence of having read his narrative?

Strategies/Structures

1. Douglass's account begins with Friday afternoon and ends with Monday morning, but some events receive considerable emphasis while others are scarcely mentioned. Which ones does he focus on? Why?
2. Why is paragraph 2 so long? Should it have been divided into shorter units, or is the longer unit preferable? Justify your answer.
3. Douglass provides considerable details about his appearance after his first beating by Covey (¶ 2), but scarcely any about the appearance of either Covey or Master Thomas. Why?
4. Would slave owners have been likely to read Douglass's autobiography? Why or why not? Would Douglass's emphasis have been likely to change for an audience of Northern post–Civil War blacks? Southern antebellum whites?

Language

1. How sophisticated is Douglass's level of diction? Is it appropriate for the narrative he tells? How is this related to his self-characterization?
2. Why does Douglass explain his changed self-image as a "resurrection, from the tomb of slavery, to the heaven of freedom"?

For Writing

1. Write a narrative in which you recount and explain the significance of an event in which you participated that provided you with an important change of self-image, or of status in the eyes of others. (See Patricia

grew up in two worlds, the tropical island and the cold city, and
that would later surface in my dreams and in my poetry.

One of these tales was about the woman who was left at the   3
altar. Mamá liked to tell that one with histrionic intensity. I
remember the rise and fall of her voice, the sighs, and her constantly gesturing hands, like two birds swooping through her
words. This particular story usually would come up in a conversation as a result of someone mentioning a forthcoming engagement
or wedding. The first time I remember hearing it, I was sitting on
the floor at Mamá's feet, pretending to read a comic book. I may
have been eleven or twelve years old, at that difficult age when a
girl was no longer a child who could be ordered to leave the room
if the women wanted freedom to take their talk into forbidden
zones, nor really old enough to be considered a part of their con-
clave. I could only sit quietly, pretending to be in another world,
while absorbing it all in a sort of unspoken agreement of my status
as silent auditor. On this day, Mamá had taken my long, tangled
mane of hair into her ever-busy hands. Without looking down at
me and with no interruption of her flow of words, she began braid-
ing my hair, working at it with the quickness and determination
that characterized all her actions. My mother was watching us
impassively from her rocker across the room. On her lips played a
little ironic smile. I would never sit still for *her* ministrations, but
even then, I instinctively knew that she did not possess Mamá's
matriarchal power to command and keep everyone's attention.
This was never more evident than in the spell she cast when telling
a story.

"It is not like it used to be when I was a girl," Mamá an-   4
nounced. "Then, a man could leave a girl standing at the church
altar with a bouquet of fresh flowers in her hands and disappear
off the face of the earth. No way to track him down if he was from
another town. He could be a married man, with maybe even two
or three families all over the island. There was no way to know.
And there were men who did this. Hombres with the devil in
their flesh who would come to a pueblo, like this one, take a job
at one of the haciendas, never meaning to stay, only to have a
good time and to seduce the women."

The whole time she was speaking, Mamá would be weav-   5
ing my hair into a flat plait that required pulling apart the two

sections of hair with little jerks that made my eyes water; but knowing how grandmother detested whining and *boba* (sissy) tears, as she called them, I just sat up as straight and stiff as I did at La Escuela San Jose, where the nuns enforced good posture with a flexible plastic ruler they bounced off of slumped shoulders and heads. As Mamá's story progressed, I noticed how my young Aunt Laura lowered her eyes, refusing to meet Mamá's meaningful gaze. Laura was seventeen, in her last year of high school, and already engaged to a boy from another town who had staked his claim with a tiny diamond ring, then left for Los Nueva Yores to make his fortune. They were planning to get married in a year. Mamá had expressed serious doubts that the wedding would ever take place. In Mamá's eyes, a man set free without a legal contract was a man lost. She believed that marriage was not something men desired, but simply the price they had to pay for the privilege of children and, of course, for what no decent (synonymous with "smart") woman would give away for free.

6   "María La Loca was only seventeen when *it* happened to her." I listened closely at the mention of this name. María was a town character, a fat middle-aged woman who lived with her old mother on the outskirts of town. She was to be seen around the pueblo delivering the meat pies the two women made for a living. The most peculiar thing about María, in my eyes, was that she walked and moved like a little girl though she had the thick body and wrinkled face of an old woman. She would swing her hips in an exaggerated, clownish way, and sometimes even hop and skip up to someone's house. She spoke to no one. Even if you asked her a question, she would just look at you and smile, showing her yellow teeth. But I had heard that if you got close enough, you could hear her humming a tune without words. The kids yelled out nasty things at her, calling her *La Loca,* and the men who hung out at the bodega playing dominoes sometimes whistled mockingly as she passed by with her funny, outlandish walk. But María seemed impervious to it all, carrying her basket of *pasteles* like a grotesque Little Red Riding Hood through the forest.

7   María La Loca interested me, as did all the eccentrics and crazies of our pueblo. Their weirdness was a measuring stick I used in my serious quest for a definition of normal. As a Navy brat

shuttling between New Jersey and the pueblo, I was constantly made to feel like an oddball by my peers, who made fun of my two-way accent: a Spanish accent when I spoke English, and when I spoke Spanish I was told that I sounded like a *Gringa*. Being the outsider had already turned my brother and me into cultural chameleons. We developed early on the ability to blend into a crowd, to sit and read quietly in a fifth story apartment building for days and days when it was too bitterly cold to play outside, or, set free, to run wild in Mamá's realm, where she took charge of our lives, releasing Mother for a while from the intense fear for our safety that our father's absences instilled in her. In order to keep us from harm when Father was away, Mother kept us under strict surveillance. She even walked us to and from Public School No. 11, which we attended during the months we lived in Paterson, New Jersey, our home base in the states. Mamá freed all three of us like pigeons from a cage. I saw her as my liberator and my model. Her stories were parables from which to glean the *Truth*.

"María La Loca was once a beautiful girl. Everyone thought 8 she would marry the Méndez boy." As everyone knew, Rogelio Méndez was the richest man in town. "But," Mamá continued, knitting my hair with the same intensity she was putting into her story, "this *macho* made a fool out of her and ruined her life." She paused for the effect of her use of the word "macho," which at that time had not yet become a popular epithet for an unliberated man. This word had for us the crude and comical connotation of "male of the species," stud; a *macho* was what you put in a pen to increase your stock.

I peeked over my comic book at my mother. She too was 9 under Mamá's spell, smiling conspiratorially at this little swipe at men. She was safe from Mamá's contempt in this area. Married at an early age, an unspotted lamb, she had been accepted by a good family of strict Spaniards whose name was old and respected, though their fortune had been lost long before my birth. In a rocker Papá had painted sky blue sat Mamá's oldest child, Aunt Nena. Mother of three children, stepmother of two more, she was a quiet woman who liked books but had married an ignorant and abusive widower whose main interest in life was accumulating wealth. He too was in the mainland working on his dream of returning home rich and triumphant to buy the *finca* of his dreams. She was waiting for him to send for her. She would leave her children with Mamá for several years while the two of them slaved away in factories. He would one day be a rich man, and she a sadder woman. Even now her life-light was dimming. She spoke little, an aberration in Mamá's house, and she read avidly, as if storing up spiritual food for the long winters that awaited her in Los Nueva Yores without her family. But even Aunt Nena came alive to Mamá's words, rocking gently, her hands over a thick book in her lap.

10   Her daughter, my cousin Sara, played jacks by herself on the tile porch outside the room where we sat. She was a year older than I. We shared a bed and all our family's secrets. Collaborators in search of answers, Sara and I discussed everything we heard the women say, trying to fit it all together like a puzzle that, once assembled, would reveal life's mysteries to us. Though she and I still enjoyed taking part in boys' games—chase, volleyball, and even *vaqueros,* the island version of cowboys and Indians involving cap-gun battles and violent shoot-outs under the mango tree in Mamá's backyard—we loved best the quiet hours in the afternoon when the men were still at work, and the boys had gone to play serious baseball at the park. Then Mamá's house belonged only to us women. The aroma of coffee perking in the kitchen, the mesmerizing creaks and groans of the rockers, and the women telling their lives in *cuentos* are forever woven into the fabric of my imagination, braided like my hair that day I felt my grandmother's hands teaching me about strength, her voice convincing me of the power of storytelling.

11   That day Mamá told how the beautiful María had fallen prey to a man whose name was never the same in subsequent versions of the story; it was Juan one time, José, Rafael, Diego, another. We understood that neither the name nor any of the *facts* were important, only that a woman had allowed love to defeat her. Mamá put each of us in Mariá's place by describing her wedding dress in loving detail: how she looked like a princess in her lace as she waited at the altar. Then, as Mamá approached the tragic denouement of her story, I was distracted by the sound of my Aunt Laura's violent rocking. She seemed on the verge of

tears. She knew the fable was intended for her. That week she was going to have her wedding gown fitted, though no firm date had been set for the marriage. Mamá ignored Laura's obvious discomfort, digging out a ribbon from the sewing basket she kept by her rocker while describing María's long illness, "a fever that would not break for days." She spoke of a mother's despair: "that woman climbed the church steps on her knees every morning, wore only black as a *promesa* to the Holy Virgin in exchange for her daughter's health." By the time María returned from her honeymoon with death, she was ravished, no longer young or sane. "As you can see, she is almost as old as her mother already," Mamá lamented while tying the ribbon to the ends of my hair, pulling it back with such force that I just knew I would never be able to close my eyes completely again.

"That María's getting crazier every day." Mamá's voice 12
would take a lighter tone now, expressing satisfaction, either for the perfection of my braid, or for a story well told—it was hard to tell. "You know that tune María is always humming?" Carried away by her enthusiasm, I tried to nod, but Mamá still had me pinned between her knees.

"Well that's the wedding march." Surprising us all, Mamá 13
sang out, "Da, da, dara . . . da, da, dara." Then lifting me off the floor by my skinny shoulders, she would lead me around the room in an impromptu waltz—another session ending with the laughter of women, all of us caught up in the infectious joke of our lives.

Content

1. How does the community of Puerto Rican women, grandmother, mother, and aunts, use storytelling to teach the young girls in their family "what it [is] like to be a woman, more specifically, a Puerto Rican woman" (¶ 2)? Are there comparable informal communities in which boys learn what it means to be men?

2. What features of the storytelling context (such as where it takes place, the storyteller's status and authority) reinforce the messages of the *cuentos?*

3. Under what circumstances is Cofer an outsider as a child (see ¶ 7)? An insider?

4. How does Cofer's dual status as an insider/outsider contribute to her childhood understanding of the story of María La Loca (¶s 6–13)? Does the fact that she is writing the story as an adult contribute any new dimensions, understanding to the tale?

Strategies/Structures

In "*Casa*," Cofer conveys a number of points of view: her own, as a child and as an adult, her grandmother's, her mother's, Aunt Nena's, and Aunt Laura's—the seventeen-year-old fiancée at whom the cautionary tale is directed. In what ways does she do this, even though some characters, such as Nena and Laura, never speak?

Language

1. "*Casa*" is written primarily in English, with a sprinkling of Spanish words. Where do these come? With what effect? Under what circumstances does the author define them? When does she expect the reader to infer their meaning?

2. What does an author gain or lose by incorporating foreign words and phrases into a primarily English text? (Assume that the author is not using these to show off!)

For Writing

1. Tell, for an audience of your peers or for younger teenagers or adolescents, a real-life cautionary tale drawn preferably from your own experience or that of someone you know well. Let the characterization and the plot make the point; you don't have to state the moral explicitly.

2. Retell for the same audience as in the previous writing suggestion a well-known fable (such as one by Aesop, Joel Chandler Harris, or James Thurber) in a contemporary context, substituting characters you know for those in the original tale.

3. Have you ever felt, as Cofer did, "like an oddball" (¶ 7)? Did you try to fit in, were you pleased to be different, or were you ambivalent about your status? How do you feel about the same characteristics—of yourself, your language or dialect, your culture, your family—now? Tell a story, for people who don't know you, that depicts yourself as an outsider and that illustrates your past and present feelings about your status.

PATRICIA J. WILLIAMS

> Williams (b. 1951) identifies herself as "the great-great-granddaughter of a slave and a white southern lawyer." She herself is a professor of commercial law at Columbia University, having also taught at CUNY School of Law and the University of Wisconsin.
>
> Her writings on a wide range of public issues have appeared in *Ms.* magazine and *The Nation.* Her autobiographical *The Alchemy of Race and Rights* (1991) broke new ground as an autobiographical meditation on the relation of race, gender, class, and the law. In a review in *The Nation* (1991), Henry Louis Gates, director of African-American studies at Harvard, praised the book for its subject, its perspective, and its style: "The first person has always been troublesome in the language of law. . . . Our judges are, in short, ventriloquists: Their decisions voice only what the law says. If they are well trained, in fact, we hardly notice their lips move. Williams, spoilsport that she is, won't play along. She moves her lips and makes sure you notice." Gates notes that unlike many critics, "Williams wants to build on liberalism, not just bash it." Moreover, he says, "Williams eschews up-against-the-wall-style rhetoric in favor of dialogue and diagnosis." These characteristics are evident in the chapter included here, "The Death of the Profane," in which Williams tells her "sad tale of exclusion from Soho's most glitzy boutique," a Benetton store. She writes from several perspectives to make, as her subtitle indicates, "a commentary on the genre of legal writing."

The Death of the Profane
(a commentary on the genre of legal writing)

B uzzers are big in New York City. Favored particularly by smaller stores and boutiques, merchants throughout the city have installed them as screening devices to reduce the incidence of robbery: if the face at the door looks desirable, the buzzer is pressed and the door is unlocked. If the face is that of an undesirable, the door stays locked. Predictably, the issue of undesirability 1 has revealed itself to be a racial determination. While controversial enough at first, even civil-rights organizations backed down eventually in the face of arguments that the buzzer system is a "necessary evil," that it is a "mere inconvenience" in comparison to the risks of being murdered, that suffering discrimination is not as bad as being assaulted, and that in any event it is not all blacks who are barred, just "17-year-old black males wearing running shoes and hooded sweatshirts."[1]

2   The installation of these buzzers happened swiftly in New York; stores that had always had their doors wide open suddenly became exclusive or received people by appointment only. I discovered them and their meaning one Saturday in 1986. I was shopping in Soho and saw in a store window a sweater that I wanted to buy for my mother. I pressed my round brown face to the window and my finger to the buzzer, seeking admittance. A narrow-eyed, white teenager wearing running shoes and feasting on bubble gum glared out, evaluating me for signs that would pit me against the limits of his social understanding. After about five seconds, he mouthed, "We're closed," and blew pink rubber at me. It was two Saturdays before Christmas, at one o'clock in the afternoon; there were several white people in the store who appeared to be shopping for things for *their* mothers.

3   I was enraged. At that moment I literally wanted to break all the windows of the store and *take* lots of sweaters for my mother. In the flicker of his judgmental gray eyes, that saleschild had transformed my brightly sentimental, joy-to-the-world, pre-Christmas spree to a shambles. He snuffed my sense of humanitarian catholicity, and there was nothing I could do to snuff his, without making a spectacle of myself.

4   I am still struck by the structure of power that drove me into such a blizzard of rage. There was almost nothing I could do, short of physically intruding upon him, that would humiliate him the way he humiliated me. No words, no gestures, no prejudices of my own would make a bit of difference to him; his refusal to let me into the store—it was Benetton's, whose colorfully punnish ad

---

[1] "When 'By Appointment' Means Keep Out," *New York Times*, December 17, 1986, p. B1. Letter to the Editor from Michael Levin and Marguerita Levin, *New York Times*, January 11, 1987, p. E32.

campaign is premised on wrapping every one of the world's peoples in its cottons and woolens—was an outward manifestation of his never having let someone like me into the realm of his reality. He had no compassion, no remorse, no reference to me; and no desire to acknowledge me even at the estranged level of arm's-length transactor. He saw me only as one who would take his money and therefore could not conceive that I was there to give him money.

In this weird ontological imbalance, I realized that buying 5 something in that store was like bestowing a gift, the gift of my commerce, the lucre of my patronage. In the wake of my outrage, I wanted to take back the gift of appreciation that my peering in the window must have appeared to be. I wanted to take it back in the form of unappreciation, disrespect, defilement. I wanted to work so hard at wishing he could feel what I felt that he would never again mistake my hatred for some sort of plaintive wish to be included. I was quite willing to disenfranchise myself, in the heat of my need to revoke the flattery of my purchasing power. I was willing to boycott Benetton's, random white-owned businesses, and anyone who ever blew bubble gum in my face again.

My rage was admittedly diffuse, even self-destructive, but it 6 was symmetrical. The perhaps loose-ended but utter propriety of that rage is no doubt lost not just to the young man who actually barred me, but to those who would appreciate my being barred only as an abstract precaution, who approve of those who would bar even as they deny that they would bar *me*.

The violence of my desire to burst into Benetton's is prob- 7 ably quite apparent. I often wonder if the violence, the exclusionary hatred, is equally apparent in the repeated public urgings that blacks understand the buzzer system by putting themselves in the shoes of white storeowners—that, in effect, blacks look into the mirror of frightened white faces for the reality of their undesirability; and that then blacks would "just as surely conclude that [they] would not let [themselves] in under similar circumstances."[2] (That some blacks might agree merely shows that some of us have learned too well the lessons of privatized intimacies of

---

[2] *New York Times,* January 11, 1987, p. E32.

self-hatred and rationalized away the fullness of our public, participatory selves.)

8   On the same day I was barred from Benetton's, I went home and wrote the above impassioned account in my journal. On the day after that, I found I was still brooding, so I turned to a form of catharsis I have always found healing. I typed up as much of the story as I have just told, made a big poster of it, put a nice colorful border around it, and, after Benetton's was truly closed, stuck it to their big sweater-filled window. I exercised my first-amendment right to place my business with them right out in the street.

9   So that was the first telling of this story. The second telling came a few months later, for a symposium on Excluded Voices sponsored by a law review. I wrote an essay summing up my feelings about being excluded from Benetton's and analyzing "how the rhetoric of increased privatization, in response to racial issues, functions as the rationalizing agent of public unaccountability and, ultimately, irresponsibility." Weeks later, I received the first edit. From the first page to the last, my fury had been carefully cut out. My rushing, run-on-rage had been reduced to simple declarative sentences. The active personal had been inverted in favor of the passive impersonal. My words were different; they spoke to me upsidedown. I was afraid to read too much of it at a time—meanings rose up at me oddly, stolen and strange.

10   A week and a half later, I received the second edit. All reference to Benetton's had been deleted because, according to the editors and the faculty adviser, it was defamatory; they feared harassment and liability; they said printing it would be irresponsible. I called them and offered to supply a footnote attesting to this as my personal experience at one particular location and of a buzzer system not limited to Benetton's; the editors told me that they were not in the habit of publishing things that were unverifiable. I could not but wonder, in this refusal even to let me file an affadavit, what it would take to make my experience verifiable. The testimony of an independent white bystander? (a requirement in fact imposed in U.S. Supreme Court holdings through the first part of the century[3]).

---

[3] See generally *Blyew v. U.S.*, 80 U.S. 581 (1871), upholding a state's right to forbid blacks to testify against whites.

Two days *after* the piece was sent to press, I received copies   11
of the final page proofs. All reference to my race had been eliminated because it was against "editorial policy" to permit descriptions of physiognomy. "I realize," wrote one editor, "that this was
a very personal experience, but any reader will know what you
must have looked like when standing at that window." In a telephone conversation to them, I ranted wildly about the significance
of such an omission. "It's irrelevant," another editor explained in
a voice gummy with soothing and patience; "It's nice and poetic,"
but it doesn't "advance the discussion of any principle . . . This is
a law review, after all." Frustrated, I accused him of censorship;
calmly he assured me it was not. "This is just a matter of style," he
said with firmness and finality.

Ultimately I did convince the editors that mention of my   12
race was central to the whole sense of the subsequent text; that
my story became one of extreme paranoia without the information that I am black, or that it became one in which the reader had
to fill in the gap by assumption, presumption, prejudgment, or
prejudice. What was most interesting to me in this experience was
how the blind application of principles of neutrality, through the
device of omission, acted either to make me look crazy or to make
the reader participate in old habits of cultural bias.

That was the second telling of my story. The third telling   13
came last April, when I was invited to participate in a law-school
conference on Equality and Difference. I retold my sad tale of exclusion from Soho's most glitzy boutique, focusing in this version
on the law-review editing process as a consequence of an ideology of style rooted in a social text of neutrality. I opined:

> Law and legal writing aspire to formalized, color-blind,
> liberal ideals. Neutrality is the standard for assuring these
> ideals; yet the adherence to it is often determined by refer-
> ence to an aesthetic of uniformity, in which difference is
> simply omitted. For example, when segregation was eradi-
> cated from the American lexicon, its omission led many to
> actually believe that racism therefore no longer existed.
> Race-neutrality in law has become the presumed antidote
> for race bias in real life. With the entrenchment of the
> notion of race-neutrality came attacks on the concept of
> affirmative action and the rise of reverse discrimination

suits. Blacks, for so many generations deprived of jobs based on the color of our skin, are now told that we ought to find it demeaning to be hired, based on the color of our skin. Such is the silliness of simplistic either-or inversions as remedies to complex problems.

What is truly demeaning in this era of double-speak-no-evil is going on interviews and not getting hired because someone doesn't think we'll be comfortable. It is demeaning not to get promoted because we're judged " too weak," then putting in a lot of energy the next time and getting fired because we're "too strong." It is demeaning to be told what we find demeaning. It is very demeaning to stand on street corners unemployed and begging. It is downright demeaning to have to explain why we haven't been employed for months and then watch the job go to someone who is "more experienced." It is outrageously demeaning that none of this can be called racism, even if it happens only to, or to large numbers of, black people; as long as it's done with a smile, a handshake and a shrug; as long as the phantom-word "race" is never used.

The image of race as a phantom-word came to me after I moved into my late godmother's home. In an attempt to make it my own, I cleared the bedroom for painting. The following morning the room asserted itself, came rushing and raging at me through the emptiness, exactly as it had been for twenty-five years. One day filled with profuse and overwhelming complexity, the next day filled with persistently recurring memories. The shape of the past came to haunt me, the shape of the emptiness confronted me each time I was about to enter the room. The force of its spirit still drifts like an odor throughout the house.

The power of that room, I have thought since, is very like the power of racism as status quo: it is deep, angry, eradicated from view, but strong enough to make everyone who enters the room walk around the bed that isn't there, avoiding the phantom as they did the substance, for fear of bodily harm. They do not even know they are avoiding; they defer to the unseen shapes of things with subtle responsiveness, guided by an impulsive awareness of

nothingness, and the deep knowledge and denial of witch-
craft at work.

The phantom room is to me symbolic of the emptiness
of formal equal opportunity, particularly as propounded
by President Reagan, the Reagan Civil Rights Commission
and the Reagan Supreme Court. Blindly formalized constructions of equal opportunity are the creation of a space
that is filled in by a meandering stream of unguided
hopes, dreams, fantasies, fears, recollections. They are the
presence of the past in imaginary, imagistic form—the
phantom-roomed exile of our longing.

It is thus that I strongly believe in the efficacy of
programs and paradigms like affirmative action. Blacks
are the objects of a constitutional omission which has been
incorporated into a theory of neutrality. It is thus that
omission is really a form of expression as oxymoronic as
that sounds: racial omission is a literal part of original
intent; it is the fixed, reiterated prophecy of the Founding
Fathers. It is thus that affirmative action is an affirmation;
the affirmative act of hiring—or hearing—blacks is a recognition of individuality that re-places blacks as a social
statistic, that is profoundly interconnective to the fate of
blacks and whites either as sub-groups or as one group.
In this sense, affirmative action is as mystical and beyond-
the-self as an initiation ceremony. It is an act of verification
and of vision. It is an act of social as well as professional
responsibility.

The following morning I opened the local newspaper, to 14
find that the event of my speech had commanded two columns
on the front page of the Metro section. I quote only the opening
lines: "Affirmative action promotes prejudice by denying the status of women and blacks, instead of affirming them as its name
suggests. So said New York City attorney Patricia Williams to an
audience Wednesday."[4]

---

[4] "Attorney Says Affirmative Action Denies Racism, Sexism," *Dominion Post*,
(Morgantown, West Virginia), April 8, 1988, p. B1.

15   I clipped out the article and put it in my journal. In the margin there is a note to myself: eventually, it says, I should try to pull all these threads together into yet another law-review article. The problem, of course, will be that in the hierarchy of law-review citation, the article in the newspaper will have more authoritative weight about me, as a so-called "primary resource," than I will have; it will take precedence over my own citation of the unverifiable testimony of my speech.

16   I have used the Benetton's story a lot in speaking engagements at various schools. I tell it whenever I am too tired to whip up an original speech from scratch. Here are some of the questions I have been asked in the wake of its telling:

17   Am I not privileging a racial perspective, by considering only the black point of view? Don't I have an obligation to include the "salesman's side" of the story?

18   · Am I not putting the salesman on trial and finding him guilty of racism without giving him a chance to respond to or cross-examine me?

19   Am I not using the store window as a "metaphorical fence" against the potential of his explanation in order to represent my side as "authentic"?

20   How can I be sure I'm right?

21   What makes my experience the real black one anyway?

22   Isn't it possible that another black person would disagree with my experience? If so, doesn't that render my story too unempirical and subjective to pay any attention to?

23   Always a major objection is to my having put the poster on Benetton's window. As one law professor put it: "It's one thing to publish this in a law review, where no one can take it personally, but it's another thing altogether to put your own interpretation right out there, just like that, uncontested, I mean, with nothing to counter it."

Content

1. In the relatively brief space of twenty-three paragraphs, Williams tells the story of her exclusion from a Benetton store four times, in several different ways, for several different purposes and audiences: paragraphs

1–7, 8; 9–12; 13–15. Why does she tell and retell this story? Identify these different purposes and different audiences.

2. In what ways does Williams's story change each time she tells it? What does Williams expect her readers to come to understand about this story in each of the successive retellings?

3. Do you personally read any or all of the versions as Williams wants you to? What experiences and values of your own do you bring to your reading of this essay? To what extent has Williams anticipated these? To what extent can Williams—or any other writer—be reasonably expected to anticipate readers' reactions to her work?

Strategies / Structures

1. For which audience does Williams intend each version? Which version are you most likely to remember? Why?

2. In paragraphs 17–23 Williams lists some objections listeners have raised in response to her story, but she offers no rebuttal to any of them. Why not?

Language

1. Williams says that the law review editors edited her story and "carefully cut out" evidence of her fury and her race (¶ 9–11), reducing her "run-on-rage" to "simple declarative sentences," and inverting "the active personal . . . in favor of the passive impersonal" (¶ 9). Why did they do this? Was it ethical for the editors to make such significant changes? Or was Williams herself in error, as the editors charged (¶ 10)? What evidence does she offer in the first telling of the story (¶s 1–5) to allow you to interpret her story?

2. Why does Williams call "race" a "phantom-word" (¶ 13)?

3. As a metaphor for racism, Williams uses the image of a "phantom room" (¶ 13), filled with the spirit of its former occupant, "deep, angry, eradicated from view, but strong enough to make everyone who enters the room . . . [avoid] the phantom as they did the substance." Explain how the metaphor works to reinforce Williams's argument.

For Writing

1. Tell a true story whose point implies or illustrates the definition of some abstract term, such as *truth, justice, racism, prejudice, discrimination.* You will need to target your intended readers so you can anticipate what

their understanding of the term is likely to be—particularly if your own definition expands the dimensions of the term, or differs from its common usage. Even if you start with a dictionary definition, your paper will go well beyond it.

2.   What does Williams mean by asserting that "when segregation was eradicated from the American lexicon, its omission led many to actually believe that racism therefore no longer existed" (¶ 13)? Does the disappearance of a word necessarily mean that what it implies has also disappeared? Explain, by analyzing one or two illustrations from either your own experience or historical accounts.

ANN UPPERCO DOLMAN

Ann Upperco Dolman (born, 1960) grew up in Arlington, Virginia, and majored in religion at the College of William and Mary (B.A., 1982). She then worked in Chicago as a textbook editor, and after marriage and a move to Wilson, North Carolina, as communications manager for the local Chamber of Commerce, where she wrote all the time—brochures, a newsletter, "even speeches. . . . I've come a long way from my undergraduate days when crying over writing papers was almost as natural to me as breathing. A big help," she says, "is the use of a word processor [for I] realize that whatever I have written is not engraved in stone. I can experiment with a variety of organizational schemes and words with just a push of a few buttons, so editing has become a breeze." In 1996 she earned a master's degree in library science from the University of North Carolina.

Dolman had been a highly anxious writer, procrastinating for long periods of time and then spending miserable, long hours trying to grind out a paper in time to meet a deadline. However, in writing "Learning to Drive" for an undergraduate composition course, she explains, "I wrote it at one sitting, then revised it. I think this method of sitting down and writing something and then going back to revise is what enabled me to get over my fear of writing." She says, "I had originally intended to write a series of comic vignettes on the individual driving styles of each member of my family. But the more I thought about it, the more comfortable I felt with the idea of poking fun at myself instead. . . . Writing this essay was almost fun."

Dolman has captured a common set of experiences participated in by a set of familiar figures, comical to contemplate from
the safe distance of time, however painful the traumas of a new
driver may have been when they occurred. The tense, skittish
novice driver is counterpointed against the patient teacher, her
reassuring father, with the nervous figure of her mother hovering
uneasily in the background.

❆ *Learning to Drive*

G reater love hath no man for his children than to teach them   1
how to drive. As soon as I turned 15 years and 8 months—
the requisite age for obtaining a learner's permit—my father
took me around our neighborhood to let me get a feel for the
huge Chevrolet we own. The quiet, tree-shaded, narrow streets
of the neighborhood witnessed the blunders of yet another new
driver: too-wide (or too-narrow) turns; sudden screeching halts
(those power brakes take some getting used to); defoliation of
low-hanging trees by the radio antenna or the car too close to the
curb; driving on the wrong side of the street to avoid the parked
cars on the right side.

Through it all my father murmured words of advice and   2
encouragement, drawing on a seemingly bottomless well of patience which I never before knew he possessed. One day while
driving on the highway, I drifted dangerously close to a car in the
lane to my right, almost scraping the shiny chrome strip right off
its side. Dad looked nonchalantly into the terrified face of the
other driver—a mere six inches away—then turned back to me
and said, "You might want to steer to the left a bit; you're just a
little close on this side." A mile further down the road, Dad
chuckled and said, "I think you gave that poor lady a scare—her
eyes were as big as golfballs!" Here was he, not only unperturbed,
but actually amused by the whole incident while I watched my
whole life pass before my eyes.

Not long after this incident I had another near miss, this   3
time while intentionally changing lanes. I still was not accustomed to using the rearview mirror, so Dad had told me to glance

over my shoulder to make sure all was clear. Being right-handed, I automatically looked over my right shoulder, and not seeing anything, proceeded to veer left. Not until I almost plowed into another car did I realize that when turning left, I needed to glance over my left shoulder to avoid causing a wreck. Despite the danger, Dad stuck it out, continuing to give me tips to improve my driving.

4   Confident now of my driving prowess, I cajoled my parents into letting me drive every chance I got. Dad usually sat up front with me, to the relief of Mom, an uneasy driver herself whose nerves were still recovering from my brother's driving apprenticeship two years earlier. This arrangement suited me perfectly; Mom's behavior in the front seat tended to make me a trifle nervous. Gripping the dashboard as if it would fall off if she let go, and frequently pressing to the floor the nonexistent brake on her side of the car, Mom would periodically utter spine-chilling gasps at the slightest provocation—none of which increased my newly-won confidence behind the wheel. Whether Dad never suffered from such a case of jitters or whether he merely hid it better, I'm not sure. But whatever the reasons, he managed to remain calm, at least outwardly, when riding with me.

5   When I had mastered (in a manner of speaking) the skill of driving our full-size, power-steering, power-brake tank, Dad proceeded to show me the secrets of operating the small, standard-shift rattle-trap-of-a-Pinto which adorned the curb in front of our house. Had I known at the time the humiliation and tribulation I'd have to endure at the wheel of that car, I'm not sure I would have embarked as willingly on the adventure. But Dad, glutton for punishment that he is, knew what was in store; as he buckled his seat belt he braced both feet against the floor and said, "Okay, let's give it a try." For at least an hour, I lurched up and down our driveway, trying to get a feel for "slipping the clutch." (Poor Dad didn't realize I hardly even knew which was the clutch, much less what "slipping" it entailed.) After one particularly violent jolt that almost sent us through the garage door, Dad decided to let me try taking the car around the block. Ostensibly, he wanted me to practice driving in all four gears, though I really think he was more concerned about the fate of the garage door than anything else.

Once out on the street (after a bristly encounter with the 6
forsythia bush which unfortunately stood at the end of the driveway), I embarrassed myself completely. To keep from stalling, I'd
rev the engine while I tried to slip the clutch. I couldn't even pretend to be a racing driver; the car didn't have the decency to sound
like a high-powered race car, it just roared like an outraged lion
with a thorn in its paw. Feeling conspicuous about making all this
noise, I let the clutch out too soon, which either stalled the car, or,
worse still, made it jerk down the street like a bucking bronco. The
poor car looked like a seesaw with the front end first taking a nose-
dive while the rear end flew up, then leaping into the air as the rear
end came back down. Jolting around the block with tires screeching and rubber burning, I provided my neighbors with the best
free entertainment they'd seen in a long time, since the days when
my brother was learning how to drive that beastly little car.

With this display of ineptitude, I tumbled from the pedestal 7
of special privilege which a driver's permit had given me; once
again the kids too young to drive regarded me as simply the klutz
I was. Good ol' Dad stuck by me through the ignominy of it all,
assuring me that everybody who learned to drive a stick-shift
underwent the same ordeal. It still amazes me that with all that
lurching around, he was willing to go with me again.

Now that I have several years' experience behind me, I 8
actually enjoy driving—especially driving a stick-shift. I'll often
take to the road to relax, emptying my mind by concentrating on
the mechanics of driving. Had it not been for Dad's patient, calm
perseverance, I might still be the public menace today that I was
three years ago. As for Dad, he lucked out—I'm the last kid in
the family.

Content

1. This essay combines the telling of a story with the explanation of a
process. Which is dominant? How do you know?

2. Could one learn how to drive—or how not to drive—from reading
this essay? If not, what is its point?

3. What is the point of the last paragraph? What impact does the fact
that not only did Dolman learn to drive but to enjoy it have on the rest
of the essay?

Strategies/Structures

1. How can you tell that Dolman is writing from the perspective of someone who has mastered the skill of driving, rather than from the viewpoint of a learner? What effect does this have on the tone of the essay?

2. Much of Dolman's humor is visual. What comic scenes does she create and how does she help readers to see them? Why should close escapes from accidents provoke laughter instead of terrified relief?

Language

1. What does Dolman's terminology reveal about her intended readers? Are they experienced drivers? Novices? Unable to drive at all?

2. Find some instances where Dolman uses overstated language, understated language, and slang to enhance the humor. What is the effect of the occasional direct quotation of Mr. Upperco's comments (¶s 2, 5)?

For Writing

1. Write an essay in which you explain the process by which you learned or are still learning to do something fairly complicated. You can write it either (1) to explain to your readers how to do the same thing or (2) to entertain your readers by showing, as Dolman does, the amusing pitfalls of the learning process.

2. Write a narrative essay in which you at your present age and level of maturity are narrating an incident in which you at a younger age and a different level of maturity are one of the principal characters. See Sanders, "Under the Influence" (pp. 420–433), Zitkala-Sa, excerpts from *The School Days of an Indian Girl* (pp. 254–262), and White, "Once More to the Lake" (pp. 142–148). You may use this dual characterization and split point of view as the basis for humor, though the essay could also be serious.

6 Process Analysis

Analysis involves dividing something into its component parts and explaining what they are, on the assumption that it is easier to consider and to understand the subject in smaller segments than in a large, complicated whole (see Division and Classification [pp. 353–356]). To analyze the human body, you could divide it into systems—skeletal, circulatory, respiratory, digestive—before identifying and defining the components of each. Of the digestive system, for instance, you would discuss the mouth, pharynx, esophagus, stomach, and large and small intestines.

You can analyze a process in the same way, focusing on *how* rather than *what*. A *directive process analysis* identifies the steps in how to make or do something: how to sail a catamaran; how to get to Kuala Lumpur; how to make brownies; or "how to get exercise into your life" (see Jane Brody [pp. 216–227]).

An *informative process analysis* can identify the stages by which something is created or formed, or how something is done. In "Those Crazy Ideas" (pp. 184–195), Isaac Asimov analyzes two "styles" of scientific investigation by comparing and contrasting the ways in which Charles Darwin (see also pp. 487–493) and Alfred Russel Wallace arrived "independently and simultaneously" at the theory of evolution. A process analysis can also explain how something functions or works, as Tom and Ray Magliozzi do in "Inside the Engine" (pp. 209–215), and as does the first half of Jane Brody's "Exercise: A New Dietary Requirement" (pp. 216–227): "Exercise Adjusts the Caloric Equation," ". . . Resets the Body Thermostat," ". . . Burns Body Fat." Or a process analysis can explain the meanings and implications of a concept, system, or mechanism as the basis for a philosophy that incorporates the process in question. Thus in the process of explaining how readers can follow a process, "How to Get Exercise into Your Life," "How to Start an Exercise Program," Brody offers not just a philosophy of exercise, but a philosophy of life. An analysis can also incorporate a critique of a process, sometimes as a way to advocate an alternative, as Scott Russell Sanders does in showing the deleterious effects of alcoholism on alcoholics' families in "Under the Influence" (pp. 420–433).

Thus, to write an informative analysis of how the digestive system works, you could explain the process by which food is ingested and broken down as it passes through the esophagus, stomach, and small and large intestines. The complexity of your analysis would depend on the sophistication of your audience. For general readers you might explain the peristaltic movement as "a strong, wave-like motion that forces food through the digestive tract." Medical students would require a far more detailed explanation of the same phenomenon—in far more technical language.

The following suggestions for writing an essay of process analysis are in themselves—you guessed it—a process analysis.

To write about a process, for whatever audience, you first have to *make sure you understand it yourself.* If it's a process you can perform, such as parallel parking or hitting a good tennis forehand, try it out before you begin to write, and note the steps and possible variations from start to finish.

Early on you'll need to *identify the purpose or function of the process and its likely outcome:* "How to lose twenty pounds in ten weeks." Then the steps or stages in the process occur in a given sequence; it's helpful to *list them in their logical or natural order* and to *provide time markers* so your readers will know what comes first, second, and thereafter. "First have a physical exam. Next: work out a sensible diet, under medical supervision. Then. . . ."

If the process involves many simultaneous operations, for clarity you may need to *classify all aspects of the process and discuss each one separately.* For instance, since playing the violin requires bowing with the right hand and fingering with the left, it makes sense to consider each by itself. After you've done this, however, be sure to *indicate how all of the separate elements of the process fit together.* To play the violin successfully the right hand has to know what the left hand is doing. If the process you're discussing is cyclic or circular—as in the life cycle of a plant, or the water cycle, involving evaporation, condensation, and precipitation—start with whatever seems to you most logical or most familiar to your readers.

If you're using specialized or technical language, *define your terms* unless you're writing for an audience of experts. You'll also need to *identify specialized equipment* and *be explicit about whatever techniques and measurements your readers need to know.* For example, an essay on how to throw a pot would need to tell a reader who had never potted what the proper consistency of the clay should be before one begins to wedge it, or how to tell when all the air bubbles have been wedged out. But how complicated should an explanation be? The more your reader knows about your subject, the more sophisticated your analysis can be, with less emphasis, if any, on the basics. How thin can the pot's walls be without collapsing? Does the type of clay (white, red, with or without grog) make any difference? The reverse is true if you're writing for novices—keep it simple to start with.

If subprocesses are involved in the larger process, you can either *explain these where they would logically come in the sequence,* or *consider them in footnotes or an appendix.* You don't want to sidetrack your reader from the main thrust. For instance, if you were to explain the process of Prank Day, an annual ritual at Cal Tech, you might begin with the time by which all seniors have to be out of their residence halls for the day, 8 A.M. You might then follow a typical prank from beginning to end: the selection of a senior's parked car to disassemble; the transportation of its parts to the victim's dorm room; the reassembling of the vehicle; the victim's consternation when he encounters it in his room with the motor running. If the focus is on the process of playing the prank, you probably wouldn't want to give directions on how to disassemble and reassemble the car; to do so would require a hefty manual. But you might want to supplement your discussion with helpful hints on how to pay (or avoid paying) for the damage.

After you've finished your essay, if it explains how to perform a process, ask a friend, preferably one who's unfamiliar with the subject, to try it out. (Even people who know how to tie shoelaces can get all tangled up in murky directions.) She can tell you what's unclear, what needs to be explained more fully—and even point out where you're belaboring the obvious. If your paper is an informative analysis of a process, as is Thomas S. Kuhn's "The Route to Normal Science" (pp. 197–208), ask your reader to tell you how well she understands what you've said. If, by the end, she's still asking you what the fundamental concept is, you'll know you've got to run the paper through your typewriter or computer once again.

Process analysis can serve as a vehicle for explaining personal relationships. For example, an analysis of the sequential process of performing some activity can serve as the framework for explaining a complicated relationship among the people involved in performing the same process or an analogous one. In such essays the relationship among the participants or the character of the person performing the process is more important than the process itself; whether or not the explanation is sufficient to enable the readers to actually perform the process is beside the point. Craig Swanson's "The Turning Point" (pp. 229–232) is typical of such writing. In this case, making a pot is the catalytic activity uniting Swanson, the admiring son, and his father, the potter. Although Mr. Swanson's process of pot-making is described in detail, readers would still need more information about potting itself to be able to learn to wedge the clay and throw the pot (as indicated above [p. 181]).

Writing parodies of processes, particularly those that are complicated, mysterious, or done badly—may be the ideal revenge of the novice learner (see Ann Upperco Dolman's "Learning to Drive" [pp. 174–177]) or the person obsessed with or defeated by a process, as in Craig Swanson's "It's the Only Videogame My Mom Lets Me Chew" (pp. 233–234). Parodies such as these may include a critique of the process, a satire of the novice or victim (often the author), or both.

STRATEGIES FOR WRITING—
PROCESS ANALYSIS

1. Is the purpose of my essay to provide directions—a step-by-step explanation of how to do or make something? Or is the essay's purpose informative—to explain how something happens or works? Do I know my subject well enough to explain it clearly and accurately?

2. If I'm providing directions, how much does my audience already know about performing the process? Should I start with definitions of basic terms ("sauté," "dado") and explanations of subprocesses, or can I focus on the main process at hand? Should I simplify the process for a naive audience, or are my readers sophisticated enough to understand its complexities? Likewise, if I'm providing an informative explanation, where will I start? How complicated will my explanation become? The assumed expertise of my audience will help determine my answers.

3. Have I presented the process in logical or chronological sequence (first, second, third . . .)? Have I furnished an overview so that my readers will have the outcome (or desired results) and major aspects of the process in mind before they immerse themselves in the particulars of the individual steps?

4. Does my language fit both the subject, however general or technical, and the audience? Do I use technical terms when necessary? Which of these do I need to define or explain for my intended readers?

5. What tone will I use in my essay? A serious or matter-of-fact tone will indicate that I'm treating my subject "straight." An ironic, exaggerated, or understated tone will indicate that I'm treating it humorously.

ISAAC ASIMOV

Asimov (1920–1992) said that his talent lay in his ability to "read a dozen dull books and make one interesting book out of them." He amplified, "I'm on fire to explain, and happiest when it's something reasonably intricate which I can make clear step by step." From these motives, Asimov wrote nearly five hundred books, averaging one every six weeks for over thirty-five years. Although Asimov held a doctorate in chemistry from Columbia University (1948), his subjects ranged from astronomy, biology, biochemistry, mathematics, and physics, to history, literature, the Bible, limericks, and a two-volume autobiography. Nevertheless, he is probably best known for his science fiction— stories and novels; "Nightfall" has been called "the best science fiction work of all time." In 1973 he won both the Hugo and Nebula Awards.

Even before the advent of word processors, Asimov wrote ninety words a minute, up to twelve hours a day, a superhuman pace. His demanding schedule allowed two—and only two— drafts of everything, the first on a typewriter, and in his final years, the second on a computer. He said, "But I have a completely unadorned style. I aim to be accurate and clear—whether for an audience of sci-fi fans or general readers, including children." Asimov has been praised for being "encyclopedic, witty, with a gift for colorful and illuminating examples and explanations"— qualities apparent in "Those Crazy Ideas." There he explains the creative processes by which two scientists, Charles Darwin and Alfred Russel Wallace, arrived independently at the theory of evolution. Then he analyzes how they worked to illustrate the common characteristics of the creative process, a combination of education, intelligence, intuition, courage—and luck.

Those Crazy Ideas

1   Time and time again I have been asked (and I'm sure others who have, in their time, written science fiction have been asked too): "Where do you get your crazy ideas?"

2   Over the years, my answers have sunk from flattered confusion to a shrug and a feeble smile. Actually, I don't really know,

and the lack of knowledge doesn't really worry me, either, as long as the ideas keep coming.

But then some time ago, a consultant firm in Boston, en- 3 gaged in a sophisticated space-age project for the government, got in touch with me.

What they needed, it seemed, to bring their project to a 4 successful conclusion were novel suggestions, startling new principles, conceptual breakthroughs. To put it into the nutshell of a well-turned phrase, they needed "crazy ideas."

Unfortunately, they didn't know how to go about getting 5 crazy ideas, but some among them had read my science fiction, so they looked me up in the phone book and called me to ask (in essence), "Dr. Asimov, where do you get your crazy ideas?"

Alas, I still didn't know, but as speculation is my profession, 6 I am perfectly willing to think about the matter and share my thoughts with you.

The question before the house, then, is: How does one go 7 about creating or inventing or dreaming up or stumbling over a new and revolutionary scientific principle?

For instance—to take a deliberately chosen example—how 8 did Darwin come to think of evolution?

To begin with, in 1831, when Charles Darwin was twenty- 9 two, he joined the crew of a ship called the *Beagle*. This ship was making a five-year voyage about the world to explore various coast lines and to increase man's geographical knowledge. Darwin went along as ship's naturalist, to study the forms of life in far-off places.

This he did extensively and well, and upon the return of the 10 *Beagle* Darwin wrote a book about his experiences (published in 1840) which made him famous. In the course of this voyage, numerous observations led him to the conclusion that species of living creatures changed and developed slowly with time; that new species descended from old. This, in itself, was not a new idea. Ancient Greeks had had glimmerings of evolutionary notions. Many scientists before Darwin, including Darwin's own grandfather, had theories of evolution.

The trouble, however, was that no scientist could evolve an 11 explanation for the *why* of evolution. A French naturalist, Jean Baptiste de Lamarck, had suggested in the early 1800s that it came about by a kind of conscious effort or inner drive. A tree-grazing animal, attempting to reach leaves, stretched its neck over the years and transmitted a longer neck to its descendants. The process was repeated with each generation until a giraffe in full glory was formed.

12   The only trouble was that acquired characteristics are not inherited and this was easily proved. The Lamarckian explanation did not carry conviction.

13   Charles Darwin, however, had nothing better to suggest after several years of thinking about the problem.

14   But in 1798, eleven years before Darwin's birth, an English clergyman named Thomas Robert Malthus had written a book entitled *An Essay on the Principle of Population*. In this book Malthus suggested that the human population always increased faster than the food supply and that the population had to be cut down by either starvation, disease, or war; that these evils were therefore unavoidable.

15   In 1838 Darwin, still puzzling over the problem of the development of species, read Malthus's book. It is hackneyed to say "in a flash" but that, apparently, is how it happened. In a flash, it was clear to Darwin. Not only human beings increased faster than the food supply; all species of living things did. In every case, the surplus population had to be cut down by starvation, by predators, or by disease. Now no two members of any species are exactly alike; each has slight individual variations from the norm. Accepting this fact, which part of the population was cut down?

16   Why—and this was Darwin's breakthrough—those members of the species who were less efficient in the race for food, less adept at fighting off or escaping from predators, less equipped to resist disease, went down.

17   The survivors, generation after generation, were better adapted, on the average, to their environment. The slow changes toward a better fit with the environment accumulated until a new (and more adapted) species had replaced the old. Darwin thus postulated the reason for evolution as being the action of *natural selection*. In fact, the full title of his book is *On the Origin of Species by Means of Natural Selection, or the Preservation of Favoured Races in the Struggle for Life*. We just call it *The Origin of Species* and miss the full flavor of what it was he did.

18   It was in 1838 that Darwin received this flash and in 1844 that he began writing his book, but he worked on for fourteen

years gathering evidence to back up his thesis. He was a method-ical perfectionist and no amount of evidence seemed to satisfy him. He always wanted more. His friends read his preliminary manuscripts and urged him to publish. In particular, Charles Lyell (whose book *Principles of Geology,* published in 1830–1833, first convinced scientists of the great age of the earth and thus first showed there was *time* for the slow progress of evolution to take place) warned Darwin that someone would beat him to the punch.

While Darwin was working, another and younger English 19 naturalist, Alfred Russel Wallace, was traveling in distant lands. He too found copious evidence to show that evolution took place and he too wanted to find a reason. He did not know that Darwin had already solved the problem.

He spent three years puzzling, and then in 1858, he too came 20 across Malthus's book and read it. I am embarrassed to have to become hackneyed again, but in a flash he saw the answer. Unlike Darwin, however, he did not settle down to fourteen years of gathering and arranging evidence.

Instead, he grabbed pen and paper and at once wrote up his 21 theory. He finished this in two days.

Naturally, he didn't want to rush into print without having 22 his notions checked by competent colleagues, so he decided to send it to some well-known naturalist. To whom? Why, to Charles Darwin. To whom else?

I have often tried to picture Darwin's feeling as he read 23 Wallace's essay which, he afterward stated, expressed matters in almost his own words. He wrote to Lyell that he had been fore-stalled "with a vengeance."

Darwin might easily have retained full credit. He was well 24 known and there were many witnesses to the fact that he had been working on his project for a decade and a half. Darwin, how-ever, was a man of the highest integrity. He made no attempt to suppress Wallace. On the contrary, he passed on the essay to others and arranged to have it published along with a similar essay of his own. The year after, Darwin published his book.

Now the reason I chose this case was that here we have two 25 men making one of the greatest discoveries in the history of sci-ence independently and simultaneously and under precisely the same stimulus. Does that mean *anyone* could have worked out the theory of natural selection if they had but made a sea voyage and combined that with reading Malthus?

26   Well, let's see. Here's where the speculation starts.

27   To begin with, both Darwin and Wallace were thoroughly grounded in natural history. Each had accumulated a vast collection of facts in the field in which they were to make their breakthrough. Surely this is significant.

28   Now every man in his lifetime collects facts, individual pieces of data, items of information. Let's call these "bits" (as they do, I think, in information theory). The "bits" can be of all varieties: personal memories, girls' phone numbers, baseball players' batting averages, yesterday's weather, the atomic weights of the chemical elements.

29   Naturally, different men gather different numbers of different varieties of "bits." A person who has collected a larger number than usual of those varieties that are held to be particularly difficult to obtain—say, those involving the sciences and the liberal arts—is considered "educated."

30   There are two broad ways in which the "bits" can be accumulated. The more common way, nowadays, is to find people who already possess many "bits" and have them transfer those "bits" to your mind in good order and in predigested fashion. Our schools specialize in this transfer of "bits" and those of us who take advantage of them receive a "formal education."

31   The less common way is to collect "bits" with a minimum amount of live help. They can be obtained from books or out of personal experience. In that case you are "self-educated." (It often happens that "self-educated" is confused with "uneducated." This is an error to be avoided.)

32   In actual practice, scientific breakthroughs have been initiated by those who were formally educated, as for instance by Nicolaus Copernicus, and by those who were self-educated, as for instance by Michael Faraday.

33   To be sure, the structure of science has grown more complex over the years and the absorption of the necessary number of "bits" has become more and more difficult without the guidance of someone who has already absorbed them. The self-educated genius is therefore becoming rarer, though he has still not vanished.

However, without drawing any distinction according to the   34
manner in which "bits" have been accumulated, let's set up the
first criterion for scientific creativity:

1) The creative person must possess as many "bits" of infor-   35
mation as possible; i.e., he must be educated.

Of course, the accumulation of "bits" is not enough in itself.   36
We have probably all met people who are intensely educated, but
who manage to be abysmally stupid, nevertheless. They have the
"bits," but the "bits" just lie there.

But what is there one can do with "bits"?   37

Well, one can combine them into groups of two or more.   38
Everyone does that; it is the principle of the string on the finger.
You tell yourself to remember *a* (to buy bread) when you observe
b (the string). You enforce a combination that will not let you
forget *a* because *b* is so noticeable.

That, of course, is a conscious and artificial combination of   39
"bits." It is my feeling that every mind is, more or less unconsciously, continually making all sorts of combinations and per-
mutations of "bits," probably at random.

Some minds do this with greater facility than others; some   40
minds have greater capacity for dredging the combinations out of
the unconscious and becoming consciously aware of them. This
results in "new ideas," in "novel outlooks."

The ability to combine "bits" with facility and to grow con-   41
sciously aware of the new combinations is, I would like to suggest, the measure of what we call "intelligence." In this view, it is
quite possible to be educated and yet not intelligent.

Obviously, the creative scientist must not only have his   42
"bits" on hand but he must be able to combine them readily and
more or less consciously. Darwin not only observed data, he also
made deductions—clever and far-reaching deductions—from
what he observed. That is, he combined the "bits" in interesting
ways and drew important conclusions.

So the second criterion of creativity is: 43

2) The creative person must be able to combine "bits" with   44
facility and recognize the combinations he has formed; i.e., he
must be intelligent.

Even forming and recognizing new combinations is insuffi-   45
cient in itself. Some combinations are important and some are

trivial. How do you tell which are which? There is no question but that a person who cannot tell them apart must labor under a terrible disadvantage. As he plods after each possible new idea, he loses time and his life passes uselessly.

46   There is also no question but that there are people who somehow have the gift of seeing the consequences "in a flash" as Darwin and Wallace did; of feeling what the end must be without consciously going through every step of the reasoning. This, I suggest, is the measure of what we call "intuition."

47   Intuition plays more of a role in some branches of scientific knowledge than others. Mathematics, for instance, is a deductive science in which, once certain basic principles are learned, a large number of items of information become "obvious" as merely consequences of those principles. Most of us, to be sure, lack the intuitive powers to see the "obvious."

48   To the truly intuitive mind, however, the combination of the few necessary "bits" is at once extraordinarily rich in consequences. Without too much trouble they see them all, including some that have not been seen by their predecessors.[1]

49   It is perhaps for this reason that mathematics and mathematical physics has seen repeated cases of first-rank breakthroughs by youngsters. Evariste Galois evolved group theory at twenty-one. Isaac Newton worked out calculus at twenty-three. Albert Einstein presented the theory of relativity at twenty-six, and so on.

50   In those branches of science which are more inductive and require larger numbers of "bits" to begin with, the average age of the scientists at the time of the breakthrough is greater. Darwin was twenty-nine at the time of his flash, Wallace was thirty-five.

51   But in any science, however inductive, intuition is necessary for creativity. So:

52   3) The creative person must be able to see, with as little delay as possible, the consequences of the new combinations of "bits" which he has formed; i.e., he must be intuitive.

53   But now let's look at this business of combining "bits" in a little more detail. "Bits" are at varying distances from each other.

---

[1] The Swiss mathematician, Leonhard Euler, said that to the true mathematician, it is at once obvious that $e^{\pi i} = -1$.

The more closely related two "bits" are, the more apt one is to be reminded of one by the other and to make the combination. Consequently, a new idea that arises from such a combination is made quickly. It is a "natural consequence" of an older idea, a "corollary." It "obviously follows."

The combination of less related "bits" results in a more startling idea; if for no other reason than that it takes longer for such a combination to be made, so that the new idea is therefore less "obvious." For a scientific breakthrough of the first rank, there must be a combination of "bits" so widely spaced that the random chance of the combination being made is small indeed. (Otherwise, it will be made quickly and be considered but a corollary of some previous idea which will then be considered the "breakthrough.") 54

But then, it can easily happen that two "bits" sufficiently widely spaced to make a breakthrough by their combination are not present in the same mind. Neither Darwin nor Wallace, for all their education, intelligence, and intuition, possessed the key "bits" necessary to work out the theory of evolution by natural selection. Those "bits" were lying in Malthus's book, and both Darwin and Wallace had to find them there. 55

To do this, however, they had to read, understand, and appreciate the book. In short, they had to be ready to incorporate other people's "bits" and treat them with all the ease with which they treated their own. 56

It would hamper creativity, in other words, to emphasize intensity of education at the expense of broadness. It is bad enough to limit the nature of the "bits" to the point where the necessary two would not be in the same mind. It would be fatal to mold a mind to the point where it was incapable of accepting "foreign bits." 57

I think we ought to revise the first criterion of creativity, then, to read: 58

1) The creative person must possess as many "bits" as possible, falling into as wide a variety of types as possible; i.e., he must be broadly educated. 59

As the total amount of "bits" to be accumulated increases with the advance of science, it is becoming more and more difficult to gather enough "bits" in a wide enough area. Therefore, the 60

practice of "brain-busting" is coming into popularity; the notion of collecting thinkers into groups and hoping that they will cross-fertilize one another into startling new breakthroughs.

61   Under what circumstances could this conceivably work? (After all, anything that will stimulate creativity is of first importance to humanity.)

62   Well, to begin with, a group of people will have more "bits" on hand than any member of the group singly since each man is likely to have some "bits" the others do not possess.

63   However, the increase in "bits" is not in direct proportion to the number of men, because there is bound to be considerable overlapping. As the group increases, the smaller and smaller addition of completely new "bits" introduced by each additional member is quickly outweighed by the added tensions involved in greater numbers; the longer wait to speak, the great likelihood of being interrupted, and so on. It is my (intuitive) guess that five is as large a number as one can stand in such a conference.

64   Now of the three criteria mentioned so far, I feel (intuitively) that intuition is the least common. It is more likely that none of the group will be intuitive than that none will be intelligent or none educated. If no individual in the group is intuitive, the group as a whole will not be intuitive. You cannot add non-intuition and form intuition.

65   If one of the group is intuitive, he is almost certain to be intelligent and educated as well, or he would not have been asked to join the group in the first place. In short, for a brain-busting group to be creative, it must be quite small and it must possess at least one creative individual. But in that case, does that one individual need the group? Well, I'll get back to that later.

66   Why did Darwin work fourteen years gathering evidence for a theory he himself must have been convinced was correct from the beginning? Why did Wallace send his manuscript to Darwin first instead of offering it for publication at once?

67   To me it seems that they must have realized that any new idea is met by resistance from the general population who, after all, are not creative. The more radical the new idea, the greater the dislike and distrust it arouses. The dislike and distrust aroused by a first-class breakthrough are so great that the author must be prepared for unpleasant consequences (sometimes for expulsion

from the respect of the scientific community; sometimes, in some societies, for death).

Darwin was trying to gather enough evidence to protect 68 himself by convincing others through a sheer flood of reasoning. Wallace wanted to have Darwin on his side before proceeding.

It takes courage to announce the results of your creativity. 69 The greater the creativity, the greater the necessary courage in much more than direct proportion. After all, consider that the more profound the breakthrough, the more solidified the previous opinions; the more "against reason" the new discovery seems, the more against cherished authority.

Usually a man who possesses enough courage to be a scien- 70 tific genius seems odd. After all, a man who has sufficient courage or irreverence to fly in the face of reason or authority must be odd, if you define "odd" as "being not like most people." And if he is courageous and irreverent in such a colossally big thing, he will certainly be courageous and irreverent in many small things so that being odd in one way, he is apt to be odd in others. In short, he will seem to the non-creative, conforming people about him to be a "crackpot."

So we have the fourth criterion: 71

4) The creative person must possess courage (and to the 72 general public may, in consequence, seem a crackpot).

As it happens, it is the crackpottery that is most often most 73 noticeable about the creative individual. The eccentric and absent-minded professor is a stock character in fiction; and the phrase "mad scientist" is almost a cliché.

(And be it noted that I am never asked where I get my inter- 74 esting or effective or clever or fascinating ideas. I am invariably asked where I get my *crazy* ideas.)

Of course, it does not follow that because the creative indi- 75 vidual is usually a crackpot, that any crackpot is automatically an unrecognized genius. The chances are low indeed, and failure to recognize that the proposition cannot be so reversed is the cause of a great deal of trouble.

Then, since I believe that combinations of "bits" take place 76 quite at random in the unconscious mind, it follows that it is quite possible that a person may possess all four of the criteria I have mentioned in superabundance and yet may never happen to make the necessary combination. After all, suppose Darwin had never read Malthus. Would he ever have thought of natural selection? What made him pick up the copy? What if someone had come in at the crucial time and interrupted him?

77   So there is a fifth criterion which I am at a loss to phrase in any other way than this:

78   5) A creative person must be lucky.

79   To summarize:

80   A creative person must be 1) broadly educated, 2) intelligent, 3) intuitive, 4) courageous, and 5) lucky.

81   How, then, does one go about encouraging scientific creativity? For now, more than ever before in man's history, we must; and the need will grow constantly in the future.

82   Only, it seems to me, by increasing the incidence of the various criteria among the general population.

83   Of the five criteria, number 5 (luck) is out of our hands. We can only hope; although we must also remember Louis Pasteur's famous statement that "Luck favors the prepared mind." Presumably, if we have enough of the four other criteria, we shall find enough of number five as well.

84   Criterion 1 (broad education) is in the hands of our school system. Many educators are working hard to find ways of increasing the quality of education among the public. They should be encouraged to continue doing so.

85   Criterion 2 (intelligence) and 3 (intuition) are inborn and their incidence cannot be increased in the ordinary way. However, they can be more efficiently recognized and utilized. I would like to see methods devised for spotting the intelligent and intuitive (particularly the latter) early in life and treating them with special care. This, too, educators are concerned with.

86   To me, though, it seems that it is criterion 4 (courage) that receives the least concern, and it is just the one we may most easily be able to handle. Perhaps it is difficult to make a person more courageous than he is, but that is not necessary. It would be equally effective to make it sufficient to be less courageous; to adopt an attitude that creativity is a permissible activity.

87   Does this mean changing society or changing human nature? I don't think so. I think there are ways of achieving the end that do

not involve massive change of anything, and it is here that brain-busting has its greatest chance of significance.

Suppose we have a group of five that includes one creative individual. Let's ask again what that individual can receive from the non-creative four.   88

The answer to me, seems to be just this: Permission!   89

They must permit him to create. They must tell him to go ahead and be a crackpot.[2]   90

How is this permission to be granted? Can four essentially non-creative people find it within themselves to grant such permission? Can the one creative person find it within himself to accept it?   91

I don't know. Here, it seems to me, is where we need experimentation and perhaps a kind of creative breakthrough about creativity. Once we learn enough about the whole matter, who knows—I may even find out where I get those crazy ideas.   92

Content

1. How does Asimov define "crazy ideas"? Is he using "crazy idea" as a synonym for a "new and revolutionary scientific principle"? How would Asimov (or you) distinguish between a "crazy idea" and a "crackpot" idea? Or the insane notion of a "mad scientist"?

2. Compare and contrast the creative processes by which Charles Darwin and Alfred Russel Wallace arrived independently at the theory of evolution.

3. How appropriate is it for Asimov to generalize about scientific creativity on the basis of two examples from a particular field?

4. Identify the five qualities Asimov says are necessary for the creative process to operate. Has he covered all the essentials? To what extent must the "climate be right" for the creative process to function effectively? What becomes of "crazy ideas" too advanced for their time?

---

[2] Always with the provision, of course, that the crackpot creation that results survives the test of hard inspection. Though many of the products of genius seem crackpot at first, very few of the creations that seem crackpot turn out, after all, to be products of genius. (Author's note)

Strategies/Structures

1. Show how Asimov's essay is an example of inductive reasoning—beginning with evidence, assessing that evidence, and drawing conclusions from it.

2. Although Asimov identifies the fifth quality in a successful creative process as luck (¶ 78), he doesn't define it, says it's "out of our hands" (¶ 83), and blithely assures us that "if we have enough of the four other criteria" we'll find enough luck as well (¶ 83). Is Asimov irresponsible here?

Language

1. Asimov uses a conversational tone and vocabulary, as well as two extended narrative examples (of Darwin and Wallace). Would you expect to find such literary techniques in scientific writing? If so, for what kind of audience? (Compare Darwin, "Understanding Natural Selection" [pp. 487–493] and Gould, "Evolution as Fact and Theory" [pp. 513–522].)

2. Asimov always identifies the scientists to whom he is referring when he first introduces them (Lamarck, ¶ 11; Malthus, ¶ 14; Lyell, ¶ 18). What does this practice reveal about the amount of scientific knowledge Asimov expects his readers to have?

For Writing

What does it take to be successful? Identify and define the essential criteria (four or five items) for an outstanding performance in one of the fields or roles below. Illustrate your definition with a detailed example or two from the lives of successful people in that field or role, perhaps people you know:

   a. Parent or grandparent
   b. Medicine (doctor, nurse, social worker, medical researcher)
   c. Politics, military, and the law (police or military officer, lawyer, elected official, bureaucrat, judge)
   d. Athletics (player of team or individual sports, coach)
   e. Education (student, teacher, or administrator)
   f. The fine arts (painter, sculptor, musician, writer)
   g. Business (self-made man or woman, salesperson, manager, executive, accountant, broker)
   h. Another profession or occupation of your choice.

THOMAS S. KUHN

Kuhn's writings as a professor of philosophy and history of science approach the ways scientists think and work from a philosophical and humanistic perspective. Kuhn (1922–1996) was educated as a physicist at Harvard (B.A., 1943; M.A., 1946; Ph.D., 1949), and taught at Harvard (1948–1956), the University of California, Berkeley (1958–1964), Princeton (1964–1979), and thereafter at the Massachusetts Institute of Technology. His illuminating books, profoundly influential on the ways scientists and humanists alike understand their own and each other's work, include *The Copernican Revolution: Planetary Astronomy in the Development of Western Thought* (1957) and *The Essential Tension* (1977). The idea for *The Structure of Scientific Revolutions* (1962), from which this classic essay is taken, had been germinating for fifteen years, beginning when Kuhn as a graduate student taught historical case studies of scientists and concluded that Aristotle's physics were not "bad Newton," but simply different. "I sweated blood and blood and blood, and finally I had a breakthrough," he said.

Nothing is as practical as a good theory, or in this case, a good definition of a theory. Kuhn begins by defining paradigms— structures or patterns that allow scientists to share a common set of assumptions, theories, laws, applications as they look at their fields. Scientists whose research is based on shared paradigms, who "learned the bases of their field from the same concrete models . . . are committed to the same rules and standards for scientific practice" and do not disagree over the fundamentals. The rest of this essay explains how and why this is so, and shows the random state of any scientific field before the emergence of a workable paradigm, the effects of competing paradigms on the discipline, and the consequences to the field of shifting from one paradigm to another.

The Route to Normal Science

In this essay, "normal science" means research firmly based upon one or more past scientific achievements, achievements that some particular scientific community acknowledges for a time as supplying the foundation for its further practice. Today such achievements are recounted, though seldom in their original form, by science textbooks, elementary and advanced. These textbooks expound the body of accepted theory, illustrate many or all of its successful applications, and compare these applications with exemplary observations and experiments. Before such books became popular early in the nineteenth century (and until even more recently in the newly matured sciences), many of the famous classics of science fulfilled a similar function. Aristotle's *Physica*, Ptolemy's *Almagest*, Newton's *Principia* and *Opticks*, Franklin's *Electricity*, Lavoisier's *Chemistry*, and Lyell's *Geology*—these and many other works served for a time implicitly to define the legitimate problems and methods of a research field for succeeding generations of practitioners. They were able to do so because they shared two essential characteristics. Their achievement was sufficiently unprecedented to attract an enduring group of adherents away from competing modes of scientific activity. Simultaneously, it was sufficiently open-ended to leave all sorts of problems for the redefined group of practitioners to resolve.

2   Achievements that share these two characteristics I shall henceforth refer to as "paradigms," a term that relates closely to "normal science." By choosing it, I mean to suggest that some accepted examples of actual scientific practice—examples which include law, theory, application, and instrumentation together— provide models from which spring particular coherent traditions of scientific research. These are the traditions which the historian describes under such rubrics as "Ptolemaic astronomy" (or "Copernican"), "Aristotelian dynamics" (or "Newtonian"), "corpuscular optics" (or "wave optics"), and so on. The study of paradigms, including many that are far more specialized than those named illustratively above, is what mainly prepares the student for membership in the particular scientific community with which he will later practice. Because he there joins men who learned the bases of their field from the same concrete models, his subsequent practice will seldom evoke overt disagreement over fundamentals. Men whose research is based on shared paradigms are committed to the same rules and standards for scientific practice. That commitment and the apparent consensus it produces are prerequisites for normal science, i.e., for the genesis and continuation of a particular research tradition.

Because in this essay the concept of a paradigm will often 3 substitute for a variety of familiar notions, more will need to be said about the reasons for its introduction. Why is the concrete scientific achievement, as a locus of professional commitment, prior to the various concepts, laws, theories, and points of view that may be abstracted from it? In what sense is the shared paradigm a fundamental unit for the student of scientific development, a unit that cannot be fully reduced to logically atomic components which might function in its stead? There can be a sort of scientific research without paradigms, or at least without any so unequivocal and so binding as the ones named above. Acquisition of a paradigm and of the more esoteric type of research it permits is a sign of maturity in the development of any given scientific field.

If the historian traces the scientific knowledge of any se- 4 lected group of related phenomena backward in time, he is likely to encounter some minor variant of a pattern here illustrated from the history of physical optics. Today's physics textbooks tell the student that light is photons, i.e., quantum-mechanical entities that exhibit some characteristics of waves and some of particles. Research proceeds accordingly, or rather according to the more elaborate and mathematical characterization from which this usual verbalization is derived. That characterization of light is, however, scarcely half a century old. Before it was developed by Planck, Einstein, and others early in this century, physics texts taught that light was transverse wave motion, a conception rooted in a paradigm that derived ultimately from the optical writings of Young and Fresnel in the early nineteenth century. Nor was the wave theory the first to be embraced by almost all practitioners of optical science. During the eighteenth century the paradigm for this field was provided by Newton's *Opticks*, which taught that light was material corpuscles. At that time physicists sought evidence, as the early wave theorists had not, of the pressure exerted by light particles impinging on solid bodies.

These transformations of the paradigms of physical optics 5 are scientific revolutions, and the successive transition from one paradigm to another via revolution is the usual developmental pattern of mature science. It is not, however, the pattern characteristic of the period before Newton's work, and that is the contrast that concerns us here. No period between remote antiquity

and the end of the seventeenth century exhibited a single generally accepted view about the nature of light. Instead there were
a number of competing schools and sub-schools, most of them
espousing one variant or another of Epicurean, Aristotelian, or
Platonic theory. One group took light to be particles emanating
from material bodies; for another it was a modification of the
medium that intervened between the body and the eye; still another explained light in terms of an interaction of the medium with
an emanation from the eye; and there were other combinations and
modifications besides. Each of the corresponding schools derived
strength from its relation to some particular metaphysic, and each
emphasized, as paradigmatic observations, the particular cluster
of optical phenomena that its own theory could do most to explain.
Other observations were dealt with by *ad hoc* elaborations, or they
remained as outstanding problems for further research.

6   At various times all these schools made significant contributions to the body of concepts, phenomena, and techniques
from which Newton drew the first nearly uniformly accepted
paradigm for physical optics. Any definition of the scientist that
excludes at least the more creative members of these various
schools will exclude their modern successors as well. Those men
were scientists. Yet anyone examining a survey of physical optics
before Newton may well conclude that, though the field's practitioners were scientists, the net result of their activity was
something less than science. Being able to take no common body
of belief for granted, each writer on physical optics felt forced to
build his field anew from its foundations. In doing so, his choice
of supporting observation and experiment was relatively free, for
there was no standard set of methods or of phenomena that every
optical writer felt forced to employ and explain. Under these circumstances, the dialogue of the resulting books was often
directed as much to the members of other schools as it was to
nature. That pattern is not unfamiliar in a number of creative
fields today, nor is it incompatible with significant discovery and
invention. It is not, however, the pattern of development that
physical optics acquired after Newton and that other natural
sciences make familiar today.

7   The history of electrical research in the first half of the
eighteenth century provides a more concrete and better known
example of the way a science develops before it acquires its first

universally received paradigm. During that period there were almost as many views about the nature of electricity as there were important electrician experimenters, men like Haukshee, Gray, Desaguliers, Du Fay, Nollett, Watson, Franklin, and others. All their numerous concepts of electricity had something in common—they were partially derived from one or another version of the mechanico-corpuscular philosophy that guided all scientific research of the day. In addition, all were components of real scientific theories, of theories that had been drawn in part from experiment and observation that partially determined the choice and interpretation of additional problems undertaken in research. Yet though all the experiments were electrical and though most of the experimenters read each other's works, their theories had no more than a family resemblance.

One early group of theories, following seventeenth-century practice, regarded attraction and frictional generation as the fundamental electrical phenomena. This group tended to treat repulsion as a secondary effect due to some sort of mechanical rebounding and also to postpone for as long as possible both discussion and systematic research on Gray's newly discovered effect, electrical conduction. Other "electricians" (the term is their own) took attraction and repulsion to be equally elementary manifestations of electricity and modified their theories and research accordingly. (Actually, this group is remarkably small—even Franklin's theory never quite accounted for the mutual repulsion of two negatively charged bodies.) But they had as much difficulty as the first group in accounting simultaneously for any but the simplest conduction effects. Those effects, however, provided the starting point for still a third group, one which tended to speak of electricity as a "fluid" that could run through conductors rather than as an "effluvium" that emanated from non-conductors. This group, in its turn, had difficulty reconciling its theory with a number of attractive and repulsive effects. Only through the work of Franklin and his immediate successors did a theory arise that could account with something like equal facility for very nearly all these effects and that therefore could and did provide a subsequent generation of "electricians" with a common paradigm for its research.

Excluding those fields, like mathematics and astronomy, in which the first firm paradigms date from prehistory and also those, like biochemistry, that arose by division and recombination of specialties already matured, the situations outlined above are historically typical. Though it involves my continuing to employ the unfortunate simplification that tags an extended historical episode with a single and somewhat arbitrarily chosen name (e.g., Newton or Franklin), I suggest that similar fundamental disagreements characterized, for example, the study of motion before Aristotle and of statics before Archimedes, the study of heat before Black, of chemistry before Boyle and Boerhaave, and of historical geology before Hutton. In parts of biology—the study of heredity, for example—the first universally received paradigms are still more recent; and it remains an open question what parts of social science have yet acquired such paradigms at all. History suggests that the road to a firm research consensus is extraordinarily arduous.

10   History also suggests, however, some reasons for the difficulties encountered on the road. In the absence of a paradigm or some candidate for paradigm, all of the facts that could possibly pertain to the development of a given science are likely to seem equally relevant. As a result, early fact-gathering is a far more nearly random activity than the one that subsequent scientific development makes familiar. Furthermore, in the absence of a reason for seeking some particular form of more recondite information, early fact-gathering is usually restricted to the wealth of data that lie ready to hand. The resulting pool of facts contains those accessible to casual observation and experiment together with some of the more esoteric data retrievable from established crafts, medicine, calendar making, and metallurgy. Because the crafts are one readily accessible source of facts that could not have been casually discovered, technology has often played a vital role in the emergence of new sciences.

11   But though this sort of fact-collecting has been essential to the origin of many significant sciences, anyone who examines, for example, Pliny's encyclopedic writings or the Baconian natural histories of the seventeenth century will discover that it produces a morass. One somehow hesitates to call the literature that results scientific. The Baconian "histories" of heat, color, wind, mining, and so on, are filled with information, some of it recondite. But they juxtapose facts that will later prove revealing (e.g., heating by mixture) with others (e.g., the warmth of dung heaps) that will

for some time remain too complex to be integrated with theory at all. In addition, since any description must be partial, the typical natural history often omits from its immensely circumstantial accounts just those details that later scientists will find sources of important illumination. Almost none of the early "histories" of electricity, for example, mention that chaff, attracted to a rubbed glass rod, bounces off again. That effect seemed mechanical, not electrical. Moreover, since the casual fact-gatherer seldom possesses the time or the tools to be critical, the natural histories often juxtapose descriptions like the above with others, say, heating by antiperistasis (or by cooling), that we are now quite unable to confirm.[1] Only very occasionally, as in the case of ancient statics, dynamics, and geometrical optics, do facts collected with so little guidance from pre-established theory speak with sufficient clarity to permit the emergence of a first paradigm.

This is the situation that creates the schools characteristic of the early stages of a science's development. No natural history can be interpreted in the absence of at least some implicit body of intertwined theoretical and methodological belief that permits selection, evaluation, and criticism. If that body of belief is not already implicit in the collection of facts—in which case more than "mere facts" are at hand—it must be externally supplied, perhaps by a current metaphysic, by another science, or by personal and historical accident. No wonder, then, that in the early stages of the development of any science different men confronting the same range of phenomena, but not usually all the same particular phenomena, describe and interpret them in different ways. What is surprising, and perhaps also unique in its degree to the fields we call science, is that such initial divergences should ever largely disappear. 12

For they do disappear to a very considerable extent and then apparently once and for all. Furthermore, their disappearance is usually caused by the triumph of one of the pre-paradigm schools, which, because of its own characteristic beliefs and preconceptions, emphasized only some special part of the too sizable 13

---

[1] Bacon [in the *Novum Organum*] says, "Water slightly warm is more easily frozen than quite cold"; *antiperistasis:* an old word meaning a reaction caused by the action of an opposite quality or principle—here, heating through cooling.

and inchoate pool of information. Those electricians who thought electricity a fluid and therefore gave particular emphasis to conduction provide an excellent case in point. Led by this belief, which could scarcely cope with the known multiplicity of attractive and repulsive effects, several of them conceived the idea of bottling the electrical fluid. The immediate fruit of their efforts was the Leyden jar, a device which might never have been discovered by a man exploring nature casually or at random, but which was in fact independently developed by at least two investigators in the early 1740's. Almost from the start of his electrical researches, Franklin was particularly concerned to explain that strange and, in the event, particularly revealing piece of special apparatus. His success in doing so provided the most effective of the arguments that made his theory a paradigm, though one that was still unable to account for quite all the known cases of electrical repulsion.[2] To be accepted as a paradigm, a theory must seem better than its competitors, but it need not, and in fact never does, explain all the facts with which it can be confronted.

14   What the fluid theory of electricity did for the subgroup that held it, the Franklinian paradigm later did for the entire group of electricians. It suggested which experiments would be worth performing and which, because directed to secondary or to overly complex manifestations of electricity, would not. Only the paradigm did the job far more effectively, partly because the end of interschool debate ended the constant reiteration of fundamentals and partly because the confidence that they were on the right track encouraged scientists to undertake more precise, esoteric, and consuming sorts of work.[3] Freed from the concern with any and all electrical phenomena, the united group of elec-

---

[2] The troublesome case was the mutual repulsion of negatively charged bodies.

[3] It should be noted that the acceptance of Franklin's theory did not end quite all debate. In 1759 Robert Symmer proposed a two-fluid version of that theory, and for many years thereafter electricians were divided about whether electricity was a single fluid or two. But the debates on this subject only confirm what has been said above about the manner in which a universally recognized achievement unites the profession. Electricians, though they continued divided on this point, rapidly concluded that no experimental tests could distinguish the two versions of the theory and that they were therefore equivalent. After that, both schools could and did exploit all the benefits that the Franklinian theory provided.

tricians could pursue selected phenomena in far more detail, designing much special equipment for the task and employing it more stubbornly and systematically than electricians had ever done before. Both fact collection and theory articulation became highly directed activities. The effectiveness and efficiency of electrical research increased accordingly, providing evidence for a societal version of Francis Bacon's acute methodological dictum: "Truth emerges more readily from error than from confusion."

We shall be examining the nature of this highly directed or 15 paradigm-based research in the next section, but must first note briefly how the emergence of a paradigm affects the structure of the group that practices the field. When, in the development of a natural science, an individual or group first produces a synthesis able to attract most of the next generation's practitioners, the older schools gradually disappear. In part their disappearance is caused by their members' conversion to the new paradigm. But there are always some men who cling to one or another of the older views, and they are simply read out of the profession, which thereafter ignores their work. The new paradigm implies a new and more rigid definition of the field. Those unwilling or unable to accommodate their work to it must proceed in isolation or attach themselves to some other group.[4] Historically, they have often simply stayed in the departments of philosophy from which so many of the special sciences have been spawned. As these indications hint, it is sometimes just its reception of a paradigm that transforms a group previously interested merely in the study of nature into a profession or, at least, a discipline. In the sciences (though not in fields like medicine, technology, and law, of which the principal *raison d'être* is an external social need), the formation of specialized journals, the foundation of specialists' societies,

---

[4] The history of electricity provides an excellent example which could be duplicated from the careers of Priestley, Kelvin, and others. Franklin reports that Nollet, who at mid-century was the most influential of the Continental electricians, "lived to see himself the last of his Sect, except Mr. B.—his *Eleve* [pupil] and immediate Disciple." More interesting, however, is the endurance of whole schools in increasing isolation from professional science. Consider, for example, the case of astrology, which was once an integral part of astronomy. Or consider the continuation in the late eighteenth, and early nineteenth centuries of a previously respected tradition of "romantic" chemistry.

and the claim for a special place in the curriculum have usually been associated with a group's first reception of a single paradigm. At least this was the case between the time, a century and a half ago, when the institutional pattern of scientific specialization first developed and the very recent time when the paraphernalia of specialization acquired a prestige of their own.

16   The more rigid definition of the scientific group has other consequences. When the individual scientist can take a paradigm for granted, he need no longer, in his major works, attempt to build his field anew, starting from first principles and justifying the use of each concept introduced. That can be left to the writer of textbooks. Given a textbook, however, the creative scientist can begin his research where it leaves off and thus concentrate exclusively upon the subtlest and most esoteric aspects of the natural phenomena that concern his group. And as he does this, his research communiqués will begin to change in ways whose evolution has been too little studied but whose modern end products are obvious to all and oppressive to many. No longer will his researches usually be embodied in books addressed, like Franklin's *Experiments . . . on Electricity* or Darwin's *Origin of Species,* to anyone who might be interested in the subject matter of the field. Instead they will usually appear as brief articles addressed only to professional colleagues, the men whose knowledge of a shared paradigm can be assumed and who prove to be the only ones able to read the papers addressed to them.

17   Today in the sciences, books are usually either texts or retrospective reflections upon one aspect or another of the scientific life. The scientist who writes one is more likely to find his professional reputation impaired than enhanced. Only in the earlier, pre-paradigm, stages of the development of the various sciences did the book ordinarily possess the same relation to professional achievement that it still retains in other creative fields. And only in those fields that still retain the book, with or without the article, as a vehicle for research communication are the lines of professionalization still so loosely drawn that the layman may hope to follow progress by reading the practitioners' original reports. Both in mathematics and astronomy, research reports had ceased already in antiquity to be intelligible to a generally educated audience. In dynamics, research became similarly esoteric

in the latter Middle Ages, and it recaptured general intelligibility only briefly during the early seventeenth century when a new paradigm replaced the one that had guided medieval research. Electrical research began to require translation for the layman before the end of the eighteenth century, and most other fields of physical science ceased to be generally accessible in the nineteenth. During the same two centuries similar transitions can be isolated in the various parts of the biological sciences. In parts of the social sciences they may well be occurring today. Although it has become customary, and is surely proper, to deplore the widening gulf that separates the professional scientist from his colleagues in other fields, too little attention is paid to the essential relationship between that gulf and the mechanisms intrinsic to scientific advance.

Ever since prehistoric antiquity one field of study after another has crossed the divide between what the historian might call its prehistory as a science and its history proper. These transitions to maturity have seldom been so sudden or so unequivocal as my necessarily schematic discussion may have implied. But neither have they been historically gradual, coextensive, that is to say, with the entire development of the fields within which they occurred. Writers on electricity during the first four decades of the eighteenth century possessed far more information about electrical phenomena than had their sixteenth-century predecessors. During the half-century after 1740, few new sorts of electrical phenomena were added to their lists. Nevertheless, in important respects, the electrical writings of Cavendish, Coulomb, and Volta in the last third of the eighteenth century seem further removed from those of Gray, Du Fay, and even Franklin than are the writings of these early eighteenth-century electrical discoverers from those of the sixteenth century.[5] Sometime between 1740 and 1780, electricians were for the first time enabled to take the foundations of their field for granted. From that point they pushed on to more

18

---

[15] The post-Franklinian developments include an immense increase in the sensitivity of charge detectors, the first reliable and generally diffused techniques for measuring charge, the evolution of the concept of capacity and its relation to a newly refined notion of electric tension, and the quantification of electrostatic force.

concrete and recondite problems, and increasingly they then reported their results in articles addressed to other electricians rather than in books addressed to the learned world at large. As a group they achieved what had been gained by astronomers in antiquity and by students of motion in the Middle Ages, of physical optics in the late seventeenth century, and of historical geology in the early nineteenth. They had, that is, achieved a paradigm that proved able to guide the whole group's research. Except with the advantage of hindsight, it is hard to find another criterion that so clearly proclaims a field a science.

Content

1. What does Kuhn mean by "normal science" (¶ 1 and elsewhere)? What is "the route to normal science," as he explains it in this essay?
2. What does Kuhn mean by a "paradigm" in science (¶ 2 and elsewhere)? What is the relation of "paradigm" to "normal science" (¶ 2 and elsewhere)?
3. What is a pre-paradigmatic state (¶s 10–13)? What is the relation of the development of a paradigm and the emergence of "some implicit body of intertwined theoretical and methodological belief that permits selection, evaluation, and criticism" (¶ 12)?
4. What is the process by which one paradigm replaces another (¶ 15)?
5. What is the relation of innovative scientists to writers of textbooks (¶s 16–17)? Who reads scientific articles? Who reads textbooks of science (¶s 16–17)?

Language

1. Why is it necessary for Kuhn to define his key terms, "paradigms" and "normal science" (¶ 2) before he proceeds with the rest of the essay? Paraphrase them to make sure you understand what he's talking about.
2. Kuhn uses relatively nontechnical language throughout to explain complicated and technical phenomena. What does this choice of language reveal about Kuhn's intended audience?
3. When Kuhn does use such illustrative concepts as "photons," he defines them immediately afterward (¶ 4). Is this adequate for nonscientific readers?

For Writing

1. Explain in your own words the prevailing paradigm in one of the sciences Kuhn uses for illustrative purposes in this essay: physics, chemistry, biology, psychology. What is the prevailing paradigm in another science you know about? Use a scientific article in a field of your choice to help illustrate your analysis. How does the search for or finding of paradigms in the sciences help you (or people new to the field) understand the field? Or explain the prevailing paradigm in another field you know, such as business, education, engineering, a fine art, or a humanistic subject.

2. Explain what Kuhn means by the following: "When the individual scientists can take a paradigm for granted, he need no longer, in his major works, attempt to build his field anew, starting from first principles and justifying the use of each concept introduced. That can be left to the writer of textbooks" (¶ 16). What paradigms do your natural science, social science, or other textbooks exemplify?

=====================================

TOM AND RAY MAGLIOZZI

Tom (born, 1938) and Ray (born, 1947) Magliozzi were born in East Cambridge, Massachusetts, and educated at the Massachusetts Institute of Technology. Tom worked in marketing; Ray was a VISTA volunteer, and taught junior high school. In 1973 the brothers opened the Good News garage in Cambridge, which Ray continues to operate while Tom teaches business at Suffolk University. Three years later their career as Click and Clack, the Tappet Brothers, began with a local call-in radio show on car repair, "Car Talk," which was syndicated through National Public Radio in 1987.

Speaking, as one commentator has observed, "pure Bostonese that sounds a lot like a truck running over vowels," and with considerable humor, including unrestrained (some say "maniacal") laughter at their own jokes, the brothers dispense realistic, easy-to-understand advice about how cars work and what to do when they don't, both on the radio and in *Car Talk* (1991), in which the following explanation of "Inside the Engine" appears.

Inside the Engine

1   A customer of ours had an old Thunderbird that he used to drive back and forth to New York to see a girlfriend every other weekend. And every time he made the trip he'd be in the shop the following Monday needing to get something fixed because the car was such a hopeless piece of trash. One Monday he failed to show up and Tom said, "Gee, that's kind of unusual." I said jokingly, "Maybe he blew the car up."

2   Well, what happened was that he was on the Merritt Parkway in Connecticut when he noticed that he had to keep the gas pedal all the way to the floor just to go 30 m.p.h., with this big V-8 engine, and he figured something was awry.

3   So he pulled into one of those filling stations where they sell gasoline and chocolate-chip cookies and milk. And he asked the attendant to look at the engine and, of course, the guy said, "I can't help you. All I know is cookies and milk." But the guy agreed to look anyway since our friend was really desperate. His girlfriend was waiting for him and he needed to know if he was going to make it. Anyway, the guy threw open the hood and jumped back in terror. The engine was glowing red. Somewhere along the line, probably around Hartford, he must have lost all of his motor oil. The engine kept getting hotter and hotter, but like a lot of other things in the car that didn't work, neither did his oil pressure warning light. As a result, the engine got so heated up that it fused itself together. All the pistons melted, and the cylinder heads deformed, and the pistons fused to the cylinder walls, and the bearings welded themselves to the crankshaft—oh, it was a terrible sight! When he tried to restart the engine, he just heard a *click, click, click* since the whole thing was seized up tighter than a drum.

4   That's what can happen in a case of extreme engine neglect. Most of us wouldn't do that, or at least wouldn't do it knowingly. Our friend didn't do it knowingly either, but he learned a valuable lesson. He learned that his girlfriend wouldn't come and get him if his car broke down. Even if he offered her cookies and milk.

5   The oil is critical to keeping things running since it not only acts as a lubricant, but it also helps to keep the engine cool. What happens is that the oil pump sucks the oil out of what's called the

sump (or the crankcase or the oil pan), and it pushes that oil, under pressure, up to all of the parts that need lubrication.

The way the oil works is that it acts as a cushion. The molecules of oil actually separate the moving metal parts from one another so that they don't directly touch; the crankshaft *journals*, or the hard parts of the crankshaft, never touch the soft connecting-rod *bearings* because there's a film of oil between them, forced in there under pressure. From the pump. 6

It's pretty high pressure too. When the engine is running at highway speed, the oil, at 50 or 60 pounds or more per square inch (or about 4 bars, if you're of the metric persuasion—but let's leave religion out of this), is coursing through the veins of the engine and keeping all these parts at safe, albeit microscopic, distances from each other. 7

But if there's a lot of dirt in the oil, the dirt particles get embedded in these metal surfaces and gradually the dirt acts as an abrasive and wears away these metal surfaces. And pretty soon the engine is junk. 8

It's also important that the motor oil be present in sufficient quantity. In nontechnical terms, that means there's got to be enough of it in there. If you have too little oil in your engine, there's not going to be enough of it to go around, and it will get very hot, because four quarts will be doing the work of five, and so forth. When that happens, the oil gets overheated and begins to burn up at a greater than normal rate. Pretty soon, instead of having four quarts, you have three and a half quarts, then three quarts doing the work of five. And then, next thing you know, you're down to two quarts and your engine is glowing red, just like that guy driving to New York, and its's chocolate-chip cookie time. 9

In order to avoid this, some cars have gauges and some have warning lights; some people call them "idiot lights." Actually, we prefer to reverse it and call them "idiot gauges." I think gauges are bad. When you drive a car—maybe I'm weird about this—I think it's a good idea to look at the road most of the time. And you can't look at the road if you're busy looking at a bunch of gauges. It's the same objection we have to these stupid radios today that have so damn many buttons and slides and digital scanners and so forth that you need a copilot to change stations. Remember when you just turned a knob? 10

11   Not that gauges are bad in and of themselves. I think if you have your choice, what you want is idiot lights—or what we call "genius lights"—and gauges too. It's nice to have a gauge that you can kind of keep an eye on for an overview of what's going on. For example, if you know that your engine typically runs at 215 degrees and on this particular day, which is not abnormally hot, it's running at 220 or 225, you might suspect that something is wrong and get it looked at before your radiator boils over.

12   On the other hand, if that gauge was the only thing you had to rely on and you didn't have a light to alert you when something was going wrong, then you'd look at the thing all the time, especially if your engine had melted on you once. In that case, why don't you take the bus? Because you're not going to be a very good driver, spending most of your time looking at the gauges.

13   Incidentally, if that oil warning light ever comes on, shut the engine off! We don't mean that you should shut it off in rush-hour traffic when you're in the passing lane. Use all necessary caution and get the thing over to the breakdown lane. But don't think you can limp to the next exit, because you can't. Spend the money to get towed and you may save the engine.

14   It's a little-known fact that the oil light does *not* signify whether or not you have oil in the engine. The oil warning light is really monitoring the oil *pressure.* Of course, if you have no oil, you'll have no oil pressure, so the light will be on. But it's also possible to have plenty of oil and an oil pump that's not working for one reason or another. In this event, a new pump would fix the problem, but if you were to drive the car (saying, "It must be a bad light, I just checked the oil!") you'd melt the motor.

15   So if the oil warning light comes on, even if you just had an oil change and the oil is right up to the full mark on the dipstick and is nice and clean—don't drive the car!

16   Here's another piece of useful info. When you turn the key to the "on" position, all the little warning lights *should light up:* the temperature light, the oil light, whatever other lights you may have. Because that is the *test mode* for these lights. If those lights *don't* light up when you turn the key to the "on" position (just before you turn it all the way to start the car), does that mean you're out

of oil? No. It means that something is wrong with the warning light itself. If the light doesn't work then, it's not going to work at all. Like when you need it, for example.

One more thing about oil: overfilling is just as bad as underfilling. Can you really have too much of a good thing? you ask. Yes. If you're half a quart or even a quart overfilled, it's not a big deal, and I wouldn't be afraid to drive the car under those circumstances. But if you're a quart and a half or two quarts or more overfilled, you could have so much oil in the crankcase that the spinning crankshaft is going to hit the oil and turn it into suds. It's impossible for the pump to pump suds, so you'll ruin the motor. It's kind of like a front-loading washing machine that goes berserk and spills suds all over the floor when you put too much detergent in. That's what happens to your motor oil when you overfill it. 17

With all this talk about things that can go wrong, let's not forget that modern engines are pretty incredible. People always say, "You know, the cars of yesteryear were wonderful. They built cars rough and tough and durable in those days." 18

Horsefeathers. 19

The cars of yesteryear were nicer to look at because they were very individualistic. They were all different, and some were even beautiful. In fact, when I was a kid, you could tell the year, make, and model of a car from a hundred paces just by looking at the taillights or the grille. 20

Nowadays, they all look the same. They're like jellybeans on wheels. You can't tell one from the other. But the truth is, they've never made engines as good as they make them today. Think of the abuse they take! None of the cars of yesteryear was capable of going 60 or 70 miles per hour all day long and taking it for 100,000 miles. 21

Engines of today—and by today I mean from the late '60s on up—are far superior. What makes them superior is not only the design and the metallurgy, but the lubricants. The oil they had thirty years ago was lousy compared to what we have today. There are magic additives and detergents and long-chain polymers and what-have-you that make them able to hold dirt in suspension and to neutralize acids and to lubricate better than oils of the old days. 22

23   There aren't too many things that will go wrong, because the engines are made so well and the tolerances are closer. And aside from doing stupid things like running out of oil or failing to heed the warning lights or overfilling the thing, you shouldn't worry.

24   But here's one word of caution about cars that have timing belts: Lots of cars these days are made with overhead camshafts. The camshaft, which opens the valves, is turned by a gear and gets its power from the crankshaft. Many cars today use a notched rubber *timing belt* to connect the two shafts instead of a chain because it's cheaper and easy to change. And here's the caveat: *if you don't change it and the belt breaks, it can mean swift ruin to the engine.* The pistons can hit the valves and you'll have bent valves and possibly broken pistons.

25   So you can do many hundreds of dollars' worth of damage by failing to heed the manufacturer's warning about changing the timing belt in a timely manner. No pun intended. For most cars, the timing belt replacement is somewhere between $100 and $200. It's not a big deal.

26   I might add that there are many cars that have rubber timing belts that will *not* cause damage to the engine when they break. But even if you have one of those cars, make sure that you get the belt changed, at the very least, when the manufacturer suggests it. If there's no specific recommendation and you have a car with a rubber belt, we would recommend that you change it at 60,000 miles. Because even if you don't do damage to the motor when the belt breaks, you're still going to be stuck somewhere, maybe somewhere unpleasant. Maybe even Cleveland! So you want to make sure that you don't fall into that situation.

27   Many engines that have rubber timing belts also use the belt to drive the water pump. On these, don't forget to change the water pump when you change the timing belt, because the leading cause of premature belt failure is that the water pump seizes. So if you have a timing belt that drives the water pump, get the water pump out of there at the same time. You don't want to put a belt in and then have the water pump go a month later, because it'll break the new belt and wreck the engine.

28   The best way to protect all the other pieces that you can't get to without spending a lot of money is through frequent oil changes.

The manufacturers recommend oil changes somewhere between seven and ten thousand miles, depending upon the car. We've always recommended that you change your oil at 3,000 miles. We realize for some people that's a bit of an inconvenience, but look at it as cheap insurance. And change the filter every time too.

And last but not least, I want to repeat this because it's important: Make sure your warning lights work. The oil pressure and engine temperature warning lights are your engine's life-line. Check them every day. You should make it as routine as checking to see if your zipper's up. You guys should do it at the same time. 29

What you do is, you get into the car, check to see that your zipper's up, and then turn the key on and check to see if your oil pressure and temperature warning lights come on. 30

I don't know what women do. 31

Content

1. Are you convinced that the Magliozzi brothers know their subject? Does their explanation of how a car engine works contain sufficient information for you to trust their authority? Why or why not?

2. What assumptions do the authors make about their readers' technical knowledge? Why do they provide basic information (such as how oil works in an engine, ¶s 5–9)? How are they able to do this without either offending their readers' intelligence or boring them?

3. Why do the Magliozzi brothers make a point of dispelling myths about "the cars of yesteryear" in comparison with the "engines of today" (¶s 18–22)?

Strategies/Structures

1. Why do the authors begin their explanation of a process with a story—in this case, a cautionary tale of the guy whose beat-up old Thunderbird had a meltdown on the Merritt Parkway?

2. When writing about science and technology, why is it important to define fundamental terms, even terms readers have heard—and used—many times, such as *motor oil* (¶s 5–9), *gauges* (or *idiot gauges* ¶s 10–12), and *oil warning light* (¶s 13–15)?

3. What part do cookies and milk play in this story? Does the author's use of humor reinforce or undermine the authority of their explanations? Does their humor help you to understand how an engine works?

Language

1. Typical of science writers, the authors use a number of analogies to explain how oil keeps an engine in good working order ("cushion," ¶ 6; "veins," ¶ 7; "front-loading washing machine" and "suds," ¶ 17). If these analogies help you to understand the subject, explain why they do. If they don't help, why don't they?

2. The authors give commands, such as "don't drive the car!" when the oil warning light is on (¶ 15), and "Make sure your warning lights work" (¶ 29). Why can they expect readers to react to such commands without being offended?

3. There are two authors. Sometimes they refer to themselves in the plural ("A customer of ours," ¶ 1); but most of the time they use the singular pronoun "I" (¶s 11, 20, and throughout). With what effect? What's the effect of addressing their readers as "you"—which Jane Brody, another advice-giver, also does (see pp. 216–227)?

For Writing

1. Write an essay for a nonspecialized audience explaining how a tool, mechanical object, or more abstract process (about which you know a great deal) works and how to get maximum performance from it. Possible topics include: a racing bicycle, a particular exercise machine, a power tool, a kitchen implement, a spread sheet, a particular computer program, management of a particular small business, an election campaign.

2. Authors in the physical or social sciences customarily work in teams, reporting on their collaborative research. In the spirit of this model, collaborate with another equally knowledgeable person or team to explain a technical process for a specialized audience in the same field.

JANE BRODY

Brody, born in Brooklyn in 1941, earned a B.S. from Cornell in 1962 and an M.A. in journalism from the University of Wisconsin in 1963. She began writing the *New York Times* personal health column in 1965. Among her numerous honors are the 1978 Science Writer's Award and a doctorate from Princeton (1987). Brody's books include *You Can Fight Cancer and Win* (with Arthur Holleb, 1978), *Jane Brody's Nutrition Book* (1981), *Jane Brody's The*

New York Times Guide to Personal Health (1982), and *Jane Brody's Good Seafood Book* (1994). All focus positively on how ordinary people can attain or maintain good health—with professional guidance but in large measure through their own common sense. Describing herself as "an inveterate jogger, tennis player, swimmer, walker, gardener, and cook," she practices what she preaches. This essay is from *Jane Brody's Good Food Book* (1985), written, she says "for the average American who likes to *eat* and likes to *live*." Her total health philosophy is one, she says, "of simple moderation. . . . Americans really don't want to give up their special passions [such as rich ice cream]. I say it is okay to indulge them now and then if you lead a healthy life the rest of the time."

Typical of writings on scientific or technical subjects for general readers, Brody begins by explaining a fundamental premise, in this case, the superiority of exercise over dieting for losing weight. Her explanation provides the background information for her analysis of the process of "how to get exercise into your life." First, realize the importance of exercise and make a commitment to exercise regularly. Then, select one or more activities you enjoy and that fit your temperament and state of health and schedule them for convenience and optimum use of calories. Like many such analyses, this essay makes the process sound easier (and simpler) than it may actually be, especially for a novice. Yet Brody's philosophy of exercise is opposed to "no pain, no gain"; she concludes with the reassuring recommendation, "Give yourself time to enjoy it."

Exercise: A New Dietary Requirement

Our species evolved on the move. Recent research on the effects of exercise and the consequences of sedentary living has shown that physical activity is crucial to the proper processing of foods that we eat. In fact, most of the chronic and often life-threatening ailments that besiege Americans in epidemic proportions could be tempered by regular exercise. Among them are heart disease, diabetes, high blood pressure, arthritis, and osteoporosis. But let's face it: most people are not motivated to exercise by what it may do for them 20 years down the pike. What gets people like me out moving every day is what exercise does for me right now, especially how it allows me to enjoy eating without gaining. I, along with millions of Americans, have discovered that exercise is the key to permanent and painless weight control.

2   After hearing a description of my usual daily exercise schedule—a morning run or bike ride and an evening swim, sometimes with an hour of tennis in between—some people remark, "Wouldn't it be a lot easier to eat one less bagel a day and skip all that exercise?" My answer is, "Easier, yes, but not nearly as effective nor as much fun." Here's why exercise, not dieting, is the best route to a leaner, lighter you.

Exercise Adjusts the Caloric Equation

3   Most of us are familiar with the basic biological "rule" that if calories *in* exceed calories *out*, you get fat. A small daily error in caloric intake—say, 100 extra calories, the equivalent of one large apple—can add up to 10 extra pounds on your frame within a year. Yet without counting every calorie they consume and use, most people are able to maintain a relatively stable weight—albeit sometimes more weight than they want—year in and year out even though caloric intake and output can vary greatly from day to day. There seems to be a built-in mechanism for balancing the calories you consume with the calories your body uses. But the available evidence indicates, *the mechanism only works properly when you are reasonably active.* Sedentary individuals tend to over-estimate their caloric needs, eating more than their bodies require and slowly acquiring excess pounds. . . .

4   According to one prevalent theory of weight control, your normal (that is, usual) body weight is like water—it constantly seeks its own level. The weight at which you stabilize when you make no special effort to gain or lose is called your body's *set point.* When your weight drops below that set point, chemical signals of starvation seem to trigger a corrective system into action to bring you back to "normal," even though normal by your definition means fat. This may be a major reason behind the failure of diets to produce long-lasting weight loss for most people. Only a few highly controlled individuals seem able to fight their set point indefinitely. But before you conclude that

keeping weight off is hopeless if it means a constant battle against an unseen biochemical enemy, the set-point theory offers you an out. Through exercise, you can safely and permanently lower your set point (as long as you keep exercising) so that you will now stabilize at a lower weight.

Exercise Resets the Body Thermostat

Everybody knows that exercise uses calories, and that the harder 5 and longer you exercise, the more calories your body will burn. But when people look at how hard they would have to work to get rid of the calories in just one piece of pie à la mode (running fast for an hour or sawing wood for 2), not to mention what it takes to lose a pound (walking for 16 hours or swimming hard for 7), many sit down in self-defeat. The effort required hardly seems to pay. But what most people don't realize is that exercise does far more than just burn calories while you're exercising. Vigorous exercise also revs up the body engine—raises its idling speed, as it were—so that *your body continues to use extra calories for up to 15 hours after you stop exercising.* If you exercise twice a day—once in the morning and once in the evening—you get the calorie-burning bonus all day long, even while you sleep. Even if your metabolism is normally on the slow side, exercise can boost it permanently by 20 percent to 30 percent.

But that's not all. According to recent studies directed by Dr. 6 David Levitsky at Cornell University, exercise provides a further calorie-burning benefit, especially after you've overeaten. The research showed that exercise done within 2 to 3 hours of a meal uses up more calories than the same exercise done on an empty stomach. Exercise does this by producing extra body heat, as would happen if you raised the thermostat in your home. . . .

Exercise Burns Body Fat

. . . Far better for your health and your future to lose primarily fat 7 in the first place. The only way to do that is through exercise, which uses body fat as its main source of energy. You may not see that initial rapid (but false) weight loss, but what you lose will be what you *want* to lose—fat, not muscle or water. Your loss will be slow but steady, and, if you make exercise a regular part of your life, chances are your loss will be permanent, too. If it's any consolation, studies have shown that in most cases, the faster people lose weight, the more likely they are to regain it. Slow loss, then, is the secret to lasting success.

8   Several studies have demonstrated the effectiveness of exercise as a weight-loss tool. One study involved 25 women who were 20 to 40 pounds overweight. They were divided into three groups: the women in one group cut 500 calories from their daily diet without changing their level of physical activity; those in the second group cut down by 250 calories and added enough exercise to use 250 extra calories a day; and those in the third group made no dietary changes but added activity that burned 500 extra calories a day. After 16 weeks, all three groups had lost weight, but the two groups that included exercise had lost significantly more fat and less muscle tissue than the diet-only group. . . .

9   If you want to lose weight faster than you can with just exercise, simply combine exercise with a reduced-calorie diet. Researchers at the University of California, Davis, showed that exercise can counter the metabolism-lowering effect of a low-calorie diet in many people. It also seems to curb the adverse caloric effect of aging on body metabolism. Whereas ordinarily your metabolism would slow down as you get older (which is one reason people get fatter in middle age even though they don't eat more), if you continue to exercise regularly, you may keep your youthful metabolic rate by maintaining a muscular body instead of losing muscle and putting on pounds of fat.

Other Benefits of Exercise

10   The weight-control benefits of exercise go far beyond its direct effect on how many calories your body uses. Vigorous exercise also suppresses your appetite. After a hard run or an hour of tennis, for example, you may find you don't get hungry for an hour or more. And although you may eat more when you exercise, chances are the extra calories will be significantly less than what you used up through exercise. A study by Dr. Peter Wood at Stanford University Medical School showed that very active people consume about 600 calories more than their sedentary counterparts but weigh on the average 20 percent less.

Furthermore, exercise is a natural relaxant and produces a [11] lasting euphoric effect. This, in turn, reduces the chance that you'll eat to relieve such emotions as tension, anxiety, anger, frustration, boredom, and depression. The good feelings induced by vigorous exercise most likely result from a natural tranquilizing chemical, beta-endorphin, that is released in the brain in response to exercise. This chemical is the body's equivalent of morphine or Valium but lacks the expense and adverse side effects associated with drugs. The release of beta-endorphin may account for the addictive quality of exercise and the fact that many exercise enthusiasts report that they don't feel as good when they are not able to exercise.

Finally, there are the many health and other benefits of ex- [12] ercise beyond weight control.

- Exercise counters heart disease and stroke by lowering serum cholesterol levels and blood pressure and by improving the ability of the heart to pump more blood with less effort.
- By enhancing muscle tone in the legs, exercise can prevent and sometimes reverse the symptoms of varicose veins.
- By facilitating the use of blood sugar by muscle tissue, exercise helps to lower blood sugar. This effect, along with exercise-induced improvements in blood circulation and weight control, helps to counter diabetes.
- Exercise strengthens bones by preventing the loss of calcium that weakens bones as people age.
- Exercise—as long as it's not abusive—helps to keep joints mobile and ward off the crippling effects of arthritis.
- Exercise is an important weapon against depression, and a growing number of therapists now insist that their depressed patients include daily exercise in their treatment program.
- Exercise improves the quality of sleep, and many people find that once they start a regular exercise program, they need less sleep than they used to because the sleep they now get is more restful.
- People who exercise regularly report that it improves their work efficiency and organization, probably because it establishes a daily routine and helps to free them of distractions and inhibitions caused by emotional tension. Thus, they are able to get more done in less time and with less effort.

- Exercise can enhance your sex life, perhaps because you feel better about your body when it has good muscle tone. However, if you become an exercise addict or marathon runner, you may not have time for sex!

How to Get Exercise into Your Life

13   The real problem with exercise for most people is not a failure to realize that it's good for them but an unwillingness to work it into their daily lives, the most common excuse being "I don't have time." My answer to such people is (if you'll pardon the pun) "That's a lame excuse." People have always managed to find time for the things they really want to do. Finding time for exercise, then, starts with a realization of its importance and a decision—a commitment—to make it a regular part of your life. Just as you brush your teeth every day, eat every day, and sleep every day, you can exercise every day. After a while, you may find, as I did, with regular moderate exercise you get more rest from less sleep and you work so much more efficiently that you actually have *more* time now that you've given up some time to exercise.

14   To maximize the weight control benefits of exercise, do three ½-hour sessions a week of an aerobic activity that uses at least 600 calories an hour or do more of a less vigorous activity. During an aerobic activity, your body uses oxygen, which is needed when fat is burned to produce body energy. Most effective are continuous-movement activities like fast walking, jogging, cycling, swimming, skating, rope jumping, aerobic dancing, cross-country skiing, hiking, and rowing. (These are the kinds of activities that "condition" your heart, improving its ability to withstand physical stress.) To be most effective, the activity should be done continuously for 20 minutes or longer three or more times a week, and you should work hard enough to get your pulse rate in the "target-zone." This zone, counted as beats per minute, can be calculated roughly by first subtracting your age from the number 220 (the resulting number represents your theoretical maximum heart rate), then multiplyling the result first by 70 percent (0.70) and then by 85 percent (0.85). The two numbers that result represent the range of heart beats per minute that you should try to maintain during your aerobic exercise session. For example, if you are 40 years old, your maximum

heart rate would be 220 minus 40, or 180, and your target heart rate for aerobic exercise would range from 126 (which is 70 percent of 180) to 153 (which is 84 percent of 180).

You can also use a lot of calories aerobically during such 15 activities as tennis, squash, handball, basketball, football, volleyball, and downhill skiing, even though these sports don't involve continuous motion for 30 consecutive minutes. However, *anaerobic* activities, like weight lifting and sprinting, that leave you breathless are not effective fat-burning exercises. Nor are they good for the heart (they increase blood pressure by causing muscles to clamp down on blood vessels), although they can certainly increase your muscle strength.

If your chosen activity uses fewer than 300 calories in ½ 16 hour, then it should be done for a longer time. And, if you're really serious about reaping the health benefits of exercise, it's best to make it part of your daily life, not just a few times a week, perhaps alternating two or more kinds of activities to reduce the risk of injury, boredom, and exercise "burnout." That way you never have to face the decision "*Should* I exercise today?" Your only daily decision needs to be "*How* should I exercise today?" And if on occasion your daily exercise is disrupted by matters beyond your control, you won't find yourself slipping back to two or even one exercise session a week.

In addition to setting aside time for a period of concentrated 17 exercise each day, you can also incorporate more activity into the routine of your daily life. Here are some possibilities:

- Walk all or part of the way to a destination instead of always hopping into a car, taxi, bus, or train. If you must take transportation to work, park the car some distance away, or get off the bus or train one stop before, and walk the rest of the way. If, while you're walking briskly for 20 minutes, you carry a heavy briefcase, shopping bag, or backpack (one that weighs 6 pounds or more), you can get enough exercise to condition your heart, Israeli researchers have shown.
- Take the stairs instead of the elevator or escalator. If you're going up more than three flights, ride only part of the way. If you're going down eight flights or less, walk.
- Use a hand mower and an old-fashioned hedge clipper instead of tools powered by gas or electricity.

- Prepare food by hand instead of always relying on a blender or food processor.
- If you bake bread, use your own power to knead it rather than an electrified dough hook. I can't promise you it will taste better, but it will be a more satisfying achievement.
- Carry your golf clubs, or pull them along, instead of riding in a motorized cart.
- Saw wood by hand, rather than using an electric saw for the entire job.

18   The possibilities are limited only by your imagination and the particular demands of your life. If for everything you do you think exercise, you'll doubtless find many enjoyable ways to get your body to use the energy it has in excess at the same time that you save some of the energy that the world has in short supply.

How to Start an Exercise Program

19   There are probably more people who have started an exercise program and dropped out than you could line up ten across along the entire course of the New York City Marathon. If you add in the people who have *thought* about getting into exercise but haven't yet done it, you could probably cover every available inch of space in all 365 square miles of the Big Apple. Yet, millions of Americans do manage to exercise regularly, and most of them would not dream of giving it up. How do they do it? It's a lot easier than you may think. If you adopt a rational approach to exercise, you're likely to find yourself eagerly anticipating your workout and resentful of anything that threatens to interfere. Here are some guidelines to help you get moving toward a slimmer, trimmer you—with pleasure, not pain.

20   *Pick an activity (or activities) you enjoy.* Exercise is not some kind of punishment for dietary transgressions. It is a positive force, to be enjoyed, not suffered through. If you try to make yourself do something you truly dislike, you'll have no trouble finding a dozen excuses to keep from doing it. Think back to what you enjoyed doing as a child. Was it biking, skating, swimming, dancing? Chances are you'll still find them fun. If you were an inactive child or one who always hated sports, try something simple and non-

competitive, like brisk walking, jogging, or bicycling. Think, too, about your native abilities. An uncoordinated person or someone who never could see the ball can find activities like rope jumping or a racket sport to be frustrating. If that's you, walking, jogging, or swimming might be more appropriate. Also consider whether you'd prefer to exercise alone (this has the advantage of not having to coordinate your schedule with anyone else's) or whether working out with a friend would be more fun and more likely to keep you at it. When you make a commitment to join someone else, you'll be less likely to skip your exercise session for trivial reasons.

Consider your time and schedule. If you have to leave for work 21 at 7 A.M. and don't get home until after the sun sets, you may be reluctant to exercise outdoors in the dark. For you, exercising at home on a stationary bicycle or rowing machine, jumping rope, swimming in a pool, or taking an aerobic dance class might be more suitable. If you think you can only spare ½ hour a day from start to finish, don't get into a sport like tennis that can easily chop 1½ to 2 hours out of your day for 1 hour's worth of exercise. Intense exercises that require minimal preparation, like jogging or rope jumping or working out on an exercise machine, would be more suitable. If you do have the time, you can use as many calories walking briskly as you would jogging over the same distance. Just remember that, for the same caloric benefit, it takes about twice as much time to walk the distance as to jog it.

Think about the cost and convenience. If money is tight, buying 22 expensive equipment or a club membership or paying high court fees may be out of the question. On the other hand, jumping rope, walking briskly, or jogging need not cost much more than the protective shoes you should have on your feet. You may have an old bicycle that can be fixed up for a few dollars, or you may be able to pick up a used bike inexpensively. Check out your local Y or community center for low-cost exercise programs, such as swimming or aerobic dancing. Make sure you can tolerate the transportation and arranging involved in your chosen activity. If, for example, you have to search for tennis partners, juggle a complicated schedule, and then drive several miles to the court, that can discourage regular participation.

Take your current health into account. If you have physical lim- 23 itations, these should be considered when you choose an exercise.

A person with asthma or foot problems, for example, may not be able to jog, but could do very well with a swimming program. If you have any chronic illness or muscle or joint problem, consult your physician first. Similarly, if you are over 35 and have been inactive, it's wise to check with your doctor before starting a program of vigorous exercise. If you are over 40, an exercise stress test may be advisable to determine what level of activity your cardiovascular system can withstand. If you are over 50, it may be best to start with a walking program to get your body into condition *before* you get into something more vigorous.

24   *Select a time for exercise.* And stick to it every day. If you want exercise to be a habit, you have to make it one, just as other daily activities are habits that you do pretty much at the same time each day without having to think about them. If you can never get up in the morning, then try exercising at lunchtime or before supper. If you're a morning person who peters out after 4 P.M., exercising soon after you get up in the morning may better suit your biological clock, although if you can get yourself to exercise in the afternoon, you may find that it renews your energy and you get more done in the evening.

25   *Give yourself time to enjoy it.* Don't expect to love your new activity the moment you start it. It can take a while—months sometimes—before you begin to feel really good about what you're doing. Make a commitment to stick with your activity for at least 3 months before deciding whether it's for you. And don't try to do too much too soon. Work up gradually to your full-length exercise program to avoid muscle soreness and injury. When I started swimming, I could do only 10 lengths of the pool at first, but by the end of a year, I was swimming 44. The same with jogging: I started with ½ mile and gradually worked up to my present level of 3- to 4-mile runs. If you've been sedentary for years and now want to get into jogging, start with a jog-walk program by alternating walking and jogging in each workout, emphasizing walking at first and gradually increasing the proportion of jogging. . . .

How Many Calories Will You Use?

26   Every movement of your body uses calories, and the harder and longer you use your muscles, the more calories you will use up.

You can use as many calories scrubbing floors as cycling around the park. Walking briskly for 3 miles uses the same number of calories as jogging that distance. Remember, too, that you're not likely to perform all activities for the same amount of time. You'd probably play tennis for at least 1 hour but jump rope for perhaps 15 minutes, swim for 30, and jog for 40. Even for the same activity done over the same period of time, different people use different amounts of calories. The number of calories your body will use to perform a particular activity depends on many factors, among them:

- How big you are to begin with. Heavier people use more calories than thinner ones to do the same activity. If you weigh 90 pounds, in 1 hour of vigorous tennis you will use about 350 calories. But if you weigh 190 pounds, in the same hour you will use twice that amount of calories.
- The temperature of the air or water. The colder it is, the more calories used because some are expended to maintain body temperature. Of course, if you dress warmly, you counteract some of this effect.
- How hard you work. Tennis players who "get everything" and hit the ball hard use more calories than those who never run after balls and just tap them back over the net. When you swim a fast crawl, you use more calories than when you do a leisurely backstroke. Lifting up your feet when you jog uses more calories than shuffling along. Riding a three-speed bike over hilly terrain requires more energy, and thus uses more calories, than riding a 10-speed bike at the same pace.

Content

1. Brody devotes half the essay (¶s 1–12) to an argument promoting the benefits of exercise before she discusses "how to get exercise into your life" (¶s 13–24). Why does she spend so much space defending a proposition that many readers would be willing to accept at face value?

2. What other benefits of exercise besides burning up calories does Brody cite (¶s 10–12)? For a number of these (¶ 12) she offers no evidence, only assertion. Should she have explained these more fully? Why or why not?

3. This essay is a chapter, slightly abridged, from *Jane Brody's Good Food Book: Living the High Carbohydrate Way* (Norton, 1985). What's it doing in a cookbook? Does it belong there?

Strategies/Structures

Brody uses a number of familiar techniques to argue her case. Find examples of the following in addition to those cited, and comment on the purpose and appropriateness of each:

   a. *Statements of general principles.* Example: If you are committed to exercising, "You never have to face the decision '*Should* I exercise today?' Your only daily decision needs to be '*How* should I exercise today?'" (¶ 16).
   b. *Definitions of key terms.* Example: The body's set point (¶ 4).
   c. *Analogies.* Example: The concept that "exercise resets the body thermostat" (¶s 5–6) to explain how exercise uses up extra calories.
   d. *Personal experience.* Example: Brody's increased endurance in swimming and jogging (¶ 24).
   e. *Mathematical formulas and calculations.* Example: How to calculate your "target zone" for aerobic exercise (¶ 14).
   f. *Bandwagon.* Example: "Millions of Americans manage to exercise regularly, and most of them would not dream of giving it up" (¶ 18).

Language

Typical of advice givers, Brody is unfailingly cheerful and optimistic. Cite some examples. Does this attitude give you (or other readers) the confidence it is intended to inspire?

For Writing

1. Propose a five- or six-point plan to enable your readers to incorporate a healthful activity into their lives (balanced meals, enough sleep, planned leisure, "good" reading, abstinence from smoking or drug use). If necessary, precede this with an explanation of why the outcome will be beneficial, and follow it with a realistic timetable of how long it will take to accomplish the desired benefits. Will this be a plan for a lifetime, or only for a limited period? Your audience should be people who are not

currently engaging in the health-promoting activity and who therefore will need to make some changes in their current behavior, as well as to be convinced of its benefits.

2. Write a satiric or comic essay defending the individual's right *not* to exercise, or the right to continue some other unhealthful practice (such as smoking or overeating). Be sure to take into account the opposing arguments.

CRAIG SWANSON

Swanson says of his life, "I was born in Ridgewood, New Jersey, in the year 1961. Not since 1881 has there been a year that can be read the same upside-down as right side up. And there won't be another until 6009. I grew up in the rural town of Hopewell, New Jersey, strikingly similar to the Lionel Train town, Plasticville. I studied at Rutgers and Syracuse universities before completing my bachelor's of mathematics/computer science at Virginia Commonwealth University in 1984. If I could write all day long"—he wrote the following essays as an undergraduate—"I'd be a very happy man. But alas, one cannot write all day, presuming he has financial obligations," so Swanson returned to Virginia Commonwealth University for graduate work in artificial intelligence. Both of the following essays, one serious, one satiric, devote most of their space to explaining processes, though in each the discussion of the process itself is the means to a different end.

Ostensibly, "The Turning Point" is an essay about making a pot; indeed, directions for the process occupy two-thirds of the text. With the addition of a few more specific details, such as what was used for the slip (¶ 6), and what the "finishing touches" were (¶ 8), the process is fairly complete. But the essay is about much more than potting. Sometimes writers describe a process in great detail as a way of focusing on the person performing it or on the people affected by either the process or the performance. Here, the activity of making the pot is the catalyst that draws the son and his father together. The first two paragraphs place the father's potting in its painful context; the potter's wheel is the consolation for the loss of his job, and he can engage in the potting itself because he has no formal claim on his time. Through Swanson's appreciation of his father's skill as a potter we recognize his respect, love, and concern for the man who performs this process so well. And so we come to appreciate the pain and the pleasure, as well as the process, in this essay with the wonderfully ambiguous title.

❄ *The Turning Point*

1   Dad lost his job last summer. They say that it was due to political reasons. After twenty years in the government it was a shock to us all. Dad never talked much about what he did at work, although it took up enough of his time. All I really know was his position: Deputy Assistant Commissioner of the State Department of Education. I was impressed by his title, though he rarely seemed to enjoy himself. Just the same, it was a job. These days it's hard enough to support a family without being out of work.

2   Apparently his co-workers felt so badly about the situation that they held a large testimonial dinner in his honor. People came from all over the east coast. I wish I could have gone. Everyone who went said it was really nice. It's a good feeling to know that your Dad means a lot to so many people. As a farewell present they gave Dad a potter's wheel. Dad says it's the best wheel he's ever seen, and to come from someone who's done pottery for as long as he has, that's saying a lot. Over the years Dad used to borrow potter's wheels from friends. That's when I learned how to "throw" a pot.

3   When I came home for Thanksgiving vacation the first thing I did was rush down to the basement to check it out. I was quite surprised. Dad had fixed the whole corner of the basement with a big table top for playing with the clay; an area set up for preparing the clay, including a plaster bat and a wedging board; the kiln Walt built for Dad one Christmas; one hundred and fifty pounds of clay; nine different glazes; hand tools for sculpting, and the brand new potter's wheel. It had a tractor seat from which you work the clay. It could be turned manually or by motor, and it offered lots of surface area, which always comes in handy. Dad

was right, it was beautiful. He had already made a couple dozen pots. I couldn't wait to try it.

The next day I came down into the basement to find Dad in [4] his old gray smock preparing the clay. I love to watch Dad do art, whether it's drawing, painting, lettering, or pottery. I stood next to him as he wedged a ball of clay the size of a small canteloupe. He'd slice it in half on the wire and slam one half onto the wedging board, a canvas-covered slab of plaster; then he'd slam the other half on top of the first. He did this to get all the air bubbles out of the clay. You put a pot with air bubbles in the kiln, the pot'll explode in the heat and you've got yourself one heck of a mess to clean up. Dad wedged the clay, over and over.

When he was finished he sat down, wet the wheelhead, and [5] pressed the clay right in the center of the wheel. Dad hit the accelerator and the clay started turning. He wet his hands and leaned over the clay. Bracing his elbows on his knees he began centering the clay. Steady right hand on the sides of the clay. Steady left hand pushing down on the clay. Centering the clay is the toughest part for me. The clay spins around and around and you have to shape it into a perfectly symmetric form in the center by letting the wheel do all the moving. Your hands stay motionless until the clay is centered. It takes me ten or fifteen minutes to do this. It takes Dad two. I shake my head and smile amazement.

Dad's hands cup the clay, thumbs together on top. He wets [6] his hands again and pushes down with his thumbs. Slowly, steadily. Once's he's as far down as he wants to go he makes the bottom of the pot by spreading his thumbs. His hands relax and he pulls them out of the pot. Every motion is deliberate. If you move your hands quickly or carelessly you can be sure you will have to start again. Dad wipes the slip, very watery clay, off his hands with a sponge. It is extremely messy.

To make the walls Dad hooks his thumbs and curls all of his [7] fingers except for his index fingers. Holding them like forceps, he reaches into the pot to mold the walls to just the right thickness. He starts at the bottom and brings them up slowly, making the walls of the pot thin and even all the way up, about twelve inches.

Dad sponges off his hands, wets them, and then cups his [8] hands around the belly of the pot. Slowly, as the pot spins around, he squeezes his hands together, causing it to bevel slightly. Dad spends five minutes on the finishing touches. He's got himself a real nice skill.

9   It is a rare treat to watch Dad do something that he enjoys so much.

Content

1. What are the meanings of the title, "The Turning Point"? How do they reinforce one another? What is the essay's main subject? Its secondary subject?
2. What other information would Swanson need to provide to complete his explanation of the process of making a pot? Given the essay's main subject, does it matter whether he explains the process of making a pot as fully as he could?

Strategies/Structures

1. In what ways does Swanson convey his attitude toward his father? Why doesn't he just come right out and say directly that he loves him and feels sorry for him?
2. How does Swanson's attitude toward his father function as a catalyst to integrate the main and secondary subjects?

Language

What is the tone of this essay? Why has Swanson chosen understatement rather than a more emotional means to make his point?

For Writing

Explain how to make or do something for an audience unfamiliar with the process. This may be the primary focus of your paper or, as in "The Turning Point," an explanation of the process may be subordinate to your discussion of something else—a relationship between the performer of the process and another person (as in Swanson and his father), or a group of people (see Zitkala-Sa [pp. 254–262]) or animals (see Cunningham [pp. 617–625]).

✳   ✳   ✳

In the following essay Swanson presents himself as a character addicted to the very process he criticizes, as we realize from the opening salvo with its implicit comparison of the video parlor to a men's room. Although his intellectual focus is on the process whereby video games extract money from the hapless player "as long as his twenty-five cent pieces last," Swanson's emotional focus is on the mindless possibility of winning: "bonus gobblers, shooters, racers, fighters. . . ."

❄ It's the Only Video Game My Mom Lets Me Chew[1]

E ven before I walk into the room I feel the electronic presence   1
sink to my bones. The beeps, twoozers, fanfares, and fugues
of the video games compete for dominance. As I enter the game
room I notice how much the machines look like urinals. People
fill the room, each playing "their" game.

My game is Tron. It is the only video game that is also a   2
movie. I do expect, however, to someday see a series of Pacman
films—"The Return of the Son of Pacman," Part II. Although I
play Tron often, I have never seen the movie. I just don't have the
money. I place my two hundredth quarter on the control panel to
reserve the next game.

Before it's my turn I have some time to watch the other   3
people within the parlor. All video players develop their own ways
of playing the games. Inexperienced players handle the controls
spasmodically and nervously. To make up for their slow reaction
time they slam the joystick much harder than necessary, under the
assumption that if they can't beat the machine through skill, then
they'll win out of brute strength. This often includes kicking the

---

[1] The title is a takeoff on a sugarless gum commercial.

coin return or beating upon the screen. Of course this is exactly what the machine wants. The sarcastic whines or droning catcalls that accompany the flashing "game over" sign are designed to antagonize the player. The angrier you get when you play these games, the worse you play. The worse you play the more games you play. Determined to get even, you pop quarter after quarter into the gaping coin slot.

4   A more experienced video player rarely shows emotion. A casual stance, a plop of the coin, a flip of an eyebrow, and he's ready. If he happens to win bonus gobblers, shooters, racers, fighters, markers, flippers, diggers, jugglers, rollers, or air ships, he does not carry on with a high-pitched, glass-shattering scream. When he loses a man, he doesn't get worked up or display fits of violence. He simply stares mindlessly into the video screen as long as his twenty-five-cent pieces last.

5   In goes my quarter. The machine sings out its familiar song of thanks, remarkably similar to Bach's Toccata in D-Minor. I am then attacked by spider-like "grid-bugs," an army of tanks, zooming "light cycles," and descending blocks that disintegrate me into a rainbow of dust particles. When my last player is played, Tron tells me the game is over by casting out the celebrated raspberry, then slowly droning out "Taps."

6   I walk out relieved. My pockets are quarterless. My vision is distorted and I am devoid of all intelligent thought. I step out, ready to avoid reality for another day.

Content

1. Is Swanson writing this to criticize video parlors? To criticize himself for his addiction to Tron? To help himself overcome his addiction? To caution others? To entertain his readers? Or some combination of these?

2. Is there a danger that explaining a process, even if one despises or has problems with it, will teach readers how to perform an offensive or problematic action? Explain your answer.

Strategies/Structures

1. What does the title signal to readers about the subject? About the way Swanson will treat the subject?

2. What kind of character is Swanson in this narrative? How do you know that Swanson as an author is exaggerating this character? Is he really "devoid of all intelligent thought"?

Language

In what respects is the narrator's language—precise, varied, and vivid throughout—at variance with video-game jargon? How does this discrepancy add to the humor and convince us of the narrator's analytic ability (see ¶ 3, for instance)?

For Writing

1. Write a parody of a process that others use straightforwardly, as a way to warn them against a mindless or self-destructive practice.

2. The technique of self-satire enables many writers to criticize potentially sensitive subjects; if they show themselves to be personally affected by the problem, their critique may seem more valid. Write a paper in which you satirize yourself in the process of providing a critique of some social, political, educational, or other phenomenon. It doesn't matter whether your intended audience knows you, but if they are unfamiliar with the object of your satire you'll need to provide enough information to make your essay self-contained.

Additional Topics for Writing
Process Analysis   (For process strategies, see page 182)

1. Write an essay in which you provide directions on how to perform a process—how to do or make something at which you are particularly skilled. In addition to the essential steps, you may wish to explain your own special technique or strategy that makes your method unique or better. Some possible subjects (which may be narrowed or adapted as you and your instructor wish) are these:

    a. How to get a good job, permanent or summer
    b. How to reduce stress
    c. How to scuba dive, hang-glide, rappel, jog, lift weights, train for a marathon or triathlon
    d. How to make a good first impression (on a prospective employer, on a date, on your date's parents)
    e. How to study for a test
    f. How to be happy
    g. How to build a library of books, tapes, videocassettes, or CDs
    h. How to lose (or gain) weight
    i. How to shop at a garage sale or secondhand store
    j. How to repair your own car, bicycle, or other machine
    k. How to live cheaply (but enjoyably)
    l. How to rope a calf, drive a tractor, ride a horse
    m. How to administer first aid for choking, drowning, burns, or some other medical emergency
    n. How to get rich
    o. Anything else you know that others might want to learn

2. Write an informative essay in which you explain how one of the following occurs or works. Although you should pick a subject you know something about, you may need to supplement your information by consulting outside sources.

    a. How I made a major decision (to be—or not to be—a member of a particular profession, to practice a particular religion or lifestyle . . .)
    b. How a computer (or amplifier, piano, microwave oven, or other machine) works
    c. How a solar (or other) heating system works
    d. How a professional develops skill in his or her chosen field; i.e., how one becomes a skilled electrical engineer, geologist, chef, tennis coach, surgeon . . . ; pick a field in which you're interested

e. How birds fly (or learn to fly), or some other process in the natural world
f. How a system of the body (circulatory, digestive, respiratory, skeletal, neurological) works
g. How the earth (or the solar system) was formed
h. How the scientific method (or a particular variation of it) functions
i. How a well-run business (pick one of your choice—manufacturing, restaurant, clothing or hardware store, television repair service . . .) functions
j. How advertisers appeal to prospective customers
k. How our federal government (or your particular local or state government) came into existence, or has changed over time
l. How a particular drug or other medicine was developed
m. How a great idea (on the nature of love, justice, truth, beauty . . .) found acceptance
n. How a particular culture (ethnic, regional, tribal, religious) or subculture (preppies, yuppies, pacifists, punk rockers, motorcycle gangs . . .) developed

3. Write a humorous paper explaining a process of the kind identified below. You will need to provide a serious analysis of the method you propose, even though the subject itself is intended to be amusing.

a. How to get good grades without actually studying
b. How to be popular
c. How to survive in college
d. How to withstand an unhappy love affair
e. How to be a model babysitter/son/daughter/student/employee/lover/spouse/parent
f. How to become a celebrity
g. Any of the topics in writing suggestions 1 or 2 above

4. Write a seemingly objective account of a social phenomenon or some other aspect of human behavior of which you actually disapprove, either because the form and context seem at variance (see Joan Didion's interpretation of Las Vegas weddings, [pp. 329–333], or because the phenomenon itself seems to you wrong, or to cause problems, or otherwise inappropriate. Justify your opinion (and convince your readers) through your choice of details and selection of a revealing incident or several vignettes (brief glimpses of scenes or actions, such as Swanson provides in "It's the Only Video Game . . ." [pp. 233–234]). Social and cultural phenomena are particularly suitable subjects for such an essay—nerd or geek or yuppie or twentysomething behavior, ways of spending money and leisure time (and foolish, trivial, or wasteful things to spend it on).

7 | *Cause and Effect*

Writers concerned with cause and effect relationships ask, "*Why* did something happen?" or "*What* are its consequences?" or both. Why did the United States develop as a democracy rather than as some other form of government? What have the effects of this form of government been on its population? Or you, as a writer may choose to examine a chain reaction in which, like a Rube Goldberg cartoon device, Cause *A* produces Effect *B* which in turn causes *C* which produces Effect *D*: Peer pressure (Cause *A*) causes young men to drink to excess (Effect *B*), which causes them to drive unsafely (Cause *C*, a corollary of Effect *B*) and results in high accident rates in unmarried males under twenty-five (Effect *D*).

Although process analysis also deals with events or phenomena in sequence, it's concerned with the *how* rather than the *why*. To focus on the process of drinking and driving would be to explain, as an accident report might, how Al C. O'Hall became intoxicated (he drank seventeen beers and a bourbon chaser in two hours at the Dun Inn); how he then roared off at ninety miles an hour, lost control of his lightweight sports car on a curve, and plowed into an oncoming sedan.

Two conditions have to be met to prove a given cause:

B cannot occur without *A*.
Whenever *A* occurs, *B* must also occur.

Thus a biologist who observed, repeatedly, that photosynthesis (*B*) occurred in green plants whenever a light source (*A*) was present, and that it only occurred under this condition could infer that light causes photosynthesis. This would be the immediate cause. The more *remote* or *ultimate cause* might be the source of the light if it were natural (the sun). Artificial light (electricity) would have a yet more remote cause, such as water or nuclear power.

But don't be misled by a coincidental time sequence. Just because *A* preceded *B* in time doesn't necessarily mean that *A* caused *B*. Although it may appear to rain every time you wash your car, the car wash doesn't cause the rain. To blame the car wash would be an example of the *post hoc, ergo propter hoc* fallacy (Latin for "after this, therefore because of this").

Indeed, in cause and effect papers ultimate causes may be of greater significance than immediate ones, especially when you're considering social, political, or psychological causes rather than exclusively physical phenomena. Looking for possible causes from multiple perspectives is a good way to develop ideas to write about. It's also a sure way to avoid oversimplification, attributing a single cause to an effect that results from several. Thus if you wanted to probe the causes of Al C. O'Hall's excessive drinking, looking at the phenomenon from the following perspectives would give you considerable breadth for discussion.

Perspective	*Reason (Attributed cause)*
Al, a twenty-one-year-old unmarried male:	"Because I like the taste."
Al's best friend:	"Because he thinks drinking is cool."
Al's mother:	"Because Al wants to defy me."
Al's father:	"Because Al wants to be my pal."
Physician:	"Because Al is addicted to alcohol. There's a strong probability that this is hereditary."
Sociologist:	"Because 79.2 percent of American males twenty-one and under drink at least once a week. It's a social trend encouraged by peer pressure."
Criminologist:	"Because Al derives antisocial pleasure from breaking the law."
Brewer or distiller:	"Because of my heavy advertising campaign."

All of these explanations may be partly right; none—not even the genetic explanation—is in itself sufficient. (Even if Al were genetically predisposed to alcoholism as the child of an alcoholic parent, he'd have to drink to become an alcoholic.) Taken together they, and perhaps still other explanations, can be considered the complex cause of Al's behavior. To write a paper on the subject, using Al as a case in point, you might decide to discuss all the causes. Or you might concentrate on the most important causes and weed out those that seem irrelevant or less significant. Or, to handle a large, complex subject in a short paper you could limit your discussion to a particular cause or type of causes, say, the social or the psychological. You have the same options for selectivity in discussing multiple effects.

The essays that follow treat cause and effect in a variety of ways. Because causes and effects are invariably intertwined, writers usually acknowledge the causes even when they're emphasizing the effects, and vice versa.

Four of the six essays in this section deal with the causes and effects of education, formal and informal, on the students involved; and with the consequences of that education—or lack of it—not only to the individual but to society. In "I Just Wanna Be Average" (pp. 243–252), Mike Rose reflects on the social, cultural, psychological, and educational causes that singly but more likely in combination would make a student decide he just wanted to be average, rather than to be the high achiever that middle-class society assumes and expects its children to be. "If you're a working-class kid in the vocational track," says Rose, your options are constrained: "You're defined by your school as 'slow'" and treated as slow by teachers and other students; "you're placed in a curriculum that isn't designed to liberate you but to occupy you" or to train you for work "society does not esteem" (p. 249). All these factors have to change for students to be able to change their mind, self-image, and aspirations. Zitkala-Sa's excerpts from *The School Days of an Indian Girl* (pp. 254–260) illustrate other constraints that are placed on Native American children uprooted from their homes and sent far away to boarding schools run by whites. Whether the efforts to acclimate these children to white middle-class culture (symbolized by cutting off their braids, making them wear Anglo clothing, and obliging them to speak English rather than their tribal languages) were made from benign or more sinister motives, the effects were the same: alienation from and marginalization in both cultures. In re-creating the child's point of view, intended to represent all children in such schools, the author does not offer solutions, though she implies them.

Jonathan Kozol's "The Human Cost of an Illiterate Society" (pp. 264–273) focuses on the enormous social costs—effects—of illiteracy on the 16 million Americans who cannot read or do math well enough to read or interpret prescriptions, insurance policies, medical warnings, bank regulations, telephone books, cookbooks, and a host of other printed materials that provide directions and information for everyday living. Illiteracy causes people to involuntarily relinquish their freedom of choice, their independence, their self-respect, their citizenship. The costs, in human, ethical, social, economic, and political terms, are enormous. In "Framing My Father" (pp. 282–287), Leslie Moore offers a portrait of a complex man, "who has made a name for himself as a son-of-a-bitch." His uncompromising perfectionism as a teacher of his young daughter produces contradictory effects—anger, exhaustion, resistance—and in the process, a high level of learning and respect.

In "A Nation of Welfare Families" (pp. 275–280), Stephanie Coontz argues that for two centuries Americans have confused effect with cause, and altogether denied the cause of the country's success. The American myth, that "dependence reflects some kind of individual or family failure, and that the ideal family is the self-reliant unit of traditional lore" is contradicted by the facts. The reality is that government policies help everybody (the rich far more than the poor) through the "abolition of child labor," putting governmental "pressure on industrialists to negotiate with unions, federal arbitration, expansion of compulsory schooling," federal subsidies of home mortgages, settlement lands, and highways. The *effect*, a seemingly self-reliant, independent citizenry, should appropriately be attributed to its *cause*, the variety of federal government policies in the nineteenth and twentieth centuries that have supported the "the well-being of its citizens."

A paper of cause and effect analysis requires you, as a thoughtful and careful writer, to know your subject well enough to avoid oversimplification and to shore up your analysis with specific, convincing details. You won't be expected to explain all the causes or effects of a particular phenomenon; that might be impossible for most humans, even the experts. But you can do a sufficiently thorough job with your chosen segment of the subject to satisfy yourself and help your readers to see it your way. Maybe they'll even come to agree with your interpretation. Why? Because. . . .

STRATEGIES FOR WRITING— CAUSE AND EFFECT

1. What is the purpose of my cause and effect paper? Will I be focusing on the cause(s) of something, or its effect(s), short- or long-term? Will I be using cause and effect to explain a process? Analyze a situation? Present a prediction or an argument?

2. How much does my audience know about my subject? Will I have to explain some portions of the cause and effect relationship in more detail than others to compensate for their lack of knowledge? Or do they have sufficient background so I can focus primarily on new information or interpretations?

3. Is the cause and effect relationship I'm writing about valid? Or might there be other possible causes (or effects) that I'm overlooking? If I'm emphasizing causes, how far back do I want to go? If I'm focusing on effects, how many do I wish to discuss, and with how many examples?

4. Will I be using narration, description, definition, process analysis, argument, or other strategies in my explanation or analysis of cause(s) and effect(s)?

5. How technical or nontechnical will my language be? Will I need to qualify any of my claims or conclusions with "probably," or "in most cases," or other admissions that what I'm saying is not absolutely certain? What will my tone be—explanatory, persuasive, argumentative, humorous?

MIKE ROSE

In the award-winning *Lives on the Boundary* (1989), Mike Rose (born, 1944) explains his firsthand understanding of the book's subtitle, *The Struggles and Achievements of America's Underprepared.* Its sequel *Possible Lives* (1995) focuses on, as the subtitle indicates, *The Promise of Public Education in America.* He was reared in the 1950s in Los Angeles in a poor neighborhood. Rose remembers his early years, when his father was ill and disabled and his mother worked as a waitress, as "a peculiar mix of physical warmth and barrenness"—"quiet, lazy, lonely." Only reading "opened up the world." For two years Rose was mistakenly placed in the bottom level vocational track, amidst classmates who could claim, with sincere indifference, "I just wanna be average." The vocational curriculum, "a dumping ground for the disaffected," was designed not to liberate the students but to occupy their time. As "I Just Wanna Be Average" makes clear, Rose and his peers reacted defensively, using their collective indifference as a defense against learning.

It took a tough, demanding, caring teacher to crack this armor of ignorance. Prodded by his sophomore biology teacher, who recognized his intellectual potential, Rose switched from the vocational to the college prep track, graduated in 1966 from Loyola University (Los Angeles), and earned a Ph.D. in education (1981) from UCLA. Rose, now a professor, has remained at UCLA ever since, directing the UCLA Writing Programs. At UCLA he tutored veterans and Chicano, Asian, and African-American students, which provided firsthand research for *Lives on the Boundary.* This excerpt is taken from Chapter 2, "I Just Wanna Be Average."

"I Just Wanna Be Average"

My rhapsodic and prescientific astronomy carried me into my teens, consumed me right up till high school, losing out finally, and only, to the siren call of pubescence—that endocrine hoodoo that transmogrifies nice boys into gawky flesh fiends. My mother used to bring home *Confidential* magazine, a peep-show rag specializing in the sins of the stars, and it beckoned me mercilessly: Jayne Mansfield's cleavage, Gina Lollobrigida's eyes, innuendos about deviant sexuality, ads for Frederick's of Hollywood—spiked heels, lacy brassieres, the epiphany of silk panties on a mannequin's hips. Along with Phil Everly, I was through with counting the stars above.

2   Budding manhood. Only adults talk about adolescence budding. Kids have no choice but to talk in extremes; they're being wrenched and buffeted, rabbit-punched from inside by systemic thugs. Nothing sweet and pastoral here. Kids become ridiculous and touching at one and the same time: passionate about the trivial, fixed before the mirror, yet traversing one of the most important rites of passage in their lives—liminal people, silly and profoundly human. Given my own expertise, I fantasized about concocting the fail-safe aphrodisiac that would bring Marianne Bilpusch, the cloakroom monitor, rushing into my arms or about commanding a squadron of bosomy, linguistically mysterious astronauts like Zsa Zsa Gabor. My parents used to say that their son would have the best education they could afford. Maybe I would be a doctor. There was a public school in our neighborhood and several Catholic schools to the west. They had heard that quality schooling meant private, Catholic schooling, so they somehow got the money together to send me to Our Lady of Mercy, fifteen or so miles southwest of Ninety-first and Vermont. So much for my fantasies. Most Catholic secondary schools then were separated by gender.

3   It took two buses to get to Our Lady of Mercy. The first started deep in South Los Angeles and caught me at midpoint. The second drifted through neighborhoods with trees, parks, big lawns, and lots of flowers. The rides were long but were livened up by a group of South L.A. veterans whose parents also thought that Hope had set up shop in the west end of the county. There was Christy Biggars, who, at sixteen, was dealing and was, according to rumor, a pimp as well. There were Bill Cobb and Johnny Gonzales, grease-pencil artists extraordinaire, who left Nembutal-enhanced swirls of "Cobb" and "Johnny" on the corrugated walls of the bus. And then there was Tyrrell Wilson. Tyrrell was the coolest kid I

knew. He ran the dozens like a metric halfback, laid down a rap that outrhymed and outpointed Cobb, whose rap was good but not great—the curse of a moderately soulful kid trapped in white skin. But it was Cobb who would sneak a radio onto the bus, and thus underwrote his patter with Little Richard, Fats Domino, Chuck Berry, the Coasters, and Ernie K. Doe's mother-in-law, an awful woman who was "sent from down below." And so it was that Christy and Cobb and Johnny G. and Tyrrell and I and assorted others picked up along the way passed our days in the back of the bus, a funny mix brought together by geography and parental desire.

Entrance to school brings with it forms and releases and 4 assessments. Mercy relied on a series of tests, mostly the Stanford-Binet, for placement, and somehow the results of my tests got confused with those of another student named Rose. The other Rose apparently didn't do very well, for I was placed in the vocational track, a euphemism for the bottom level. Neither I nor my parents realized what this meant. We had no sense that Business Math, Typing, and English-Level D were dead ends. The current spate of reports on the schools criticizes parents for not involving themselves in the education of their children. But how would someone like Tommy Rose, with his two years of Italian schooling, know what to ask? And what sort of pressure could an exhausted waitress apply? The error went undetected, and I remained in the vocational track for two years. What a place.

My homeroom was supervised by Brother Dill, a troubled 5 and unstable man who also taught freshman English. When his class drifted away from him, which was often, his voice would rise in paranoid accusations, and occasionally he would lose control and shake or smack us. I hadn't been there two months when one of his brisk, face-turning slaps had my glasses sliding down the aisle. Physical education was also pretty harsh. Our teacher was a stubby ex-lineman who had played old-time pro ball in the Midwest. He routinely had us grabbing our ankles to receive his stinging paddle across our butts. He did that, he said, to make men of us. "Rose," he bellowed on our first encounter; me standing geeky in line in my baggy shorts. "'Rose'? What the hell kind of name is that?"

6   "Italian, sir," I squeaked.

7   "Italian! Ho. Rose, do you know the sound a bag of shit makes when it hits the wall?"

8   "No, sir."

9   "Wop!"

10   Sophomore English was taught by Mr. Mitropetros. He was a large, bejeweled man who managed the parking lot at the Shrine Auditorium. He would crow and preen and list for us the stars he'd brushed against. We'd ask questions and glance knowingly and snicker, and all that fueled the poor guy to brag some more. Parking cars was his night job. He had little training in English, so his lesson plan for his day work had us reading the district's required text, *Julius Caesar*, aloud for the semester. We'd finish the play way before the twenty weeks was up, so he'd have us switch parts again and again and start again: David Snyder, the fastest guy at Mercy, muscling through Caesar to the breathless squeals of Calpurnia, as interpreted by Steve Fusco, a surfer who owned the school's most envied paneled wagon. Week ten and Dave and Steve would take on new roles, as would we all, and render a water-logged Cassius and a Brutus that are beyond my powers of description.

11   Spanish I—taken in the second year—fell into the hands of a new recruit. Mr. Montez was a tiny man, slight, five foot six at the most, soft-spoken and delicate. Spanish was a particularly rowdy class, and Mr. Montez was as prepared for it as a doily maker at a hammer throw. He would tap his pencil to a room in which Steve Fusco was propelling spitballs from his heavy lips, in which Mike Dweetz was taunting Billy Hawk, a half-Indian, half-Spanish, reed-thin, quietly explosive boy. The vocational track at Our Lady of Mercy mixed kids traveling in from South L.A. with South Bay surfers and a few Slavs and Chicanos from the harbors of San Pedro. This was a dangerous miscellany: surfers and hodads and South-Central blacks all ablaze to the metronomic tapping of Hector Montez's pencil.

12   One day Billy lost it. Out of the corner of my eye I saw him strike out with his right arm and catch Dweetz across the neck. Quick as a spasm, Dweetz was out of his seat, scattering desks, cracking Billy on the side of the head, right behind the eye.

Snyder and Fusco and others broke it up, but the room felt hot and close and naked. Mr. Montez's tenuous authority was finally ripped to shreds, and I think everyone felt a little strange about that. The charade was over, and when it came down to it, I don't think any of the kids really wanted it to end this way. They had pushed and pushed and bullied their way into a freedom that both scared and embarrassed them.

Students will float to the mark you set. I and the others in the voca- 13
tional classes were bobbing in pretty shallow water. Vocational education has aimed at increasing the economic opportunities of students who do not do well in our schools. Some serious programs succeed in doing that, and through exceptional teachers—like Mr. Gross in *Horace's Compromise*—students learn to develop hypotheses and troubleshoot, reason through a problem, and communicate effectively—the true job skills. The vocational track, however, is most often a place for those who are just not making it, a dumping ground for the disaffected. There were a few teachers who worked hard at education; young Brother Slattery, for example, combined a stern voice with weekly quizzes to try to pass along to us a skeletal outline of world history. But mostly the teachers had no idea of how to engage the imaginations of us kids who were scuttling along at the bottom of the pond.

And the teachers would have needed some inventiveness, 14
for none of us was groomed for the classroom. It wasn't just that I didn't know things—didn't know how to simplify algebraic fractions, couldn't identify different kinds of clauses, bungled Spanish translations—but that I had developed various faulty and inadequate ways of doing algebra and making sense of Spanish. Worse yet, the years of defensive tuning out in elementary school had given me a way to escape quickly while seeming at least half alert. During my time in Voc. Ed., I developed further into a mediocre student and a somnambulant problem solver, and that affected the subjects I did have the wherewithal to handle: I detested Shakespeare; I got bored with history. My attention flitted here and there. I fooled around in class and read my books indifferently—the intellectual equivalent of playing with your food. I did what I had to do to get by, and I did it with half a mind.

15   But I did learn things about people and eventually came into my own socially. I liked the guys in Voc. Ed. Growing up where I did, I understood and admired physical prowess, and there was an abundance of muscle here. There was Dave Snyder, a sprinter and halfback of true quality. Dave's ability and his quick wit gave him a natural appeal, and he was welcome in any clique, though he always kept a little independent. He enjoyed acting the fool and could care less about studies, but he possessed a certain maturity and never caused the faculty much trouble. It was a testament to this independence that he included me among his friends—I eventually went out for track, but I was no jock. Owing to the Latin alphabet and a dearth of *R*s and *S*s, Snyder sat behind Rose, and we started exchanging one-liners and became friends.

16   There was Ted Richard, a much-touted Little League pitcher. He was chunky and had a baby face and came to Our Lady of Mercy as a seasoned street fighter. Ted was quick to laugh and he had a loud, jolly laugh, but when he got angry he'd smile a little smile, the kind that simply raises the corner of the mouth a quarter of an inch. For those who knew, it was an eerie signal. Those who didn't found themselves in big trouble, for Ted was very quick. He loved to carry on what we would come to call philosophical discussions: What is courage? Does God exist? He also loved words, enjoyed picking up big ones like *salubrious* and *equivocal* and using them in our conversations—laughing at himself as the word hit a chuckhole rolling off his tongue. Ted didn't do all that well in school—baseball and parties and testing the courage he'd speculated about took up his time. His textbooks were *Argosy* and *Field and Stream,* whatever newspapers he'd find on the bus stop—from the *Daily Worker* to pornography—conversations with uncles or hobos or businessmen he'd meet in a coffee shop, *The Old Man and the Sea.* With hindsight, I can see that Ted was developing into one of those rough-hewn intellectuals whose sources are a mix of the learned and the apocryphal, whose discussions are both assured and sad.

17   And then there was Ken Harvey. Ken was good-looking in a puffy way and had a full and oily ducktail and was a car enthusiast . . . a hodad. One day in religion class, he said the sentence that turned out to be one of the most memorable of the hundreds

of thousands I heard in those Voc. Ed. years. We were talking about the parable of the talents, about achievement, working hard, doing the best you can do, blah-blah-blah, when the teacher called on the restive Ken Harvey for an opinion. Ken thought about it, but just for a second, and said (with studied, minimal affect), "I just wanna be average." That woke me up. Average?! Who wants to be average? Then the athletes chimed in with clichés that make you want to laryngectomize them, and the exchange became a platitudinous melee. At the time, I thought Ken's assertion was stupid, and I wrote him off. But his sentence has stayed with me all these years, and I think I am finally coming to understand it.

Ken Harvey was gasping for air. School can be a tremen- 18 dously disorienting place. No matter how bad the school, you're going to encounter notions that don't fit with the assumptions and beliefs that you grew up with—maybe you'll hear these dissonant notions from teachers, maybe from the other students, and maybe you'll read them. You'll also be thrown in with all kinds of kids from all kinds of backgrounds, and that can be unsettling—this is especially true in places of rich ethnic and linguistic mix, like the L.A. basin. You'll see a handful of students far excel you in courses that sound exotic and that are only in the curriculum of the elite: French, physics, trigonometry. And all this is happening while you're trying to shape an identity, your body is changing, and your emotions are running wild. If you're a working-class kid in the vocational track, the options you'll have to deal with this will be constrained in certain ways: You're defined by your school as "slow"; you're placed in a curriculum that isn't designed to liber- ate you but to occupy you, or, if you're lucky, train you, though the training is for work the society does not esteem; other students are picking up the cues from your school and your curriculum and interacting with you in particular ways. If you're a kid like Ted Richard, you turn your back on all this and let your mind roam where it may. But youngsters like Ted are rare. What Ken and so many others do is protect themselves from such suffocating mad- ness by taking on with a vengeance the identity implied in the vocational track. Reject the confusion and frustration by openly defining yourself as the Common Joe. Champion the average. Rely on your own good sense. Fuck this bullshit. Bullshit, of course, is everything you—and the others—fear is beyond you: books, essays, tests, academic scrambling, complexity, scientific reasoning, philosophical inquiry.

19   The tragedy is that you have to twist the knife in your own gray matter to make this defense work. You'll have to shut down, have to reject intellectual stimuli or diffuse them with sarcasm, have to cultivate stupidity, have to convert boredom from a malady into a way of confronting the world. Keep your vocabulary simple, act stoned when you're not or act more stoned than you are, flaunt ignorance, materialize your dreams. It is a powerful and effective defense—it neutralizes the insult and the frustration of being a vocational kid and, when perfected, it drives teachers up the wall, a delightful secondary effect. But like all strong magic, it exacts a price.

20 My own deliverance from the Voc. Ed. world began with sopho-more biology. Every student, college prep to vocational, had to take biology, and unlike the other courses, the same person taught all sections. When teaching the vocational group, Brother Clint probably slowed down a bit or omitted a little of the fundamental biochemistry, but he used the same book and more or less the same syllabus across the board. If one class got tough, he could get tougher. He was young and powerful and very handsome, and looks and physical strength were high currency. No one gave him any trouble.

21   I was pretty bad at the dissecting table, but the lectures and the textbook were interesting: plastic overlays that, with each turned page, peeled away skin, then veins and muscle, then organs, down to the very bones that Brother Clint, pointer in hand, would tap out on our hanging skeleton. Dave Snyder was in big trouble, for the study of life—versus the living of it—was sticking in his craw. We worked out a code for our multiple-choice exams. He'd poke me in the back: once for the answer under *A*, twice for *B*, and so on; and when he'd hit the right one, I'd look up to the ceiling as though I were lost in thought. Poke: cytoplasm. Poke, poke: methane. Poke, poke, poke: William Harvey. Poke, poke, poke, poke: islets of Langerhans. This didn't work out perfectly, but Dave passed the course, and I mastered the dreamy look of a

guy on a record jacket. And something else happened. Brother Clint puzzled over this Voc. Ed. kid who was racking up 98s and 99s on his tests. He checked the school's records and discovered the error. He recommended that I begin my junior year in the College Prep program. According to all I've read since, such a shift, as one report put it, is virtually impossible. Kids at that level rarely cross tracks. The telling thing is how chancy both my placement into and exit from Voc. Ed. was; neither I nor my parents had anything to do with it. I lived in one world during spring semester, and when I came back to school in the fall, I was living in another.

Switching to College Prep was a mixed blessing. I was an   22
erratic student. I was undisciplined. And I hadn't caught onto the rules of the game: Why work hard in a class that didn't grab my fancy? I was also hopelessly behind in math. Chemistry was hard; toying with my chemistry set years before hadn't prepared me for the chemist's equations. Fortunately, the priest who taught both chemistry and second-year algebra was also the school's athletic director. Membership on the track team covered me; I knew I wouldn't get lower than a C. U.S. history was taught pretty well, and I did okay. But civics was taken over by a football coach who had trouble reading the textbook aloud—and reading aloud was the centerpiece of his pedagogy. College Prep at Mercy was certainly an improvement over the vocational program—at least it carried some status—but the social science curriculum was weak, and the mathematics and physical sciences were simply beyond me. I had a miserable quantitative background and ended up copying some assignments and finessing the rest as best I could. Let me try to explain how it feels to see again and again material you should once have learned but didn't.

You are given a problem. It requires you to simplify alge-   23
braic fractions or to multiply expressions containing square roots. You know this is pretty basic material because you've seen it for years. Once a teacher took some time with you, and you learned how to carry out these operations. Simple versions, anyway. But that was a year or two or more in the past, and these are more complex versions, and now you're not sure. And this, you keep telling yourself, is ninth- or even eighth-grade stuff.

24   Next it's a word problem. This is also old hat. The basic elements are as familiar as story characters: trains speeding so many miles per hour or shadows of buildings angling so many degrees. Maybe you know enough, have sat through enough explanations, to be able to begin setting up the problem: "If one train is going this fast . . ." or "This shadow is really one line of a triangle. . . ." then: "Let's see . . ." "How did Jones do this?" "Hmmmm." "No." "No, that won't work." Your attention wavers. You wonder about other things: a football game, a dance, that cute new checker at the market. You try to focus on the problem again. You scribble on paper for a while, but the tension wins out and your attention flits elsewhere. You crumple the paper and begin daydreaming to ease the frustration.

25   The particulars will vary, but in essence this is what a number of students go through, especially those in so-called remedial classes. They open their textbooks and see once again the familiar and impenetrable formulas and diagrams and terms that have stumped them for years. There is no excitement here. *No* excitement. Regardless of what the teacher says, this is not a new challenge. There is, rather, embarrassment and frustration and, not surprisingly, some anger in being reminded once again of long-standing inadequacies. No wonder so many students finally attribute their difficulties to something inborn, organic: "That part of my brain just doesn't work." Given the troubling histories many of these students have, it's miraculous that any of them can lift the shroud of hopelessness sufficiently to make deliverance from these classes possible.

Content

1. In Rose's view, what is there about school itself—student placement, courses, teachers' and students' expectations and attitudes—that causes students to be indifferent as to whether they learn anything or not? Do you agree? Why or why not?
2. Rose demonstrates the immediate effects of deficient or inadequate schooling on the students in the classroom; these range from boredom to anarchy, and are not conducive to learning. What long-range effects, extending well beyond the schools themselves, does Rose project or imply as the consequences of short-term inadequacies?

3. In what ways is this as much an essay about social class and economic marginality as it is about education? How are these themes intertwined?

Strategies/Structures

1. Rose often re-creates the students' point of view ("I just wanna be average") to help his readers understand the learning problems typical of such disaffected, discouraged students (see, for instance, ¶s 24 and 25). What does this point of view reveal that the perspectives of teachers or parents are likely to miss?

2. Rose personifies the problems of inadequate schools by characterizing some of their presumably typical teachers (Brother Dill, Mr. Mitropetros, Mr. Montez) and students (Mike Dweetz, Billy Hawk, Dave Snyder, Ted Richard, Ken Harvey, and Rose himself). What are some of the problems associated with each character? Does such characterization make the problems more memorable? More understandable? Does it run the risk of oversimplifying them? Explain your answers.

3. Writings about education often portray one or two teachers as life-savers, rescuing their students who would otherwise drown in a sea of mediocrity, indifference, or worse. What teacher performs this function in "I Just Wanna Be Average"? Why is he successful?

Language

1. How can you tell that Rose cares passionately about whether or not students learn and want to learn?

2. What is Rose's characteristic language in this essay? How does it reinforce his subject and his thesis? How compatible is this language with the speech of the high school students he's writing about?

For Writing

1. Explain, candidly, to readers who don't know your family or your hometown, what it was like to be a student in your high school. If you wish, compare your experiences with those of Zitkala-Sa (pp. 254–262), Shirley Lim (pp. 364–373), or Richard Wright (pp. 409–418). What factors, in your home, school, or community environment contributed to your decision to attend college? If there were any factors that worked against this decision, what were they, and how compelling did you find them? If you're convinced that you made the right decision, explain why; if not, why are you unconvinced or uncertain?

2. Have you ever dropped out of school? If so, why did you do so? What were the consequences? Why did you return to school? What do you expect the consequences, short- and long-range, to be?

ZITKALA-SA

Zitkala-Sa (1878–1938) was the first Native American woman to write her autobiography by herself, without the help of an intermediary, such as an ethnographer, translator, editor, or oral historian. This unmediated authenticity gives her work unusual authority. She was a Yankton, born on the Pine Ridge Reservation in South Dakota, daughter of a full-blooded Sioux and a white father.

Zitkala-Sa wrote a number of autobiographical essays to call attention to the cultural dislocation and hardships caused when whites sent Native American children to boarding schools hundreds of miles away from home and imposed white culture on them. In her own case, as she explains in "The Land of Red Apples" (pp. 255–257), at the age of eight she left the reservation to attend a boarding school in Wabash, Indiana, run by Quaker missionaries. On her return, "neither a wild Indian nor a tame one" (¶ 25), her distress and cultural displacement were acute, as "Four Strange Summers" (pp. 259–262) makes clear. These were originally published in *Atlantic Monthly* (1900), as portions of *Impressions of an Indian Childhood* and *The School Days of an Indian Girl.*

Zitkala-Sa remained unhappily on the reservation for four years, then returned to the Quaker school, and at nineteen enrolled in the Quaker-run Earlham College in Indiana. Her marriage to Raymond Bonnin, a Sioux, enhanced her activism for Indian rights. She served as secretary of the Society of American Indians, and also edited *American Indian Magazine.* As a lobbyist and spokesperson for the National Council of American Indians, which she founded in 1926, she helped to secure passage of the Indian Citizenship Bill and other reforms. Yet she was an integrationist, not a separatist, and attempted to forge meaningful connections between cultures.

from The School Days of an Indian Girl

I   The Land of Red Apples

There were eight in our party of bronzed children who were going East with the missionaries. Among us were three young braves, two tall girls, and we three little ones, Judéwin, Thowin, and I.

We had been very impatient to start on our journey to the Red Apple Country, which, we were told, lay a little beyond the great circular horizon of the Western prairie. Under a sky of rosy apples we dreamt of roaming as freely and happily as we had chased the cloud shadows on the Dakota plains. We had anticipated much pleasure from a ride on the iron horse, but the throngs of staring palefaces disturbed and troubled us.

On the train, fair women, with tottering babies on each arm, stopped their haste and scrutinized the children of absent mothers. Large men, with heavy bundles in their hands, halted near by, and riveted their glassy blue eyes upon us.

I sank deep into the corner of my seat, for I resented being watched. Directly in front of me, children who were no larger than I hung themselves upon the backs of their seats, with their bold white faces toward me. Sometimes they took their forefingers out of their mouths and pointed at my moccasined feet. Their mothers, instead of reproving such rude curiosity, looked closely at me, and attracted their children's further notice to my blanket. This embarrassed me, and kept me constantly on the verge of tears.

I sat perfectly still, with my eyes downcast, daring only now and then to shoot long glances around me. Chancing to turn to the window at my side, I was quite breathless upon seeing one familiar object. It was the telegraph pole which strode by at short paces. Very near my mother's dwelling, along the edge of a road thickly bordered with wild sunflowers, some poles like these had been planted by white men. Often I had stopped, on my way down the road, to hold my ear against the pole, and, hearing its low moaning, I used to wonder what the paleface had done to hurt it. Now I sat watching for each pole that glided by to be the last one.

6   In this way I had forgotten my uncomfortable surroundings, when I heard one of my comrades call out my name. I saw the missionary standing very near, tossing candies and gums into our midst. This amused us all, and we tried to see who could catch the most of the sweet-meats. The missionary's generous distribution of candies was impressed upon my memory by a disastrous result which followed. I had caught more than my share of candies and gums, and soon after our arrival at the school I had a chance to disgrace myself, which, I am ashamed to say, I did.

7   Though we rode several days inside of the iron horse, I do not recall a single thing about our luncheons.

8   It was night when we reached the school grounds. The lights from the windows of the large buildings fell upon some of the icicled trees that stood beneath them. We were led toward an open door, where the brightness of the lights within flooded out over the heads of the excited palefaces who blocked the way. My body trembled more from fear than from the snow I trod upon.

9   Entering the house, I stood close against the wall. The strong glaring light in the large whitewashed room dazzled my eyes. The noisy hurrying of hard shoes upon a bare wooden floor increased the whirring in my ears. My only safety seemed to be in keeping next to the wall. As I was wondering in which direction to escape from all this confusion, two warm hands grasped me firmly, and in the same moment I was tossed high in midair. A rosy-checked paleface woman caught me in her arms. I was both frightened and insulted by such trifling. I stared into her eyes, wishing her to let me stand on my own feet, but she jumped me up and down with increasing enthusiasm. My mother had never made a plaything of her wee daughter. Remembering this I began to cry aloud.

10   They misunderstood the cause of my tears, and placed me at a white table loaded with food. There our party were united again. As I did not hush my crying, one of the older ones whispered to me, "Wait until you are alone in the night."

11   It was very little I could swallow besides my sobs, that evening.

12   "Oh, I want my mother and my brother Dawée! I want to go to my aunt!" I pleaded; but the ears of the palefaces could not hear me.

came nearer and nearer. Woman and girls entered the room. I held my breath, and watched them open closet doors and peep behind large trunks. Some one threw up the curtains, and the room was filled with sudden light. What caused them to stoop and look under the bed I do not know. I remember being dragged out, though I resisted by kicking and scratching wildly. In spite of myself, I was carried downstairs and tied fast in a chair.

I cried aloud, shaking my head all the while until I felt the cold blades of the scissors against my neck, and heard them 23 gnaw off one of my thick braids. Then I lost my spirit. Since the day I was taken from my mother I had suffered extreme indignities. People had stared at me. I had been tossed about in the air like a wooden puppet. And now my long hair was shingled like a coward's! In my anguish I moaned for my mother, but no one came to comfort me. Not a soul reasoned quietly with me, as my own mother used to do: for now I was only one of many little animals driven by a herder. . . .

VI Four Strange Summers[1]

After my first three years of school, I roamed again in the Western 24 country through four strange summers.

During this time I seemed to hang in the heart of chaos, be- 25 yond the touch or voice of human aid. My brother, being almost ten years my senior, did not quite understand my feelings. My mother had never gone inside of a schoolhouse, and so she was not capable of comforting her daughter who could read and write. Even nature seemed to have no place for me. I was neither a wee girl nor a tall one; neither a wild Indian nor a tame one. This deplorable situation was the effect of my brief course in the East, and the unsatisfactory "teenth" in a girl's years.

It was under these trying conditions that, one bright after- 26 noon, as I sat restless and unhappy in my mother's cabin, I caught the sound of the spirited step of my brother's pony on the road which passed by our dwelling. Soon I heard the wheels of a light

---

[1] Sections III, IV, and V are omitted.

buckboard, and Dawée's familiar "Ho!" to his pony. He alighted upon the bare ground in front of our house. Tying his pony to one of the projecting corner logs of the low-roofed cottage, he stepped upon the wooden doorstep.

27   I met him there with a hurried greeting, and, as I passed by, he looked a quiet "What?" into my eyes.

28   When he began talking with my mother, I slipped the rope from the pony's bridle. Seizing the reins and bracing my feet against the dashboard, I wheeled around in an instant. The pony was ever ready to try his speed. Looking backward, I saw Dawée waving his hand to me. I turned with the curve in the road and disappeared. I followed the winding road which crawled upward between the bases of little hillocks. Deep water-worn ditches ran parallel on either side. A strong wind blew against my cheeks and fluttered my sleeves. The pony reached the top of the highest hill, and began an even race on level lands. There was nothing moving within that great circular horizon of the Dakota prairies save the tall grasses, over which the wind blew and rolled off in long, shadowy waves.

29   Within this vast wigwam of blue and green I rode reckless and insignificant. It satisfied my small consciousness to see the white foam fly from the pony's mouth.

30   Suddenly, out of the earth a coyote came forth at a swinging trot that was taking the cunning thief toward the hills and the village beyond. Upon the moment's impulse, I gave him a long chase and a wholesome fright. As I turned away to go back to the village, the wolf sank down upon his haunches for a rest, for it was a hot summer day; and as I drove slowly homeward, I saw his sharp nose still pointed at me, until I vanished below the margin of the hilltops.

31   In a little while I came in sight of my mother's house. Dawée stood in the yard, laughing at an old warrior who was pointing his forefinger, and again waving his whole hand, toward the hills. With his blanket drawn over one shoulder, he talked and motioned excitedly. Dawée turned the old man by the shoulder and pointed me out to him.

32   "Oh han!" (Oh yes) the warrior muttered, and went his way. He had climbed the top of his favorite barren hill to survey the surrounding prairies, when he spied my chase after the coyote.

His keen eyes recognized the pony and driver. At once uneasy for my safety, he had come running to my mother's cabin to give her warning. I did not appreciate his kindly interest, for there was an unrest gnawing at my heart.

As soon as he went away, I asked Dawée about some-   33
thing else.

"No, my baby sister. I cannot take you with me to the party   34
to-night," he replied. Though I was not far from fifteen, and I felt that before long I should enjoy all the privileges of my tall cousin, Dawée persisted in calling me his baby sister.

That moonlight night, I cried in my mother's presence when   35
I heard the jolly young people pass by our cottage. There were no more young braves in blankets and eagle plumes, nor Indian maids with prettily painted cheeks. They had gone three years to school in the East, and had become civilized. The young men wore the white man's coat and trousers, with bright neckties. The girls wore tight muslin dresses, with ribbons at neck and waist. At these gatherings they talked English. I could speak English almost as well as my brother, but I was not properly dressed to be taken along. I had no hat, no ribbons, and no close-fitting gown. Since my return from school I had thrown away my shoes, and wore again the soft moccasins.

While Dawée was busily preparing to go I controlled my   36
tears. But when I heard him bounding away on his pony, I buried my face in my arms and cried hot tears.

My mother was troubled by my unhappiness. Coming to   37
my side, she offered me the only printed matter we had in our home. It was an Indian Bible, given her some years ago by a mis-sionary. She tried to console me. "Here, my child, are the white man's papers. Read a little from them," she said most piously.

I took it from her hand, for her sake; but my enraged spirit   38
felt more like burning the book, which afforded me no help, and was a perfect delusion to my mother. I did not read it, but laid it unopened on the floor, where I sat on my feet. The dim yellow light of the braided muslin burning in a small vessel of oil flick-ered and sizzled in the awful silent storm which followed my rejection of the Bible.

Now my wrath against the fates consumed my tears before   39
they reached my eyes. I sat stony, with a bowed head. My mother

threw a shawl over her head and shoulders, and stepped out into the night.

40   After an uncertain solitude, I was suddenly aroused by a loud cry piercing the night. It was my mother's voice wailing among the barren hills which held the bones of buried warriors. She called aloud for her brothers' spirits to support her in her helpless misery. My fingers grew icy cold, as I realized that my unrestrained tears had betrayed my suffering to her, and she was grieving for me.

41   Before she returned, though I knew she was on her way, for she had ceased her weeping, I extinguished the light, and leaned my head on the window sill.

42   Many schemes of running away from my surroundings hovered about in my mind. A few more moons of such a turmoil drove me away to the Eastern school. I rode on the white man's iron steed, thinking it would bring me back to my mother in a few winters, when I should be grown tall, and there would be congenial friends awaiting me. . . .

Content

1. To an extent, leaving the security of home and its familiar culture to go to school, with its inevitably somewhat different culture, presents problems for any child. To what extent are Zitkala-Sa's memories of being uprooted and sent away to school similar to those of any child in a similar circumstance, and to what extent are they exacerbated by the alien culture to which she is expected to adapt?

2. What was the whites' rationale for sending Native American children away to boarding school? Why did parents allow their children to be sent away (see "The Land of Red Apples")? In what ways did this contribute to the adulteration and breakup of Native American culture (see all sections)?

3. Historically, the Quakers have a reputation for being respectful of civil rights and very sympathetic to the preservation of minority cultures. Quaker households, for instance, were often places of shelter for slaves escaping along the Underground Railway. Was the Quaker school to which Zitkala-Sa went an exception? What factors influenced her perception of the school when she was in residence and later when she wrote about it?

Strategies / Structures

1.   Zitkala-Ša is writing in English for a white audience in 1900, many of whom might never have met a Native American, and who would have known very little about their schooling. What information does she need to supply to make the context of her narrative clear? Has she done this?

2.   Zitkala-Ša's readers might be expected to share the viewpoint of the school personnel, in opposition to her own point of view, both as a character in her own story and the narrator of it. By what means does she try to win readers to her point of view? Is she successful?

Language

1.   Why did Zitkala-Ša choose to write primarily in standard English, omitting the stereotypical features whites attribute, rightly or wrongly, to Native American speakers of English as a second language?

2.   What are the effects of occasional passages in the language whites attribute to Native Americans? See, for example, "palefaces" (¶ 2 and *passim*); "A few *more moons* . . . I rode on the white man's *iron steed,* thinking it would bring me back to my mother in a *few winters*" (¶ 42).

3.   Examine the language of the last paragraph of "The Cutting of My Long Hair" and analyze it in light of your answers to 1 and 2.

For Writing

1.   Today many Native American children living on reservations can go to school there. On some reservations, college students can even earn degrees in such subjects as education. Write an essay for parents trying to decide what's best for their children in which you weigh the advantages of cultural integrity versus ghettoization that are inherent in this, or any system, of a closed-culture education—public or private (including parochial schooling). Feel free to draw on your own experiences in school. You may need to do some research on a particular school system to provide information for your argument.

2.   As Zitkala-Ša does, tell the story of an experience of cultural displacement that you or someone you know well has experienced. Identify its causes and interpret its consequences, short- and long-term.

JONATHAN KOZOL

During the course of his career as a critic of American schools, Kozol (born, 1936) has metamorphosed from an angry young man to an aging man with no diminution of anger in sight. His first critique of American education, *Death at an Early Age: The Destruction of the Hearts and Minds of Negro Children in the Boston Public Schools* (1967), won the National Book Award. Written during the civil rights and school desegregation movements in the 1960s, this book documents the repressive teaching methods in Boston's unintegrated public schools, designed, Kozol claimed, to reinforce a system that would keep the children separate but unequal. Kozol, himself a Harvard graduate (1958), Rhodes Scholar, and recipient of numerous prestigious fellowships (Gugenheim, Rockefeller, and Ford foundations), transcends his privileged background to address what he considers to be the failure of American education to reach minorities and the poor. Even his book on middle-class education, *The Night Is Dark and I Am Far from Home* (1975), expounds on his claim that because the schools reflect the inequities in society at large, the more affluent are educated at the expense of the poor. His most recent book, *Savage Inequalities: Children in America's Schools* (1991), extends and reinforces these concerns.

Illiterate America (1985) analyzes the nature, causes, and effects of illiteracy, the ultimate and pervasive failure that, says Kozol, denies sixty million people "significant participation" in the government that "is neither of, nor for, nor by, the people." Kozol concludes with a call to action, a nationwide army of neighborhood volunteers who would teach people to read. Part of his strategy in arousing his own readers to action is to make them understand what it's like to be illiterate, on which this chapter (reprinted in full) focuses. Characteristically, Kozol interprets both the causes of illiteracy and the effects—discussed here—in human, moral terms. Kozol says, "I write as a witness. . . . this is what we have done. This is what we have permitted."

The Human Cost of an Illiterate Society

PRECAUTIONS. READ BEFORE USING.   1
Poison: Contains sodium hydroxide (caustic soda-lye).
Corrosive: Causes severe eye and skin damage, may cause blindness.
Harmful or fatal if swallowed.
If swallowed, give large quantities of milk or water.
Do not induce vomiting.
Important: Keep water out of can at all times to prevent contents from violently erupting . . .

—warning on a can of Drāno

We are speaking here no longer of the dangers faced by passengers   2
on Eastern Airlines or the dollar costs incurred by U.S. corporations and taxpayers. We are speaking now of human suffering and of the ethical dilemmas that are faced by a society that looks upon such suffering with qualified concern but does not take those actions which its wealth and ingenuity would seemingly demand.

Questions of literacy, in Socrates' belief, must at length be   3
judged as matters of morality. Socrates could not have had in mind the moral compromise peculiar to a nation like our own. Some of our Founding Fathers did, however, have this question in their minds. One of the wisest of those Founding Fathers (one who may not have been most compassionate but surely was more prescient than some of his peers) recognized the special dangers that illiteracy would pose to basic equity in the political construction that he helped to shape.

"A people who mean to be their own governors," James   4
Madison wrote, "must arm themselves with the power knowledge gives. A popular government without popular information or the means of acquiring it, is but a prologue to a farce or a tragedy, or perhaps both."

Tragedy looms larger than farce in the United States today.   5
Illiterate citizens seldom vote. Those who do are forced to cast a vote of questionable worth. They cannot make informed decisions

based on serious print information. Sometimes they can be alerted to their interests by aggressive voter education. More frequently, they vote for a face, a smile, or a style, not for a mind or character or body of beliefs.

6   The number of illiterate adults exceeds by 16 million the entire vote cast for the winner in the 1980 presidential contest. If even one third of all illiterates could vote, and read enough and do sufficient math to vote in their self-interest, Ronald Reagan would not likely have been chosen president. There is, of course, no way to know for sure. We do know this: Democracy is a mendacious term when used by those who are prepared to countenance the forced exclusion of one third of our electorate. So long as 60 million people are denied significant participation, the government is neither of, nor for, nor by, the people. It is a government, at best, of those two thirds whose wealth, skin color, or parental privilege allows them opportunity to profit from the provocation and instruction of the written word.

7   The undermining of democracy in the United States is one "expense" that sensitive Americans can easily deplore because it represents a contradiction that endangers citizens of all political positions. The human price is not so obvious at first.

8   Since I first immersed myself within this work I have often had the following dream: I find that I am in a railroad station or a large department store within a city that is utterly unknown to me and where I cannot understand the printed words. None of the signs or symbols is familiar. Everything looks strange: like mirror writing of some kind. Gradually I understand that I am in the Soviet Union. All the letters on the walls around me are Cyrillic. I look for my pocket dictionary but I find that it has been mislaid. Where have I left it? Then I recall that I forgot to bring it with me when I packed my bags in Boston. I struggle to remember the name of my hotel. I try to ask somebody for directions. One person stops and looks at me in a peculiar way. I lose the nerve to ask. At last I reach into my wallet for an ID card. The card is missing. Have I lost it? Then I remember that my card was confiscated for some reason, many years before. Around this point, I wake up in a panic.

9   This panic is not so different from the misery that millions of adult illiterates experience each day within the course of their routine existence in the U.S.A.

Illiterates cannot read the menu in a restaurant.   10

They cannot read the cost of items on the menu in the   11
window of the restaurant before they enter.

Illiterates cannot read the letters that their children bring   12
home from their teachers. They cannot study school department
circulars that tell them of the courses that their children must be
taking if they hope to pass the SAT exams. They cannot help with
homework. They cannot write a letter to the teacher. They are
afraid to visit in the classroom. They do not want to humiliate
their child or themselves.

Illiterates cannot read instructions on a bottle of prescription   13
medicine. They cannot find out when a medicine is past the year of
safe consumption; nor can they read of allergenic risks, warnings to
diabetics, or the potential sedative effect of certain kinds of non-
prescription pills. They cannot observe preventive health care ad-
monitions. They cannot read about "the seven warning signs of
cancer" or the indications of blood-sugar fluctuations or the risks of
eating certain foods that aggravate the likelihood of cardiac arrest.

Illiterates live, in more than literal ways, an uninsured ex-   14
istence. They cannot understand the written details on a health
insurance form. They cannot read the waivers that they sign
preceding surgical procedures. Several women I have known in
Boston have entered a slum hospital with the intention of obtaining a tubal ligation and have emerged a few days later after having been subjected to a hysterectomy. Unaware of their rights,
incognizant of jargon, intimidated by the unfamiliar air of fear
and atmosphere of ether that so many of us find oppressive in
the confines even of the most attractive and expensive medical
facilities, they have signed their names to documents they could
not read and which nobody, in the hectic situation that prevails
so often in those overcrowded hospitals that serve the urban
poor, had even bothered to explain.

Childbirth might seem to be the last inalienable right of any   15
female citizen within a civilized society. Illiterate mothers, as we
shall see, already have been cheated of the power to protect their
progeny against the likelihood of demolition in deficient public
schools and, as a result, against the verbal servitude within which
they themselves exist. Surgical denial of the right to bear that child
in the first place represents an ultimate denial, an unspeakable

metaphor, a final darkness that denies even the twilight gleamings of our own humanity. What greater violation of our biological, our biblical, our spiritual humanity could possibly exist than that which takes place nightly, perhaps hourly these days, within such overburdened and benighted institutions as the Boston City Hospital? Illiteracy has many costs; few are so irreversible as this.

16   Even the roof above one's head, the gas or other fuel for heating that protects the residents of northern city slums against the threat of illness in the winter months become uncertain guarantees. Illiterates cannot read the lease that they must sign to live in an apartment which, too often, they cannot afford. The cannot manage check accounts and therefore seldom pay for anything by mail. Hours and entire days of difficult travel (and the cost of bus or other public transit) must be added to the real cost of whatever they consume. Loss of interest on the check accounts they do not have, and could not manage if they did, must be regarded as another of the excess costs paid by the citizen who is excluded from the common instruments of commerce in a numerate society.

17   "I couldn't understand the bills," a woman in Washington, D.C., reports, "and then I couldn't write the checks to pay them. We signed things we didn't know what they were."

18   Illiterates cannot read the notices that they receive from welfare offices or from the IRS. They must depend on word-of-mouth instruction from the welfare worker—or from other persons whom they have good reason to mistrust. They do not know what rights they have, what deadlines and requirements they face, what options they might choose to exercise. They are half-citizens. Their rights exist in print but not in fact.

19   Illiterates cannot look up numbers in a telephone directory. Even if they can find the names of friends, few possess the sorting skills to make use of the yellow pages; categories are bewildering and trade names are beyond decoding capabilities for millions of nonreaders. Even the emergency numbers listed on the first page of the phone book—"Ambulance," "Police," and "Fire"—are too frequently beyond the recognition of nonreaders.

20   Many illiterates cannot read the admonition on a pack of cigarettes. Neither the Surgeon General's warning nor its reproduction on the package can alert them to the risks. Although most people learn by word of mouth that smoking is related to a number of grave physical disorders, they do not get the chance to

read the detailed stories which can document this danger with the vividness that turns concern into determination to resist. They can see the handsome cowboy or the slim Virginia lady lighting up a filter cigarette; they cannot heed the words that tell them that this product is (not "may be") dangerous to their health. Sixty million men and women are condemned to be the unalerted, high-risk candidates for cancer.

Illiterates do not buy "no-name" products in the super-   21 markets. They must depend on photographs or the familiar logos that are printed on the packages of brand-name groceries. The poorest people, therefore, are denied the benefits of the least costly products.

Illiterates depend almost entirely upon label recognition.   22 Many labels, however, are not easy to distinguish. Dozens of different kinds of Campbell's soup appear identical to the nonreader. The purchaser who cannot read and does not dare to ask for help, out of the fear of being stigmatized (a fear which is unfortunately realistic), frequently comes home with something which she never wanted and her family never tasted.

Illiterates cannot read instructions on a pack of frozen food.   23 Packages sometimes provide an illustration to explain the cooking preparations; but illustrations are of little help to someone who must "boil water, drop the food—*within* its plastic wrapper—in the boiling water, wait for it to simmer, instantly remove."

Even when labels are seemingly clear, they may be easily   24 mistaken. A woman in Detroit brought home a gallon of Crisco for her children's dinner. She thought that she had bought the chicken that was pictured on the label. She had enough Crisco now to last a year—but no more money to go back and buy the food for dinner.

Recipes provided on the packages of certain staples some-   25 times tempt a semiliterate person to prepare a meal her children have not tasted. The longing to vary the uniform and often starchy content of low-budget meals provided to the family that relies on food stamps commonly leads to ruinous results. Scarce funds have been wasted and the food must be thrown out. The same applies to distribution of food-surplus produce in emergency conditions. Government inducements to poor people to "explore the ways" by which to make a tasty meal from tasteless noodles, surplus cheese, and powdered milk are useless to nonreaders. Intended as benevolent advice, such recommendations mock reality and foster deeper feelings of resentment and of inability to cope. (Those, on the other hand, who cautiously refrain from "innovative" recipes in preparation of their children's meals must suffer the opprobrium of "laziness," "lack of imagination . . .")

26   Illiterates cannot travel freely. When they attempt to do so, they encounter risks that few of us can dream of. They cannot read traffic signs and, while they often learn to recognize and to decipher symbols, they cannot manage street names which they haven't seen before. The same is true for bus and subway stops. While ingenuity can sometimes help a man or woman to discern directions from familiar landmarks, buildings, cemeteries, churches, and the like, most illiterates are virtually immobilized. They seldom wander past the streets and neighborhoods they know. Geographical paralysis becomes a bitter metaphor for their entire existence. They are immobilized in almost every sense we can imagine. They can't move up. They can't move out. They cannot see beyond. Illiterates may take an oral test for drivers' permits in most sections of America. It is a questionable concession. Where will they go? How will they get there? How will they get home? Could it be that some of us might like it better if they stayed where they belong?

27   Travel is only one of many instances of circumscribed existence. Choice, in almost all of its facets, is diminished in the life of an illiterate adult. Even the printed TV schedule, which provides most people with the luxury of preselection, does not belong within the arsenal of options in illiterate existence. One consequence is that the viewer watches only what appears at moments when he happens to have time to turn the switch. Another consequence, a lot more common, is that the TV set remains in operation night and day. Whatever the program offered at the hour when he walks into the room will be the nutriment that he accepts and swallows. Thus, to passivity, is added frequency—indeed, almost uninterrupted continuity. Freedom to select is no more possible here than in the choice of home or surgery or food.

28   "You don't choose," said one illiterate woman. "You take your wishes from somebody else." Whether in perusal of a menu, selection of highways, purchase of groceries, or determination of

affordable enjoyment, illiterate Americans must trust somebody else: a friend, a relative, a stranger on the street, a grocery clerk, a TV copywriter.

"All of our mail we get, it's hard for her to read. Settin' down and writing a letter, she can't do it. Like if we get a bill . . . we take it over to my sister-in-law . . . My sister-in-law reads it." 29

Billing agencies harass poor people for the payment of the bills for purchases that might have taken place six months before. Utility companies offer an agreement for a staggered payment schedule on a bill past due. "You have to trust them," one man said. Precisely for this reason, you end up by trusting no one and suspecting everyone of possible deceit. A submerged sense of distrust becomes the corollary to a constant need to trust. "They are cheating me . . . I have been tricked . . . I do not know . . ." 30

Not knowing: This is a familiar theme. Not knowing the right word for the right thing at the right time is one form of subjugation. Not knowing the world that lies concealed behind those words is a more terrifying feeling. The longitude and latitude of one's existence are beyond all easy apprehension. Even the hard, cold stars within the firmament above one's head begin to mock the possibilities for self-location. Where am I? Where did I come from? Where will I go? 31

"I've lost a lot of jobs," one man explains. "Today, even if you're a janitor, there's still reading and writing . . . They leave a note saying, 'Go to room so-and-so . . .' You can't do it. You can't read it. You don't know." 32

"The hardest thing about it is that I've been places where I didn't know where I was. You don't know where you are . . . You're lost." 33

"Like I said: I have two kids. What do I do if one of my kids starts choking? I go running to the phone . . . I can't look up the hospital phone number. That's if we're at home. Out on the street, I can't read the sign. I get to a pay phone. 'Okay, tell us where you are. We'll send an ambulance.' I look at the street sign. Right there, I can't tell you what it says. I'd have to spell it out, letter for letter. By that time, one of my kids would be dead . . . These are the kinds of fears you go with, every single day . . ." 34

"Reading directions, I suffer with. I work with chemicals . . . That's scary to begin with . . ." 35

36   "You sit down. They throw the menu in front of you. Where do you go from there? Nine times out of ten you say, 'Go ahead. Pick out something for the both of us.' I've eaten some weird things, let me tell you!"

37   Menus. Chemicals. A child choking while his mother searches for a word she does not know to find assistance that will come too late. Another mother speaks about the inability to help her kids to read: "I can't read to them. Of course that's leaving them out of something they should have. Oh, it matters. You *believe* it matters! I ordered all these books. The kids belong to a book club. Donny wanted me to read a book to him. I told Donny: 'I can't read.' He said: 'Mommy, you sit down. I'll read it to you.' I tried it one day, reading from the pictures. Donny looked at me. He said, 'Mommy, that's not right.' He's only five. He knew I couldn't read . . ."

38   A landlord tells a woman that her lease allows him to evict her if her baby cries and causes inconvenience to her neighbors. The consequence of challenging his words conveys a danger which appears, unlikely as it seems, even more alarming than the danger of eviction. Once she admits that she can't read, in the desire to maneuver for the time in which to call a friend, she will have defined herself in terms of an explicit impotence that she cannot endure. Capitulation in this case is preferable to self-humiliation. Resisting the definition of oneself in terms of what one cannot do, what others take for granted, represents a need so great that other imperatives (even one so urgent as the need to keep one's home in winter's cold) evaporate and fall away in face of fear. Even the loss of home and shelter, in this case, is not so terrifying as the loss of self.

39   "I come out of school. I was sixteen. They had their meetings. The directors meet. They said that I was wasting their school paper. I was wasting pencils . . ."

40   Another illiterate, looking back, believes she was not worthy of her teacher's time. She believes that it was wrong of her to take up space within her school. She believes that it was right to leave in order that somebody more deserving could receive her place.

41   Children choke. Their mother chokes another way: on more than chicken bones.

People eat what others order, know what others tell them, 42
struggle not to see themselves as they believe the world perceives
them. A man in California speaks about his own loss of identity,
of self-location, definition:

"I stood at the bottom of the ramp. My car had broke down 43
on the freeway. There was a phone. I asked for the police. They
was nice. They said to tell them where I was. I looked up at the
signs. There was one that I had seen before. I read it to them: ONE
WAY STREET. They thought it was a joke. I told them I couldn't read.
There was other signs above the ramp. They told me to try. I
looked around for somebody to help. All the cars was going by
real fast. I couldn't make them understand that I was lost. The cop
was nice. He told me: 'Try once more.' I did my best. I couldn't
read. I only knew the sign above my head. The cop was trying to
be nice. He knew that I was trapped. 'I can't send out a car to you
if you can't tell me where you are.' I felt afraid. I nearly cried. I'm
forty-eight years old. I only said: 'I'm on a one-way street . . .'"

Perhaps we might slow down a moment here and look at the 44
realities described above. This is the nation that we live in. This is
a society that most of us did not create but which our President
and other leaders have been willing to sustain by virtue of malign
neglect. Do we possess the character and courage to address a
problem which so many nations, poorer than our own, have found
it natural to correct?

The answers to these questions represent a reasonable test 45
of our belief in the democracy to which we have been asked in
public school to swear allegiance.

Content

1. In earlier eras, explanations for illiteracy often implied considerable
blame for the victims—they were seen as stupid, lazy, shiftless, impru-
dent, living only for the day but with no concern for the future. To what
extent do these explanations confuse the effects of illiteracy with the
causes? In what ways does Kozol's essay refute these stereotypes? In his
opinion, who's to blame?

2. How does Kozol's chapter illustrate his assertion that 60 million
illiterates in America are "denied significant participation" in the government "of those two thirds whose wealth, skin color, or parental privilege

allows them the opportunity to profit from the provocation and instruction of the written word" (¶ 6)? What's provocative about literacy?

Strategies/Structures

1. Why does Kozol begin his chapter on the costs of illiteracy with the warning on a can of Drāno (a caustic chemical to unclog drains)? Why doesn't he say anything more about it—or about a great many of his other examples? To what extent can these (or any) examples be counted on to speak for themselves?

2. Kozol constructs his argument by using a myriad of examples of the effects of illiteracy. What determines the order of the examples? Which are the most memorable? Where in this chapter do they appear?

Language

1. Why does Kozol use so many direct quotations from the illiterate people whose experiences he cites as examples?

2. What clues in Kozol's language let his readers know that he's sympathetic toward his subjects and angry at the conditions that cause the class of people his readers represent?

For Writing

1. "Questions of literacy, in Socrates' belief, must at length be judged as matters of morality" (¶ 3). Write an essay in which you explain the connection between literacy and a moral society (and the converse, illiteracy and an immoral society), either for an audience you expect to agree with you or for readers who will disagree.

2. In the concluding vignette of the man unable to read the road signs to guide the police to his disabled car on the freeway (¶s 42–43), Kozol implicitly equates literacy with a sense of self-identity, self-location, self-definition. Write an essay exploring the question, How does being literate enable one to become a full human being? When you're thinking about this, imagine what your life would be like if you couldn't read, write, or do math.

STEPHANIE COONTZ

Coontz (born, 1944) earned a B.A. at the University of California, Berkeley (1966), and an M.A. at the University of Washington (1970). A faculty member since 1975 at Evergreen State College in Olympia, Washington, her research in history and women's studies coalesce in work intended to correct misconceptions about American families. She is critical of the nostalgia that she sees as "very tempting to political and economic elitists who would like to avoid grappling with new demographic challenges. My favorite example," she told an interviewer, "is when people get nostalgic about the way elders were cared for in the past. Well, good Lord! Elders were the poorest, most abused sector of the population until the advent of Social Security."

The mythical American family, autonomous and independent, lives in legends from the early Puritans to the midwestern homesteaders to the rugged ranchers who "tamed" the Wild West. But people confuse the effect with the cause; the mythological characteristics of hard work and self-reliance are at odds with the facts—that the American family actually succeeded only with considerable outside help, particularly through federal policies. Thus in this essay, originally published in *Harper's Magazine* (1992) and in the book *The Way We Never Were: American Families and the Nostalgia Trap* (1992), Coontz identifies the numerous ways in which "assisting families is, simply, what government does."

A Nation of Welfare Families

T he current political debate over family values, personal re- 1
sponsibility, and welfare takes for granted the entrenched American belief that dependence on government assistance is a recent and destructive phenomenon. Conservatives tend to blame this dependence on personal irresponsibility aggravated by a swollen welfare apparatus that saps individual initiative. Liberals are more likely to blame it on personal misfortune magnified by the harsh lot that falls to losers in our competitive market economy. But both sides believe that "winners" in America make it on

their own, that dependence reflects some kind of individual or family failure, and that the ideal family is the self-reliant unit of traditional lore—a family that takes care of its own, carves out a future for its children, and never asks for handouts. Politicians at both ends of the ideological spectrum have wrapped themselves in the mantle of these "family values," arguing over *why* the poor have not been able to make do without assistance, or whether aid has exacerbated their situation, but never questioning the assumption that American families traditionally achieve success by establishing their independence from the government.

2   The myth of family self-reliance is so compelling that our actual national and personal histories often buckle under its emotional weight. "We always stood on our own two feet," my grandfather used to say about his pioneer heritage, whenever he walked me to the top of the hill to survey the property in Washington State that his family had bought for next to nothing after it had been logged off in the early 1900s. Perhaps he didn't know that the land came so cheap because much of it was part of a federal subsidy originally allotted to the railroad companies, which had received 183 million acres of the public domain in the nineteenth century. These federal giveaways were the original source of most major Western logging companies' land, and when some of these logging companies moved on to virgin stands of timber, federal lands trickled down to a few early settlers who were able to purchase them inexpensively.

3   Like my grandparents, few families in American history— whatever their "values"—have been able to rely solely on their own resources. Instead, they have depended on the legislative, judicial, and social support structures set up by governing authorities, whether those authorities were the clan elders of Native American societies, the church courts and city officials of colonial America, or the judicial and legislative bodies established by the Constitution.

4   At America's inception, this was considered not a dirty little secret but the norm, one that confirmed our social and personal interdependence. The idea that the family should have the sole or even primary responsibility for educating and socializing its members, finding them suitable work, or keeping them from

poverty and crime was not only ludicrous to colonial and revolutionary thinkers but dangerously parochial.

Historically, one way that government has played a role in the well-being of its citizens is by regulating the way that employers and civic bodies interact with families. In the early twentieth century, for example, as a response to rapid changes ushered in by a mass-production economy, the government promoted a "family wage system." This system was designed to strengthen the ability of the male breadwinner to support a family without having his wife or children work. This family wage system was not a natural outgrowth of the market. It was a *political* response to conditions that the market had produced: child labor, rampant employment insecurity, recurring economic downturns, an earnings structure in which 45 percent of industrial workers fell below the poverty level and another 40 percent hovered barely above it, and a system in which thousands of children had been placed in orphanages or other institutions simply because their parents could not afford their keep. The state policies involved in the establishment of the family wage system included abolition of child labor, government pressure on industrialists to negotiate with unions, federal arbitration, expansion of compulsory schooling—and legislation discriminating against women workers.

But even such extensive regulation of economic and social institutions has never been enough: government has always supported families with direct material aid as well. The two best examples of the government's history of material aid can be found in what many people consider the ideal models of self-reliant families: the Western pioneer family and the 1950s suburban family. In both cases, the ability of these families to establish and sustain themselves required massive underwriting by the government.

Pioneer families, such as my grandparents, could never have moved west without government-funded military mobilizations against the original Indian and Mexican inhabitants or state-sponsored economic investment in transportation systems. In addition, the Homestead Act of 1862 allowed settlers to buy 160 acres for $10—far below the government's cost of acquiring the land—if the homesteader lived on and improved the land for five years. In the twentieth century, a new form of public assistance became crucial to Western families: construction of dams and other federally subsidized irrigation projects. During the 1930s, for example, government electrification projects brought pumps, refrigeration, and household technology to millions of families.

8   The suburban family of the 1950s is another oft-cited example of familial self-reliance. According to legend, after World War II a new, family-oriented generation settled down, saved their pennies, worked hard, and found well-paying jobs that allowed them to purchase homes in the suburbs. In fact, however, the 1950s suburban family was far more dependent on government assistance than any so-called underclass family of today. Federal GI benefit payments, available to 40 percent of the male population between the ages of twenty and twenty-four, permitted a whole generaticn of men to expand their education and improve their job prospects without forgoing marriage and children. The National Defense Education Act retooled science education in America, subsidizing both American industry and the education of individual scientists. Government-funded research developed the aluminum clapboards, prefabricated walls and ceilings, and plywood paneling that comprised the technological basis of the postwar housing revolution. Government spending was also largely responsible for the new highways, sewer systems, utility services, and traffic-control programs that opened up suburbia.

9   In addition, suburban home ownership depended on an unprecedented expansion of federal regulation and financing. Before the war, banks often required a 50 percent down payment on homes and normally issued mortgages for five to ten years. In the postwar period, however, the Federal Housing Authority, supplemented by the GI bill, put the federal government in the business of insuring and regulating private loans for single-home construction. FHA policy required down payments of only 5 to 10 percent of the purchase price and guaranteed mortgages of up to thirty years at interest rates of just 2 to 3 percent. The Veterans Administration required a mere dollar down from veterans. Almost half the housing in suburbia in the 1950s depended on such federal programs.

10   The drawback of these aid programs was that although they worked well for recipients, nonrecipients—disproportionately

poor and urban—were left far behind. While the general public financed the roads that suburbanites used to commute, the street-cars and trolleys that served urban and poor families received almost no tax revenues, and our previously thriving rail system was allowed to decay. In addition, federal loan policies, which were a boon to upwardly mobile white families, tended to systematize the pervasive but informal racism that had previously characterized the housing market. FHA redlining practices, for example, took entire urban areas and declared them ineligible for loans, while the government's two new mortgage institutions, the Federal National Mortgage Association and the Government National Mortgage Association (Fannie Mae and Ginny Mae) made it possible for urban banks to transfer savings out of the cities and into new suburban developments in the South and West.

Despite the devastating effects on families and regions that 11 did not receive such assistance, government aid to suburban residents during the 1950s and 1960s produced in its beneficiaries none of the demoralization usually presumed to afflict recipients of government handouts. Instead, federal subsidies to suburbia encouraged family formation, residential stability, upward occupational mobility, and rising educational aspirations among youth who could look forward to receiving such aid. Seen in this light, the idea that government subsidies intrinsically induce dependence, undermine self-esteem, or break down family ties is exposed as no more than a myth.

I am not suggesting that the way to solve the problems of poverty 12 and urban decay in America is to quadruple our spending on welfare. Certainly there are major reforms needed in our current aid policies to the poor. But the debate over such reform should put welfare in the context of *all* federal assistance programs. As long as we pretend that only poor or single-parent families need outside assistance, while normal families "stand on their own two feet," we will shortchange poor families, overcompensate rich ones, and fail to come up with effective policies for helping out families in the middle. Current government housing policies are a case in point. The richest 20 percent of American households receives three times as much federal housing aid—mostly in tax subsidies—as the poorest 20 percent receives in expenditures for low-income housing.

13   Historically, the debate over government policies toward families has never been over *whether* to intervene but *how:* to rescue or to warehouse, to prevent or to punish, to moralize about values or mobilize resources for education and job creation. Today's debate, lacking such historical perspective, caricatures the real issues. Our attempt to sustain the myth of family self-reliance in the face of all the historical evidence to the contrary has led policymakers into theoretical contortions and practical miscalculations that are reminiscent of efforts by medieval philosophers to maintain that the earth and not the sun was the center of the planetary system. In the sixteenth century, leading European thinkers insisted that the planets and the sun all revolved around the earth—much as American politicians today insist that our society revolves around family self-reliance. When evidence to the contrary mounted, defenders of the Ptolemaic universe postulated all sorts of elaborate planetary orbits in order to reconcile observed reality with their cherished theory. Similarly, rather than admit that all families need some kind of public support, we have constructed ideological orbits that explain away each instance of middle-class dependence as "exception," an "abnormality," or even an illusion. We have distributed public aid to families through convoluted bureaucracies that have become impossible to track; in some cases the system has become so cumbersome that it threatens to collapse around our ears. It is time to break through the old paradigm of self-reliance and substitute a new one that recognizes that assisting families is, simply, what government does.

Content

1. How could the Great American Myth—if myth it is—"that American families traditionally achieve success by establishing their independence from the government" (¶ 1) have arisen?
2. Why has this myth remained, in spite of the evidence to the contrary that Coontz cites throughout the essay?
3. What sorts of dependence on the government do Western pioneers and "the 1950s suburban family" (¶ 6) have in common (¶s 6–10)?

4. Is it accurate to say, as Coontz does, that "assisting families is, simply, what government does"? Explain your answer, in light of both this essay and your own experience.

Strategies/Structures

1. Coontz is a historian. How does her professional orientation govern the sorts of examples she uses? The way she organizes the essay?

2. Much of Coontz's evidence is expressed in percentages, as in paragraphs 8, 9, 12, and multiples, as in, "The richest 20 percent of American households receives three times as much federal housing aid—mostly in tax subsidies—as the poorest 20 percent receives in expenditures for low-income housing" (¶ 12). Is this evidence convincing? More or less convincing than evidence expressed in terms of numbers of people and dollar amounts?

3. The stereotype of welfare dependence is essentially negative. What sorts of evidence does Coontz use to replace this powerful stereotype with a positive one? Does she succeed in changing your mind?

Language

1. In what ways do the language and illustrations of the essay imply that Coontz is writing for an audience of the very same middle-class American families that she identifies as dependent on federal assistance?

2. Define "family values," "personal irresponsibility," "welfare," "family self-reliance" (used in the first two paragraphs and throughout the essay) as they are used by one or another vested interest group and as Coontz uses them. To what extent are all these definitions value-laden? Can you think of any neutral definitions for these terms?

For Writing

1. Most people believe, says Coontz, that "'winners' in America make it on their own, that dependence reflects some kind of individual or family failure, and that the ideal family is the self-reliant unit of traditional lore—a family that takes care of its own, carves out a future for its children, and never asks for handouts" (¶ 1). Does "A Nation of Welfare Families" convince you that this is, as Coontz says, a "myth"? Write a paper for an audience that shares this belief, in which you either reinforce or dispute Coontz's claim. You will need to take into account the evidence she provides and to supplement it with evidence from your own and your family's experience.

2. Compare and contrast the conventional stereotypes of welfare recipients with the typical middle-class welfare family that Coontz describes. Do you think that the politicians who promise to end welfare as we know it have the middle class in mind? Explain, for a middle-class readership, using evidence from Coontz (feel free to consult her book, *The Way We Never Were*) and from either local or national politicians.

===

LESLIE S. MOORE

Moore (born, 1954) grew up in California and majored in English at the University of California at Santa Cruz and at Berkeley, earning a B.A. in 1976 and an M.A.T. in 1982. She has served twice in the Peace Corps, first teaching English in Korea, 1977–1979. Six years later, she and her husband joined the Peace Corps together and were sent to Bamako, Mali, to teach composition and literature at the Ecole Normale Supérieure. In 1982 the couple moved to Princeton, Massachusetts, where Moore first worked as a newspaper feature writer and photographer and then taught high school English.

Two writers influenced Moore's prizewinning "Framing My Father," Eudora Welty (see pp. 29–34) and Scott Russell Sanders. She explains, "I used what Welty said in *One Writer's Beginnings* about the increasing importance of framing scene, situation, implication, and finally, 'a single, entire human being,' as a challenge to push me beyond merely describing scenes and situations to considering implications and to capturing more of the entire human being. Thus, Welty provided the shape for my essay. Sanders taught me another lesson in point of view with his two essays about his father: 'The Inheritance of Tools' (pp. 319–328) and 'Under the Influence: Paying the Price of My Father's Booze' (pp. 420–433). By first eulogizing his father as a mentor in carpentry and then lamenting his father's alcoholism, Sanders showed me two ways of looking at the same man and the divergent lessons he taught his son. In 'Framing My Father,' I used Sanders' two-pronged approach in reverse, first presenting my father and the lessons he taught me in a negative light, then shifting my perspective to the positive."

❄ Framing My Father

The frame through which I viewed the world changed too, with time.
Greater than scene, I came to see, is situation. Greater than situation is
implication. Greater than all of these is a single, entire human being,
who will never be confined in any frame.

EUDORA WELTY, *One Writer's Beginnings*

First Frame: The Scene

My father, fierce as ever, sits in the center of our living room   1
folded into the low-slung chair, his long frame scooped to its
elliptical contours, his thin shoulders hunched around his ears, his
white beard bristling against his chest. He's reading *The Bourne
Ultimatum* by Robert Ludlum. "#1 New York Times Bestseller"
announces the front cover; "VINTAGE LUDLUM" proclaims the back.
He's wearing white leather athletic shoes, gray warm-up pants, a
red-knit shirt with the collar turned up, and black-rimmed reading glasses—full-sized, not half glasses. At his right elbow a com-
puterized chess set stands ready, the little plastic players guarding
their squares: black king on white, white king on black, queens,
bishops, knights, castles, and pawns ranged around them. To his
left the wood stove ticks.

Second Frame: The Situation

On his visit to New England from California with his wife of only   2
two months, my father commandeers the best chair in the house.
An heirloom from my husband's side of the family, the chair is a
citadel of security that no one vacates willingly. "Out!" my father
orders the Scottie and she thumps down with a suffering sidelong
glance. The Westie suffers his eviction with a great show of terrier
ferocity that delights my father. My stepmother keeps out of the
fray, opting for the second best chair in the house. Neither my
husband nor I have a minute to dispute the chair with my father.
My husband's not on vacation. When he's not reading or writing
or teaching, he's harvesting firewood, loading stove lengths into
the wheelbarrow in the woodlot then wheeling it to the woodshed

in our garage. And I'm too busy entertaining—orchestrating meals and planning itineraries. I don't have the leisure to sit in the chair. So my father monopolizes the house favorite for ten days—from Friday, the eve of my April vacation, to Monday, the day I go back to teaching school. He gets up early each morning, brings one armload of wood in from the garage, stokes the stove next to the chair, and folds into it. Then he shifts his attention from bestsellers to chess problems.

Third Frame: The Implication

3   My father dominates our living room with his inertia. He forces us to move around him—around his feet, his books, his games—around a lifestyle that we don't share. Of course my husband and I both read. We have to. We read for the courses we teach and take. We read our students' papers. We read each other's writing. We read with pencils in hand, underlining, taking notes, commenting in the margins. We read as a discipline. My father reads to escape. He has always read. He warned my mother early that marriage wasn't going to get in the way of his reading; the marriage ended in divorce. He reads widely and eclectically, balancing history, philosophy, and science on the one hand, science fiction, spy thrillers, and mysteries on the other. He used to read with a drink in one hand and a cigar in the other, but he has given up both—for health, not sociability. He avoids what he calls "classical literature," the sort I read. In a bookstore I point out Toni Morrison's *Beloved* but he ignores the suggestion and heads for the bestseller rack.

4   While my father sits folded into our favorite chair, my husband and I fret over the school work we have to get done this week. My husband is writing papers, working on images of pride in seventeenth-century country house poems and analyzing Hawthorne's rhetorical stance in the introduction to *The Scarlet Letter*. He wants me to critique his writing. I have to wrench my thoughts from hostess problems—how much fresh pasta it takes to feed four, whether my stepmother has enough Swiss almond coffee beans to last the week, when I'll get to the store to buy my father his newspapers—to concentrate on houses of pride and phrases embedded within phrases. Plus I have my own work to do—*Romeo and Juliet* papers to grade and a high school murder

mystery I've promised my students I'd write with them—but I don't have the psychic space to start either. Meanwhile my father gives up another game of chess to the computer, stokes the fire, and goes back to *The Bourne Ultimatum.*

"Why doesn't he put on a sweater?" asks my husband. ⁵ "We've burned more wood this week than we did in January."

We heat our house with wood that my husband cuts on our ⁶ property. It's a process that he works at year long and enjoys—felling oak, hickory, and maple with his chainsaw, limbing the trees, pulling and piling the brush to burn later, cutting the wood into stove lengths, stacking it to dry, splitting the dry wood with a sledge and steel wedges, then wheeling it into the woodshed. Once he leaves the full wheelbarrow nosed half-way into the garage. My father doesn't offer to help unload it.

We wait for my father to take an interest in us—to ask what ⁷ we are teaching, to inquire about books we have read, to wonder what we have written. Instead, near the end of his visit, he offers to buy us things. A microwave. We decline. A telephone answering machine. We shudder. We suggest rose bushes for our garden and he writes a check, then returns to his chair and his thriller.

Fourth Frame: The Human Being

My father has made a name for himself as a son-of-a-bitch. He ⁸ has spent a lifetime cultivating a fierceness that intimates adults and terrorizes children. That's one reason, I'm sure, he gave up pediatrics to go into public health. He honed this fierceness on his own four children. When my brothers and I were growing up, his favorite phrase was "Stop crying or I'll spank you again." His favorite epithet was "You dumb stupe!" We cringed at the sound of his explosive "God-damn-it-all-to-hells!" and ducked out of the reach of his backhands. Recently my father admitted to me that the way he treated us as children would be considered child abuse today.

The lessons my father taught me were stamped in fear and ⁹ humiliation. Somehow I survived. Somehow the lessons stuck. Somehow I am grateful for the things I learned.

My father taught me how to body surf at Laguna Beach in ¹⁰ Southern California. One moment I would be patting wet sand onto a castle, the next I would be tucked under his arm like a football and carried full speed into the surf kicking and screaming and swallowing salt water. Yet I learned how to body surf. I learned how to get out past the breakers, diving under walls of thundering surf. I learned what to look for in a wave—the green swell on the horizon, the slow build, the fingers of foam tickling the top. I learned how to time my take-off, poised under the wave's foaming lip, arms cocked for their furious windmilling, feet set to kick. I learned how to let the wave take me, my body rigid and horizontal, head jutting out of the wave, one arm straight-fisted before me, the other clasped to my side. Finally I learned how to finish, tucking and rolling out of the breaker as it ground its way onto the shore.

11   When I was an awkward thirteen-year-old seeking acceptance in a new school, my father taught me to throw a softball so that I could try out for Miss Sparks' all-star team. He began our first lesson with an insult. "You throw the ball just like a girl," he told me. "Here!" he ordered. "Hold it like this. Like *this*, I said. *Look* at me!" He taught me to hold the ball between my thumb and two fingers, to draw it back behind my ear, cocking my elbow, curling my arm like a snake ready to strike, then whipping it from my shoulder to my wrist. He also taught me to catch: to scoop up the grounders that skittered across the pavement, to glove the fast balls without flinching, to judge the high flies and get underneath them, to dive for the balls that curved out of reach. Finally he taught me to catch and throw in the same instant, to fire the ball back at him faster than thought, only a short skip between the crack in my mitt and its sendoff.

12   I don't know when I first showed my father my school papers, but by the time I was in high school we had established regular editing sessions. I slaved over my manuscripts in longhand, leaving margins where my father wrote my literary pretensions clean off the page. He never commented on content—he'd rarely read the "classical literature" I was writing about—but he always had plenty to say about my style. None of it was complimentary. He muttered my sentences out loud, his pencil poised over the page, ready to attack my excesses—"You don't need *this*. Get rid of *that*."—my obscurities—"What in the hell is *that*

supposed to mean?"—my stumblings—"You dumb stupe!"—my misspellings—"Look it up." He jabbed holes through the paper where I used big words to conceal incomplete thoughts and demanded that I sort out my ideas on the spot. And so we worked our way through my papers, paragraph by painful paragraph, page after painful page. By the end of an editing session with my father, my papers and my pretensions were returned to me, battered and bleeding, and I limped back to my room to start the rewrites.

My father's fierceness has cut both ways. It has cut all of his 13 children, leaving scars on each. Some of the scars have healed. It has also cut him off, isolated him from human kindness, left him lonely and needy. And so, like King Lear in his retirement, my father invites himself to his grown children's houses. He commandeers the best chairs. He surrounds himself with books and games. And then he folds in upon himself. He has spent much of his fierceness and now he needs friends. Oscar Wilde says, "Children begin by loving their parents; then they judge them; sometimes they forgive them." As I trip over my father's feet in my living room, I wonder if I've forgiven him.

I remember those editing sessions—my father's lessons in 14 brevity, clarity, grace, and precision. They were lessons in honesty, too. "Well then, why in the hell don't you say what you mean?" I can still hear my father demanding. And so I say it and I edit it and I rewrite it and I say it again.

I remember those softball practices—my father and I standing at opposite ends of stinging fast balls, the clap of leather 15 against leather echoing off houses, our own special pattern of plays back and forth, the pain that numbed my throwing arm, yet still the "Just a few more, Dad, please?" and the weight of acceptance that lone ball carried on its fleeting course from hand to glove.

And I remember my brothers and me at Laguna Beach, 16 called out of the water at dusk and pleading to stay longer—"Just till the sun goes down, please, Daddy?" Then we'd bob out there past the breakers, watching the sun sigh into the Pacific, firing its dark surface with one last breath, until only a whisper of red remained, and we rode our last waves in triumphantly.

Content

1. Was Dr. Smith, Moore's father, a good or bad teacher of his own children? Does Moore view his lessons differently as an adult than she did at the time he was teaching her?

2. Is it possible to sort out single causes and single effects from among the complex factors that influence the ways we learn anything and everything? Explain your answer with reference to Moore's essay.

3. Moore says, "Recently my father admitted to me that the way he treated us as children would be considered child abuse today" (¶ 8). Do you agree? Why do you think Dr. Smith, a pediatrician and public health physician, treated his children so harshly? What was their reaction to him at the time?

Strategies/Structures

1. How does Moore's use, and labeling, of the four frames provide structure for her essay?

2. What does Moore think of her father? How do you know? Does she want you to share her opinion? Does her opinion actually change as the essay proceeds, or does she complicate it by showing more facets of a complicated parent-child relationship?

Language

1. Moore uses quotations from her father in all but the first of the essay's frames. What are these, how do they change as the essay proceeds, and what do they convey to you about the ambivalent relationship of Moore and her father?

2. If you (or anyone) had Dr. Smith for a writing tutor, would you have learned to write well? What is the effect of working one's way through a paper, under a mentor's unforgiving scrutiny, "paragraph by painful paragraph, page after painful page"?

For Writing

1. What makes parents good, or bad, teachers of their own children? Can they be both concurrently? Address this question, for an audience that doesn't know your parents (or other significant mentor) by identifying two or three of your major personal characteristics (such as honesty, curiosity, perseverance, loyalty, athletic ability, whatever) and show how

a parent or mentor strongly influenced these while you were growing up. Show, as Moore does, through some characteristic incidents, what this person did (or did not do) to cause these effects. Do you consider the results good, bad, or a mixture? Explain why.

2. Try writing an essay by using a series of several frames, as Moore does, to establish and interpret a relationship, either between an older and younger person or between two age peers—grandparent-grandchild, teacher-student, a married couple, two friends or enemies of the same or opposite sex, or others. Whether or not you write about yourself, you should know both of your subjects very well. The frames may be the same as Moore's (scene, situation, implication, character) or others of your own choice.

3. Throughout America's history, harshness has alternated with gentleness as being for children's own good. Is the adage "No pain, no gain" a valid assertion, in teaching children or in learning anything else? What teaching/learning style suits you best? Why?

BOBBIE ANN MASON

Mason's writings capture the people, the accents, and the culture of the countryside in which she was born (in 1940) and reared—rural and small town Kentucky. After graduating from the University of Kentucky in 1962, Mason worked briefly as a magazine writer in New York, contributing to *Movie Stars, Movie Life*, and *T.V. Star Parade*. She continued her education in the northeast, earning an M.A. from the State University of New York at Binghamton in 1966, and a Ph.D from the University of Connecticut in 1972. Mason stopped teaching English after five years to concentrate on fiction writing, encouraged by *New Yorker* fiction editor Roger Angell. Her first collection of short stories, *Shiloh and Other Stories* (1982) received nominations for a host of literary prizes, and fellowships to support her writing soon followed. *In Country* (1985), her first novel, treats themes comparable to those in her stories, the "dislocations wrought on ordinary blue-collar lives by recent history," in this case, the Vietnam War. Her later novels are *Spence + Lila* (1988) and *Feather Crowns* (1993).

As with all major writers, her works transcend the immediate locale in their engagement with the concerns of American culture at large. As the old South rapidly becomes the New South, Mason's Kentucky is in a state of flux and change. Her characters have to contend, each in his or her own way, with events in their lives that lead to the acceptance of new ways or the rejection—or loss—of the old. They are uneasy, frightened; they haven't the power to avoid or escape the forces at work in the culture. As Mason observes in a comment that applies to many of her works, including "Shiloh," "Some people will stay at home and be content there, others are born to run. It's the conflict"—between fixity and change, acceptance of the status quo and ambition—"that fascinates me."

Shiloh

1   Leroy Moffitt's wife, Norma Jean, is working on her pectorals. She lifts three-pound dumbbells to warm up, then progresses to a twenty-pound barbell. Standing with her legs apart, she reminds Leroy of Wonder Woman.

2   "I'd give anything if I could just get these muscles to where they're real hard," says Norma Jean. "Feel this arm. It's not as hard as the other one."

3   "That's 'cause you're right-handed," says Leroy, dodging as she swings the barbell in an arc.

4   "Do you think so?"

5   "Sure."

6   Leroy is a truckdriver. He injured his leg in a highway accident four months ago, and his physical therapy, which involves weights and a pulley, prompted Norma Jean to try building herself up. Now she is attending a body-building class. Leroy has been collecting temporary disability since his tractor-trailer jackknifed in Missouri, badly twisting his left leg in its socket. He has a steel pin in his hip. He will probably not be able to drive his rig again. It sits in the backyard, like a gigantic bird that has flown home to roost. Leroy has been home in Kentucky for three months, and his leg is almost healed, but the accident frightened

him and he does not want to drive any more long hauls. He is not sure what to do next. In the meantime, he makes things from craft kits. He started by building a miniature log cabin from notched Popsicle sticks. He varnished it and placed it on the TV set, where it remains. It reminds him of a rustic Nativity scene. Then he tried string art (sailing ships on black velvet), a macramé owl kit, a snap-together B–17 Flying Fortress, and a lamp made out of a model truck, with a light fixture screwed on the top of the cab. At first the kits were diversions, something to kill time, but now he is thinking about building a full-scale log house from a kit. It would be considerably cheaper than building a regular house, and besides, Leroy has grown to appreciate how things are put together. He has begun to realize that in all the years he was on the road he never took time to examine anything. He was always flying past scenery.

"They won't let you build a log cabin in any of the new sub- 7 divisions," Norma Jean tells him.

"'They will if I tell them it's for you," he says, teasing her. 8 Ever since they were married, he has promised Norma Jean he would build her a new home one day. They have always rented, and the house they live in is small and nondescript. It does not even feel like a home, Leroy realizes now.

Norma Jean works at the Rexall drugstore, and she has ac- 9 quired an amazing amount of information about cosmetics. When she explains to Leroy the three stages of complexion care, involving creams, toners, and moisturizers, he thinks happily of other petroleum products—axle grease, diesel fuel. This is a connection between him and Norma Jean. Since he has been home, he has felt unusually tender about his wife and guilty over his long absences. But he can't tell what she feels about him. Norma Jean has never complained about his traveling; she has never made hurt remarks, like calling his truck a "widow-maker." He is reasonably certain she has been faithful to him, but he wishes she would celebrate his permanent homecoming more happily. Norma Jean is often startled to find Leroy at home, and he thinks she seems a little disappointed about it. Perhaps he reminds her too much of the early days of their marriage, before he went on the road. They had a child who died as an infant, years ago. They never speak about their memories of Randy, which have almost faded, but now that Leroy is home all the time, they sometimes feel awkward around each other, and Leroy wonders if one of them should mention the child. He has the feeling that they are waking up out of a dream together—that they must create a new marriage, start afresh. They are lucky they are still married. Leroy has read that for most people losing a child destroys the marriage—or else he heard this on *Donahue*. He can't always remember where he learns things anymore.

10   At Christmas, Leroy bought an electric organ for Norma Jean. She used to play the piano when she was in high school. "It don't leave you," she told him once. "It's like riding a bicycle."

11   The new instrument had so many keys and buttons that she was bewildered by it at first. She touched the keys tentatively, pushed some buttons, then pecked out "Chopsticks." It came out in an amplified fox-trot rhythm, with marimba sounds.

12   "It's an orchestra!" she cried.

13   The organ had a pecan-look finish and eighteen preset chords, with optional flute, violin, trumpet, clarinet, and banjo accompaniments. Norma Jean mastered the organ almost immediately. At first she played Christmas songs. Then she bought *The Sixties Songbook* and learned every tune in it, adding variations to each with the rows of brightly colored buttons.

14   "I didn't like these old songs back then," she said. "But I have this crazy feeling I missed something."

15   "You didn't miss a thing," said Leroy.

16   Leroy likes to lie on the couch and smoke a joint and listen to Norma Jean play "Can't Take My Eyes Off You" and "I'll Be Back." He is back again. After fifteen years on the road, he is finally settling down with the woman he loves. She is still pretty. Her skin is flawless. Her frosted curls resemble pencil trimmings.

17   Now that Leroy has come home to stay, he notices how much the town has changed. Subdivisions are spreading across western Kentucky like an oil slick. The sign at the edge of town says "Pop: 11,500"—only seven hundred more than it said twenty years before. Leroy can't figure out who is living in all the new houses. The farmers who used to gather around the courthouse square on Saturday afternoons to play checkers and spit tobacco juice have gone. It has been years since Leroy has thought about the farmers, and they have disappeared without his noticing.

Leroy meets a kid named Stevie Hamilton in the parking lot 18
at the new shopping center. While they pretend to be strangers
meeting over a stalled car, Stevie tosses an ounce of marijuana
under the front seat of Leroy's car. Stevie is wearing orange
jogging shoes and a T-shirt that says CHATTAHOOCHEE SUPER-RAT.
His father is a prominent doctor who lives in one of the expensive
subdivisions in a new white-columned brick house that looks like
a funeral parlor. In the phone book under his name there is a
separate number, with the listing "Teenagers."

"Where do you get this stuff?" asks Leroy. "From your 19
pappy?"

"That's for me to know and you to find out," Stevie says. He 20
is slit-eyed and skinny.

"What else you got?" 21

"What you interested in?" 22

"Nothing special. Just wondered." 23

Leroy used to take speed on the road. Now he has to go 24
slowly. He needs to be mellow. He leans back against the car and
says, "I'm aiming to build me a log house, soon as I get time. My
wife, though, I don't think she likes the idea."

"Well, let me know when you want me again," Stevie says. 25
He has a cigarette in his cupped palm, as though sheltering it
from the wind. He takes a long drag, then stomps it on the asphalt
and slouches away.

Stevie's father was two years ahead of Leroy in high school. 26
Leroy is thirty-four. He married Norma Jean when they were both
eighteen, and their child Randy was born a few months later, but
he died at the age of four months and three days. He would be
about Stevie's age now. Norma Jean and Leroy were at the drive-
in, watching a double feature (*Dr. Strangelove* and *Lover Come
Back*), and the baby was sleeping in the back seat. When the first
movie ended, the baby was dead. It was sudden infant death
syndrome. Leroy remembers handing Randy to a nurse at the
emergency room, as though he were offering her a large doll as a
present. A dead baby feels like a sack of flour. "It just happens
sometimes," said the doctor, in what Leroy always recalls as a non-
chalant tone. Leroy can hardly remember the child anymore, but
he still sees vividly a scene from *Dr. Strangelove* in which the President of the United States was talking in a folksy voice on the hot

line to the Soviet premier about the bomber accidentally headed toward Russia. He was in the War Room, and the world map was lit up. Leroy remembers Norma Jean standing catatonically beside him in the hospital and himself thinking: Who is this strange girl? He had forgotten who she was. Now scientists are saying that crib death is caused by a virus. Nobody knows anything, Leroy thinks. The answers are always changing.

27   When Leroy gets home from the shopping center, Norma Jean's mother, Mabel Beasley, is there. Until this year, Leroy has not realized how much time she spends with Norma Jean. When she visits, she inspects the closets and then the plants, informing Norma Jean when a plant is droopy or yellow. Mabel calls the plants "flowers," although there are never any blooms. She always notices if Norma Jean's laundry is piling up. Mabel is a short, overweight woman whose tight, brown-dyed curls look more like a wig that the actual wig she sometimes wears. Today she has brought Norma Jean an off-white dust ruffle she made for the bed; Mabel works in a custom-upholstery shop.

28   "This is the tenth one I made this year," Mabel says. "I got started and couldn't stop."

29   "It's real pretty," says Norma Jean.

30   "Now we can hide things under the bed," says Leroy, who gets along with his mother-in-law primarily by joking with her. Mabel has never really forgiven him for disgracing her by getting Norma Jean pregnant. When the baby died, she said that fate was mocking her.

31   "What's that thing?" Mabel says to Leroy in a loud voice, pointing to a tangle of yarn on a piece of canvas.

32   Leroy holds it up for Mabel to see. "It's my needlepoint," he explains. "This is a *Star Trek* pillow cover."

33   "That's what a woman would do," says Mabel. "Great day in the morning!"

34   "All the big football players on TV do it," he says.

35   "Why, Leroy, you're always trying to fool me. I don't believe you for one minute. You don't know what to do with yourself—that's the whole trouble. Sewing!"

36   "I'm aiming to build us a log house," says Leroy. "Soon as my plans come."

"Like *heck* you are," says Norma Jean. She takes Leroy's 37 needlepoint and shoves it into a drawer. "You have to find a job first. Nobody can afford to build now anyway."

Mabel straightens her girdle and says, "I still think before 38 you get tied down y'all ought to take a little run to Shiloh."

"One of these days, Mama," Norma Jean says impatiently. 39

Mabel is talking about Shiloh, Tennessee. For the past few 40 years, she has been urging Leroy and Norma Jean to visit the Civil War battleground there. Mabel went there on her honeymoon—the only real trip she ever took. Her husband died of a perforated ulcer when Norma Jean was ten, but Mabel, who was accepted into the United Daughters of the Confederacy in 1975, is still preoccupied with going back to Shiloh.

"I've been to kingdom come and back in that truck out 41 yonder," Leroy says to Mabel, "but we never yet set foot in that battleground. Ain't that something? How did I miss it?"

"It's not even that far," Mabel says. 42

After Mabel leaves, Norma Jean reads to Leroy from a list 43 she has made. "Things you could do," she announces. "You could get a job as a guard at Union Carbide, where they'd let you set on a stool. You could get on at the lumberyard. You could do a little carpenter work, if you want to build so bad. You could—"

"I can't do something where I'd have to stand up all day." 44

"You ought to try standing up all day behind a cosmetics 45 counter. It's amazing that I have strong feet, coming from two parents that never had strong feet at all." At the moment Norma Jean is holding on to the kitchen counter, raising her knees one at a time as she talks. She is wearing two-pound ankle weights.

"Don't worry," says Leroy. "I'll do something." 46

"You could truck calves to slaughter for somebody. You 47 wouldn't have to drive any big old truck for that."

"I'm going to build you this house," says Leroy. "I want to 48 make you a real home."

"I don't want to live in any log cabin." 49

"It's not a cabin. It's a house." 50

"I don't care. It looks like a cabin." 51

"You and me together could lift those logs. It's just like lift- 52 ing weights."

53   Norma Jean doesn't answer. Under her breath, she is counting. Now she is marching through the kitchen. She is doing goose
steps.

54 Before his accident, when Leroy came home he used to stay in the
house with Norma Jean, watching TV in bed and playing cards.
She would cook fried chicken, picnic ham, chocolate pie—all his
favorites. Now he is home alone much of the time. In the mornings, Norma Jean disappears, leaving a cooling place in the bed.
She eats a cereal called Body Buddies, and she leaves the bowl on
the table, with the soggy tan balls floating in a milk puddle. He
sees things about Norma Jean that he never realized before. When
she chops onions, she stares off into a corner, as if she can't bear
to look. She puts on her house slippers almost precisely at nine
o'clock every evening and nudges her jogging shoes under the
couch. She saves bread heels for the birds. Leroy watches the birds
at the feeder. He notices the peculiar way goldfinches fly past the
window. They close their wings, then fall, then spread their wings
to catch and lift themselves. He wonders if they close their eyes
when they fall. Norma Jean closes her eyes when they are in bed.
She wants the lights turned out. Even then, he is sure she closes
her eyes.

55   He goes for long drives around town. He tends to drive a
car rather carelessly. Power steering and an automatic shift make
a car feel so small and inconsequential that his body is hardly
involved in the driving process. His injured leg stretches out com-
fortably. Once or twice he has almost hit something, but even the
prospect of an accident seems minor in a car. He cruises the new
subdivisions, feeling like a criminal rehearsing for a robbery.
Norma Jean is probably right about a log house being inappropriate here in the new subdivisions. All the houses look grand
and complicated. They depress him.

56   One day when Leroy comes home from a drive he finds
Norma Jean in tears. She is in the kitchen making a potato and
mushroom-soup casserole, with grated-cheese topping. She is
crying because her mother caught her smoking.

57   "I didn't hear her coming. I was standing here puffing away
pretty as you please," Norma Jean says, wiping her eyes.

"I knew it would happen sooner or later," says Leroy, 58
putting his arm around her.

"She don't know the meaning of the word 'knock,'" says 59
Norma Jean. "It's a wonder she hadn't caught me years ago."

"Think of it this way," Leroy says. "What if she caught me 60
with a joint?"

"You better not let her!" Norma Jean shrieks. "I'm warning 61
you, Leroy Moffitt!"

"I'm just kidding. Here, play me a tune. That'll help you 62
relax."

Norma Jean puts the casserole in the oven and sets the timer. 63
Then she plays a ragtime tune, with horns and banjo, as Leroy
lights up a joint and lies on the couch, laughing to himself about
Mabel's catching him at it. He thinks of Stevie Hamilton—a doctor's son pushing grass. Everything is funny. The whole town
seems crazy and small. He is reminded of Virgil Mathis, a boast-
ful policeman Leroy used to shoot pool with. Virgil recently led a
drug bust in a back room at a bowling alley, where he seized ten
thousand dollars' worth of marijuana. The newspaper had a picture of him holding up the bags of grass and grinning widely.
Right now, Leroy can imagine Virgil breaking down the door and
arresting him with a lungful of smoke. Virgil would probably have
been alerted to the scene because of all the racket Norma Jean is
making. Now she sounds like a hard-rock band. Norma Jean is ter-
rific. When she switches to a Latin-rhythm version of "Sunshine
Superman," Leroy hums along. Norma Jean's foot goes up and
down, up and down.

"Well, what do you think?" Leroy says, when Norma Jean 64
pauses to search through her music.

"What do I think about what?" 65

His mind had gone blank. Then he says, "I'll sell my rig and 66
build us a house." That wasn't what he wanted to say. He wanted
to know what she thought—what she *really* thought—about them.

"Don't start in on that again," says Norma Jean. She begins 67
playing "Who'll Be the Next in Line?"

Leroy used to tell hitchhikers his whole life story—about his 68
travels, his hometown, the baby. He would end with a question:
"Well, what do you think?" It was just a rhetorical question. In

time, he had the feeling that he'd been telling the same story over and over to the same hitchhikers. He quit talking to hitchhikers when he realized how his voice sounded—whining and self-pitying, like some teenage-tragedy song. Now Leroy has the sudden impulse to tell Norma Jean about himself, as if he had just met her. They have known each other so long they have forgotten a lot about each other. They could become reacquainted. But when the oven timer goes off and she runs to the kitchen, he forgets why he wants to do this.

69   The next day, Mabel drops by. It is Saturday and Norma Jean is cleaning. Leroy is studying the plans for his log house, which have finally come in the mail. He has them spread out on the table—big sheets of stiff blue paper, with diagrams and numbers printed in white. While Norma Jean runs the vacuum, Mabel drinks coffee. She sets her coffee cup on a blueprint.

70   "I'm just waiting for time to pass," she says to Leroy, drumming her fingers on the table.

71   As soon as Norma Jean switches off the vacuum, Mabel says in a loud voice, "Did you hear about the datsun dog that killed the baby?"

72   Norma Jean says, "The word is 'dachshund.'"

73   "They put the dog on trial. It chewed the baby's legs off. The mother was in the next room all the time." She raises her voice. "They thought it was neglect."

74   Norma Jean is holding her ears. Leroy manages to open the refrigerator and get some Diet Pepsi to offer Mabel. Mabel still has some coffee and she waves away the Pepsi.

75   "Datsuns are like that," Mabel says. "They're jealous dogs. They'll tear a place to pieces if you don't keep an eye on them."

76   "You better watch out what you're saying, Mabel," says Leroy.

77   "Well, facts is facts."

78   Leroy looks out the window at his rig. It is like a huge piece of furniture gathering dust in the backyard. Pretty soon it will be an antique. He hears the vacuum cleaner. Norma Jean seems to be cleaning the living room rug again.

79   Later, she says to Leroy, "She just said that about the baby because she caught me smoking. She's trying to pay me back."

"What are you talking about?" Leroy says, nervously shuf- 80
fling blueprints.

"You know good and well," Norma Jean says. She is sitting 81
in a kitchen chair with her feet up and her arms wrapped around
her knees. She looks small and helpless. She says, "The very idea,
her bringing up a subject like that! Saying it was neglect."

"She didn't mean that," Leroy says. 82

"She might not have *thought* she meant it. She always says 83
things like that. You don't know how she goes on."

"But she didn't really mean it. She was just talking." 84

Leroy opens a king-sized bottle of beer and pours it into two 85
glasses, dividing it carefully. He hands a glass to Norma Jean and
she takes it from him mechanically. For a long time, they sit by the
kitchen window watching the birds at the feeder.

Something is happening. Norma Jean is going to night school. 86
She has graduated from her six-week body-building course and
now she is taking an adult-education course in composition at
Paducah Community College. She spends her evenings outlining
paragraphs.

"First you have a topic sentence," she explains to Leroy. 87
"Then you divide it up. Your secondary topic has to be connected
to your primary topic."

To Leroy, this sounds intimidating. "I never was any good in 88
English," he says.

"It makes a lot of sense." 89

"What are you doing this for, anyhow?" 90

She shrugs. "It's something to do." She stands up and lifts 91
her dumbbells a few times.

"Driving a rig, nobody cared about my English." 92

"I'm not criticizing your English." 93

Norma Jean used to say, "If I lose ten minutes' sleep, I just 94
drag all day." Now she stays up late, writing compositions. She got
a B on her first paper—a how-to theme on soup-based casseroles.
Recently Norma Jean has been cooking unusual foods—tacos,
lasagna, Bombay chicken. She doesn't play the organ anymore,
though her second paper was called "Why Music Is Important to
Me." She sits at the kitchen table, concentrating on her outlines,
while Leroy plays with his log house plans, practicing with a set

of Lincoln Logs. The thought of getting a truckload of notched, numbered logs scares him, and he wants to be prepared. As he and Norma Jean work together at the kitchen table, Leroy has the hopeful thought that they are sharing something, but he knows he is a fool to think this. Norma Jean is miles away. He knows he is going to lose her. Like Mabel, he is just waiting for time to pass.

95   One day Mabel is there before Norma Jean gets home from work, and Leroy finds himself confiding in her. Mabel, he realizes, must know Norma Jean better than he does.

96   "I don't know what's got into that girl," Mabel says. "She used to go to bed with the chickens. Now you say she's up all hours. Plus her a-smoking. I like to died."

97   "I want to make her this beautiful home," Leroy says, indicating the Lincoln Logs. "I think she even wants it. Maybe she was happier with me gone."

98   "She don't know what to make of you, coming home like this."

99   "Is that it?"

100   Mabel takes the roof off his Lincoln Log cabin. "You couldn't get *me* in a log cabin," she says. "I was raised in one. It's no picnic, let me tell you."

101   "They're different now," says Leroy.

102   "I tell you what," Mabel says, smiling oddly at Leroy.

103   "What?"

104   "Take her down to Shiloh. Y'all need to get out together, stir a little. Her brain's all balled up over them books."

105   Leroy can see traces of Norma Jean's features in her mother's face. Mabel's worn face has the texture of crinkled cotton, but suddenly she looks pretty. It occurs to Leroy that Mabel has been hinting all along that she wants them to take her with them to Shiloh.

106   "Let's all go to Shiloh," he says. "You and me and her. Come Sunday."

107   Mabel throws up her hand in protest. "Oh, no, not me. Young folks want to be by themselves."

108   When Norma Jean comes in with groceries, Leroy says excitedly, "Your mama here's been dying to go to Shiloh for thirty-five years. It's about time we went, don't you think?"

109   "I'm not going to butt in on anybody's second honeymoon," Mabel says.

"Who's going on a honeymoon, for Christ's sake?" Norma   110
Jean says loudly.

"I never raised no daughter of mine to talk that-a-way,"   111
Mabel says.

"You ain't seen nothing yet," says Norma Jean. She starts   112
putting away boxes and cans, slamming cabinet doors.

"There's a log cabin at Shiloh," Mabel says. "It was there   113
during the battle. There's bullet holes in it."

"When are you going to *shut up* about Shiloh, Mama?" asks   114
Norma Jean.

"I always thought Shiloh was the prettiest place, so full of   115
history," Mabel goes on. "I just hoped y'all could see it once
before I die, so you could tell me about it." Later, she whispers to
Leroy, "You do what I said. A little change is what she needs."

"Your name means 'the king,'" Norma Jean says to Leroy that   116
evening. He is trying to get her to go to Shiloh, and she is reading
a book about another century.

"Well, I reckon I ought to be right proud."   117

"I guess so."   118

"Am I still king around here?"   119

Norma Jean flexes her biceps and feels them for hardness.   120
"I'm not fooling around with anybody, if that's what you mean,"
she says.

"Would you tell me if you were?"   121

"I don't know."   122

"What does *your* name mean?"   123

"It was Marilyn Monroe's real name."   124

"No kidding!"   125

"Norma comes from the Normans. They were invaders,"   126
she says. She closes her book and looks hard at Leroy. "I'll go to
Shiloh with you if you'll stop staring at me."

On Sunday, Norma Jean packs a picnic and they go to Shiloh. To   127
Leroy's relief, Mabel says she does not want to come with them.
Norma Jean drives, and Leroy, sitting beside her, feels like some
boring hitchhiker she has picked up. He tries some conversation,
but she answers him in monosyllables. At Shiloh, she drives aim-
lessly through the park, past bluffs and trails and steep ravines.

Shiloh is an immense place, and Leroy cannot see it as a battle-ground. It is not what he expected. He thought it would look like a golf course. Monuments are everywhere, showing through the thick clusters of trees. Norma Jean passes the log cabin Mabel mentioned. It is surrounded by tourists looking for bullet holes.

128   "That's not the kind of log house I've got in mind," says Leroy apologetically.

129   "I know *that*."

130   "This is a pretty place. Your mama was right."

131   "It's O.K." says Norma Jean. "Well, we've seen it. I hope she's satisfied."

132   They burst out laughing together.

133   At the park museum, a movie on Shiloh is shown every half hour, but they decide that they don't want to see it. They buy a souvenir Confederate flag for Mabel, and then they find a picnic spot near the cemetery. Norma Jean has brought a picnic cooler, with pimento sandwiches, soft drinks, and Yodels. Leroy eats a sandwich and then smokes a joint, hiding it behind the picnic cooler. Norma Jean has quit smoking altogether. She is picking cake crumbs from the cellophane wrapper, like a fussy bird.

134   Leroy says, "So the boys in gray ended up in Corinth. The Union soldiers zapped 'em finally. April 7, 1862."

135   They both know that he doesn't know any history. He is just talking about some of the historical plaques they have read. He feels awkward, like a boy on a date with an older girl. They are still just making conversation.

136   "Corinth is where Mama eloped to," says Norma Jean.

137   They sit in silence and stare at the cemetery for the Union dead and, beyond, at a tall cluster of trees. Campers are parked nearby, bumper to bumper, and small children in bright clothing are cavorting and squealing. Norma Jean wads up the cake wrapper and squeezes it tightly in her hand. Without looking at Leroy, she says, "I want to leave you."

138   Leroy takes a bottle of Coke out of the cooler and flips off the cap. He holds the bottle poised near his mouth but cannot remember to take a drink. Finally he says, "No, you don't."

139   "Yes, I do."

140   "I won't let you."

141   "You can't stop me."

"Don't do me that way."   142

Leroy knows Norma Jean will have her own way. "Didn't I   143
promise to be home from now on?" he says.

"In some ways, a woman prefers a man who wanders," says   144
Norma Jean. "That sounds crazy, I know."

"You're not crazy."   145

Leroy remembers to drink from his Coke. Then he says, "Yes,   146
you *are* crazy. You and me could start all over again. Right back at
the beginning."

"We *have* started all over again." says Norma Jean. "And   147
this is how it turned out."

"What did I do wrong?"   148

"Nothing."   149

"Is this one of those women's lib things?" Leroy asks.   150

"Don't be funny."   151

The cemetery, a green slope dotted with white markers,   152
looks like a subdivision site. Leroy is trying to comprehend that
his marriage is breaking up, but for some reason he is wondering
about white slabs in a graveyard.

"Everything was fine till Mama caught me smoking," says   153
Norma Jean, standing up. "That set something off."

"What are you talking about?"   154

"She won't leave me alone—*you* won't leave me alone."   155
Norma Jean seems to be crying, but she is looking away from him.
"I feel eighteen again. I can't face that all over again." She starts
walking away. "No, it *wasn't* fine. I don't know what I'm saying.
Forget it."

Leroy takes a lungful of smoke and closes his eyes as Norma   156
Jean's words sink in. He tries to focus on the fact that thirty-five
hundred soldiers died on the grounds around him. He can only
think of that war as a board game with plastic soldiers. Leroy
almost smiles, as he compares the Confederates' daring attack on
the Union camps and Virgil Mathis's raid on the bowling alley.
General Grant, drunk and furious, shoved the southerners back to
Corinth, where Mabel and Jet Beasley were married years later,
when Mabel was still thin and good-looking. The next day, Mabel
and Jet visited the battleground, and then Norma Jean was born,
and then she married Leroy and they had a baby, which they lost,
and now Leroy and Norma Jean are here at the same battleground.

Leroy knows he is leaving out a lot. He is leaving out the insides of history. History was always just names and dates to him. It occurs to him that building a house out of logs is similarly empty—too simple. And the real inner workings of a marriage, like most of history, have escaped him. Now he sees that building a log house is the dumbest idea he could have had. It was clumsy of him to think Norma Jean would want a log house. It was a crazy idea. He'll have to think of something else, quickly. He will wad the blueprints into tight balls and fling them into the lake. Then he'll get moving again. He opens his eyes. Norma Jean has moved away and is walking through the cemetery, following a serpentine brick path.

157   Leroy gets up to follow his wife, but his good leg is asleep and his bad leg still hurts him. Norma Jean is far away, walking rapidly toward the bluff by the river, and he tries to hobble toward her. Some children run past him, screaming noisily. Norma Jean has reached the bluff, and she is looking out over the Tennessee River. Now she turns toward Leroy and waves her arms. Is she beckoning to him? She seems to be doing an exercise for her chest muscles. The sky is unusually pale—the color of the dust ruffle Mabel made for their bed.

Additional Topics for Writing
Cause and Effect   (For process strategies, see page 242)

Write an essay, adapted to an audience of your choice, explaining either the causes or the effects of one of the following:

1. Substance abuse by teenagers, young adults, or another group
2. America's 50 percent divorce rate
3. Genetic engineering
4. Teenage pregnancy
5. The popularity of a given television show, movie or rock star, film, book, or type of book (such as romance, Gothic, Western)
6. Current taste in clothing, food, cars, architecture, interior decoration
7. The Civil War, the Great Depression, World War II, the Vietnam War, or other historical event
8. The popularity of a particular spectator or active sport
9. Your personality or temperament
10. Success in college or in business
11. Being "born again" or losing one's religious faith
12. Racial, sexual, or religious discrimination
13. An increasingly highier proportion of women and mothers who also work outside the home
14. The computer revolution
15. The American Dream that "if you work hard you're bound to succeed"
16. America's disappearing farm land, and/or the decrease in the number of family farms (see Keifer, "The Death of a Farm" [pp. 662–665])
17. The actual or potential consequences of nuclear leaks, meltdowns
18. Vanishing animal or plant species; or the depletion of natural resources (see Cunningham, "The Struggle to Save Endangered Species" [pp. 617–625])
19. Decrease in the number of people in training for skilled labor—electricians, plumbers, carpenters, tool and die makers, and others
20. A sudden change in personal status (from being a high school student to being a college freshman; from living at home to living away from home; from being dependent to being self-supporting; from being single to being married; from being childless to being a parent; from being married to being divorced . . .)

Part III

Clarifying Ideas

8 Description

When you describe a person, place, thing, or phenomenon, you want your readers to see it as you do, and to experience its sounds, tastes, smells, or textures. You may or may not wish to interpret it for them as well.

If you don't, you can describe something with seeming objectivity, impartially, sticking to the facts without evaluating them and letting your readers infer what they wish. (But bear in mind that by your very *selection and organization* of the facts you are implicitly evaluating them, deciding that some deserve emphasis, or mention, for whatever reasons, and others don't). Technical and scientific descriptions usually aim for objectivity, as would the author of a manual describing the components of a home computer, or an astronaut explaining the size, appearance, and composition of a newly discovered crater on the moon. So do some travel guides when describing places, for the authors cannot afford to let their personal preferences influence their presentations of Altoona and Oshkosh, which (bigosh!) must be described as impartially as San Francisco and New Orleans. *corny!*

If you do want to interpret something for your readers, your writing is bound to be subjective. For example, Joan Didion's "Marrying Absurd" (pp. 329–333), an indictment of Las Vegas weddings, condemns the place and its venal inhabitants as well as the practice mentioned in her judgmental title. The desert setting is a "moonscape of rattlesnakes and mesquite." Las Vegas, Didion says,

> is the most extreme and allegorical of American settlements, bizarre and beautiful in its venality and in its devotion to immediate gratification, a place the tone of which is set by mobsters and call girls and ladies' room attendants with amyl nitrite poppers in their uniform pockets. . . . There is no "time" in Las Vegas, no night and no day and no past and no future. . . .

Its values, she says, are hedonistic and money-oriented, as reflected by the only people she identifies, "mobsters," "call girls," and "ladies' room attendants." It is a place so "extreme," so weird, that even the ordinary measurements of time do not function. It is horrible, she implies.

In contrast to Didion's thorough distaste for Las Vegas, Mark Twain wants us to relish the joys of his "Uncle John's Farm" (pp. 312–318). Thus, he shows us how "inviting" a "prize watermelon" looks "when it is cooling itself in a tub of water under the bed waiting." He lets us hear its "crackling sound" on being cut open, and offers a taste of the illicit succulence of a watermelon "acquired by art," as opposed to one that "has been honestly come by."

Kathleen Norris sets herself a harder task in "The Beautiful Places" (pp. 334–343), a chapter from *Dakota: A Spiritual Geography*. Writing about the spiritual quality of anything—person, experience, or landscape—is difficult because the spirituality, though felt, is ineffable. So her description approaches the subject from a variety of angles: geography (¶ 1), climate (¶s 2, 4), driving through the area (¶ 3), through family history (¶ 7), and more. Taken together, the external features of this barren but beautiful landscape of extremes become emblematic of its inner character, its fundamental spirituality that Norris finds in St. Hilary's observation, "Everything that seems empty is full of the angels of God."

In "Why I write in a language my mother does not speak" (pp. 344–349) Genevieve Brassard uses an account of her development as a writer in English to describe the relationship between herself and her mother, a free-spirited French-speaking woman from Montreal. In "The Inheritance of Tools" (pp. 319–328) Scott Russell Sanders interprets the character of his father, who has just died. Although both essays describe a parent's character and major family relationships, Brassard and Sanders don't tell us what their parents look like; we don't need appearance to recognize the parents' personalities, values, ways of behaving.

As Sanders's essay becomes a tribute to his father, and to the extended family of which his father was a member, Sanders describes his legacy, the carpenters' tools ("the hammer [that] had belonged to him, and to his father before him") and the knowledge of how to use them, transmitted through years of patient teaching and an insistence on high-quality work, "making sure before I drove the first nail that every line was square and true." This type of description consists of stories embedded within stories: How Sanders's father taught him to use the hammer (¶s 6, 9), the saw (¶s 10, 12), the square (¶s 14–16). Still more stories incorporate the current use to which Sanders puts this knowledge (he's building a bedroom in the basement), the incident of the gerbil escaping behind the new bedroom wall (¶s 17, 22), learning of his father's death (¶s 26, 28)—all embedded in the matrix of the stories of four generations of the Sanders family.

Thus through details, carefully chosen and arranged, description offers an interpretation, an understanding of its varied subjects. The subjects may be *places*—both natural (the Dakota terrain) and constructed by humans (Twain's Uncle John's farm, Las Vegas). The subjects may be *people,* as characters in their own right or in relation to others (Brassard's mother, Sanders's father). People are usually seen in relation to a particular place or other context, and as characters experiencing change or understanding (or some other state of being) as a consequence of their reactions to or adventures in a particular setting, as Kathleen Norris does continually throughout her residence in Dakota. The organizational pattern of details may be fairly obvious, even when implied; Norris's spare and harsh "beautiful place," Dakota, is understood in relation to lusher, greener, more accommodating terrain. Twain's deliciously long list of the succulent foods served at the "sumptuous meals" on Uncle John's farm proceeds in the order that the meal would be eaten and remembered, with the entrees (meat and game) first, side dishes (hot breads, vegetables) next, and desserts (homegrown fruits and homemade pies and cobblers) last.

Rarely do any literary techniques occur in isolation. Although the organization of *The Essay Connection* is intended to highlight many of the major techniques of nonfiction writing, it would be unrealistic to present pure types, for they rarely exist. Even when you write an essay to experiment with a particular technique, such as description or narration, you're bound to employ others, as well.

Thus none of the essays in this chapter is purely descriptive. Note, for instance, the extensive comparisons and contrasts in people, territory, ways of life implied in the essays by Sanders, Didion, Norris, and Brassard. All of these essays involve narration, as the writers tell of their personal involvement with the subject, through conversation, scene setting, and actions of people and animals. Twain and Norris use a great deal of exposition (explanations about their subject) to interpret them favorably: "[E]specially in western Dakota we live in tension between myth and truth. Are we cowboys or farmers? Are we fiercely independent frontier types or community builders? . . . The land around us was divided neatly in 160-acre rectangular sections. . . . But our human geography has never been as orderly." Brassard's and Sanders's family stories coalesce to present a multigenerational portrait of their respective families. While Brassard and her mother are both integrated and separated by language, Sanders's family is bound together by "the inheritance of tools," each physical object embodying the legacy of respect, use, and care of not only the implements, but pride of craftsmanship, integrity of family. In contrast, Didion uses extensive description to present implied arguments against what she sees as the dominant Las Vegas lifestyle and values: "Las Vegas seems to offer something other than 'convenience'; it is merchandising 'niceness,' the facsimile of proper ritual, to children who do not know how else to find it, how to make the arrangements, how to do it 'right.'"

STRATEGIES FOR WRITING— DESCRIPTION

1. What is my main purpose in writing this descriptive essay? To present and interpret factual information about the subject? To recreate its essence as I have experienced it, or the person, as I have known him or her? To form the basis for a narrative, or an argument—overt or implied? What mixture of objective information and subjective impressions will best fit my purpose?

2. If my audience is completely unfamiliar with the subject, how much and what kinds of basic information will I have to provide so they can understand what I'm talking about? (Can I assume that they've seen lakes, but not necessarily Lake Tahoe, the subject of my paper? Or that they know other grandmothers, but not mine, about whom I'm writing?) If my readers are familiar with the subject, in what ways can I describe it so they'll discover new aspects of it?

3. What particular characteristics of my subject do I wish to emphasize? Will I use in this description details revealed by the senses—sight, sound, taste, smell, touch? Any other sort of information, such as a person's characteristic behavior, gestures, ways of speaking or moving or dressing, values, companions, possessions, occupation, residence, style of spending money, beliefs, hopes, vulnerabilities? Non-sensory details will be particularly necessary in describing an abstraction, such as somebody's temperament or state of mind.

4. How will I organize my description? From the most dominant to the least dominant details? From the most to the least familiar aspects (or vice versa)? According to what an observer is likely to notice first, second . . . last? Or according to some other pattern?

5. Will I use much general language, or will my description be highly specific throughout? Do I want to evoke a clear, distinct image of the subject? Or a mood—nostalgic, thoughtful, happy, sad, or otherwise?

MARK TWAIN

For Mark Twain's biography, see page 80. *Autobiography,* published in 1924, fourteen years after Twain's death, presents an idyllic but comically realistic picture of a country childhood, specific in time (pre–Civil War) and place ("in the country four miles from Florida," Missouri), yet timeless and ubiquitous. The *Autobiography* presents two central characters, the boy Sam Clemens, who enjoyed every aspect of his Uncle John Quarles's farm, and Mark Twain, the older, wiser, and sometimes more cynical author, who writes these reminiscences after alerting readers to bear in mind that he can "remember anything, whether it had happened or not." What he remembers is the spirit of the farm, of the people who lived there, white and black, and how they lived in abiding harmony.

Twain reinforces that spirit with an abundance of sensory details—often the mainstay of description, as they are here. Thus he evokes sound ("I know the crackling sound [a ripe watermelon] makes when the carving knife enters its end"), smell ("I can call back . . . the mystery of the deep woods, the earthy smells"), touch ("I can feel the thumping rain, upon my head, of hickory nuts and walnuts when we were out in the frosty dawn"), and especially of taste ("I know the taste of the watermelon which has been honestly come by, and I know the taste of the watermelon which has been acquired by art"), and sight ("I know the look of Uncle Dan'l's kitchen as it was on the privileged nights, when I was a child, and I can see the white and black children grouped on the hearth, with the firelight playing on their faces and the shadows flickering up on the walls . . .").

Uncle John's Farm[1]

1   For many years I believed that I remembered helping my grandfather drink his whisky toddy when I was six weeks old, but I do not tell about that any more, now; I am grown old and my memory is not as active as it used to be. When I was younger I could remember anything, whether it had happened

---

[1] Title supplied.

or not; but my faculties are declining now, and soon I shall be so I cannot remember any but the things that never happened. It is sad to go to pieces like this, but we all have to do it.

My uncle, John A. Quarles, was a farmer, and his place was in the country four miles from Florida. He had eight children and fifteen or twenty negroes, and was also fortunate in other ways, particularly in his character. I have not come across a better man than he was. I was his guest for two or three months every year, from the fourth year after we removed to Hannibal till I was eleven or twelve years old. I have never consciously used him or his wife in a book, but his farm has come very handy to me in literature once or twice. In *Huck Finn* and *Tom Sawyer, Detective* I moved it down to Arkansas. It was all of six hundred miles, but it was no trouble; it was not a very large farm—five hundred acres, perhaps—but I could have done it if it had been twice as large. And as for the morality of it, I cared nothing for that; I would move a state if the exigencies of literature required it.

It was a heavenly place for a boy, that farm of my uncle John's. The house was a double log one, with a spacious floor (roofed in) connecting it with the kitchen. In the summer the table was set in the middle of that shady and breezy floor, and the sumptuous meals—well, it makes me cry to think of them. Fried chicken, roast pig; wild and tame turkeys, ducks, and geese; venison just killed; squirrels, rabbits, pheasants, partridges, prairie-chickens; biscuits, hot batter cakes, hot buckwheat cakes, hot "wheat bread," hot rolls, hot corn pone; fresh corn boiled on the ear, succotash, butter-beans, stringbeans, tomatoes, peas, Irish potatoes, sweet potatoes; butter-milk, sweet milk, "clabber"; watermelons, muskmelons, cantaloupes—all fresh from the garden; apple pie, peach pie, pumpkin pie, apple dumplings, peach cobbler—I can't remember the rest. . . .

The farmhouse stood in the middle of a very large yard, and the yard was fenced on three sides with rails and on the rear side with high palings; against these stood the smokehouse; beyond the palings was the orchard; beyond the orchard were the negro quarters and the tobacco fields. The front yard was entered over a stile made of sawed-off logs of graduated heights; I do not remember any gate. In a corner of the front yard were a dozen lofty hickory trees and a dozen black walnuts, and in the nutting season riches were to be gathered there.

5   Down a piece, abreast the house, stood a little log cabin against the rail fence; and there the woody hill fell sharply away, past the barns, the corncrib, the stables, and the tobacco-curing house, to a limpid brook which sang along over its gravelly bed and curved and frisked in and out and here and there and yonder in the deep shade of overhanging foliage and vines—a divine place for wading, and it had swimming pools, too, which were forbidden to us and therefore much frequented by us. For we were little Christian children and had early been taught the value of forbidden fruit. . . .

6   I can see the farm yet, with perfect clearness. I can see all its belongings, all its details; the family room of the house, with a "trundle" bed in one corner and a spinning-wheel in another—a wheel whose rising and falling wail, heard from a distance, was the mournfulest of all sounds to me, and made me homesick and low spirited, and filled my atmosphere with the wandering spirits of the dead; the vast fireplace, piled high, on winter nights, with flaming hickory logs from whose ends a sugary sap bubbled out, but did not go to waste, for we scraped it off and ate it; the lazy cat spread out on the rough hearthstones; the drowsy dogs braced against the jambs and blinking; my aunt in one chimney corner, knitting; my uncle in the other, smoking his corn-cob pipe; the slick and carpetless oak floor faintly mirroring the dancing flame tongues and freckled with black indentations where fire coals had popped out and died a leisurely death; half a dozen children romping in the background twilight; "split"-bottomed chairs here and there, some with rockers; a cradle—out of service, but waiting, with confidence; in the early cold mornings a snuggle of children, in shirts and chemises, occupying the hearthstone and procrastinating—they could not bear to leave that comfortable place and go out on the wind-swept floor space between the house and kitchen where the general tin basin stood, and wash.

7   Along outside of the front fence ran the country road, dusty in the summertime, and a good place for snakes—they liked to lie in it and sun themselves; when they were rattlesnakes or puff adders, we killed them; when they were black snakes, or racers, or belonged to the fabled "hoop" breed, we fled, without shame; when they were "house snakes," or "garters," we carried them home and put them in Aunt Patsy's work basket for a surprise; for she was prejudiced against snakes, and always when she took the

basket in her lap and they began to climb out of it it disordered her mind. She never could seem to get used to them; her opportunities went for nothing. And she was always cold toward bats, too, and could not bear them; and yet I think a bat is as friendly a bird as there is. My mother was Aunt Patsy's sister and had the same wild superstitions. A bat is beautifully soft and silky; I do not know any creature that is pleasanter to the touch or is more grateful for caressings, if offered in the right spirit. I know all about these coleoptera, because our great cave, three miles below Hannibal, was multitudinously stocked with them, and often I brought them home to amuse my mother with. It was easy to manage if it was a school day, because then I had ostensibly been to school and hadn't any bats. She was not a suspicious person, but full of trust and confidence; and when I said, "There's something in my coat pocket for you," she would put her hand in. But she always took it out again, herself; I didn't have to tell her. It was remarkable, the way she couldn't learn to like private bats. The more experience she had, the more she could not change her views. . . .

Beyond the road where the snakes sunned themselves was a dense young thicket, and through it a dim-lighted path led a quarter of a mile; then out of the dimness one emerged abruptly upon a level great prairie which was covered with wild strawberry plants, vividly starred with prairie pinks, and walled in on all sides by forests. The strawberries were fragrant and fine, and in the season we were generally there in the crisp freshness of the early morning, while the dew beads still sparkled upon the grass and the woods were ringing with the first songs of the birds.

Down the forest slopes to the left were the swings. They were made of bark stripped from hickory saplings. When they became dry they were dangerous. They usually broke when a child was forty feet in the air, and this was why so many bones had to be mended every year. I had no ill luck myself, but none of my cousins escaped. There were eight of them, and at one time and another they broke fourteen arms among them. But it cost next to nothing, for the doctor worked by the year—twenty-five dollars for the whole family. I remember two of the Florida doctors, Chowning and Meredith. They not only tended an entire family for twenty-five dollars a year, but furnished the medicine themselves. Good measure, too. Only the largest persons could hold a whole dose. Castor oil was the principal beverage. . . .

10   The country schoolhouse was three miles from my uncle's farm. It stood in a clearing in the woods and would hold about twenty-five boys and girls. We attended the school with more or less regularity once or twice a week, in summer, walking to it in the cool of the morning by the forest paths, and back in the gloaming at the end of the day. All the pupils brought their dinners in baskets—corn dodger, buttermilk, and other good things—and sat in the shade of the trees at noon and ate them. It is the part of my education which I look back upon with the most satisfaction. My first visit to the school was when I was seven. A strapping girl of fifteen, in the customary sunbonnet and calico dress, asked me if I "used tobacco"—meaning did I chew it. I said no. It roused her scorn. She reported me to all the crowd, and said:

11   "Here is a boy seven years old who can't chew tobacco."

12   By the looks and comments which this produced I realized that I was a degraded object, and was cruelly ashamed of myself. I determined to reform. But I only made myself sick; I was not able to learn to chew tobacco. I learned to smoke fairly well, but that did not conciliate anybody and I remained a poor thing, and characterless. I longed to be respected, but I never was able to rise. Children have but little charity for one another's defects.

13   As I have said, I spent some part of every year at the farm until I was twelve or thirteen years old. The life which I led there with my cousins was full of charm and so is the memory of it yet. I can call back the solemn twilight and mystery of the deep woods, the earthy smells, the faint odors of the wild flowers, the sheen of rain-washed foliage, the rattling clatter of drops when the wind shook the trees, the far-off hammering of woodpeckers and the muffled drumming of wood pheasants in the remoteness of the forest, the snapshot glimpses of disturbed wild creatures scurrying through the grass—I can call it all back and make it as real as it ever was, and as blessed. I can call back the prairie, and its loneliness and peace, and a vast hawk hanging motionless in the sky, with his wings spread wide and the blue of the vault showing through the fringe of their end feathers. I can see the woods in their autumn dress, the oaks purple, the hickories washed with gold, the maples and the sumachs luminous with crimson fires, and I can hear the rustle made by the fallen leaves as we plowed through them. I can see the blue clusters of wild

grapes hanging among the foliage of the saplings, and I remember the taste of them and the smell. I know how the wild blackberries looked, and how they tasted, and the same with the pawpaws, the hazelnuts, and the persimmons; and I can feel the thumping rain, upon my head, of hickory nuts and walnuts when we were out in the frosty dawn to scramble for them with the pigs, and the gusts of wind loosed them and sent them down. I know the stain of blackberries, and how pretty it is, and I know the stain of walnut hulls, and how little it minds soap and water, also what grudged experience it had of either of them. I know the taste of maple sap, and when to gather it, and how to arrange the troughs and the delivery tubes, and how to boil down the juice, and how to hook the sugar after it is made, also how much better hooked sugar tastes than any that is honestly come by, let bigots say what they will. I know how a prize watermelon looks when it is sunning its fat rotundity among pumpkin vines and "simblins"; I know how to tell when it is ripe without "plugging" it; I know how inviting it looks when it is cooling itself in a tub of water under the bed, waiting; I know how it looks when it lies on the table in the sheltered great floor space between house and kitchen, and the children gathered for the sacrifice and their mouths watering; I know the crackling sound it makes when the carving knife enters its end, and I can see the split fly along in front of the blades as the knife cleaves its way to the other end; I can see its halves fall apart and display the rich red meat and the black seeds, and the heart standing up, a luxury fit for the elect; I know how a boy looks behind a yard-long slice of that melon, and I know how he feels; for I have been there. I know the taste of the watermelon which has been honestly come by, and I know the taste of the watermelon which has been acquired by art. Both taste good, but the experienced know which tastes best. I know the look of green apples and peaches and pears on the trees, and I know how entertaining they are when they are inside of a person. I know how ripe ones look when they are piled in pyramids under the trees, and how pretty they are and how vivid their colors. I know how a frozen apple looks, in a barrel down cellar in the wintertime, and how hard it is to bite, and how the frost makes the teeth ache, and yet how good it is, notwithstanding. I know the disposition of elderly people to select the specked apples for the children, and I once knew ways to beat the game. I know the look of an apple that is roasting and sizzling on a hearth on a winter's evening, and I know the comfort that comes of eating it hot, along with some sugar and a drench of cream. I know the delicate art and mystery of so cracking hickory nuts and walnuts on a flatiron with a hammer that the kernels will be delivered whole, and I know how the nuts, taken in conjunction with winter apples, cider, and doughnuts, make old people's old tales and old jokes sound fresh and crisp and enchanting, and juggle an evening away before you know what went with the time. I know the look of Uncle Dan'l's kitchen as it was on the privileged nights, when I was a child, and I can see the white and black children grouped on the hearth, with the firelight playing on their faces and the shadows flickering upon the walls, clear back toward the cavernous gloom of the rear, and I can hear Uncle Dan'l telling the immortal tales which Uncle Remus Harris was to gather into his book and charm the world with, by and by; and I can feel again the creepy joy which quivered through me when the time for the ghost story was reached—and the sense of regret, too, which came over me, for it was always the last story of the evening and there was nothing between it and the unwelcome bed. . . .

Content

1. Even though Twain's opening two paragraphs warn that he is quite capable of remembering anything, "whether it had happened or not," what he says throughout this essay appears true and convincing. Why? Does anything seem too good to be true?

2. Twain recalls how the farm was a "heavenly place for a boy." What made it so? Do his memories of children's broken bones (¶ 9) and his childhood shame at being unable to chew tobacco (¶s 11–12) diminish his pleasant recollections?

Strategies/Structures

1. In places Twain's description involves long lists or catalogs—of foods (¶ 3), of the sights and sounds and activities of farm life (¶s 3–13). How does he vary the lists to keep them appealing?

2. Why does Twain pack so many details into such a long paragraph (¶ 13)? If he had broken it up, where could he have done so? With what effects?

3. Twain also employs some very long sentences. Paragraph 6 consists of two sentences, one of 9 words, the other of 234 words. What devices does he use in long sentences to provide unity? Variety?

4. In this largely descriptive account, Twain provides characterizations of the local doctors (¶ 9), many interpretations ("The life was . . . full of charm," [¶ 13]), and narration of incidents, for instance, of Aunt Patsy and the snakes (¶ 7). Explain how these techniques contribute to the overall picture of life on the farm.

Language

1. Twain uses the language of an adult to recall events from his childhood. Find a typical passage in which he enables us to see the experience as a child would but to imply or offer an adult's interpretation.

2. In the last paragraph (¶ 13) Twain's reminiscences are identified by many sentences beginning with parallel constructions, "I can call back," "I know," "I remember." What is the effect of this much repetition?

For Writing

1. Identify a place that had considerable significance—pleasant or unpleasant—for you as a child, and describe it for an unfamiliar reader to emphasize your attitude toward it. Use sensory details, where appropriate, to help your readers to recreate your experiences.

2. Pick an aspect of your childhood relationship with a parent or other adult, or a critical experience in your elementary schooling, and describe it so the reader shares your experience. Compare, if you wish, with Welty (pp. 29–34), Zikala-Sa (pp. 254–262), Lim (pp. 365–373), or Wright (pp. 409–418).

SCOTT RUSSELL SANDERS

Sanders (born, 1945) grew up in Ohio, earned a Ph.D. in English from Cambridge University in 1971, and has taught ever since at Indiana University. His dozen books include fiction, science fiction, a biography of Audubon, and several collections of personal essays. The essay collections, *In Limestone Country* (1985), *Secrets of the Universe* (1991), *Staying Put* (1993), and *Writing from the Center* (1995), focus on living and writing in the Midwest. Sanders interprets his seemingly diverse work as an integrated whole: "I have long been divided, in my life and in my work, between science and the arts." As a novelist, Sanders focused on "many of the fundamental questions that scientists ask," seeking "to understand our place in nature, trace the sources of our violence, and speculate about the future evolution of our species. My writing . . . is bound together by a web of questions," which he continues to ask in personal essays dealing with "the ways in which human beings come to terms with the practical problems of living on a small planet, in nature and in communities. I am concerned with the life people make together, in marriages and families and towns. . . ."

The elegiac "The Inheritance of Tools" appeared in the award-winning *The Paradise of Bombs* (1987), a collection of personal essays mainly about the American culture of violence. This essay reveals Sanders's concerns, as a writer and as a son, husband, and father, with the inheritance of skills and values through the generations. Here description is explanation, as Sanders shows how tools become not just extensions of the hand and brain, but of the human heart, as the knowledge of how to use and care for them is transmitted from grandfather to father to son to grandchildren— a girl as well as a boy. The ways in which people use tools, and think about tools and care for them, reflect their values and personalities; "each hammer and level and saw is wrapped in a cloud of knowing."

The Inheritance of Tools

1   At just about the hour when my father died, soon after dawn one February morning when ice coated the windows like cataracts, I banged my thumb with a hammer. Naturally I swore at the hammer, the reckless thing, and in the moment of swearing I thought of what my father would say: "If you'd try hitting the nail it would go in a whole lot faster. Don't you know your thumb's not as hard as that hammer?" We both were doing carpentry that day, but far apart. He was building cupboards at my brother's place in Oklahoma; I was at home in Indiana, putting up a wall in the basement to make a bedroom for my daughter. By the time my mother called with news of his death—the long distance wires whittling her voice until it seemed too thin to bear

the weight of what she had to say—my thumb was swollen. A week or so later a white scar in the shape of a crescent moon began to show above the cuticle and month by month it rose across the pink sky of my thumbnail. It took the better part of a year for the scar to disappear, and every time I noticed it I thought of my father.

The hammer had belonged to him, and to his father before   2 him. The three of us have used it to build houses and barns and chicken coops, to upholster chairs and crack walnuts, to make doll furniture and bookshelves and jewelry boxes. The head is scratched and pockmarked, like an old plowshare that has been working rocky fields, and it gives off the sort of dull sheen you see on fast creek water in the shade. It is a finishing hammer, about the weight of a bread loaf, too light, really, for framing walls, too heavy for cabinet work, with a curved claw for pulling nails, a rounded head for pounding, a fluted neck for looks, and a hickory handle for strength.

The present handle is my third one, bought from a lumber-   3 yard in Tennessee, down the road from where my brother and I were helping my father build his retirement house. I broke the previous one by trying to pull sixteen-penny nails out of floor joists—a foolish thing to do with a finishing hammer, as my father pointed out. "You ever hear of a crowbar?" he said. No telling how many handles he and my grandfather had gone through before me. My grandfather used to cut down hickory trees on his farm, saw them into slabs, cure the planks in his hayloft, and carve handles with a drawknife. The grain in hickory is crooked and knotty, and therefore tough, hard to split, like the grain in the two men who owned this hammer before me.

After proposing marriage to a neighbor girl, my grandfather   4 used this hammer to build a house for his bride on a stretch of river bottom in northern Mississippi. The lumber for the place, like the hickory for the handle, was cut on his own land. By the day of the wedding he had not quite finished the house, and so right after the ceremony he took his wife home and put her to work. My grandmother had worn her Sunday dress for the wedding, with a fringe of lace tacked on around the hem in honor of the occasion. She removed this lace and folded it away before going out to help my grandfather nail siding on the house. "There she was in her good dress," he told me some fifty-odd years after that wedding day, "holding up them long pieces of clapboard while I hammered, and together we got the place covered up before dark." As the family grew to four, six, eight, and eventually thirteen, my grandfather used this hammer to enlarge his house room by room, like a chambered nautilus expanding its shell.

5   By and by the hammer was passed along to my father. One day he was up on the roof of our pony barn nailing shingles with it, when I stepped out the kitchen door to call him for supper. Before I could yell, something about the sight of him straddling the spine of that roof and swinging the hammer caught my eye and made me hold my tongue. I was five or six years old, and the world's commonplaces were still news to me. He would pull a nail from the pouch at his waist, bring the hammer down, and a moment later the *thunk* of the blow would reach my ears. And that is what had stopped me in my tracks and stilled my tongue, that momentary gap between seeing and hearing the blow. Instead of yelling from the kitchen door, I ran to the barn and climbed two rungs up the ladder—as far as I was allowed to go—and spoke quietly to my father. On our walk to the house he explained that sound takes time to make its way through air. Suddenly the world seemed larger, the air more dense, if sound could be held back like any ordinary traveler.

6   By the time I started using this hammer, at about the age when I discovered the speed of sound, it already contained houses and mysteries for me. The smooth handle was one my grandfather had made. In those days I needed both hands to swing it. My father would start a nail in a scrap of wood, and I would pound away until I bent it over.

7   "Looks like you got ahold of some of those rubber nails," he would tell me. "Here, let me see if I can find you some stiff ones." And he would rummage in a drawer until he came up with a fistful of more cooperative nails. "Look at the head," he would tell me. "Don't look at your hands, don't look at the hammer. Just look at the head of that nail and pretty soon you'll learn to hit it square."

8   Pretty soon I did learn. While he worked in the garage cutting dovetail joints for a drawer or skinning a deer or tuning an engine, I would hammer nails. I made innocent blocks of wood look like porcupines. He did not talk much in the midst of his

tools, but he kept up a nearly ceaseless humming, slipping in and out of a dozen tunes in an afternoon, often running back over the same stretch of melody again and again, as if searching for a way out. When the humming did cease, I knew he was faced with a task requiring great delicacy or concentration, and I took care not to distract him.

He kept scraps of wood in a cardboard box—the ends of   9 two-by-fours, slabs of shelving and plywood, odd pieces of molding—and everything in it was fair game. I nailed scraps together to fashion what I called boats or houses, but the results usually bore only faint resemblance to the visions I carried in my head. I would hold up these constructions to show my father, and he would turn them over in his hands admiringly, speculating about what they might be. My cobbled-together guitars might have been alien spaceships, my barns might have been models of Aztec temples, each wooden contraption might have been anything but what I had set out to make.

Now and again I would feel the need to have a chunk of   10 wood shaped or shortened before I riddled it with nails, and I would clamp it in a vise and scrape at it with a handsaw. My father would let me lacerate the board until my arm gave out, and then he would wrap his hand around mine and help me finish the cut, showing me how to use my thumb to guide the blade, how to pull back on the saw to keep it from binding, how to let my shoulder do the work.

"Don't force it," he would say, "just drag it easy and give the   11 teeth a chance to bite."

As the saw teeth bit down, the wood released its smell, each   12 kind with its own fragrance, oak or walnut or cherry or pine— usually pine because it was the softest, easiest for a child to work. No matter how weathered and gray the board, no matter how warped and cracked, inside there was this smell waiting, as of something freshly baked. I gathered every smidgen of sawdust and stored it away in coffee cans, which I kept in a drawer of the workbench. When I did not feel like hammering nails, I would dump my sawdust on the concrete floor of the garage and landscape it into highways and farms and towns, running miniature cars and trucks along miniature roads. Looming as huge as a colossus, my father worked over and around me, now and again bending down to inspect my work, careful not to trample my creations. It was a landscape that smelled dizzyingly of wood. Even after a bath my skin would carry the smell, and so would my father's hair, when he lifted me for a bedtime hug.

13   I tell these things not only from memory but also from recent observation, because my own son now turns blocks of wood into nailed porcupines, dumps cans full of sawdust at my feet and sculpts highways on the floor. He learns how to swing a hammer from the elbow instead of the wrist, how to lay his thumb beside the blade to guide a saw, how to tap a chisel with a wooden mallet, how to mark a hole with an awl before starting a drill bit. My daughter did the same before him, and even now, on the brink of teenage aloofness, she will occasionally drag out my box of wood scraps and carpenter something. So I have seen my apprenticeship to wood and tools reenacted in each of my children, as my father saw his own apprenticeship renewed in me.

14   The saw I use belonged to him, as did my level and both of my squares, and all four tools had belonged to his father. The blade of the saw is the bluish color of gun barrels, and the maple handle, dark from the sweat of hands, is inscribed with curving leaf designs. The level is a shaft of walnut two feet long, edged with brass and pierced by three round windows in which air bubbles float in oil-filled tubes of glass. The middle window serves for testing if a surface is horizontal, the others for testing if a surface is plumb or vertical. My grandfather used to carry this level on the gun rack behind the seat in his pickup, and when I rode with him I would turn around to watch the bubbles dance. The larger of the two squares is called a framing square, a flat steel elbow, so beat up and tarnished you can barely make out the rows of numbers that show how to figure the cuts on rafters. The smaller one is called a try square, for marking right angles, with a blued steel blade for the shank and a brass-faced block of cherry for the head.

15   I was taught early on that a saw is not to be used apart from a square: "If you're going to cut a piece of wood," my father insisted, "you owe it to the tree to cut it straight."

16   Long before studying geometry, I learned there is a mystical virtue in right angles. There is an unspoken morality in seeking the level and the plumb. A house will stand, a table will bear weight,

the sides of a box will hold together, only if the joints are square and the members upright. When the bubble is lined up between two marks etched in the glass tube of a level, you have aligned yourself with the forces that hold the universe together. When you miter the corners of a picture frame each angle must be exactly forty-five degrees, as they are in the perfect triangles of Pythagoras, not a degree more or less. Otherwise the frame will hang crookedly, as if ashamed of itself and of its maker. No matter if the joints you are cutting do not show. Even if you are butting two pieces of wood together inside a cabinet, where no one except a wrecking crew will ever see them, you must take pains to ensure that the ends are square and the studs are plumb.

I took pains over the wall I was building on the day my   17
father died. Not long after that wall was finished—paneled with tongue-and-groove boards of yellow pine, the nail holes filled with putty and the wood all stained and sealed—I came close to wrecking it one afternoon when my daughter ran howling up the stairs to announce that her gerbils had escaped from their cage and were hiding in my brand new wall. She could hear them scratching and squeaking behind her bed. Impossible! I said. How on earth could they get inside my drum-tight wall? Through the heating vent, she answered. I went downstairs, pressed my ear to the honey-colored wood, and heard the *scritch scritch* of tiny feet.

"What can we do?" my daughter wailed. "They'll starve to   18
death, they'll die of thirst, they'll suffocate."

"Hold on," I soothed. "I'll think of something."   19

While I thought and she fretted, the radio on her bedside   20
delivered us the headlines: Several thousand people had died in a city in India from a poisonous cloud that had leaked overnight from a chemical plant. A nuclear-powered submarine had been launched. Rioting continued in South Africa. An airplane had been hijacked in the Mediterranean. Authorities calculated that several thousand homeless people slept on the streets within sight of the Washington Monument. I felt my usual helplessness in the face of all these calamities. But here was my daughter, weeping because her gerbils were holed up in a wall. This calamity I could handle.

"Don't worry," I told her. "We'll set food and water by the   21
heating vent and lure them out. And if that doesn't do the trick, I'll tear the wall apart until we find them."

22   She stopped crying and gazed at me. "You'd really tear it apart? Just for my gerbils? The *wall?*" Astonishment slowed her down only for a second, however, before she ran to the workbench and began tugging at drawers, saying, "Let's see, what'll we need? Crowbar. Hammer. Chisels. I hope we don't have to use them—but just in case."

23   We didn't need the wrecking tools. I never had to assault my handsome wall, because the gerbils eventually came out to nibble at a dish of popcorn. But for several hours I studied the tongue-and-groove skin I had nailed up on the day of my father's death, considering where to begin prying. There were no gaps in that wall, no crooked joints.

24   I had botched a great many pieces of wood before I mastered the right angle with a saw, botched even more before I learned to miter a joint. The knowledge of these things resides in my hands and eyes and the webwork of muscles, not in the tools. There are machines for sale—powered miter boxes and radial-arm saws, for instance—that will enable any casual soul to cut proper angles in boards. The skill is invested in the gadget instead of the person who uses it, and this is what distinguishes a machine from a tool. If I had to earn my keep by making furniture or building houses, I suppose I would buy powered saws and pneumatic nailers; the need for speed would drive me to it. But since I carpenter only for my own pleasure or to help neighbors or to remake the house around the ears of my family, I stick with hand tools. Most of the ones I own were given to me by my father who also taught me how to wield them. The tools in my workbench are a double inheritance, for each hammer and level and saw is wrapped in a cloud of knowing.

25   All of these tools are a pleasure to look at and to hold. Merchants would never paste NEW NEW NEW! signs on them in stores. Their designs are old because they work, because they serve their purpose well. Like folk songs and aphorisms and the grainy bits of language, these tools have been pared down to essentials. I look at my claw hammer, the distillation of a hundred generations of carpenters, and consider that it holds up well beside those other classics—Greek vases, Gregorian chants, *Don Quixote,* barbed fish hooks, candles, spoons. Knowledge of hammering stretches back to the earliest humans who squatted beside fires, chipping flints.

Anthropologists have a lovely name for those unworked rocks that served as the earliest hammers. "Dawn stones," they are called. Their only qualification for the work, aside from hardness, is that they fit the hand. Our ancestors used them for grinding corn, tapping awls, smashing bones. From dawn stones to this claw hammer is a great leap in time, but no great distance in design or imagination.

On that iced-over February morning when I smashed my thumb   26
with the hammer, I was down in the basement framing the wall that my daughter's gerbils would later hide in. I was thinking of my father, as I always did whenever I built anything, thinking how he would have gone about the work, hearing in memory what he would have said about the wisdom of hitting the nail instead of my thumb. I had the studs and plates nailed together all square and trim, and was lifting the wall into place when the phone rang upstairs. My wife answered, and in a moment she came to the basement door and called down softly to me. The stillness in her voice made me drop the framed wall and hurry upstairs. She told me my father was dead. Then I heard the details over the phone from my mother. Building a set of cupboards for my brother in Oklahoma, he had knocked off work early the previous afternoon because of cramps in his stomach. Early this morning, on his way into the kitchen of my brother's trailer, maybe going for a glass of water, so early that no one else was awake, he slumped down on the linoleum and his heart quit.

For several hours I paced around inside my house, upstairs   27
and down, in and out of every room, looking for the right door to open and knowing there was no such door. My wife and children followed me and wrapped me in arms and backed away again, circling and staring as if I were on fire. Where was the door, the door, the door? I kept wondering. My smashed thumb turned purple and throbbed, making me furious. I wanted to cut it off and rush outside and scrape away at the snow and hack a hole in the frozen earth and bury the shameful thing.

I went down into the basement, opened a drawer in my   28
workbench, and stared at the ranks of chisels and knives. Oiled and sharp, as my father would have kept them, they gleamed at me like teeth. I took up a clasp knife, pried out the longest blade, and tested

the edge on the hair of my forearm. A tuft came away cleanly, and I saw my father testing the sharpness of tools on his own skin, the blades of axes and knives and gouges and hoes, saw the red hair shaved off in patches from his arms and the backs of his hands. "That will cut bear," he would say. He never cut a bear with his blades, now my blades, but he cut deer, dirt, wood. I closed the knife and put it away. Then I took up the hammer and went back to work on my daughter's wall, snugging the bottom plate against a chalk line on the floor, shimming the top plate against the joists overhead, plumbing the studs with my level, making sure before I drove the first nail that every line was square and true.

Content

1. Sanders characterizes his father, and grandfather, and himself by showing how they used tools and transmitted this knowledge to their children. What characteristics do they have in common? Why does he omit any differences they might have, focusing on their similarities?

2. Sanders distinguishes between a machine and a tool, saying "The skill is invested in the gadget instead of the person who uses it" (¶ 24). Why does he favor tools over machines? Do you agree with his definition? With his preference?

Strategies/Structures

1. What is the point of this essay? Why does Sanders begin and end with the relation between banging his thumb with a hammer and his father's death?

2. Why does Sanders include the vignette of his daughter and her gerbils, which escaped inside the "drum-tight wall" he had just built (¶ 17–23)? Would he really have wrecked the wall to get the gerbils out?

3. For what audience is Sanders writing? Does it matter whether or not his readers know how to use tools?

Language

1. Sanders occasionally quotes his father's advice (¶s 7, 11, 15). What do these quotations reveal about his father?

2. Show, through specific examples, how Sanders's language fits his subject, tools, and the people who use them. Consider phrases such as "ice coated the windows like cataracts" (¶ 1) and "making sure before I drove the first nail that every line was square and true" (¶ 28).

For Writing

1. Sanders defines the "inheritance" of tools as, "So I have seen my apprenticeship to wood and tools re-enacted in each of my children, as my father saw his own apprenticeship renewed in me." (¶ 13). Tell the story of your own apprenticeship with a tool or collection of tools (kitchen utensils, art supplies, a sewing machine, computer, skis, or other equipment). The explanation of your increasing skill in learning to use it should be intertwined with your relationship with the person who taught you how to use it (not necessarily a family member) and the manner of the teaching—and of the learning. How many generations of teachers and learners does your inheritance involve? If you have taught others how to use it, incorporate this as well.

2. Sanders says that the classic designs of tools "are old because they work, because they serve their purpose well . . . pared down to essentials" (¶ 25). Pick another classic or type of classic (Sanders mentions "Greek vases, Gregorian chants, *Don Quixote,* barbed fish hooks, candles, spoons") and explain why, in your experience and opinion, it's a classic. (How much your intended audience knows about the subject will determine how extensively you need to explain its characteristics.) Then, use your explanation to define a "classic."

JOAN DIDION

Novelist and essayist Didion was born (1934) in Sacramento, California, and educated at the University of California, Berkeley. Since 1964 she and her husband, writer John Gregory Dunne, have collaborated on screenplays, including *A Star Is Born* (1976) and *Up Close and Personal* (1996). In her novels, including *A Book of Common Prayer* (1977) and *Democracy* (1984), and two essay collections, *Slouching Towards Bethlehem* (1968) and *The White Album* (1979), Didion writes to confound the moral vacuum she finds in people estranged from the traditional values of religion, family, and society.

Estrangement from tradition permeates "Marrying Absurd," as Didion focuses on the discrepancy between our exalted expectations of marriage as a sacrament and the reality of this experience in Las Vegas, where "marriage, like craps, is a game to be played when the table seems hot." Didion uses a number of examples to make her point: the speedy judge who compresses the ceremony from five minutes into three; the commercial Las Vegas wedding chapels, as divorced from life in the rest of the world as Las Vegas itself is; the 11 p.m. wedding of a drunken bride rushing to perform in "the midnight show"; and the oddly formal weddings of innocents who confuse the accessories (formal clothes and pink champagne) with the essence of a personally significant ceremony. Through vivid, compelling examples Didion defines a city and a travesty of a ceremony—and the people who partake of both. In accord with her own advice, *"listen to me, see it my way, change your mind,"* Didion promotes her moral vision.

Marrying Absurd

1   To be married in Las Vegas, Clark County, Nevada, a bride must swear that she is eighteen or has parental permission and a bridegroom that he is twenty-one or has parental permission. Someone must put up five dollars for the license. (On Sundays and holidays, fifteen dollars. The Clark County Courthouse issues marriage licenses at any time of the day or night except between noon and one in the afternoon, between eight and nine in the evening, and between four and five in the morning.) Nothing else is required. The State of Nevada, alone among these United States, demands neither a premarital blood test nor a waiting period before or after the issuance of a marriage license. Driving in across the Mojave from Los Angeles, one sees the signs way out on the desert, looming up from that moonscape of rattlesnakes and mesquite, even before the Las Vegas lights appear like a mirage on the horizon: "GETTING MARRIED? Free License Information First Strip Exit." Perhaps the Las Vegas wedding industry achieved its peak operational efficiency between 9:00 p.m. and midnight of August 26, 1965, an otherwise unremarkable Thursday which happened to be, by Presidential order, the last day on which anyone could improve his draft status merely by getting married. One hundred and seventy-one couples were pronounced man and wife in the name of Clark County and the State of Nevada that night, sixty-seven of them by a single justice of the

peace, Mr. James A. Brennan. Mr. Brennan did one wedding at the Dunes and the other sixty-six in his office, and charged each couple eight dollars. One bride lent her veil to six others. "I got it down from five to three minutes," Mr. Brennan said later of his feat. "I could've married them *en masse*, but they're people, not cattle. People expect more when they get married."

What people who get married in Las Vegas actually do 2 expect—what, in the largest sense, their "expectations" are— strikes one as a curious and self-contradictory business. Las Vegas is the most extreme and allegorical of American settlements, bizarre and beautiful in its venality and in its devotion to immediate gratification, a place the tone of which is set by mobsters and call girls and ladies' room attendants with amyl nitrite poppers in their uniform pockets. Almost everyone notes that there is no "time" in Las Vegas, no night and no day and no past and no future (no Las Vegas casino, however, has taken the obliteration of the ordinary time sense quite so far as Harold's Club in Reno, which for a while issued, at odd intervals in the day and night, mimeographed "bulletins" carrying news from the world outside); neither is there any logical sense of where one is. One is standing on a highway in the middle of a vast hostile desert looking at an eighty-foot sign which blinks "STARDUST" or "CAESAR'S PALACE." Yes, but what does that explain? This geographical implausibility reinforces the sense that what happens there has no connection with "real" life; Nevada cities like Reno and Carson are ranch towns, Western towns, places behind which there is some historical imperative. But Las Vegas seems to exist only in the eye of the beholder. All of which makes it an extraordinarily stimulating and interesting place, but an odd one in which to want to wear a candlelight satin Priscilla of Boston wedding dress with Chantilly lace insets, tapered sleeves and a detachable modified train.

And yet the Las Vegas wedding business seems to appeal to 3 precisely that impulse. "Sincere and Dignified Since 1954," one wedding chapel advertises. There are nineteen such wedding chapels in Las Vegas, intensely competitive, each offering better, faster, and, by implication, more sincere services than the next: Our Photos Best Anywhere, Your Wedding on A Phonograph Record, Candlelight with Your Ceremony, Honeymoon Accommodations, Free Transportation from Your Motel to Courthouse to Chapel and Return to Motel, Religious or Civil Ceremonies, Dressing Rooms, Flowers, Rings, Announcements, Witnesses Available, and Ample Parking. All of these services, like most others in Las Vegas (sauna baths, payroll-check cashing, chinchilla coats for sale or rent) are offered twenty-four hours a day, seven days a week, presumably on the premise that marriage, like craps, is a game to be played when the table seems hot.

4   But what strikes one most about the Strip chapels, with their wishing wells and stained-glass paper windows and their artificial bouvardia, is that so much of their business is by no means a matter of simple convenience, of late-night liaisons between show girls and baby Crosbys. Of course there is some of that. (One night about eleven o'clock in Las Vegas I watched a bride in an orange minidress and masses of flame-colored hair stumble from a Strip chapel on the arm of her bridegroom, who looked the part of the expendable nephew in movies like *Miami Syndicate*. "I gotta get the kids," the bride whimpered. "I gotta pick up the sitter, I gotta get to the midnight show." "What you gotta get," the bridegroom said, opening the door of a Cadillac Coupe de Ville and watching her crumple on the seat, "is sober.") But Las Vegas seems to offer something other than "convenience"; it is merchandising "niceness," the facsimile of proper ritual, to children who do not know how else to find it, how to make the arrangements, how to do it "right." All day and evening long on the Strip, one sees actual wedding parties, waiting under the harsh lights at a crosswalk, standing uneasily in the parking lot of the Frontier while the photographer hired by The Little Church of the West ("Wedding Place of the Stars") certifies the occasion, takes the picture: the bride in a veil and white satin pumps, the bridegroom usually in a white dinner jacket, and even an attendant or two, a sister or a best friend in hot-pink *peau de soie*, a flirtation veil, a carnation nosegay. "When I Fall in Love It Will Be Forever," the organist plays, and then a few bars of Lohengrin. The mother cries; the stepfather, awkward in his role, invites the chapel hostess to join them for a drink at the Sands. The hostess declines with a professional smile; she has already transferred her interest to the group waiting outside. One bride out, another in, and again the sign goes up on the chapel door: "One moment please—Wedding."

I sat next to one such wedding party in a Strip restaurant the 5
last time I was in Las Vegas. The marriage had just taken place; the
bride still wore her dress, the mother her corsage. A bored waiter
poured out a few swallows of pink champagne ("on the house")
for everyone but the bride, who was too young to be served.
"You'll need something with more kick than that," the bride's
father said with heavy jocularity to his new son-in-law; the ritual
jokes about the wedding night had a certain Panglossian character, since the bride was clearly several months pregnant. Another
round of pink champagne, this time not on the house, and the
bride began to cry. "It was just as nice," she sobbed, "as I hoped
and dreamed it would be."

Content

1. How does Didion's essay illustrate her observation that "there is no
'time' in Las Vegas, no night and no day and no past and no future" (¶ 2)?
2. How does Didion illustrate her point that in Las Vegas there is no
"logical sense of where one is" (¶ 2)? That Las Vegas is geographically
implausible (¶ 2)?
3. Do you think that Didion agrees with the Las Vegas assumption that
"marriage, like craps, is a game to be played when the table seems hot"
(¶ 3)? What illustrations does she provide to demonstrate that the patrons
of Las Vegas believe this?
4. Does the concluding illustration of the pregnant, underage bride sob-
bing with pleasure at the "niceness" of her wedding (¶ 5) support Didion's
assertion that Las Vegas is "merchandising 'niceness,' the facsimile of
proper ritual, to children who do not know how else to find it" (¶ 4)?

Strategies/Structures

1. Why does Didion emphasize so early in the essay the juxtaposition of
the "moonscape of rattlesnakes and mesquite" with the "Getting Married"
signs (¶ 1)? The hasty weddings and the view of the justice of the peace
who married sixty-seven couples in three hours (¶ 1)?
2. What is Didion's prevailing tone? Find some instances of it. Can she
count on her readers to share her attitude toward Las Vegas weddings?
Does Didion's intended audience include the kind of people who might
get married in Las Vegas?

Language

1. What language is Didion imitating when she refers to "a candlelight satin Priscilla of Boston wedding dress with Chantilly lace insets, tapered sleeves and a detachable modified train" (¶ 2)? Why does she employ only one comma in this heavily modified sequence that might ordinarily use many more?

2. In paragraph 3 Didion quotes or paraphrases many advertising slogans. For what purposes? With what effects?

For Writing

1. Describe, for people who haven't been there, a place—either an entertainment spot, a college, a whole city or town—(as Didion does Las Vegas), or a family property (as Twain does in "Uncle John's Farm" [pp. 312–318]). Through carefully selected details, convey not only an impression of the place, but your attitude toward it, favorable or otherwise.

2. Connect two or three anecdotes or vignettes to illustrate a thesis, as Didion does with the sixty-seven speedy weddings (¶ 1), the wedding of the showgirl and the "expendable nephew" (¶ 4), and the wedding of the underage pregnant bride (¶ 5).

KATHLEEN NORRIS

"The Beautiful Places" is the first chapter of *Dakota: A Spiritual Geography* (1993), the book Norris (born, 1947) wrote as "an invitation to a land of little rain and few trees, dry summer winds and harsh winters, a land rich in grass and sky and surprises." She and her husband, fellow poet David Dwyer, moved in 1973 from New York City to "the small house in Lemmon, South Dakota"—still an "isolated" frontier town "on the border between North and South Dakota"—that her grandparents built in 1923. Norris, like the monks with whom she identifies, "made a counter-cultural choice to live in what the rest of the world considers a barren waste."

For Norris, the Plains are essential to her "growth as a writer, they have formed [her] spiritually" and "have made [her] a human being." After indifference to religion for much of her life, for the past dozen years Norris has been a Benedictine oblate (as well as a lay Presbyterian preacher)—a lay person attracted to the Benedictine "family spirit of religious community," ideal of moderation, and "no unusual austerity in religious life." The "rhythms of monasticism" gave her "a heightened sense of the power of language," as reflected in both her poetry, *Little Girls in Church* (1995), and her prose, *The Cloister Walk* (1996), as well as in *Dakota*. In this essay, the description of spirituality is embedded in the description of the landscape. They are reciprocal metaphors, expressing Norris's view that natural phenomena remind us of our own uncertainty and inability to control nature: "Most of us can have some kind of faith that the seed is going to grow, but we don't know how it happens. We have to let it sit there in the dark and germinate itself."

The Beautiful Places

The Scarecrow sighed. "Of course I cannot understand it," he said. "If your heads were stuffed with straw like mine, you would probably all live in the beautiful places, and then Kansas would have no people at all. It is fortunate for Kansas that you have brains."

L. FRANK BAUM, *The Wizard of Oz*

T he high plains, the beginning of the desert West, often act as   1
a crucible for those who inhabit them. Like Jacob's angel, the region requires that you wrestle with it before it bestows a blessing. This can mean driving through a snowstorm on icy roads, wondering whether you'll have to pull over and spend the night in your car, only to emerge under tag ends of clouds into a clear sky blazing with stars. Suddenly you know what you're seeing: the earth has turned to face the center of the galaxy, and many more stars are visible than the ones we usually see on our wing of the spiral.

Or a vivid double rainbow marches to the east, following the   2
wild summer storm that nearly blew you off the road. The storm sky is gunmetal gray, but to the west the sky is peach streaked with crimson. The land and sky of the West often fill what Thoreau termed our "need to witness our limits transgressed." Nature, in Dakota, can indeed be an experience of the holy.

3   More Americans than ever, well over 70 percent, now live in urban areas and tend to see Plains land as empty. What they really mean is devoid of human presence. Most visitors to Dakota travel on interstate highways that will take them as quickly as possible through the region, past our large cities to such attractions as the Badlands and the Black Hills. Looking at the expanse of land in between, they may wonder why a person would choose to live in such a barren place, let alone love it. But mostly they are bored: they turn up the car stereo, count the miles to civilization, and look away.

4   Dakota is a painful reminder of human limits, just as cities and shopping malls are attempts to deny them. This book is an invitation to a land of little rain and few trees, dry summer winds and harsh winters, a land rich in grass and sky and surprises. On a crowded planet, this is a place inhabited by few, and by the circumstance of inheritance, I am one of them. Nearly twenty years ago I returned to the holy ground of my childhood summers; I moved from New York City to the house my mother had grown up in, in an isolated town on the border between North and South Dakota.

5   More than any other place I lived as a child or young adult—Virginia, Illinois, Hawaii, Vermont, New York—this is my spiritual geography, the place where I've wrestled my story out of the circumstances of landscape and inheritance. The word "geography" derives from the Greek words for earth and writing, and writing about Dakota has been my means of understanding that inheritance and reclaiming what is holy in it. Of course Dakota has always been such a matrix for its Native American inhabitants. But their tradition is not mine, and in returning to the Great Plains, where two generations of my family lived before me, I had to build my own traditions, those of the Christian West.

6   When a friend referred to the western Dakotas as the Cappadocia of North America, I was handed an essential connection between the spirituality of the landscape I inhabit and that of the fourth-century monastics who set up shop in Cappadocia and the deserts of Egypt. Like those monks, I made a countercultural choice to live in what the rest of the world considers a barren waste. Like them, I had to stay in this place, like a scarecrow in a field, and hope for the brains to see its beauty. My idea of what makes a place beautiful had to change, and it has. The city no

longer appeals to me for the cultural experiences and possessions I might acquire there, but because its population is less homogenous than Plains society. Its holiness is to be found in being open to humanity in all its diversity. And the western Plains now seem bountiful in their emptiness, offering solitude and room to grow.

I want to make it clear that my move did not take me "back 7 to the land" in the conventional sense. I did not strike out on my own to make a go of it with "an acre and a cow," as a Hungarian friend naively imagined. As the homesteaders of the early twentieth century soon found out, it is not possible to survive on even 160 acres in western Dakota. My move was one that took me deep into the meaning of inheritance, as I had to try to fit myself into a complex network of long-established relationships.

My husband and I live in the small house in Lemmon, South 8 Dakota, that my grandparents built in 1923. We moved there after they died because my mother, brother, and sisters, who live in Honolulu, did not want to hold an estate auction, the usual procedure when the beneficiaries of an inheritance on the Plains live far away. I offered to move there and manage the farm interests (land and a cattle herd) that my grandparents left us. David Dwyer, my husband, also a poet, is a New York City native who spent his childhood summers in the Adirondacks, and he had enough sense of adventure to agree to this. We expected to be in Dakota for just a few years.

It's hard to say why we stayed. A growing love of the prairie 9 landscape and the quiet of a small town, inertia, and because as freelance writers, we found we had the survival skills suitable for a frontier. We put together a crazy quilt of jobs: I worked in the public library and as an artist-in-residence in both Dakotas; I also did freelance writing and bookkeeping. David tended bar, wrote computer programs for a number of businesses in the region, and did freelance translation of French literature for several publishers. In 1979 we plunged into the cable television business with some friends, one of whom is an electronics expert. David learned how to climb poles and put up the hardware, and I kept the books. It was a good investment; after selling the company we found that we had bought ourselves a good three years to write. In addition, I still do bookkeeping for my family's farm business: the land is leased to people I've known all my life, people who have rented our land for two generations and also farm their own land and maintain their own cattle herds, an arrangement that is common in western Dakota.

10   In coming to terms with my inheritance, and pursuing my vocation as a writer, I have learned, as both farmers and writers have discovered before me, that it is not easy to remain on the Plains. Only one of North Dakota's best-known writers—Richard Critchfield, Louise Erdrich, Lois Hudson, Thomas McGrath, and Larry Woiwode—currently lives in the state. And writing the truth about the Dakota experience can be a thankless task. I recently discovered that Lois Hudson's magnificent novel of the Dakota Dust Bowl, *The Bones of Plenty*, a book arguably better than *The Grapes of Wrath*, was unknown to teachers and librarians in a town not thirty miles from where the novel is set. The shame of it is that Hudson's book could have helped these people better understand their current situation, the economic crisis forcing many families off the land. Excerpts from *The Grapes of Wrath* were in a textbook used in the school, but students could keep them at a safe distance, part of that remote entity called "American literature" that has little relation to their lives.

11   The Plains are full of what a friend here calls "good telling stories," and while our sense of being forgotten by the rest of the world makes it all the more important that we preserve them and pass them on, instead we often neglect them. Perversely, we do not even claim those stories which have attracted national attention. Both John Neihardt and Frederick Manfred have written about Hugh Glass, a hunter and trapper mauled by a grizzly bear in 1823 at the confluence of the Little Moreau and Grand rivers just south of Lemmon. Left for dead by his companions, he crawled and limped some two hundred miles southeast, to the trading post at Fort Kiowa on the Missouri River. Yet when Manfred wanted to give a reading in Lemmon a few years ago, the publicist was dismissed by a high school principal who said, "Who's he? Why would our students be interested?" Manfred's audience of eighty—large for Lemmon—consisted mainly of the people who remembered him from visits he'd made in the early 1950s while researching his novel *Lord Grizzly*.

12   Thus are the young disenfranchised while their elders drown in details, "story" reduced to the social column of the weekly newspaper that reports on family reunions, card parties, even shopping

excursions to a neighboring town. But real story is as hardy as grass, and it survives in Dakota in oral form. Good storytelling is one thing rural whites and Indians have in common. But Native Americans have learned through harsh necessity that people who survive encroachment by another culture need story to survive. And a storytelling tradition is something Plains people share with both ancient and contemporary monks: we learn our ways of being and reinforce our values, by telling tales about each other.

One of my favorite monastic stories concerns two fourth-century monks who "spent fifty years mocking their temptations by saying 'After this winter, we will leave here.' When the summer came, they said, 'After this summer, we will go away from here.' They passed all their lives in this way." These ancient monks sound remarkably like the farmers I know in Dakota who live in what they laconically refer to as "next-year country." We hold on to hopes for next year every year in western Dakota: hoping that droughts will end; hoping that our crops won't be hailed out in the few rainstorms that come; hoping that it won't be too windy on the day we harvest, blowing away five bushels an acre; hoping (usually against hope) that if we get a fair crop, we'll be able to get a fair price for it. Sometimes survival is the only blessing that the terrifying angel of the Plains bestows. Still, there are those born and raised here who can't imagine living anywhere else. There are also those who are drawn here—teachers willing to take the lowest salaries in the nation; clergy with theological degrees from Princeton, Cambridge, and Zurich who want to serve small rural churches—who find that they cannot remain for long. Their professional mobility sets them apart and becomes a liability in an isolated Plains community where outsiders are treated with an uneasy mix of hospitality and rejection.

"Extremes," John R. Milton suggests in his history of South Dakota, is "perhaps the key word for Dakota . . . What happens to extremes is that they come together, and the result is a kind of tension." I make no attempt in this book to resolve the tensions and contradictions I find in the Dakotas between hospitality and insularity, change and inertia, stability and instability, possibility and limitation, between hope and despair, between open hearts and closed minds.

I suspect that these are the ordinary contradictions of human life, and that they are so visible in Dakota because we are

13

14

15

340   *Description*

so few people living in a stark landscape. We are at the point of
transition between East and West in America, geographically and
psychically isolated from either coast, and unlike either the Midwest or the desert West. South Dakota has been dubbed both the
Sunshine State and the Blizzard State, and both designations have
a basis in fact. Without a strong identity we become a mythic
void; "the Great Desolation" as novelist Ole Rolvaag wrote early
in this century, or "The American Outback," as *Newsweek* designated us a few years ago.

16   Geographical and cultural identity is confused even within
the Dakotas. The eastern regions of both states have more in
common with each other than with the area west of the Missouri,
colloquially called the "West River." Although I commonly use the
term "Dakota" to refer to both Dakotas, most of my experience is
centered in this western region, and it seems to me that, especially
in western Dakota we live in tension between myth and truth. Are
we cowboys or farmers? Are we fiercely independent frontier
types or community builders? One myth that haunts us is that the
small town is a stable place. The land around us was divided
neatly in 160-acre rectangular sections, following the Homestead
Act of 1863 (creating many section-line roads with 90-degree
turns). But our human geography has never been as orderly. The
western Dakota communities settled by whites are, and always
have been, remarkably unstable. The Dakotas have always been
a place to be *from:* some 80 percent of homesteaders left within
the first twenty years of settlement, and our boom-and-bust agricultural and oil industry economy has kept people moving in and
out (mostly out) ever since. Many small-town schools and pulpits
operate with revolving doors, adding to the instability.

17   When I look at the losses we've sustained in western Dakota
since 1980 (about one fifth of the population in Perkins County,
where I live, and a full third in neighboring Corson County) and
at the human cost in terms of anger, distrust, and grief, it is the
prairie descendants of the ancient desert monastics, the monks
and nuns of Benedictine communities in the Dakotas, who inspire
me to hope. One of the vows a Benedictine makes is *stability:* commitment to a particular community, a particular place. If this vow
is countercultural by contemporary American standards, it is
countercultural in the way that life on the Plains often calls us
to be. Benedictines represent continuity in the boom-and-bust

cycles of the Plains; they incarnate, and can articulate, the reasons people want to stay.

Terrence Kardong, a monk at an abbey in Dakota founded 18 roughly a thousand years after their European motherhouse, has termed the Great Plains "a school for humility," humility being one goal of Benedictine life. He writes, "in this eccentric environment . . . certainly one is made aware that things are not entirely in control." In fact, he says, the Plains offer constant reminders that "we are quite powerless over circumstance." His abbey, like many Great Plains communities with an agricultural base, had a direct experience of powerlessness, going bankrupt in the 1920s. Then, and at several other times in the community's history, the monks were urged to move to a more urban environment.

Kardong writes, "We may be crazy, but we are not neces- 19 sarily stupid . . . We built these buildings ourselves. We've cultivated these fields since the turn of the century. We watched from our dining room window the mirage of the Killdeer Mountains rise and fall on the horizon. We collected a library full of local history books and they belong here, not in Princeton. Fifty of our brothers lie down the hill in our cemetery. We have become as indigenous as the cottonwood trees . . . If you take us somewhere else, we lose our character, our history—maybe our soul."

A monk does not speak lightly of the soul, and Kardong 20 finds in the Plains the stimulus to develop an inner geography. "A monk isn't supposed to need all kinds of flashy surroundings. We're supposed to have a beautiful inner landscape. Watching a storm pass from horizon to horizon fills your soul with reverence. It makes your soul expand to fill the sky."

Monks are accustomed to taking the long view, another 21 countercultural stand in our fast-paced, anything-for-a-buck society which has corrupted even the culture of farming into "agribusiness." Kardong and many other writers of the desert West, including myself, are really speaking of values when they find beauty in this land no one wants. He writes: "We who are permanently camped here see things you don't see at 55 m.p.h. . . . We see white-faced calves basking in the spring grass like the lilies of the field. We see a chinook wind in January make rivulets run. We see dust-devils and lots of little things. We are grateful."

The so-called emptiness of the Plains is full of such miracu- 22 lous "little things." The way native grasses spring back from a drought, greening before your eyes; the way a snowy owl sits on a fencepost, or a golden eagle hunts, wings outstretched over grassland that seems to go on forever. Pelicans rise noisily from a lake; an antelope stands stock-still, its tattooed neck like a message in unbreakable code; columbines, their long stems beaten down by hail, bloom in the mud, their whimsical and delicate flowers intact. One might see a herd of white-tailed deer jumping a fence; fox cubs wrestling at the door of their lair; cock pheasants stepping out of a medieval tapestry into windrowed hay; cattle bunched in the southeast corner of a pasture, anticipating a storm in the approaching thunderheads. And above all, one notices the quiet, the near-absence of human noise.

23   My spiritual geography is a study in contrasts. The three places with which I have the deepest affinity are Hawaii, where I spent my adolescent years; New York City, where I worked after college; and western South Dakota. Like many Americans of their generation, my parents left their small-town roots in the 1930s and moved often. Except for the family home in Honolulu—its yard rich with fruits and flowers (pomegranate, tangerine, lime, mango, plumeria, hibiscus, lehua, ginger, and bird-of-paradise)—and my maternal grandparents' house in a remote village in western Dakota—its modest and hard-won garden offering columbine, daisies and mint—all my childhood places are gone.

24   When my husband and I moved nearly twenty years ago from New York to that house in South Dakota, only one wise friend in Manhattan understood the inner logic of the journey. Others, appalled, looked up Lemmon, South Dakota (named for George Lemmon, a cattleman and wheeler-dealer of the early 1900s, and home of the Petrified Wood Park—the world's largest—a gloriously eccentric example of American folk art) in their atlases and shook their heads. How could I leave the artists' and writers' community in which I worked, the diverse and stimulating environment of a great city, for such barrenness? Had I lost my mind? But I was young, still in my twenties, an apprentice poet certain of the rightness of returning to the place where I suspected I would find my stories. As it turns out, the Plains have been essential not only for my growth as a writer, they have formed me spiritually. I would even say they have made me a human being.

St. Hilary, a fourth-century bishop (and patron saint against   25
snake bites) once wrote, "Everything that seems empty is full of
the angels of God." The magnificent sky above the Plains sometimes seems to sing this truth; angels seem possible in the wind-
filled expanse. A few years ago a small boy named Andy who had
recently moved to the Plains from Pennsylvania told me he knew
an angel named Andy Le Beau. He spelled out the name for me
and I asked him if the angel had visited him here. "Don't you
know?" he said in the incredulous tone children adopt when
adults seem stupefyingly ignorant. "Don't you know?" he said,
his voice rising, "*This* is where angels drown."

Andy no more knew that he was on a prehistoric sea bed   26
than he knew what *le beau* means in French, but some ancient
wisdom in him had sensed great danger here; a terrifying but
beautiful landscape in which we are at the mercy of the unexpected, and even angels proceed at their own risk.

Content

1. What does Norris mean by "Dakota is a painful reminder of human
limits, just as cities and shopping malls are attempts to deny them" (¶ 4)?
2. Why does Norris quote with approval Terrence Kardong's observation that the Great Plains is "a school for humility," where the geography
reminds us that "we are quite powerless over circumstance" (¶ 18)?
Norris implies that everyone, not only monks, should learn humility
(¶s 18–22). Do you agree? Why or why not?
3. Norris says, "One myth that haunts us is that the small town is a
stable place" (¶ 16). What evidence does she provide to counter this myth?
4. What is the "inner logic" of Norris's move from New York City to
"that house in South Dakota" (¶ 24)?

Strategies/Structures

1. What does Norris mean by "spiritual geography" (¶ 5 and throughout)? In what ways is her description of the Great Plains also a definition? How does her definition contradict popular images of the Plains?
Is spirituality necessarily proportionate to the severity of the location?
2. To what extent is Norris's definition of the territory also a definition
of herself? Since Norris is in fact holier than many of her readers, if not
"thou," does she expect her readers to find her self-definition appealing
or not?

Language

1. Find language, including figures of speech, that indicate Norris is defensive about both the Dakotas and her choice to return there to live. Is Norris writing primarily for Dakotans, or for people unfamiliar with the Dakotas?

2. In paragraphs 3–6 Norris mentions a number of places: The Badlands, the Black Hills, New York City, Virginia, Illinois, Hawaii, Vermont, the Great Plains, the Christian West, the deserts of Egypt. What connotations—of the physical and spiritual geography of each place, does she expect readers to have? Norris agreed with a friend who referred to "the western Dakotas as the Cappadocia of North America" (¶ 4). What does she mean by the comparison?

For Writing

1. Norris says, "I make no attempt in this book to resolve the tensions and contradictions I find in the Dakotas between hospitality and insularity, change and inertia, stability and instability, possibility and limitation, between hope and despair, between open hearts and closed minds" (¶ 14). Pick one antithetical pair that pertains to a place you're familiar with (it could be a country, state, region, city, town, neighborhood) and write an essay explaining its contradictory nature to an outsider. Do the contradictions reside in the physical place, the geography, the inhabitants? Is this a good place to live, or to visit? Explain why or why not.

2. What does it mean to make a "commitment to a particular community, a particular place," as Norris says the Benedictines do (¶ 17)? In your own life or in the lives of people you know, in what ways could such a commitment be translated into action?

GENEVIEVE BRASSARD

Brassard writes, "I was born French and Catholic in Quebec City in 1965, four years before French joined English to become the other official language of supposedly bilingual Canada. I never realized, growing up as I did in my French Catholic cocoon, that I was a minority in my own country. My childhood was spent negotiating my position between competing opposites. My mother spoke only French and campaigned for Quebec's independence. My father was bilingual, believed in the unity of Canada, and encouraged me to learn English." Although her parents divorced when she was six, Brassard did in fact learn English. After attending Université Laval in Quebec and Concordia University in Montreal, Brassard earned a B.A. in English literature from San Francisco State University (1995) and an M.A. in English from the University of Connecticut (1997). "Sometimes," she says, "I feel like a traitor to my culture and my language: how can a Quebecoise deeply attached to her roots move to the United States, study English literature, and write in English? But my self-exile has only heightened my sense of belonging to the Quebec culture. Coming to the U.S., I've only traveled from one minority status to another."

"I could say, as many writers do, that I write to find out what I think, to engage in a dialogue with the reader, or to express what I believe. But deep down, if I'm brutally honest with myself, I'm really motivated by a mixture of insecurity and bravado: my insecure Quebec self, and my brash new American persona."

"I write to have the last word." And here it is.

❄ Why I write in a language my mother does not speak

I remember the tight knot of identification I felt when I read   1
this brief passage in Margaret Atwood's *Cat's Eye:* "I live in a
house . . . in British Columbia, which is as far away from Toronto
as I could get without drowning . . . on good days it still feels like
a vacation, an evasion." I read this in Los Angeles, where I had
lived for the past two years. The character's sentiment and my
own were almost eerily identical, in spirit if not actual geography. I felt as if Atwood were speaking to me; the small miracle of
recognition that makes reading and writing worthwhile had
happened. Like her character, in a journey akin to an escape, I
had run away as far as I could to finally dig my heels in the sand
of a Pacific beach.

2   The particulars of why I left country, culture, language, family, and friends behind armed with only two bags, an adequate knowledge of English and a head full of dreams don't matter. I may have told people I wanted to be a movie star and almost convinced myself as well, but I know now that I left to shake off the labels that stuck to my skin, and reinvent myself. I lost a daily routine conducted in my native French to find one where events had to be negotiated, people's alien codes deciphered, and places tamed to be hospitable. I lost daily contact with the members of my tribe—close friends as well as mere acquaintances like radio announcers and corner store owners, backdrop people weaved into the fabric of my past life—but I found a different way to communicate with those who mattered to me most. Letter-writing became my lifeline, the essential link connecting me to the mother country. It became my preferred mode of communication, originally imposed by my limited income, but more suitable to my introspective temperament than hurried long-distance calls. Without knowing John Donne, I had instinctively embraced his phrase "letters mingle souls."

3   In Los Angeles I felt divided, torn, neither here nor there, as if I was slowly losing my old self and picking up new fragments of identity along the way. I would spend my days interacting with people in English, slowly losing my accent, learning to use slang words, and discovering the intoxicating power of making people laugh in a language I was barely mastering. I was becoming someone who lived in a language her mother did not speak. At night, I would still dream in French, although my new tongue slowly insinuated itself in my sleeping hours as it pervaded my waking ones. I still felt "Quebecoise" and loyal to the independence cause, I could revert to colloquialisms and inside jokes when I talked with friends or parents on the phone, and write letters in fluid French. But I wasn't sure who I was anymore.

4   When I was eight years old, I began writing novels. I liked to call them so, even though they were merely pale imitations of the adventure books in the Nancy Drew vein I was avidly reading at the time. I may have been innocent and deluded but I was also practical: I wrote my stories in small, longhand script on sheets of paper the size of my books, "ready to bound" as I liked to declare proudly to my mother and her friends, as if publication

was imminent. This writing habit became an almost daily routine for a few years, a refuge from reality, but I eventually hit my first snag as a budding writer: I could not finish my stories. Instead, I would begin a new installment of my heroine/alter-ego's adventures, change the locale, create a new villian, introduce a compelling plot, and I was entranced again. I was creating a world; I felt powerful. I did not see my incomplete stories as a problem until my mother started referring to my bulging folders as my "great incomplete works," with a playful but in my eyes sarcastic smile. I stopped writing stories and never believed I could be a fiction writer again despite the writing workshops I attended in a vain attempt to fill the need I had to express myself.

My mother and I looked alike but our temperaments were so different we could only irritate and antagonize each other for years. She was a popular divorcée with a string of lovers and a large circle of friends. I was an introverted teenager, an only child continually being compared to an ideal, my mother, and found lacking. I began to learn English for obvious practical reasons but I also think it offered me a chance to set myself apart from her. She may have been the sexy, vibrant, and sought-after one, but *I* was the one who could speak English.

I had developed an affinity with British and American authors in translation in high school and naturally gravitated towards literary studies in college, but a look back at my freshman courseload hints at the divided self to come. I studied stories by Wharton and Lawrence, and English grammar, but I also enrolled in creative writing courses in French. As if I couldn't quite let go of my mother('s) tongue yet. The following year, more secure in my reading comprehension, I moved to Montreal, enrolled in an English university, and devoted my entire schedule to literature in English. By this time, my mother could not read what I wrote anymore, which also meant she could not mock it. I had no sense of victory; instead, I felt as if I had finally swum to shore. I could barely breathe but at least I was a person separate from her. Fleeing and then staying in California merely sealed a separateness already begun with language.

The language that allows me to write this also frees me from reproach or criticism, since my mother cannot read it. It doesn't free me from guilt, however. I know I'm criticizing her, no matter what language I use. Ironically, my mother and I grew closer the further apart we were geographically. She's one of my favorite correspondents, and I hide very little from her in writing. One half of my divided self becomes a Quebec native again when I write her a letter or when I go back home to visit. (This phrase "go back home" seems to imply a regression, a movement in time, as if a visit becomes a journey into childhood.) There is always a period of adjustment, however; I must first enter a linguistic no-man's-land where I peel off my English-speaking skin. Some small incident of my life across the border cannot be adequately translated; words may exist, but the context, background history, and players involved are too complex to explain. I need a few days to find my cultural bearings, leave my other life behind, and in effect become a different person.

8   But the thing is, I do find my bearings. I find my old voice, reconnect with the family lore and my tribe's habits, and slip back into my native tongue as naturally as I switch back to English at the border. My self may be divided, but the separation between my French and English sides is as thin as a layer of skin. I may start a diary entry in English and end it in French. I can discuss literature with an American professor one day, and talk with my grandmother the next without feeling alien to myself anymore. It's as if I've safely navigated to a place where I can be two people speaking a different language and still be myself.

9   Today, I wish my mother could read English and she envies my fluency in a tongue she would love to speak. I may one day revert back to writing in French, this time by translating books by English authors I love and would like to share with her. This could be a concrete way to unite my divided self, and finally present her with a completed manuscript, one she would enjoy and respect because it would not be a child's self-aggrandizing prose but the fiction of an accomplished writer adapted for her by her daughter.

10   I can't imagine doing anything else but read and write. I hesitate to add "for a living" since that part is so uncertain and up to fate. I think I write in French to reconnect not only with my correspondents but also with the eight-year-old who wrote for the pure joy of living exciting adventures vicariously. And I write in English because it's the language of writers I admire. I don't use

their language to emulate them, but rather to enter the dialogue between writer and reader implied in literary criticism, and to share my love of literature with others similarly afflicted. I no longer write in English to set myself apart from my mother. Instead, English and its literature have become a different sort of family, a welcoming tribe in which I feel at home.

Content

1. Explain how Brassard learns English and uses her new language to distance herself from her French-speaking mother.

2. Why, then, did mother and daughter grow "closer the further apart we were geographically" (¶ 7)?

3. What does Brassard mean by "My self may be divided, but the separation between my French and English sides is as thin as a layer of skin" (¶ 8)? Using the examples of Amy Tan's mother (pp. 21–28), Judith Ortiz Cofer (pp. 157–163), and Ning Yu (pp. 389–401), explain ways in which one can be both bilingual and bicultural.

4. What sense of each culture, French Canadian and American, does Brassard's essay provide?

Strategies/Structures

This essay is shaped like a conch shell, with mother and daughter far apart at the beginning and gradually drawing closer until at the end they are united. What conditions in their relationship contribute to this shape, somewhat irregular but spiraling to an integrated focal point?

Language

1. Although Brassard writes about being bilingual, her essay is written exclusively in English; she doesn't use any French. Why not?

2. How can one write about writing without sounding self-conscious? Has Brassard succeeded in doing this?

For Writing

1. If you're bilingual, write an essay explaining why being bilingual means being bicultural. What relationship do your cultures have in your

life—a harmonious blend (in some or all dimensions), an antagonism or conflict (in some or all dimensions), or some combination of both? Do you use one language for certain purposes and the other for others? What determines which language you associate with particular people or places? (See also Amy Tan, "Mother Tongue" [pp. 21–28] and Ning Yu, "One English Major's Beginnings" [pp. 389–402].)

2. Brassard explains that she "left country, culture, language, family and friends behind" for a new country and culture where "events had to be negotiated, people's alien codes deciphered, and places tamed to be hospitable" (¶ 2). Under what circumstances might a person choose such exile, despite its difficulties (again, see essays by Tan and Yu)?

Choose 3 for Tuesday

Additional Topics for Writing
Description   (For process strategies, see page 311)

1. Places, for readers who haven't been there:

    a. Your dream house (or room)
    b. Your favorite spot on earth
    c. A ghost town, or a dying or decaying neighborhood
    d. A foreign city or country you have visited
    e. A shopping mall
    f. A factory, farm, store, or other place where you've worked
    g. The waiting room of a bus station, airport, hospital, or dentist's office
    h. A mountain, beach, lake, forest, desert, field, or other natural setting you know well
    i. Or, compare and contrast two places you know well—two churches, houses, restaurants, vacation spots, schools, or any of the places identified in parts a–h, above

2. People, for readers who don't know them:

    a. A close relative or friend
    b. A friend or relative with whom you were once very close but from whom you are presently separated, physically or psychologically
    c. An antagonist
    d. Someone with an occupation or skill you want to know more about—you may want to interview the person to learn what skills, training, and personal qualities the job or activity requires
    e. Someone who has participated, voluntarily or involuntarily, in a significant historical event
    f. A bizarre or eccentric person, a "character"
    g. A high achiever—in business, sports, the arts or sciences, politics, religion
    h. A person whose reputation, public or private, has changed dramatically, for better or worse

3. Situations or events, for readers who weren't there:

    a. A holiday, birthday, or community celebration
    b. A high school or college party
    c. A farmer's market, flea market, garage sale, swap meet, or auction

    d. An athletic event

    e. A performance of a play or concert

    f. A ceremony—a graduation, wedding, christening, bar or bat mitzvah, an initiation, the swearing-in of a public official

    g. A family or school reunion

    h. A confrontation—between team members and referees or the coach, strikers and scabs, protesters and police

4. Experiences or feelings, for readers with analogous experiences:

    a. Love—romantic, familial, patriotic, or religious

    b. Isolation or rejection

    c. Fear

    d. Aspiration

    e. Success

    f. Anger

    g. Peace, contentment, or happiness

    h. An encounter with birth or death

    i. Coping with a handicap or disability—yours or that of someone close to you (see Nancy Mairs, pp. 472–485)

9 | *Division and Classification*

To divide something is to separate it into its component parts. As a writer you can divide a large, complex subject into smaller segments, easier for you and your readers to deal with individually than to consider in a large, complicated whole. As the section on process analysis indicates (see pp. 179–182), writers usually employ division to explain the individual stages of a process—how the earth was formed; how a professional jockey (or potter or surgeon) performs his or her job; how a heat pump works. Process analysis also underlies explanations of how to make or do something, how to train your dog, or make a cake, or cut gems.

You could also divide your subject in other ways—according to types of dogs, cakes, or gems. And there would be still different ways to divide a discussion of dogs—by their size (miniature, small, medium, large); by the length of their hair (short or long); or according to their suitability as working dogs, pets, or show dogs.

As you start to divide your subject, you almost naturally begin to *classify* it as well, to sort it into categories of groups or families. You'll probably determine the subcategories according to some logical principle or according to characteristics common to members of particular subgroups. Don't stretch to create esoteric groupings (dogs by hair color, for example) if your common sense suggests a more natural way. Some categories simply make more sense than others. A discussion of dogs by breeds could be logically arranged in alphabetical order—Afghan, borzoi, bulldog, collie, weimaraner. But a discussion that grouped dogs by type first and then breed would be easier to understand and more economical to write. For instance, you could consider all the common features of spaniels first, before dividing them into breeds of spaniels—cocker, springer, water—and discussing the differences.

Again, how minutely you refine the subcategories of your classification system depends on the length of your writing, your focus, and your emphasis. You could use a *binary* (two-part) *classification.* This is a favorite technique of classifiers who wish to sort things into two categories, those with a particular characteristic and those without it (drinkers and nondrinkers, swimmers and nonswimmers). Thus, in a essay discussing the components of a large structure or organization—a farm, a corporation, a university—a binary classification might lead you to focus on management and labor, or the university's academic and nonacademic functions. In "None of This Is Fair" (pp. 375–380), Richard Rodriguez adopts two binary classification systems, first dividing students into ethnic minorities and majorities to argue against affirmative action; then in the last two paragraphs dividing all children into two classes— the poor, irrespective of race, who "lack the confidence to assume their right to a good education," and all other people, who feel entitled to a good education. Likewise, Ning Yu's "Red and Black, or One English Major's Beginning" (pp. 389–401) uses the Chinese Communists' classification of Chinese citizens into "reds" (and therefore good, proletarian party loyalists) and "blacks" (and therefore subversive intellectuals and political dissenters) as the basis for showing two very different ways of teaching English to children who speak only Chinese. Embedded in these political labels are two very different cultures and sets of values, each claiming to promote what is good for China and its people.

In "Pomegranates and English Education,"(pp. 364–373) Shirley Geok-lin Lim, a Chinese born and reared in Malacca, Malaysia, examines the multiple influences on her elementary and high school education of the French-oriented convent school whose curriculum followed that of an English private school in which the students studied English books and therefore English culture: She writes, "No one asked why Indian, Eurasian, Malay, and Chinese children should be singing" Scottish and Irish ballads. "What was the place of Celt ballads in a Malayan future?" The nuns, European and Eurasian, exhibited a hierarchy of jobs and power which, "despite their uniform habits and sisterly titles," was "a ranking regulated by race." The same racial basis for status was replicated among the pupils, who valued above all European appearance and clothing. And why not? "To every schoolgirl," sensitive to all nuances and caste distinctions, "it was obvious that something about a white child made the good nuns benevolent." Only the orphans, "girls abandoned as babies on the convent doorsteps," had a lower status than the Chinese; they were "a class to be shunned."

Another type of classification is to construct three categories or subcategories. In "The Technology of Medicine" (pp. 358–363), Lewis Thomas classifies his subject as "nontechnology," "halfway technology," and the "genuinely decisive technology of modern medicine," arranged from the least to the most genuine technology. Each of these has specific functions, causes, and effects. As he classifies, Thomas also analyzes his subject by comparing the first two categories, which deal with medical problems after they have occurred and are very costly and difficult to deliver. He contrasts these with the last category; decisive technology, he demonstrates, is preventive, "relatively inexpensive and relatively easy to deliver."

Obviously, you can create as many categories and subcategories as are useful in enabling you and your readers to understand and interpret the subject. If you wanted to concentrate on the academic aspects of your own university, you might categorize them according to academic divisions—arts and sciences, business, education, music, public health. A smaller classification would examine the academic disciplines within a division—biology, English, history, mathematics. Or smaller yet, depending on your purpose—English literature, American literature, creative writing, linguistics—*ad infinitum,* as the anonymous jingle observes:

> Big fleas have little fleas, and these
> Have littler fleas to bite 'em,
> And these have fleas, and these have fleas,
> And so on *ad infinitum.*

James Thurber's caricatures of various student types in "University Days" (pp. 381–387) lend themselves to ready classifications: nerds, jocks, dullards, the militarily challenged; the faculty are likewise typecast. While serious essays, such as Lim's

"Pomegranates and English Education" (pp. 364–373) and Rodriguez's "None of This Is Fair" (pp. 375–380) argue against stereotypes, humorous essays often exploit them for comic purposes. Humorists can count on their readers to recognize and even embellish their caricatures of people, even if such caricatures are limited and unfair; although straightforward argumentative writing needs to play fair, humor doesn't. Thus Thurber caricatures the overzealous botany professor, so wedded to his subject that he is intolerant of any perspective other than that favored by his discipline ("We are not concerned with beauty in this course. . . . We are concerned solely with what I may call the *mechanics* of flars"), so devoted to imparting the necessary information "with every adjustment of the microscope known to man," that he "quivers all over" in rage, finally losing his temper when Thurber, in the self-caricature of a laboratory incompetent, once again fails to see cells: "You've drawn your eye!"

In all five of the essays in this chapter, the classification system provides the basis for the overall organization; but here as in most essays, the authors use many other techniques of writing in addition—narration, definition, description, analysis, illustration, and comparison and contrast.

In writing essays based on division, you might ask the following questions to help organize your materials: What are the parts of the total unit? How can these be subdivided to make the subject more understandable to my readers? In essays of classification, where you're sorting or grouping two or more things, you can ask: Into what categories can I sort these items? According to what principles—of logic, common characteristics, "fitness"? Do I want my classification to emphasize the similarities among groups or their differences? Once I've determined the groupings, am I organizing my discussion of each category in the same way, considering the same features in the same order? In many instances divisions and classifications are in the mind of the beholder. Is the glass half full or half empty? Your job as a writer is to help your readers recognize and accept the order of your universe.

STRATEGIES FOR WRITING— DIVISION AND CLASSIFICATION

1. Am I going to explain an existing system of classification, or am I going to invent a new one? Do I want to define a system by categorizing its components? Explain a process by dividing it into stages? Argue in favor of one category or another? Entertain through an amusing classification?
2. Do my readers know my subject but not my classification system? Know both subject and system? Or are they unacquainted with either? How will their knowledge (or lack of knowledge) of the subject or system influence how much I say about either? Will this influence the simplicity or complexity of my classification system?
3. According to what principle am I classifying or dividing my subject? Is it sensible? Significant? Does it emphasize the similarities or the differences among groups? Have I applied the principle consistently with respect to each category? How have I integrated my paper (to keep it from being just a long list), through providing interconnections among the parts and transitions between the divisions?
4. Have I organized my discussion of each category in the same way, considering the same features in the same order? Have I illustrated each category? Are the discussions of each category the same length? Should they be? Why or why not?
5. Have I used language similar in vocabulary level (equally technical, or equally informal) in each category? Have I defined any needed terms?

LEWIS THOMAS

Thomas (1913–1993) who earned a B.S. from Princeton (1933) and an M.D. from Harvard (1937), was the author of some two hundred research papers on immunology and pathology. As he explained in his autobiography, *The Youngest Science* (1983), these were written "in the relentlessly flat style required for absolute unambiguity." He is better known to the public, however, for his witty monthly columns in the *New England Journal of Medicine* that have been collected in *The Lives of a Cell: Notes of a Biology Watcher* (1974), winner of a 1974 National Book Award; *The Medusa and the Snail: More Notes of a Biology Watcher* (1979); and *Late Night Thoughts on Listening to Mahler's Ninth Symphony* (1983). Writing late at night, "usually on the weekend two days after I'd already passed the deadline," never outlining "or planning in advance," Thomas created graceful, informal personal essays using scientific knowledge, particularly from cell biology, as a source of metaphors for understanding human experience and the natural world.

Thomas taught at Johns Hopkins, the School of Medicine at New York University, and the Yale Medical School; from 1973 to 1980 he was president of the Memorial Sloan-Kettering Cancer Center, thereafter, president emeritus.

This essay, from *The Lives of a Cell* (1974), categorizes three levels of medical technology (supportive, "halfway," and preventive) and demonstrates Thomas's talent for explaining medical phenomena in terms general readers—and potential beneficiaries of this technology—can understand. Thomas uses the classification he has established as the basis for his argument, that "the real high technology of medicine . . . comes as the result of a genuine understanding of disease mechanisms" and is the least dramatic, the least obtrusive, and "relatively inexpensive, and relatively easy to deliver."

The Technology of Medicine

1 Technology assessment has become a routine exercise for the scientific enterprises on which the country is obliged to spend vast sums for its needs. Brainy committees are continually evalu-

ating the effectiveness and cost of doing various things in space, defense, energy, transportation, and the like, to give advice about prudent investments for the future.

Somehow medicine, for all the $80-odd billion that it is said to cost the nation, has not yet come in for much of this analytical treatment. It seems taken for granted that the technology of medicine simply exists, take it or leave it, and the only major technologic problem which policy-makers are interested in is how to deliver today's kind of health care, with equity, to all the people.

When, as is bound to happen sooner or later, the analysts get around to the technology of medicine itself, they will have to face the problem of measuring the relative cost and effectiveness of all the things that are done in the management of disease. They make their living at this kind of thing, and I wish them well, but I imagine they will have a bewildering time. For one thing, our methods of managing disease are constantly changing—partly under the influence of new bits of information brought in from all corners of biologic science. At the same time, a great many things are done that are not so closely related to science, some not related at all.

In fact, there are three quite different levels of technology in medicine, so unlike each other as to seem altogether different undertakings. Practitioners of medicine and the analysts will be in trouble if they are not kept separate.

1. First of all, there is a large body of what might be termed "nontechnology," impossible to measure in terms of its capacity to alter either the natural course of disease or its eventual outcome. A great deal of money is spent on this. It is valued highly by the professionals as well as the patients. It consists of what is sometimes called "supportive therapy." It tides patients over through diseases that are not, by and large, understood. It is what is meant by the phrases "caring for" and "standing by." It is indispensable. It is not, however, a technology in any real sense, since it does not involve measures directed at the underlying mechanism of disease.

It includes the large part of any good doctor's time that is taken up with simply providing reassurance, explaining to patients who fear that they have contracted one or another lethal disease that they are, in fact, quite healthy.

7   It is what physicians used to be engaged in at the bedside of patients with diphtheria, meningitis, poliomyelitis, lobar pneumonia, and all the rest of the infectious diseases that have since come under control.

8   It is what physicians must now do for patients with intractable cancer, severe rheumatoid arthritis, multiple sclerosis, stroke, and advanced cirrhosis. One can think of at least twenty major diseases that require this kind of supportive medical care because of the absence of an effective technology. I would include a large amount of what is called mental disease, and most varieties of cancer, in this category.

9   The cost of this nontechnology is very high, and getting higher all the time. It requires not only a great deal of time but also very hard effort and skill on the part of physicians; only the very best of doctors are good at coping with this kind of defeat. It also involves long periods of hospitalization, lots of nursing, lots of involvement of nonmedical professionals in and out of the hospital. It represents, in short, a substantial segment of today's expenditures for health.

10   2. At the next level up is a kind of technology best termed "halfway technology." This represents the kinds of things that must be done after the fact, in efforts to compensate for the incapacitating effects of certain diseases whose course one is unable to do very much about. It is a technology designed to make up for disease, or to postpone death.

11   The outstanding examples in recent years are the transplantations of hearts, kidneys, livers, and other organs, and the equally spectacular inventions of artificial organs. In the public mind, this kind of technology has come to seem like the equivalent of the high technologies of the physical sciences. The media tend to present each new procedure as though it represented a breakthrough and therapeutic triumph, instead of the makeshift that it really is.

12   In fact, this level of technology is, by its nature, at the same time highly sophisticated and profoundly primitive. It is the kind of thing that one must continue to do until there is a genuine understanding of the mechanisms involved in disease. In chronic glomerulonephritis, for example, a much clearer insight will be needed into the events leading to the destruction of glomeruli by the immunologic reactants that now appear to govern this disease, before one will know how to intervene intelligently to prevent the

process, or turn it around. But when this level of understanding has been reached, the technology of kidney replacement will not be much needed and should no longer pose the huge problem of logistics, cost, and ethics that it poses today.

An extremely complex and costly technology for the management of coronary heart disease has evolved—involving specialized ambulances and hospital units, all kinds of electronic gadgetry, and whole platoons of new professional personnel—to deal with the end results of coronary thrombosis. Almost everything offered today for the treatment of heart disease is at this level of technology, with the transplanted and artificial hearts as ultimate examples. When enough has been learned to know what really goes wrong in heart disease, one ought to be in a position to figure out ways to prevent or reverse the process, and when this happens the current elaborate technology will probably be set to one side.

Much of what is done in the treatment of cancer, by surgery, irradiation, and chemotherapy, represents halfway technology, in the sense that these measures are directed at the existence of already established cancer cells, but not at the mechanisms by which cells become neoplastic.

It is a characteristic of this kind of technology that it costs an enormous amount of money and requires a continuing expansion of hospital facilities. There is no end to the need for new, highly trained people to run the enterprise. And there is really no way out of this, at the present state of knowledge. If the installation of specialized coronary-care units can result in the extension of life for only a few patients with coronary disease (and there is no question that this technology is effective in a few cases), it seems to me an inevitable fact of life that as many of these as can be will be put together, and as much money as can be found will be spent. I do not see that anyone has much choice in this. The only thing that can move medicine away from this level of technology is new information, and the only imaginable source of this information is research.

3. The third type of technology is the kind that is so effective that it seems to attract the least public notice; it has come to be taken for granted. This is the genuinely decisive technology of modern medicine, exemplified best by modern methods for immunization against diphtheria, pertussis, and the childhood virus

diseases, and the contemporary use of antibiotics and chemo-therapy for bacterial infections. The capacity to deal effectively with syphilis and tuberculosis represents a milestone in human endeavor, even though full use of this potential has not yet been made. And there are, of course, other examples: the treatment of endocrinologic disorders with appropriate hormones, the prevention of hemolytic disease of the newborn, the treatment and prevention of various nutritional disorders, and perhaps just around the corner the management of Parkinsonism and sickle-cell anemia. There are other examples, and everyone will have his favorite candidates for the list, but the truth is that there are nothing like as many as the public has been led to believe.

17   The point to be made about this kind of technology—the real high technology of medicine—is that it comes as the result of a genuine understanding of disease mechanisms, and when it becomes available, it is relatively inexpensive, and relatively easy to deliver.

18   Offhand, I cannot think of any important human disease for which medicine possesses the outright capacity to prevent or cure where the cost of the technology is itself a major problem. The price is never as high as the cost of managing the same diseases during the earlier stages of no-technology or halfway technology. If a case of typhoid fever had to be managed today by the best methods of 1935, it would run to a staggering expense. At, say, around fifty days of hospitalization, requiring the most demanding kind of nursing care, with the obsessive concern for details of diet that characterized the therapy of that time, with daily laboratory monitoring, and, on occasion, surgical intervention for abdominal catastrophe, I should think $10,000 would be a conservative estimate for the illness, as contrasted with today's cost of a bottle of chloramphenicol and a day or two of fever. The halfway technology that was evolving for poliomyelitis in the early 1950s, just before the emergence of the basic research that made the vaccine possible, provides another illustration of the point. Do you remember Sister Kenny, and the cost of those institutes for rehabilitation, with all those ceremonially applied hot fomentations, and the debates about whether the affected limbs should be totally immobilized or kept in passive motion as frequently as possible, and the masses of statistically tormented data mobilized to support one view or the other? It is the cost of that kind of technology,

and its relative effectiveness, that must be compared with the cost and effectiveness of the vaccine.

Pulmonary tuberculosis had similar episodes in its history. There was a sudden enthusiasm for the surgical removal of infected lung tissue in the early 1950s, and elaborate plans were being made for new and expensive installations for major pulmonary surgery in tuberculosis hospitals, and then INH and streptomycin came along and the hospitals themselves were closed up. 19

It is when physicians are bogged down by their incomplete technologies, by the innumerable things they are obliged to do in medicine when they lack a clear understanding of disease mechanisms, that the deficiencies of the health-care system are most conspicuous. If I were a policy-maker, interested in saving money for health care over the long haul, I would regard it as an act of high prudence to give high priority to a lot more basic research in biologic science. This is the only way to get the full mileage that biology owes to the science of medicine, even though it seems, as used to be said in the days when the phrase still had some meaning, like asking for the moon. 20

Content

1. What is "supportive therapy" (¶ 5)? Why isn't it a technology?
2. Why does Thomas term the second level of technology "halfway technology" (¶ 10)? Why does this technology "make up for disease, or postpone death" (¶ 10)? Why is it "profoundly primitive" (¶ 12)?
3. Why does Thomas most strongly favor the third type of technology, the "genuinely decisive technology of modern medicine" (¶ 16)? Why does he say that preventive technology is unobtrusive, taken for granted?
4. What does Thomas mean by "basic research in biologic science" (¶ 20)? Why does he believe that basic research will ultimately save money for health care "over the long haul"? What evidence does he provide to demonstrate this?

Strategies/Structures

1. What is the basis for Thomas's three-part classification? Show how Thomas uses the three categories of technology (or nontechnology) in medicine as the three stages of an argument that he builds as the essay progresses. Could these have been arranged in any other order?

2. Thomas's thesis takes issue with the conventional views about health care delivery that he states in the first two paragraphs. Where does he state his thesis? Why does he wait until so late in the essay to present it?

Language

1. What does Thomas mean by the "technology" of medicine? Why does he continually use the term "technology" rather than "science" except in the last sentence of the essay?

2. Would a general audience understand the examples Thomas provides to illustrate each category? How does the simplicity or technicality of his language affect that understanding?

For Writing

1. Thomas refers briefly to past ("halfway technology") treatments of tuberculosis and polio and compares them to current ("high technology") treatments of the same disease. Pick a disease whose treatment and cure has changed dramatically over the years and analyze its history to illustrate the truth of Thomas's assertion about "The Technology of Medicine."

2. Write an essay, intended to convince skeptics, in which you explain and advocate the benefits of prevention (of alcoholism, drug abuse, unwanted pregnancies, obesity) over prolonged treatment or cure.

SHIRLEY GEOK-LIN LIM

Lim was born in 1944 in Malacca, Malaysia, and immigrated to the United States in 1969 after enrolling in Brandeis University, where she earned a Ph.D. in 1973. She married a Jewish-American professor in 1972 and has taught at Hostos Community College in New York City; at Westchester Community College, in Valhalla, New York; and since 1990 at the University of California Santa Barbara. Ever conscious of her complicated heritage, "Chinese/Malaysian/American," she explains, "Much of my writing life is composed of negotiating multiple identities, multiple societies, multiple desires, and multiple genres." She has published poetry (*Crossing the Peninsula and Other Poems* won the Commonwealth Poetry Prize in 1980), short stories (*Another Country and Other Stories*, 1982), criticism, and an autobiography, *Among the White Moon Faces: An Asian-American Memoir Of Homelands* (1996), of which "Pomegranates and English Education" is a partial chapter.

Although Lim as an adult insists on the importance of an integrated multicultural life, she grew up in a colonial society that was based on a distinct social and political hierarchy and thus embedded complicated systems of divisions and classifications. As she says, "My Chinese life in Malaysia up to 1969 was a pomegranate, thickly seeded"; she appropriated those aspects of "British colonial culture" that she learned from French-accented Chinese nuns in her convent school as a way to "break out of the pomegranate shell of being Chinese and girl."

Pomegranates and English Education

A pomegranate tree grew in a pot on the open-air balcony at the back of the second floor. It was a small skinny tree, even to a small skinny child like me. It had many fruits, marble-sized, dark green, shiny like overwaxed coats. Few grew to any size. The branches were sparse and graceful, as were the tear-shaped leaves that fluttered in the slightest breeze. Once a fruit grew round and large, we watched it every day. It grew lighter, then streaked with yellow and red. Finally we ate it, the purple and crimson seeds bursting with a tart liquid as we cracked the dry tough skin into segments to be shared by our many hands and mouths.

We were many. Looking back it seems to me that we had always been many. Beng was the fierce brother, the growly eldest son. Chien was the gentle second brother, born with a squint eye. Seven other children followed after me: Jen, Wun, Wilson, Hui, Lui, Seng, and Marie, the last four my half-siblings. I was third, the only daughter through a succession of eight boys and, as far as real life goes, measured in rice bowls and in the bones of morning, I have remained an only daughter in my memory.

3   We were as many as the blood-seeds we chewed, sucked, and spat out, the indigestible cores pulped and gray while their juice ran down our chins and stained our mouths with triumphant color. I still hold that crimson in memory, the original color of Chinese prosperity and health, now transformed to the berry shine of wine, the pump of blood in test tubes and smeared on glass plates to prophesy one's future from the wriggles of a virus. My Chinese life in Malaysia up to 1969 was a pomegranate, thickly seeded.

4   When Beng and Chien began attending the Bandar Hilir Primary School, they brought home textbooks, British readers with thick linen-rag covers, strong slick paper, and lots of short stories and poems accompanied by colorful pictures in the style of Aubrey Beardsley. The story of the three Billy Goats Gruff who killed the Troll under the bridge was stark and compressed, illustrated by golden kids daintily trotting over a rope bridge and a dark squat figure peering from the ravine below. Wee Willie Winkie ran through a starry night wearing only a white night cap and gown. The goats, the troll, and Willie Winkie were equally phantasms to me, for whoever saw anything like a flowing white gown on a boy or a pointy night cap in Malaya?

5   How to explain the disorienting power of story and picture? Things never seen or thought of in Malayan experience took on a vividness that ordinary life could not possess. These British childhood texts materialized for me, a five- and six-year-old child, the kind of hyper-reality that television images hold for a later generation, a reality, moreover, that was consolidated by colonial education.

6   At five, I memorized the melody and lyrics to "The Jolly Miller" from my brother's school rendition:

> There lived a jolly miller once
> Along the River Dee.
> He worked and sang from morn till night,
> No lark more blithe than he.
> And this the burden of his song
> As always used to be,
> I care for nobody, no not I,
> And nobody cares for me.

It was my first English poem, my first English song, and my   7
first English lesson. The song ran through my head mutely, obses-
sively, on hundreds of occasions. What catechism did I learn as I
sang the words aloud? I knew nothing of millers or of larks. As a
preschool child, I ate bread, that exotic food, only on rare and
unwelcome occasions. The miller working alone had no analogue
in the Malayan world. In Malacca, everyone was surrounded by
everyone else. A hawker needed his regular customers, a store-
front the stream of pedestrians who shopped on the move. Caring
was not a concept that signified. Necessity, the relations between
and among many and diverse people, composed the bonds of
Malaccan society. Caring denoted a field of choice, of individual
voluntary action, that was foreign to family, the place of compulsory relations. Western ideological subversion, cultural colonialism, whatever we call those forces that have changed societies
under forced political domination, for me began with something
as simple as an old English folk song.

The pomegranate is a fruit of the East, coming originally from   8
Persia. The language of the West, English, and all its many manifestations in stories, songs, illustrations, films, school, and government, does not teach the lesson of the pomegranate. English taught
me the lesson of the individual, the miller who is happy alone, and
who affirms the principle of not caring for community. Why was it
so easy for me to learn that lesson? Was it because within the
pomegranate's hundreds of seeds is also contained the drive for
singularity that will finally produce one tree from one seed? Or
was it because my grandparents' Hokkien and *nonya* societies had
become irremediably damaged by British colonial domination,
their cultural confidence never to be recovered intact, so that Western notions of the individual took over collective imaginations,
making of us, as V. S. Naipaul has coined it, "mimic" people?

But I resist this reading of colonialist corruption of an origi-   9
nal pure culture. Corruption is inherent in every culture, if we
think of corruption as a will to break out, to rupture, to break
down, to decay, and thus to change. We are all mimic people, born
to cultures that push us, shape us, and pummel us; and we are all
agents, with the power of the subject, no matter how puny or inar-
ticulate, to push back and to struggle against such shaping. So I
have seen myself not so much sucking at the teat of British colonial

culture as actively appropriating those aspects of it that I needed to escape that other familial/gender/native culture that violently hammered out only one shape for self. I actively sought corruption to break out of the pomegranate shell of being Chinese and girl.

10   It was the convent school that gave me the first weapons with which to wreck my familial culture. On the first day, Ah Chan took me, a six-year-old, in a trishaw to the Convent of the Holy Infant Jesus. She waited outside the classroom the entire day with a *chun*, a tiffin carrier, filled with steamed rice, soup, and meat, fed me this lunch at eleven-thirty, then took me home in a trishaw at two. I wore a starched blue pinafore over a white cotton blouse and stared at the words, *See Jane run. Can Jane run? Jane can run.* After the first week, I begged to attend school without Ah Chan present. Baba drove me to school after he dropped my older brothers at their school a mile before the convent; I was now, like my brothers, free of domestic female attachment.

11   The convent school stood quiet and still behind thick cement walls that hid the buildings and its inhabitants from the road and muffled the sounds of passing traffic. The high walls also serve to snuff out the world once you entered the gates, which were always kept shut except at the opening and closing of the school day. Shards of broken bottles embedded in the top of the walls glinted in the hot tropical sunshine, a provocative signal that the convent women were daily conscious of dangers intruding on their seclusion. For the eleven years that I entered through those gates, I seldom met a man on the grounds, except for the Jesuit brought to officiate at the annual retreat. A shared public area was the chapel, a small low dark structure made sacred by stained glass windows, hard wooden benches, and the sacristy oil lamp whose light was never allowed to go out. The community was allowed into the chapel every Sunday to attend the masses held for the nuns and the orphans who lived in the convent.

12   But if the convent closed its face to the town of men and unbelievers, it lay open at the back to the Malacca Straits. Every recess I joined hundreds of girls milling at the canteen counters for little plates of noodles, curry puffs stuffed with potatoes, peas and traces of meat, and vile orange-colored sugared drinks. The food never held me for long. Instead I spent recess by the sea wall, a

stone barrier free of bristling glass. Standing before the sandy ground that separated the field and summer house from the water, I gazed at high tide as the waves threw themselves against the wall with the peculiar repeated whoosh and sigh that I never wearied of hearing. Until I saw the huge pounding surf of the Atlantic Ocean, I believed all the world's water to be dancing, diamond-bright surfaced, a hypnotic meditative space in which shallow and deep seemed one and the same. Once inside the convent gates, one was overtaken by a similar sense of an overwhelming becalmedness, as if one had fallen asleep, out of worldliness, and entered the security of a busy dream.

During recess the little girls sang, "In and out the window, 13 in and out the window, as we have done before," and skipped in and out of arching linked hands, in a mindless pleasure of repeated movement, repeating the desire for safety, for routine, and for the linked circular enclosure of the women's community that would take me in from six to seventeen.

I also learned to write the alphabet. At first, the gray pencil 14 wouldn't obey my fingers. When the little orange nub at the end of the pencil couldn't erase the badly made letter, I wetted a finger with spit, rubbed hard, and then blubbered at the hole I had made in the paper. Writing was fraught with fear. I cried silently as I wrestled with the fragile paper that wouldn't sit still and that crushed and tore under my palm.

My teacher was an elderly nun of uncertain European 15 nationality, perhaps French, who didn't speak English well. She spoke with a lisp, mispronounced my name, called me "chérie" instead of "Shirley," and, perhaps accordingly, showed more affection to me than to the other children in her class. Sister Josie was the first European I knew. Even in her voluminous black robes and hood, she was an image of powder-white and pink smiles. Bending over my small desk to guide my fingers, and peering into my teary eyes, she spoke my name with a tender concern. She was my first experience of an enveloping, unconditional, and safe physical affection. She smelled sweet, like fresh yeast, and as I grew braver each day and strayed from my desk, she would upbraid me in the most remorseful of tones, "Chérie," which carried with it an approving smile.

16   In return I applied myself to Jane and Dick and Spot and to copying the alphabet letter by letter repeatedly. Sister Josie couldn't teach anything beyond the alphabet and simple vocabulary. In a few years, she was retired to the position of gatekeeper at the chapel annex. When I visited her six years later, as a child of twelve, at the small annex in which a store of holy pictures, medals, and lace veils were displayed for sale, Sister Josie's smile was still as fond. But to my mature ears, her English speech was halting, her grammar and vocabulary fractured. It was only to a six-year-old new to English that dear Sister Josie could have appeared as a native speaker of the English language.

17   It was my extreme good fortune to have this early missionary mother. Her gentle, undemanding care remains memorialized as a type of human relation not found in the fierce self-involvements of my family. My narrowly sensory world broadened not only with the magical letters she taught that spelled lives beyond what my single dreaming could imagine, but differently with her gentle greetings, in her palpable affection.

18   Nurturing is a human act that overleaps categories, but it is not free of history. It is not innocent. For the next eleven years nuns like Sister Josie broke down the domain of my infancy. Leaving the Bata shop and entering the jagged-glass-edged walls of the convent, I entered a society far removed from Baba and Emak.

19   The nuns wore the heavy wool habit of the missionary, full black blouses with wide sleeves like bat wings, long voluminous black skirts, black stockings, and shoes. Deep white hoods covered their heads and fell over their shoulders, and a white skull cap came down over their brows. Inexplicably they were collectively named "the French Convent," like a French colony or the foreign legion, but they were not chiefly white or European. Even in the early 1950s, some were Chinese and Eurasian "sisters."

20   Yet, despite their uniform habits and sisterly titles, a ranking regulated by race was obvious, even to the youngest Malayan child. Mother Superior was always white. A few white sisters, Sister Sean, Sister Patricia, and Sister Peter, taught the upper grades; or they performed special duties, like Sister Maria who gave singing lessons, or Sister Bernadette, who taught cooking and controlled the kitchen and the canteen.

Sister Maria was the only woman who was recognizably   21
French. Her accent was itself music to us as she led us through
years of Scottish and Irish ballads. No one asked why "Ye Banks
and Braes of Bonnie Doon" or "The Minstrel Boy" formed our
music curriculum, why Indian, Eurasian, Malay, and Chinese
children should be singing, off-key, week after week in a faintly
French-accented manner the melancholic attitudes of Celtic
gloom. What was the place of Celt ballads in a Malayan future?
What did they instruct of a history of feelings, of British blood-
shed and patriotism? Or were the curriculum setters in the Colonial Office in London reproducing in fortissimo an imperial
narrative—the tragedy of failed Scottish and Irish nationalism,
the first of England's colonies—in the physical pulses of the
newly colonized?

Of the nonmissionary teachers from Malacca, many were   22
Eurasian, and a few were Indian, and Chinese. The sole Malay
teacher appeared only after the British ceded independence to the
Federation of Malaya in 1957. Chik Guru taught us the Malay
language in my last two years at the convent, just as now in the
United States in many colleges and universities, the only African-
American or Latino or Asian-American professor a student may
meet teaches African-American or Latino or Asian-American
studies. Up to the end of the 1950s, and perhaps right up to the
violence of the May 13 race riots in 1969, the educational structure
in Malaya was British colonial.

My first inkling of race preference was formed by these   23
earliest teachers. In primary school, my teachers were almost all
European expatriates or native-born Eurasian Catholics bearing
such Hispanic and Dutch names as De Souza, De Witt, Minjoot,
Aerea, and De Costa. They were the descendants of Portuguese
soldiers and sailors who had captured Malacca from the Malay
Sultanate in 1511, when Portugal was a small, poorly populated
state. Expanding into the Spice Islands in the East, the Governor-
Generals of the Indies encouraged intermarriage between Portu-
guese males and native women, thus seeding the loyal settler
population with Portuguese mestizos. The Portuguese governed
Malacca for 130 years. When the forces of the Dutch East India
Company captured the port and its fortress in 1641, they found a

garrison there of some 260 Portuguese soldiers, reinforced with a mestizo population of about two to three thousand fighting men. For over four hundred years, the mestizos of Malacca had identified themselves as Portuguese.

24   The Eurasian teachers were physically distinguished from me. I learned this in Primary Two with Mrs. Damien, a white-haired, very large woman whose fat dimpled arms fascinated me. While she demonstrated how to embroider a daisy stitch as we crowded around her chair, I poked my finger into the dimples and creases that formed in the pale flesh that flowed over her shoulders and sagged in her upper arms. She was a fair Eurasian who dressed as a British matron, in sleeveless flowered print frocks with square-cut collars for coolness. Her exposed arms and chest presented dazzling mounds of white flesh that aroused my ardent admiration. I do not remember learning anything else in her class.

25   A few Eurasian girls were among my classmates. While they were not as coddled as the white daughters of plantation managers, they had an air of ease and inclusion that I envied. Their hair, which often had a copper sheen to it, was braided, while we Chinese girls had black, pudding-bowl cropped hair. By the time we were twelve and thirteen, and still flatchested, they had budded into bosomy women whose presence in Sunday masses attracted the attention of young Catholic males. The royal blue pleated pinafores that covered our prim skinny bodies like cardboard folded teasingly over their chests and hips. The difference between us and the early maturity of Eurasian girls was a symptom of the difference between our Chinese Malaccan culture and that dangerous Western culture made visible in their lushness. They were overtly religious, controlled by their strict mothers and the Ten Commandments that we had all memorized by pre-adolescence. But their breasts and hips that made swing skirts swing pronounced them ready for that unspoken but pervasive excitement we knew simply as "boys."

26   The convent held a number of orphans, girls abandoned as babies on the convent doorsteps, or given over to the nuns to raise by relatives too poor to pay for their upkeep. During school hours these "orphaned" girls were indistinguishable from the rest of us. They wore the school uniforms, white short-sleeved blouses under

sleeveless blue linen smocks that were fashioned with triple over-pleats on both sides so that burgeoning breasts were multiply overlayered with folds of starched fabric. But once school hours were over they changed into pink or blue gingham dresses that buttoned right up to the narrow Peter Pan collars. Those loose shapeless dresses, worn by sullen girls who earned their keep by helping in the kitchen and laundry, formed some of my early images of a class to be shunned.

Instead I longed to be like the privileged boarders, almost all of whom were British, whose parents lived in remote and danger-ous plantations or administrative outposts in the interior. These girls wore polished black leather shoes and fashionable skirts and blouses after school. In our classes, they sang unfamiliar songs, showed us how to dance, jerking their necks like hieroglyphic Egyptians. In the convent classroom where silence and stillness were enforced as standard behavior, they giggled and joked, shift-ing beams of sunshine, and were never reprimanded. To every schoolgirl it was obvious that something about a white child made the good nuns benevolent.

27

Content

1. Lim explains her early life as dominated by numerous divisions and classifications—by race, ethnicity, gender, religion, age, educational status, family background. Explain in what ways these influenced her thinking, behavior, and self-esteem as she was growing up.

2. Why were Chinese children in a Malaysian Catholic school run by French nuns educated in British culture about "things never seen or thought of in Malayan experience" (¶ 5; see also ¶ 21)? What effects did such a school have on Lim as a girl?

3. Many Americans are descendants of colonial peoples, either the col-onizers or the colonized. What, if any, connections might Lim's readers make between her experience of a colonial education (being obliged to learn the colonizers' language, literature, history, and values) and their own life history or cultural history?

Strategies/Structures

1. Lim uses the pomegranate tree (¶s 1, 3, 8) to symbolize her "Chinese life in Malaysia up to 1969" (¶ 3). Does this symbol do the work she

expects it to? Why or why not? Identify other symbols (such as the nuns' missionary clothing, ¶ 19) and explain how they work to reinforce Lim's point about colonialism.

2. In one sense, Lim's school world is self-contained and cloistered from the rest of the world by "thick cement walls" with "shards of broken bottles embedded in the top" (¶ 11). In another sense, the internal world is as full of categories and divisions as the outer world from which the schoolgirls are sheltered. Explain. Is the same true of any or all schools everywhere?

Language

1. In what language was Lim educated? In what culture? For what purposes?

2. In what language and for what readers does Lim write about her education? For what purposes?

For Writing

1. Lim says, "Corruption is inherent in every culture, if we think of corruption as a will to break out, to rupture, to break down, to decay, and thus to change. We are all mimic people, born to cultures that push us, shape us, and pummel us; and we are all agents, with the power . . . to push back and to struggle against such shaping" (¶ 9). Identify a culture (of family, gender, race, class, occupation, nationality) that shaped you and which to an extent you have resisted. What did you take from it and what about it did you resist? If you made deliberate choices, on what basis did you do so? If the shaping was unavoidable, explain why this was so.

2. All of us are continually in the process of shaping and being shaped by a particular culture or cultures; identify some of the major features of this process and explain how this process works. You could refer not only to Lim's essay, but to essays by any of the following: Rose (pp. 243–252), Zitkala-Sa (pp. 254–262), Sanders (pp. 319–328 and 420–433), Norris (pp. 334–343), Rodriguez (pp. 375–380).

RICHARD RODRIGUEZ

How Richard Rodriguez, born in San Francisco in 1944, the son of Mexican immigrants, should and can deal with his dual heritage is the subject of his autobiographical *Hunger of Memory: The Education of Richard Rodriguez* (1982). He spoke Spanish at home and didn't learn English until he began grammar school in Sacramento. Although for a time he refused to speak Spanish, he studied that language in high school as if it were a foreign language. Nevertheless, classified as Mexican-American, Rodriguez benefited from Affirmative Action programs, and on scholarships he earned a B.A. from Stanford (1967), and an M.A. from Columbia (1969). After that he studied Renaissance literature at the University of California, Berkeley—the site of the climactic event described in the following essay, later incorporated into *Hunger of Memory.* In 1992 he published *Days of Obligation: An Argument with my Mexican Father,* another collection of autobiographical essays focusing on his complicated relations to the cultures of the Catholic Church, San Francisco's gay Castro District, and Mexico.

For two decades Rodriguez, now an educational consultant and freelance writer, has consistently—and controversially— argued against bilingual education, other programs that would separate minority students from the mainstream, and Affirmative Action. In this essay Rodriguez argues against the arbitrary—and divisive—classification of people into categories, by race, religion, or ethnic origin, for the purposes of Affirmative Action. But he concludes with a different classification of people on the basis of income, which lumps together "white, black, brown. Always poor. Silent." Hopeless. And untouched by Affirmative Action. He will be their spokesperson, too.

None of This Is Fair

M y plan to become a professor of English—my ambition during long years in college at Stanford, then in graduate school at Columbia and Berkeley—was complicated by feelings of embarrassment and guilt. So many times I would see other Mexican-Americans and know we were alike only in race. And yet, simply because our race was the same, I was, during the last years of my schooling, the beneficiary of their situation. Affirmative Action programs had made it all possible. The disadvantages of others permitted my promotion; the absence of many Mexican-Americans from academic life allowed my designation as a "minority student."

2   For me opportunities had been extravagant. There were fellowships, summer research grants, and teaching assistantships. After only two years in graduate school, I was offered teaching jobs by several colleges. Invitations to Washington conferences arrived and I had the chance to travel abroad as a "Mexican-American representative." The benefits were often, however, too gaudy to please. In three published essays, in conversations with teachers, in letters to politicians and at conferences, I worried the issue of Affirmative Action. Often I proposed contradictory opinions. Though consistent was the admission that—because of an early, excellent education—I was no longer a principal victim of racism or any other social oppression. I said that but still I continued to indicate on applications for financial aid that I was a Hispanic-American. It didn't really occur to me to say anything else, or to leave the question unanswered.

3   Thus I complied with and encouraged the odd bureaucratic logic of Affirmative Action. I let government officials treat the disadvantaged condition of many Mexican-Americans with my advancement. Each fall my presence was noted by Health, Education, and Welfare department statisticians. As I pursued advanced literary studies and learned the skill of reading Spenser and Wordsworth and Empson, I would hear myself numbered among the culturally disadvantaged. Still, silent, I didn't object.

4   But the irony cut deep. And guilt would not be evaded by averting my glance when I confronted a face like my own in a crowd. By late 1975, nearing the completion of my graduate studies at Berkeley, I was so wary of the benefits of Affirmative Action that I feared my inevitable success as an applicant for a teaching position. The months of fall—traditionally that time of academic job-searching—passed without my applying to a single school. When one of my professors chanced to learn this in late November, he was astonished, then furious. He yelled at me: Did I think that because I was a minority student jobs would just come

looking for me? What was I thinking? Did I realize that he and several other faculty members had already written letters on my behalf? Was I going to start acting like some other minority students he had known? They struggled for success and then, when it was almost within reach, grew strangely afraid and let it pass. Was that it? Was I determined to fail?

I did not respond to his questions. I didn't want to admit to   5 him, and thus to myself, the reason I delayed.

I merely agreed to write to several schools. (In my letter I   6 wrote: "I cannot claim to represent disadvantaged Mexican-Americans. The very fact that I am in a position to apply for this job should make that clear.") After two or three days, there were telegrams and phone calls, invitations to interviews, then airplane trips. A blur of faces and the murmur of their soft questions. And, over someone's shoulder, the sight of campus buildings shadowing pictures I had seen years before when I leafed through Ivy League catalogues with great expectations. At the end of each visit, interviewers would smile and wonder if I had any questions. A few times I quietly wondered what advantage my race had given me over other applicants. But that was an impossible question for them to answer without embarrassing me. Quickly, several persons insisted that my ethnic identity had given me no more than a "foot inside the door"; at most, I had a "slight edge" over other applicants. "We just looked at your dossier with extra care and we like what we saw. There was never any question of having to alter our standards. You can be certain of that."

In the early part of January, offers arrived on stiffly elegant   7 stationery. Most schools promised terms appropriate for any new assistant professor. A few made matters worse—and almost more tempting—by offering more: the use of university housing; an unusually large starting salary; a reduced teaching schedule. As the stack of letters mounted, my hesitation increased. I started calling department chairmen to ask for another week, then 10 more days—"more time to reach a decision"—to avoid the decision I would need to make.

At school, meantime, some students hadn't received a single   8 job offer. One man, probably the best student in the department, did not even get a request for his dossier. He and I met outside a classroom one day and he asked about my opportunities. He seemed happy for me. Faculty members beamed. They said they had expected it. "After all, not many schools are going to pass up getting a Chicano with a Ph.D. in Renaissance literature," somebody said laughing. Friends wanted to know which of the offers I was going to accept. But I couldn't make up my mind. February came and I was running out of time and excuses. (One chairman guessed my delay was a bargaining ploy and increased his offer with each of my calls.) I had to promise a decision by the 10th; the 12th at the very latest.

9   On the 18th of February, late in the afternoon, I was in the office I shared with several other teaching assistants. Another graduate student was sitting across the room at his desk. When I got up to leave, he looked over to say in an uneventful voice that he had some big news. He had finally decided to accept a position at a faraway university. It was not a job he especially wanted, he admitted. But he had to take it because there hadn't been any other offers. He felt trapped, and depressed, since his job would separate him from his young daughter.

10   I tried to encourage him by remarking that he was lucky at least to have found a job. So many others hadn't been able to get anything. But before I finished speaking I realized that I had said the wrong thing. And I anticipated his next question.

11   "What are your plans?" he wanted to know. "Is it true you've gotten an offer from Yale?"

12   I said that it was. "Only, I still haven't made up my mind."

13   He stared at me as I put on my jacket. And smiling, then unsmiling, he asked if I knew that he too had written to Yale. In his case, however, no one had bothered to acknowledge his letter with even a postcard. What did I think of that?

14   He gave me no time to answer.

15   "Damn!" he said sharply and his chair rasped the floor as he pushed himself back. Suddenly, it was to *me* that he was complaining. "It's just not right, Richard. None of this is fair. You've done some good work, but so have I. I'll bet our records are just about equal. But when we look for jobs this year, it's a different story. You get all of the breaks."

16   To evade his criticism, I wanted to side with him. I was about to admit the injustice of Affirmative Action. But he went on, his voice hard with accusation. "It's all very simple this year.

You're a Chicano. And I am a Jew. That's the only real difference between us."

His words stung me: there was nothing he was telling me 17 that I didn't know. I had admitted everything already. But to hear someone else say these things, and in such an accusing tone, was suddenly hard to take. In a deceptively calm voice, I responded that he had simplified the whole issue. The phrases came like bubbles to the tip of my tongue: "new blood"; "the importance of cultural diversity"; "the goal of racial integration." These were all the arguments I had proposed several years ago—and had long since abandoned. Of course the offers were unjustifiable. I knew that. All I was saying amounted to a frantic self-defense. I tried to find an end to a sentence. My voice faltered to a stop.

"Yeah, sure," he said. "I've heard all that before. Nothing 18 you say really changes the fact that Affirmative Action is unfair. You see that, don't you? There isn't any way for me to compete with you. Once there were quotas to keep my parents out of certain schools; now there are quotas to get you in and the effect on me is the same as it was for them."

I listened to every word he spoke. But my mind was really 19 on something else. I knew at that moment that I would reject all of the offers. I stood there silently surprised by what an easy conclusion it was. Having prepared for so many years to teach, having trained myself to do nothing else, I had hesitated out of practical fear. But now that it was made, the decision came with relief. I immediately knew I had made the right choice.

My colleague continued talking and I realized that he was 20 simply right. Affirmative Action programs *are* unfair to white students. But as I listened to him assert his rights, I thought of the seriously disadvantaged. How different they were from white, middle-class students who come armed with the testimony of their grades and aptitude scores and self-confidence to complain about the unequal treatment they now receive. I listen to them. I do not want to be careless about what they say. Their rights are important to protect. But inevitably when I hear them or their lawyers, I think about the most seriously disadvantaged, not simply Mexican-Americans, but of all those who do not ever imagine themselves going to college or becoming doctors: white, black, brown. Always poor. Silent. They are not plaintiffs before the court or against the misdirection of Affirmative Action. They lack the confidence (my confidence!) to assume their right to a good education. They lack the confidence and skills a good primary and secondary education provides and which are prerequisites for informed public life. They remain silent.

21   The debate drones on and surrounds them in stillness. They are distant, faraway figures like the boys I have seen peering down from freeway overpasses in some other part of town.

Content

1. What does Rodriguez mean by his fundamental premise, "None of this is fair" (¶ 15)?
2. What is Affirmative Action? What is reverse discrimination? What does Rodriguez's comparison of his job-seeking experience with those of his white male classmates illustrate about these terms?
3. Does Rodriguez intend that his readers generalize on the basis of the job-seeking experiences of himself and his two white male classmates, one Jewish?
4. What categories of people does Rodriguez claim are currently benefiting from Affirmative Action programs? What categories of people are the victims of reverse discrimination?
5. In Rodriguez's opinion, which people truly need Affirmative Action (¶ 20)? Why aren't they getting what they need? Why does he wait so long to get to this point?

Strategies/Structures

1. If Rodriguez believes that Affirmative Action doesn't benefit the "most seriously disadvantaged" of all races (¶ 20), why doesn't he illustrate the point with an example of such people? And devote more space to them?
2. Show how Rodriguez employs division and classification to conduct his argument.

For Writing

1. If you or someone you know has either benefited from Affirmative Action or experienced reverse discrimination, write an essay about that experience to illustrate a general point about it for readers unfamiliar with the issue.

2. Rodriguez has been attacked as an Uncle Juan (a Chicano Uncle Tom) for claiming that he and other middle-class minority students improperly benefit from Affirmative Action programs that do not aid "all those who do not ever imagine themselves going to college or becoming doctors: white, black, brown. Always poor. Silent" (¶ 20). Write an essay to convince your opposition in which you agree either with Rodriguez or with his critics.

===

JAMES THURBER

Thurber's sense of the ridiculous is sublime. Some of the funniest of his comic sketches are derived from his childhood in Columbus, Ohio, where he was born in 1894, and from his college days at Ohio State University. After working briefly as a reporter for the *Columbus Dispatch,* Thurber migrated to New York via Paris, where he was a reporter for the Paris edition of the *Chicago Tribune.* At the *New Yorker* he was first hired as managing editor, but within six months he had managed to work himself "down to a more comfortable position." For the next forty years—despite progressive blindness—Thurber contributed articles, stories, fables, and quirky line drawings (Dorothy Parker called them "unbaked cookies") to the magazine, until his death in 1961. He mines the bizarre commonplaces of ordinary people in ordinary life in such books as *Is Sex Necessary?* (1929), with E. B. White, and the autobiographical *My Life and Hard Times* (1933). Among his other twenty volumes are a play, *The Male Animal* (1939), with Elliott Nugent; a cartoon book, *Men, Women, and Dogs* (1943); several children's books, among them *The Wonderful O* (1957); and *The Years with Ross* (1959), an account of the magical, symbiotic relationship between the *New Yorker* and its crusty, perfectionist editor, Harold Ross.

"University Days" is Thurber's wry interpretation of his experiences at Ohio State University, which he attended from 1913 to 1918, but left without earning a degree. His caricature portraits of student and faculty types have been discussed (pp. 355–356). Another way to read this as an essay of classification is according to the types of student ineptitude displayed by Thurber and others: academic (Thurber's failure to "see cells" in biology), athletic (Thurber's failure to pass gym, except by cheating), extracurricular (Haskins's inability to write appealing stories for the student paper), and military drill. Although the commanding officer claims that Thurber was right and the other hundred and nine men marching in the opposite direction were wrong, we know whom to believe.

University Days

1   I passed all the other courses that I took at my University, but I could never pass botany. This was because all botany students had to spend several hours a week in a laboratory looking through a microscope at plant cells, and I could never see through a microscope. I never once saw a cell through a microscope. This used to enrage my instructor. He would wander around the laboratory pleased with the progress all the students were making in drawing the involved and, so I am told, interesting structure of flower cells, until he came to me. I would just be standing there. "I can't see anything," I would say. He would begin patiently enough, explaining how anybody can see through a microscope, but he would always end up in a fury; claiming that I could *too* see through a microscope but just pretended that I couldn't. "It takes away from the beauty of flowers anyway," I used to tell him. "We are not concerned with beauty in this course," he would say. "We are concerned solely with what I may call the *mechanics* of flars." "Well," I'd say. "I can't see anything." "Try it just once again," he'd say, and I would put my eye to the microscope and see nothing at all, except now and again a nebulous milky substance—a phenomenon of maladjustment. You were supposed to see a vivid, restless clockwork of sharply defined plant cells. "I see what looks like a lot of milk," I would tell him. This he claimed, was the result of my not having adjusted the microscope properly, so he would readjust it for me, or rather, for himself. And I would look again and see milk.

2   I finally took a deferred pass, as they called it, and waited a year and tried again. (You had to pass one of the biological sciences or you couldn't graduate.) The professor had come back from vacation brown as a berry, bright-eyed, and eager to explain cell-structure again to his classes. "Well," he said to me, cheerily, when we met in the first laboratory hour of the semester, "we're going to

see cells this time, aren't we?" "Yes, sir," I said. Students to the right of me and left of me and in front of me were seeing cells; what's more, they were quietly drawing pictures of them in their notebooks. Of course, I didn't see anything.

"We'll try it," the professor said to me, grimly, "with every 3 adjustment of the microscope known to man. As God is my witness, I'll arrange this glass so that you see cells through it or I'll give up teaching. In twenty-two years of botany, I—" He cut off abruptly for he was beginning to quiver all over, like Lionel Barrymore, and he genuinely wished to hold onto his temper; his scenes with me had taken a great deal out of him.

So we tried it with every adjustment of the microscope 4 known to man. With only one of them did I see anything but blackness or the familiar lacteal opacity, and that time I saw, to my pleasure and amazement, a variegated constellation of flecks, specks, and dots. These I hastily drew. The instructor, noting my activity, came from an adjoining desk, a smile on his lips and his eyebrows high in hope. He looked at my cell drawing. "What's that?" he demanded, with a hint of squeal in his voice. "That's what I saw," I said. "You didn't, you didn't, you *did*n't!" he screamed, losing control of his temper instantly, and he bent over and squinted into the microscope. His head snapped up. "That's your eye!" he shouted. "You've fixed the lens so that it reflects! You've drawn your eye!"

Another course that I didn't like, but somehow managed to 5 pass, was economics. I went to that class straight from the botany class, which didn't help me any in understanding either subject. I used to get them mixed up. But not as mixed up as another student in my economics class who came there direct from a physics laboratory. He was a tackle on the football team, named Bolenciecwcz. At that time Ohio State University had one of the best football teams in the country, and Bolenciecwcz was one of its outstanding stars. In order to be eligible to play it was necessary for him to keep up in his studies, a very difficult matter, for while he was not dumber than an ox he was not any smarter. Most of his professors were lenient and helped him along. None gave him more hints, in answering questions, or asked him simpler ones than the economics professor, a thin, timid man named Bassum. One day when we were on the subject of transportation and distribution, it came

Bolenciecwcz's turn to answer a question. "Name one means of transportation," the professor said to him. No light came into the big tackle's eyes. "Just any means of transportation," said the professor. Bolenciecwcz sat staring at him. "That is," pursued the professor, "any medium, agency, or method of going from one place to another." Bolenciecwcz had the look of a man who is being led into a trap. "You may choose among steam, horsedrawn, or electrically propelled vehicles," said the instructor. "I might suggest the one which we commonly take in making long journeys across land." There was a profound silence in which everybody stirred uneasily, including Bolenciecwcz and Mr. Bassum. Mr. Bassum abruptly broke this silence in an amazing manner. "Choo-choo-choo," he said, in a low voice, and turned instantly scarlet. He glanced appealingly around the room. All of us, of course, shared Mr. Bassum's desire that Bolenciecwcz should stay abreast of the class in economics, for the Illinois game, one of the hardest and most important of the season, was only a week off. "Toot, toot, too-toooooooot!" some student with a deep voice moaned, and we all looked encouragingly at Bolenciecwcz. Somebody else gave a fine imitation of a locomotive letting off steam. Mr. Bassum himself rounded off the little show. "Ding, dong, ding, dong," he said, hopefully. Bolenciecwcz was staring at the floor now, trying to think, his great brow furrowed, his huge hands rubbing together, his face red.

6   "How did you come to college this year, Mr. Bolenciecwcz? asked the professor. "*Chuffa* chuffa, *chuffa* chuffa."

7   "M'father sent me," said the football player.

8   "What on?" asked Bassum.

9   "I git an 'lowance," said the tackle, in a low, husky voice, obviously embarrassed.

10   "No, no," said Bassum. "Name a means of transportation. What did you *ride* here on?"

11   "Train," said Bolenciecwcz.

12   "Quite right," said the professor. "Now, Mr. Nugent, will you tell us—"

13   If I went through anguish in botany and economics—for different reasons—gymnasium work was even worse. I don't even like to think about it. They wouldn't let you play games or join in the exercises with your glasses on and I couldn't see with mine off. I bumped into professors, horizontal bars, agricultural students,

and swinging iron rings. Not being able to see, I could take it but I couldn't dish it out. Also, in order to pass gymnasium (and you had to pass it to graduate) you had to learn to swim if you didn't know how. I didn't like the swimming pool, I didn't like swimming, and I didn't like the swimming instructor, and after all these years I still don't. I never swam but I passed my gym work anyway, by having another student give my gymnasium number (978) and swim across the pool in my place. He was a quiet, amiable blonde youth, number 473, and he would have seen through a microscope for me if we could have got away with it, but we couldn't get away with it. Another thing I didn't like about gymnasium work was that they made you strip the day you registered. It is impossible for me to be happy when I am stripped and being asked a lot of questions. Still, I did better than a lanky agricultural student who was cross-examined just before I was. They asked each student what college he was in—that is, whether Arts, Engineering, Commerce, or Agriculture. "What college are you in?" the instructor snapped at the youth in front of me. "Ohio State University," he said promptly.

It wasn't that agricultural student but it was another a whole 14
lot like him who decided to take up journalism, possibly on the ground that when farming went to hell he could fall back on newspaper work. He didn't realize, of course, that that would be very much like falling back full-length on a kit of carpenter's tools. Haskins didn't seem cut out for journalism, being too embarrassed to talk to anybody and unable to use a typewriter, but the editor of the college paper assigned him to the cow barns, the sheep house, the horse pavilion, and the animal husbandry department generally. This was a genuinely big "beat," for it took up five times as much ground and got ten times as great a legislative appropriation as the College of Liberal Arts. The agricultural student knew animals, but nevertheless his stories were dull and colorlessly written. He took all afternoon on each one of them, on account of having to hunt for each letter on the typewriter. Once in a while he had to ask somebody to help him hunt. "C" and "L", in particular, were hard letters for him to find. His editor finally got pretty much annoyed at the farmer-journalist because his pieces were so uninteresting. "See here, Haskins," he snapped at him one day, "why is it we never have anything hot from you on the horse pavilion? Here we have two hundred head of horses on this campus—more

than any other university in the Western Conference except Purdue—and yet you never get any real lowdown on them. Now shoot over to the horse barns and dig up something lively." Haskins shambled out and came back in about an hour; he said he had something. "Well, start it off snappily," said the editor. "Something people will read." Haskins set to work and in a couple of hours brought a sheet of typewritten paper to the desk; it was a two-hundred word story about some disease that had broken out among the horses. Its opening sentence was simple but arresting. It read: "Who has noticed the sores on the tops of the horses in the animal husbandry building?"

15   Ohio State was a land grant university and therefore two years of military drill was compulsory. We drilled with old Springfield rifles and studied the tactics of the Civil War even though the World War was going on at the time. At 11 o'clock each morning thousands of freshmen and sophomores used to deploy over the campus, moodily creeping up on the old chemistry building. It was good training for the kind of warfare that was waged at Shiloh but it had no connection with what was going on in Europe. Some people used to think there was German money behind it, but they didn't dare say so or they would have been thrown in jail as German spies. It was a period of muddy thought and marked, I believe, the decline of higher education in the Middle West.

16   As a soldier I was never any good at all. Most of the cadets were glumly indifferent soldiers, but I was no good at all. Once General Littlefield, who was commandant of the cadet corps, popped up in front of me during regimental drill and snapped, "You are the main trouble with this university!" I think he meant that my type was the main trouble with the university but he may have meant me individually. I was mediocre at drill, certainly— that is, until my senior year. By that time, I had drilled longer than anybody else in the Western Conference, having failed at military at the end of each preceding year so that I had to do it all over again. I was the only senior still in uniform. The uniform which, when new, had made me look like an interurban railway conductor, now that it had become faded and too tight made me look like Bert Williams in his bellboy act. This had a definitely bad effect on my morale. Even so, I had become by sheer practice little short of wonderful at squad manoeuvres.

One day General Littlefield picked our company out of the   17
whole regiment and tried to get it mixed up by putting it through
one movement after another as fast as we could execute them:
squads right, squads left, squads on right into line, squads right
about, squads left front into line etc. In about three minutes one
hundred and nine men were marching in one direction and I
was marching away from them at an angle of forty degrees, all
alone. "Company, halt!" shouted General Littlefield, "That man
is the only man who has it right!" I was made a corporal for my
achievement.

The next day General Littlefield summoned me to his office.   18
He was swatting flies when I went in. I was silent and he was
silent too, for a long time. I don't think he remembered me or why
he had sent for me, but he didn't want to admit it. He swatted
some more flies, keeping his eyes on them narrowly before he let
go with the swatter. "Button up your coat!" he snapped. Looking
back on it now I can see that he meant me although he was looking at a fly, but I just stood there. Another fly came to rest on a
paper in front of the general and began rubbing its hind legs
together. The general lifted the swatter cautiously. I moved rest-
lessly and the fly flew away. "You startled him!" barked General
Littlefield, looking at me severely. I said I was sorry. "That won't
help the situation!" snapped the General, with cold military logic.
I didn't see what I could do except offer to chase some more flies
toward his desk, but I didn't say anything. He stared out the window at the faraway figures of co-eds crossing the campus toward
the library. Finally, he told me I could go. So I went. He either
didn't know which cadet I was or else he forgot what he wanted
to see me about. I may have been that he wished to apologize for
having called me the main trouble with the university; or maybe
he had decided to compliment me on my brilliant drilling of the
day before and then at the last minute decided not to. I don't
know. I don't think about it much anymore.

Content

1. Thurber's essay discusses several of his experiences as a college student between 1913 and 1918. What details reveal this time period? What
in this classic essay transcends the period in which it was written? Are

students significantly different now from those in Thurber's day? Why or why not?

2. What kind of character does Thurber portray himself as when he was a student? Are Bolenciecwcz and Haskins similar to each other or to Thurber? Have the three any conspicuous differences? Do these characters remain funny in an era of political correctness?

3. What are Thurber's professors like? In what ways is their behavior stereotypical of college professors? What characteristics are exaggerated? For what purposes does Thurber use such exaggerated features?

Strategies/Structures

1. What determines the basis for Thurber's categories?

2. In retrospect Thurber as author can laugh at some of his experiences as an undergraduate at Ohio State which were not funny at the time. Why? Does he expect his readers to laugh, too? Why or why not?

3. Thurber presents several incidents in the form of dramatic vignettes. Identify these incidents.

4. What is the thesis of Thurber's essay? Is it explicit or implicit? Why might an essay composed of distinct categories be likely to have an implicit rather than an explicit thesis?

Language

Why, in an essay of fairly simple language, does Thurber use "the familiar lacteal opacity" in paragraph 4? Does he use any other complicated language? If so, where? For what purposes?

For Writing

1. Present, for readers who don't know you, a significant aspect of your college days through narration of an incident or two in which you are the main character. If you wish, you may use dialogue and describe other students or professors. And if you want to write humorously, you may exaggerate actions, gestures, speech mannerisms, or other features.

2. Write, for the next generation, a straightforward essay about your college days in which you classify one or more major aspects of your experience—your courses, professors, fellow students, extracurricular activities, successes or failures. Use the classification as the basis for organizing your essay.

NING YU

Ning Yu was born in 1955 in Beijing, People's Republic of China, and came to the United States in 1986 for graduate study. He earned a Ph.D. in English from the University of Connecticut in 1993 and now teaches at Western Washington University.

Ning Yu recounts some of the significant events of his youth in the following prizewinning essay, "Red and Black, or One English Major's Beginning." When he was in fourth grade, his school was closed down as a consequence of the "Great Proletarian Cultural Revolution," which overturned the existing social order. The intellectual class (the "blacks," in Ning's classification scheme) to which Yu's family belonged because his father was a professor of Chinese language and literature, were replaced on their jobs by members of the People's Liberation Army, "the reds," whose status—as we can see from Ning Yu's teachers—was determined by their political loyalty rather than their academic training.

So Ning Yu learned one kind of English at school, the rote memorization of political slogans: "Long live Chairman Mao! Down with the Soviet Neo-Czarists!" He explains that because the Cultural Revolution stifled originality of language, as of thought, "the Cultural Revolution was rightly called the decade of clichés, when people couldn't say what they really wanted to say and therefore used trite phrases to say what they didn't want to say. "Consequently," he says, "I used the clichés deliberately to create a realistic atmosphere for my story, and also ironically to attack the decade of clichés."

Ning Yu learned another kind of English, the rich, imaginative language of high-culture literature, from his father. On the verge of his fourth imprisonment as an intellectual (and therefore by definition subversive), Dr. Yu taught his teenage son the alphabet, some rules for pronunciation, spelling, and grammar, and how to use a dictionary. As he went to prison, he gave Yu a copy of Jane Austen's *Pride and Prejudice* and an old English-Chinese dictionary and told him to translate the novel—which Ning Yu "struggled through from cover to cover" during the nineteen months of his father's incarceration. Ning Yu's essay makes clear the relations among politics, social class, and education under the Maoist regime.

❄ Red and Black, or One English Major's Beginning

1   I have always told my friends that my first English teacher was
my father. That is the truth, but not the whole truth. It was a
freezing morning more than twenty years ago, we, some fifty-odd
boys and girls, were shivering in a poorly heated classroom when
the door was pushed open and in came a gust of wind and Comrade Chang Hong-gen, our young teacher. Wrapped in an elegant
army overcoat, Comrade Chang strode in front of the blackboard
and began to address us in outrageous gibberish. His gestures, his
facial expressions, and his loud voice unmistakably communi-
cated that he was lecturing us as a People's Liberation Army captain would address his soldiers before a battle—in revolutionary
war movies, that is. Of course we didn't understand a word of the
speech until he translated it into Chinese later:

> Comrades, red-guards, and revolutionary pupils:
> The Great Revolutionary Teacher Marx teaches us:
> "A foreign language is an important weapon in the
> struggle of human life." Our Great Leader, Great Teacher,
> Great Supreme-Commander, and Great Helmsman, Chair-
> man Mao, has also taught us that it is not too difficult to
> learn a foreign language. "Nothing in the world is too
> difficult if you are willing to tackle it with the same spirit
> in which we conquered this mountain."
> Now, as you know, the Soviet Social Imperialists and
> the U.S. Imperialists have agreed on a venomous scheme
> to enslave China. For years the U.S. Imperialists have
> brought war and disaster to Vietnam; and you must have
> heard that the Soviet troops invaded our Jewel Island in
> Heilongjiang Province last month. Their evil purpose is
> obvious—to invade China, the Soviets from the north and
> the Americans from the south through Vietnam.
> We are not afraid of them, because we have the
> leadership of Chairman Mao, the invincible Mao Zedong
> Thought, and seven hundred million people. But we need
> to be prepared. As intellectual youth, you must not only

prepare to sacrifice your lives for the Party and the Motherland, but also learn to stir up our people's patriotic zeal and
to shatter the morale of the enemy troops. To encourage our
own people, you must study Chairman Mao's works very
hard and learn your lessons well with your teacher of
Chinese; to crush the enemy, you must learn your English
lessons well with me.

Then Comrade Chang paused, his face red and sweat bead- 2
ing on the tip of his nose. Though nonplussed, we could see that
he was genuinely excited, but we were not sure whether his excitement was induced by "patriotic zeal" or the pleasure of hearing
grandiose sounds issued from his own lips. For my part, I suspected that verbal intoxication caused his excitement. Scanning
the classroom, he seemed to bask in our admiration rather than to
urge us to sacrifice our lives for the Party. He then translated the
speech into Chinese and gave us another dose of eloquence:

> From now on, you are not pupils anymore, but soldiers—
> young, intellectual soldiers fighting at a special front.
> Neither is each English word you learn a mere word any-
> more. Each new word is a bullet shot at the enemy's chest,
> and each sentence a hand grenade.

Comrade Chang was from a "red" family. His name *hong* 3
means red in Chinese, and *gen* means root, so literally, he was
"Chang of Red Root." Students said that his father was a major in
the People's Liberation Army, and his grandfather a general, and
that both the father and the grandfather had "contributed a great
deal to the Party, the Motherland, and the Chinese working
people." When the "Great Proletarian Cultural Revolution" started,
Mr. Chang had just graduated from the Beijing Foreign Languages
Institute, a prestigious university in the capital where some thirty
languages were taught to people "of red roots." Red youngsters
were trained there to serve in the Foreign Ministry, mostly in
Chinese embassies and consulates in foreign countries. We understood that Comrade Chang would work only for a token period in
our ghetto middle school. At the time, the Foreign Ministry was
too busy with the Cultural Revolution to hire new translators,
but as soon as the "Movement" was over and everything back to

normal, Comrade Chang, we knew, would leave us and begin his diplomatic career.

4   In the late 1960s the Revolution defined "intellectual" as "subversive." So my father, a university professor educated in a British missionary school in Tianjin, was regarded as a "black" element, an enemy of the people. In 1967, our family was driven out of our university faculty apartment, and I found myself in a ghetto middle school, an undeserving pupil of the red expert Comrade Chang.

5   In a shabby and ill-heated schoolroom I began my first English lesson, not "from the very beginning" by studying the alphabet, but with some powerful "hand grenades":

> Give up; no harm!
> Drop your guns!
> Down with the Soviet Neo-Czarists!
> Down with U.S. Imperialism!
> Long live Chairman Mao!
> We wish Chairman Mao a long, long life!
> Victory belongs to our people!

6   These sentences turned out to be almost more difficult and more dangerous to handle than real grenades, for soon the words became mixed up in our heads. So much so that not a few "revolutionary pupils" reconstructed the slogans to the hearty satisfactions of themselves but to the horror of Comrade Chang:

> Long live the Soviet Neo-Czarists!
> Victory belongs to your guns!

Upon hearing this, Comrade Chang turned pale and shouted at us, "You idiots! Had you uttered anything like that in Chinese, young as you are, you could have been thrown into jail for years. Probably me too! Now you follow me closely: Long live Chairman Mao!"

7   "Long live Chairman Mao!" we shouted back.
8   "Long live Chairman Mao!"
9   "Long live Chairman Mao!"
10   "Down with the Soviet Neo-Czarists!"
11   "Down with the Soviet Neo-Czarists!"

Comrade Chang decided that those two sentences were enough for idiots to learn in one lesson, and he told us to forget the other sentences for the moment. Then he wrote the two sentences on the chalkboard and asked us to copy them in our English exercise books. Alas, how could anybody in our school know what that was!

I wrote the two sentences on my left palm and avoided putting my left hand in my pocket or mitten for the rest of the day. I also remembered what Comrade Chang said about being thrown into jail, for as the son of a "black, stinking bourgeois intellectual," I grasped the truth in his warning. The two English sentences were a long series of meaningless, unutterable sounds. Comrade Chang had the power to impose some Chinese meaning on my mind. So, before I forgot or confused the sounds, I invented a makeshift transliteration in Chinese for the phonetically difficult and politically dangerous parts of the sentences. I put the Chinese words *qui, mian,* and *mao* (cut, noodle, hair) under "Chairman Mao," and *niu za sui* (beef organ meat) under "Neo-Czarists." "Down with" were bad words applied to the enemies; "long live" were good words reserved for the great leader. These were easy to remember. So I went home with a sense of security, thinking the device helped me distinguish the Great Leader from the enemy.

The next morning, Comrade "Red Roots" asked us to try our weapons before the blackboard. Nobody volunteered. Then Comrade Chang began calling us by name. My friend "Calf" was the first to stand up. He did not remember anything. He didn't try to learn the words, and he told me to "forget it" when I was trying to memorize the weird sounds. In fact, none of my classmates remembered the sentences.

My fellow pupils were all "red" theoretically. But they were not Comrade Chang's type of red. Their parents were coolies, candy-peddlers, or bricklayers. Poor and illiterate. Before the 1949 revolution, these people led miserable lives. Even the revolution didn't improve their lives much, and parents preferred their children to do chores at home rather than fool around with books, especially after the "Great Proletarian Cultural Revolution" started in 1966. Books were dangerous. Those who read books often ran into trouble for having ideas the Party didn't want them to have. "Look at the intellectuals," they said. "They suffer even more than us illiterates." They also knew that their children could not become "red experts" like Comrade Chang, because they themselves were working people who didn't contribute to the Party, the Motherland—or to the liberation of the working people themselves.

16   Thus my friends didn't waste time in remembering nonsense. Still Comrade Chang's questions had to be answered. Since I was the only one in class not from a red family, my opinion was always the last asked, if asked at all. I stood up when Comrade Chang called my name. I had forgotten the English sounds too, for I took Calf's advice. But before I repeated the apology already repeated fifty times by my friends, I glanced at my left palm and inspiration lit up my mind. "Long live *qie mian mao!* Down with *niu za sui!*" My friends stared, and Comrade Chang glared at me. He couldn't believe his ears. "Say that again." I did. This time my classmates burst into a roar of laughter. "Cut noodle hair! Beef organ meat!" they shouted again and again.

17   "Shut up!" Comrade Chang yelled, trembling with anger and pointing at me with his right index finger. "What do you mean by 'cut noodle hair'? That insults our great leader Chairman Mao." Hearing that, the class suddenly became silent. The sons and daughters of the "Chinese working people" knew how serious an accusation that could be. But Calf stood up and said: "Comrade Teacher, it is truly a bad thing that Ning Yu should associate Chairman Mao with such nonsense as 'cut noodle hair.' But he didn't mean any harm. He was trying to throw a hand grenade at the enemy. He also called the Soviets 'beef organ meat.' He said one bad thing (not enough respect for Chairman Mao) but then said a good thing (condemning the Soviets). One take away one is zero. So he didn't really do anything wrong, right?"

18   Again the room shook with laughter.

19   Now Comrade Chang flew into a rage and began to lecture us about how class enemies often say good things to cover up evil intentions. Calf, Chang said, was a red boy and should draw a line between himself and me, the black boy. He also threatened to report my "evil words" to the revolutionary committee of the middle school. He said that in the "urgent state of war" what I said could not be forgiven or overlooked. He told me to examine my mind and conduct severe self-criticism before being punished.

"The great proletarian dictatorship," he said, "is all-powerful. All good will be rewarded and all evil punished when the right time comes." He left the classroom in anger without giving us any new hand grenades.

I felt ruined. Destroyed. Undone. I could feel icy steel hand- 20 cuffs closing around my wrists. I could hear the revolutionary slogans that the mobs would shout at me when I was dragged off by the iron hand of the Proletarian Dictatorship. My legs almost failed me on my way home.

Calf knew better. "You have nothing to worry about, Third 21 Ass."

I am the third child in my family, and it is a tradition of old 22 Beijing to call a boy by number. So usually my family called me Thirdy. But in my ghetto, when the kids wanted to be really friendly, they added the word "ass" to your number or name. This address upset me when I first moved into the neighborhood. I was never comfortable with that affix during the years I lived there, but at that moment I appreciated Calf's kindness in using that affix. Words are empty shells. It's the feeling that people attach to a word that counts.

"I'll be crushed like a rotten egg by the iron fist of the Great 23 Proletarian Dictatorship," I said.

"No way. Red Rooty is not going to tell on you. Don't you 24 know he was more scared than you? He was responsible. How could you say such things if he had not taught you? You get it? You relax. *Qie mian mao!* You know, you really sounded like Rooty." Calf grinned.

Although Calf's wisdom helped me to "get it," relax I could 25 not. My legs were as stiff as sticks and my heart beat against my chest so hard that I could hardly breathe. For many years I had tried to get rid of my "blackness" by hard work and good manners. But I could not succeed. No matter how hard I tried I could not change the fact that I was not "red." The Party denied the existence of intermediate colors. If you were not red, logically you could only be black. What Chang said proved what I guessed. But, when cornered, even a rabbit may bite. Comrade Chang, I silently imagined, if I have to be crushed, you can forget about your diplomatic career. I created a drama in which Comrade Chang, the red root, and I, the black root, were crushed into such fine powder that one could hardly tell the red from the black. All one could see was a dark, devilish purple.

26   The next morning, I went to school with a faltering heart, expecting to be called out of the classroom and cuffed. Nothing happened. Comrade Chang seemed to have forgotten my transgression and gave us three handfuls of new "bullets." He slowed down too, placing more emphasis on pronunciation. He cast the "bullets" into hand grenades only after he was sure that we could shoot the "bullets" with certainty.

27   Nothing happened to me that day, or the next day, or the week after. Calf was right. As weeks passed, my dislike of Chang dwindled and I began to feel something akin to gratitude to him. Before learning his English tongue twisters, we only recited Chairman Mao's thirty-six poems. We did that for so long that I memorized the annotations together with the text. I also memorized how many copies were produced for the first, the second, and the third printing. I was bored, and Teacher Chang's tongue twisters brought me relief. Granted they were only old slogans in new sounds. But the mere sounds and the new way of recording the sounds challenged me. Still, as an old Chinese saying goes, good luck never lasts long.

28   Forty hand grenades were as many as the Party thought proper for us to hold. Before I mastered the fortieth tongue twister—"Revolutionary committees are fine"—our "fine" revolutionary committee ordered Comrade Chang to stop English lessons and to make us dig holes for air raid shelters. Comrade Chang approached this new task with just as much "patriotic zeal" as he taught English. In truth he seemed content to let our "bullets" and "hand grenades" rust in the bottom of the holes we dug. But I was not willing to let my only fun slip away easily. When digging the holes I repeated the forty slogans silently. I even said them at home in bed. One night I uttered a sentence as I climbed onto my top bunk. Reading in the bottom bunk, my father heard me and was surprised. He asked where I had learned the words. Then for the first time I told him about Comrade Chang's English lessons.

29   Now it may seem strange for a middle school boy not to turn to his family during a "political crisis." But at that time, it was not strange at all. By then my mother, my sister, and my

brother had already been sent to the countryside in two different remote provinces. Getting help from them was almost impossible, for they had enough pressing problems themselves. Help from my father was even more impractical: he was already "an enemy of the people," and therefore whatever he said or did for me could only complicate my problems rather than resolve them. So I kept him in the dark. Since we had only each other in the huge city of eight million people, we shared many things, but not political problems.

Our home in the working class neighborhood was a single seventeen-square-meter room. Kitchen, bathroom, sitting room, study, bedroom, all in one. There was no ceiling, so we could see the black beams and rafters when we lay in bed. The floor was a damp and sticky dirt, which defied attempts at sweeping and mopping. The walls were yellow and were as damp as the dirt floor. To partition the room was out of the question. Actually my parents had sold their king-sized bed and our single beds, and bought two bunk beds in their stead. My mother and sister each occupied a top bunk, my father slept in one bottom bunk, and my brother and I shared the other. Red Guards had confiscated and burned almost all of my father's Chinese books, but miraculously they left his English books intact. The English books were stuffed under the beds on the dirt floor. We lived in this manner for more than a year till the family members were scattered all over China, first my siblings to a province in the northwest, and then my mother to southern China. They were a thousand miles from us and fifteen hundred miles from each other. After they left, I moved to the top bunk over my father, and we piled the books on the other bed. Thanks to the hard covers, only the bottom two layers of the books had begun to mold.

That evening, after hearing me murmuring in English, my father gestured for me to sit down on his bunk. He asked me whether I knew any sentences other than the one he had heard. I jumped at the opportunity to go through the inventory of my English arsenal. After listening to my forty slogans my father said: "You have a very good English teacher. He has an excellent pronunciation, standard Oxford pronunciation. But the sentences are not likely to be found in any books written by native English speakers. Did he teach you how to read?"

32   "I can read all those sentences if you write them out."

33   "If *I* write them? But can't *you* write them by yourself?"

34   "No."

35   "Did he teach you grammar?"

36   "No."

37   "Did he teach you the alphabet?"

38   "No."

39   My father looked amused. Slowly he shook his head and then asked: "Can you recognize the words, the separate words, when they appear in different contexts?"

40   "I think so, but I'm not sure."

41   He re-opened the book that he was reading and turned to the first page and pointed with his index finger at the first word in the first sentence, signaling me to identify it.

42   I shook my head.

43   He moved the finger to the next word. I didn't know that either. Nor did I know the third word, the shortest word in the line, the word made up of a single letter. My father traced the whole sentence slowly, hoping that I could identify some words. I recognized the bullet "in" and at once threw a hand grenade at him: "Beloved Chairman Mao, you are the red sun *in* our hearts." Encouraged, my father moved his finger back to the second word in the sentence. This time I looked at the word more closely but couldn't recognize it. "It's an 'is,'" he said. "You know 'are' but not 'is'! The third word in this sentence is an 'a'. It means 'one.'" It is the first letter in the alphabet and you don't know that either! What a teacher! A well-trained one too!" He then cleared his throat and read the whole sentence aloud: "It is a truth universally acknowledged that a man in possession of a good fortune, must be in want of a wife."

44   The sounds he uttered reminded me of Chang's opening speech, but they flowed out of my father's mouth smoothly. Without bothering about the meaning of the sentence, I asked my father to repeat it several times because I liked the rhythm. Pleased with my curiosity, my father began to explain the grammatical structure of the sentence. His task turned out to be much harder than he expected, for he had to explain terms such as "subject," "object," "nouns," "verbs" and "adjectives." To help me under-

stand the structure of the English sentence, he had to teach me Chinese grammar first. He realized that the Great Proletarian Culture Revolution had made his youngest son literally illiterate, in Chinese as well as English.

That night, our English lessons started. He taught me the letters A through F. By the end of the week, I had learned my alphabet. Afterward he taught the basics of grammar, sometimes using my hand grenades to illustrate the rules. He also taught me the international phonetic symbols and the way to use a dictionary. For reading materials, he excerpted simple passages from whatever books were available. Some were short paragraphs while others just sentences. We started our lessons at a manageable pace, but after a couple of months, for reasons he didn't tell me till the very last, he speeded up the pace considerably. The new words that I had to memorize increased from twenty words per day to fifty. To meet the challenge, I wrote the new words on small, thin slips of paper and hid them in the little red book of Chairman Mao, so that I could memorize them during the political study hours at school. In hole-digging afternoons I recited the sentences and sometimes even little paragraphs—aloud when I was sure that Chang was not around.

Before the sounds and shapes of English words became less elusive, before I could confidently study by myself, my father told me that I would have to continue on my own. He was going to join the "Mao Zedong Thought Study Group" at his university. In those years, "Mao Zedong Thought Study Group" was a broad term that could refer to many things. Used in reference to my father and people like him, it had only one meaning: a euphemism for imprisonment. He had been imprisoned once when my mother and siblings were still in Bejing. Now it had come again. I asked, "Are you detained or arrested?" "I don't know," he said. "It's just a Study Group." "Oh," I said, feeling the weight of the words. Legally, detention couldn't be any longer than fifteen days; arrest had to be followed by a conviction and a sentence, which also had a definite term. "Just a Study Group" could be a week or a lifetime. I was on my own in a city of eight million people, my English lessons indefinitely postponed. What was worse, some people never returned alive from "Study Groups."

47   "When are you joining them?"

48   "Tomorrow."

49   I pretended to be "man" enough not to cry, but my father's eyes were wet when he made me promise to finish *Pride and Prejudice* by the time he came back.

50   After he left for the "Study Group," bedding roll on his shoulder, I took my first careful look at the book he had thrust into my hands. It was a small book with dark green cloth covers and gilt designs and letters on its spine. I lifted the front cover; the frontispiece had a flowery design and a woman figure on the upper right corner. Floating in the middle of the flowery design and as a mother, holding a baby, she held an armful of herbs, two apples or peaches, and a scroll. Her head tilted slightly toward her right, to an opened scroll intertwined with the flowers on the other side of the page. On the unrolled scroll, there were some words. I was thrilled to find that I could understand all the words in the top two lines with no difficulty except the last word: EVERYMAN, / I WILL GO WITH THEE. . . .

51   Two months after father entered the "Study Group," I stopped going to his university for my monthly allowance. The Party secretary of the bursar's office wore me out by telling me that my father and I didn't deserve to be fed by "working people." "Your father has never done any positive work," meaning the twenty years my father taught at the university undermined rather than contributed to socialist ideology. To avoid starvation, I picked up horse droppings in the streets and sold them to the farming communes in the suburb. Between the little cash savings my father left me and what I earned by selling dung, I managed an independent life. Meanwhile, I didn't forget my promise to my father. When I saw him again nineteen months later, I boasted of having thumbed his dictionary to shreds and struggled through Austen's novel from cover to cover. I hadn't understood the story but I had learned many words.

52   My father was not surprised to find that I took pleasure in drudgery. He knew that looking up English words in a dictionary and wrestling with an almost incomprehensible text could be an exciting challenge. It provided an intellectual relief for a teenager living at a time when the entire country read nothing but Chairman Mao's works. "Don't worry whether you are red or black,"

my father said. "Just be yourself. Just be an ordinary everyman. Keep up with your good work, and when you learn English well enough, you'll be sure of a guide 'in your most need.'"

Content

1. An essay of division and classification often draws rigid boundaries between its categories, so that they are mutually exclusive. Is that true in Ning Yu's essay? Are the "reds" in total opposition to the "blacks"? If there is any overlap or intermingling among these groups, where does it occur (see, for instance, ¶ 15)? Explain your answer.

2. Ning Yu is writing this essay for an American audience that he assumes is relatively unfamiliar with Red Chinese culture. What sorts of information does he need to supply each time he introduces an unfamiliar concept? Has he done this successfully? (An examination of ¶s 1–3 will help focus your answer.)

Strategies/Structures

1. Ning Yu can count on his American readers to make implicit comparisons between his childhood, schooling, and living conditions and their own. What sorts of comparisons do you make, and how do these enhance your understanding of "Red and Black"?

2. Ning Yu depends on Western readers, for political and cultural reasons, to be on the side of those persecuted by the People's Liberation Army, such as his father and, as a consequence, himself. Is this assumption accurate? What evidence from the text corroborates your answer? In what ways do your sympathies determine how you react to the characters and events in Ning Yu's account?

3. This essay gradually shifts from humor to somberness. In what ways does Ning Yu prepare his readers for this shift, and consequently, for the essay's conclusion?

Language

1. Much of the humor in "Red and Black" depends on the students' lack of understanding of the English slogans they are obliged to memorize, and their teacher's failure to teach them how to learn the language. Find some examples of this linguistic humor; why would it strike English-speaking readers as funny, but not the pupils who are trying to memorize the slogans?

2. Ning Yu's essay was written in English, not Chinese. Does his writing give any clues that his native language was not English? Explain your answer.

For Writing

1. Have you ever been given a "label"—based on your race, social class, gender, political or religious affiliation, place of residence (street or area, city or town, state)? If so, what was (or is) that label? How accurate are its connotations? Are they favorable, unfavorable, or a mixture? Does the label stereotype or limit the ways people are expected to react to it? Did (or do) you feel comfortable with that label? If not, what can you do to change it? Write a paper exploring these issues for an audience which includes at least some people whom that label doesn't fit.

2. Have you or anyone you know well ever experienced persecution or harassment—intellectual, political, economic, racial, religious, or for other reasons? If so, write a paper explaining the causes, effects, and resolution (if any) of the problem. If it's extremely complex, select one or two aspects to concentrate on in your paper. Can you count on your audience to be sympathetic to your point of view? If not, what will you need to do to win them to your side?

Additional Topics for Writing
Division and Classification

(For process strategies, see page 357)

1. Write an essay in which you use division to analyze one of the subjects below. Explain or illustrate each of the component parts, showing how each part functions or relates to the functioning or structure of the whole. Remember to adapt your analysis to your reader's assumed knowledge of the subject. Is it extensive? Meager? Or somewhere in between?

   a. The organization of the college or university you attend
   b. An organization of which you are a member—team, band or orchestra, fraternity or sorority, social or political action group
   c. A typical (or atypical) weekday or weekend in your life
   d. Your budget, or the federal budget
   e. Your family
   f. A farm, kibbutz, or factory
   g. Geologic periods
   h. A poem
   i. A provocative short story, novel, play, or television or film drama
   j. A hospital, city hall, bank, restaurant, supermarket, shopping mall

2. Write an essay, adapted to your reader's assumed knowledge of the subject, in which you classify members of one of the following subjects. Make the basis of your classification apparent, consistent, and logical. You may want to identify each group or subgroup by a name or relevant term, actual or invented.

   a. Types of cars (or sports cars), boats, or bicycles
   b. People's temperaments or personality types
   c. Vacations or holidays
   d. Styles of music, or types of a particular kind of music (classical, country and western, folk, rock)
   e. People's styles of spending money
   f. Types of restaurants, or subcategories (such as types of fast-food restaurants)
   g. Individual or family lifestyles
   h. Types of post–high school educational institutions, or types of courses a given school offers
   i. Clothing styles for your age group

    j. Tennis players, skiers, golfers, runners, or other sports stars; or television or movie stars
    k. Computers
    l. Types of stores or shopping malls
   m. Some phenomenon, activity, types of people or literature or entertainment that you like or dislike a great deal
    n. Social or political groups

10 | *Illustration and Example*

If generalizations are an essay's superstructure, illustrations are its building blocks, reinforcing and filling in the skeletal outline. Writers use examples or illustrations to clarify a general point, to make abstractions concrete, to give their general ideas focus, to show readers what they have in mind rather than letting them guess. Suppose you're writing a paper with the general thesis, "Women have been a powerful force in twentieth-century politics." You'll need to identify some of the women you have in mind by adding, for instance, "among them are Eleanor Roosevelt, Golda Meir, Indira Gandhi, Margaret Thatcher, and Aung San Suu Kyi." Each of these references is an example.

But is a simple allusion sufficient? An illustration is meaningful to the extent that your readers understand it. Can you count on them to understand your reference to Eleanor Roosevelt? If not, you'll have to provide enough detail so they'll recognize why you've included her—perhaps because she was the first American ambassador to the United Nations. How much space you spend on the explanation depends on how important the example is to the point you're illustrating. It might warrant a sentence or two, or in an expanded version become the focus of the whole essay.

The essays in this section illustrate the variety of types of examples writers can use, and the varied techniques for using them. "The Power of Books" (pp. 409–418) could be seen as a single, extended narrative illustration of the crucial importance of reading on Richard Wright's development as an independent-minded thinker, writer, and human being who would rather die than lead a slave's life in the South. This illustration itself incorporates a number of significant examples of the particular books and authors who most strongly influenced Wright. H. L. Mencken gets the most space, and consequently the greatest emphasis, because his work was the first that Wright borrowed clandestinely from the public library (which denied access to African-Americans), and its impact was electrifying: "[T]he impulse to dream . . . surged up again and I hungered for books, new ways of looking and seeing." Sinclair Lewis's *Main Street*, the "first serious novel" Wright read, gets the second largest amount of space. Except for including the titles of two Dreiser novels which revived Wright's "vivid sense of [his] mother's suffering," Wright does not differentiate among the other books he read, but treats them as a group (and therefore as a single example), concentrating on their collective impact: "Reading was like a drug, a dope. The novels created moods in which I lived for days."

How many examples do you need to illustrate a point? Enough to make it clear, without become redundant or boring. Sometimes a single example, with or without interpretation or analysis (depending on how obvious it is) will suffice. In "Under the Influence" (pp. 420–433), Scott Russell Sanders uses the single case of his father's alcoholism (and its many manifestations) and his family's reaction to it to represent the problem of alcoholism as it affects the entire alcoholic population of our country. Even though the particulars may vary, Sanders implies, the characteristics of the alcoholic—the drinking, the bravado, the lying and losing control—and of his cowering, continually betrayed family are common enough to be representative of the entire population.

In contrast to the negative discoveries Sanders made about his father's alcoholism and the ambiguous discoveries Wright made in the process of learning to read, in "What's in a Name?" (pp. 448–450) Seung Hee Suh tells a positive story—about how she learned to accept her national origin—through two contrasting examples of her appearance before and after she learned to value her Korean features.

Both Alan Dershowitz and Patricia J. Williams question the conventional use and common interpretations of particular examples. In "The Saints of Servitude" (pp. 435–439) Williams objects to the public welfare policy that stereotypes recipients as lazy loafers who need to learn "the lessons of hard work." She criticizes those who use the example of laundress Oseola McCarty, "a poor black woman of sufficient sacrificial thrift to amass a small fortune" and then give it away for scholarships. "Do we really want to romanticize a system of indentured servitude" for black women? "[A]re there really people in the world who believe that it never occurred to Oseola McCarty that washing clothes was a dead-end job?" In "Shouting 'Fire!'" (pp. 440–446) Dershowitz offers an extended critique of Oliver Wendell Holmes's claim that a given utterance is "just like" falsely shouting "Fire!" in a crowded theater—an analogy often quoted to justify the curtailment of free speech. It's a bad example, argues Dershowitz, inapt, dishonest, misleading, and so often used (or, in Dershowitz's view, misused) that it "may well be the only jurisprudential analogy that has assumed the status of a folk argument."

When you're seeking examples for your own writing, as the motto of the state of Michigan advises, "look about you." Ask "What do I want to illustrate?" "Why?" "Is this a good illustration?" If someone throws an abstraction at you—"What is Truth? Beauty? Justice?"—you can toss it back, without striking out on the curve, if you examine your own experience. Who is the most beautiful person you ever knew? Was the beauty skin-deep? Internal? Or both? Why? What, in your view, is the most beautiful place on earth (including perhaps your own home, a favorite grandparent's kitchen, or . . .)? What makes it so attractive? Other examples might come from what you know about the lives of your family and friends; from conversations, reading, radio, and television.

But, as Dershowitz and Williams remind us, examples can be misleading, and they can be subject to multiple interpretations—and misinterpretations. Choose your examples with care, and anticipate in your analysis how others of differing points of view might interpret them. To control the illustrations, instead of leaving vague, general gaps for your readers to fill in, is to enable your readers to experience the subject your way. With revealing examples, carefully interpreted, you're in charge.

STRATEGIES FOR WRITING— ILLUSTRATION AND EXAMPLE

1. Is my essay a single, extended illustration? Or a combination of several? What am I using the illustration(s) for—to clarify a point? To make an abstraction or a relationship concrete? To provide a definition? To imply or promote an argument?

2. Is my audience familiar with my example(s) or not? How much detail and background information must I provide to be sure the audience understands what I'm saying? How many examples will make my point most effectively? When will they become redundant or boring? Have I chosen the most appropriate examples I could use?

3. What kinds of illustrations or examples am I using? Positive? Negative? Or both? Simple or complicated? What are the sources of my examples—my own or others' personal experiences, a knowledge of history or some other subject, reading? My imagination? Are they to be interpreted literally, symbolically, or on multiple levels?

4. If I'm using more than one illustration or example, in what order will I arrange them? From the most to the least memorable, or vice versa? From the simplest to the most elaborate, or the reverse? In the order in which they occur naturally, historically, or in which they are arranged spatially or geographically? Or by some other means?

5. Are the illustrations or examples self-evident? To what extent must I analyze them to explain their meaning? Does my analysis anticipate objections readers might have to the example(s) I've chosen? Will my language (sarcastic, nostalgic, sentimental, objective) help to provide an interpretation? Does the language fit the example?

RICHARD WRIGHT

Wright was born in 1908 in a sharecropper's cabin on a plantation near Natchez, Mississippi. After a childhood plagued by the poverty, violence, racial discrimination, and family instability that Wright movingly chronicled in *Black Boy* (1945), the first volume of his autobiography, he moved to Memphis and then to Chicago, where he worked in the post office. He found conditions in the North as discriminatory as those in the South, as *American Hunger* (1977), the second—and even angrier—part of his autobiography demonstrates. (Current editions of *Black Boy* include both parts.) In Chicago and later in New York he wrote for a time for radical left publications, the *New Masses* and the *Daily Worker,* but soon chose to concentrate instead on tales of individuals as a literary mode of social protest. His first works, *Uncle Tom's Children* (1938), a collection of short stories, and *Native Son* (1940), established the international reputation he maintained until his death in 1960 in Paris, to which he had expatriated in 1946 in search of a more congenial racial and political environment.

"The Power of Books," from *Black Boy,* powerfully illustrates the liberating effects of reading on Wright as a young man, particularly the works of social iconoclast H. L. Mencken. Fortunately, Wright was unaware of Mencken's racist and anti-Semitic attitudes, made explicit with the publication in 1989 of Mencken's *Diary*. Indeed, these attitudes were at variance with Mencken's own enduring friendships with Jews and with his support of Harlem cultural life in the 1920s.

The Power of Books[1]

One morning I arrived early at work and went into the bank 1
lobby where the Negro porter was mopping. I stood at a counter and picked up the Memphis *Commercial Appeal* and began my free reading of the press. I came finally to the editorial page and saw an article dealing with one H. L. Mencken. I knew by hearsay that he was the editor of the *American Mercury,* but aside

---

[1] Title supplied.

from that I knew nothing about him. The article was a furious denunciation of Mencken, concluding with one, hot, short sentence: Mencken is a fool.

2   I wondered what on earth this Mencken had done to call down upon him the scorn of the South. The only people I had ever heard denounced in the South were Negroes, and this man was not a Negro. Then what ideas did Mencken hold that made a newspaper like the *Commercial Appeal* castigate him publicly? Undoubtedly he must be advocating ideas that the South did not like. Were there, then, people other than Negroes who criticized the South? I knew that during the Civil War the South had hated northern whites, but I had not encountered such hate during my life. Knowing no more of Mencken than I did at that moment, I felt a vague sympathy for him. Had not the South, which had assigned me the role of a nonman, cast at him its hardest words?

3   Now, how could I find out about this Mencken? There was a huge library near the riverfront, but I knew that Negroes were not allowed to patronize its shelves any more than they were the parks and playgrounds of the city. I had gone into the library several times to get books for the white men on the job. Which of them would now help me to get books? And how could I read them without causing concern to the white men with whom I worked? I had so far been successful in hiding my thoughts and feelings from them, but I knew that I would create hostility if I went about this business of reading in a clumsy way.

4   I weighed the personalities of the men on the job. There was Don, a Jew; but I distrusted him. His position was not much better than mine and I knew that he was uneasy and insecure; he had always treated me in an offhand, bantering way that barely concealed his contempt. I was afraid to ask him to help me to get books; his frantic desire to demonstrate a racial solidarity with the whites against Negroes might make him betray me.

5   Then how about the boss? No, he was a Baptist and I had the suspicion that he would not be quite able to comprehend why a black boy would want to read Mencken. There were other white men on the job whose attitudes showed clearly that they were Kluxers or sympathizers, and they were out of the question.

6   There remained only one man whose attitude did not fit into an anti-Negro category, for I had heard the white men refer to him as a "Pope lover." He was an Irish Catholic and was hated by the

white Southerners. I knew that he read books, because I had got him volumes from the library several times. Since he, too, was an object of hatred, I felt that he might refuse me but would hardly betray me. I hesitated, weighing and balancing the imponderable realities.

One morning I paused before the Catholic fellow's desk.   7

"I want to ask you a favor," I whispered to him.   8

"What is it?"   9

"I want to read. I can't get books from the library. I wonder   10
if you'd let me use your card?"

He looked at me suspiciously.   11

"My card is full most of the time," he said.   12

"I see," I said and waited, posing my question silently.   13

"You're not trying to get me into trouble, are you, boy?" he   14
asked, starting at me.

"Oh, no, sir."   15

"What book do you want?"   16

"A book by H. L. Mencken."   17

"Which one?"   18

"I don't know. Has he written more than one?"   19

"He has written several."   20

"I didn't know that."   21

"What makes you want to read Mencken?"   22

"Oh, I just saw his name in the newspaper," I said.   23

"It's good of you to want to read," he said. "But you ought   24
to read the right things."

I said nothing. Would he want to supervise my reading?   25

"Let me think," he said. "I'll figure out something."   26

I turned from him and he called me back. He stared at me   27
quizzically.

"Richard, don't mention this to the other white men," he said.   28

"I understand," I said, "I won't say a word."   29

A few days later he called me to him.   30

"I've got a card in my wife's name," he said. "Here's mine."   31

"Thank you, sir."   32

"Do you think you can manage it?"   33

"I'll manage fine," I said.   34

"If they suspect you, you'll get in trouble," he said.   35

"I'll write the same kind of notes to the library that you   36
wrote when you sent me for books," I told him. "I'll sign your
name."

37   He laughed.

38   "Go ahead. Let me see what you get," he said.

39   That afternoon I addressed myself to forging a note. Now, what were the names of books written by H. L. Mencken? I did not know any of them. I finally wrote what I thought would be a fool-proof note: *Dear Madam: Will you please let this nigger boy*—I used the word "nigger" to make the librarian feel that I could not possibly be the author of the note—*have some books by H. L. Mencken?* I forged the white man's name.

40   I entered the library as I had always done when on errands for whites, but I felt that I would somehow slip up and betray myself. I doffed my hat, stood a respectful distance from the desk, look as unbookish as possible, and waited for the white patrons to be taken care of. When the desk was clear of people, I still waited. The white librarian looked at me.

41   "What do you want, boy?"

42   As though I did not possess the power of speech, I stepped forward and simply handed her the forged note, not parting my lips.

43   "What books by Mencken does he want?" she asked.

44   "I don't know, ma'am," I said, avoiding her eyes.

45   "Who gave you this card?"

46   "Mr. Falk," I said.

47   "Where is he?"

48   "He's at work, at the M——— Optical Company," I said. "I've been in here for him before."

49   "I remember," the woman said. "But he never wrote notes like this."

50   Oh, God, she's suspicious. Perhaps she would not let me have the books? If she had turned her back at that moment, I would have ducked out the door and never gone back. Then I thought of a bold idea.

51   "You can call him up, ma'am," I said, my heart pounding.

52   "You're not using these books, are you?" she asked pointedly.

53   "Oh, no, ma'am. I can't read."

54   "I don't know what he wants by Mencken," she said under her breath.

55   I knew now that I had won; she was thinking of other things and the race question had gone out of her mind. She went to the

shelves. Once or twice she looked over her shoulder at me, as though she was still doubtful. Finally she came forward with two books in her hand.

"I'm sending him two books," she said. "But tell Mr. Falk to come in next time, or send me the names of the books he wants. I don't know what he wants to read."

56

I said nothing. She stamped the card and handed me the books. Not daring to glance at them, I went out of the library, fearing that the woman would call me back for further questioning. A block away from the library I opened one of the books and read a title: *A Book of Prefaces*. I was nearing my nineteenth birthday and I did not know how to pronounce the word *preface*. I thumbed the pages and saw strange words and strange names. I shook my head, disappointed. I looked at the other book; it was called *Prejudices*. I knew what that word meant; I had heard it all of my life. And right off I was on guard against Mencken's books. Why would a man want to call a book *Prejudices?* The word was so stained with all my memories of racial hate that I could not conceive of anybody using it for a title. Perhaps I had made a mistake about Mencken? A man who had prejudices must be wrong.

57

When I showed the books to Mr. Falk, he looked at me and frowned.

58

"That librarian might telephone you," I warned him.

59

"That's all right," he said. "But when you're through reading those books, I want you to tell me what you get out of them."

60

That night in my rented room, while letting the hot water run over my can of pork and beans in the sink, I opened *A Book of Prefaces* and began to read. I was jarred and shocked by the style, the clear, clean, sweeping sentences. Why did he write like that? And how did one write like that? I pictured the man as a raging demon, slashing with his pen, consumed with hate, denouncing everything American, extolling everything European or German, laughing at the weaknesses of people, mocking God, authority. What was this? I stood up, trying to realize what reality lay behind the meaning of the words. . . . Yes, this man was fighting, fighting with words. He was using words as a weapon, using them as one would use a club. Could words be weapons? Well, yes, for here they were. Then, maybe, perhaps, I could use them as a weapon? No. It frightened me. I read on and what amazed

61

me was not what he said, but how on earth anybody had the courage to say it.

62   Occasionally I glanced up to reassure myself that I was alone in the room. Who were these men about whom Mencken was talking so passionately? Who was Anatole France? Joseph Conrad? Sinclair Lewis, Sherwood Anderson, Dostoevski, George Moore, Gustave Flaubert, Maupassant, Tolstoy, Frank Harris, Mark Twain, Thomas Hardy, Arnold Bennett, Stephen Crane, Zola, Norris, Gorky, Bergson, Ibsen, Balzac, Bernard Shaw, Dumas, Poe, Thomas Mann, O. Henry, Dreiser, H. G. Wells, Gogol, T. S. Eliot, Gide, Baudelaire, Edgar Lee Masters, Stendhal, Turgenev, Huneker, Nietzsche, and scores of others? Were these men real? Did they exist or had they existed? And how did one pronounce their names?

63   I ran across many words whose meanings I did not know, and I either looked them up in a dictionary or, before I had a chance to do that, encountered the word in a context that made its meaning clear. But what strange world was this? I concluded the book with the conviction that I had somehow overlooked something terribly important in life. I had once tried to write, had once reveled in feeling, had let my crude imagination roam, but the impulse to dream had been slowly beaten out of me by experience. Now it surged up again and I hungered for books, new ways of looking and seeing. It was not a matter of believing or disbelieving what I read, but of feeling something new, of being affected by something that made the look of the world different.

64   As dawn broke I ate my pork and beans, feeling dopey, sleepy. I went to work, but the mood of the book would not die; it lingered, coloring everything I saw, heard, did. I now felt that I knew what the white men were feeling. Merely because I had read a book that had spoken of how they lived and thought, I identified myself with that book, I felt vaguely guilty. Would I, filled with bookish notions, act in a manner that would make the whites dislike me?

65   I forged more notes and my trips to the library became frequent. Reading grew into a passion. My first serious novel was Sinclair Lewis's *Main Street*. It made me see my boss, Mr. Gerald, and identify him as an American type. I would smile when I saw him lugging his golf bags into the office. I had always felt a vast

distance separating me from the boss, and now I felt closer to him, though still distant. I felt now that I knew him, that I could feel the very limits of his narrow life. And this had happened because I had read a novel about a mythical man called George F. Babbitt.

The plots and stories in the novels did not interest me so much as the point of view revealed. I gave myself over to each novel without reserve, without trying to criticize it; it was enough for me to see and feel something different. And for me, everything was something different. Reading was like a drug, a dope. The novels created moods in which I lived for days. But I could not conquer my sense of guilt, my feeling that the white men around me knew that I was changing, that I had begun to regard them differently. 66

Whenever I brought a book to the job, I wrapped it in newspaper—a habit that was to persist for years in other cities and under other circumstances. But some of the white men pried into my packages when I was absent and they questioned me. 67

"Boy, what are you reading those books for?" 68

"Oh, I don't know, sir." 69

"That's deep stuff you're reading, boy." 70

"I'm just killing time, sir." 71

"You'll addle your brains if you don't watch out." 72

I read Dreiser's *Jennie Gerhardt* and *Sister Carrie* and they revived in me a vivid sense of my mother's suffering; I was overwhelmed, I grew silent, wondering about the life around me. It would have been impossible for me to have told anyone what I derived from these novels, for it was nothing less than a sense of life itself. All my life had shaped me for the realism, the naturalism of the modern novel, and I could not read enough of them. 73

Steeped in new moods and ideas, I bought a ream of paper and tried to write; but nothing would come, or what did come was flat beyond telling. I discovered that more than desire and feeling were necessary to write and I dropped the idea. Yet I still wondered how it was possible to know people sufficiently to write about them? Could I ever learn about life and people? To me, with my vast ignorance, my Jim Crow station in life, it seemed a task impossible of achievement. I now knew what being a Negro meant. I could endure the hunger. I had learned to live with hate. But to feel that there were feelings denied me, that the 74 very breath of life itself was beyond my reach, that more than anything else hurt, wounded me. I had a new hunger.

75   In buoying me up, reading also cast me down, made me see what was possible, what I had missed. My tension returned, new, terrible, bitter, surging, almost too great to be contained. I no longer *felt* that the world about me was hostile, killing; I *knew* it. A million times I asked myself what I could do to save myself, and there were no answers. I seemed forever condemned, ringed by walls.

76   I did not discuss my reading with Mr. Falk, who had lent me his library card; it would have meant talking about myself and that would have been too painful. I smiled each day, fighting desperately to maintain my old behavior, to keep my disposition seemingly sunny. But some of the white men discerned that I had begun to brood.

77   "Wake up there, boy!" Mr. Olin said one day.

78   "Sir!" I answered for the lack of a better word.

79   "You act like you've stolen something," he said.

80   I laughed in the way I knew he expected me to laugh, but I resolved to be more conscious of myself, to watch my every act, to guard and hide the new knowledge that was dawning within me.

81   If I went north, would it be possible for me to build a new life then? But how could a man build a life upon vague, unformed yearnings? I wanted to write and I did not even know the English language. I bought English grammars and found them dull. I felt that I was getting a better sense of the language from novels than grammars. I read hard, discarding a writer as soon as I felt that I had grasped his point of view. At night the printed page stood before my eyes in sleep.

82   Mrs. Moss, my landlady, asked me one Sunday morning:

83   "Son, what is this you keep on reading?"

84   "Oh, nothing. Just novels."

85   "What you get out of 'em?"

86   "I'm just killing time," I said.

87   "I hope you know your own mind," she said in a tone which implied that she doubted if I had a mind.

88   I knew of no Negroes who read the books I liked and I wondered if any Negroes ever thought of them. I knew that there were Negro doctors, lawyers, newspapermen, but I never saw any of

them. When I read a Negro newspaper I never caught the faintest echo of my preoccupation in its pages. I felt trapped and occasionally, for a few days, I would stop reading. But a vague hunger would come over me for books, books that opened up new avenues of feeling and seeing, and again I would forge another note to the white librarian. Again I would read and wonder as only the naive and unlettered can read and wonder, feeling that I carried a secret, criminal burden about with me each day.

That winter my mother and brother came and we set up   89
housekeeping, buying furniture on the installment plan, being cheated and yet knowing no way to avoid it. I began to eat warm food and to my surprise found the regular meals enabled me to read faster. I may have lived through many illnesses and survived them, never suspecting that I was ill. My brother obtained a job and we began to save toward the trip north, plotting our time, setting tentative dates for departure. I told none of the white men on the job that I was planning to go north; I knew that the moment they felt I was thinking of the North they would change toward me. It would have made them feel that I did not like the life I was living, and because my life was completely conditioned by what they said or did, it would have been tantamount to challenging them.

I could calculate my chances for life in the South as a Negro   90
fairly clearly now.

I could fight the southern whites by organizing with other   91
Negroes, as my grandfather had done. But I knew that I could never win that way; there were many whites and there were but few blacks. They were strong and we were weak. Outright black rebellion could never win. If I fought openly I would die and I did not want to die. News of lynchings were frequent.

I could submit and live the life of a genial slave, but that was   92
impossible. All of my life had shaped me to live by my own feelings and thoughts. I could make up to Bess and marry her and inherit the house. But that, too, would be the life of a slave; if I did that, I would crush to death something within me, and I would hate myself as much as I knew the whites already hated those who had submitted. Neither could I ever willingly present myself to be kicked, as Shorty had done. I would rather have died than do that.

I could drain off my restlessness by fighting with Shorty and   93
Harrison. I had seen many Negroes solve the problem of being

black by transferring their hatred of themselves to others with a black skin and fighting them. I would have to be cold to do that, and I was not cold and I could never be.

94   I could, of course, forget what I had read, thrust the whites out of my mind, forget them; and find release from anxiety and longing in sex and alcohol. But the memory of how my father had conducted himself made that course repugnant. If I did not want others to violate my life, how could I voluntarily violate it myself?

95   I had no hope whatever of being a professional man. Not only had I been so conditioned that I did not desire it, but the fulfillment of such an ambition was beyond my capabilities. Well-to-do Negroes lived in a world that was almost as alien to me as the world inhabited by whites.

96   What, then, was there? I held my life in my mind, in my consciousness each day, feeling at times that I would stumble and drop it, spill it forever. My reading had created a vast sense of distance between me and the world in which I lived and tried to make a living, and that sense of distance was increasing each day. My days and nights were one long, quiet, continuously contained dream of terror, tension, and anxiety. I wondered how long I could bear it.

Content

1. This essay, a self-contained section of Wright's autobiography, is an extended illustration of "the power of books." What sorts of power did books hold and promise for Wright, a poor, black, undereducated teenage laborer in Memphis in the 1920s?

2. This essay is also an example of problem-solving. What is Wright's immediate problem (¶s 1–3)? How does he go about solving it? Why does the solution require lying, deception, and manipulation of others?

3. How does Wright expect his readers to react to this behavior? What moral standards does he expect them to apply? (Remember that he published this some twenty years before the passage of the 1964 Civil Rights Act; would his initial readers, southern or northern, have been receptive to his defiance of the law?)

4. How do both the problem and the solution reflect the larger problematic condition of Wright's life? In what ways does solving the immediate problem raise larger, profound issues that require long-term solutions? What options and possible solutions does he contemplate (¶s 90–95)?

Strategies/Structures

1. Why does Wright single out only H. L. Mencken, Sinclair Lewis, and Theodore Dreiser (¶s 61–73) for individual commentary as powerful influences on his "new ways of looking and seeing"? Why does he treat the rest of his vast reading collectively rather than individually?

2. Wright alternates between analytic narrative and scenes, short and long, involving characters and dialogue. Identify some of the key scenes and explain what each scene or character illustrates. What is the effect of these scenes, which show—rather than tell—us what happened?

Language

1. Wright saw Mencken "using words as a weapon, using them as one would use a club" (¶ 61). How does this influence his decision to become a writer? Why, having been overcome with "desire and feeling," can't he just plunge in and write (¶ 74)?

2. Reading gave Wright much of the vocabulary with which he has written "The Power of Books." Identify some words Wright the author uses here that the teenage Wright might not have known. Why does this more sophisticated vocabulary seem natural in the mature Wright's presentation of himself as a teenager?

For Writing

1. In this essay, Wright makes an implicit case for civil disobedience. (Compare this with King's explicit argument for civil disobedience in "Letter from Birmingham Jail" [pp. 569–586]). Write an essay for a generally law-abiding audience in which, using an example from your life or the life of someone you know well (or perhaps have read about), you justify breaking the law (presumably, a "bad" civil law—you'll have to define that) or violating some accepted standards of conduct to support some higher moral principle. The principle(s) involved should be apparent from the example.

2. For Wright, the hard-won opportunity to read provocative and stimulating books not only revolutionized his thinking but gave him the energy to completely change his life. Write an essay on "the power of . . ." for people who would benefit from such power. Focus on a hard-won privilege, opportunity, or relationship and its implications for your life, actual or potential. If the implications have been realized (or are in the process of realization), what enabled you to accomplish them (your own efforts, help from others, luck)? (See Asimov, "Those Crazy Ideas" [pp. 184–195].)

If the potential "power of . . ." has not been fulfilled, what has kept it from coming to fruition? Were there any social or political factors (such as discrimination on account of race, religion, gender, national origin) that influenced the outcome? Jealously from rivals? Your own inadequacies? Will you get a second chance?

SCOTT RUSSELL SANDERS

"Under the Influence," from *Secrets of the Universe* (1991), is full of examples of the effects of alcoholism—on the alcoholic father, on his wife, alternately distressed and defiant, and on his children, cowering with guilt and fear. Sanders uses especially the example of himself, the eldest son, who felt responsible for his father's drinking, guilty because he couldn't get him to stop, and obligated to atone for his father's sins through his own perfection and accomplishment. Although at the age of forty-four Sanders knows that his father was "consumed by disease rather than by disappointment," he writes to understand "the corrosive mixture of helplessness, responsibility, and shame that I learned to feel as the son of an alcoholic." Through the highly specific example of his family's behavior, Sanders illustrates the general problem of alcoholism that afflicts some "ten or fifteen million people." He expects his readers to generalize and to learn from his understanding. (For more information about Sanders, see page 319).

Under the Influence: Paying the Price of My Father's Booze

1   My father drank. He drank as a gut-punched boxer gasps for breath, as a starving dog gobbles food—compulsively, secretly, in pain and trembling. I use the past tense not because he ever quit drinking but because he quit living. That is how the story ends for my father, age sixty-four, heart bursting, body cooling, slumped and forsaken on the linoleum of my brother's

trailer. The story continues for my brother, my sister, my mother, and me, and will continue as long as memory holds.

In the perennial present of memory, I slip into the garage or 2 barn to see my father tipping back the flat green bottles of wine, the brown cylinders of whiskey, the cans of beer disguised in paper bags. His Adam's apple bobs, the liquid gurgles, he wipes the sandy-haired back of a hand over his lips, and then, his blood-shot gaze bumping into me, he stashes the bottle or can inside his jacket, under the workbench, between two bales of hay, and we both pretend the moment has not occurred.

"What's up, buddy?" he says, thick-tongued and edgy. 3

"Sky's up," I answer, playing along. 4

"And don't forget prices," he grumbles. "Prices are always 5 up. And taxes."

In memory, his white 1951 Pontiac with the stripes down the 6 hood and the Indian head on the snout lurches to a stop in the driveway; or it is the 1956 Ford station wagon, or the 1963 Rambler shaped like a toad, or the sleek 1969 Bonneville that will do 120 miles per hour on straightaways; or it is the robin's-egg-blue pickup, new in 1980, battered in 1981, the year of his death. He climbs out, grinning dangerously, unsteady on his legs, and we children interrupt our game of catch, our building of snow forts, our picking of plums, to watch in silence as he weaves past us into the house, where he drops into his overstuffed chair and falls asleep. Shaking her head, our mother stubs out a cigarette he has left smoldering in the ashtray. All evening, until our bedtimes, we tiptoe past him, as past a snoring dragon. Then we curl fearfully in our sheets, listening. Eventually he wakes with a grunt, Mother slings accusations at him, he snarls back, she yells, he growls, their voices clashing. Before long, she retreats to their bedroom, sob-bing—not from the blows of fists, for he never strikes her, but from the force of his words.

Left alone, our father prowls the house, thumping into furni- 7 ture, rummaging in the kitchen, slamming doors, turning the pages of the newspaper with a savage crackle, muttering back at the late-night drivel from television. The roof might fly off, the walls might buckle from the pressure of his rage. Whatever my brother and sister and mother may be thinking on their own rumpled pillows, I lie there hating him, loving him, fearing him, knowing I have failed him. I tell myself he drinks to ease the ache that gnaws at his belly, an ache I must have caused by disappointing him somehow, a murderous ache I should be able to relieve by doing all my chores, earning A's in school, winning baseball games, fixing the broken washer and the burst pipes, bringing in the money to fill his empty wallet. He would not hide the green bottles in his toolbox, would not sneak off to the barn with a lump under his coat, would not fall asleep in the daylight, would not roar and fume, would not drink himself to death, if only I were perfect.

8   I am forty-four, and I know full well now that my father was an alcoholic, a man consumed by disease rather than by disappointment. What had seemed to me a private grief is in fact, of course, a public scourge. In the United States alone, some ten or fifteen million people share his ailment, and behind the doors they slam in fury or disgrace, countless other children tremble. I comfort myself with such knowledge, holding it against the throb of memory like an ice pack against a bruise. Other people have keener sources of grief: poverty, racism, rape, war. I do not wish to compete to determine who has suffered most. I am only trying to understand the corrosive mixture of helplessness, responsibility, and shame that I learned to feel as the son of an alcoholic. I realize now that I did not cause my father's illness, nor could I have cured it. Yet for all this grownup knowledge, I am still ten years old, my own son's age, and as that boy I struggle in guilt and confusion to save my father from pain.

9   Consider a few of our synonyms for *drunk:* tipsy, tight, pickled, soused, and plowed; stoned and stewed, lubricated and inebriated, juiced and sluiced; three sheets to the wind, in your cups, out of your mind, under the table; lit up, tanked up, wiped out; besotted, blotto, bombed, and buzzed; plastered, polluted, putrefied; loaded or looped, boozy, woozy, fuddled, or smashed; crocked and shit-faced, corked and pissed, snockered and sloshed.

10   It is a mostly humorous lexicon, as the lore that deals with drunks—in jokes and cartoons, in plays, films and television skits—is largely comic. Aunt Matilda nips elderberry wine from the sideboard and burps politely during supper. Uncle Fred slouches to the table glassy-eyed, wearing a lampshade for a hat and murmuring, "Candy is dandy, but liquor is quicker." Inspired by cocktails, Mrs. Somebody recounts the events of her day in a

fuzzy dialect, while Mr. Somebody nibbles her ear and croons a bawdy song. On the sofa with Boyfriend, Daughter Somebody giggles, licking gin from her lips, and loosens the bows in her hair. Junior knocks back some brews with his chums at the Leopard Lounge and stumbles home to the wrong house, wonders foggily why he cannot locate his pajamas, and crawls naked into bed with the ugliest girl in school. The family dog slurps from a neglected martini and wobbles to the nursery, where he vomits in Baby's shoe.

It is all great fun. But if in the audience you notice a few   11 laughing faces turn grim when the drunk lurches onstage, don't be surprised, for these are the children of alcoholics. Over the grinning mask of Dionysus, the leering face of Bacchus, these children cannot help seeing the bloated features of their own parents. Instead of laughing, they wince, they mourn. Instead of celebrating the drunk as one freed from constraints, they pity him as one enslaved. They refuse to believe *in vino veritas*, having seen their befuddled parents skid away from truth toward folly and oblivion. And so these children bite their lips until the lush staggers into the wings.

My father, when drunk, was neither funny nor honest; he   12 was pathetic, frightening, deceitful. There seemed to be a leak in him somewhere, and he poured in booze to keep from draining dry. Like a torture victim who refuses to squeal, he would never admit that he had touched a drop, not even in his last year, when he seemed to be dissolving in alcohol before our very eyes. I never knew him to lie about anything, ever, except about this one ruinous fact. Drowsy, clumsy, unable to fix a bicycle tire, balance a grocery sack, or walk across a room, he was stripped of his true self by drink. In a matter of minutes, the contents of a bottle could transform a brave man into a coward, a buddy into a bully, a gifted athlete and skilled carpenter and shrewd businessman into a bumbler. No dictionary of synonyms for *drunk* would soften the anguish of watching our prince turn into a frog.

Father's drinking became the family secret. While growing   13 up, we children never breathed a word of it beyond the four walls of our house. To this day, my brother and sister rarely mention it, and then only when I press them. I did not confess the ugly, bewildering fact to my wife until his wavering and slurred speech forced me to. Recently, on the seventh anniversary of my father's death, I asked my mother if she ever spoke of his drinking to friends. "No, no, never," she replied hastily. "I couldn't bear for anyone to know."

14   The secret bores under the skin, gets in the blood, into the bone, and stays there. Long after you have supposedly been cured of malaria, the fever can flare up, the tremors can shake you. So it is with the fevers of shame. You swallow the bitter quinine of knowledge, and you learn to feel pity and compassion toward the drinker. Yet the shame lingers and, because of it, anger.

15 For a long stretch of my childhood we lived on a military reservation in Ohio, an arsenal where bombs were stored underground in bunkers and vintage airplanes burst into flames and unstable artillery shells boomed nightly at the dump. We had the feeling, as children, that we played within a minefield, where a heedless footfall could trigger an explosion. When Father was drinking, the house, too, became a minefield. The least bump could set off either parent.

16   The more he drank, the more obsessed Mother became with stopping him. She hunted for bottles, counted the cash in his wallet, sniffed at his breath. Without meaning to snoop, we children blundered left and right into damning evidence. On afternoons when he came home from work sober, we flung ourselves at him for hugs and felt against our ribs the telltale lump in his coat. In the barn we tumbled on the hay and heard beneath our sneakers the crunch of broken glass. We tugged open a drawer in his workbench, looking for screwdrivers or crescent wrenches, and spied a gleaming six-pack among the tools. Playing tag, we darted around the house just in time to see him sway on the rear stoop and heave a finished bottle into the woods. In his goodnight kiss we smelled the cloying sweetness of Clorets, the mints he chewed to camouflage his dragon's breath.

17   I can summon up that kiss right now by recalling Theodore Roethke's lines about his own father:

> The whiskey on your breath
> Could make a small boy dizzy;
> But I hung on like death:
> Such waltzing was not easy.

Such waltzing was hard, terribly hard, for with a boy's scrawny arms I was trying to hold my tipsy father upright.

For years, the chief source of those incriminating bottles and 18 cans was a grimy store a mile from us, a cinderblock place called Sly's, with two gas pumps outside and a mangy dog asleep in the window. Inside, on rusty metal shelves or in wheezing coolers, you could find pop and Popsicles, cigarettes, potato chips, canned soup, raunchy postcards, fishing gear, Twinkies, wine, and beer. When Father drove anywhere on errands, Mother would send us along as guards, warning us not to let him out of our sight. And so with one or more of us on board, Father would cruise up to Sly's, pump a dollar's worth of gas or plump the tires with air, and then, telling us to wait in the car, he would head for the doorway.

Dutiful and panicky, we cried, "Let us go with you!"   19

"No," he answered. "I'll be back in two shakes."   20

"Please!"   21

"No!" he roared. "Don't you budge or I'll jerk a knot in your 22 tails!"

So we stayed put, kicking the seats, while he ducked inside. 23 Often, when he had parked the car at a careless angle, we gazed in through the window and saw Mr. Sly fetching down from the shelf behind the cash register two green pints of Gallo wine. Father swigged one of them right there at the counter, stuffed the other in his pocket, and then out he came, a bulge in his coat, a flustered look on his reddened face.

Because the mom and pop who ran the dump were neigh- 24 bors of ours, living just down the tar-blistered road, I hated them all the more for poisoning my father. I wanted to sneak in their store and smash the bottles and set fire to the place. I also hated the Gallo brothers, Ernest and Julio, whose jovial faces beamed from the labels of their wine, labels I would find, torn and curled, when I burned the trash. I noted the Gallo brothers' address in California and studied the road atlas to see how far that was from Ohio, because I meant to go out there and tell Ernest and Julio what they were doing to my father, and then, if they showed no mercy, I would kill them.

While growing up on the back roads and in the country schools 25 and cramped Methodist churches of Ohio and Tennessee, I never heard the word *alcoholic,* never happened across it in books or magazines. In the nearby towns, there were no addiction-treatment programs, no community mental-health centers, no Alcoholics Anonymous chapters, no therapists. Left alone with our grievous secret, we had no way of understanding Father's drinking except as an act of will, a deliberate folly or cruelty, a moral weakness, a sin. He drank because he chose to, pure and simple. Why our father, so playful and competent and kind when sober, would choose to ruin himself and punish his family we could not fathom.

26   Our neighborhood was high on the Bible, and the Bible was hard on drunkards. "Woe to those who are heroes at drinking wine and valiant men in mixing strong drink," wrote Isaiah. "The priest and the prophet reel with strong drink, they are confused with wine, they err in vision, they stumble in giving judgment. For all tables are full of vomit, no place is without filthiness." We children had seen those fouled tables at the local truck stop where the notorious boozers hung out, our father occasionally among them. "Wine and new wine take away the understanding," declared the prophet Hosea. We had also seen evidence of that in our father, who could multiply seven-digit numbers in his head when sober but when drunk could not help us with fourth-grade math. Proverbs warned: "Do not look at wine when it is red, when it sparkles in the cup and goes down smoothly. At the last it bites like a serpent and stings like an adder. Your eyes will see strange things, and your mind utter perverse things." Woe, woe.

27   Dismayingly often, these biblical drunkards stirred up trouble for their own kids. Noah made fresh wine after the flood, drank too much of it, fell asleep without any clothes on, and was glimpsed in the buff by his son Ham, whom Noah promptly cursed. In one passage—it was so shocking we had to read it under our blankets with flashlights—the patriarch Lot fell down drunk and slept with his daughters. The sins of the fathers set their children's teeth on edge.

28   Our ministers were fond of quoting St. Paul's pronouncement that drunkards would not inherit the kingdom of God. These grave preachers assured us that the wine referred to in the Last Supper was in fact grape juice. Bible and sermons and hymns combined to give us the impression that Moses should have brought down from the mountain another stone tablet, bearing the Eleventh Commandment: Thou shalt not drink.

The scariest and most illuminating Bible story apropos of 29
drunkards was the one about the lunatic and the swine. We knew
it by heart: When Jesus climbed out of his boat one day, this lunatic came charging up from the graveyard, stark naked and filthy,
frothing at the mouth, so violent that he broke the strongest
chains. Nobody would go near him. Night and day for years, this
madman had been wailing among the tombs and bruising himself
with stones. Jesus took one look at him and said, "Come out of the
man, you unclean spirits!" for he could see that the lunatic was
possessed by demons. Meanwhile, some hogs were conveniently
rooting nearby. "If we have to come out," begged the demons, "at
least let us go into those swine." Jesus agreed, the unclean spirits
entered the hogs, and the hogs raced straight off a cliff and
plunged into a lake. Hearing the story in Sunday school, my
friends thought mainly of the pigs. (How big a splash did they
make? Who paid for the lost pork?) But I thought of the redeemed
lunatic, who bathed himself and put on clothes and calmly sat at
the feet of Jesus, restored—so the Bible said— to "his right mind."

When drunk, our father was clearly in his wrong mind. He 30
became a stranger, as fearful to us as any graveyard lunatic, not
quite frothing at the mouth but fierce enough, quick-tempered,
explosive; or else he grew maudlin and weepy, which frightened
us nearly as much. In my boyhood despair, I reasoned that maybe
he wasn't to blame for turning into an ogre: Maybe, like the
lunatic, he was possessed by demons.

If my father was indeed possessed, who would exorcise 31
him? If he was a sinner, who would save him? If he was ill, who
would cure him? If he suffered, who would ease his pain? Not
ministers or doctors, for we could not bring ourselves to confide
in them; not the neighbors, for we pretended they had never seen
him drunk; not Mother, who fussed and pleaded but could not
budge him; not my brother and sister, who were only kids. That
left me. It did not matter that I, too, was only a child, and a bewildered one at that. I could not excuse myself.

On first reading a description of delirium tremens—in a book on 32
alcoholism I smuggled from a university library—I thought immediately of the frothing lunatic and the frenzied swine. When I
read stories or watched films about grisly metamorphoses—Dr.
Jekyll and Mr. Hyde, the mild husband changing into a werewolf,

the kindly neighbor inhabited by a brutal alien—I could not help but see my own father's mutation from sober to drunk. Even today, knowing better, I am attracted by the demonic theory of drink, for when I recall my father's transformation, the emergence of his ugly second self, I find it easy to believe in being possessed by unclean spirits. We never knew which version of Father would come home from work, the true or the tainted, nor could we guess how far down the slope toward cruelty he would slide.

33   How far a man *could* slide we gauged by observing our back-road neighbors—the out-of-work miners who had dragged their families to our corner of Ohio from the desolate hollows of Appalachia, the tightfisted farmers, the surly mechanics, the balked and broken men. There was, for example, whiskey-soaked Mr. Jenkins, who beat his wife and kids so hard we could hear their screams from the road. There was Mr. Lavo the wino, who fell asleep smoking time and again, until one night his disgusted wife bundled up the children and went outside and left him in his easy chair to burn; he awoke on his own, staggered out coughing into the yard, and pounded her flat while the children looked on and the shack turned to ash. There was the truck driver, Mr. Sampson, who tripped over his son's tricycle one night while drunk and got mad, jumped into his semi, and drove away, shifting through the dozen gears, and never came back. We saw the bruised children of these fathers clump onto our school bus, we saw the abandoned children huddle in the pews at church, we saw the stunned and battered mothers begging for help at our doors.

34   Our own father never beat us, and I don't think he beat Mother, but he threatened often. The Old Testament Yahweh was not more terrible in His rage. Eyes blazing, voice booming, Father would pull out his belt and swear to give us a whipping, but he never followed through, never needed to, because we could imagine it so vividly. He shoved us, pawed us with the back of his hand, not to injure, just to clear a space. I can see him grabbing Mother by the hair as she cowers on a chair during a nightly quarrel. He twists her neck back until she gapes up at him, and then he lifts over her skull a glass quart bottle of milk, and milk spilling down his forearm, and he yells at her, "Say just one more word, one goddamn word, and I'll shut you up!" I fear she will prick him with her sharp tongue, but she is terrified into silence, and so am

I, and the leaking bottle quivers in the air, and milk seeps through the red hair of my father's uplifted arm, and the entire scene is there to this moment, the head jerked back, the club raised.

When the drink made him weepy, Father would pack, kiss each of us children on the head, and announce from the front door that he was moving out. "Where to?" we demanded, fearful each time that he would leave for good, as Mr. Sampson had roared away for good in his diesel truck. "Someplace where I won't get hounded every minute," Father would answer, his jaw quivering. He stabbed a look at Mother, who might say, "Don't run into the ditch before you get there," or "Good riddance," and then he would slink away. Mother watched him go with arms crossed over her chest, her face closed like the lid on a box of snakes. We children bawled. Where could he go? To the truck stop, that den of iniquity? To one of those dark, ratty flophouses in town? Would he wind up sleeping under a railroad bridge or on a park bench or in a cardboard box, mummied in rags like the bums we had seen on our trips to Cleveland and Chicago? We bawled and bawled, wondering if he would ever come back.

He always did come back, a day or a week later, but each time there was a sliver less of him.

In Kafka's *Metamorphosis*, which opens famously with Gregor Samsa waking up from uneasy dreams to find himself transformed into an insect, Gregor's family keep reassuring themselves that things will be just fine again "when he comes back to us." Each time alcohol transformed our father we held out the same hope, that he would really and truly come back to us, our authentic father, the tender and playful and competent man, and then all things would be fine. We had grounds for such hope. After his tearful departures and chapfallen returns, he would sometimes go weeks, even months, without drinking. Those were glad times. Every day without the furtive glint of bottles, every meal without a fight, every bedtime without sobs encouraged us to believe that such bliss might go on forever.

Mother was fooled by such a hope all during the forty-odd years she knew Greeley Ray Sanders. Soon after she met him in a Chicago delicatessen on the eve of World War II and fell for his butter-melting Mississippi drawl and his wavy red hair, she learned that he drank heavily. But then so did a lot of men. She would soon coax or scold him into breaking the nasty habit. She would point out to him how ugly and foolish it was, this bleary drinking, and then he would quit. He refused to quit during their engagement, however, still refused during the first years of marriage, refused until my older sister came along. The shock of fatherhood sobered him, and he remained sober through my birth at the end of the war and right on through until we moved in 1951 to the Ohio arsenal. The arsenal had more than its share of alcoholics, drug addicts, and other varieties of escape artists. There I turned six and started school and woke into a child's flickering awareness, just in time to see my father begin sneaking swigs in the garage.

39   He sobered up again for most of a year at the height of the Korean War, to celebrate the birth of my brother. But aside from that dry spell, his only breaks from drinking before I graduated from high school were just long enough to raise and then dash our hopes. Then during the fall of my senior year—the time of the Cuban Missile Crisis, when it seemed that the nightly explosions at the munitions dump and the nightly rages in our household might spread to engulf the globe—Father collapsed. His liver, kidneys, and heart all conked out. The doctors saved him, but only by a hair. He stayed in the hospital for weeks, going through a withdrawal so terrible that Mother would not let us visit him. If he wanted to kill himself, the doctors solemnly warned him, all he had to do was hit the bottle again. One binge would finish him.

40   Father must have believed them, for he stayed dry the next fifteen years. It was an answer to prayer, Mother said, it was a miracle. I believe it was a reflex of fear, which he sustained over the years through courage and pride. He knew a man could die from drink, for his brother Roscoe had. We children never laid eyes on doomed Uncle Roscoe, but in the stories Mother told us he became a fairy-tale figure, like a boy who took the wrong turn in the woods and was gobbled up by the wolf.

41   The fifteen-year dry spell came to an end with Father's retirement in the spring of 1978. Like many men, he gave up his identity along with his job. One day he was a boss at the factory, with a brass plate on his door and a reputation to uphold; the next day he was a nobody at home. He and Mother were leaving Ontario, the

last of the many places to which his job had carried them, and they were moving to a new house in Mississippi, his childhood stomping ground. As a boy in Mississippi, Father sold Coca-Cola during dances while the moonshiners peddled their brew in the parking lot; as a young blade, he fought in bars and in the ring, winning a state Golden Gloves championship; he gambled at poker, hunted pheasant, raced motorcycles and cars, played semiprofessional baseball, and, along with all his buddies—in the Black Cat Saloon, behind the cotton gin, in the woods—he drank hard. It was a perilous youth to dream of recovering.

After his final day of work, Mother drove on ahead with a 42 car full of begonias and violets, while Father stayed behind to oversee the packing. When the van was loaded, the sweaty movers broke open a six-pack and offered him a beer.

"Let's drink to retirement!" they crowed. "Let's drink to 43 freedom! to fishing! hunting! loafing! Let's drink to a guy who's going home!"

At least I imagine some such words, for that is all I can do, 44 imagine, and I see Father's hand trembling in midair as he thinks about the fifteen sober years and about the doctors' warning, and he tells himself, *Goddamnit, I am a free man,* and *Why can't a free man drink one beer after a lifetime of hard work?* and I see his arm reaching, his fingers closing, the can tilting to his lips. I even supply a label for the beer, a swaggering brand that promises on television to deliver the essence of life. I watch the amber liquid pour down his throat, the alcohol steal into his blood, the key turn in his brain.

Soon after my parents moved back to Father's treacherous stomp- 45 ing ground, my wife and I visited them in Mississippi with our four-year-old daughter. Mother had been too distraught to warn me about the return of the demons. So when I climbed out of the car that bright July morning and saw my father napping in the hammock, I felt uneasy, and when he lurched upright and blinked his bloodshot eyes and greeted us in a syrupy voice, I was hurled back into childhood.

"What's the matter with Papaw?" our daughter asked. 46

"Nothing," I said. "Nothing!" 47

Like a child again, I pretended not to see him in his stupor, 48 and behind my phony smile I grieved. On that visit and on the few that remained before his death, once again I found bottles in the workbench, bottles in the woods. Again his hands shook too much for him to run a saw, to make his precious miniature furniture, to drive straight down back roads. Again he wound up in the ditch, in the hospital, in jail, in the treatment center. Again he shouted and wept. Again he lied. "I never touched a drop," he swore. "Your mother's making it up."

49   I no longer fancied I could reason with the men whose names I found on the bottles—Jim Beam, Jack Daniel's—but I was able now to recall the cold statistics about alcoholism: ten million victims, fifteen million, twenty. And yet, in spite of my age, I reacted in the same blind way as I had in childhood, by vainly seeking to erase through my efforts whatever drove him to drink. I worked on their place twelve and sixteen hours a day, in the swelter of Mississippi summers, digging ditches, running electrical wires, planting trees, mowing grass, building sheds, as though what nagged at him was some list of chores, as though by taking his worries upon my shoulders I could redeem him. I was flung back into boyhood, acting as though my father would not drink himself to death if only I were perfect.

50   I failed of perfection; he succeeded in dying. To the end, he considered himself not sick but sinful. "Do you want to kill yourself?" I asked him. "Why not?" he answered. "Why the hell not? What's there to save?" To the end, he would not speak about his feelings, would not or could not give a name to the beast that was devouring him.

51   In silence, he went rushing off to the cliff. Unlike the biblical swine, however, he left behind a few of the demons to haunt his children. Life with him and the loss of him twisted us into shapes that will be familiar to other sons and daughters of alcoholics. My brother became a rebel, my sister retreated into shyness, I played the stalwart and dutiful son who would hold the family together. If my father was unstable, I would be a rock. If he squandered money on drink, I would pinch every penny. If he wept when drunk—and only when drunk—I would not let myself weep at all. If he roared at the Little League umpire for calling my pitches balls, I would throw nothing but strikes. Watching him flounder and rage, I came to dread the loss of control. I would go through life without making anyone mad. I vowed never to put in my mouth or veins any chemical that would banish my everyday self. I would

never make a scene, never lash out at the ones I loved, never hurt a soul. Through hard work, relentless work, I would achieve something dazzling—in the classroom, on the basketball court, in the science lab, in the pages of books—and my achievement would distract the world's eyes from his humiliation. I would become a worthy sacrifice, and the smoke of my burning would please God.

It is far easier to recognize these twists in my character than to undo them. Work has become an addiction for me, as drink was an addiction for my father. Knowing this, my daughter gave me a placard for the wall: WORKAHOLIC. The labor is endless and futile, for I can no more redeem myself through work than I could redeem my father. I still panic in the face of other people's anger, because his drunken temper was so terrible. I shrink from causing sadness or disappointment even to strangers, as though I were still concealing the family shame. I still notice every twitch of emotion in those faces around me, having learned as a child to read the weather in faces, and I blame myself for their least pang of unhappiness or anger. In certain moods I blame myself for everything. Guilt burns like acid in my veins. 52

I am moved to write these pages now because my own son, at the age of ten, is taking on himself the griefs of the world, and in particular the griefs of his father. He tells me that when I am gripped by sadness, he feels responsible; he feels there must be something he can do to spring me from depression, to fix my life and that crushing sense of responsibility is exactly what I felt at the age of ten in the face of my father's drinking. My son wonders if I, too, am possessed. I write, therefore, to drag into the light what eats at me—the fear, the guilt, the shame—so that my own children may be spared. 53

I still shy away from nightclubs, from bars, from parties where the solvent is alcohol. My friends puzzle over this, but it is no more peculiar than for a man to shy away from the lions' den after seeing his father torn apart. I took my own first drink at the age of twenty-one, half a glass of burgundy. I knew the odds of my becoming an alcoholic were four times higher than for the children of nonalcoholic fathers. So I sipped warily. 54

I still do—once a week, perhaps, a glass of wine, a can of beer, nothing stronger, nothing more. I listen for the turning of a key in my brain. 55

Content

1. This essay abounds in examples of alcoholism. Which examples are the most memorable? Are these also the most painful? The most powerful? Explain why.

2. Sanders says that in spite of all his "grown-up knowledge" of alcoholism, "I am still ten years old, my own son's age" (¶ 8) as he writes this essay. What does he mean by this? What kind of a character is Sanders in this essay? What kind of a character is his father? Is there any resemblance between father and son?

Strategies/Structures

1. Is Sanders writing for alcoholic readers? Their families? People unfamiliar with the symptoms of alcoholism? Or is he writing mostly for himself, to try to come to terms with the effects of his father's alcoholism on him then and now?

2. Each section of this essay (¶s 1–8, 9–14, 15–24, 25–31, 32–36, 37–44, 45–52, 53–55) focuses on a different sort of example. What are they, and why are they arranged in this particular order?

3. Why does Sanders wait until late in the essay (¶ 39) to discuss his father's sobriety, and then devote only three paragraphs to a state that lasted fifteen years?

Language

What is the tone of this essay? How does Sanders, one of the victims of alcoholism as both a child and an adult, avoid being full of self-pity? Is he angry at his father? How can you tell?

For Writing

1. "Father's drinking became the family secret," says Sanders (¶ 13). Every family has significant secrets. Explain one of your family secrets, illustrating its effects on various family members, particularly on yourself. If you wish to keep the secret, don't show your essay to anyone; the point of writing this is to help yourself understand or come to terms with the matter.

2. Define an economic, political, ecological, social, or personal problem (unemployment, waste disposal, AIDS, hunger, housing, racism, or another subject of your choice) so your readers can understand it from an unusual perspective—your own or that of your sources. Illustrate its causes, effects, or implications with several significant examples.

PATRICIA J. WILLIAMS

In "The Saints of Servitude," an op-editorial first published
in the *New York Times* (October 13, 1996), Williams employs a
technique common in making arguments. She uses a specific,
single-case example—in this instance, the life, hard work, and
generosity of Mississippi laundress Oseola McCarty (born,
1908)—to illustrate a principle that presumably applies to a very
large (though unspecified) number of supposedly similar cases.
What is true of Oseola McCarty, the argument goes, is true of all
others in this class. Indeed, Williams criticizes an alternative
interpretation of the same example. In making her own argument that opposes a fundamental premise of workfare programs
(all the poor "have to do to improve themselves is to work
hard . . . and then try harder, harder, harder"), Williams attacks
another columnist's "simplistic" analysis of McCarty's seventy-
five years of taking in laundry: "It never occurred to her that
she had a claim on the taxpayers for the money she hadn't
earned. . . . Or that society owed her anything except . . . the
freedom to make herself useful." The same story, two versions.

And still more versions. A front-page story in the *New
York Times* (November 12, 1996) explains how Ms. McCarty's
unselfish gift—she did not even ask for so much as a brick to be
dedicated in her name—has inspired others not only to multiply
her gift, but to honor her. Ms. McCarty, so isolated that at times
she talked mostly to her dog (named Dog), her pig (named
Hog), and her cow (named Hazel), has found a voice as people
have acknowledged her generosity. Before she made her gift,
she had been out of Mississippi only once; she had never been
on an airplane or in a tall building. Within a year of establishing
the scholarship fund, she had been given an honorary doctorate
by Harvard, a gold medal by the National Institute of Social
Sciences, won the Wallenberg Humanitarian Award, carried the
Olympic Torch, and dined at the White House. "It has been
like watching a flower open," says a university spokeswoman.
"Nothing of value was lost in the transformation." People make
pilgrimages to her tiny house because "they want to be close
to someone good" and to share in the sense of peace and yes,
humility, that she conveys. Does the fact that so many have
been so moved by Ms. McCarty's generosity negate Williams's
critique? (For biographical information on Williams, see
page 165.)

The Saints of Servitude

1   There's a lot in the press these days about "the lessons of hard work." I'm thinking of the pictures of those women sweating rivers as they tote those bales on the newly equal-opportunity chain gangs in Arizona. No romantic dew of perspiration upon their sopping brows; they atone for their sins in a way that all of the viewing public can enjoy.

2   Elsewhere, welfare recipients are channeled into workfare programs insuring that the poor never sit around twiddling the thumbs of their otherwise idle hands—surely the prelude to reproductive devilment. Make work, not babies, is the message to those on welfare—and indeed make-work is the best the poor can expect from this most wealthy nation's most recent welfare package.

3   Meanwhile, children in gutted inner cities are told that all they have to do to improve themselves is to work hard, just stop complaining—and a smile now and then wouldn't hurt—and then try harder, harder, harder.

4   Now, I'm a fan of work as much as the next person, but I do wonder what lessons are being imparted. In New York City, the poor—many of whom are the descendants of hard-working slaves, or the grandchildren of hard-working sharecroppers, or the children of coal miners, dirt farmers and sweatshop laborers—are to be uplifted from their purportedly lazy ways through the rehabilitative effort of cleaning the subways. Subways in which some of them are living. Their instructors will be unionized workers who have spent decades organizing to improve their own lot, yet whose livelihoods are threatened by workfare's nonunionized, below-minimum-wage pools of labor.

5   The use of work as "lesson" in an economy that offers the least skilled few options is quite troubling. Is it significant, I wonder, that the rush to embrace the least attractive norms of the Industrial Revolution is occurring at a moment when Americans are working harder and harder and harder and harder? Deep resentments are developing toward those who are not busy every single moment of the day. The resentment is deepest, perhaps, among baby boomers who grew up thinking of themselves as the leisure class yet whom Charles Reich has aptly renamed "the

anxious class"—overworked, overwrought, so overwhelmed by debt that even real prisoners in real prisons seem like they're enjoying a vacation just because they have time to sit down and have dinner together.

While much publicity has focused on teaching the poor 6 "discipline" and exposing them to "real work," much of this labor bears little relation either to saving taxpayer dollars or to the lessons of any labor market. The Governor of Alabama, for example, ordered prisoners' vegetable gardens to be plowed under and then imported rock for chain gangs to crush—even in the absence of any need for crushed rock.

Alabama's chain gangs were recently abandoned in the face 7 of pending lawsuits, but the theme of display labor has played on in the several states where chain gangs persist. I begin to wonder if there is not some theatrical stake in the phenomenon of a public excited by stereotyped and overwhelmingly fictional images of luxurious prisons and indolent welfare recipients, lounging about watching cable TV. I grow concerned about a thirst for hard labor.

Not long ago, there were news reports about Oseola McCarty, 8 a woman who had "taken in wash" for more than 75 years and who, having no family, had saved some $150,000 from wages that never exceeded a few dollars a week. At the age of 87, desiring to put her affairs in order, she donated the money to the University of Southern Mississippi for a scholarship fund for black students.

The media made much of the marvel of a poor black woman 9 of sufficient sacrificial thrift to amass a small fortune—and then to hand it on to others. "There was nothing I wanted for myself," she was quoted as saying time and again, patiently, to reporters who seemed awestruck and slightly appalled by the simplicity of her life and by her humility. "I just wanted to do nice . . . something for the children to get an education. Because I didn't get mine, but I want them to have theirs."

Many hailed Ms. McCarty's story with a kind of nostalgia for 10 the good old days when blacks valued a *real* work ethic, eschewed having babies and didn't go to white people for a handout. Jeff Jacoby, a newspaper columnist, wrote: "No one ever notified her that she was one of life's losers, unable to survive without help from Big Brother. It never occurred to her that she was fit only to receive, not to give, to be assisted, never to assist. For that matter, it never occurred to her that she had a claim on the taxpayers for the money she hadn't earned. Or that washing clothes was a 'dead-end' job. Or that society owed her anything except respect, and the freedom to make herself useful."

11   It's a doozy, this phrase: "the freedom to make herself useful." This oddly expressed "freedom" of servitude is, I suppose, a twisted reference to the notion that underlies the common law concept of employment-at-will and much historical resistance to organized labor. The premise is a simple—dare I say simplistic—one. The employer hires a worker. The employer can fire the worker at any time. The worker can quit at any time. Employment at will.

12   But assume that there comes a moment when there is little movement of wealth, when mobility is considerably more limited than this ideal economic model.

13   Assume that poisonous work environments and Dickensian labor conditions exist in a world of free trade zones, of manufacturing islands whose operations can shift almost overnight from North Carolina to Mexico, Thailand or the Philippines. Assume further that the problem of labor is overlaid with unparalleled migrations from rural to urban locations, immigration across national boundaries and the general suspension of civil rights laws.

14   With all these complications in mind, I'll turn to Oseola McCarty, whose genuinely heroic story is so overlaid with easy finger-shaking bromides about self-discipline. It is probably worth asking just a few questions.

15   Do we really want to romanticize a system of indentured servitude that left the vast majority of black women in Miss McCarty's generation actually envying those who did laundry because it was a better job than most? And before making generalizations about what Miss McCarty may have "not earned" in benefits from the Government, isn't it worth asking what she ought to have earned in the private sector, given the great likelihood that she was grossly underpaid? Forgive my naïveté, but are there really people in the world who believe that it never occurred to Oseola McCarty that washing clothes was a dead-end job?

16   Why the rush to declare 75 years of washing other people's dirty drawers a blessing? As though never getting "mine" were the answer to every one else's prayers?

We are faced today with a challenge not to forget the insights   17
of those who worked to create the occupational protections that
many of us take for granted and that many more struggle to retain.
Perhaps if we listened closely to the voices of so many who slaved
their lives away, we might find not only the tenaciously held faith
that there was, at the end of the line, a heaven for them but also a
vision of a future that would be different for us all, the children of
their inconceivably generous aspirations.

Content

1. In using the example of Oseola McCarty as the "Saint of Servitude,"
what does Williams imply about the working poor? About working
women? About the nonworking poor? About relations between employers
and employees throughout the world?

2. What are Williams's objections to reporter Jeff Jacoby's interpretation of the example of Oseola McCarty (¶s 10, 11, 15–17)?

Strategies/Structures

1. Is it appropriate for Williams, in constructing her argument, to treat
Ms. McCarty as representative of numerous other comparable cases?
Why or why not?

2. Both Williams and Jacoby interpret the example of Oseola McCarty,
but neither directly asks McCarty for her opinion. "Forgive my naïveté,"
says Williams, "but are there really people in the world who believe that
it never occurred to Oseola McCarty [in 75 years] that washing clothes
was a dead-end job?" (¶ 15) Given the way each writer uses the example,
would McCarty's explicitly stated opinion matter to either argument?

3. Williams uses irony throughout this essay. Other than the example
cited in the previous question (from ¶ 15), identify other instances of
irony (see, for example, ¶s 1–5) and evaluate their effectiveness in making Williams's case.

Language

1. The success of Williams's argument depends, in part, on changing
readers' stereotypes about "welfare recipients" and "workfare." She uses
fragmentary examples to implicitly define these terms. Are these definitions sufficient to dispel the stereotypes? To convince her readers?

2. What does Williams mean by "equal-opportunity chain gangs" (¶ 1), "workfare" (¶ 2), "display labor" (¶ 7), "sacrificial thrift" (¶ 9), "employment-at-will" (¶ 11)? She doesn't define any of these terms; can she correctly assume that their meaning is clear in context?

For Writing

1. To construct an argument using a single example as the focal point is to make an implicit analogy between that example and all other unspecified cases that the author generalizes about. Write an essay in which you analyze the technique of the single-example argument and either affirm or reject its effectiveness. However, don't rely solely on Williams's "The Saints of Servitude"; analyze one or two additional essays as well. You might consider, for instance, Williams's other essay, "The Death of the Profane" (pp. 165–172), Richard Rodriguez's "None of This Is Fair" (pp. 375–380), Richard Wright's "The Power of Books" (pp. 409–418), Scott Russell Sanders's "Under the Influence" (pp. 420–433), Amy Jo Keifer's "The Death of a Farm" (pp. 662–665), or any other reading of your choice.

2. Write a definition of *welfare* as you have come to know it from Williams's essay and from Stephanie Coontz's "A Nation of Welfare Families" (pp. 275–280). To illustrate your definition, use and interpret the example of one federal, state, or local government policy of which you approve and from which you or your family benefit personally.

ALAN M. DERSHOWITZ

> Dershowitz (born, 1938) earned a B.A. from Brooklyn College and a law degree from Yale. In 1964, after law clerkships with U.S. Appellate Judge David Bazelon and Supreme Court Justice Arthur J. Goldberg, he joined the faculty of Harvard Law School. His academic career has been eclipsed by the high-profile court cases he takes on appeal, as the nearly invincible "defense attorney of last resort for the desperate and despised, counselor for lost causes and forlorn hopes." His passionate defense of civil liberties, articulated in such books as *The Best Defense* (1982) and *Taking Liberties: A Compendium of Hard Cases, Legal Dilemmas and Bum Raps* (1988), has been subordinated in the press by his defense of

celebrity clients, including Soviet dissident Anatoly Shcharansky, kidnap victim-turned-terrorist Patty Hearst, televangelist Jim Bakker, actress Mia Farrow, and former football star O. J. Simpson. In "Shouting 'Fire!'" (*Atlantic*, 1989), Dershowitz analyzes the often-used legal analogy that some speech should be suppressed because it is "just like" falsely shouting "Fire!" in a crowded theater. He contends that both opponents and proponents of censorship have consistently misused this analogy, that was "inapt . . . even in the context in which it was originally offered."

Shouting "Fire!"

W hen the Reverend Jerry Falwell learned that the Supreme   1
Court had reversed his $200,000 judgment against *Hustler* magazine for the emotional distress that he had suffered from an outrageous parody, his response was typical of those who seek to censor speech: "Just as no person may scream 'Fire!' in a crowded theater when there is no fire, and find cover under the First Amendment, likewise, no sleazy merchant like Larry Flynt should be able to use the First Amendment as an excuse for maliciously and dishonestly attacking public figures, as he has so often done."

Justice Oliver Wendell Holmes's classic example of unpro-   2
tected speech—falsely shouting "Fire!" in a crowded theater—has been invoked so often, by so many people, in such diverse contexts, that it has become part of our national folk language. It has even appeared—most appropriately—in the theater: in Tom Stoppard's play *Rosencrantz and Guildenstern Are Dead* a character shouts at the audience, "Fire!" He then quickly explains: "It's all right—I'm demonstrating the misuse of free speech." Shouting "Fire!" in the theater may well be the only jurisprudential analogy that has assumed the status of a folk argument. A prominent historian recently characterized it as "the most brilliantly persuasive expression that ever came from Holmes' pen." But in spite of its hallowed position in both the jurisprudence of the First Amendment and the arsenal of political discourse, it is and was an inapt analogy, even in the context in which it was originally offered. It has lately become—despite, perhaps even because of, the frequency and

promiscuousness of its invocation—little more than a caricature of logical argumentation.

3   The case that gave rise to the "Fire!"-in-a-crowded-theater analogy, *Schenck* v. *United States*, involved the prosecution of Charles Schenck, who was the general secretary of the Socialist party in Philadelphia, and Elizabeth Baer, who was its recording secretary. In 1917 a jury found Schenck and Baer guilty of attempting to cause insubordination among soldiers who had been drafted to fight in the First World War. They and other party members had circulated leaflets urging draftees not to "submit to intimidation" by fighting in a war being conducted on behalf of "Wall Street's chosen few."

4   Schenck admitted, and the Court found, that the intent of the pamphlets' "impassioned language" was to "influence" draftees to resist the draft. Interestingly, however, Justice Holmes noted that nothing in the pamphlet suggested that the draftees should use unlawful or violent means to oppose conscription: "In form at least [the pamphlet] confined itself to peaceful measures, such as a petition for the repeal of the act" and an exhortation to exercise "your right to assert your opposition to the draft." Many of its most impassioned words were quoted directly from the Constitution.

5   Justice Holmes acknowledged that "in many places and in ordinary times the defendants, in saying all that was said in the circular, would have been within their constitutional rights." "But," he added, "the character of every act depends upon the circumstances in which it is done." And to illustrate that truism he went on to say:

> The most stringent protection of free speech would not protect a man in falsely shouting fire in a theater, and causing a panic. It does not even protect a man from an injunction against uttering words that may have all the effect of force.

6   Justice Holmes then upheld the convictions in the context of a wartime draft, holding that the pamphlet created "a clear and present danger" of hindering the war effort while our soldiers were fighting for their lives and our liberty.

7   The example of shouting "Fire!" obviously bore little relationship to the facts of the Schenck case. The Schenck pamphlet contained a substantive political message. It urged its draftee

readers to *think* about the message and then—if they so chose—to act on it in a lawful nonviolent way. The man who shouts "Fire!" in a crowded theater is neither sending a political message nor inviting his listener to think about what he has said and decide what to do in a rational, calculated manner. On the contrary, the message is designed to force action *without* contemplation. The message "Fire!" is directed not to the mind and the conscience of the listener but, rather, to his adrenaline and his feet. It is a stimulus to immediate *action,* not thoughtful reflection. It is—as Justice Holmes recognized in his follow-up sentence—the functional equivalent of "uttering words that may have all the effect of force."

Indeed, in that respect the shout of "Fire!" is not even speech, 8 in any meaningful sense of that term. It is a *clang* sound, the equivalent of setting off a nonverbal alarm. Had Justice Holmes been more honest about his example, he would have said that freedom of speech does not protect a kid who pulls a fire alarm in the absence of a fire. But that obviously would have been irrelevant to the case at hand. The proposition that pulling an alarm is not protected speech certainly leads to the conclusion that shouting the word "fire" is also not protected. But the core analogy is the nonverbal alarm, and the derivative example is the verbal shout. By cleverly substituting the derivative shout for the core alarm, Holmes made it possible to analogize one set of words to another—as he could not have done if he had begun with the self-evident proposition that setting off an alarm bell is not free speech.

The analogy is thus not only inapt but also insulting. Most Amer- 9 icans do not respond to political rhetoric with the same kind of automatic acceptance expected of schoolchildren responding to a fire drill. Not a single recipient of the Schenck pamphlet is known to have changed his mind after reading it. Indeed, one draftee, who appeared as a prosecution witness, was asked whether reading the pamphlet asserting that the draft law was unjust would make him "immediately decide that you must erase that law." Not surprisingly, he replied, "I do my own thinking." A theatergoer would probably not respond similarly if asked how he would react to a shout of "Fire!"

Another important reason why the analogy is inapt is that 10 Holmes emphasizes the factual falsity of the shout "Fire!" The

Schenck pamphlet, however, was not factually false. It contained political opinions and ideas about the causes of the war and about appropriate and lawful responses to the draft. As the Supreme Court recently reaffirmed (in *Falwell* v. *Hustler*), "The First Amendment recognizes no such thing as a 'false' idea." Nor does it recognize false opinions about the causes of or cures for war.

11   A closer analogy to the facts of the Schenck case might have been provided by a person's standing outside a theater, offering the patrons a leaflet advising them that in his opinion the theater was structurally unsafe, and urging them not to enter but to complain to the building inspectors. That analogy, however, would not have served Holmes's argument for punishing Schenck. Holmes needed an analogy that would appear relevant to Schenck's political speech but that would invite the conclusion that censorship was appropriate.

12   Unsurprisingly, a war-weary nation—in the throes of a know-nothing hysteria over immigrant anarchists and socialists—welcomed the comparison between what was regarded as a seditious political pamphlet and a malicious shout of "Fire!" Ironically, the "Fire!" analogy is nearly all that survives from the Schenck case; the ruling itself is almost certainly not good law. Pamphlets of the kind that resulted in Schenck's imprisonment have been circulated with impunity during subsequent wars.

13   Over the past several years I have assembled a collection of instances—cases, speeches, arguments—in which proponents of censorship have maintained that the expression at issue is "just like" or "equivalent to" falsely shouting "Fire!" in a crowded theater and ought to be banned, "just as" shouting "Fire!" ought to be banned. The analogy is generally invoked, often with self-satisfaction, as an absolute argument-stopper. It does, after all, claim the high authority of the great Justice Oliver Wendell Holmes. I have rarely heard it invoked in a convincing, or even particularly relevant, way. But that, too, can claim lineage from the great Holmes.

14   Not unlike Falwell, with his silly comparison between shouting "Fire!" and publishing an offensive parody, courts and commentators have frequently invoked "Fire!" as an analogy to expression that is not an automatic stimulus to panic. A state supreme court held that "Holmes' aphorism . . . applies with equal

force to pornography"—in particular to the exhibition of the movie *Carmen Baby* in a drive-in theater in close proximity to highways and homes. Another court analogized "picketing . . . in support of a secondary boycott" to shouting "Fire!" because in both instances "speech and conduct are brigaded." In the famous Skokie case one of the judges argued that allowing Nazis to march through a city where a large number of Holocaust survivors live "just might fall into the same category as one's 'right' to cry fire in a crowded theater."

Outside court the analogies become even more badly stretched. A spokesperson for the New Jersey Sports and Exposition Authority complained that newspaper reports to the effect that a large number of football players had contracted cancer after playing in the Meadowlands—a stadium atop a landfill—were the "journalistic equivalent of shouting fire in a crowded theater." An insect researcher acknowledged that his prediction that a certain amusement park might become roach-infested "may be tantamount to shouting fire in a crowded theater." The philosopher Sidney Hook, in a letter to the *New York Times* bemoaning a Supreme Court decision that required a plaintiff in a defamation action to prove that the offending statement was actually false, argued that the First Amendment does not give the press carte blanche to accuse innocent persons "anymore than the First Amendment protects the right of someone falsely to shout fire in a crowded theater."

Some close analogies to shouting "Fire!" or setting off an alarm are, of course, available: calling in a false bomb threat; dialing 911 and falsely describing an emergency; making a loud, gun-like sound in the presence of the President; setting off a voice-activated sprinkler system by falsely shouting "Fire!" In one case in which the "Fire!" analogy was directly to the point, a creative defendant tried to get around it. The case involved a man who calmly advised an airline clerk that he was "only here to hijack the plane." He was charged, in effect, with shouting "Fire!" in a crowded theater, and his rejected defense—as quoted by the court—was as follows: "If we built fire-proof theaters and let people know about this, then the shouting of 'Fire!' would not cause panic."

Here are some more-distant but still related examples: the recent incident of the police slaying in which some members of an onlooking crowd urged a mentally ill vagrant who had taken an officer's gun to shoot the officer; the screaming of racial epithets during a tense confrontation; shouting down a speaker and preventing him from continuing his speech.

18   Analogies are, by their nature, matters of degree. Some are closer to the core example than others. But any attempt to analogize political ideas in a pamphlet, ugly parody in a magazine, offensive movies in a theater, controversial newspaper articles, or any of the other expressions and actions catalogued above to the very different act of shouting "Fire!" in a crowded theater is either self-deceptive or self-serving.

19   The government does, of course, have some arguable legitimate bases for suppressing speech which bears no relationship to shouting "Fire!" It may ban the publication of nuclear-weapon codes, of information about troop movements, and of the identity of undercover agents. It may criminalize extortion threats and conspiratorial agreements. These expressions may lead directly to serious harm, but the mechanisms of causation are very different from that at work when an alarm is sounded. One may also argue—less persuasively, in my view—against protecting certain forms of public obscenity and defamatory statements. Here, too, the mechanisms of causation are very different. None of these exceptions to the First Amendment's exhortation that the government "shall make no law . . . abridging the freedom of speech, or of the press" is anything like falsely shouting "Fire!" in a crowded theater; they all must be justified on other grounds.

20   A comedian once told his audience, during the stand-up routine, about the time he was standing around a fire with a crowd of people and got in trouble for yelling "Theater, theater!" That, I think, is about as clear and productive a use as anyone has ever made of Holmes's flawed analogy.

Content

1. Why does Dershowitz consider Holmes's "inapt analogy" of "unprotected speech—falsely shouting 'Fire!' in a crowded theater"—as "little more than a caricature of logical argumentation" (¶ 2)?

2. Why does Dershowitz consider the "'Fire!'-in-a-crowded-theater analogy" (¶ 3) "insulting" (¶ 9)?

3. If this analogy is false, "inapt," and insulting, why is it so commonly used in court cases and in popular discourse (¶s 13–17)?

4. Assuming that you knew the "'Fire!'-in-a-crowded-theater analogy" before you read this essay, has Dershowitz offered new ways to think about the use of this familiar analogy? Has he changed your mind about how to use it?

Strategies/Structures

1. When you hear "Fire!" what do you think is going on? Do you react as Dershowitz says people do (¶ 7)? To what extent does Dershowitz's argument depend on the reader's personal experience with such a shout of alarm to corroborate his explanation (¶ 8)?

2. Why does Dershowitz always use an exclamation point when he says "Fire!" in this essay?

Language

1. The essay begins (¶ 2) and ends (¶ 20) with "'Fire!'-in-a-crowded-theater" jokes. Presumably Dershowitz believes the humor will reinforce his serious points. Does it? Or is "'Fire!'-in-a-crowded-theater" too serious to joke about? Are there any taboo subjects for jokes, or does the joke always reside in the way the material is handled and the ways in which it is understood?

2. Dershowitz, a Harvard law professor, summarizes a number of complicated legal cases in language for a general readership. If he has done this successfully, you should be able to understand his argument without recourse to a law dictionary. How well has he succeeded?

For Writing

1. "Analogies are, by their nature, matters of degree. Some are closer to the core example than others," says Dershowitz (¶ 18). Write an essay in which you use an extended analogy to make a point. The analogy should be true, appropriate, and germane to the relevant points of the comparison, implied or overt.

2. Define "free speech," using the First Amendment to the Constitution and Dershowitz's commentary on it as the basis of your definition. Provide three examples, of at least a paragraph in length each, that illustrate your definition.

SEUNG HEE SUH

At the age of ten, Seung Hee Suh moved to the United States in 1980 with her family, in pursuit of her parents' American Dream, to provide their six children, all girls, with a better opportunity for education than they could find in Korea. Her father, who had given up a successful journalistic career in Korea to emigrate, ran a convenience store, and her mother worked on an assembly line "so their daughters could live in a house in the suburbs of Connecticut and wear clothes like the doctors' and lawyers' kids."

But despite the clothes, writes Suh, "I still looked and felt different. I felt so ugly because I did not have the eyes, the hair, and the bright skin like the American kids. To be an American, I thought I had to look white. My funny sounding name reminded them and me that I did not belong in their group." She continues, "I had been denying all along who I was and where I was from. As a result, I also deprived others of what I could share and teach about another world. This essay was written as somewhat of a catharsis. My parents are living out their 'American Dream.' This fall they will be sending their youngest child to college. I graduated from the University of Connecticut in 1993 and I too am fulfilling my dream of living in New York and pursuing a career in journalism."

❄ *What's in a Name?*

1   O kay then, I'm Erin," I said, "Yun, you're Katie, and Jong, your name is Allison." My two younger sisters and I decided on our new American names while we waited for the principal of our new school to come out and greet us. Unlike the other Korean kids we knew, our parents made us keep our Korean names when they enrolled us in our first American school. I grew tired of the puzzled faces when I told my name. Teachers got stuck when my name came up in the attendance call. People always asked me to repeat the name two or three times and no one ever got the pronunciation right. Attending a new school in a new town was my chance to take on a new identity. I could be more American with

my new name. Adults won't bother me with questions about my name, then ask me to tell them stories of Korea. When they learn my new American name, I won't be singled out as the Asian kid. I could be another Jennifer, Kathy, or Mary.

However, the name wasn't enough to make me an Ameri- 2
can. My five sisters and I all took turns getting our hair permed. Mom sat us down and carefully rolled our straight hairs and soaked them with chemicals. As a result, my hair-do was bigger than my body, but it was curly like the American girls'. No one will finger my hair and say, "It's so straight," as if straight hairs didn't belong in this country.

Rippled hair-do still didn't complete the look. In the class- 3
room, the black-haired girl always stood out. In order to cure that problem, I brushed a syrup-like brown solution on to my hair. In minutes, the syrup gave me amber highlights, like the solution box said.

A girl named Erin with curly-brown hair still didn't look 4
like the other kids. You could always find her face. That changed when I was old enough to wear make-up. Dark eyeliner outlined around the eyes and the brush of blue eyeshadow made my eyes bigger. Touch of peach blush on the cheeks narrowed my face. Before drawing my face, I pasted the skin with an ivory skin-tone cream. Now I was painted in colors and shapes like the other girls did in the bathroom before every class period.

In the morning, my sisters and I crowded around the bath- 5
room mirror, curling our hair and layering on the make-up. Dad would look at us frowning and say, "Asian girls shouldn't wear blue paint and red lipstick, and why do you perm your hair?" I immediately dismissed his scolding. What does he know about modern girls anyway? He doesn't know about America. Mom understood why we clustered in front of the mirror. She bought us the make-up and permed our hair.

Later, Mom didn't have time to play with my hair, so I let the 6
curls go straight. My hair was back in proportion to my body and it looked like the women on the cover of Mom's Korean maga-zines. But I was surprised; the girls at school commented, "you have such pretty hair; I wish my hair was straight." Strangers compared my hair with silk and wanted to caress it.

7   Also, the highlights dimmed after several washes. Someone asked me, "How do you get your hair color to be so black? I tried coloring but it didn't come out right." A smile came over me knowing that an American girl admired and wanted what I had as an Asian.

8   A man at my father's store told me, "You have very pretty eyes." The compliment surprised me because of the jokes and the ridicule I had heard about slanty-thin oriental eyes. I threw away the blush; the broken eyeshadow was never replaced, and I washed the white skin off my face.

9   On the college applications I wrote Seung Hee Suh and checked off the box for *Asian/Islander.* "What a pretty name. It sounds like 'song.'" People loved repeating my name. They wanted to hear it roll off their tongue. "Seung. What a great name. What does it mean?" they asked. "Endurance, never giving up," I replied and they would say, "I wish my name had a meaning."

10   My younger sister Yun said to me once, "I used to be ashamed and embarrassed to be an Asian, but I'm so glad now that I'm different. I like that people remember me and I can stick out in the crowd. I am glad my name is Yun." In few words, she had summed up what I had gone through and my attitude from the experience. It brought me comfort to know that my insecurities and pride were shared.

Content

1. What indeed is in a name? Or a culture?
2. Why did Seung Hee Suh's mother collaborate with her daughters in their attempt to become physically Americanized?
3. Why does it comfort the author to know that her sister shared her insecurities and pride?

Strategies/Structures

1. At what point in Seung Hee Suh's story do you know she's going to change her mind and accept her Korean origin?
2. Is it necessary to state the moral of the story explicitly in the last paragraph?

Language

What features of Seung Hee Suh's language reveal the influence of an Asian language?

For Writing

1. Have you ever tried to adopt the mask or mannerisms of a race, culture, or class other than the one you were born into? Explain why and how you did this, whether the adoptive guise was temporary or (to date) permanent, and what the consequences were. What were the costs and benefits of your transformation, attempted or actual? Because a paper on this subject could be very long, for the sake of economy you could restrict your discussion to one or two interpreted illustrations.

2. Seung Hee Suh's illustrations could be divided into before/after; foolishness/wisdom; innocence/experience; resistance/acceptance; shame/pride; adolescence/maturity. Pick one pair and use it as the basis for writing an essay, for readers who don't know you, about a comparable theme as it played out in your own life or in the life of someone you know well.

Additional Topics for Writing Illustration and Example

(For process strategies, see page 408)

1. Write an essay that takes as its thesis one of the general statements below, or your adaptation, variation, or disagreement with it. To make the point, use an extended illustration or several shorter ones, based on your own experience, reading, knowledge of history or current events, or other information. Assume that you have to convince a skeptical audience.

    a. Actions speak louder than words.
    b. To err is human.
    c. The only thing we have to fear is fear itself.
    d. And you shall know the truth and the truth shall set you free.
    e. Two heads are better than one.
    f. A house divided against itself cannot stand.
    g. You can lead a horse to water but you can't make him drink.
    h. Time is money.
    i. There never was a good war or a bad peace.
    j. The style is the person.
    k. Early to bed and early to rise, makes a man healthy, wealthy, and wise.
    l. Without justice, courage is weak.
    m. An ounce of prevention is worth a pound of cure.
    n. Self-love is the greatest of all flatterers.
    o. Those who can, do; those who can't, teach.
    p. Vision is the art of seeing things invisible.
    q. A little learning is a dangerous thing.
    r. Some books are to be tasted, others to be swallowed, and some few to be chewed and digested.
    s. Love is blind.
    t. Knowledge is power.
    u. All's fair in love and war.
    v. A winner never quits; a quitter never wins.

2. In an essay, for readers of the dominant ethnic majority, make a generalization about what it means (or meant) to be a member of an ethnic minority in the United States, either in the nineteenth or twentieth century, or before or after certain landmark events, such as the Civil War or the 1964 Civil Rights Act. Use illustrative examples from your own experience, outside reading, or two or three of the following essays in

The Essay Connection: Marshall, "The Making of a Writer" (pp. 42–50); Watanabe (pp. 98–99); Douglass, "Resurrection" (pp. 150–156); Williams, "The Death of the Profane" (pp. 165–172); Zitkala-Sa, excerpts from *The School Days of an Indian Girl* (pp. 254–262); Lim, "Pomegranates and English Education" (pp. 364–373); Rodriguez, "None of This Is Fair" (pp. 375–380); Yu, "Red and Black" (pp. 389–401); Wright, "The Power of Books" (pp. 409–418); Williams, "The Saints of Servitude" (pp. 435–439); Kingston, "On Discovery" (pp. 132–135); Suh, "What's in a Name?" (pp. 448–450); Mairs, "On Being a Cripple" (pp. 472–485); King, "Letter from Birmingham Jail" (pp. 569–586); and Guinier, "The Tyranny of the Majority"(pp. 588–595).

Or, write a comparable essay on what it means to be a writer, or to try to become a writer. Among the essays you might consider, for example, are Tan, "Mother Tongue" (pp. 21–28); Welty, "In Love with Books" (pp. 29–34); Marshall, "The Making of a Writer" (pp. 42–50); Weisel, "Why I Write: Making No Become Yes" (pp. 51–57); Plath, "Sylvia Plath at Seventeen" (pp. 88–90); Student Writer's Notebooks (pp. 90–100); Murray, "The Maker's Eye" (pp. 106–115); and Wright, "The Power of Books" (pp. 409–418).

11 | Definition

A definition can set limits or expand them. An objective definition may settle an argument; a subjective definition can provoke one. In either case, they answer the definer's fundamental question, What is X? The easiest way to define something is to identify it as a member of a class and then specify the characteristics that make it distinctive from all the other members of that class. You could define yourself as a "student," but that wouldn't be sufficient to discriminate between you as a college undergraduate and pupils in kindergarten, elementary, junior high, or high school, graduate students, or, for that matter, a person independently studying aardvarks, gourmet cooking, or the nature of the universe.

As you make any kind of writing more specific, you lower the level of abstraction, usually a good idea in definition. So you could identify—and thereby define—yourself by specifying "college student," or more specifically yet, your class status, "college freshman." That might be sufficient for some contexts, such as filling out an application blank. Or you might need to indicate where you go to school "at Cuyahoga Community College" or "Michigan State University." (Initials won't always work—readers might think MSU means Memphis State, or Mississippi, or Montana.)

But if you're writing an entire essay devoted to defining exactly what kind of student you are, a phrase or sentence will be insufficient, even if expanded to include "a computer science major" or "a business major with an accounting specialty, and a varsity diver." Although the details of that definition would separate and thereby distinguish you from, certainly, most other members of your class, they wouldn't convey the essence of what you as a person are like in your student role.

You could consider that sentence your core definition, and expand each key word into a separate paragraph to create an essay-length definition that could include "college student," "accounting major," and "varsity diver." By that still might not cover it. You could approach the subject through considering *cause-and-effect*. Why did you decide to go to college? Because you love to learn? Because you need to get specialized training for your chosen career? To get away from home? What have been the short-term effects of your decision to attend college? What are the long-term effects likely to be—on yourself, on your chosen field, perhaps on the world?

Or you might define yourself as a college student by *comparing and contrasting* your current life with that of a friend still in high school, or with someone who hasn't gone to college, or with a person you admire who has already graduated. If you work part- or full-time while attending college, you could write an *analysis* of its effect on your studying; or an *argument*, using yourself as an *extended example*, stating why it's desirable (or undesirable) for college students to work. Or, among many other possibilities, you could write a *narrative* of a typical week or semester at college. Each of these modes of writing could be an essay of definition. Each could be only partial, unless you wrote a book, for every definition is, by definition, selective. But each would serve your intended purpose. Each essay in this section represents a different common type of definition, but most use other types as well.

Definition According to Purpose. A definition according to purpose specifies the fundamental qualities an object, principle or policy, role, or literary or artistic work has—or should have—in order to fulfill its potential. Thus, such a definition might explicitly answer such questions as, What is the purpose of X? ("A parable is a simple story designed to teach a moral truth.") What is X for? ("Horror movies exist to scare the spectators.") Judy Brady's "I Want a Wife" (pp. 468–471) concentrates on two other aspects of definition according to purpose, What does X do? and What is the role of X? An ideal wife, says Brady, will serve as a wage-earner, secretary, housekeeper, "nurturant attendant" of the children, hostess, entertainer, and sexual companion, among other roles. Brady defines by both negative and positive examples: "I want a wife who will not bother me with rambling complaints about a wife's duties. But I want a wife who will listen to me when I feel the need to explain a rather difficult point I have come across in my course of studies." Because Brady is writing satirically, however, it is possible to interpret the positive examples as negative and vice versa, and still to agree with the emphatic conclusion of her definition, "My God, who *wouldn't* want a wife?"

Descriptive Definition.   A descriptive definition identifies the distinctive characteristics of an individual or group that set it apart from others. Thus a descriptive definition may begin by *naming* something, answering the question, What is X called? A possible answer might be Eudora Welty (unique among all other women); a walnut (as opposed to all other species of nuts); or *The Sound and the Fury* (and no other novel by William Faulkner). A descriptive definition may also *specify the relationship among the parts of a unit or group*, responding to the questions, What is the structure of X? How is X organized? How is X put together? Or it may *identify or describe the obvious traits of something*, What is X made of? Kelly Shea's "Acid Rain" (pp. 495–498) fulfills many of these functions. In naming "acid rain" she identifies other forms of this acid precipitation, "snow, hail, sleet, water vapor, mist and even dew." She refers to it by its unique name, *acid*, and shows how it differs from normal precipitation. She then moves to a process definition, showing the effects of acid rain on the environment: "Acids can leach essential nutrients from lakes, streams, and soils. They can also increase the ability of toxic metals (lead and mercury, for example) to dissolve into a medium." Shea uses this extended definition of acid rain (which comprises seven of the essay's nine paragraphs) as the basis for her concluding argument, "What can we do about the problem?"

Essential or Existential Definition.   An essential definition might be considered a variation of a descriptive definition as it answers the question, "What is the essence, the fundamental nature of X?"—love, beauty, truth, justice, for instance. An existential definition presents the essence of its subject by answering the question, "What does it mean to be X?" or "What does it mean to live as an X" or "in a state of X?"—perhaps Chinese, supremely happy, married, an AIDS victim, handicapped—or as Nancy Mairs says, "crippled." In "On Being a Cripple" (pp. 472–485) Mairs's definition is as complex rhetorically as it is in human terms. In the process of defining what it means to live with multiple sclerosis, Mairs uses a series of illustrations to show what she can do (cook, write, be a wife, mother, teacher, and friend) and what she can't do (run, walk easily, vacuum). Some of these have a narrative structure that states a problem, shows the complications of the problem, and resolves it—all within a paragraph, such as the paragraph that opens the essay with a dramatic fall which Mairs transforms into a comic pratfall—"the old beetle-on-its-back routine." Together these illustrations comprise a partial autobiography that also incorporates thumbnail sketches of Mairs's husband and children. A major aspect of Mairs's definition is her attitude toward MS; she treats her subject as she treats herself, with honesty, anger, sardonic humor, and considerable vigor. Mairs's own life, her reactions to it, and her interpretations of it comprise her existential definition of multiple sclerosis.

Process Definitions.   These are concerned with how things or phenomena get to be the way they are. How is X produced? What causes X? How does it work? What does it do, or not do? With what effects? How does change affect X itself? Such questions are often the basis for scientific definitions, as "Acid Rain," Lewis Thomas's "The Technology of Medicine" (pp. 358–363) and Charles Darwin's "Understanding Natural Selection" (pp. 487–493) illustrate. Darwin's definition is composed of a series of illustrations of natural phenomena and processes (such as stags' horns, cocks' spurs, lions' manes, male peacocks' plumage) that lead to demonstrable effects, such as the propagation and survival of the species. However, Maxine Hong Kingston addresses these questions through a narrative that defines as it explains and analyzes. Kingston's parable, "On Discovery" (pp. 132–135), graphically demonstrates the painful processes by which the traditional, male-dominated Chinese society defined and created female "beauty": plucking out women's facial and eyebrow hairs; piercing their ears by poking and probing the delicate layers of skin; binding their feet by bending the toes so far backward that the arched foot cracked, and squeezing each foot to break the "many tiny bones along the sides." Each illustration in this feminist definition becomes an implicit protest.

Logical Definitions.   Logical definitions answer two related questions: Into what general category does X fall? and How does it differ from all other members of that category? ("A porpoise is a marine mammal but differs from whales, seals, dolphins, and the others in its. . . .") Logical definitions are often used in scientific and philosophical writing, and indeed form the basis for Susanne K. Langer's "Signs and Symbols" (pp. 460–467).

Langer's essay demonstrates the five key principles for writing logical definitions:

1. For economy's sake, use the most specific category to which the item to be defined belongs, rather than broader categories. Thus, Langer confines her discussion to communication among higher animals; her analysis does not encompass the entire animal kingdom.

2. Any division of a class must include all members of that class. In such statements as "Animals think, but they think *of* and *at* things; men think primarily *about* things," Langer is referring to all humans and all higher animals. *Negative definitions* explain what is excluded from a given classification and what is not. Langer says: "A symbol differs from a sign in that it does not announce the presence of the object . . . which is its meaning, but merely *brings this thing to mind*. It is not a mere "'substitute sign' to which we react as though it were the object itself."

3. Subdivisions must be smaller than the class divided. Language and dreaming are two kinds of symbolic behavior.

4. Categories should be mutually exclusive; they should not overlap. A sign is not a symbol.

5. The basis for subdividing categories must be consistent throughout each stage of subdivision. "A sign is always embedded in reality, . . . but a symbol may be divorced from reality altogether."

Ultimately, when you're writing an extended definition, you'll need to make it as clear, real, and understandable as possible. You could define a dog as "a clawed, domesticated carnivorous mammal, *Canis familiaris.*" But would that abstract, technical definition get at your intended focus on working dogs (for instance, sheepherding border collies or seeing-eye German shepherds), or convey the essence of the family setter, Serendipity, who rescued you from drowning when you were five and has been your security blanket ever since? Your choices of specific details, illustrations, analogies, anecdotes, and the like will enable your readers to accept your definition, the ways you see the subject, the boundaries you set.

STRATEGIES FOR WRITING—DEFINITION

1. What is the purpose of the definition (or definitions) I'm writing about? Do I want to explain the subject's particular characteristics? Identify its nature? Persuade readers of my interpretation of its meaning? Entertain readers with a novel, bizarre, or highly personal meaning? How long will my essay be? (A short essay will require a restricted subject that you can cover in the limited space.)

2. For whom am I providing the definition? Why are they reading it? Do they know enough about the background of the subject to enable me to deal with it in a fairly technical way? Or must I stick to the basics— or at least begin there? If I wish to persuade or entertain my readers, can I count on them to have a pre-existing definition in mind against which I can match my own?

3. Will my entire essay be a definition, or will I incorporate definition(s) as part of a different type of essay? What proportion of my essay will be devoted to definition? Where will I include definitions? As I introduce new terms or concepts? Where else, if at all?

4. What techniques of definition will I use: naming; providing examples, brief or extended; comparing and contrasting; considering cause and effect; analysis; argument; narrative; analogy; or a mixture? Will I employ primarily positive or negative means (i.e., X is, or X is not)?

5. How much denotative (objective) definition will I use in my essay? How much connotative (subjective) definition? Will my tone be serious? Authoritative? Entertaining? Sarcastic? Or otherwise?

SUSANNE K. LANGER

Langer (1895–1985), a philosopher, was born in New York City. She earned three degrees from Radcliffe (Ph.D., 1926), taught at Columbia University from 1945 to 1950, and thereafter at Connecticut College until her retirement in 1962. Her concern with the ability of humans to symbolize integrates her research on topics as seemingly different as aesthetics, examined in *Feeling and Form: A Theory of Art* (1953); the nature of the human mind, explored in *Mind: An Essay on Human Feeling* (2 vols., 1957–1972); and symbolic logic, analyzed in the landmark *Philosophy in a New Key: A Study in the Symbols of Reason, Rite, and Art* (1942), which includes "Signs and Symbols." *Mind* focuses on "the nature and origin of the veritable gulf that divides human from animal mentality," and makes human nature unique in the animal kingdom.

"Signs and Symbols" epitomizes this view; "Language is the . . . most amazing achievement of the symbolistic human mind. . . . [W]ithout it anything properly called 'thought' is impossible. . . . The line between man and beast . . . is the language line." Langer offers extended definitions that distinguish signs (which animals use and respond to) from symbols (uniquely human), and illustrates these with numerous examples of human and animal behavior.

Signs and Symbols

1   The trait that sets human mentality apart from every other is its preoccupation with symbols, with images and names that *mean* things, rather than with things themselves. This trait may have been a mere sport of nature once upon a time. Certain creatures do develop tricks and interests that seem biologically unimportant. Pack rats, for instance, and some birds of the crow family take a capricious pleasure in bright objects and carry away such things for which they have, presumably, no earthly use. Perhaps man's tendency to see certain forms as *images,* to hear certain sounds not only as signals but as expressive tones, and to be excited by sunset colors or starlight, was originally just a peculiar sensitivity in a rather highly developed brain. But whatever its

cause, the ultimate destiny of this trait was momentous; for all human activity is based on the appreciation and use of symbols. Language, religion, mathematics, all learning, all science and superstition, even right and wrong, are products of symbolic expression rather than direct experience. Our commonest words, such as "house" and "red" and "walking," are symbols; the pyramids of Egypt and the mysterious circles of Stonehenge are symbols; so are dominions and empires and astronomical universes. We live in a mind-made world, where the things of prime importance are images or words that embody ideas and feelings and attitudes.

The animal mind is like a telephone exchange; it receives 2 stimuli from outside through the sense organs and sends out appropriate responses through the nerves that govern muscles, glands, and other parts of the body. The organism is constantly interacting with its surroundings, receiving messages and acting on the new state of affairs that the messages signify.

But the human mind is not a simple transmitter like a tele- 3 phone exchange. It is more like a great projector; for instead of merely mediating between an event in the outer world and a creature's responsive action, it transforms or, if you will, distorts the event into an image to be looked at, retained, and contemplated. For the images of things that we remember are not exact and faithful transcriptions even of our actual sense impressions. They are made as much by what we think as by what we see. It is a well-known fact that if you ask several people the size of the moon's disk as they look at it, their estimates will vary from the area of a dime to that of a barrel top. Like a magic lantern, the mind projects its ideas of things on the screen of what we call "memory"; but like all projections, these ideas are transformations of actual things. They are, in fact, *symbols* of reality, not pieces of it.

A symbol is not the same thing as a sign; that is a fact that 4 psychologists and philosophers often overlook. All intelligent animals use signs; so do we. To them as well as to us sounds and smells and motions are signs of food, danger, the presence of other beings, or of rain or storm. Furthermore, some animals not only attend to signs but produce them for the benefit of others. Dogs bark at the door to be let in; rabbits thump to call each other; the cooing of doves and the growl of a wolf defending his kill are unequivocal signs of feelings and intentions to be reckoned with by other creatures.

5   We use signs just as animals do, though with considerably more elaboration. We stop at red lights and go on green; we answer calls and bells, watch the sky for coming storms, read trouble or promise or anger in each other's eyes. That is animal intelligence raised to the human level. Those of us who are dog lovers can probably all tell wonderful stories of how high our dogs have sometimes risen in the scale of clever sign interpretation and sign using.

6   A sign is anything that announces the existence or the imminence of some event, the presence of a thing or a person, or a change in a state of affairs. There are signs of the weather, signs of danger, signs of future good or evil, signs of what the past has been. In every case a sign is closely bound up with something to be noted or expected in experience. It is always a part of the situation to which it refers, though the reference may be remote in space and time. In so far as we are led to note or expect the signified event we are making correct use of a sign. This is the essence of rational behavior, which animals show in varying degrees. It is entirely realistic, being closely bound up with the actual objective course of history—learned by experience, and cashed in or voided by further experience.

7   If man had kept to the straight and narrow path of sign using, he would be like the other animals, though perhaps a little brighter. He would not talk, but grunt and gesticulate and point. He would make his wishes known, give warnings, perhaps develop a social system like that of bees and ants, with such a wonderful efficiency of communal enterprise that all men would have plenty to eat, warm apartments—all exactly alike and perfectly convenient—to live in, and everybody could and would sit in the sun or by the fire, as the climate demanded, not talking but just basking, with every want satisfied, most of his life. The young would romp and make love, the old would sleep, the middle-aged would do the routine work almost unconsciously and eat a great deal. But that would be the life of a social, superintelligent, purely sign-using animal.

8   To us who are human, it does not sound very glorious. We want to go places and do things, own all sorts of gadgets that we do not absolutely need, and when we sit down to take it easy we want to talk. Rights and property, social position, special talents

and virtues, and above all our ideas, are what we live for. We have gone off on a tangent that takes us far away from the mere biological cycle that animal generations accomplish; and that is because we can use not only signs but symbols.

A symbol differs from a sign in that it does not announce the   9 presence of the object, the being, condition, or whatnot, which is its meaning, but merely *brings this thing to mind.* It is not a mere "substitute sign" to which we react as though it were the object itself. The fact is that our reaction to hearing a person's name is quite different from our reaction to the person himself. There are certain rare cases where a symbol stands directly for its meaning: in religious experience, for instance, the Host is not only a symbol but a Presence. But symbols in the ordinary sense are not mystic. They are the same sort of thing that ordinary signs are; only they do not call our attention to something necessarily present or to be physically dealt with—they call up merely a conception of the thing they "mean."

The difference between a sign and a symbol is, in brief, that a   10 sign causes us to think or act *in face of* the thing signified, whereas a symbol causes us to think *about* the thing symbolized. Therein lies the great importance of symbolism for human life, its power to make this life so different from any other animal biography that generations of men have found it incredible to suppose that they were of purely zoological origin. A sign is always embedded in reality, in a present that emerges from the actual past and stretches to the future; but a symbol may be divorced from reality altogether. It may refer to what is *not* the case, to a mere idea, a figment, a dream. It serves, therefore, to liberate thought from the immediate stimuli of a physically present world; and that liberation marks the essential difference between human and nonhuman mentality. Animals think, but they think *of* and *at* things; men think primarily *about* things. Words, pictures, and memory images are symbols that may be combined and varied in a thousand ways. The result is a symbolic structure whose meaning is a complex of all their respective meanings, and this kaleidoscope of *ideas* is the typical product of the human brain that we call the "stream of thought."

The process of transforming all direct experience into   11 imagery or into that supreme mode of symbolic expression, language, has so completely taken possession of the human mind that it is not only a special talent but a dominant, organic need. All our sense impressions leave their traces in our memory not only as signs disposing our practical reactions in the future but also as symbols, images representing our *ideas* of things; and the tendency to manipulate ideas, to combine and abstract, mix and extend them by playing with symbols, is man's outstanding characteristic. It seems to be what his brain most naturally and spontaneously does. Therefore his primitive mental function is not judging reality, but *dreaming his desires.*

12   Dreaming is apparently a basic function of human brains, for it is free and unexhausting like our metabolism, heartbeat, and breath. It is easier to dream than not to dream, as it is easier to breathe than to refrain from breathing. The symbolic character of dreams is fairly well established. Symbol mongering, on this ineffectual, uncritical level, seems to be instinctive, the fulfillment of an elementary need rather than the purposeful exercise of a high and difficult talent.

13   The special power of man's mind rests on the evolution of this special activity, not on any transcendently high development of animal intelligence. We are not immeasurably higher than other animals; we are different. We have a biological need and with it a biological gift that they do not share.

14   Because man has not only the ability but the constant need of *conceiving* what has happened to him, what surrounds him, what is demanded of him—in short, of symbolizing nature, himself, and his hopes and fears—he has a constant and crying need of *expression.* What he cannot express, he cannot conceive; what he cannot conceive is chaos, and fills him with terror.

15   If we bear in mind this all-important craving for expression we get a new picture of man's behavior; for from this trait spring his powers and his weaknesses. The process of symbolic transformation that all our experiences undergo is nothing more nor less than the process of *conception,* which underlies the human faculties of abstraction and imagination.

16   When we are faced with a strange or difficult situation, we cannot react directly, as other creatures do, with flight, aggression, or any such simple instinctive pattern. Our whole reaction depends on how we manage to conceive the situation—whether we cast it in a definite dramatic form, whether we see it as a disaster,

a challenge, a fulfillment of doom, or a fiat of the Divine Will. In words or dreamlike images, in artistic or religious or even in cynical form, we must *construe* the events of life. There is great virtue in the figure of speech, "I can *make* nothing of it," to express a failure to understand something. Thought and memory are processes of *making* the thought content and the memory image; the pattern of our ideas is given by the symbols through which we express them. And in the course of manipulating those symbols we inevitably distort the original experience, as we abstract certain features of it, embroider and reinforce those features with other ideas, until the conception we project on the screen of memory is quite different from anything in our real history.

Conception is a necessary and elementary process; what we 17 do with our conceptions is another story. That is the entire history of human culture—of intelligence and mortality, folly and super- stition, ritual, language, and the arts—all the phenomena that set man apart from, and above, the rest of the animal kingdom. As the religious mind has to make all human history a drama of sin and salvation in order to define its own moral attitudes, so a scientist wrestles with the mere presentation of "the facts" before he can reason about them. The process of *envisaging* facts, values, hopes, and fears underlies our whole behavior pattern; and this process is reflected in the evolution of an extraordinary phenomenon found always, and only, in human societies—the phenomenon of language.

Language is the highest and most amazing achievement of 18 the symbolistic human mind. The power it bestows is almost inestimable, for without it anything properly called "thought" is impossible. The birth of language is the dawn of humanity. The line between man and beast—between the highest ape and the lowest savage—is the language line. Whether the primitive Neanderthal man was anthropoid or human depends less on his cranial capacity, his upright posture, or even his use of tools and fire, than on one issue we shall probably never be able to settle— whether or not he spoke.

In all physical traits and practical responses, such as skills 19 and visual judgments, we can find certain continuity between animal and human mentality. Sign using is an ever evolving, ever improving function throughout the whole animal kingdom, from the lowly worm that shrinks into his hole at the sound of an approaching foot, to the dog obeying his master's command, and even to the learned scientist who watches the movements of an index needle.

20   This continuity of the sign-using talent has led psychologists to the belief that language is evolved from the vocal expressions, grunts and coos and cries, whereby animals vent their feelings or signal their fellows; that man has elaborated this sort of communication to the point where it makes a perfect exchange of ideas possible.

21   I do not believe that this doctrine of the origin of language is correct. The essence of language is symbolic, not signific; we use it first and most vitally to formulate and hold ideas in our own minds. Conception, not social control, is its first and foremost benefit.

22   Watch a young child that is just learning to speak play with a toy; he says the name of the object, e.g.,: "Horsey! horsey! horsey!" over and over again, looks at the object, moves it, always saying the name to himself or to the world at large. It is quite a time before he talks to anyone in particular; he talks first of all to himself. This is his way of forming and fixing the *conception* of the object in his mind, and around this conception all his knowledge of it grows. *Names* are the essence of language; for the *name* is what abstracts the conception of the horse from the horse itself, and lets the mere idea recur at the speaking of the name. This permits the conception gathered from one horse experience to be exemplified again by another instance of a horse, so that the notion embodied in the name is a general notion.

23   To this end, the baby uses a word long before he *asks for* the object; when he wants his horsey he is likely to cry and fret, because he is reacting to an actual environment, not forming ideas. He uses the animal language of *signs* for his wants; talking is still a purely symbolic process—its practical value has not really impressed him yet.

24   Language need not be vocal; it may be purely visual, like written language, or even tactual, like the deaf-mute system of speech; but it *must be denotative*. The sounds, intended or unintended, whereby animals communicate do not constitute a language, because they are signs, not names. They never fall into an

organic pattern, a meaningful syntax of even the most rudimentary sort, as all language seems to do with a sort of driving necessity. That is because signs refer to actual situations, in which things have obvious reactions to each other that require only to be noted; but symbols refer to ideas, which are not physically there for inspection, so their connections and features have to be represented. This gives all true language a natural tendency toward growth and development, which seems almost like a life of its own. Languages are not invented; they grow with our need for expression.

In contrast, animal "speech" never has a structure. It is 25 merely an emotional response. Apes may greet their ration of yams with a shout of "Nga!" But they do not say "Nga" between meals. If they could *talk about* their yams instead of just saluting them, they would be the most primitive men instead of the most anthropoid of beasts. They would have ideas, and tell each other things true or false, rational or irrational; they would make plans and invent laws and sing their own praises, as men do.

Content

1. How does Langer define signs and symbols? Why are these definitions, and the distinctions between them, important to an understanding of human mentality?

2. Do the ongoing experiments in which chimpanzees and gorillas "talk" in American Sign Language or by pressing word or symbol keys on special typewriters, and even teach what they've learned to others of their species, threaten the definition of mankind as the exclusively symbol-using species?

Strategies/Structures

Find examples of the following common techniques of definition, and comment on their effectiveness in conveying the meanings of *signs, symbols,* or both:

   a. Illustration
   b. Comparison and contrast
   c. Negation (saying what something is not)
   d. Analysis
   e. Explanation of a process (how something is made, or works)

    f. Identification of cause or effects
    g. Simile, metaphor, and/or analogy
    h. Reference to authority and/or writer's own expertise
    i. Reference to writer's or others' personal experience or observation

Language

1. Why are *names* "the essence of language" (¶ 22)?
2. "Language need not be vocal; it may be purely visual, like written language, or even tactual, like the deaf-mute system of speech; but it *must be denotative*" (¶ 24). Explain.
3. Why does all language "fall into an organic pattern, a meaningful syntax" (¶ 24)? How does this "driving necessity" distinguish human language from animal sounds?

For Writing

1. Write a definition of an abstract term for readers who may not have thought much about the term but who have probably used it often in everyday life—something intangible that can be identified in terms of its effects, causes, manifestations, or other nonphysical properties, such as love, truth, justice, greed, stubbornness, or pride. Illustrate your definition with one or two specific examples with which you are familiar; use the examples as a basis for making generalizations that apply to other aspects of the term.
2. Analyze the literal and symbolic meanings of an action, social phenomenon, poem, novel, or film to interpret what it's saying. Do the literal meanings reinforce the symbolic meanings, or are they at variance with one another?

JUDY BRADY

Brady was born in 1937 in San Francisco and earned a bachelor's degree in painting from the University of Iowa in 1962. Married in 1960 and now divorced, she raised two daughters as a "disenfranchised and fired housewife" while working full-time as a secretary and attending night school. Her activities in the women's movement led to political activism and a trip to Cuba in 1973 to study the influence of class relationships on social change.

Brady's definition of a wife, in the essay below, was first published in December 1971 in the inaugural issue of the feminist magazine *Ms.* That it has been widely reprinted ever since testifies to its appeal to a much wider audience than originally intended. This definition is comprehensive, though ironic, covering wifely behavior; temperament; domestic, social, and sexual tasks; and projected life span of eternal servitude; it justifies the title as well as the closing exclamation, "My God, who *wouldn't* want a wife?"

I Want a Wife

I belong to that classification of people known as wives. I am a 1
Wife. And, not altogether incidentally, I am a mother.

Not too long ago a male friend of mine appeared on the 2
scene fresh from a recent divorce. He had one child, who is, of course, with his ex-wife. He is obviously looking for another wife. As I thought about him while I was ironing one evening, it suddenly occurred to me that I, too, would like to have a wife. Why do I want a wife?

I would like to go back to school so that I can become eco- 3
nomically independent, support myself, and, if need be, support those dependent upon me. I want a wife who will work and send me to school. And while I am going to school I want a wife to take care of my children. I want a wife to keep track of the children's doctor and dentist appointments. And to keep track of mine, too. I want a wife to make sure my children eat properly and are kept clean. I want a wife who will wash the children's clothes and keep them mended. I want a wife who is a good nurturant attendant to my children, who arranges for their schooling, makes sure that they have an adequate social life with their peers, takes them to the park, the zoo, etc. I want a wife who takes care of the children when they are sick, a wife who arranges to be around when the children need special care, because, of course, I cannot miss classes at school. My wife must arrange to lose time at work and not lose the job. It may mean a small cut in my wife's income from time to time, but I guess I can tolerate that. Needless to say, my wife will arrange and pay for the care of the children while my wife is working.

4   I want a wife who will take care of *my* physical needs. I want a wife who will keep my house clean. A wife who will pick up after me. I want a wife who will keep my clothes clean, ironed, mended, replaced when need be, and who will see to it that my personal things are kept in their proper place so that I can find what I need the minute I need it. I want a wife who cooks the meals, a wife who is a *good* cook. I want a wife who will plan the menus, do the necessary grocery shopping, prepare the meals, serve them pleasantly, and then do the cleaning up while I do my studying. I want a wife who will care for me when I am sick and sympathize with my pain and loss of time from school. I want a wife to go along when our family takes a vacation so that someone can continue to care for me and my children when I need a rest and change of scene.

5   I want a wife who will not bother me with rambling complaints about a wife's duties. But I want a wife who will listen to me when I feel the need to explain a rather difficult point I have come across in my course of studies. And I want a wife who will type my papers for me when I have written them.

6   I want a wife who will take care of the details of my social life. When my wife and I are invited out by my friends, I want a wife who will take care of the babysitting arrangements. When I meet people at school that I like and want to entertain, I want a wife who will have the house clean, will prepare a special meal, serve it to me and my friends, and not interrupt when I talk about the things that interest me and my friends. I want a wife who will have arranged that the children are fed and ready for bed before my guests arrive so that the children do not bother us. I want a wife who takes care of the needs of my guests so that they feel comfortable, who makes sure that they have an ashtray, that they are passed the hors d'oeuvres, that they are offered a second helping of the food, that their wine glasses are replenished when necessary, that their coffee is served to them as they like it. And I want a wife who knows that sometimes I need a night out by myself.

7   I want a wife who is sensitive to my sexual needs, a wife who makes love passionately and eagerly when I feel like it, a wife who makes sure that I am satisfied. And, of course, I want a wife who will not demand sexual attention when I am not in the mood for it. I want a wife who assumes the complete responsi-

bility for birth control, because I do not want more children. I want a wife who will remain sexually faithful to me so that I do not have to clutter up my intellectual life with jealousies. And I want a wife who understands that *my* sexual needs may entail more than strict adherence to monogamy. I must, after all, be able to relate to people as fully as possible.

If, by chance, I find another person more suitable as a wife   8
than the wife I already have, I want the liberty to replace my present wife with another one. Naturally, I will expect a fresh, new life; my wife will take the children and be solely responsible for them so that I am left free.

When I am through with school and have a job, I want my   9
wife to quit working and remain at home so that my wife can more fully and completely take care of a wife's duties.

My God, who *wouldn't* want a wife?   10

Content

1. Brady defines *wife* in terms of the purpose(s), activities, and personality traits of a person functioning in a wife's many roles. What are some of these?

2. What is the purpose of Brady's definition of *wife?* How could she expect her intended audience of feminist women to react to this definition? How would more traditional women be expected to respond to this definition? Would men be expected to react in ways similar to those of their female counterparts?

Strategies/Structures

1. In what order does Brady list the wife's expected services?

2. How do you know that Brady does not always mean what she says— for instance, that she does not really favor the sexual double standard identified in paragraphs 7 and 8?

Language

1. Brady always calls a *wife* by that label and never uses the pronouns *he* or *she.* Why not?

2. Why does Brady use the short, simple (almost simplistic) phrase "I want a wife," and why does she repeat it so often?

For Writing

1. Write your own ironic version of "I want a wife," or "I want a husband," aimed at your significant other, actual or imagined. Identify, as Brady does, the spouse's most important roles, activities, personality traits; this should imply or state the reciprocal way you would function as a spouse, for better or worse.

2. Write an essay in which you define the ideal relationship between husband and wife. How likely is this ideal to be realized? If you are married or engaged in a serious courtship, ask your partner to comment on a draft before you revise it.

=====

NANCY MAIRS

Nancy Mairs (born, 1943) defies conventional autobiography as she defies conventional life. In her major works, *Plaintext* (1986), *Remembering the Bone House* (1989), and *Ordinary Time* (1993), all autobiographical, this candid writer presents herself as bitchy, whiny, self-indulgent—but with a redeeming spirituality and wry humor. Married at nineteen, Mairs finished college (Wheaton, 1964), and bore two children. Her reaction to marriage and motherhood ("I didn't know how to do it") resulted in a suicidal mixture of agoraphobia and anorexia. Hospitalized for six months, she has ever since coped with panic attacks and the worsening symptoms of multiple sclerosis. Yet she refuses to sentimentalize her physical state ("I hate it"), or to equate herself with MS: "I am not a disease. What I hate is not me but a disease."

In "On Being a Cripple" Mairs provides for an audience of healthy people a searing comprehensive definition of what it means to be "a cripple," the word she chooses to define herself— instead of "disabled," handicapped," or "differently abled." She examines head-on the symptoms from which those who can "pick up babies, play the piano" too often avert their eyes in embarrassment, ignorance, or fear. With humor and uncompromising integrity, this gutsy woman shows herself in action, grotesque ("I carry one arm bent in front of me, the fingers curled into a claw"), clumsy (falling over backward in a public toilet), fearful of others' pity: "If I had to have MS, by God I was going to do it well. This is a class act, ladies and gentlemen." In the process of explaining what it's like to live with MS, Mairs also shows what it's like to be a wife, a mother, a teacher, a writer. Her initial sense of "grief and fury and terror" has given way, over the years, to acceptance of the "change and loss" that are part of the human condition. Thus Mairs's thoroughly human definition of a particular disease expands to encompass a definition of what it means to be human.

On Being a Cripple

To escape is nothing. Not to escape is nothing.

LOUISE BOGAN

The other day I was thinking of writing an essay on being a cripple. I was thinking hard in one of the stalls of the women's room in my office building, as I was shoving my shirt into my jeans and tugging up my zipper. Preoccupied, I flushed, picked up my book bag, took my cane down from the hook, and unlatched the door. So many movements unbalanced me, and as I pulled the door open I fell over backward, landing fully clothed on the toilet seat with my legs splayed in front of me: the old beetle-on-its-back routine. Saturday afternoon, the building deserted, I was free to laugh aloud as I wriggled back to my feet, my voice bouncing off the yellowish tiles from all directions. Had anyone been there with me, I'd have been still and faint and hot with chagrin. I decided that it was high time to write the essay.

First, the matter of semantics. I am a cripple. I choose this word to name me. I choose from among several possibilities, the most common of which are "handicapped" and "disabled." I made the choice a number of years ago, without thinking, unaware of my motives for doing so. Even now, I'm not sure what those motives are, but I recognize that they are complex and not entirely flattering. People—crippled or not—wince at the word "cripple," as they do not at "handicapped" or "disabled." Perhaps I want them to wince. I want them to see me as a tough customer, one to whom the fates/gods/viruses have not been kind, but who can face the brutal truth of her existence squarely. As a cripple, I swagger.

3   But, to be fair to myself, a certain amount of honesty underlies my choice. "Cripple" seems to me a clean word, straightforward and precise. It has an honorable history, having made its
first appearance in the Lindisfarne Gospel in the tenth century. As
a lover of words, I like the accuracy with which it describes my
condition: I have lost the full use of my limbs. "Disabled," by contrast, suggests any incapacity, physical or mental. And I certainly
don't like "handicapped," which implies that I have deliberately
been put at a disadvantage, by whom I can't imagine (my God is
not a Handicapper General), in order to equalize chances in the
great race of life. These words seem to me to be moving away from
my condition, to be widening the gap between word and reality.
Most remote is the recently coined euphemism "differently abled,"
which partakes of the same semantic hopefulness that transformed
countries from "undeveloped" to "underdeveloped," then to "less
developed," and finally to "developing" nations. People have continued to starve in those countries during the shift. Some realities
do not obey the dictates of language.

4   Mine is one of them. Whatever you call me, I remain
crippled. But I don't care what you call me, so long as it isn't "differently abled," which strikes me as pure verbal garbage designed,
by its ability to describe anyone, to describe no one. I subscribe to
George Orwell's thesis that "the slovenliness of our language
makes it easier for us to have foolish thoughts." And I refuse to
participate in the degeneration of the language to the extent that
I deny that I have lost anything in the course of this calamitous
disease; I refuse to pretend that the only differences between you
and me are the various ordinary ones that distinguish any one
person from another. But call me "disabled" or "handicapped" if
you like. I have long since grown accustomed to them; and if they
are vague, at least they hint at the truth. Moreover, I use them
myself. Society is no readier to accept crippledness than to accept
death, war, sex, sweat, or wrinkles. I would never refer to another
person as a cripple. It is the word I use to name only myself.

5   I haven't always been crippled, a fact for which I am soundly
grateful. To be whole of limb is, I know from experience, infinitely
more pleasant and useful than to be crippled; and if that knowledge leaves me open to bitterness at my loss, the physical soundness I once enjoyed (though I did not enjoy it half enough) is well

worth the occasional stab of regret. Though never any good at sports, I was a normally active child and young adult. I climbed trees, played hopscotch, jumped rope, skated, swam, rode my bicycle, sailed. I despised team sports, spending some of the wretchedest afternoons of my life, sweaty and humiliated, behind a field-hockey stick and under a basketball hoop. I tramped alone for miles along the bridle paths that webbed the woods behind the house I grew up in. I swayed through countless dim hours in the arms of one man or another under the scattered shot of light from mirrored balls, and gyrated through countless more as Tab Hunter and Johnny Mathis gave way to the Rolling Stones, Creedence Clearwater Revival, Cream. I walked down the aisle. I pushed baby carriages, changed tires in the rain, marched for peace.

When I was twenty-eight I started to trip and drop things. 6 What at first seemed my natural clumsiness soon became too pronounced to shrug off. I consulted a neurologist, who told me that I had a brain tumor. A battery of tests, increasingly disagreeable, revealed no tumor. About a year and a half later I developed a blurred spot in one eye. I had, at last, the episodes "disseminated in space and time" requisite for a diagnosis: multiple sclerosis. I have never been sorry for the doctor's initial misdiagnosis, however. For almost a week, until the negative results of tests were in, I thought that I was going to die right away. Every day for the past nearly ten years, then, has been a kind of gift. I accept all gifts.

Multiple sclerosis is a chronic degenerative disease of the 7 central nervous system, in which the myelin that sheathes the nerves is somehow eaten away and scar tissue forms in its place, interrupting the nerves' signals. During its course, which is unpredictable and uncontrollable, one may lose vision, hearing, speech, the ability to walk, control of bladder and/or bowels, strength in any or all extremities, sensitivity to touch, vibration, and/or pain, potency, coordination of movements—the list of possibilities is lengthy and yes, horrifying. One may also lose one's sense of humor. That's the easiest to lose and the hardest to survive without.

In the past ten years, I have sustained some of these losses. 8 Characteristic of MS are sudden attacks, called exacerbations, followed by remissions, and these I have not had. Instead, my disease has been slowly progressive. My left leg is now so weak that I walk with the aid of a brace and a cane; and for distances I use an Amigo, a variation on the electric wheelchair that looks rather like an electrified kiddie car. I no longer have much use of my left hand. Now my right side is weakening as well. I still have the blurred spot in my right eye. Overall, though, I've been lucky so far. My world has, of necessity, been circumscribed by my losses, but the terrain left me has been ample enough for me to continue many of the activities that absorb me: writing, teaching, raising children and cats and plants and snakes, reading, speaking publicly about MS and depression, even playing bridge with people patient and honorable enough to let me scatter cards every which way without sneaking a peek.

9   Lest I begin to sound like Pollyanna, however, let me say that I don't like having MS. I hate it. My life holds realities—harsh ones, some of them—that no right-minded human being ought to accept without grumbling. One of them is fatigue. I know of no one with MS who does not complain of bone-weariness; in a disease that presents an astonishing variety of symptoms, fatigue seems to be a common factor. I wake up in the morning feeling the way most people do at the end of a bad day, and I take it from there. As a result, I spend a lot of time *in extremis* and, impatient with limitation, I tend to ignore my fatigue until my body breaks down in some way and forces rest. Then I miss picnics, dinner parties, poetry readings, the brief visits of old friends from out of town. The offspring of a puritanical tradition of exceptional venerability, I cannot view these lapses without shame. My life often seems a series of small failures to do as I ought.

10   I lead, on the whole, an ordinary life, probably rather like the one I would have led had I not had MS. I am lucky that my predilections were already solitary, sedentary, and bookish—unlike the world-famous French cellist I have read about, or the young woman I talked with one long afternoon who wanted only to be a jockey. I had just begun graduate school when I found out something was wrong with me, and I have remained, interminably, a graduate student. Perhaps I would not have if I'd thought I had the stamina to return to a full-time job as a technical editor; but I've enjoyed my studies.

11   In addition to studying, I teach writing courses. I also teach medical students how to give neurological examinations. I pick up freelance editing jobs here and there. I have raised a foster son and

sent him into the world, where he has made me two grandbabies, and I am still escorting my daughter and son through adolescence. I go to Mass every Saturday. I am a superb, if messy, cook. I am also an enthusiastic laundress, capable of sorting a hamper full of clothes into five subtly differentiated piles, but a terrible house-keeper. I can do italic writing and, in an emergency, bathe an oil-soaked cat. I play a fiendish game of Scrabble. When I have the time and money, I like to sit on my front steps with my husband, drinking Amaretto and smoking a cigar, as we imagine our counter-parts in Leningrad and make sure that the sun gets down once more behind the sharp childish scrawl of the Tucson Mountains.

This lively plenty has its bleak complement, of course, in all 12 the things I can no longer do. I will never run again, except in dreams, and one day I may have to write that I will never walk again. I like to go camping, but I can't follow George and the chil-dren along the trails that wander out of a campsite through the desert or into the mountains. In fact, even on the level I've learned never to check the weather or try to hold a coherent conversation: I need all my attention for my wayward feet. Of late, I have begun to catch myself wondering how people can propel themselves without canes. With only one usable hand, I have to select my clothing with care not so much for style as for ease of ingress and egress, and even so, dressing can be laborious. I can no longer do fine stitchery, pick up babies, play the piano, braid my hair. I am immobilized by acute attacks of depression, which may or may not be physiologically related to MS but are certainly its logical concomitant.

These two elements, the plenty and the privation, are never 13 pure, nor are the delight and wretchedness that accompany them. Almost every pickle that I get into as a result of my weakness and clumsiness—and I get into plenty—is funny as well as madden-ing and sometimes painful. I recall one May afternoon when a friend and I were going out for a drink after finishing up at school. As we were climbing into opposite sides of my car, chat-ting, I tripped and fell, flat and hard, onto the asphalt parking lot, my abrupt departure interrupting him in mid-sentence. "Where'd you go?" he called as he came around the back of the car to find me hauling myself up by the door frame. "Are you all right?" Yes, I told him, I was fine, just a bit ratty, and we drove off to find a shady patio and some beer. When I got home an hour or so later, my daughter greeted me with "What have you done to yourself?" I looked down. One elbow of my white turtleneck with the green froggies, one knee of my white trousers, one white kneesock were bloodsoaked. We peeled off the clothes and inspected the damage, which was nasty enough but not alarming. That part wasn't funny: The abrasions took a long time to heal, and one got a little infected. Even so, when I think of my friend talking earnestly, suddenly, to the hot thin air while I dropped from his view as though through a trap door, I find the image as silly as something from a Marx Brothers movie.

14   I may find it easier than other cripples to amuse myself because I live propped by the acceptance and the assistance and, sometimes, the amusement of those around me. Grocery clerks tear my checks out of my checkbook for me, and sales clerks find chairs to put into dressing rooms when I want to try on clothes. The people I work with make sure I teach at times when I am least likely to be fatigued, in places I can get to, with the materials I need. My students, with one anonymous exception (in an end-of-the-semester evaluation), have been unperturbed by my disability. Some even like it. One was immensely cheered by the information that I paint my own fingernails; she decided, she told me, that if I could go to such trouble over fine details, she could keep on writing essays. I suppose I became some sort of bright-fingered muse. She wrote good essays, too.

15   The most important struts in the framework of my existence, of course, are my husband and children. Dismayingly few marriages survive the MS test, and why should they? Most twenty-two- and nineteen-year-olds, like George and me, can vow in clear conscience, after a childhood of chickenpox and summer colds, to keep one another in sickness and in health so long as they both shall live. Not many are equipped for catastrophe: the dismay, the depression, the extra work, the boredom that a degenerative disease can insinuate into a relationship. And our society, with its emphasis on fun and its association of fun with physical performance, offers little encouragement for a whole spouse to stay with a crippled partner. Children experience similar stresses when faced with a crippled parent, and they are more helpless, since parents and children can't usually get divorced. They hate, of

course, to be different from their peers, and the child whose mother is tacking down the aisle of a school auditorium packed with proud parents like a Cape Cod dinghy in a stiff breeze jolly well stands out in a crowd. Deprived of legal divorce, the child can at least deny the mother's disability, even her existence, forgetting to tell her about recitals and PTA meetings, refusing to accompany her to stores or church or the movies, never inviting friends to the house. Many do.

But I've been limping along for ten years now, and so far 16 George and the children are still at my left elbow, holding tight. Anne and Matthew vacuum floors and dust furniture and haul trash and rake up dog droppings and button my cuffs and bake lasagna and Toll House cookies with just enough grumbling so I know that they don't have brain fever. And far from hiding me, they're forever dragging me by racks of fancy clothes or through teeming school corridors, or welcoming gaggles of friends while I'm wandering through the house in Anne's filmy pink babydoll pajamas. George generally calls before he brings someone home, but he does just as many dumb thankless chores as the children. And they all yell at me, laugh at some of my jokes, write me funny letters when we're apart—in short, treat me as an ordinary human being for whom they have some use. I think they like me. Unless they're faking. . . .

Faking. There's the rub. Tugging at the fringes of my con- 17 sciousness always is the terror that people are kind to me only because I'm a cripple. My mother almost shattered me once, with that instinct mothers have—blind, I think, in this case, but unerring nonetheless—for striking blows along the fault-lines of their children's hearts, by telling me, in an attack on my selfishness, "We all have to make allowances for you, of course, because of the way you are." From the distance of a couple of years, I have to admit that I haven't any idea just what she meant, and I'm not sure that she knew either. She was awfully angry. But at the time, as the words thudded home, I felt my worst fear, suddenly realized. I could bear being called selfish: I am. But I couldn't bear the corroboration that those around me were doing in fact what I'd always suspected them of doing, professing fondness while silently putting up with me because of the way I am. A cripple. I've been a little cracked ever since.

18   Along with this fear that people are secretly accepting shoddy goods comes a relentless pressure to please—to prove myself worth the burdens I impose, I guess, or to build a substantial account of goodwill against which I may write drafts in times of need. Part of the pressure arises from social expectations. In our society, anyone who deviates from the norm had better find some way to compensate. Like fat people, who are expected to be jolly, cripples must bear their lot meekly and cheerfully. A grumpy cripple isn't playing by the rules. And much of the pressure is self-generated. Early on I vowed that, if I had to have MS, by God I was going to do it well. This is a class act, ladies and gentlemen. No tears, no recriminations, no faint-heartedness.

19   One way and another, then, I wind up feeling like Tiny Tim, peering over the edge of the table at the Christmas goose, waving my crutch, piping down God's blessing on us all. Only sometimes I don't want to play Tiny Tim. I'd rather be Caliban, a most scurvy monster. Fortunately, at home no one much cares whether I'm a good cripple or a bad cripple as long as I make vichyssoise with fair regularity. One evening several years ago, Anne was reading at the dining-room table while I cooked dinner. As I opened a can of tomatoes, the can slipped in my left hand and juice spattered me and the counter with bloody spots. Fatigued and infuriated, I bellowed, "I'm so sick of being crippled!" Anne glanced at me over the top of her book. "There now," she said, "do you feel better?" "Yes," I said, "yes, I do." She went back to her reading. I felt better. That's about all the attention my scurviness ever gets.

20   Because I hate being crippled, I sometimes hate myself for being a cripple. Over the years I have come to expect—even accept—attacks of violent self-loathing. Luckily, in general our society no longer connects deformity and disease directly with evil (though a charismatic once told me that I have MS because a devil is in me) and so I'm allowed to move largely at will, even among small children. But I'm not sure that this revision of attitude has been particularly helpful. Physical imperfection, even freed of moral disapprobation, still defies and violates the ideal, especially for women, whose confinement in their bodies as objects of desire is far from over. Each age, of course, has its ideal, and I doubt that ours is any better or worse than any other. Today's ideal woman, who lives on the glossy pages of dozens of magazines, seems to be

between the ages of eighteen and twenty-five; her hair has body, her teeth flash white, her breath smells minty, her underarms are dry, she has a career but is still a fabulous cook, especially of meals that take less than twenty minutes to prepare; she does not ordinarily appear to have a husband or children; she is trim and deeply tanned; she jogs, swims, plays tennis, rides a bicycle, sails, but does not bowl; she travels widely, even to out-of-the-way places like Finland and Samoa, always in the company of the ideal man, who possesses a nearly identical set of characteristics. There are a few exceptions. Though usually white and often blonde, she may be black, Hispanic, Asian, or Native American, so long as she is unusually sleek. She may be old, provided she is selling a laxative or is Lauren Bacall. If she is selling a detergent, she may be married and have a flock of strikingly messy children. But she is never a cripple.

Like many women I know, I have always had an uneasy 21
relationship with my body. I was not a popular child, largely, I think now, because I was peculiar: intelligent, intense, moody, shy, given to unexpected actions and inexplicable notions and emotions. But as I entered adolescence, I believed myself unpopular because I was homely: my breasts too flat, my mouth too wide, my hips too narrow, my clothing never quite right in fit or style. I was not, in fact, particularly ugly, old photographs inform me, though I was well off the ideal; but I carried this sense of self-alienation with me into adulthood, where it regenerated in response to the depredations of MS. Even with my brace I walk with a limp so pronounced that, seeing myself on the videotape of a television program on the disabled, I couldn't believe that anything but an inchworm could make progress humping along like that. My shoulders droop and my pelvis thrusts forward as I try to balance myself upright, throwing my frame into a bony S. As a result of contractures, one shoulder is higher than the other and I carry one arm bent in front of me, the fingers curled into a claw. My left arm and leg have wasted into pipe-stems, and I try always to keep them covered. When I think about how my body must look to others, especially to men, to whom I have been trained to display myself, I feel ludicrous, even loathsome.

At my age, however, I don't spend much time thinking 22
about my appearance. The burning egocentricity of adolescence,

which assures one that all the world is looking all the time, has passed, thank God, and I'm generally too caught up in what I'm doing to step back, as I used to, and watch myself as though upon a stage. I'm also too old to believe in the accuracy of self-image. I know that I'm not a hideous crone, that in fact, when I'm rested, well dressed, and well made up, I look fine. The self-loathing I feel is neither physically nor intellectually substantial. What I hate is not me but a disease.

23   I am not a disease.

24   And a disease is not—at least not singlehandedly—going to determine who I am, though at first it seemed to be going to. Adjusting to a chronic incurable illness, I have moved through a process similar to that outlined by Elizabeth Kübler-Ross in *On Death and Dying.* The major difference—and it is far more significant than most people recognize—is that I can't be sure of the outcome, as the terminally ill cancer patient can. Research studies indicate that, with proper medical care, I may achieve a "normal" life span. And in our society, with its vision of death as the ultimate evil, worse even than decrepitude, the response to such news is, "Oh well, at least you're not going to *die*." Are there worse things than dying? I think that there may be.

25   I think of two women I know, both with MS, both enough older than I to have served me as models. One took to her bed several years ago and has been there ever since. Although she can sit in a high-backed wheelchair, because she is incontinent she refuses to go out at all, even though incontinent pants, which are readily available at any pharmacy, could protect her from embarrassment. Instead, she stays at home and insists that her husband, a small quiet man, a retired civil servant, stay there with her except for a quick weekly foray to the supermarket. The other woman, whose illness was diagnosed when she was eighteen, a nursing student engaged to a young doctor, finished her training, married her doctor, accompanied him to Germany when he was in the service, bore three sons and a daughter, now grown and gone. When she can, she travels with her husband; she plays bridge, embroiders, swims regularly; she works, like me, as a symptomatic-patient instructor of medical students in neurology. Guess which woman I hope to be.

26   At the beginning, I thought about having MS almost incessantly. And because of the unpredictable course of the disease, my

thoughts were always terrified. Each night I'd get into bed wondering whether I'd get out again the next morning, whether I'd be
able to see, to speak, to hold a pen between my fingers. Knowing
that the day might come when I'd be physically incapable of
killing myself, I thought perhaps I ought to do so right away,
while I still had the strength. Gradually I came to understand that
the Nancy who might one day lie inert under a bedsheet, arms and
legs paralyzed, unable to feed or bathe herself, unable to reach out
for a gun, a bottle of pills, was not the Nancy I was at present, and
that I could not presume to make decisions for that future Nancy,
who might well not want in the least to die. Now the only provision I've made for the future Nancy is that when the time comes—
and it is likely to come in the form of pneumonia, friend to the
weak and the old—I am not to be treated with machines and
medications. If she is unable to communicate by then, I hope she
will be satisfied with these terms.

Thinking all the time about having MS grew tiresome and   27
intrusive, especially in the large and tragic mode in which I was
accustomed to considering my plight. Months and even years
went by without catastrophe (at least without one related to MS),
and really I was awfully busy, what with George and children
and snakes and students and poems, and I hadn't the time, let
alone the inclination, to devote myself to being a disease. Too, the
richer my life became, the funnier it seemed, as though there were
some connection between largesse and laughter, and so my tragic
stance began to waver until, even with the aid of a brace and cane,
I couldn't hold it for very long at a time.

After several years I was satisfied with my adjustment. I had   28
suffered my grief and fury and terror, I thought, but now I was at
ease with my lot. Then one summer day I set out with George and
the children across the desert for a vacation in California. Part way
to Yuma I became aware that my right leg felt funny. "I think
I've had an exacerbation," I told George. "What shall we do?" he
asked. "I think we'd better get the hell to California," I said,
"because I don't know whether I'll ever make it again." So we
went on to San Diego and then to Orange, and up the Pacific Coast
Highway to Santa Cruz, across to Yosemite, down to Sequoia and
Joshua Tree, and so back over the desert to home. It was a fine two-
week trip, filled with friends and fair weather, and I wouldn't

have missed it for the world, though I did in fact make it back to California two years later. Nor would there have been any point in missing it, since in MS, once the symptoms have appeared, the neurological damage has been done, and there's no way to predict or prevent that damage.

29   The incident spoiled my self-satisfaction, however. It renewed my grief and fury and terror, and I learned that one never finishes adjusting to MS. I don't know now why I thought one would. One does not, after all, finish adjusting to life, and MS is simply a fact of my life—not my favorite fact, of course—but as ordinary as my nose and my tropical fish and my yellow Mazda station wagon. It may at any time get worse, but no amount of worry or anticipation can prepare me for a new loss. My life is a lesson in losses. I learn one at a time.

30   And I had best be patient in the learning, since I'll have to do it like it or not. As any rock fan knows, you can't always get what you want. Particularly when you have MS. You can't, for example, get cured. In recent years researchers and the organizations that fund research have started to pay MS some attention even though it isn't fatal; perhaps they have begun to see that life is something other than a quantitative phenomenon, that one may be very much alive for a very long time in a life that isn't worth living. The researchers have made some progress toward understanding the mechanism of the disease: It may well be an autoimmune reaction triggered by a slow-acting virus. But they are nowhere near its prevention, control, or cure. And most of us want to be cured. Some, unable to accept incurability, grasp at one treatment after another, no matter how bizarre: megavitamin therapy, gluten-free diet, injections of cobra venom, hypothermal suits, lymphocyto-pharesis, hyperbaric chambers. Many treatments are probably harmless enough, but none are curative.

31   The absence of a cure often makes MS patients bitter toward their doctors. Doctors are, after all, the priests of modern society, the new shamans, whose business is to heal, and many an MS patient roves from one to another, searching for the "good" doctor who will make him well. Doctors too think of themselves as healers, and for this reason many have trouble dealing with MS patients, whose disease in its intransigence defeats their aims and mocks their skills. Too few doctors, it is true, treat their patients as

whole human beings, but the reverse is also true. I have always tried to be gentle with my doctors, who often have more at stake in terms of ego than I do. I may be frustrated, maddened, depressed by the incurability of my disease, but I am not diminished by it, and they are. When I push myself up from my seat in the waiting room and stumble toward them, I incarnate the limitation of their powers. The least I can do is refuse to press on their tenderest spots.

This gentleness is part of the reason that I'm not sorry to be a 32 cripple. I didn't have it before. Perhaps I'd have developed it any-way—how could I know such a thing?—and I wish I had more of it, but I'm glad of what I have. It has opened and enriched my life enormously, this sense that my frailty and need must be mirrored in others, that in searching for and shaping a stable core in a life wrenched by change and loss, change and loss, I must recognize the same process, under individual conditions, in the lives around me. I do not deprecate such knowledge, however I've come by it.

All the same, if a cure were found, would I take it? In a 33 minute. I may be a cripple, but I'm only occasionally a loony and never a saint. Anyway, in my brand of theology God doesn't give bonus points for a limp. I'd take a cure; I just don't need one. A friend who also has MS startled me once by asking, "Do you ever say to yourself, 'Why me, Lord?'" "No, Michael, I don't," I told him, "because whenever I try, the only response I can think of is 'Why not?'" If I could make a cosmic deal, who would I put in my place? What in my life would I give up in exchange for sound limbs and a thrilling rush of energy? No one. Nothing. I might as well do the job myself. Now that I'm getting the hang of it.

Content

1. Mairs uses a number of illustrations to compose her definition of "being a cripple," many of them involving physical failure or physical difficulty. Identify some of these. Given the fact that they represent re-curring problems that will only get worse and will never be solved, how do you account for the ultimately positive, affirmative tone of the essay?

2. Mairs is very candid about her body, with which she has "always had an uneasy relationship" (¶ 21). What features of American culture and values cause people to be dissatisfied with their bodies? Is this as true of men as of women, of adults as well as teenagers? How has Mairs come to

terms with her appearance, which is, in fact, continuing to deteriorate (¶ 22)? What could others, "crippled" or not, learn from her example?

Strategies/Structures

1. This essay involves considerable comparison and contrast, overt and implied, between being crippled and not crippled. Why is it important for Mairs to establish the fact that she "was a normally active child and young adult" (¶ 5)? How can we tell that she is writing for an audience "whole of limb," who will as they read be comparing their state with hers?

2. This essay is full of examples of Mairs in a variety of roles—wife, mother, friend, teacher, writer. What examples of activities does Mairs use to characterize herself in these roles as an adult with MS? Why are these varied examples important to her definition of "being crippled"?

Language

1. Why does Mairs choose for herself the label of "cripple" (¶s 2–4) rather than the alterative labels—"disabled," "handicapped," "differently abled"—that she rejects? Why does she put that word, sure to offend some readers, in the title?

2. Mairs wants our sympathetic understanding but not our pity. What language does she use to obtain this? What is her essay's prevailing tone? Is Mairs a person you'd like to know? Why or why not? Which of your reasons are related to her handicap?

For Writing

1. A handicap of any kind makes the victim different from people without that handicap. Mairs's essay shows the positive as well as negative effects of being different, and she also shows how these differences can be transcended, in spirit and in action. Have you ever felt different enough from your peers to be uncomfortable? If so, for mainstream readers, write a definition of "being different," and illustrate its effects, for better and/or worse. Make some connections between your case and larger groups.

2. Mairs says, "Every day for the past ten years," since her symptoms were diagnosed as MS rather than a malignant brain tumor, "has been a kind of gift" (¶ 6). If you (or someone you know well) have had an experience that has made you grateful for every day thereafter, explain the nature of that experience and show why its effects have been so profound.

CHARLES DARWIN

Darwin (1809–1882) descended from a distinguished British scientific family; his father was a physician, and his grandfather was the renowned Erasmus Darwin, amateur naturalist. As a youth Darwin was most alert when studying natural phenomena, particularly beetles, even popping a rare specimen into his mouth to preserve it when his hands were full of other newly collected insects. So, despite his lackadaisical study of medicine at Edinburgh University (1825–1828) and equally indifferent preparation for the clergy at Cambridge (B.A. 1831), he shipped aboard the HMS *Beagle* on a scientific expedition around South America, 1831–1836. As the ship's naturalist, he recorded careful observations of plants, animals, and human behavior that were published in *The Voyage of the Beagle* (1839), and eventually led to his theories of natural selection (roughly translated as "the survival of the fittest") and evolution. The publication of the earthshaking *On the Origin of Species by Means of Natural Selection, or the Preservation of Favored Races in the Struggle for Life* (1859) was based on his painstaking observations of animals and plants, on land and sea and in the air.

"Understanding Natural Selection," a small portion of this work, contains the essence of Darwin's best-known and most revolutionary principles, that in natural selection those variations, "infinitesimally small inherited modifications," endure if they aid in survival. The claim that these modifications occur gradually, rather than being produced at a single stroke by a divine creator, is the basis for Darwin's theory of evolution, extended to humans in *The Descent of Man* (1871). Darwin's theories provoked the enormous controversy between theologians and scientists that continues to this day—as Gould's "Evolution as Fact and Theory" (pp. 513–522) makes clear.

Darwin's work continues to be read, as much for its clear and elegant literary style as for its content. Using the techniques of popular literature to explain sophisticated scientific concepts and to present mountains of detailed information, Darwin is a highly engaging writer. He uses the first person, metaphors, anecdotes, and numerous illustrations that overlap and reinforce one another—here as ways to define his subject. Because he is explaining a theory and concepts totally new to his audience, he has to ground them in the reality of numerous natural phenomena that can be seen and studied.

Understanding Natural Selection

1   It may be said that natural selection is daily and hourly scruti-
nizing, throughout the world, every variation, even the slightest; rejecting that which is bad, preserving and adding up all that
is good; silently and insensibly working, whenever and wherever
opportunity offers, at the improvement of each organic being in
relation to its organic and inorganic conditions of life. We see
nothing of these slow changes in progress, until the hand of time
has marked the long lapses of ages, and then so imperfect is our
view into long past geological ages, that we only see that the
forms of life are now different from what they formerly were.

2   Although natural selection can act only through and for the
good of each being, yet characters and structures, which we are apt
to consider as of very trifling importance, may thus be acted on.
When we see leaf-eating insects green, and bark-feeders mottled-
grey; the alpine ptarmigan white in winter, the red-grouse the
color of heather, and the black-grouse that of peaty earth, we must
believe that these tints are of service to these birds and insects in
preserving them from danger. Grouse, if not destroyed at some
period of their lives, would increase in countless numbers; they
are known to suffer largely from birds of prey; and hawks are
guided by eyesight to their prey—so much so, that on parts of the
Continent persons are warned not to keep white pigeons, as being
the most liable to destruction. Hence I can see no reason to doubt
that natural selection might be most effective in giving the proper
color to each kind of grouse, and in keeping that color, when once
acquired, true and constant. Nor ought we to think that the occasional destruction of an animal of any particular color would produce little effect: we should remember how essential it is in a
flock of white sheep to destroy every lamb with the faintest trace
of black. In plants the down on the fruit and the color of the flesh
are considered by botanists as characters of the most trifling importance: yet we hear from an excellent horticulturist, Downing,
that in the United States smooth-skinned fruits suffer far more
from a beetle, a curculio, than those with down; that purple
plums suffer far more from a certain disease than yellow plums;
whereas another disease attacks yellow-fleshed peaches far more
than those with other colored flesh. If, with all the aids of art,

these slight differences make a great difference in cultivating the several varieties, assuredly, in a state of nature, where the trees would have to struggle with other trees and with a host of enemies, such differences would effectually settle which variety, whether a smooth or downy, a yellow or purple fleshed fruit, should succeed.

In looking at many small points of difference between species, which, as far as our ignorance permits us to judge, seem to be quite unimportant, we must not forget that climate, food, and so on probably produce some slight and direct effect. It is, however, far more necessary to bear in mind that there are many unknown laws of correlation to growth, which, when one part of the organization is modified through variation, and the modifications are accumulated by natural selection for the good of the being, will cause other modifications, often of the most unexpected nature.

As we see that those variations which under domestication appear at any particular period of life, tend to reappear in the offspring of the same period; for instance, in the seeds of the many varieties of our culinary and agricultural plants; in the caterpillar and cocoon stages of the varieties of the silkworm; in the eggs of poultry, and in the color of the down of their chickens; in the horns of our sheep and cattle when nearly adult; so in a state of nature, natural selection will be enabled to act on and modify organic beings at any age, by the accumulation of profitable variations at that age, and by their inheritance at a corresponding age. If it profit a plant to have its seeds more and more widely disseminated by the wind, I can see no greater difficulty in this being effected through natural selection, than in the cotton-planter increasing and improving by selection the down in the pods on his cotton-trees. Natural selection may modify and adapt the larva of an insect to a score of contingencies, wholly different from those which concern the mature insect. These modifications will no doubt affect, through the laws of correlation, the structure of the adult; and probably in the case of those insects which live only for a few hours, and which never feed, a large part of their structure is merely the correlated result of successive changes in the structure of their larvae. So, conversely, modifications in the adult will probably often affect the structure of the larva; but in all cases natural selection will ensure that modifications consequent on other modifications at a different period of life, shall not be in the least degree injurious: for if they became so, they would cause the extinction of the species.

5   Natural selection will modify the structure of the young in relation to the parent, and of the parent in relation to the young. In social animals it will adapt the structure of each individual for the benefit of the community; if each in consequence profits by the selected change. What natural selection cannot do, is to modify the structure of one species, without giving it any advantage, for the good of another species; and though statements to this effect may be found in works of natural history, I cannot find one case which will bear investigation. A structure used only once in an animal's whole life, if of high importance to it, might be modified to any extent by natural selection; for instance, the great jaws possessed by certain insects, and used exclusively for opening the cocoon—or the hard tip to the beak of nestling birds, used for breaking the egg. It has been asserted, that of the best short-beaked tumbler pigeons more perish in the egg than are able to get out of it; so that fanciers assist in the act of hatching. Now, if nature had to make the beak of a full-grown pigeon very short for the bird's own advantage, the process of modification would be very slow, and there would be simultaneously the most rigorous selection of the young birds within the egg, which had the most powerful and hardest beaks, for all with weak beaks would inevitably perish: or, more delicate and more easily broken shells might be selected, the thickness of the shell being known to vary like every other structure.

Sexual Selection

6   Inasmuch as peculiarities often appear under domestication in one sex and become hereditarily attached to that sex, the same fact probably occurs under nature, and if so, natural selection will be able to modify one sex in its functional relations to the other sex, or in relation to wholly different habits of life in the two sexes, as is sometimes the case with insects. And this leads me to say a few words on what I call sexual selection. This depends, not on a struggle for existence, but on a struggle between the males for possession of the females; the result is not death to the unsuccessful competitor, but few or no offspring. Sexual selection is,

therefore, less rigorous than natural selection. Generally, the most vigorous males, those which are best fitted for their places in nature, will leave most progeny. But in many cases, victory will depend not on general vigor, but on having special weapons, confined to the male sex. A hornless stag or spurless cock would have a poor chance of leaving offspring. Sexual selection by always allowing the victor to breed might surely give indomitable courage, length to the spur, and strength to the wing to strike in the spurred leg, as well as the brutal cock-fighter, who knows well that he can improve his breed by careful selection of the best cocks. How low in the scale of nature this law of battle descends, I know not; male alligators have been described as fighting, bellowing, and whirling round, like Indians in a war dance, for the possession of the females; male salmons have been seen fighting all day long; male stag-beetles often bear wounds from the huge mandibles of other males. The war is, perhaps, severest between the males of polygamous animals, and these seem oftenest provided with special weapons. The males of carnivorous animals are already well armed; though to them and to others, special means of defence may be given through means of sexual selection, as the mane to the lion, the shoulder-pad to the boar, and the hooked jaw to the male salmon, for the shield may be as important for victory, as the sword or spear.

Amongst birds, the contest is often of a more peaceful character. All those who have attended to the subject, believe that there is the severest rivalry between the males of many species to attract by singing the females. The rock-thrush of Guiana, birds of Paradise, and some others, congregate; and successive males display their gorgeous plumage and perform strange antics before the females, which standing by as spectators, as last choose the most attractive partner. Those who have closely attended to birds in confinement well know that they often take individual preferences and dislikes: thus Sir R. Heron has described how one pied peacock was eminently attractive to all his hen birds. It may appear childish to attribute any effect to such apparently weak means: I cannot here enter on the details necessary to support this view; but if man can in a short time give elegant carriage and beauty to his bantams, according to his standard of beauty, I can see no good reason to doubt that female birds, by selecting, during thousands of generations, the most melodious or beautiful males, according to their standard of beauty, might produce a marked effect. I strongly suspect that some well-known laws with respect to the plumage of male and female birds, in comparison with the plumage of the young, can be explained on the view of plumage having been chiefly modified by sexual selection, acting when the birds have come to the breeding age or during the breeding season; the modifications thus produced being inherited at corresponding ages or seasons, either by the males alone, or by the males and females; but I have not space here to enter on this subject.

8   Thus it is, as I believe, that when the males and females of any animal have the same general habits of life, but differ in structure, color, or ornament, such differences have been mainly caused by sexual selection; that is, individual males have had, in successive generations, some slight advantage over other males, in their weapons, means of defence, or charms; and have transmitted these advantages to their male offspring. Yet, I would not wish to attribute all such sexual differences to this agency: for we see peculiarities arising and becoming attached to the male sex in our domestic animals (as the wattle in male carriers, horn-like protuberances in the cocks of certain fowls, and so on), which we cannot believe to be either useful to the males in battle, or attractive to the females. We see analogous cases under nature, for instance, the tuft of hair on the breast of the turkey-cock, which can hardly be either useful or ornamental to this bird; indeed, had the tuft appeared under domestication, it would have been called a monstrosity.

Illustration of the Action of Natural Selection

9   . . . Let us take the case of a wolf, which preys on various animals, securing some by craft, some by strength, and some by fleetness; and let us suppose that the fleetest prey, a deer for instance, had from any change in the country increased in numbers, or that other prey had decreased in numbers, during that season of the year when the wolf is hardest pressed for food. I can under such circumstances see no reason to doubt that the swiftest and slimmest wolves would have the best chance of surviving, and so be preserved or selected—provided always that they retain strength to master their prey at this or at some other period of the year, when

they might be compelled to prey on other animals. I can see no more reason to doubt this, than that man can improve the fleetness of his greyhounds by careful and methodical selection, or by that unconscious selection which results from each man trying to keep the best dogs without any thought of modifying the breed.

Even without any change in the proportional numbers of the 10 animals on which our wolf preyed, a cub might be born with an innate tendency to pursue certain kinds of prey. Nor can this be thought very improbable; for we often observe great differences in the natural tendencies of our domestic animals; one cat, for instance, taking to catch rats, another mice; one cat . . . bringing home winged game, another hares or rabbits, and another hunting on marshy ground and almost nightly catching woodcocks or snipes. The tendency to catch rats rather than mice is known to be inherited. Now, if any slight innate change of habit or of structure benefited an individual wolf, it would have the best chance of surviving and of leaving offspring. Some of its young would probably inherit the same habits or structure, and by the repetition of this process, a new variety might be formed which would either supplant or coexist with the parent-form of wolf. Or, again, the wolves inhabiting a mountainous district, and those frequenting the lowlands, would naturally be forced to hunt different prey; and from the continued preservation of the individuals best fitted for the two sites, two varieties might slowly be formed. These varieties would cross and blend where they met; but to this subject of intercrossing we shall soon have to return. I may add, that . . . there are two varieties of the wolf inhabiting the Catskill Mountains in the United States, one with a light greyhoundlike form, which pursues deer, and the other more bulky, with shorter legs, which more frequently attacks the shepherd's flocks.

Content

1. What does Darwin mean by "natural selection" (¶s 1–5)? How does "natural selection" differ from "sexual selection" (¶s 6–8)?

2. Although Darwin doesn't use the term "evolution," this piece clearly illustrates that concept. Define that term, using some of Darwin's illustrations. Does your definition anticipate creationists' objections? Should it? If you believe in creationism, how does this belief influence the way you define "evolution"?

3. Distinguish between theory, opinion, and fact in Darwin's presentation of the concepts of natural selection (¶s 1–5, 9–10).

Strategies/Structures

1. Darwin offers arguments on behalf of both natural selection and sexual selection. Which argument has the better supporting evidence? Which argument makes its case more compellingly? Why?
2. Darwin builds his case for the existence of natural selection by using numerous illustrations. Identify some. Explain how an argument can also, as in this case, be a definition.
3. What kind of authorial persona does Darwin present? In what ways is this "scientist figure" familiar today? How does this persona differ from the stereotype of the "mad scientist"?

Language

1. Is Darwin writing for an audience of other scientists? For a general readership? Or for both? What aspects of his language (choice of vocabulary, familiar or unfamiliar language and illustrations), tone, and sentence structure reinforce your answer?
2. Are there features of Darwin's language, and sentence and paragraph structure, that indicates that this excerpt was written in the nineteenth rather than the twentieth century? Illustrate your answer.

For Writing

1. Write a definition of something (a natural phenomenon, human or animal behavior you have observed carefully over time) for an audience of nonscientists. If you are writing about the behavior of college students in a particular type of situation—for example, some aspect(s) of test-taking, dating, dressing, eating—record your observations in as objective and "scientific" a manner as you can.
2. Every definition is an argument, overt or implied, for the definer's particular way of looking at the subject (for example, see Gould's "Evolution as Fact and Theory" [pp. 513–522]). For readers who might disagree with you, write a controversial definition of a subject about which you feel passionate—friendship, love, marriage, violence, war, an ideal— you name it (place to live, job to have, family life, public policy). If you are dealing in abstractions, as you are likely to do in an extended definition, you will need to shore up your generalizations with specific information and illustrations.

KELLY SHEA

Shea (born, 1960), a 1982 graduate of the College of William and Mary, worked as a national park ranger, and then as an editor for *Computerworld* magazine. After earning a master's degree in educational administration at Harvard she became dean of students at Centenary College. "Acid Rain" reflects her double major in English and biology. Here, in a common type of scientific writing, she explains a natural phenomenon for a general audience. First, she defines the central term, "acid rain," using a general chemistry textbook as her source of information, and devotes the first third of her paper to explaining that phenomenon in clear, nontechnical language. This explanation becomes the basis for the next third of the paper, a comparison between the buffering that occurs with rain of "normal" acidity, and the more devastating effects of acid rain; definitions often employ comparison and contrast. The last third of the paper analyzes the causes of acid rain, projects even more devastating long-term consequences, examines possible solutions, and ends with a brief argument advocating cleaner air.

The structure and strategy of Shea's essay are typical of some writing in the natural and social sciences: beginning with an extended definition; using that definition as the basis for the paper's next section; and concluding by examining the consequences of the phenomenon—in this case, negative and potentially even worse—and an appeal for responsible social action and reform. See Jonathan Kozol's "The Human Cost of an Illiterate Society" (pp. 264–273) as well as the arguments in Chapter 13 by Martin Luther King, Jr. (pp. 569–586); Lani Guinier (pp. 588–595), John Kenneth Galbraith (pp. 596–603), and Robert Reich (pp. 604–615).

❄ *Acid Rain*

We live in an era that has ostensibly become concerned with the natural environment, conservation, and pollution. Every day there is something new to be worried about in the resources we use, including the air we breathe, the food we eat, the water we drink. If we destroy what we have, use it up, or pollute it, we will inevitably lose these valuable natural resources.

Among the many possible victims of environmental exploitation are lakes, streams, soils, buildings, monuments, statues, and ancient ruins. All of these static, vulnerable treasures are in danger of being eaten away by a recently recognized phenomenon called acid precipitation.

2   Although acid precipitation includes snow, hail, sleet, water vapor, mist and even dew, it is often termed simply, "acid rain." Describing the "acid" portion of the phrase is more complicated. A general chemistry textbook defines an acid as a substance dissolved in water producing a solution of pH less than seven. So what does pH mean? The pH scale is one which describes the concentration of hydrogen ions in substances. The more ions, the more "acid," the fewer ions the more "basic." A lower pH value indicates high acidity, while a higher pH indicates high alkalinity (basicity). The pH scale goes from one to fourteen. One is highly acidic, fourteen is highly basic, and seven is neutral (neither acidic nor basic)—the ions are in balance.

3   Normal precipitation has an average pH of 5.6, already on the acidic side of the scale, but not dangerously so. The various "rained on" substrates can handle this slight acidity, mainly because they possess a "buffering capacity." That is, they contain enough of certain materials which can, in effect, combine with the acids to produce harmless substances, and thus decrease the acidity. They "buffer" the medium (lake, soil, even a statue) against the acid by neutralizing the effects it can have.

4   What are these effects? What do acids do to lakes, streams, and other substances? Acids have different effects on different materials. In the case of statues, monuments, and stone buildings, acids simply break down the composition of minerals—slowly, for certain, but there is a definite breakdown. If you pour soda onto a hard crust of bread, the crust will hold up for a while, but soon it will start to melt away and will eventually fall apart. Of course the presence of buffers combats the destruction but if, somehow, the acids become stronger (or the buffers weaker), the defense will be less powerful. More immediately noticeable effects can be seen in aquatic and terrestrial environments. Acids can leach essential nutrients from lakes, streams and soils. They can also increase the ability of toxic metals (lead and mercury, for example) to dissolve into a medium. When these metals are released into water, for

example, they can cause pipes to corrode faster, fish to become contaminated and die, and plants to be destroyed. Whole habitats can be wiped out and have been. There are lakes in the Adirondacks which have become completely barren of all life due to the devastation of acid rain.

How, then, do acids get into the atmospheric precipitation? 5 Now we come to the core of the problem—the source of the acids. There are certain substances which, when added to rain, dew, and mist, can decrease the pH to 4.5 through 4, and lower, which means increased acidity. This precipitation falls from the sky into lakes, onto soil, and pelts monuments such as the Lincoln Memorial, wreaking its havoc.

The "certain substances" added are pollutants, namely sulfur 6 and nitrogen oxides, formed from smelting and the burning of coal, oil, and gas. When these fossil fuels are burned, the oxides are evolved. When combined with water in *any* form, the oxides produce—surprise!—sulfuric and nitric acids. So when the oxides are emitted into the atmosphere, and then precipitation comes down through them, the acids are formed, causing acid rain.

So, how are lakes and streams affected, when most industrial 7 smelting factories and comparable industries are located in and around cities? How can the Parthenon be endangered when there are obviously no factories in the immediate area? First, don't forget automobiles, crafty culprits contributing to the emission of the dangerous oxides. But the four-wheeled demons represent only a small part of the whole picture. The major instigator, ironically, is one which evolved to protect human beings from air pollution. The Clean Air Act of 1977 set up standards by which many industries had to somehow decrease the pollution released at ground level where air is breathed by humans. In response to these mandates, incredibly tall (typically 1000 feet) smokestacks were developed to remove the offensive oxides from the local area. So, the oxides are emitted higher in the sky and are easily carried away by winds from the cities to the air high above the typically endangered areas. Winds can carry oxides for five days over thousands of miles, causing acid rain to be deposited anywhere and everywhere.

Thus an initially local problem (air pollution) has become a 8 devastating phenomenon of global significance. Reports of ever-decreasing pH levels of rain come from all over the world. For example, a 1974 Scotland storm produced rain of pH 2.4, the same pH as vinegar. And as the pH deceases, the deleterious effects increase.

9   The most urgent question now is: What can we do about the problem? Devices called scrubbers have been installed in some smokestacks. These are units which can trap most of the sulfur oxides and prevent their atmospheric getaway. But not all factories are required to install them, and they don't eliminate the other major group of pollutants, the nitrogen oxides. The burning of low-sulfur coal and oil is another alternative solution, but that still doesn't eliminate all the emissions. The real solution lies in con-trolled technology, the conservation of fuel, and an increased awareness by the general public. Yes, these common solutions used to combat most types of pollution reveal that they can be consis-tently and accurately applied to any environmental nuisance. The only way our society is ever going to solve the problems of pollu-tion is for us to wake up and examine the world around us. It is slowly and silently falling apart and one day, when we do notice its deterioration and wish we tried to prevent it sooner, it will be too late. We'll have lost much of the beauty, history, and integrity of nature, as well as of man's creativity.

Content

1. What are the purposes of Shea's introduction to a very large and complicated subject? What are her main topics? What are the limitations of this or any introduction to a subject?

2. Why is it necessary for Shea to explain at the outset that "acid rain" really means "acid precipitation," and "includes snow, hail, sleet, water vapor, mist and even dew"?

3. In a single sentence, Shea offers solutions to the problems that are caused by acid rain (¶ 9). Although the paper is short, should she have elaborated more fully on her conclusion? Or would development of any one of her ideas have required a new paper?

Strategies/Structures

1. "Acid Rain" can be divided into three parts: definition, comparison, and contrast, and cause and effect. Where does each part begin?

2. Why is the definition of acid rain a necessary preface to the rest of the essay? What readers would need this definition?

3. Since Shea is writing as an undergraduate student, how does she establish her authority on the subject?

Language

1. Shea uses rhetorical questions to begin paragraphs 4, 5, 7, and 9. Why? What do these questions require her to do as an author?

2. Is it necessary to discuss a serious, scientific subject in a ponderous style? Or does that depend on the purpose of the discussion and the personality and stylistic preferences of the writer?

For Writing

1. Write an essay providing brief definitions of five or six terms or concepts central to the understanding of a specific area of a discipline, field, or subject you're interested in (such as molecular biology, not just biology in general; French country cooking, not all cooking; white-water canoeing; artificial intelligence). Explain, either in your introduction or conclusion, why these definitions are indispensable.

2. Write an essay in which your definition of a key term or concept becomes the basis for exploring a problem or controversy that the definition raises (for instance, pornography, apartheid, genocide, creationism, biological warfare, athletic scholarships, the greenhouse effect, toxic waste).

Additional Topics for Writing
Definition   (For process strategies, see page 459)

1. Write an extended definition of one or more of the following trends, concepts, abstractions, phenomena, or institutions. Be sure to identify your audience, limit your subject, and illustrate your essay with specific examples.

    a. Physical fitness
    b. Personality
    c. Character
    d. Optimism
    e. Depression (economic or psychological)
    f. The nature of friendship
    g. Marriage (either, the ideal marriage, or the ideal versus the reality—see Judy Brady, pp. 468–471)
    h. Parenthood
    i. Education—formal or informal
    j. A good job or profession
    k. Comedy, tragedy, romance, or satire
    l. A sport, game, hobby, or recreational activity
    m. A Northerner, Southerner, Midwesterner, Texan, Californian, or person from some other state or region
    n. A scientific or technical phenomenon of your choice (an eclipse, the "big bang" theory of creation, genetic engineering, DNA, the MX missile; see Kelly Shea pp. 495–498)

2. Explain a particular value system or belief system, such as:

    a. Democracy, communism, socialism, or some other political theory or form of government
    b. Protestantism (or a particular sect), Catholicism, Judaism (or a particular branch—Orthodox, Conservative, Reform), Buddhism (or a particular sort), Islam, or some other religion
    c. A theoretical system and some of its major ramifications (feminism, post-colonialism, Freudianism)

3. Prepare a dictionary of ten jargon or slang words used in your academic major, in your hobby, or in some other activity you enjoy, such as playing a particular sport or game, listening to a specific type of music, or working on a computer system.

12 | Comparison and Contrast

Writers compare people, places, things, or qualities to identify their similarities, and contrast them to identify the differences. What you say about one subject usually helps to illuminate or explain the other; such explanations have the added advantage of answering questions that hinge on the similarities and differences under consideration. Your commentary can also provide the basis for judging the relative merits and demerits of the subject at hand.

For instance, comparison and contrast can help you determine whether to choose a liberal arts or technical education, and what your future will be like with whichever you select. It can help you explain the resemblances between the works of Faulkner and Hemingway, and the differences—and to justify your preference for one author over the other. Comparison and contrast can help you decide whom to vote for, what movie to see (or avoid), where to spend your next vacation, what car to buy, which person to marry. A thoroughgoing, detailed comparison and contrast of the reasons for the quality of life with and without handguns, conservation of natural resources, or nuclear power can provide a convincing argument for your choice.

But not everything will work. The subjects you select should have some obvious qualities in common to make the comparison and contrast fruitful. If you try to compare very dissimilar things, as the Mad Hatter does in *Alice in Wonderland* ("Why is a raven like a writing desk?"), you'll have to stretch for an answer ("Because they both begin with an *r* sound.") that may be either silly or irrelevant. But other comparisons by their very nature can command appropriate contrasts. Susanne K. Langer's "Signs and

Symbols' (pp. 460–467) uses a discussion of both signs and symbols to illuminate the meaning of each. Deborah Tannen's "Communication Styles" (pp. 505–511) is based on an extended exploration of differences in the way men and women students behave in the classroom.

In writing an essay of comparison and contrast you'll need to justify your choice of subject, unless the grounds for comparison are obvious. Thus in "Evolution as Fact and Theory" (pp. 513–522), Stephen Jay Gould explains a contrast that is not necessarily apparent to general readers—that evolution as a theory and evolution as a fact are "different things, not rungs in a hierarchy of increasing certainty." Facts are the data which theories try to explain, as evolutionists have always made clear "from the very beginning, if only because we have always acknowledged how far we are from completely understanding the mechanisms (theory) by which evolution (fact) occurred." He then uses these definitions as the basis for refuting the contrasting view of "scientific creationism," a "self-contradictory, nonsense" set of beliefs.

You'll also have to limit your comparison. It would take a book or more to compare and contrast all the relevant aspects of the People's Republic of China and Taiwan. In an essay—short or long, or even treatise-length—on the subject you could focus instead on their relative educational systems, on their relations with the United Sates, or on the everyday life of the average worker in each country. Likewise, in a short paper, you're better off to compare the relevant aspects of two entities. The more items you add, the more complicated the comparison becomes, as you try to deal with the political system in the People's Republic of China, and Taiwan, and Russia, and Poland, and Romania, and....

There are three common ways to organize an essay of comparison and contrast. Let's say you're comparing several places where you've lived, as Leslie S. Moore does in "Homes Away from Home" (pp. 540–546). You could discuss each of them separately, as Moore does, describing in turn three "homes away from home" in Mali. Because the discussion of each is short, not more than five paragraphs, it's easy for readers to keep in mind everything Moore has said about each house while they're reading about the others. Furthermore, because in her second paragraph Moore has described her home in Massachusetts, she sets up a continuing point of contrast between the familiar, comfortable home and the succession of unfamiliar, uncomfortable dwellings on which the essay focuses. Bailey White uses the same organizational pattern in "Mortality" (pp. 536–539) to discuss her two cars. The description of the "real" (old) car sets up a continuing basis of contrast between that familiar, idiosyncratic, yet venerable vehicle and the slightly disconcerting, mechanically perfect new car.

The longer the discussion, the less easy it is for readers to remember what they need to. In a longer essay, therefore, it's preferable to compare and contrast one point at a time, alternating between subjects: the setting of house *A*, the setting of house *B*, the floor plan of house *A*, the floor plan of house *B*, and so on. If you've evaluated each point as you went along, the conclusion, having evolved naturally, might simply sum up the logical outcome of the comparison: "Although my grandparents' house is larger and has many attractive nooks and crannies, my smaller, newer house is more energy efficient and easier to maintain." Or you could group all the similarities of houses *A* and *B* in one section of a paper, and all the differences in another.

Whatever pattern of comparison and contrast you use, a topic outline can help you to organize such papers, and to make sure you've covered equivalent points for each item in the comparison. However you organize the paper, you don't have to give such equal emphasis to the similarities and to the differences; some may simply be more important than others. But you do have to make your chosen points of comparison relevant. Comparison and contrast is particularly useful as a technique in explanations. You can compare something that readers don't know much about (dwellings in Mali) with something that's familiar (a New England house).

Contrast is also the basis of many types of argumentation; we tend to think in terms of a "right" versus a "wrong" side even when issues are more complicated than they might seem in a simple opposition. In "What's Wrong with Animal Rights?" (pp. 524–534), Vicki Hearne turns the conventional argument on its head. The animal rights advocates have "got it all wrong," she argues, for they build their advocacy "upon a misconceived premise that rights were created to prevent us from unnecessary suffering"; they view death, perhaps through a "humane" society, as positive, "the ultimate release." This sentimental stereotype of animals as "Helpless Fluff" and "Agonized Fluff" contrasts significantly with Hearne's experienced and unsentimental animal trainer's view that animals are ethical creatures who are happiest when doing good work. The appropriate rights for animals, in Hearne's view, are the positive Jeffersonian rights to "life, liberty, and the pursuit of happiness."

As we've seen, essays of comparison and contrast may include other types of writing, particularly description, narration, and analysis. Classification and division often determine the points to be covered in such essays: my actual life versus my ideal life, country living versus city living, life on the East (or West) coast versus life in the Midwest, middle-class life versus upper-class life. . . . And essays of comparison and contrast themselves become, at times, illustrations or arguments, direct or indirect, overt or more subtle. Long live the differences and the zest they provide.

STRATEGIES FOR WRITING— COMPARISON AND CONTRAST

1. Will my essay focus on the similarities between two or more things (comparison) or the differences (contrast), or will I be discussing both similarities and differences? Why do I want to make the comparison or contrast? To find, explore, or deny overt or less apparent resemblances among the items? To decide which one of a pair or group is better or preferable? Or to use the comparison or contrast to argue for my preference?
2. Are my readers familiar with one or more of the objects of my comparison? If they are familiar with them all, then can I concentrate on the unique features of my analysis? (If they are familiar with only one item, start with the known before discussing the unknown. If they are unacquainted with everything, for purposes of explanation you might wish to begin with a comparison that focuses on the common elements among the items under discussion.)
3. How global or minute will my comparison be (i.e., do I want to make only a few points of comparison or contrast, or many)? Will my essay make more sense to my readers if I present each subject as a complete unit before discussing the next? Or will the comparison or contrast be more meaningful if I proceed point by point?
4. Have I ruled out trivial and irrelevant comparisons? Does each point have a counterpart that I have treated in an equivalent manner, through comparable analysis or illustration, length, and language?
5. Suppose I like or favor one item of the comparison or contrast over the others? Am I obliged to treat every item equally in language and tone, or can my tone vary to reinforce my interpretation?

DEBORAH TANNEN

Tannen, born in Brooklyn in 1945, was partially deafened by a childhood illness. Her consequent interest in nonverbal communication and other aspects of conversation led ultimately to a doctorate in linguistics (University of California, Berkeley, 1979) and professorship at Georgetown University. Tannen's numerous studies of gender-related speech patterns draw on the combined perspectives of anthropology, sociology, psychology, and women's studies, as well as linguistics. A poet and short story writer (*Greek Icons*) as well, Tannen brings a sensitive ear and keen analysis to *Gender and Conversational Interaction* (1993) among students from preschool through junior high, high school, and college. She also explores aspects of communication related to gender, power, and status in the best-selling *That's Not What I Meant!: How Conversational Style Makes or Breaks Your Relations with Others* (1986), *You Just Don't Understand: Women and Men in Conversation* (1990), and *Talking from 9 to 5* (1994).

Much of Tannen's research, like her writing, is based on comparative analyses of the contrasting behavior of men and women in a variety of situations. "Communication Styles" was originally published as "Teachers' Classroom Strategies Should Recognize that Men and Women Use Language Differently" in the *Chronicle of Higher Education* (June 19, 1991). Here Tannen explores differences in the ways that men and women students interact, and how the size, informality, and composition of the group influences who speaks up and who remains silent.

Communication Styles

W hen I researched and wrote my book, *You Just Don't Understand: Women and Men in Conversation*, the furthest thing from my mind was reevaluating my teaching strategies. But that has been one of the direct benefits of having written the book.

The primary focus of my linguistic research always has been the language of everyday conversation. One facet of this is conversational style: how different regional, ethnic, and class backgrounds, as well as age and gender, result in different ways of using language to communicate. *You Just Don't Understand* is about the conversational styles of women and men. As I gained more insight into typically male and female ways of using language, I began to suspect some of the causes of the troubling facts that women who go to single-sex schools do better in later life, and that when young women sit next to young men in classrooms, the males talk more. This is not to say that all men talk in class, nor that no women do. It is simply that a greater percentage of discussion time is taken by men's voices.

3   The research of sociologists and anthropologists such as Janet Lever, Marjorie Harness Goodwin, and Donna Eder has shown that girls and boys learn to use language differently in their sex-separate peer groups. Typically, a girl has a best friend with whom she sits and talks, frequently telling secrets. It's the telling of secrets, the fact and the way that they talk to each other, that makes them best friends. For boys, activities are central: Their best friends are the ones they do things with. Boys also tend to play in larger groups that are hierarchical. High-status boys give orders and push low-status boys around. So boys are expected to use language to seize center stage: by exhibiting their skills, displaying their knowledge, and challenging and resisting challenges.

4   These patterns have stunning implications for classroom interaction. Most faculty members assume that participating in class discussion is a necessary part of successful performance. Yet speaking in a classroom is more congenial to boys' language experience than to girls', since it entails putting oneself forward in front of a large group of people, many of whom are strangers and at least one of whom is sure to judge speakers' knowledge and intelligence by their verbal display.

5   Another aspect of many classrooms that makes them more hospitable to most men than to most women is the use of debate-like formats as a learning tool. Our educational system, as Walter Ong argues persuasively in his book *Fighting for Life* (Cornell University Press, 1981), is fundamentally male in that the pursuit of knowledge is believed to be achieved by ritual opposition: public display followed by argument and challenge. Father Ong demonstrates that ritual opposition—what he calls "adversativeness" or "agonism"—is fundamental to the way most males approach almost any activity. (Consider, for example, the little boy who

shows he likes a little girl by pulling her braids and shoving her.) But ritual opposition is antithetical to the way most females learn and like to interact. It is not that females don't fight, but that they don't fight for fun. They don't *ritualize* opposition.

Anthropologists working in widely disparate parts of the world 6
have found contrasting verbal rituals for women and men. Women in completely unrelated cultures (for example, Greece and Bali) engage in ritual laments: spontaneously produced rhyming couplets that express their pain, for example, over the loss of loved ones. Men do not take part in laments. They have their own, very different verbal ritual: a contest, a war of words in which they vie with each other to devise clever insults.

When discussing these phenomena with a colleague, I com- 7
mented that I see these two styles in American conversation: Many women bond by talking about troubles, and many men bond by exchanging playful insults and put-downs, and other sorts of verbal sparring. He exclaimed: "I never thought of this, but that's the way I teach: I have students read an article, and then I invite them to tear it apart. After we've torn it to shreds, we talk about how to build a better model."

This contrasts sharply with the way I teach: I open the discus- 8
sion of readings by asking, "What did you find useful in this? What can we use in our own theory building and our own methods?" I note what I see as weaknesses in the author's approach, but I also point out that the writer's discipline and purposes might be different from ours. Finally, I offer personal anecdotes illustrating the phenomena under discussion and praise students' anecdotes as well as their critical acumen.

These different teaching styles must make our classrooms 9
wildly different places and hospitable to different students. Male students are more likely to be comfortable attacking the readings and might find the inclusion of personal anecdotes irrelevant and "soft." Women are more likely to resist discussion they perceive as hostile, and, indeed, it is women in my classes who are most likely to offer personal anecdotes.

A colleague who read my book commented that he had always 10
taken for granted that the best way to deal with students'

comments is to challenge them; this, he felt it was self-evident, sharpens their minds and helps them develop debating skills. But he had noticed that women were relatively silent in his classes, so he decided to try beginning discussion with relatively open-ended questions and letting comments go unchallenged. He found, to his amazement and satisfaction, that more women began to speak up.

11   Though some women in his class clearly liked this better, perhaps some of the men liked it less. One young man in my class wrote in a questionnaire about a history professor who gave students questions to think about and called on people to answer them: "He would then play devil's advocate . . . *i.e.,* he debated us. . . . That class *really* sharpened me intellectually. . . . We as students do need to know how to defend ourselves." This young man valued the experience of being attacked and challenged publicly. Many, if not most, women would shrink from such "challenge," experiencing it as public humiliation.

12   A professor at Hamilton College told me of a young man who was upset because he felt his class presentation had been a failure. The professor was puzzled because he had observed that class members had listened attentively and agreed with the student's observations. It turned out that it was this very agreement that the student interpreted as failure: Since no one had engaged his ideas by arguing with him, he felt they had found them unworthy of attention.

13   So one reason men speak in class more than women is that many of them find the "public" classroom setting more conducive to speaking, whereas most women are more comfortable speaking in private to a small group of people they know well. A second reason is that men are more likely to be comfortable with the debate-like form that discussion may take. Yet another reason is the different attitudes toward speaking in class that typify women and men.

14   Students who speak frequently in class, many of whom are men, assume that it is their job to think of contributions and try to get the floor to express them. But many women monitor their participation not only to get the floor but to avoid getting it. Women students in my class tell me that if they have spoken

up once or twice, they hold back for the rest of the class because they don't want to dominate. If they have spoken a lot one week, they will remain silent the next. These different ethics of participation are, of course, unstated, so those who speak freely assume that those who remain silent have nothing to say, and those who are reining themselves in assume that the big talkers are selfish and hoggish.

When I looked around my classes, I could see these differing ethics and habits at work. For example, my graduate class in analyzing conversation had 20 students, 11 women and 9 men. Of the men, four were foreign students: two Japanese, one Chinese, and one Syrian. With the exception of the three Asian men, all the men spoke in class at least occasionally. The biggest talker in the class was a woman, but there were also five women who never spoke at all, only one of whom was Japanese. I decided to try something different.

I broke the class into small groups to discuss the issues raised in the readings and to analyze their own conversational transcripts. I devised three ways of dividing the students into groups: one by the degree program they were in, one by gender, and one by conversational style, as closely as I could guess it. This meant that when the class was grouped according to conversational style, I put Asian students together, fast talkers together, and quiet students together. The class split into groups six times during the semester, so they met in each grouping twice. I told students to regard the groups as examples of interactional data and to note the different ways they participated in different groups. Toward the end of the term, I gave them a questionnaire asking about their class and group participation.

I could see plainly from my observation of the groups at work that women who never opened their mouths in class were talking away in the small groups. In fact, the Japanese woman commented that she found it particularly hard to contribute to the all-woman group she was in because "I was overwhelmed by how talkative the female students were in the female-only group." This is particularly revealing because it highlights that the same person who can be "oppressed" into silence in one context can become the talkative "oppressor" in another. No one's conversational style is absolute; everyone's style changes in response to the context and others' styles.

18   Some of the students (seven) said that they preferred the same-gender groups; others preferred the same-style groups. In answer to the question "Would you have liked to speak in class more than you did?" six of the seven who said Yes were women; the one man was Japanese. Most startlingly, this response did not come only from quiet women; it came from women who had indicated they had spoken in class never, rarely, sometimes, and often. Of the 11 students who said the amount they had spoken was fine, 7 were men. Of the four women who checked "fine," two added qualifications indicating it wasn't completely fine: One wrote in "maybe more," and one wrote, "I have an urge to participate but often feel I should have something more interesting/relevant/wonderful/intelligent to say!!"

19   I counted my experiment a success. Everyone in the class found the small groups interesting, and no one indicated he or she would have preferred that the class not break into groups. Perhaps most instructive, however, was the fact that the experience of breaking into groups, and of talking about participation in class, raised everyone's awareness about classroom participation. After we had talked about it, some of the quietest women in the class made a few voluntary contributions, though sometimes I had to insure their participation by interrupting the students who were exuberantly speaking out.

20   Americans are often proud that they discount the significance of cultural differences: "We are all individuals," many people boast. Ignoring such issues as gender and ethnicity becomes a source of pride: "I treat everyone the same." But treating people the same is not equal treatment if they are not the same.

21   The classroom is a different environment for those who feel comfortable putting themselves forward in a group than it is for those who find the prospect of doing so chastening, or even terrifying. When a professor asks, "Are there any questions?," students who can formulate statements the fastest have the greatest opportunity to respond. Those who need significant time to do so have

not really been given a chance at all, since by the time they are ready to speak, someone else has the floor.

In a class where some students speak out without raising hands, those who feel they must raise their hands and wait to be recognized do not have equal opportunity to speak. Telling them to feel free to jump in will not make them feel free; one's sense of timing, of one's rights and obligations in a classroom, are automatic, learned over years of interaction. They may be changed over time, with motivation and effort, but they cannot be changed on the spot. And everyone assumes his or her own way is best. When I asked my students how the class could be changed to make it easier for them to speak more, the most talkative woman said she would prefer it if no one had to raise hands, and a foreign student said he wished people would raise their hands and wait to be recognized. 22

My experience in this class has convinced me that small-group interaction should be part of any class that is not a small seminar. I also am convinced that having the students become observers of their own interaction is a crucial part of their education. Talking about ways of talking in class makes students aware that their ways of talking affect other students, that the motivations they impute to others may not truly reflect others' motives, and that the behaviors they assume to be self-evidently right are not universal norms. 23

The goal of complete equal opportunity in class may not be attainable, but realizing that one monolithic classroom-participation structure is not equal opportunity is itself a powerful motivation to find more-diverse methods to serve diverse students—and every classroom is diverse. 24

Content

1. In your experience, are boys (more often than girls) "expected to use language to seize center stage: by exhibiting their skill, displaying their knowledge, and challenging and resisting challenges" (¶ 3)? How does this translate into classroom performance (¶s 4, 7)? In your experience, is Walter Ong's claim true that "ritual opposition . . . is fundamental to the way most males approach almost any activity" (¶ 5)?

2.   "Treating people the same is not equal treatment if they are not the same" (¶ 20). Explain how this idea applies in a classroom.
3.   Does Tannen equate student talkativeness in class with an inquiring mind? With intelligent preparation? If so, is she justified in equating the two? Or does she base her equation exclusively on gender?
4.   Does Tannen argue that the differences between men's and women's communication styles are biologically or culturally determined? Explain your answer.

Strategies/Structures

Tannen's article follows the format of physical science and social research: statement of the problem, review of the literature, identification of research methodology, explanation of the research procedure, interpretation of the research findings, and generalizations to other situations or recommendations for either further research or practical applications or both. Show where each stage occurs in this article.

Language

"No one's conversational style is absolute; everyone's style changes in response to the context and others' styles" (¶ 17). Explain, with reference to your own experience and other students' behavior in your classes—and out.

For Writing

1.   If you go to a co-ed school, do some primary investigation to replicate Tannen's observation that "when young women sit next to [presumably she means *share the same classroom*, not necessarily *sit in immediate proximity to*] young men in classrooms, the males talk more" (¶ 2). Is this true in any or all of your classes? Typically, do men speak more than women in classes taught by men? Do women speak more or less than men in classes taught by women? Do the ages and life experiences of men and women influence the extent of their class participation? Generalize from your findings and interpret them with regard to Tannen's findings. Do you think the men and women students at your school are typical of students at all American colleges or only at colleges of the type that yours represents (private or public community college, four-year undergraduate school, research university)?
2.   Do you agree with Tannen's conclusion that "small-group interaction should be part of any class that is not a small seminar" (¶ 23)? If so,

why? If not, why not? What demands does this format place on the students? What does this format imply about the way we learn?

3. Write an essay about any of the Content questions. Base your essay on your own experience, and reinforce it with three interviews—one with a student of a different gender from yours, another with a student of a different racial background, another with a student from a different socio-economic class. (To control for teaching style and content, all the students should be enrolled in the same course at the same time.) To what extent are your conclusions influenced by your informants' class and ethnicity, in comparison with their gender?

4. Examine a class in which you wanted to talk more (or at all), but did not do so. Why were you more silent than you wanted to be? What in the class format—teacher's instructional style, other students' behavior, your own preparation or maturity—would have had to change in order for you to have been willing to talk more? Would you have gained more from the class if you'd been a more talkative (and hence, active) participant?

STEPHEN JAY GOULD

Gould (born, 1941) graduated from Antioch in 1963, earned a Ph.D. from Columbia in 1967, and since then has been a geology professor at Harvard, where he teaches paleontology, biology, and history of science. He provides exceptionally clear definitions, explanations, and arguments in his writings for students, colleagues, and general readers of his columns in *Natural History*. These have been collected in *Ever Since Darwin* (1977); *The Panda's Thumb* (1980); *Hen's Teeth and Horse's Toes* (1983); and *Bully for Brontosaurus* (1991). Gould's scientific orientation favors the underdog, as is evident in *The Mismeasure of Man* (1981). There he reinterprets two centuries of IQ testing and other quantitative ways of determining intelligence to show how flawed measurement procedures and wrong interpretations of information invariably favored educated white Anglo-Saxon males and contributed to the oppression of everyone else. Gould has received numerous honors, including the American Book Award in Science and a MacArthur Fellowship (a "genius grant").

Gould's analysis of the qualities of great scientific essayists (T. H. Huxley, J. B. S. Haldane, P. B. Medawar) applies equally well to his own writings:

All write about the simplest things and draw from them a universe of implications. . . . All maintain an unflinching commitment to rationality amid the soft attractions of an uncritical mysticism. . . . All demonstrate a deep commitment to the demystification of science by cutting through jargon; they show by example rather than exhortation that the most complex concepts can be rendered intelligible to everyone.

These qualities are apparent in "Evolution as Fact and Theory," originally published in *Discover* (1981), a journal of popular science. Gould uses the crucial definitions and distinctions between fact and theory as the basis for contrasting the evolutionists' scientific position with the creationists' pseudo-scientific position, which he argues against in most of the rest of the essay. He contends—by means of another contrast—that "'scientific creationism' is a self-contradictory, nonsense phrase precisely because it cannot be falsified."

Evolution as Fact and Theory

1   Kirtley Mather, who died last year at age 89, was a pillar of both science and the Christian religion in America and one of my dearest friends. The difference of half a century in our ages evaporated before our common interests. The most curious thing we shared was a battle we each fought at the same age. For Kirtley had gone to Tennessee with Clarence Darrow to testify for evolution at the Scopes trial of 1925. When I think that we are enmeshed again in the same struggle for one of the best documented, most compelling and exciting concepts in all of science, I don't know whether to laugh or cry.

2   According to idealized principles of scientific discourse, the arousal of dormant issues should reflect fresh data that give renewed life to abandoned notions. Those outside the current debate may therefore be excused for suspecting that creationists have come up with something new, or that evolutionists have generated some serious internal trouble. But nothing has changed; the creationists have not a single new fact or argument. Darrow and Bryan were at least more entertaining than we lesser antagonists today. The rise of creationism is politics, pure and

simple; it represents one issue (and by no means the major concern) of the resurgent evangelical right. Arguments that seemed kooky just a decade ago have re-entered the mainstream.

Creationism Is Not Science

The basic attack of the creationists falls apart on two general counts before we even reach the supposed factual details of their complaints against evolution. First, they play upon a vernacular misunderstanding of the word "theory" to convey the false impression that we evolutionists are covering up the rotten core of our edifice. Second, they misuse a popular philosophy of science to argue that they are behaving scientifically in attacking evolution. Yet the same philosophy demonstrates that their own belief is not science, and that "scientific creationism" is therefore meaningless and self-contradictory, a superb example of what Orwell called "newspeak." 3

In the American vernacular, "theory" often means "imperfect fact"—part of a hierarchy of confidence running downhill from fact to theory to hypothesis to guess. Thus the power of the creationist argument: evolution is "only" a theory, and intense debate now rages about many aspects of the theory. If evolution is less than a fact, and scientists can't even make up their minds about the theory, then what confidence can we have in it? Indeed, President Reagan echoed this argument before an evangelical group in Dallas when he said (in what I devoutly hope was campaign rhetoric): "Well, it is a theory. It is a scientific theory only, and it has in recent years been challenged in the world of science—that is, not believed in the scientific community to be as infallible as it once was." 4

Well, evolution *is* a theory. It is also a fact. And facts and theories are different things, not rungs in a hierarchy of increasing certainty. Facts are the world's data. Theories are structures of ideas that explain and interpret facts. Facts do not go away when scientists debate rival theories to explain them. Einstein's theory of gravitation replaced Newton's, but apples did not suspend themselves in mid-air pending the outcome. And human beings evolved from apelike ancestors whether they did so by Darwin's proposed mechanism or by some other, yet to be discovered. 5

6   Moreover, "fact" does not mean "absolute certainty." The final proofs of logic and mathematics flow deductively from stated premises and achieve certainty only because they are *not* about the empirical world. Evolutionists make no claim for perpetual truth, though creationists often do (and then attack us for a style of argument that they themselves favor). In science, "fact" can only mean "confirmed to such a degree that it would be perverse to withhold provisional assent." I suppose that apples might start to rise tomorrow, but the possibility does not merit equal time in physics classrooms.

7   Evolutionists have been clear about this distinction between fact and theory from the very beginning, if only because we have always acknowledged how far we are from completely understanding the mechanisms (theory) by which evolution (fact) occurred. Darwin continually emphasized the difference between his two great and separate accomplishments: establishing the fact of evolution, and proposing a theory—natural selection—to explain the mechanism of evolution. He wrote in *The Descent of Man*: "I had two distinct objects in view; firstly, to show that species had not been separately created, and secondly, that natural selection had been the chief agent of change . . . Hence if I have erred in . . . having exaggerated its [natural selection's] power . . . I have at least, as I hope, done good service in aiding to overthrow the dogma of separate creations."

8   Thus Darwin acknowledged the provisional nature of natural selection while affirming the fact of evolution. The fruitful theoretical debate that Darwin initiated has never ceased. From the 1940s through the 1960s, Darwin's own theory of natural selection did achieve a temporary hegemony that it never enjoyed in his lifetime. But renewed debate characterizes our decade, and, while no biologist questions the importance of natural selection, many now doubt its ubiquity. In particular, many evolutionists argue that substantial amounts of genetic change may not be subject to natural selection and may spread through populations at random. Others are challenging Darwin's linking of natural selection with gradual, imperceptible change through all intermediary degrees; they are arguing that most evolutionary events may occur far more rapidly than Darwin envisioned.

9   Scientists regard debates on fundamental issues of theory as a sign of intellectual health and a source of excitement. Science

is—and how else can I say it?—most fun when it plays with interesting ideas, examines their implications, and recognizes that old information may be explained in surprisingly new ways. Evolutionary theory is now enjoying this uncommon vigor. Yet amidst all this turmoil no biologist has been led to doubt the fact that evolution occurred; we are debating *how* it happened. We are all trying to explain the same thing: the tree of evolutionary descent linking all organisms by ties of genealogy. Creationists pervert and caricature this debate by conveniently neglecting the common conviction that underlies it, and by falsely suggesting that we now doubt the very phenomenon we are struggling to understand.

Using another invalid argument, creationists claim that "the dogma of separate creations," as Darwin characterized it a century ago, is a scientific theory meriting equal time with evolution in high school biology curricula. But a prevailing viewpoint among philosophers of science belies this creationist argument. Philosopher Karl Popper has argued for decades that the primary criterion of science is the falsifiability of its theories. We can never prove absolutely, but we can falsify. A set of ideas that cannot, in principle, be falsified is not science.

The entire creationist argument involves little more than a rhetorical attempt to falsify evolution by presenting supposed contradictions among its supporters. Their brand of creationism, they claim, is "scientific" because it follows the Popperian model in trying to demolish evolution. Yet Popper's argument must apply in both directions. One does not become a scientist by the simple act of trying to falsify another scientific system; one has to present an alternative system that also meets Popper's criterion—it too must be falsifiable in principle.

"Scientific creationism" is a self-contradictory, nonsense phrase precisely because it cannot be falsified. I can envision observations and experiments that would disprove any evolutionary theory I know, but I cannot imagine what potential data could lead creationists to abandon their beliefs. Unbeatable systems are dogma, not science. Lest I seem harsh or rhetorical, I quote creationism's leading intellectual, Duane Gish, Ph.D., from his recent (1978) book *Evolution? The Fossils Say No!* "By creation we mean the bringing into being by a supernatural Creator of the basic kinds of plants and animals by the process of sudden, or fiat, creation. We do not know how the Creator created, what processes He used, *for He used processes which are not now operating anywhere in the natural universe* [Gish's italics]. This is why we refer to creation as special creation. We cannot discover by scientific investigations anything about the creative processes used by the Creator." Pray tell, Dr. Gish, in the light of your last sentence, what then is "scientific" creationism?

The Fact of Evolution

13   Our confidence that evolution occurred centers upon three general arguments. First, we have abundant, direct, observational evidence of evolution in action, from both the field and the laboratory. It ranges from countless experiments on change in nearly everything about fruit flies subjected to artificial selection in the laboratory to the famous British moths that turned black when industrial soot darkened the trees upon which they rest. (The moths gain protection from sharp-sighted bird predators by blending into the background.) Creationists do not deny these observations; how could they? Creationists have tightened their act. They now argue that God only created "basic kinds," and allowed for limited evolutionary meandering within them. Thus toy poodles and Great Danes come from the dog kind and moths can change color, but nature cannot convert a dog to a cat or a monkey to a man.

14   The second and third arguments for evolution—the case for major changes—do not involve direct observation of evolution in action. They rest upon inference, but are no less secure for that reason. Major evolutionary change requires too much time for direct observation on the scale of recorded human history. All historical sciences rest upon inference, and evolution is no different from geology, cosmology, or human history in this respect. In principle, we cannot observe processes that operated in the past. We must infer them from results that still survive: living and fossil organisms for evolution, documents and artifacts for human history, strata and topography for geology.

15   The second argument—that the imperfection of nature reveals evolution—strikes many people as ironic, for they feel that evolution should be most elegantly displayed in the nearly perfect adaptation expressed by some organisms—the chamber of a gull's

wing, or butterflies that cannot be seen in ground litter because they mimic leaves so precisely. But perfection could be imposed by a wise creator or evolved by natural selection. Perfection covers the tracks of past history. And past history—the evidence of descent—is our mark of evolution.

Evolution lies exposed in the *imperfections* that record a 16 history of descent. Why should a rat run, a bat fly, a porpoise swim, and I type this essay with structures built of the same bones unless we all inherited them from a common ancestor? An engineer, starting from scratch, could design better limbs in each case. Why should all the large native mammals of Australia be marsupials, unless they descended from a common ancestor isolated on this island continent? Marsupials are not "better," or ideally suited for Australia; many have been wiped out by placental mammals imported by man from other continents. This principle of imperfection extends to all historical sciences. When we recognize the etymology of September, October, November, and December (seventh, eighth, ninth, and tenth, from the Latin), we know that two additional items (January and February) must have been added to an original calendar of ten months.

The third argument is more direct: transitions are often 17 found in the fossil record. Preserved transitions are not common— and should not be, according to our understanding of evolution (see next section)—but they are not entirely wanting, as creationists often claim. The lower jaw of reptiles contains several bones, that of mammals only one. The non-mammalian jawbones are reduced, step by step, in mammalian ancestors until they become tiny nubbins located at the back of the jaw. The "hammer" and "anvil" bones of the mammalian ear are descendants of these nubbins. How could such a transition be accomplished? the creationists ask. Surely a bone is either entirely in the jaw or in the ear. Yet paleontologists have discovered two transitional lineages or therapsids (the so-called mammal-like reptiles) with a double jaw joint—one composed of the old quadrate and articular bones (soon to become the hammer and anvil), the other of the squamosal and dentary bones (as in modern mammals). For that matter, what better transitional form could we desire than the oldest human, *Australopithecus afarensis*, with its apelike palate, its human upright stance, and a cranial capacity larger than any ape's of the same body size but a full 1,000 cubic centimeters below ours? If God made each of the half dozen human species discovered in ancient rocks, why did he create in an unbroken temporal sequence of progressively more modern features—increasing cranial capacity, reduced face and teeth, larger body size? Did he create to mimic evolution and test our faith thereby?

An Example of Creationist Argument

18   Faced with these facts of evolution and the philosophical bankruptcy of their own position, creationists rely upon distortion and innuendo to buttress their rhetorical claim. If I should sound sharp or bitter, indeed I am—for I have become a major target of these practices.

19   I count myself among the evolutionists who argue for a jerky, or episodic, rather than a smoothly gradual, pace of change. In 1972 my colleague Niles Eldredge and I developed the theory of punctuated equilibrium. We argued that two outstanding facts of the fossil record—geologically "sudden" origin of new species and failure to change thereafter (stasis)—reflect the predictions of evolutionary theory, not the imperfections of the fossil record. In most theories, small isolated populations are the source of new species, and the process of speciation takes thousands or tens of thousands of years. This amount of time, so long when measured against our lives, is a geological microsecond. It represents much less than 1 percent of the average life span for a fossil invertebrate species—more than 10 million years. Large, widespread, and well-established species, on the other hand, are not expected to change very much. We believe that the inertia of large populations explains the stasis of most fossil species over millions of years.

20   We proposed the theory of punctuated equilibrium largely to provide a different explanation for pervasive trends in the fossil record. Trends, we argued, cannot be attributed to gradual transformation within lineages, but must arise from the differential success of certain kinds of species. A trend, we argued, is more like climbing a flight of stairs (punctuations and stasis) than rolling up an inclined plane.

21   Since we proposed punctuated equilibria to explain trends, it is infuriating to be quoted again and again by creationists—

whether through design or stupidity, I do not know—as admitting that the fossil record includes no transitional forms. Transitional forms are generally lacking at the species level, but are abundant between larger groups. The evolution from reptiles to mammals, as mentioned earlier, is well documented. Yet a pamphlet entitled "Harvard Scientists Agree Evolution Is a Hoax" states: "The facts of punctuated equilibrium which Gould and Eldredge . . . are forcing Darwinists to swallow fit the picture that Bryan insisted on, and which God has revealed to us in the Bible."

Continuing the distortion, several creationists have equated   22 the theory of punctuated equilibrium with a caricature of the beliefs of Richard Goldschmidt, a great early geneticist. Goldschmidt argued, in a famous book published in 1940, that new groups can arise all at once through major mutations. He referred to these suddenly transformed creatures as "hopeful monsters." (I am attracted to some aspects of the non-caricatured version, but Goldschmidt's theory still has nothing to do with punctuated equilibrium.) Creationist Luther Sunderland talks of the "punctuated equilibrium hopeful monster theory" and tells his hopeful readers that "it amounts to tacit admission that anti-evolutionists are correct in asserting there is no fossil evidence supporting the theory that all life is connected to a common ancestor." Duane Gish writes, "According to Goldschmidt, and now apparently according to Gould, a reptile laid an egg from which the first bird, feathers and all, was produced." Any evolutionist who believed such nonsense would rightly be laughed off the intellectual stage; yet the only theory that could ever envision such a scenario for the evolution of birds is creationism—God acts in the egg.

Conclusion   •

I am both angry at and amused by the creationists; but mostly I am   23 deeply sad. Sad for many reasons. Sad because so many people who respond to creationist appeals are troubled for the right reason, but venting their anger at the wrong target. It is true that scientists have often been dogmatic and elitist. It is true that we have often allowed the white-coated, advertising image to represent us—"Scientists say that Brand X cures bunions ten times faster than . . ." We have not fought it adequately because we derive benefits from appearing as a new priesthood. It is also true that faceless bureaucratic state power intrudes more and more into our lives and removes choices that should belong to individuals and communities. I can understand that requiring that evolution be taught in schools might be seen as one more insult on all these grounds. But the culprit is not, and cannot be, evolution or any other fact of the natural world. Identify and fight your legitimate enemies by all means, but we are not among them.

24   I am sad because the practical result of this brouhaha will not be expanded coverage to include creationism (that would also make me sad), but the reduction or excision of evolution from high school curricula. Evolution is one of the half dozen "great ideas" developed by science. It speaks to the profound issues of genealogy that fascinate all of us—the "roots" phenomenon writ large. Where did we come from? Where did life arise? How did it develop? How are organisms related? It forces us to think, ponder, and wonder. Shall we deprive millions of this knowledge and once again teach biology as a set of dull and unconnected facts, without the thread that weaves diverse material into a supple unity?

25   But most of all I am saddened by a trend I am just beginning to discern among my colleagues. I sense that some now wish to mute the healthy debate about theory that has brought new life to evolutionary biology. It provides grist for creationist mills, they say, even if only by distortion. Perhaps we should lie low and rally round the flag of strict Darwinism, at least for the moment— a kind of old-time religion on our part.

26   But we should borrow another metaphor and recognize that we too have to tread a straight and narrow path, surrounded by roads to perdition. For if we ever begin to suppress our search to understand nature, to quench our own intellectual excitement in a misguided effort to present a united front where it does not and should not exist, then we are truly lost.

Content

1. Identify Gould's two different definitions of "theory," one scientific, the other vernacular (common, everyday) (¶s 3–4, and elsewhere). Define what he means by a "fact" (¶s 5–7). Using these definitions, explain what he means by "Well, evolution *is* a theory. It is also a fact." What differentiation does Gould make between evolution as a fact and evolution as a theory (¶s 5–7 and throughout)?

2. What does Gould mean by insisting that any set of scientific ideas must be able to be falsified? Why does he identify creationism as an "unbeatable system" that cannot be falsified?

3. "Scientists regard debates on fundamental issues of theory as a sign of intellectual health and a source of excitement," says Gould (¶ 9). Why is this so? Why is evolutionary theory so much fun, in Gould's view? Why would creationist theories stifle debate and take the "fun" out of doing science (¶s 9–12)?

Strategies/Structures

1. How does Gould use definitions in constructing his argument against creationism?

2. Using Gould's definitions, derive Gould's rules for scientific debate. Does he follow his own rules in this essay?

Language

1. Gould says, "The rise of creationism is politics, pure and simple" (¶ 2). What does he mean by this? How does politics influence the language we use?

2. How does the language we use influence our beliefs about a particular subject? In reference to this essay, you could talk about *science* and *creationism*, but there are many other possibilities for discussion.

3. Gould says, "I am both angry at and amused by the creationists; but mostly I am deeply sad" (¶ 23). Does the language Gould uses in addressing the ideas of his opponents (both creationists and fellow strict Darwinist geologists who dispute his theories and would suppress them for different reasons [¶s 23–26]) reflect any or all of these attitudes? Does he treat his opponents with courtesy? With respect?

For Writing

1. Science, like any other body of knowledge, is ever-changing. Facts can be reassessed, reinterpreted; intellectual constructs can be reconfigured—suppose someone redrew the constellations to represent great works of art instead of mythological stories. New contexts can be provided to enable new ways to understand familiar information. Select a definition of a term central to medicine, psychology, sociology, or an empirically oriented science, that has undergone major changes (*race, homosexual, family,* are among the possible terms). Trace the history of this

definition to highlight the changes in the word's meaning, and explore some of the implications of the old and new definitions.

2. Judging from Gould's practice in this essay, construct a set of rules for appropriate treatment of one's opponents in an argument. (You could use your answers to Language question 3 as a point of departure.) Under what, if any, circumstances are irony, sarcasm, invective, humor suitable in referring to ideas or people with whom you disagree?

VICKI HEARNE

Hearne's dual professions, writer and animal trainer, reinforce each other in unusual and enlightening ways. Hearne (born, 1946) earned a B.A. from the University of California, Riverside (1971) and studied poetry writing at Stanford on a Stegner Fellowship. She has published poetry, *Nervous Horses* (1980) and *In Absence of Horses* (1984); a novel, *The White German Shepherd* (1988); and three nonfiction works, *Adam's Task: Calling Animals by Name* (1986), *Bandit: Dossier of a Dangerous Dog* (1991), and *Animal Happiness* (1994).

As in "What's Wrong with Animal Rights?" first published in *Harper's* in 1991, Hearne's nonfiction, poetry, and fiction provide subtle interpretations, sophisticated and wise, of the complex relationships between animals and humans. Her common sense and experience as a trainer of dogs and horses is buttressed by wide reading in philosophy, literature, and natural history. In the introduction to *Adam's Task*, she explains how her unique membership in two communities enabled her to write that book:

> If I had remained firmly within the worlds of discourse provided by the stable and the kennel, I would have been content, not because there is no philosophy in those worlds, but because there is such a rich and ever-changing web of philosophies when good trainers talk and write. . . .
>
> However, my temperament regularly led me away from the kennel and tack room to university libraries and cafeterias, laboratories and classrooms. The result was that for some years I uneasily inhabited at least two completely different worlds of discourse, each using a group of languages that were intertranslatable—dog trainers can talk to horse

trainers, and philosophers can talk to linguists and psychologists, but dog trainers and philosophers can't make much sense of each other.

In bridging the gap between these different worlds, Hearne is able to see each from the point of view of the other. Her dual vision not only enables but mandates an implicit perspective of continual comparison and contrast. From this vantage point she questions the generalizations humans make about animals, and challenges what people take for granted in their stereotyping of animal behavior, even animal rights.

What's Wrong with Animal Rights?

N ot all happy animals are alike. A Doberman going over a hurdle after a small wooden dumbbell is sleek, all arcs of harmonious power. A basset hound cheerfully performing the same exercise exhibits harmonies of a more lugubrious nature. There are chimpanzees who love precision the way musicians or fanatical housekeepers or accomplished hypochondriacs do; others for whom happiness is a matter of invention and variation—chimp vaudevillians. There is a rhinoceros whose happiness, as near as I can make out, is in needing to be trained every morning, all over again, or else he "forgets" his circus routine, and in this you find a clue to the slow, deep, quiet chuckle of his happiness and to the glory of the beast. Happiness for Secretariat is in his ebullient bound, that joyful length of stride. For the draft horse or the weight-pull dog, happiness is of a different shape, more awesome and less obviously intelligent. When the pulling horse is at its most intense, the animal goes into himself, allocating all of the educated power that organizes his desire to dwell in fierce and delicate intimacy with that power, leans into the harness, AND MAKES THAT SUCKER *MOVE*.

If we are speaking of human beings and use the phrase "animal happiness," we tend to mean something like "creature comforts." The emblems of this are the golden retriever rolling in the grass, the horse with his nose deep in the oats, the kitty by the fire. Creature comforts are important to animals—"Grub first, then ethics" is a motto that would describe many a wise Labrador retriever, and I have a pit bull named Annie whose continual quest for the perfect pillow inspires her to awesome feats. But there is something more to animals, a capacity for satisfactions that come from work in the fullest sense—what is known in philosophy and in this country's Declaration of Independence as "happiness." This is a sense of personal achievement, like the satisfaction felt by a good wood-carver or a dancer or a poet or an accomplished dressage horse. It is a happiness that, like the artist's, must come from something within the animal, something trainers call "talent." Hence, it cannot be imposed on the animal. But it is also something that does not come *ex nihilo*. If it had not been a fairly ordinary thing, in one part of the world, to teach young children to play the pianoforte, it is doubtful that Mozart's music would exist.

3   Happiness is often misunderstood as a synonym for pleasure or as an antonym for suffering. But Aristotle associated happiness with ethics—codes of behavior that urge us toward the sensation of getting it right, a kind of work that yields the "click" of satisfaction upon solving a problem or surmounting an obstacle. In his *Ethics*, Aristotle wrote, "If happiness is activity in accordance with excellence, it is reasonable that it should be in accordance with the highest excellence." Thomas Jefferson identified the capacity for happiness as one of the three fundamental rights on which all others are based: "life, liberty, and the pursuit of happiness."

4   I bring up this idea of happiness as a form of work because I am an animal trainer, and work is the foundation of the happiness a trainer and an animal discover together. I bring up these words also because they cannot be found in the lexicon of the animal-rights movement. This absence accounts for the uneasiness toward the movement of most people, who sense that rights advocates have a point but take it too far when they liberate snails or charge that goldfish at the county fair are suffering. But the problem with the animal-rights advocates is not that they take it too far, it's that they've got it all wrong.

5   Animal rights are built upon a misconceived premise that rights were created to prevent us from unnecessary suffering. You can't find an animal-rights book, video, pamphlet, or rock concert in which someone doesn't mention the Great Sentence, written by

Jeremy Bentham in 1789. Arguing in favor of such rights, Bentham wrote: "The question is not, Can they *reason?* nor, can they *talk?* but, can they suffer?"

The logic of the animal-rights movement places suffering at 6 the iconographic center of a skewed value system. The thinking of its proponents—given eerie expression in a virtually sado-pornographic sculpture of a tortured monkey that won a prize for its compassionate vision—has collapsed into a perverse conundrum. Today the loudest voices calling for—demanding—the destruction of animals are the humane organizations. This is an inevitable consequence of the apotheosis of the drive to relieve suffering: Death is the ultimate release. To compensate for their contradictions, the humane movement has demonized, in this century and the last, those who made animal happiness their business: veterinarians, trainers, and the like. We think of Louis Pasteur as the man whose work saved you and me and your dog and cat from rabies, but antivivisectionists of the time claimed that rabies increased in areas where there were Pasteur Institutes.

An anti-rabies public-relations campaign mounted in Eng- 7 land in the 1880s by the Royal Society for the Prevention of Cruelty to Animals and other organizations led to orders being issued to club any dog found not wearing a muzzle. England still has her cruel and unnecessary law that requires an animal to spend six months in quarantine before being allowed loose in the country. Most of the recent propaganda about pit bulls—the crazy claim that they "take hold with their front teeth while they chew away with their rear teeth" (which would imply, incorrectly, that they have double jaws)—can be traced to literature published by the Humane Society of the United States during the fall of 1987 and earlier. If your neighbors want your dog or horse impounded and destroyed because he is a nuisance—say the dog barks, or the horse attracts flies—it will be the local Humane Society to whom your neighbors turn for action.

In a way, everyone has the opportunity to know that the 8 history of the humane movement is largely a history of miseries, arrests, prosecutions, and death. The Humane Society is the pound, the place with the decompression chamber or the lethal injections. You occasionally find worried letters about this in Ann Landers's column.

9   Animal-rights publications are illustrated largely with photographs of two kinds of animals—"Helpless Fluff" and "Agonized Fluff," the two conditions in which some people seem to prefer their animals, because any other version of an animal is too complicated for propaganda. In the introduction to his book *Animal Liberation*, Peter Singer says somewhat smugly that he and his wife have no animals and, in fact, don't much care for them. This is offered as evidence of his objectivity and ethical probity. But it strikes me as an odd, perhaps obscene, underpinning for an ethical project that encourages university and high school students to cherish their ignorance of, say, great bird dogs as proof of their devotion to animals.

10   I would like to leave these philosophers behind, for they are inept connoisseurs of suffering who might revere my Airedale for his capacity to scream when subjected to a blowtorch but not for his wit and courage, not for his natural good manners that are a gentle rebuke to ours. I want to celebrate the moment not long ago when, at his first dog show, my Airedale, Drummer, learned that there can be a public place where his work is respected. I want to celebrate his meticulousness, his happiness upon realizing at the dog show that no one would swoop down upon him and swamp him with the goo-goo excesses known as the "teddy-bear complex" but that people actually got out of his way, gave him room to work. I want to say, "There can be a six-and-a-half-month-old puppy who can care about accuracy, who can be fastidious, and whose fastidiousness will be a foundation for courage later." I want to say, "Leave my puppy alone!"

11   I want to leave the philosophers behind, but I cannot, in part because the philosophical problems that plague academicians of the animal-rights movement are illuminating. They wonder, do animals have rights or do they have interests? Or, if these rightists lead particularly unexamined lives, they dismiss that question as obvious (yes, of course, animals have rights, prima facie) and proceed to enumerate them, James Madison style. This leads to the issuance of bills of rights—the right to an environment, the right not to be used in medical experiments—and other forms of trivialization.

12   The calculus of suffering can be turned against the philosophers of festering flesh, even in the case of food animals, or exotic animals who perform in movies and circuses. It is true that it hurts

to be slaughtered by a man, but it doesn't hurt nearly as much as some of the cunningly cruel arrangements meted out by "Mother Nature." In Africa, 75 percent of the lions cubbed do not survive to the age of two. For those who make it to two, the average age at death is ten years. Asali, the movie and TV lioness, was still working at age twenty-one. There are fates worse than death, but twenty-one years of a close working relationship with Hubert Wells, Asali's trainer, is not one of them. Dorset sheep and polled Herefords would not exist at all were they not in a symbiotic relationship with human beings.

A human being living in the "wild"—somewhere, say, without the benefits of medicine and advanced social organizations— would probably have a life expectancy of from thirty to thirty-five years. A human being living in "captivity"—in, say, a middle-class neighborhood of what the Centers for Disease Control call a Metropolitan Statistical Area—has a life expectancy of seventy or more years. For orangutans in the wild in Borneo and Malaysia, the life expectancy is thirty-five years; in captivity, fifty years. The wild is not a suffering-free zone or all that frolicsome a location. [13]

The questions asked by animal-rights activists are flawed, because they are built on the concept that the origin of rights is in the avoidance of suffering rather than in the pursuit of happiness. The question that needs to be asked—and that will put us in closer proximity to the truth—is not, do they have rights? or, what are those rights? but rather, what is a right? [14]

Rights originate in committed relationships and can be found, both intact and violated, wherever one finds such relationships—in social compacts, within families, between animals, and between people and nonhuman animals. This is as true when the nonhuman animals in question are lions or parakeets as when they are dogs. It is my Airedale whose excellencies have my attention at the moment, so it is with reference to him that I will consider the question, what is a right? [15]

When I imagine situations in which it naturally arises that A defends or honors or respects B's rights, I imagine situations in which the relationship between A and B can be indicated with a possessive pronoun. I might say, "Leave her alone, she's my daughter" or, "That's what she wants, and she is my daughter. I think I am bound to honor her wants." Similarly, "Leave her alone, she's my mother." I am more tender of the happiness of my [16] mother, my father, my child, than I am of other people's family members; more tender of my friends' happiness than your friends' happiness, unless you and I have a mutual friend.

17   Possession of a being by another has come into more and more disrepute, so that the common understanding of one person possessing another is slavery. But the important detail about the kind of possessive pronoun that I have in mind is reciprocity: If I have a friend, she has a friend. If I have a daughter, she has a mother. The possessive does not bind one of us while freeing the other; it cannot do that. Moreover, should the mother reject the daughter, the word that applies is "disown." The form of disowning that most often appears in the news is domestic violence. Parents abuse children; husbands batter wives.

18   Some cases of reciprocal possessives have built-in limitations, such as "my patient/my doctor" or "my student/my teacher" or "my agent/my client." Other possessive relations are extremely limited but still remarkably binding: "my neighbor" and "my country" and "my president."

19   The responsibilities and the ties signaled by reciprocal possession typically are hard to dissolve. It can be as difficult to give up an enemy as to give up a friend, and often the one becomes the other, as though the logic of the possessive pronoun outlasts the forms it chanced to take at a given moment, as though we were stuck with one another. In these bindings, nearly inextricable, are found the origin of our rights. They imply a possessiveness but also recognize an acknowledgment by each side of the other's existence.

20   The idea of democracy is dependent on the citizens' having knowledge of the government; that is, realizing that the government exists and knowing how to claim rights against it. I know this much because I get mail from the government and see its "representatives" running about in uniforms. Whether I actually have any rights in relationship to the government is less clear, but the idea that I do is symbolized by the right to vote. I obey the government, and, in theory, it obeys me, by counting my ballot, reading the *Miranda* warning to me, agreeing to be bound by the Constitution. My friend obeys me as I obey her; the government "obeys" me to some extent, and, to a different extent, I obey it.

21   What kind of thing can my Airedale, Drummer, have knowledge of? He can know that I exist and through that knowledge can

claim his happiness, with varying degrees of success, both with me and against me. Drummer can also know about larger human or dog communities than the one that consists only of him and me. There is my household—the other dogs, the cats, my husband. I have had enough dogs on campuses to know that he can learn that Yale exists as a neighborhood or village. My older dog, Annie, not only knows that Yale exists but can tell Yalies from townies, as I learned while teaching there during labor troubles.

Dogs can have elaborate conceptions of human social struc- 22 tures, and even of something like their rights and responsibilities within them, but these conceptions are never elaborate enough to construct a rights relationship between a dog and the state, or a dog and the Humane Society. Both of these are concepts that depend on writing and memoranda, officers in uniform, plaques and seals of authority. All of these are literary constructs, and all of them are beyond a dog's ken, which is why the mail carrier who doesn't also happen to be a dog's friend is forever an intruder—this is why dogs bark at mailmen.

It is clear enough that natural rights relations can arise between 23 people and animals. Drummer, for example, can insist, "Hey, let's go outside and do something!" if I have been at my computer several days on end. He can both refuse to accept various of my suggestions and tell me when he fears for his life—such as the time when the huge, white flapping flag appeared out of nowhere, as it seemed to him, on the town green one evening when we were working. I can (and do) say to him either, "Oh, you don't have to worry about that" or "Uh oh, you're right, Drum, that guy looks dangerous." Just as the government and I—two different species of organism—have developed improvised ways of communicating, such as the vote, Drummer and I have worked out a number of ways to make our expressions known. Largely through obedience, I have taught him a fair amount about how to get responses from me. Obedience is reciprocal; you cannot get responses from a dog to whom you do not respond accurately. I have enfranchised him in a relationship to me by educating him, creating the conditions by which he can achieve a certain happiness specific to a dog, maybe even specific to an Airedale, inasmuch as this same relationship has allowed me to plumb the happiness of being a trainer and writing this article.

24   Instructions in this happiness are given terms that are alien to a culture in which liver treats, fluffy windup toys, and miniature sweaters are confused with respect and work. Jack Knox, a sheepdog trainer originally from Scotland, will shake his crook at a novice handler who makes a promiscuous move to praise a dog, and will call out in his Scottish accent, "Eh! Eh! Get back, get BACK! Ye'll no be abusin' the dogs like that in my clinic." America is a nation of abused animals, Knox says, because we are always swooping at them with praise, "no gi'ing them their freedom." I am reminded of Rainer Maria Rilke's account in which the Prodigal Son leaves—has to leave—because everyone loves him, even the dogs love him, and he has no path to the delicate and fierce truth of himself. Unconditional praise and love, in Rilke's story, disenfranchise us, distract us from what truly excites our interest.

25   In the minds of some trainers and handlers, praise is dishonesty. Paradoxically, it is a kind of contempt for animals that masquerades as a reverence for helplessness and suffering. The idea of freedom means that you do not, at least not while Jack Knox is nearby, helpfully guide your dog through the motions of, say, herding over and over—what one trainer calls "explainy-wainy." This is rote learning. It works tolerably well on some handlers, because people have vast unconscious minds and can store complex pre-programmed behaviors. Dogs, on the other hand, have almost no unconscious minds, so they can learn only by thinking. Many children are like this until educated out of it.

26   If I tell my Airedale to sit and stay on the town green, and someone comes up and burbles, "What a pretty thing you are," he may break his stay to go for a caress. I pull him back and correct him for breaking. Now he holds his stay because I have blocked his way to movement but not because I have punished him. (A correction blocks one path as it opens another for desire to work; punishment blocks desire and opens nothing.) He holds his stay now, and—because the stay opens this possibility of work, new to a heedless young dog—he watches. If the person goes on talking, and isn't going to gush with praise, I may heel Drummer out of his stay and give him an "Okay" to make friends. Sometimes something about the person makes Drummer feel that reserve is

in order. He responds to an insincere approach by sitting still, going down into himself, and thinking, "This person has no business pawing me. I'll sit very still, and he will go away." If the person doesn't take the hint from Drummer, I'll give the pup a little backup by saying, "Please don't pet him, he's working," even though he was not under any command.

The pup reads this, and there is a flicker of working trust 27 now stirring in the dog. Is the pup grateful? When the stranger leaves, does he lick my hand, full of submissive blandishments? This one doesn't. This one says nothing at all, and I say nothing much to him. This is a working trust we are developing, not a mutual-congratulation society. My backup is praise enough for him; the use he makes of my support is praise enough for me.

Listening to a dog is often praise enough. Suppose it is just 28 after dark and we are outside. Suddenly there is a shout from the house. The pup and I both look toward the shout and then toward each other: "What do you think?" I don't so much as cock my head, because Drummer is growing up, and I want to know what he thinks. He takes a few steps toward the house, and I follow. He listens again and comprehends that it's just Holly, who at fourteen is much given to alarming cries and shouts. He shrugs at me and goes about his business. I say nothing. To praise him for this performance would make about as much sense as praising a human being for the same thing. Thus:

A. *What's that?*
B. *I don't know. [Listens] Oh, it's just Holly.*
C. *What a gooooooood human being!*
D. *Huh?*

This is one small moment in a series of like moments that will 29 culminate in an Airedale who on Friday will have the discrimination and confidence required to take down a man who is attacking me with a knife and on Saturday clown and play with the children at the annual Orange Empire Dog Club Christmas party.

People who claim to speak for animal rights are increasingly 30 devoted to the idea that the very keeping of a dog or a horse or a gerbil or a lion is in and of itself an offense. The more loudly they speak, the less likely they are to be in a rights relation to any given animal, because they are spending so much time in airplanes or transmitting fax announcements of the latest Sylvester Stallone anti-fur rally. In a 1988 *Harper's* forum, for example, Ingrid Newkirk, the national director of People for the Ethical Treatment of Animals, urged that domestic pets be spayed and neutered and ultimately phased out. She prefers, it appears, wolves—and wolves someplace else—to Airedales and, by a logic whose interior structure is both emotionally and intellectually forever closed to Drummer, claims thereby to be speaking for "animal rights."

31   She is wrong. I am the only one who can own up to my Airedale's inalienable rights. Whether or not I do it perfectly at any given moment is no more refutation of this point than whether I am perfectly my husband's mate at any given moment refutes the fact of marriage. Only people who know Drummer, and whom he can know, are capable of this relationship. PETA and the Humane Society and the ASPCA and the Congress and NOW—as institutions—do have the power to affect my ability to grant rights to Drummer but are otherwise incapable of creating conditions or laws or rights that would increase his happiness. Only Drummer's owner has the power to obey him—to obey who he is and what he is capable of—deeply enough to grant him his rights and open up the possibility of happiness.

Content

1.   Compare Hearne's definition of "animal happiness" (¶s 1–3) with the view of "animal happiness" she attributes to the animal rights movement.

2.   "Animal rights," says Hearne, "are built upon a misconceived premise that rights were created to prevent us from unnecessary suffering" (¶ 5) "rather than in the pursuit of happiness" (¶ 14). Why does she say that premise is "misconceived"? What is the proper premise for ensuring animal rights?

3.   What, in Hearne's view, are the right animal rights? Why does she take issue with the conventional animal rights advocate's view that "possession of one being by another" is wrong (¶ 17 and following ¶s)?

4.   Compare and contrast Hearne's conception of a "symbiotic relationship" between animals and humans with the "cunningly cruel arrangements meted out by 'Mother Nature'" (¶ 12). Which is preferable, and why?

Strategies/Structures

1. Hearne uses numerous examples of cooperation between animals and their trainers or owners. Identify several of these and show how each reinforces her definition of "animal rights."

2. "Animal-rights publications," says Hearne, "are illustrated largely with photographs of two kinds of animals—'Helpless Fluff' and 'Agonized Fluff.'" Why does she interpret these illustrations as oversimplified "propaganda" (¶ 9)? What sorts of illustrations would be satisfactory to Hearne?

Language

1. What aspects of Hearne's language tell her readers of her deep love and respect for animals? How can she convey her strong feeling without lapsing into the sentimentality of the "Helpless Fluff" and "Agonized Fluff" views she attributes to animal rights publications (¶ 9)?

2. Hearne's seemingly straightforward language is punctuated with contemptuous references to animal-rights advocates: "inept connoisseurs of suffering" (¶ 9), "the philosophers of festering flesh" (¶ 12) who confuse "liver treats, fluffy windup toys, and miniature sweaters . . . with respect and work" (¶ 24). To what extent does this loaded language reinforce or diminish Hearne's argument? To what extent does your answer to this question depend on whether or not you agree with Hearne?

For Writing

1. "Rights," explains Hearne, "originate in committed relationships and can be found, both intact and violated, wherever one finds such relationships—in social compacts, within families, and between people and nonhuman animals" (¶ 15). Identify such a "right" that originates in a committed relationship between two individuals or groups, for instance as the Declaration of Independence asserts, "the right to life, liberty, and the pursuit of happiness." Explain the right for an audience who is likely to have taken that right for granted, and show how the mutual commitment of the parties involved reinforces that right. What could violate it? (Check with your instructor before choosing a topic; there may be some subjects with which he or she is overly familiar and would prefer not to receive papers on.)

2. "Today the loudest voices calling for—demanding—the destruction of animals are the humane organizations," says Hearne (¶ 6). How does she account for this paradox? Does she approve of this? Do you? Write a

paper arguing for or against Hearne's view. One half of the paper should be directed to an audience of conventional animal-rights advocates; another should be directed to an audience favorable to Hearne's position.

BAILEY WHITE

White, a first-grade teacher and first-rate storyteller, lives with her mother in Thomasville, Georgia, the town where she was born (1950) and reared. After graduation from Florida State University in 1973 and a decade-long sojourn (and marriage) in California, she returned to her birthplace and a deliberately simple life. She writes on an ancient portable typewriter when her computer breaks, and listens to the radio in preference to watching TV. "We do have a TV," she told an interviewer, "but we've never hooked it up. I'm not against TV, but I think the radio has a way of making you have deeper feelings for people."

Thus it is not surprising that White writes humorous stories of small-town life in a world kinder and simpler than today's, but not free of crotchets and adversities. She has told many of these stories on National Public Radio news broadcasts, and they have been collected in *Mama Makes Up Her Mind and Other Dangers of Southern Living* (1993) and *Sleeping at the Starlite Motel and Other Adventures on the Way Back Home* (1995). That many of them—including "Mortality" from *Mama Makes Up Her Mind*—have a strong, though not preachy, moral orientation is not surprising. White, in the guise of a friendly narrator, is really a kamikaze warrior for the good, the true, and the environmentally friendly.

Mortality

1   It really makes you feel your age when you get a letter from your insurance agent telling you that the car you bought, only slightly used, the year you got out of college, is now an antique. "Beginning with your next payment, your insurance premiums will reflect this change in classification," the letter said.

I went out and looked at the car. I thought back over the 2
years. I could almost hear my uncle's disapproving voice. "You
should never buy a used car," he had told me the day I brought it
home. Ten years later I drove that used car to his funeral. I drove
my sister, Louise, to the hospital in that car to have her first baby,
and I drove to Atlanta in that car when the baby graduated from
Georgia Tech with a degree in physics.

"When are you going to get a new car?" my friends asked me. 3

"I don't need a new car," I said. "This car runs fine." 4

I changed the oil often, and kept good tires on it. It always 5
got me where I wanted to go. But the stuffing came out of the backseat and the springs poked through, and the dashboard disinte-
grated. At 300,000 miles the odometer quit turning, but I didn't
really care to know how far I had driven.

A hole wore in the floor where my heel rested in front of the 6
accelerator, and the insulation all peeled off the fire wall. "Old
piece of junk," my friends whispered. The seat-belt catch wore
out, and I tied on a huge bronze hook with a fireman's knot.

Big flashy cars would zoom past me. People would shake 7
their fists out the windows. "Get that clunker off the road!" they
would shout.

Then one day on my way to work, the car coughed, sput- 8
tered, and stopped. "This is it," I thought, and I gave it a pat. "It's
been a good car."

I called the mechanic. "Tow it in," I said. "I'll have to decide 9
what to do." After work I went over there. I was feeling very glum.
The mechanic laughed at me. "It's not funny," I said. "I've had that
car a long time."

"You know what's wrong with that car?" he said. "That car 10
was out of gas." So I slopped a gallon of gas in the tank and drove
ten more years. The gas gauge never worked again after that day,
but I got to where I could tell when the gas was low by the smell.
I think it was the smell of the bottom of the tank.

There was also a little smell of brake fluid, a little smell of 11
exhaust, a little smell of oil, and after all the years a little smell
of me. Car smells. And sounds. The wonderful sound when the
engine finally catches on a cold day, and an ominous *tick tick* in
July when the radiator is working too hard. The windshield
wipers said "Gracie Allen Gracie Allen Gracie Allen." I didn't

like a lot of conversation in the car because I had to keep listening
for a little skip that meant I needed to jump out and adjust the
carburetor.

12   I kept a screwdriver close to hand—and a pint of brake fluid,
and a new rotor, just in case. "She's strange," my friends whispered. "And she drives so slow."

13   I don't know how fast I drove. The speedometer had quit
working years ago. But when I would look down through the
hole in the floor and see the pavement, a gray blur, whizzing by
just inches away from my feet, and feel the tremendous heat of
internal combustion pouring back through the fire wall into my
lap, and hear each barely contained explosion just as a heart
attack victim is able to hear his own heartbeat, it didn't feel like
slow to me. A whiff of brake fluid would remind me just what a
tiny thing I was relying on to stop myself from hurtling along the
surface of the earth at an unnatural speed, and when I finally
arrived at my destination, I would slump back, unfasten the seat
belt hook with trembling hands, and stagger out. I would gather
up my things and give the car a last look. "Thank you, sir," I
would say. "We got here one more time."

14   But after I got that letter, I began thinking about getting a
new car. I read the newspaper every night. Finally I found one
that sounded good. It was the same make as my car, but almost
new. "Call Steve," the ad said.

15   I went to see the car. It was parked in Steve's driveway. It was
a fashionable wheat color. There was carpet on the floor, and the
seats were covered with a soft, velvety-feeling stuff. It smelled like
acrylic and vinyl and Steve. The instrument panel looked like what
you would need to run a jet plane. I turned a knob. Mozart's Concerto for Flute and Harp poured out of four speakers. "But how can
you listen to the engine with music playing?" I asked Steve.

16   I turned the key. The car started instantly. No desperate
pleadings, no wild hopes, no exquisitely paired maneuvers with
the accelerator and the choke. Just instant ignition. I turned off the
radio. I could barely hear the engine running, a low, steady hum.
I fastened my seat belt. Nothing but a click.

17   Steve got in the passenger seat, and we went for a test drive.
We floated down the road. I couldn't hear a sound, but I decided
it must be time to shift gears. I stomped around on the floor and

grabbed Steve's knee before I remembered it had automatic transmission. "You mean you just put it in 'Drive' and drive?" I asked.

Steve scrunched himself way over against his door and 18 clamped his knees together. He tested his seat belt. "Have you ever driven a car before?" he asked.

I bought it for two thousand dollars. I rolled all the windows 19 up by mashing a button beside my elbow, set the air-conditioning on "Recirc," and listened to Vivaldi all the way home.

So now I have two cars. I call them my new car and my real 20 car. Most of the time I drive my new car. But on some days I go out to the barn and get in my real car. I shoo the rats out of the backseat and crank it up. Even without daily practice my hands and feet know just what to do. My ears perk up, and I sniff the air. I add a little brake fluid, a little water. I sniff again. It'll need gas next week, and an oil change.

I back it out and we roll down the road. People stop and 21 look. They smile. "Neat car!" they say.

When I pull into the parking lot, my friends shake their 22 heads and chuckle. They amble into the building. They're already thinking about their day's work. But I take one last look at the car and think what an amazing thing it is, internal combustion. And how wonderful to be still alive!

Content

1. If cars reflect their owners, what kind of person is Bailey White? Is she someone you'd like to know better? Why or why not?
2. To what extent does a car or a house or a style of dressing or eating reflect a person's values and lifestyle?
3. In what ways is White like her old car? Judging from the details she provides, what would you estimate the age of each to be?

Strategies/Structures

1. Why does this essay have so many short paragraphs? Could any have been combined? If so, which ones? With what effect?
2. Why do White's friends appear to ask, "When are you going to get a new car?" (¶ 3) Why, then, when the car is even older, an antique, do the people who see it rolling down the road smile and say, "Neat car!" (¶ 21)?

3. White casually mentions listening to "Mozart's Concerto for Flute and Harp" (¶ 15) in the new car and shooing "the rats out of the backseat" of her old car (¶ 20) so she can take it out for a drive. What is she trying to demonstrate to the readers with these observations?

Language

1. White now owns two cars, her "new car" and her "real car" (¶ 20). Why is the old car the "real car"?
2. White reads her stories aloud on National Public Radio. Judging from this essay, how do they sound?

For Writing

1. If you have any venerable object (car, house, dog or other pet, piece of furniture, book, significant item of clothing or jewelry . . .) to which you are unreasonably (in the eyes of the rest of the world) attached, write an essay for an audience unfamiliar with the specific object in which you demonstrate the force of your attachment and justify your preference for the old over the new. You may make it comic or serious, but avoid sentimentality—an excess of emotion—even if you're very devoted to the object.
2. Do cars, houses, pets, clothing, furniture, books, tastes in food and entertainment reflect the values and personalities of the owner or consumer? Write an essay comparing and contrasting a significant material object or style of yours with a comparable one of someone you know well as a way of comparing and contrasting the two people involved. (You may prefer the new to the old, the cheap to the expensive, the trendy to the classical; your companion's preference may either agree or contrast with yours.)

LESLIE S. MOORE

Of "Homes Away from Home," Moore (whose biographical information appears on page 282) explains: "I originally wrote this for a special section on 'Holden Area Homes' in the *Landmark*, a five-town weekly newspaper published in central Massachusetts. I thought the grim reality of my third-world living experiences would contrast nicely with its companion pieces: 'The Colonial Farmhouse—A Haven in the North,' 'The Scavenger's Den . . . and Living Room . . . and Garage,' and 'What Will a Million Dollars Buy in the Area?' My husband and I actually lived in more African houses than I've discussed in this essay. We house-sat for the American cultural attaché and for a Canadian hydraulic engineer, but I left these plush accommodations out because they didn't fit the types of houses I was describing or the overall tone of the piece."

By first describing the New England house she leaves behind, Moore obliges us to read about her homes in Mali through the lens of the first house she has shown us. This is a technique that travelers, strangers in strange lands, use to "ground" themselves and their readers as they remain on the move. It establishes a continuing point of contrast between the familiar home and the succession of new, unfamiliar dwellings, obliging readers to interpret each new dwelling in comparison to—and in often uncomfortable contrast with—the comforts of home. Only when Moore has returned home (¶ 15) does she begin to fully appreciate the positive features of her homes away from home.

❄ *Homes Away from Home*

I identify
well with this

S omething in me likes to pack a suitcase and say good-bye. Far 1 from feeling a sense of loss, I am enriched by each old place that I leave and by each new place that I visit. And I find that the farther my wanderings take me from comfort and familiarity, the deeper the details burn. A glow of fondness gradually surrounds them as I return to my more familiar life. Take my homes away from home in Africa.

When my husband and I left to teach English in Mali for the 2 Peace Corps, we knew and loved what we were leaving—a modest New England house that Tom had built, tucked into a slice of woods not a mile from the center of town, yet too secluded to bother with curtains. Windows were its extravagance; a wealth of light reflected off white walls and wooden floors. It rented in a snap. We drafted our own lease, packed away our belongings, and left the house swept and uncluttered. I remember admiring its clean lines as we walked out. I never suspected they would haunt me.

3   Two weeks later, in the village of Souban, between the Niger
River and the African bush, our world was transformed. Stripped
of familiar surroundings and habits like snakes that have
sloughed off their old skins, we faced this world feeling renewed,
but tender. No electricity. No running water. No transportation
beyond two feet, donkey carts, and bicycles. Our first "house"
consisted of two rooms in a mud and thatch compound. We were
the guests of Kognan Diarra and his family—his mother, two
wives, a sister-in-law, eight children, a herd of goats, a flock of
guinea fowl, a donkey, and a dog. We all lived together in the
compound, set off from the village by mud walls, millet fields,
and mango orchards.

4   Our new house was luxurious by Malian standards, but dis-
heartening by ours. Yes, Peace Corps had upgraded the accommodations by replacing our thatched roof with corrugated metal,
covering the dirt floors with concrete, slapping a thin coat of
whitewash over the mud walls, and adding two tiny windows
with screens. Yet, unlike our house in New England, these rooms
were dim and dusty, infested with termites, and stifling in the
heat. Peace Corps had also provided the furnishings: a bamboo
bed with mosquito netting, two metal trunks, two grass mats, two
kerosene lanterns, two plastic buckets, and two matching scoops.
The details linger. I remember wondering why I had felt so compelled to pack a suitcase and leave the comforts of home behind.

5   But that night we made the best of it. We put clean sheets on
the bed, hung a Monet calendar on the wall, and left our suitcases
packed. Tom wrote a letter in the living room, sitting on a grass
mat on the concrete floor, his typewriter between his knees, a
lantern smoking beside him. The murmur of Bambura came in
from the compound, goats bleated, a child cried himself to sleep,
and the guinea fowl scrabbled for footholds on the roof. In bed
the mosquito netting draped over us like a shroud. The lumpy
cotton mattress sagged in the middle. The sheets grew soggy with
sweat. Tom's stomach percolated the rice and peanut sauce we'd
finger-fed ·ourselves for dinner. We slept fitfully. I remember
dreaming of smooth sheets stretched taut over firm mattresses.

6   My dream didn't last long. At 3:00 a.m. the wind woke us, a
blowing gale that demanded all hands on deck—our landlord
battening down the shutters, Tom fumbling with their clasps, me

holding the flashlight. The first fat drops hit the metal roofing like bullets, then multiplied into a bombardment. Next morning the sun sat astride mango trees like a bloodied yolk. The compound looked shipwrecked. Guinea fowl stood knee-deep in water, mortars and pestles sank in the mud, and the grass matting over the lean-to hung in tatters. A neighbor in his field bent double over his short-handled *daba*, turning the red rain-soaked earth around fresh millet stalks. I picked my way through puddles to the bathroom—outside and uncovered, a mud-walled enclosure with a hole for a toilet, a flat stone for a tub. As I sat sluicing my-self with murky river water, the donkey cut loose with a gusty he-haaaaaaw! Recalling the bathroom I'd left back home—white porcelain, polished fixtures, hot water gushing clean from the tap—I had to laugh with him.

After nine weeks of this, Tom and I had lost ten pounds each 7 to dysentery, our Monet calendar to termites, and much of our initial enthusiasm. We weren't really sure we were being "en-riched" by our adventure so far, but we weren't ready to give up either. Having survived our initiation into Peace Corps Mali, we placed our hopes on our next residence—a house in the capital city, Bamako.

Unlike our "compound" house, our "city" house seemed 8 luxurious even by our standards—at first. It boasted two rooms, a kitchenette on the balcony, and a real bathroom. There were tile floors and electric ceiling fans, plaster walls without termites, two sinks, a bathtub, a bidet, a sit-down toilet, a hot-water heater, and running water. Bliss! We celebrated with a festival of house-keeping—sweeping the floors, scouring the sinks, polishing the fixtures. I did loads of laundry in the bathtub, scrubbing the red mud of Souban out of our clothes, while Tom jury-rigged a closet out of bamboo, string, and duct tape. We unpacked our suitcases, rounded up a table and chairs, plugged in the refrigerator Peace Corps had provided, and made ice cubes. Both of us sang in the shower that night.

We stopped singing shortly thereafter. Our city house was 9 really more like a rabbit-hutch. The two tiny rooms were claus-trophobic, and very few of the luxuries actually worked. The ceil-ing fan in the living room whirled so fast it was dangerous, the hot-water heater made no hot water, the toilet was missing its seat, and the refrigerator door barely had room to open. It was better than the compound house, but a far cry from the space and efficiencies of our own home. We drew in our elbows, settled for cold showers, and established a new routine.

10   Every morning at 5:00 a.m. the muezzin woke us, chanting the first prayer over a loudspeaker from the minaret at the local mosque. Mosquitoes clung to the netting around our bed and a cock cleared its throat on the street. I bought fresh baguettes for breakfast at the corner store and ripe fruit from a woman who balanced a pyramid of mangoes on a tray on her head. Wrapped Madonna-like in her flowered *pagne*, she gave me soft greetings— "*Ah-ni-sogoma*" ("You and your morning"), shy smiles, and both palms raised in benediction. Our morning exchange was one of the rare beauties of life in the city, but not enough to make me want to stay.

11   When we got a chance for another residence in the suburbs, "*une petite villa*," it said in the contract, we left easily. Our landlord was the 70-year-old husband of three wives, the father of 21 children (the oldest was 50, the youngest one-and-a-half), and the grandfather and great-grandfather of more than he could remember. He stood no taller than five feet, dressed in traditional white robes, wore a fez on his head, carried prayer beads in his hand, and had a billy goat b-a-a-a-ah to his voice. When he drove us downtown to put the water and electricity in our name, he spun around a traffic circle so fast that the door on my side of the Peugeot flew open, almost spilling me out. He chuckled, leaned across my lap, and slammed it shut.

12   Even without the contributions of our landlord, the "villa" was the hub of a busy neighborhood, crowded with people just one step out of their villages. They drew water from the municipal tap, cooked food over wood fires, and kept sheep, goats, and chickens in their compounds. The villa turned out to be as dim, dusty, and stifling as the compound house, so we spent most of our time in the walled-in garden under a mango tree. Both inside and out were incessantly noisy, making us long for a buffer zone of thick forest.

13   At this house too, the muezzin woke us at five o'clock in the morning. Dogs barked. Cocks crowed. We never needed an alarm clock. Across the street, girls gathered at the municipal

water faucet. Sitting on the rims of their buckets as they waited for their turns at the tap, they filled the time with chatter, then head-balanced their brimming buckets back home for the first wash. In the next compound, the dull thud of a pestle pounding millet echoed off the walls. Beneath our windows, shepherds herded their flocks to the riverbanks, the ewes bawling at recalcitrant lambs. The only neighbor who went about his business quietly was the old man who swept the street. Tall and spare, dressed in a farmer's loose trousers, a skull cap on his gray head, he bent from the waist to whisk his clutch of dried millet stalks over the ground, gathering together all the yellow blossoms the cassia trees had dropped during the night. He swept the bright petals into a pile and left them, a cache of gold in the dust.

By afternoon, when the heat and our heavy teaching loads 14 dictated naps, the children in the neighborhood took over the noise making. Tom said it was as if we'd been plunked down in the middle of a playground during recess. They rapped on our metal shutters with sticks. They spun the shutter-holders in their sockets. They shouted *"Toubaboo!"* ("Whiteman!") through the slats. Then they jiggled the handle on our gate and ran away when we opened it. The night was no better for sleeping. Everyone stayed up late. Children kicked soccer balls and played hide-and-seek. Women gathered outside to gossip. Men clustered around tiny braziers, brewing sweet tea spiced with mint. A beggar woman and her blind husband traversed the streets singing a litany of woes back and forth and rattling their alms in a tin cup. The sheep came home and Bob Marley wailed reggae on a cassette player until midnight. The insomnia of the whole neighborhood kept us awake—night after night.

By Christmas, we knew we couldn't go on with it. For lots 15 of reasons, including our problems with housing, our yearning for adventure away from home had given way to a yearning to return. We finished the school year and returned to New England in June. So today I sit in my own study, surrounded by white walls and familiar books, a Monet print above me, soft carpet at my feet, a comfortable chair, good reading light. Outside, the leaves are changing. Chickadees crack sunflower seeds at the feeder. A red squirrel drops hickory nuts from a tree. Tom splits wood in the driveway.

16   It is here that I can reflect on all those African houses. The details have burned deep—the murky water, mud walls, and mosquitoes of the compound; the broken toilet and lethal fan of the rabbit hutch; the cacophony of daily life around the villa. Yet a glow of fondness has begun to surround them. For it is also here that I can still see African sunrises over millet fields, still hear a Muslim prayer chanted at dawn, still taste the sweet flesh of ripe mangoes, still discover a clutch of gold petals in the dust. And it is these memories that will probably have me packing a suitcase again.

Content

1. In what ways is Moore "enriched" (¶ 1) by her living experiences in Mali, even though some were unpleasant? Does her essay make you want to go there, either vicariously or in actuality?

2. How can/does Moore create herself as a character critical of her Peace Corps housing (and of some aspects of the culture this represents) without sounding like an "ugly American" who critically and negatively measures everything abroad by American cultural standards?

Strategies/Structures

1. Moore doesn't say much about her New England house (¶ 2), yet we see it clearly. Why? Why does she supply many more details about her three dwellings in Mali?

2. "Show, don't tell," is advice commonly given to writers to encourage them to make their point through concrete rather than abstract means. What does each sentence in paragraph 14 show? What is the cumulative effect of all the details in that paragraph?

3. The essay's last paragraph sums up some of the contrasts, unpleasant and pleasant, that Moore experienced in Mali. Why is it necessary to include the pleasant details in this essay that largely dwells on the unpleasant ones?

Language

1. Moore's language is evocative of sights, sounds, tastes, and textures. Find some of these sensory details and show how they contribute to the overall effect of the piece.

2. Although Moore said she was aiming for a "woe-is-we" tone in "Homes Away from Home," does the essay in fact sound self-pitying? Why or why not? Would (or does) a self-pitying tone make you more— or less—sympathetic to the author as a person, and to her situation?

For Writing

1. Compare and contrast two dwellings you know intimately for an audience unfamiliar with each. Use descriptive details of each to reflect the lives and values of the inhabitants. Are there any oddities, incongruities that don't fit with the overall picture? What are they, and why are they there? In what ways are the two dwellings and their inhabitants similar? Different?

2. Define and describe your dream house in its ideal setting. In what ways is this similar to your actual residence? In what ways is it different? What lifestyles and values does each reflect? Are these compatible or quite different? Explain, for an audience who doesn't know you but who might share your aspirations.

RAYMOND CARVER

F. Scott Fitzgerald said there are no second acts in American life, but Carver's recovery from alcoholism the decade before his death at 50 in 1988 was a stunning second act. During this decade, through the examples of his own short stories, collected in more than a dozen volumes, Carver was a major influence in reviving short fiction—which some critics had left for dead after World War II— as a major form of serious literature. *Will You Please Be Quiet, Please?* (1976), *Where I'm Calling From* (1988), and *What We Talk About When We Talk About Love* (1981), from which the title story is reprinted below, are typical in their understated representations of drab and difficult lower-middle-class life in the Pacific Northwest—Carver's home territory—where, as one critic says, people worry about unemployment, bankruptcy, and "whether their old cars will start."

Carver himself knew this barren life firsthand, having married and fathered two children before he was twenty. He "picked tulips, pumped gas, swept hospital corridors, and swabbed toilets" in the process of earning a B.A. at Humboldt State College (1963) and an

M.F.A. at the University of Iowa (1966). One friend, poet Morton Marcus, says, "He was writing his worst dreams, readying himself for whatever might happen to him and his family, innocent small-town kids moving through the world like victims in search of an oppressor." Nearly felled by alcoholism in midcareer, with the advent of a new love—poet Tess Gallagher—and a new stability, Carver's life moved from liability to legend, his prolific work honored with numerous literary awards—a virtual fulfillment of the American Dream. His legacy came "at great personal expense," says Marcus, "a suitcase full of small trick mirrors in which we can see our distorted inner selves." Carver "shaped and polished those mirrors day after day after day through cigarette smoke" (he died of lung cancer), "alcohol fumes, unpaid bills, and domestic dog-fights. He came and is gone, but the gifts he made for us remain, each one a kiss on our lives."

What We Talk About
When We Talk About Love

1   My friend Mel McGinnis was talking. Mel McGinnis is a car-diologist, and sometimes that gives him the right.

2   The four of us were sitting around his kitchen table drinking gin. Sunlight filled the kitchen from the big window behind the sink. There were Mel and me and his second wife, Teresa—Terri, we called her—and my wife, Laura. We lived in Albuquerque then. But we were all from somewhere else.

3   There was an ice bucket on the table. The gin and the tonic water kept going around, and we somehow got on the subject of love. Mel thought real love was nothing less than spiritual love. He said he'd spent five years in a seminary before quitting to go to medical school. He said he still looked back on those years in the seminary as the most important years in his life.

4   Terri said the man she lived with before she lived with Mel loved her so much he tried to kill her. Then Terri said, "He beat me up one night. He dragged me around the living room by my ankles. He kept saying, 'I love you, I love you, you bitch.' He went on dragging me around the living room. My head kept knocking

on things." Terri looked around the table. "What do you do with love like that?"

She was a bone-thin woman with a pretty face, dark eyes, 5 and brown hair that hung down her back. She like necklaces made of turquoise, and long pendant earrings.

"My God, don't be silly. That's not love, and you know it," 6 Mel said. "I don't know what you'd call it, but I sure know you wouldn't call it love."

"Say what you want to, but I know it was," Terri said. "It 7 may sound crazy to you, but it's true just the same. People are different, Mel. Sure, sometimes he may have acted crazy. Okay. But he loved me. In his own way maybe, but he loved me. There was love there, Mel. Don't say there wasn't."

Mel let out his breath. He held his glass and turned to Laura 8 and me. "The man threatened to kill me," Mel said. He finished his drink and reached for the gin bottle. "Terri's a romantic. Terri's of the kick-me-so-I'll-know-you-love-me school. Terri, hon, don't look that way." Mel reached across the table and touched Terri's cheek with his fingers. He grinned at her.

"Now he wants to make up," Terri said. 9

"Make up what?" Mel said. "What is there to make up? I 10 know what I know. That's all."

"How'd we get started on this subject, anyway?" Terri said. 11 She raised her glass and drank from it. "Mel always has love on his mind," she said. "Don't you, honey?" She smiled, and I thought that was the last of it.

"I just wouldn't call Ed's behavior love. That's all I'm say- 12 ing, honey," Mel said. "What about you guys?" Mel said to Laura and me. "Does that sound like love to you?"

"I'm the wrong person to ask," I said. "I didn't even know the 13 man. I've only heard his name mentioned in passing. I wouldn't know. You'd have to know the particulars. But I think what you're saying is that love is an absolute."

Mel said, "The kind of love I'm talking about is. The kind of 14 love I'm talking about, you don't try to kill people."

Laura said, "I don't know anything about Ed, or anything 15 about the situation. But who can judge anyone else's situation?"

I touched the back of Laura's hand. She gave me a quick 16 smile. I picked up Laura's hand. It was warm, the nails polished, perfectly manicured. I encircled the broad wrist with my fingers, and I held her.

17   "When I left, he drank rat poison," Terri said. She clasped her arms with her hands. "They took him to the hospital in Santa Fe. That's where we lived then, about ten miles out. They saved his life. But his gums went crazy from it. I mean they pulled away from his teeth. After that, his teeth stood out like fangs. My God," Terri said. She waited a minute, then let go of her arms and picked up her glass.

18   "What people won't do!" Laura said.

19   "He's out of the action now," Mel said. "He's dead."

20   Mel handed me the saucer of limes. I took a section, squeezed it over my drink, and stirred the ice cubes with my finger.

21   "It gets worse," Terri said. "He shot himself in the mouth. But he bungled that too. Poor Ed," she said. Terri shook her head.

22   "Poor Ed nothing," Mel said. "He was dangerous."

23   Mel was forty-five years old. He was tall and rangy with curly soft hair. His face and arms were brown from the tennis he played. When he was sober, his gestures, all his movements, were precise, very careful.

24   "He did love me though, Mel. Grant me that," Terri said. "That's all I'm asking. He didn't love me the way you love me. I'm not saying that. But he loved me. You can grant me that, can't you?"

25   "What do you mean, he bungled it?" I said.

26   Laura leaned forward with her glass. She put her elbows on the table and held her glass in both hands. She glanced from Mel to Terri and waited with a look of bewilderment on her open face, as if amazed that such things happened to people you were friendly with.

27   "How'd he bungle it when he killed himself?" I said.

28   "I'll tell you what happened," Mel said. "He took this twenty-two pistol he'd bought to threaten Terri and me with. Oh, I'm serious, the man was always threatening. You should have seen the way we lived in those days. Like fugitives. I even bought a gun myself. Can you believe it? A guy like me? But I did. I bought one for self-defense and carried it in the glove compartment. Sometimes I'd have to leave the apartment in the middle of the night. To go to the hospital, you know? Terri and I weren't

married then, and my first wife had the house and kids, the dog, everything, and Terri and I were living in this apartment here. Sometimes, as I say, I'd get a call in the middle of the night and have to go in to the hospital at two or three in the morning. It'd be dark out there in the parking lot, and I'd break into a sweat before I could even get to my car. I never knew if he was going to come up out of the shrubbery or from behind a car and start shooting. I mean, the man was crazy. He was capable of wiring a bomb, anything. He used to call my service at all hours and say he needed to talk to the doctor, and when I'd return the call, he'd say, 'Son of a bitch, your days are numbered.' Little things like that. It was scary, I'm telling you."

"I still feel sorry for him," Terri said.   29

"It sounds like a nightmare," Laura said. "But what exactly   30
happened after he shot himself?"

Laura is a legal secretary. We'd met in a professional capacity.   31
Before we knew it, it was a courtship. She's thirty-five, three years younger than I am. In addition to being in love, we like each other and enjoy one another's company. She's easy to be with.

"What happened?" Laura said.   32

Mel said, "He shot himself in the mouth in his room. Some- 33
one heard the shot and told the manager. They came in with a passkey, saw what had happened, and called an ambulance. I happened to be there when they brought him in, alive but past recall. The man lived for three days. His head swelled up to twice the size of a normal head. I'd never seen anything like it, and I hope I never do again. Terri wanted to go in and sit with him when she found out about it. We had a fight over it. I didn't think she should see him like that. I didn't think she should see him, and I still don't."

"Who won the fight?" Laura said.   34

"I was in the room with him when he died," Terri said. "He 35
never came up out of it. But I sat with him. He didn't have any-one else."

"He was dangerous," Mel said. "If you call that love, you 36
can have it."

"It was love," Terri said. "Sure, it's abnormal in most 37
people's eyes. But he was willing to die for it. He did die for it."

38   "I sure as hell wouldn't call it love," Mel said. "I mean, no one knows what he did it for. I've seen a lot of suicides, and I couldn't say anyone ever knew what they did it for."

39   Mel put his hands behind his neck and tilted his chair back. "I'm not interested in that kind of love," he said. "If that's love, you can have it."

40   Terri said, "We were afraid. Mel even made a will out and wrote to his brother in California who used to be a Green Beret. Mel told him who to look for if something happened to him."

41   Terri drank from her glass. She said, "But Mel's right—we lived like fugitives. We were afraid. Mel was, weren't you, honey? I even called the police at one point, but they were no help. They said they couldn't do anything until Ed actually did something. Isn't that a laugh?" Terri said.

42   She poured the last of the gin into her glass and waggled the bottle. Mel got up from the table and went to the cupboard. He took down another bottle.

43   "Well, Nick and I know what love is," Laura said. "For us, I mean," Laura said. She bumped my knee with her knee. "You're supposed to say something now," Laura said, and turned her smile on me.

44   For an answer, I took Laura's hand and raised it to my lips. I made a big production out of kissing her hand. Everyone was amused.

45   "We're lucky," I said.

46   "You guys," Terri said. "Stop that now. You're making me sick. You're still on the honeymoon, for God's sake. You're still gaga, for crying out loud. Just wait. How long have you been together now? How long has it been? A year? Longer than a year?"

47   "Going on a year and a half," Laura said, flushed and smiling.

48   "Oh, now," Terri said. "Wait awhile."

49   She held her drink and gazed at Laura.

50   "I'm only kidding," Terri said.

51   Mel opened the gin and went around the table with the bottle.

52   "Here, you guys," he said. "Let's have a toast. I want to propose a toast. A toast to love. To true love," Mel said.

We touched glasses.   53

"To love," we said.   54

Outside in the backyard, one of the dogs began to bark. The   55
leaves of the aspen that leaned past the window ticked against
the glass. The afternoon sun was like a presence in this room, the
spacious light of ease and generosity. We could have been anywhere, somewhere enchanted. We raised our glasses again and
grinned at each other like children who had agreed on something
forbidden.

"I'll tell you what real love is," Mel said. "I mean, I'll give   56
you a good example. And then you can draw your own conclusions." He poured more gin into his glass. He added an ice cube
and a sliver of lime. We waited and sipped our drinks. Laura and
I touched knees again. I put a hand on her warm thigh and left
it there.

"What do any of us really know about love?" Mel said. "It   57
seems to me we're just beginners at love. We say we love each
other and we do, I don't doubt it. I love Terri and Terri loves me,
and you guys love each other too. You know the kind of love I'm
talking about now. Physical love, that impulse that drives you to
someone special, as well as love of the other person's being, his or
her essence, as it were. Carnal love and, well, call it sentimental
love, the day-to-day caring about the other person. But sometimes
I have a hard time accounting for the fact that I must have loved
my first wife too. But I did, I know I did. So I suppose I am like
Terri in that regard. Terri and Ed." He thought about it and then
he went on. "There was a time when I thought I loved my first
wife more than life itself. But now I hate her guts. I do. How do
you explain that? What happened to that love? What happened to
it, is what I'd like to know. I wish someone could tell me. Then
there's Ed. Okay, we're back to Ed. He loves Terri so much he tries
to kill her and he winds up killing himself." Mel stopped talking
and swallowed from his glass. "You guys have been together
eighteen months and you love each other. It shows all over you.
You glow with it. But you both loved other people before you met
each other. You've both been married before, just like us. And you
probably loved other people before that too, even. Terri and I have
been together five years, been married for four. And the terrible

thing, the terrible thing is, but the good thing too, the saving grace, you might say, is that if something happened to one of us—excuse me for saying this—but if something happened to one of us tomorrow I think the other one, the other person, would grieve for a while, you know, but then the surviving party would go out and love again, have someone else soon enough. All this, all of this love we're talking about, it would just be a memory. Maybe not even a memory. Am I wrong? Am I way off base? Because I want you to set me straight if you think I'm wrong. I want to know. I mean, I don't know anything, and I'm the first one to admit it."

58   "Mel, for God's sake," Terri said. She reached out and took hold of his wrist. "Are you getting drunk? Honey? Are you drunk?"

59   "Honey, I'm just talking," Mel said. "All right? I don't have to be drunk to say what I think. I mean, we're all just talking, right?" Mel said. He fixed his eyes on her.

60   "Sweetie, I'm not criticizing," Terri said.

61   She picked up her glass.

62   "I'm not on call today," Mel said. "Let me remind you of that. I am not on call," he said.

63   "Mel, we love you," Laura said.

64   Mel looked at Laura. He looked at her as if he could not place her, as if she was not the woman she was.

65   "Love you too, Laura," Mel said. "And you, Nick, love you too. You know something?" Mel said. "You guys are our pals," Mel said.

66   He picked up his glass.

67   Mel said, "I was going to tell you about something. I mean, I was going to prove a point. You see, this happened a few months ago, but it's still going on right now, and it ought to make us feel ashamed when we talk like we know what we're talking about when we talk about love."

68   "Come on now," Terri said. "Don't talk like you're drunk if you're not drunk."

69   "Just shut up for once in your life," Mel said very quietly. "Will you do me a favor and do that for a minute? So as I was saying, there's this old couple who had this car wreck out on the interstate. A kid hit them and they were all torn to shit and nobody was giving them much chance to pull through."

Terri looked at us and then back at Mel. She seemed anxious,   70
or maybe that's too strong a word.

Mel was handing the bottle around the table.   71

"I was on call that night," Mel said. "It was May or maybe   72
it was June. Terri and I just sat down to dinner when the hospital
called. There'd been this thing out on the interstate. Drunk kid,
teenager, plowed his dad's pickup into this camper with this old
couple in it. They were up in their mid-seventies, that couple. The
kid—eighteen, nineteen, something—he was DOA. Taken the
steering wheel through his sternum. The old couple, they were
alive, you understand. I mean, just barely. But they had everything. Multiple fractures, internal injuries, hemorrhaging, contu-
sions, lacerations, the works, and they each of them had
themselves concussions. They were in a bad way, believe me.
And, of course, their age was two strikes against them. I'd say
she was worse off than he was. Ruptured spleen along with
everything else. Both kneecaps broken. But they'd been wearing
their seatbelts and, God knows, that's what saved them for the
time being."

"Folks, this is an advertisement for the National Safety   73
Council," Terri said. "This is your spokesman, Dr. Melvin R.
McGinnis, talking." Terri laughed. "Mel," she said, "sometimes
you're too much. But I love you, hon," she said.

"Honey, I love you," Mel said.   74

He leaned across the table. Terri met him halfway. They   75
kissed.

"Terri's right," Mel said as he settled himself again. "Get   76
those seatbelts on. But seriously, they were in some shape, those
oldsters. By the time I got down there, the kid was dead, as I said.
He was off in a corner, laid out on a gurney. I took one look at the
old couple and told the ER nurse to get me a neurologist and an
orthopedic man and a couple of surgeons down there right away."

He drank from his glass. "I'll try to keep this short," he said.   77
"So we took the two of them up to the OR and worked like fuck
on them most of the night. They had these incredible reserves,
those two. You see that once in a while. So we did everything that
could be done, and toward morning we're giving them a fifty-
fifty chance, maybe less than that for her. So here they are, still
alive the next morning. So, okay, we move them into the ICU,
which is where they both kept plugging away at it for two weeks,

hitting it better and better on all the scopes. So we transfer them to their own room."

78   Mel stopped talking. "Here," he said, "let's drink this cheapo gin the hell up. Then we're going to dinner, right? Terri and I know a new place. That's where we'll go, to this new place we know about. But we're not going until we finish up this cut-rate, lousy gin."

79   Terri said, "We haven't actually eaten there yet. But it looks good. From the outside, you know."

80   "I like food," Mel said. "If I had it to do all over again, I'd be a chef, you know? Right, Terri?" Mel said.

81   He laughed. He fingered the ice in his glass.

82   "Terri knows," he said. "Terri can tell you. But let me say this. If I could come back again in a different life, a different time and all, you know what? I'd like to come back as a knight. You were pretty safe wearing all that armor. It was all right being a knight until gunpowder and muskets and pistols came along."

83   "Mel would like to ride a horse and carry a lance," Terri said.

84   "Carry a woman's scarf with you everywhere," Laura said.

85   "Or just a woman," Mel said.

86   "Shame on you," Laura said.

87   Terri said, "Suppose you came back as a serf. The serfs didn't have it so good in those days," Terri said.

88   "The serfs never had it good," Mel said. "But I guess even the knights were vessels to someone. Isn't that the way it worked? But then everyone is always a vessel to someone. Isn't that right? Terri? But what I liked about knights, besides their ladies, was that they had that suit of armor, you know, and they couldn't get hurt very easy. No cars in those days, you know? No drunk teenagers to tear into your ass."

89   "Vassals," Terri said.

90   "What?" Mel said.

91   "Vassals," Terri said. "They were called vassals, not vessels."

92   "Vassals, vessels," Mel said, "what the fuck's the difference? You knew what I meant anyway. All right," Mel said. "So I'm not educated. I learned my stuff. I'm a heart surgeon, sure, but I'm just a mechanic. I go in and I fuck around and I fix things. Shit," Mel said.

"Modesty doesn't become you," Terri said.   93

"He's just a humble sawbones," I said. "But sometimes they   94
suffocated in all the armor, Mel. They'd even have heart attacks if
it got too hot and they were too tired and worn out. I read somewhere that they'd fall off their horses and not be able to get up
because they were too tired to stand with all that armor on them.
They got trampled by their own horses sometimes."

"That's terrible," Mel said. "That's a terrible thing, Nicky. I   95
guess they'd just lay there and wait until somebody came along
and made a shish kebab out of them."

"Some other vessel," Terri said.   96

"That's right," Mel said. "Some vassal would come along   97
and spear the bastard in the name of love. Or whatever the fuck
it was they fought over in those days."

"Same things we fight over these days," Terri said.   98

Laura said, "Nothing's changed."   99

The color was still high in Laura's cheeks. Her eyes were   100
bright. She brought her glass to her lips.

Mel poured himself another drink. He looked at the label   101
closely as if studying a long row of numbers. Then he slowly put
the bottle down on the table and slowly reached for the tonic
water.

"What about the old couple?" Laura said. "You didn't finish that   102
story you started."

Laura was having a hard time lighting her cigarette. Her   103
matches kept going out.

The sunshine inside the room was different now, changing,   104
getting thinner. But the leaves outside the window were still shim-
mering, and I stared at the pattern they made on the panes and on
the Formica counter. They weren't the same patterns, of course.

"What about the old couple?" I said.   105

"Older but wiser," Terri said.   106

Mel stared at her.   107

Terri said, "Go on with your story, hon. I was only kidding.   108
Then what happened?"

"Terri, sometimes," Mel said.   109

"Please, Mel," Terri said. "Don't always be so serious,   110
sweetie. Can't you take a joke?"

"Where's the joke?" Mel said.   111

112   He held his glass and gazed steadily at his wife.

113   "What happened?" Laura said.

114   Mel fastened his eyes on Laura. He said, "Laura, if I didn't have Terri and if I didn't love her so much, and if Nick wasn't my best friend, I'd fall in love with you, I'd carry you off, honey," he said.

115   "Tell your story," Terri said. "Then we'll go to that new place, okay?"

116   "Okay," Mel said. "Where was I?" he said. He stared at the table and then he began again.

117   "I dropped in to see each of them every day, sometimes twice a day if I was up doing other calls anyway. Casts and bandages, head to foot, the both of them. You know, you've seen it in the movies. That's just the way they looked, just like in the movies. Little eye-holes and nose-holes and mouth-holes. And she had to have her legs slung up on top of it. Well, the husband was very depressed for the longest while. Even after he found out that his wife was going to pull through, he was still very depressed. Not about the accident, though. I mean, the accident was one thing, but it wasn't everything. I'd get up to his mouth-hole, you know, and he'd say no, it wasn't the accident exactly but it was because he couldn't see her through his eye-holes. He said that was what was making him feel so bad. Can you imagine? I'm telling you, the man's heart was breaking because he couldn't turn his goddamn head and *see* his goddamn wife."

118   Mel looked around the table and shook his head at what he was going to say.

119   "I mean, it was killing the old fart just because he couldn't *look* at the fucking woman."

120   We all looked at Mel.

121   "Do you see what I'm saying?" he said.

122   Maybe we were a little drunk by then. I know it was hard keeping things in focus. The light was draining out of the room, going back through the window where it had come from. Yet nobody made a move to get up from the table to turn on the overhead light.

123   "Listen," Mel said. "Let's finish this fucking gin. There's about enough left here for a shooter all around. Then let's go eat. Let's go to the new place."

"He's depressed," Terri said. "Mel, why don't you take a   124
pill?"

Mel shook his head. "I've taken everything there is."   125

"We all need a pill now and then," I said.   126

"Some people are born needing them," Terri said.   127

She was using her finger to rub at something on the table.   128
Then she stopped rubbing.

"I think I want to call my kids," Mel said. "Is that all right   129
with everybody? I'll call my kids," he said.

Terri said, "What if Marjorie answers the phone? You guys,   130
you've heard us on the subject of Marjorie. Honey, you know you
don't want to talk to Marjorie. It'll make you feel even worse."

"I don't want to talk to Marjorie," Mel said. "But I want to   131
talk to my kids."

"There isn't a day goes by that Mel doesn't say he wishes   132
she'd get married again. Or else die," Terri said. "For one thing,"
Terri said, "she's bankrupting us. Mel says it's just to spite him
that she won't get married again. She has a boyfriend who lives
with her and the kids, so Mel is supporting the boyfriend too."

"She's allergic to bees," Mel said. "If I'm not praying she'll   133
get married again, I'm praying she'll get herself stung to death by
a swarm of fucking bees."

"Shame on you," Laura said.   134

"Bzzzzzzz," Mel said, turning his fingers into bees and   135
buzzing them at Terri's throat. Then he let his hands drop all the
way to his sides.

"She's vicious," Mel said. "Sometimes I think I'll go up there   136
dressed like a beekeeper. You know, that hat that's like a helmet
with the plate that comes down over your face, the big gloves,
and the padded coat? I'll knock on the door and let loose a hive
of bees in the house. But first I'd make sure the kids were out, of
course."

He crossed one leg over the other. It seemed to take him a   137
lot of time to do it. Then he put both feet on the floor and leaned
forward, elbows on the table, his chin cupped in his hands.

"Maybe I won't call the kids, after all. Maybe it isn't such a   138
hot idea. Maybe we'll just go eat. How does that sound?"

"Sounds fine to me," I said. "Eat or not eat. Or keep drink-   139
ing. I could head right on out into the sunset."

140   "What does that mean, honey?" Laura said.

141   "It just means what I said," I said. "It means I could just keep going. That's all it means."

142   "I could eat something myself," Laura said. "I don't think I've ever been so hungry in all my life. Is there something to nibble on?"

143   "I'll put out some cheese and crackers," Terri said.

144   But Terri just sat there. She did not get up to get anything.

145   Mel turned his glass over. He spilled it out on the table.

146   "Gin's gone," Mel said.

147   Terri said, "Now what?"

148   I could hear my heart beating. I could hear everyone's heart. I could hear the human noise we sat there making, not one of us moving, not even when the room went dark.

Additional Topics for Writing
Comparison and Contrast

(For process strategies, see page 504)

1. Write an essay, full of examples, that compares and contrasts any of the following pairs:

    a. Two people with a number of relevant characteristics in common (two of your teachers, roommates, friends, relatives playing the same role—i.e., two of your sisters or brothers, two of your grandparents, a father or mother and a stepparent)

    b. Two cities or regions of the country you know well, or two neighborhoods you have lived in

    c. Two comparable historical figures with similar positions, such as two presidents, two senators, two generals, two explorers, or others

    d. Two religions or two sects or churches within the same religion

    e. Two utopian communities (real or imaginary)

    f. Two explanations or interpretations of the same scientific, economic, religious, psychological, or political phenomenon (for instance, creationism versus Darwinism; Freudian versus Skinnerian theory of behavior)

    g. The cuisine of two different countries or two or more parts of a country (Greek versus French cooking; Szechuan, Cantonese, and Peking Chinese food)

2. Write a balanced essay involving a comparison and contrast of one of the subjects below that justifies your preference for one over the other. Write for a reader who is likely to debate your choice.

    a. American-made versus foreign-made cars (specify the country and the manufacturer)

    b. The styles of two performers—musicians, actors or actresses, dancers, athletes participating in the same sport, comedians

    c. The work of two writers, painters, theater or film directors; or two (or three) works by the same writer or painter

    d. Two political parties, campaigns, or machines, past or present

    e. Two colleges or universities (or programs or sports teams within them) that you know well

    f. Two styles of friendship, courtship, marriage, or family (both may be contemporary, or you may compare and contrast past and present styles)

g. Two academic majors, professions, or careers
h. Life in the mainstream or on the margin (specify of which group, community, or society)

3. Write an essay, for an audience of fellow students, comparing the reality with the ideal of one of the following :

a. Dating styles
b. Your current job and the most satisfying job you could have
c. Your current accomplishment in a particular area (sports, a performing art, a skill, or a level of knowledge) with what you hope to attain
d. Friendship
e. Parenthood
f. Your present dwelling and your dream house
g. The way you currently spend your leisure time and the way you'd like to spend it
h. The present state of affairs versus the future prospects of some issue of social significance, such as world population, ecology, the control of nuclear arms, the treatment of hijackers and other international terrorists

Part **IV**

Arguing Directly and Indirectly

13 *Appealing to Reason: Deductive and Inductive Arguments*

When you write persuasively you're trying to move your readers to either belief or action or both. You can do this through appealing to their reasons, their emotions, or their sense of ethics, as you know if you've ever tried to prove a point on an exam or change an attitude in a letter to the editor. The next section discusses appeals to emotion and ethics; here we'll concentrate on argumentation.

An argument, as we're using the term here, does not mean a knockdown confrontation over an issue: "Philadelphia is the most wonderful place in the world to live!" "No, it's not. Social snobbery has ruined the City of Brotherly Love." Nor is an argument hard-sell brainwashing that admits of no alternatives: "America— love it or leave it!" When you write an argument, however, as a reasonable writer you'll present a reasonable proposition that states what you believe ("As we approach the twenty-first century,

America remains the best country in the world for freedom, democracy, and the opportunity to succeed.") You'll need to offer logic, evidence, and perhaps emotional appeals, to try to convince your readers of the merits of what you say. Sometimes, but not always, you'll also argue that they should adopt a particular course of action. ("Consequently, America should establish an 'open door' immigration policy to enable the less fortunate to enjoy these benefits, too." Or, "Consequently, America should severely restrict immigration, to prevent overcrowding and enable every citizen to enjoy these hard-won benefits.")

Unless you're writing an indirect argument that makes its point through satire, irony, an imagined character whose actions or life story illustrate a point (see Jonathan Swift, "A Modest Proposal," [pp. 637–645]), or some other oblique means, you'll probably want to identify the issue at hand and justify its significance early in the essay: "Mandatory drug-testing is essential for public officials with access to classified information." If it's a touchy subject, you may wish at this point to demonstrate good will toward readers likely to disagree with you by showing the basis for your common concern: "Most Americans would agree that it's important to protect children and adolescents from harmful influences." You could follow this by acknowledging the merits of their valid points: "And it's also true that drug abuse is currently a national crisis, and deserves immediate remedy." You'll need to follow this with an explanation of why, nevertheless, your position is better than theirs: "But mandatory drug testing for everyone would be a violation of their civil liberties, incredibly costly, and subject to abuse through misuse of the data."

There are a number of suitable ways to organize the body of your argument. If your audience is inclined to agree with much of what you say, you might want to put your strongest point first and provide the most evidence for that, before proceeding to the lesser points, arranged in order of descending importance:

1. Mandatory drug testing for everyone is unconstitutional.
   (three paragraphs)
2. Mandatory drug testing would be extremely costly, an expense grossly disproportionate to the results.
   (two paragraphs)

3. The results of mandatory drug testing would be easy to abuse—to falsify, to misreport, to misinterpret.
   (one paragraph)
4. Consequently, mandatory drug testing for everyone would cause more problems than it would solve.
   (conclusion—one paragraph)

For an antagonistic audience you could do the reverse, beginning with the points easiest to accept or agree with and concluding with the most difficult. Or you could work from the most familiar to the least familiar parts.

No matter what organizational pattern you choose, you'll need to provide supporting evidence—through specific examples, facts and figures, the opinions of experts, case histories, narratives, analogies, considerations of cause and effect. Any or all of these techniques can be employed in either *inductive* or *deductive* reasoning. Chances are that most of your arguments will proceed by induction. You might use an individual example intended as representative of the whole, as Scott Russell Sanders does in anatomizing his father's alcoholism to illustrate the alcoholic's characteristic behavior (pp. 420–433).

Or you might use a larger number of examples and apply inductive reasoning to prove a general proposition. Research scientists and detectives work this way, as do some social commentators and political theorists. Robert Reich identifies the characteristics of "The Global Elite" (pp. 604–615) and uses them both to counteract the myths that the United States is a benevolent, egalitarian society and to argue against the separatism— moral and economic secession—that upper-income Americans currently practice to dissociate themselves from responsibilities toward the rest of society. Galbraith's method of argument is disingenuous. In identifying the major ways "we" (the *haves*) behave in order to ". . . Get the Poor [the *have-nots*] off Our Conscience" (pp. 596–603), Galbraith explains five philosophical ("any form of public help to the poor only hurts the poor") and psychological ("denial") principles, with corroborating illustrations as evidence, for his argument that a compassionate social policy "remains the only one that is consistent with a totally civilized life."

Using a similar method in "The Struggle to Save Endangered Species" (pp. 617–625), Janna L. Cunningham examines the implications of a public policy in the United States and in Kenya in order to understand and interpret the issue of animal conservation. As a freshman student who has not visited Africa or been immersed in college studies at an advanced level, she is obliged to rely on the sources she cites in her essay.

An essay of deductive reasoning proceeds from a general proposition to a specific conclusion. The model for a deductive argument is the syllogism, a three-part sequence that begins with a major premise, is followed by a minor premise, and leads to a conclusion. Aristotle's classic example of this basic logical pattern is

> Major premise: All men are mortal.
> Minor premise: Socrates is a man.
> Conclusion: Therefore, Socrates is mortal.

In "Letter from Birmingham Jail" (pp. 569–586), Martin Luther King, Jr., argues for the proposition that "one has not only a legal but a moral responsibility to disobey unjust laws" and uses a vast range of resources to demonstrate his point. He uses Biblical and historical examples to explain the situation in Birmingham; illustrations from his own life and from the lives of his own children and other victims of racial segregation; and more generalized incidents of brutal treatment of "unarmed, nonviolent Negroes." Lani Guinier designs her deductive argument, "The Tyranny of the Majority" (pp. 588–595), to illustrate the thesis that the rules of fair play "should reward those who win, but they must be acceptable to those who lose"; as an acceptable alternative to a "zero-sum game" ("I win; you lose"), she substitutes "the principle of taking turns." To make her point, Guinier draws on examples from constitutional law, American history, and analogies in playing sports and games.

No matter what your argumentative strategy, you will want to avoid *logical fallacies,* errors of reasoning that can lead you to the wrong conclusion. The most common logical fallacies to be aware of are the following:

- *Arguing from analogy:* Comparing only similarities between things, concepts, or situations while overlooking significant differences that might weaken the argument. "Having a standing army is just like having a loaded gun in the house. If it's around, people will want to use it."

- *Argumentation ad hominem* (from Latin, "argument to the man"): Attacking a person's ideas or opinions by discrediting him or her as a person. "Napoleon was too short to be a distinguished general." "She was seen at the Kit Kat Lounge one night last week; she can't possibly be a good mother."
- *Argument from doubtful or unidentified authority:* Treating an unqualified, unreliable, or unidentified source as an expert on the subject at hand. "They say you can't get pregnant the first time." "'History is bunk!' said Henry Ford."
- *Begging the question:* Regarding as true from the start what you set out to prove; asserting that what is true is true. "Rapists and murderers awaiting trial shouldn't be let out on bail" assumes that the suspects have already been proven guilty, which is the point of the impending trial.
- *Arguing in a circle:* Demonstrating a premise by a conclusion and a conclusion by a premise. "People should give 10 percent of their income to charity because that is the right thing to do. Giving 10 percent of one's income to charity is the right thing to do because it is expected."
- *Either/or reasoning:* Restricting the complex aspects of a difficult problem or issue to only one of two possible solutions. "You're not getting any younger. Marry me or you'll end up single forever."
- *Hasty generalization:* Erroneously applying information or knowledge of one or a limited number of representative instances to an entire, much larger category. "Poor people on welfare cheat. Why, just yesterday I saw a Cadillac parked in front of the tenement at 9th and Main."
- *Non sequitur* (from the Latin, "it does not follow"): Asserting as a conclusion something that doesn't follow from the first premise or premises. "The Senator must be in cahoots with that shyster developer, Landphill. After all, they were college fraternity brothers."
- *Oversimplification:* Providing simplistic answers to complex problems. "Ban handguns and stop organized crime."
- *Post hoc ergo propter hoc* (from Latin, "after this, therefore because of this"): Confusing a cause with an effect and vice versa. "Bicyclists are terribly unsafe riders. They're always getting into accidents with cars." Or confusing causality with proximity: just because two events occur in sequence doesn't

necessarily mean that the first caused the second. Does war cause famine, or is famine sometimes the cause of war?

After you've written a logical argument, have someone who disagrees with you read it critically to look for loopholes. Your critic's guidelines could be the same questions you might ask yourself while writing the paper, as indicated in the process strategies below. If you can satisfy yourself and a critic, you can take on the world. Or is that a logical fallacy?

STRATEGIES FOR WRITING— APPEALING TO REASON: DEDUCTIVE AND INDUCTIVE ARGUMENTS

1. Do I want to convince my audience of the truth of a particular matter? Do I want essentially to raise their consciousness of an issue? Do I want to promote a belief or refute a theory? Or do I want to move my readers to action? If action, what kind? To change their minds, attitudes, or behavior? To right a wrong, or alter a situation?

2. At the outset, do I expect my audience to agree with my ideas? To be neutral about the issues at hand? Or to be opposed to my views? Can I build into my essay responses to my readers' anticipated reactions, such as rebuttals to their possible objections? Do I know enough about my subject to be able to do this?

3. What is my strongest (and presumably most controversial) point, and where should I put it? At the beginning, if my audience agrees with my views? At the end, after a gradual build-up, for an antagonistic audience? How much development (and consequent emphasis) should each point have? Will a deductive or inductive format best express my thesis?

4. What will be my best sources of evidence? My own experience? The experiences of people I know? Common sense or common knowledge? Opinion from experts in a relevant field? Scientific evidence? Historic records? Economic, anthropological, or statistical data?

5. What tone will best reinforce my evidence? Will my audience also find this tone appealing? Convincing? Would an appropriate tone be sincere? Straightforward? Objective? Reassuring? Confident? Placating? What language can I use to most appropriately convey this tone?

MARTIN LUTHER KING, JR.

"Letter from Birmingham Jail," a literary and humanitarian masterpiece, reveals why Martin Luther King, Jr. was the most influential leader of the American civil rights movement in the 1950s and 1960s, and, why, with Mahatma Gandhi, he was one of this century's most influential advocates for human rights. King was born in Atlanta in 1929, the son of a well-known Baptist clergyman, educated at Morehouse College, and ordained in his father's denomination.

A forceful and charismatic leader, Dr. King became at twenty-six a national spokesperson for the civil rights movement when in 1955 he led a successful boycott of the segregated bus system of Montgomery, Alabama. Dr. King became president of the Southern Christian Leadership Conference and led the sit-ins and demonstrations—including the 1964 march on Washington, D.C., which climaxed with his famous "I Have a Dream" speech—that helped to ensure passage of the 1964 Civil Rights Act and the Voting Rights Act of 1965. He received the Nobel Peace Prize in 1964. Toward the end of his life, cut short by assassination in 1968, Dr. King was increasingly concerned with improving the rights and the lives of the nation's poor, irrespective of race, and with ending the war in Vietnam. His birthday became a national holiday in 1986.

In 1963 King wrote the letter reprinted below while imprisoned for "parading without a permit." Though ostensibly replying to eight clergymen—Protestant, Catholic, and Jewish—who feared violence in the Birmingham desegregation demonstrations, King actually intended his letter for the worldwide audience his civil rights activities commanded. Warning that America had more to fear from passive moderates ("the appalling silence of good people") than from extremists, King defended his policy of "nonviolent direct action" and explained why he was compelled to disobey "unjust laws"—supporting his argument with references to Protestant, Catholic, and Jewish examples ("Was not Jesus an extremist for love. . . ."), as well as to the painful examples of segregation in his own life.

Letter from Birmingham Jail[1]

April 16, 1963

My Dear Fellow Clergymen:

1   While confined here in the Birmingham city jail, I came across your recent statement calling my present activities "unwise and untimely." Seldom do I pause to answer criticism of my work and ideas. If I sought to answer all the criticisms that cross my desk, my secretaries would have little time for anything other than such correspondence in the course of the day, and I would have no time for constructive work. But since I feel that you are men of genuine good will and that your criticisms are sincerely set forth, I want to try to answer your statement in what I hope will be patient and reasonable terms.

2   I think I should indicate why I am here in Birmingham, since you have been influenced by the view which argues against "outsiders coming in." I have the honor of serving as president of the Southern Christian Leadership Conference, an organization operating in every southern state, with headquarters in Atlanta, Georgia. We have some eighty-five affiliated organizations across the South, and one of them is the Alabama Christian Movement for Human Rights. Frequently we share staff, educational and financial resources with our affiliates. Several months ago the affiliate here in Birmingham asked us to be on call to engage in a nonviolent direct-action program if such were deemed necessary. We readily consented, and when the hour came we lived up to our promise. So I, along with several members of my staff, am here because I was invited here. I am here because I have organizational ties here.

---

[1] AUTHOR'S NOTE: This response to a published statement by eight fellow clergymen from Alabama (Bishop C. C. J. Carpenter, Bishop Joseph A. Durick, Rabbi Hilton L. Grafman, Bishop Paul Hardin, Bishop Holan B. Harmon, the Reverend George M. Murray, the Reverend Edward V. Ramage and the Reverend Earl Stallings) was composed under somewhat constricting circumstances. Begun on the margins of the newspaper in which the statement appeared while I was in jail, the letter was continued on scraps of writing paper supplied by a friendly Negro trusty, and concluded on a pad my attorneys were eventually permitted to leave me. Although the text remains in substance unaltered, I have indulged in the author's prerogative of polishing it for publication.

But more basically, I am in Birmingham because injustice 3
is here. Just as the prophets of the eighth century B.C. left their
villages and carried their "thus saith the Lord" far beyond the
boundaries of their home towns, and, just as the Apostle Paul left
his village of Tarsus and carried the gospel of Jesus Christ to the
far corners of the Greco-Roman world, so am I compelled to carry
the gospel of freedom beyond my own home town. Like Paul, I
must constantly respond to the Macedonian call for aid.

Moreover, I am cognizant of the interrelatedness of all com- 4
munities and states. I cannot sit idly by in Atlanta and not be concerned about what happens in Birmingham. Injustice anywhere is
a threat to justice everywhere. We are caught in an inescapable
network of mutuality, tied in a single garment of destiny. Whatever affects one directly, affects all indirectly. Never again can we
afford to live with the narrow, provincial "outside agitator" idea.
Anyone who lives inside the United States can never be considered an outsider anywhere within its bounds.

You deplore the demonstrations taking place in Birmingham. 5
But your statement, I am sorry to say, fails to express a similar concern for the conditions that brought about the demonstrations. I
am sure that none of you would want to rest content with the
superficial kind of social analysis that deals merely with effects
and does not grapple with underlying causes. It is unfortunate that
demonstrations are taking place in Birmingham, but it is even
more unfortunate that the city's white power structure left the
Negro community with no alternative.

In any nonviolent campaign there are four basic steps: 6
collection of the facts to determine whether injustices exist; negotiation; self-purification; and direct action. We have gone through all
these steps in Birmingham. There can be no gainsaying the fact
that racial injustice engulfs this community. Birmingham is probably the most thoroughly segregated city in the United States. An
ugly record of brutality is widely known. Negroes have experienced grossly unjust treatment in the courts. There have been more
unsolved bombings of Negro homes and churches in Birmingham
than in any other city in the nation. These are the hard brutal facts
of the case. On the basis of these conditions, Negro leaders sought
to negotiate with the city fathers. But the latter consistently refused
to engage in good-faith negotiation.

7   Then, last September, came the opportunity to talk with leaders of Birmingham's economic community. In the course of the negotiations, certain promises were made by the merchants—for example, to remove the stores' humiliating racial signs. On the basis of these promises, the Reverend Fred Shuttlesworth and the leaders of the Alabama Christian Movement for Human Rights agreed to a moratorium on all demonstrations. As the weeks and months went by, we realized that we were the victims of a broken promise. A few signs, briefly removed, returned; the others remained.

8   As in so many past experiences, our hopes had been blasted, and the shadow of deep disappointment settled upon us. We had no alternative except to prepare for direct action, whereby we would present our very bodies as a means of laying our case before the conscience of the local and the national community. Mindful of the difficulties involved, we decided to undertake a process of self-purification. We began a series of workshops on nonviolence, and we repeatedly asked ourselves: "Are you able to accept blows without retaliating?" "Are you able to endure the ordeal of jail?" We decided to schedule our direct-action program for the Easter season, realizing that except for Christmas, this is the main shopping period of the year. Knowing that a strong economic-withdrawal program would be the by-product of direct action, we felt that this would be the best time to bring pressure to bear on the merchants for the needed change.

9   Then it occurred to us that Birmingham's mayoralty election was coming up in March, and we speedily decided to postpone action until after election day. When we discovered that the Commissioner of Public Safety, Eugene "Bull" Connor, had piled up enough votes to be in the run-off, we decided again to postpone action until the day after the run-off so that the demonstrations could not be used to cloud the issues. Like many others, we waited to see Mr. Connor defeated, and to this end we endured postponement after postponement. Having aided in this community need, we felt that our direct-action program could be delayed no longer.

10   You may well ask: "Why direct action? Why sit-ins, marches and so forth? Isn't negotiation a better path?" You are quite right in calling for negotiation. Indeed this is the very purpose of direct action. Nonviolent direct action seeks to create such a crisis and foster such a tension that a community which has constantly

fears and outer resentments; when you are forever fighting a degenerating sense of "nobodiness"—then you will understand
why we find it difficult to wait. There comes a time when the cup
of endurance runs over, and men are no longer willing to be
plunged into the abyss of despair. I hope, sirs, you can understand our legitimate and unavoidable impatience.

You express a great deal of anxiety over our willingness to   15
break laws. This is certainly a legitimate concern. Since we so dili-
gently urge people to obey the Supreme Court's decision of 1954
outlawing segregation in the public schools, at first glance it may
seem rather paradoxical for us consciously to break laws. One
may well ask: "How can you advocate breaking some laws and
obeying others?" The answer lies in the fact that there are two
types of laws: just and unjust. I would be the first to advocate
obeying just laws. One has not only a legal but a moral responsibility to obey just laws. Conversely, one has a moral responsibility to disobey unjust laws. I would agree with St. Augustine that
"an unjust law is no law at all."

Now, what is the difference between the two? How does one   16
determine whether a law is just or unjust? A just law is a man-
made code that squares with the moral law or the law of God. An
unjust law is a code that is out of harmony with the moral law. To
put it in the terms of St. Thomas Aquinas: An unjust law is a
human law that is not rooted in eternal law and natural law. Any
law that uplifts human personality is just. Any law that degrades
human personality is unjust. All segregation statutes are unjust
because segregation distorts the soul and damages the personality.
It gives the segregator a false sense of superiority and the segregated a false sense of inferiority. Segregation, to use the terminology of the Jewish philosopher Martin Buber, substitutes an "I-it"
relationship for an "I-thou" relationship and ends up relegating
persons to the status of things. Hence segregation is not only
politically, economically and sociologically unsound, it is morally
wrong and sinful. Paul Tillich has said that sin is separation. Is not
segregation an existential expression of man's tragic separation,
his awful estrangement, his terrible sinfulness? Thus it is that I can
urge men to obey the 1954 decision of the Supreme Court, for it is
morally right; and I can urge them to disobey segregation ordi-
nances, for they are morally wrong.

17   Let us consider a more concrete example of just and unjust laws. An unjust law is a code that a numerical or power majority group compels a minority group to obey but does not make binding on itself. This is *difference* made legal. By the same token, a just law is a code that a majority compels a minority to follow and that it is willing to follow itself. This is *sameness* made legal.

18   Let me give another explanation. A law is unjust if it is inflicted on a minority that, as a result of being denied the right to vote, had no part in enacting or devising the law. Who can say that the legislature of Alabama which set up that state's segregation laws was democratically elected? Throughout Alabama all sorts of devious methods are used to prevent Negroes from becoming registered voters, and there are some counties in which even though Negroes constitute a majority of the population, not a single Negro is registered. Can any law enacted under such circumstances be considered democratically structured?

19   Sometimes a law is just on its face and unjust in its application. For instance, I have been arrested on a charge of parading without a permit. Now, there is nothing wrong in having an ordinance which requires a permit for a parade. But such an ordinance becomes unjust when it is used to maintain segregation and to deny citizens the First-Amendment privilege of peaceful assembly and protest.

20   I hope you are able to see the distinction I am trying to point out. In no sense do I advocate evading or defying the law, as would the rabid segregationist. That would lead to anarchy. One who breaks an unjust law must do so openly, lovingly, and with a willingness to accept the penalty. I submit that an individual who breaks a law that conscience tells him is unjust, and who willingly accepts the penalty of imprisonment in order to arouse the conscience of the community over its injustice, is in reality expressing the highest respect for the law.

21   Of course, there is nothing new about this kind of civil disobedience. It was evidenced sublimely in the refusal of Shadrach, Meshach and Abednego to obey the laws of Nebuchadnezzar, on the ground that a higher moral law was at stake. It was practiced superbly by the early Christians, who were willing to face hungry lions and the excruciating pain of chopping blocks rather than submit to certain unjust laws of the Roman Empire. To a degree,

academic freedom is a reality today because Socrates practiced civil disobedience. In our own nation, the Boston Tea Party represented a massive act of civil disobedience.

We should never forget that everything Adolf Hitler did in 22 Germany was "legal" and everything the Hungarian freedom fighters did in Hungary was "illegal." It was "illegal" to aid and comfort a Jew in Hitler's Germany. Even so, I am sure that, had I lived in Germany at the time, I would have aided and comforted my Jewish brothers. If today I lived in a Communist country where certain principles dear to the Christian faith are suppressed, I would openly advocate disobeying that country's antireligious laws.

I must make two honest confessions to you, my Christian 23 and Jewish brothers. First, I must confess that over the past few years I have been gravely disappointed with the white moderate. I have almost reached the regrettable conclusion that the Negro's great stumbling block in his stride toward freedom is not the White Citizen's Counciler or the Ku Klux Klanner, but the white moderate, who is more devoted to "order" than to justice; who prefers a negative peace which is the absence of tension to a positive peace which is the presence of justice; who constantly says: "I agree with you in the goal you seek, but I cannot agree with your methods of direct action"; who paternalistically believes he can set the timetable for another man's freedom; who lives by a mythical concept of time and who constantly advises the Negro to wait for a "more convenient season." Shallow understanding from people of good will is more frustrating than absolute misunderstanding from people of ill will. Lukewarm acceptance is much more bewildering than outright rejection.

I had hoped that the white moderate would understand that 24 law and order exist for the purpose of establishing justice and that when they fail in this purpose they become the dangerously structured dams that block the flow of social progress. I had hoped that the white moderate would understand that the present tension in the South is a necessary phase of the transition from an obnoxious negative peace, in which the Negro passively accepted his unjust plight, to a substantive and positive peace, in which all men will respect the dignity and worth of human personality. Actually, we who engage in nonviolent direct action are not the creators of tension. We merely bring to the surface the hidden tension that is already alive. We bring it out in the open, where it can be seen and dealt with. Like a boil that can never be cured so long as it is covered up but must be opened with all its ugliness to the natural medicines of air and light, injustice must be exposed, with all the tension its exposure creates, to the light of human conscience and the air of national opinion before it can be cured.

25   In your statement you assert that our actions, even though peaceful, must be condemned because they precipitate violence. But is this a logical assertion? Isn't this like condemning a robbed man because his possession of money precipitated the evil act of robbery? Isn't this like condemning Socrates because his unswerving commitment to truth and his philosophical inquiries precipitated the act by the misguided populace in which they made him drink hemlock? Isn't this like condemning Jesus because his unique God-consciousness and never-ceasing devotion to God's will precipitated the evil act of crucifixion? We must come to see that, as the federal courts have consistently affirmed, it is wrong to urge an individual to cease his efforts to gain his basic constitutional rights because the quest may precipitate violence. Society must protect the robbed and punish the robber.

26   I had also hoped that the white moderate would reject the myth concerning time in relation to the struggle for freedom. I have just received a letter from a white brother in Texas. He writes: "All Christians know that the colored people will receive equal rights eventually, but it is possible that you are in too great a religious hurry. It has taken Christianity almost two thousand years to accomplish what it has. The teachings of Christ take time to come to earth." Such an attitude stems from a tragic misconception of time, from the strangely irrational notion that there is something in the very flow of time that will inevitably cure all ills. Actually, time itself is neutral; it can be used either destructively or constructively. More and more I feel that the people of ill will have used time much more effectively than have the people of good will. We will have to repent in this generation not merely for the hateful words and actions of the bad people but for the appalling silence of the good people. Human progress never rolls in on wheels of inevitability; it comes through the tireless efforts of men willing to be coworkers with God, and without this hard work, time itself

becomes an ally of the forces of social stagnation. We must use time creatively, in the knowledge that the time is always ripe to do right. Now is the time to make real the promise of democracy and transform our pending national elegy into a creative psalm of brotherhood. Now is the time to lift our national policy from the quicksand of racial injustice to the solid rock of human dignity.

You speak of our activity in Birmingham as extreme. At first   27
I was rather disappointed that fellow clergymen would see my nonviolent efforts as those of an extremist. I began thinking about the fact that I stand in the middle of two opposing forces in the Negro community. One is a force of complacency, made up in part of Negroes who, as a result of long years of oppression, are so drained of self-respect and a sense of "somebodiness" that they have adjusted to segregation; and in part of a few middle-class Negroes who, because of a degree of academic and economic security and because in some ways they profit by segregation, have become insensitive to the problems of the masses. The other force is one of bitterness and hatred, and it comes perilously close to advocating violence. It is expressed in the various black nationalist groups that are springing up across the nation, the largest and best-known being Elijah Muhammad's Muslim movement. Nourished by the Negro's frustration over the continued existence of racial discrimination, this movement is made up of people who have lost faith in America, who have absolutely repudiated Christianity, and who have concluded that the white man is an incorrigible "devil."

I have tried to stand between these two forces, saying that   28
we need emulate neither the "do-nothingism" of the complacent nor the hatred and despair of the black nationalist. For there is the more excellent way of love and nonviolent protest. I am grateful to God that, through the influence of the Negro church, the way of nonviolence became an integral part of our struggle.

If this philosophy had not emerged, by now many streets of   29
the South would, I am convinced, be flowing with blood. And I am further convinced that if our white brothers dismiss as "rabble-rousers" and "outside agitators" those of us who employ nonviolent direct action, and if they refuse to support our nonviolent efforts, millions of Negroes will, out of frustration and despair, seek solace and security in black-nationalist ideologies—a development that would inevitably lead to a frightening racial nightmare.

30   Oppressed people cannot remain oppressed forever. The yearning for freedom eventually manifests itself, and that is what has happened to the American Negro. Something within has reminded him of his birthright of freedom, and something without has reminded him that it can be gained. Consciously or unconsciously, he has been caught up by the *Zeitgeist*, and with his black brothers of Africa and his brown and yellow brothers of Asia, South America and the Caribbean, the United States Negro is moving with a sense of great urgency toward the promised land of racial justice. If one recognizes this vital urge that has engulfed the Negro community, one should readily understand why public demonstrations are taking place. The Negro has many pent-up resentments and latent frustrations, and he must release them. So let him march; let him make prayer pilgrimages to the city hall; let him go on freedom rides—and try to understand why he must do so. If his repressed emotions are not released in nonviolent ways, they will seek expression through violence; this is not a threat but a fact of history. So I have not said to my people: "Get rid of your discontent." Rather, I have tried to say that this normal and healthy discontent can be channeled into the creative outlet of nonviolent direct action. And now this approach is being termed extremist.

31   But though I was initially disappointed at being categorized as an extremist, as I continued to think about the matter I gradually gained a measure of satisfaction from the label. Was not Jesus an extremist for love: "Love your enemies, bless them that curse you, do good to them that hate you, and pray for them which despitefully use you, and persecute you." Was not Amos an extremist for justice: "Let justice roll down like waters and righteousness like an ever-flowing stream." Was not Paul an extremist for the Christian gospel: "I bear in my body the marks of the Lord Jesus." Was not Martin Luther an extremist: "Here I stand; I cannot do otherwise, so help me God." And John Bunyan: "I will stay in jail to the end of my days before I make a butchery of my conscience." And Abraham Lincoln: "This nation cannot survive half slave and half free." And Thomas Jefferson: "We hold these truths to be self-evident, that all men are created equal. . . ." So the question is not whether we will be extremists, but what kind of extremists we will be. Will we be extremists for hate or for love? Will we be extremists for the preservation of injustice or for

the extension of justice? In that dramatic scene on Calvary's hill three men were crucified. We must never forget that all three were crucified for the same crime—the crime of extremism. Two were extremists for immorality, and thus fell below their environment. The other, Jesus Christ, was an extremist for love, truth and goodness, and thereby rose above his environment. Perhaps the South, the nation and the world are in dire need of creative extremists.

I had hoped that the white moderate would see this need. Perhaps I was too optimistic; perhaps I expected too much. I suppose I should have realized that few members of the oppressor race can understand the deep groans and passionate yearnings of the oppressed race, and still fewer have the vision to see that injustice must be rooted out by strong, persistent and determined action. I am thankful, however, that some of our white brothers in the South have grasped the meaning of this social revolution and committed themselves to it. They are still all too few in quantity, but they are big in quality. Some—such as Ralph McGill, Lillian Smith, Harry Golden, James McBride Dabbs, Ann Braden and Sarah Patton Boyle—have written about our struggle in eloquent and prophetic terms. Others have marched with us down nameless streets of the South. They have languished in filthy, roach-infested jails, suffering the abuse and brutality of policemen who view them as "dirty nigger-lovers." Unlike so many of their moderate brothers and sisters, they have recognized the urgency of the moment and sensed the need for powerful "action" antidotes to combat the disease of segregation. 32

Let me take note of my other major disappointment. I have been so greatly disappointed with the white church and its leadership. Of course, there are some notable exceptions. I am not unmindful of the fact that each of you has taken some significant stands on this issue. I commend you, Reverend Stallings, for your Christian stand on this past Sunday, in welcoming Negroes to your worship service on a nonsegregated basis. I commend the Catholic leaders of this state for integrating Spring Hill College several years ago. 33

But despite these notable exceptions, I must honestly reiterate that I have been disappointed with the church. I do not say this as one of those negative critics who can always find something wrong with the church. I say this as a minister of the gospel, who 34 loves the church; who was nurtured in its bosom; who has been sustained by its spiritual blessings and who will remain true to it as long as the cord of life shall lengthen.

35   When I was suddenly catapulted into the leadership of the bus protest in Montgomery, Alabama, a few years ago, I felt we would be supported by the white church. I felt that the white ministers, priests and rabbis of the South would be among our strongest allies. Instead, some have been outright opponents, refusing to understand the freedom movement and misrepresenting its leaders; all too many others have been more cautious than courageous and have remained silent behind the anesthetizing security of stained-glass windows.

36   In spite of my shattered dreams, I came to Birmingham with the hope that the white religious leadership of this community would see the justice of our cause and, with deep moral concern, would serve as the channel through which our just grievances could reach the power structure. I had hoped that each of you would understand. But again I have been disappointed.

37   I have heard numerous southern religious leaders admonish their worshipers to comply with a desegregation decision because it is the law, but I have longed to hear white ministers declare: "Follow this decree because integration is morally right and because the Negro is your brother." In the midst of blatant injustices inflicted upon the Negro, I have watched white churchmen stand on the sideline and mouth pious irrelevancies and sanctimonious trivialities. In the midst of a mighty struggle to rid our nation of racial and economic injustice, I have heard many ministers say: "Those are social issues, with which the gospel has no real concern." And I have watched many churches commit themselves to completely other-worldly religion which makes a strange, un-Biblical distinction between body and soul, between the sacred and the secular.

38   I have traveled the length and breadth of Alabama, Mississippi and all the other southern states. On sweltering summer days and crisp autumn mornings I have looked at the South's beautiful churches with their lofty spires pointing heavenward. I have beheld the impressive outlines of her massive religious-education buildings. Over and over I have found myself asking: "What kind of people worship here? Who is their God? Where were their voices when the lips of Governor Barnett dripped with

words of interposition and nullification? Where were they when Governor Wallace gave a clarion call for defiance and hatred? Where were their voices of support when bruised and weary Negro men and women decided to rise from the dark dungeons of complacency to the bright hills of creative protest?"

Yes, these questions are still in my mind. In deep disappoint-   39
ment I have wept over the laxity of the church. But be assured that my tears have been tears of love. There can be no deep disappointment where there is not deep love. Yes, I love the church. How could I do otherwise? I am in the rather unique position of being the son, the grandson and the great-grandson of preachers. Yes, I see the church as the body of Christ. But, oh! How we have blemished and scarred that body through social neglect and through fear of being nonconformists.

There was a time when the church was very powerful—   40
in the time when the early Christians rejoiced at being deemed worthy to suffer for what they believed. In those days the church was not merely a thermometer that recorded the ideas and principles of popular opinion; it was a thermostat that transformed the mores of society. Whenever the early Christians entered a town, the people in power became disturbed and immediately sought to convict the Christians for being "disturbers of the peace" and "outside agitators." But the Christians pressed on, in the conviction that they were "a colony of heaven," called to obey God rather than man. Small in number, they were big in commitment. They were too God-intoxicated to be "astronomically intimidated." By their effort and example they brought an end to such ancient evils as infanticide and gladiatorial contests.

Things are different now. So often the contemporary church   41
is a weak, ineffectual voice with an uncertain sound. So often it is an archdefender of the status quo. Far from being disturbed by the presence of the church, the power structure of the average community is consoled by the church's silent—and often even vocal—sanction of things as they are.

But the judgment of God is upon the church as never before.   42
If today's church does not recapture the sacrificial spirit of the early church, it will lose its authenticity, forfeit the loyalty of millions, and be dismissed as an irrelevant social club with no meaning for the twentieth century. Every day I meet young people whose disappointment with the church has turned into outright disgust.

43   Perhaps I have once again been too optimistic. Is organized religion too inextricably bound to the status quo to save our nation and the world? Perhaps I must turn my faith to the inner spiritual church, the church within the church, as the true *ekklesia* and the hope of the world. But again I am thankful to God that some noble souls from the ranks of organized religion have broken loose from the paralyzing chains of conformity and joined us as active partners in the struggle for freedom. They have left their secure congregations and walked the streets of Albany, Georgia, with us. They have gone down the highways of the South on tortuous rides for freedom. Yes, they have gone to jail with us. Some have been dismissed from their churches, have lost the support of their bishops and fellow ministers. But they have acted in the faith that right defeated is stronger than evil triumphant. Their witness has been the spiritual salt that has preserved the true meaning of the gospel in these troubled times. They have carved a tunnel of hope through the dark mountain of disappointment.

44   I hope the church as a whole will meet the challenge of this decisive hour. But even if the church does not come to the aid of justice, I have no despair about the future. I have no fear about the outcome of our struggle in Birmingham, even if our motives are at present misunderstood. We will reach the goal of freedom in Birmingham and all over the nation, because the goal of America is freedom. Abused and scorned though we may be, our destiny is tied up with America's destiny. Before the pilgrims landed at Plymouth, we were here. Before the pen of Jefferson etched the majestic words of the Declaration of Independence across the pages of history, we were here. For more than two centuries our forebears labored in this country without wages; they made cotton king; they built the homes of their masters while suffering gross injustice and shameful humiliation—and yet out of a bottomless vitality they continued to thrive and develop. If the inexpressible cruelties of slavery could not stop us, the opposition we now face will surely fail. We will win our freedom because the sacred heritage of our nation and the eternal will of God are embodied in our echoing demands.

45   Before closing I feel impelled to mention one other point in your statement that has troubled me profoundly. You warmly commended the Birmingham police force for keeping "order" and "preventing violence." I doubt that you would have so warmly

commended the police force if you had seen its dogs sinking their teeth into unarmed, nonviolent Negroes. I doubt that you would so quickly commend the policemen if you were to observe their ugly and inhumane treatment of Negroes here in the city jail; if you were to watch them push and curse old Negro women and young Negro girls; if you were to see them slap and kick old Negro men and young boys; if you were to observe them as they did on two occasions, refuse to give us food because we wanted to sing our grace together. I cannot join you in your praise of the Birmingham police department.

It is true that the police have exercised a degree of discipline   46 in handling the demonstrators. In this sense they have conducted themselves rather "nonviolently" in public. But for what purpose? To preserve the evil system of segregation. Over the past few years I have consistently preached that nonviolence demands that the means we use must be as pure as the ends we seek. I have tried to make clear that it is wrong to use immoral means to attain moral ends. But now I must affirm that it is just as wrong, or perhaps even more so, to use moral means to preserve immoral ends. Perhaps Mr. Connor and his policemen have been rather nonviolent in public, as was Chief Pritchett in Albany, Georgia, but they have used the moral means of nonviolence to maintain the immoral end of racial injustice. As T. S. Eliot has said: "The last temptation is the greatest treason: To do the right deed for the wrong reason."

I wish you had commended the Negro sit-inners and demon-   47 strators of Birmingham for their sublime courage, their willingness to suffer and their amazing discipline in the midst of great provocation. One day the South will recognize its real heroes. They will be the James Merediths, with the noble sense of purpose that enables them to face jeering and hostile mobs, and with the agonizing loneliness that characterizes the life of the pioneer. They will be old, oppressed, battered Negro women, symbolized in a seventy-two-year-old woman in Montgomery, Alabama, who rose up with a sense of dignity and with her people decided not to ride segregated buses, and who responded with ungrammatical profundity to one who inquired about her weariness: "My feet is tired, but my soul is at rest." They will be the young high school and college students, the young ministers of the gospel and a host of their elders, courageously and nonviolently sitting in at lunch counters and willingly going to jail for conscience' sake. One day the South will know that when these disinherited children of God sat down at lunch counters, they were in reality standing up for what is best in the American dream and for the most sacred values in our Judaeo-Christian heritage, thereby bringing our nation back to those great wells of democracy which were dug deep by the founding fathers in their formulation of the Constitution and the Declaration of Independence.

48   Never before have I written so long a letter. I'm afraid it is much too long to take your precious time. I can assure you that it would have been much shorter if I had been writing from a comfortable desk, but what else can one do when he is alone in a narrow jail cell, other than write long letters, think long thoughts and pray long prayers?

49   If I have said anything in this letter that overstates the truth and indicates an unreasonable impatience, I beg you to forgive me. If I have said anything that understates the truth and indicates my having a patience that allows me to settle for anything less than brotherhood, I beg God to forgive me.

50   I hope this letter finds you strong in faith. I also hope that circumstances will soon make it possible for me to meet each of you, not as an integrationist or a civil-rights leader but as a fellow clergyman and a Christian brother. Let us all hope that the dark clouds of racial prejudice will soon pass away and the deep fog of misunderstanding will be lifted from our fear-drenched communities, and in some not too distant tomorrow the radiant stars of love and brotherhood will shine over our great nation with all their scintillating beauty.

Yours for the cause of Peace and Brotherhood,
Martin Luther King, Jr.

Content

1. In paragraph 4 King makes several assertions on which he bases the rest of his argument. What are they? Does he ever prove them, or does he assume that readers will take them for granted?

2. In paragraph 5 King asserts that Birmingham's "white power structure left the Negro community with no alternative" but to commit civil disobedience. Does he ever prove this? Does he need to? Is it a debatable statement?

3. What, according to King, are the "four basic steps" in "any nonviolent campaign" (¶ 6)? What is the goal of "nonviolent direct action" (¶ 10)? What is the "constructive, nonviolent tension" (¶ 10) King favors?

4. Why has King been disappointed by white moderates (¶s 23–32)? By the white church (¶ 33–44)? What does he want white moderates to do? What does he claim that the church should do?

5. How does King deal with the argument that civil rights activists are too impatient, that they should go slow because "It has taken Christianity almost two thousand years to accomplish what it has" (¶ 26)? How does he refute the argument that he is an extremist (¶ 27)?

Strategies/Structures

1. How does King establish, in the salutation and first paragraph, his reasons for writing? The setting in which he writes? His intended audience? A sensitive, reasonable tone?

2. King's letter ostensibly replies to that of the eight clergymen. Find passages in which he addresses them, and analyze the voice he uses. In what relation to the clergymen does King see himself? He also has a secondary audience; who are its members? Locate passages that seem especially directed to this second audience. In what relation to this audience does King see himself?

3. Why does King cite the theologians Aquinas (a Catholic), Buber (a Jew), and Tillich (a Protestant) in paragraph 16? What similarities link the three?

4. After defending his actions against the criticisms of the clergymen, King takes the offensive in paragraphs 23–44. How does he signal this change?

5. Which parts of King's letter appeal chiefly to reason? To emotion? How are the two types of appeals interrelated?

6. King uses large numbers of rhetorical questions throughout this essay (see ¶s 18, 25, 31, 38, 39). Why? With what effects?

Language

1. How does King define a "just law" (¶s 16, 17)? An "unjust law" (¶s 16, 17)? Why are these definitions crucial to the argument that follows?

2. Consult your dictionary, if necessary, for the meanings of the following words or others you do not understand: cognizant (¶ 4), gainsaying (¶ 6), moratorium (¶ 7), gadflies (¶ 10), harried (¶ 14), degenerating (¶ 14), abyss (¶ 14), incorrigible (¶ 27), *Zeitgeist* (¶ 30), scintillating (¶ 47).

For Writing

1. Under what circumstances, if any, is breaking the law justifiable? If you use Dr. King's definition of just and unjust law (¶s 15–20), or make any distinction, say, between moral law and civil law, be sure to explain what you mean. You may, if you wish, use examples with which you are personally familiar. Or you may elaborate on some of the examples King uses (¶ 22) or on examples from King's own civil-rights activities, such as the boycotts in the early 1950s of the legally segregated Montgomery bus system (¶ 35).

2. If you are a member of a church, or attend a church regularly, address members of the congregation on what, if any, commitment you think your church should make to the betterment of minorities, the poor, or other groups who do not attend that church. Does this commitment extend to civil disobedience?

3. Would you ever be willing to go to jail for a cause? What cause? Under what circumstances? If you knew that a prison record might bar you from some privileges in some states (such as practicing law or medicine), would you still be willing to take such a risk?

LANI GUINIER

Guinier, the daughter of black and Jewish parents in Queens, New York, was born (1950) into a complex heritage of concern for racial equality. Her father's scholarship to Harvard had been withdrawn in the 1930s when administrators realized that Harvard had already admitted its quota of black scholarship students—one—that year. Decades later Ewart Guinier chaired Harvard's Afro-American studies department. Guinier herself received a scholarship to Harvard (B.A., 1971) and received her law degree from Yale (1974), where she was a friend and classmate of Bill Clinton and Hillary Rodham. Implications of the Voting Rights Act of 1965, central to the civil rights movement, became the legal specialty that led Guinier to four years of service as an attorney in the Civil Rights Division of the Department of Justice during the Carter administration, followed by six years with the NAACP Legal Defense Fund.

In 1988 she became a professor at the University of Pennsylvania, doing research, as she had previously practiced litigation, on ways to remedy racial discrimination: "Inspired by James Madison, I explored ways to ensure that even a self-interested majority could work with, rather than 'tyrannize,' a minority. . . . I imagined a more consensual, deliberative, and participatory democracy for all voters." In 1993, when Clinton nominated Guinier for Assistant Attorney General for Civil Rights, her even-handed record of consensus-building was distorted by opponents ("Czarina of Czeparatism") and in the ensuing controversy the nomination was withdrawn. Guinier's new visibility, however, has given her a national audience, whom she addressed in *The Tyranny of the Majority* (1994), from which the following essay is taken. She explains her philosophy: "My point is simple: 51 percent of the people should not always get 100 percent of the power [especially] if they use that power to exclude the 49 percent. In that case we do not have majority rule. We have majority tyranny."

The Tyranny of the Majority

I have always wanted to be a civil rights lawyer. This lifelong ambition is based on a deep-seated commitment to democratic fair play—to playing by the rules as long as the rules are fair. When the rules seem unfair, I have worked to change them, not subvert them. When I was eight years old, I was a Brownie. I was especially proud of my uniform, which represented a commitment to good citizenship and good deeds. But one day, when my Brownie group staged a hatmaking contest, I realized that uniforms are only as honorable as the people who wear them. The contest was rigged. The winner was assisted by her milliner mother, who actually made the winning entry in full view of all the participants. At the time, I was too young to be able to change the rules, but I was old enough to resign, which I promptly did.

To me, fair play means that the rules encourage everyone to play. They should reward those who win, but they must be acceptable to those who lose. The central theme of my academic writing is that not all rules lead to elemental fair play. Some even commonplace rules work against it.

The professional milliner competing with amateur Brownies stands as an example of rules that are patently rigged or patently subverted. Yet, sometimes, even when rules are perfectly fair in form, they serve in practice to exclude particular groups from meaningful participation. When they do not encourage everyone to play, or when, over the long haul, they do not make the losers feel as good about the outcomes as the winners, they can seem as unfair as the milliner who makes the winning hat for her daughter.

4   Sometimes, too, we construct rules that force us to be divided into winners and losers when we might have otherwise joined together. This idea was cogently expressed by my son, Nikolas, when he was four years old, far exceeding the thoughtfulness of his mother when she was an eight-year-old Brownie. While I was writing one of my law journal articles, Nikolas and I had a conversation about voting prompted by a *Sesame Street Magazine* exercise. The magazine pictured six children: four children had raised their hands because they wanted to play tag; two had their hands down because they wanted to play hide-and-seek. The magazine asked its readers to count the number of children whose hands were raised and then decide what game the children would play.

5   Nikolas quite realistically replied, "They will play both. First they will play tag. Then they will play hide-and-seek." Despite the magazine's "rules," he was right. To children, it is natural to take turns. The winner may get to play first or more often, but even the "loser" gets something. His was a positive-sum solution that many adult rule-makers ignore.

6   The traditional answer to the magazine's problem would have been a zero-sum solution: "The children—all the children—will play tag, and only tag." As a zero-sum solution, everything is seen in terms of "I win; you lose." The conventional answer relies on winner-take-all majority rule, in which the tag players, as the majority, win the right to decide for all the children what game to play. The hide-and-seek preference becomes irrelevant. The numerically more powerful majority choice simply subsumes minority preferences.

7   In the conventional case, the majority that rules gains all the power and the minority that loses gets none. For example, two years ago Brother Rice High School in Chicago held two senior proms. It was not planned that way. The prom committee at Brother Rice, a boys' Catholic school, expected just one prom when it hired a disc jockey, picked a rock band, and selected music for

the prom by consulting student preferences. Each senior was asked to list his three favorite songs, and the band would play the songs that appeared most frequently on the lists.

Seems attractively democratic. But Brother Rice is predomi- 8 nantly white, and the prom committee was all white. That's how they got two proms. The black seniors at Brother Rice felt so shut out by the "democratic process" that they organized their own prom. As one black student put it: "For every vote we had, there were eight votes for what they wanted. . . . [W]ith us being in the minority we're always outvoted. It's as if we don't count."

Some embittered white seniors saw things differently. They 9 complained that the black students should have gone along with the majority: "The majority makes a decision. That's the way it works."

In a way, both groups were right. From the white students' 10 perspective, this was ordinary decisionmaking. To the black students, majority rule sent the message: "we don't count" is the "way it works" for minorities. In a racially divided society, majority rule may be perceived as majority tyranny.

That is a large claim, and I do not rest my case for it solely 11 on the actions of the prom committee in one Chicago high school. To expand the range of argument, I first consider the ideal of majority rule itself, particularly as reflected in the writings of James Madison[1] and other founding members of our Republic. These early democrats explored the relationship between majority rule and democracy. James Madison warned, "If a majority be united by a common interest, the rights of the minority will be insecure." The tyranny of the majority, according to Madison, requires safeguards to protect "one part of the society against the injustice of the other part."

For Madison, majority tyranny represented the great danger 12 to our early constitutional democracy. Although the American revolution was fought against the tyranny of the British monarch, it soon became clear that there was another tyranny to be avoided. The accumulations of all powers in the same hands,

---

[1] Founding Father (1751–1836) and fourth president of the United States, from 1809–1817.

Madison warned, "whether of one, a few, or many, and whether hereditary, self-appointed, or elective, may justly be pronounced the very definition of tyranny."

13   As another colonist suggested in papers published in Philadelphia, "We have been so long habituated to a jealousy of tyranny from monarchy and aristocracy, that we have yet to learn the dangers of it from democracy." Despotism had to be opposed "whether it came from Kings, Lords or the people."

14   The debate about majority tyranny reflected Madison's concern that the majority may not represent the whole. In a homogeneous society, the interest of the majority would likely be that of the minority also. But in a heterogeneous community, the majority may not represent all competing interests. The majority is likely to be self-interested and ignorant or indifferent to the concerns of the minority. In such case, Madison observed, the assumption that the majority represents the minority is "altogether fictitious."

15   Yet even a self-interested majority can govern fairly if it cooperates with the minority. One reason for such cooperation is that the self-interested majority values the principle of reciprocity. The self-interested majority worries that the minority may attract defectors from the majority and become the next governing majority. The Golden Rule principle of reciprocity functions to check the tendency of a self-interested majority to act tyrannically.

16   So the argument for the majority principle connects it with the value of reciprocity: You cooperate when you lose in part because members of the current majority will cooperate when they lose. The conventional case for the fairness of majority rule is that it is not really the rule of a fixed group—The Majority— on all issues; instead it is the rule of shifting majorities, as the losers at one time or on one issue join with others and become part of the governing coalition at another time or on another issue. The result will be a fair system of mutually beneficial cooperation. I call a majority that rules but does not dominate a Madisonian Majority.

17   The problem of majority tyranny arises, however, when the self-interested majority does not need to worry about defections. When the majority is fixed and permanent, there are no checks on its ability to be overbearing. A majority that does not worry about defectors is a majority with total power.

18   In such a case, Madison's concern about majority tyranny arises. In a heterogeneous community, any faction with total

power might subject "the minority to the caprice and arbitrary decisions of the majority, who instead of consulting the interest of the whole community collectively, attend sometimes to partial and local advantages."

"What remedy can be found in a republican Government, where the majority must ultimately decide," argued Madison, but to ensure "that no one common interest or passion will be likely to unite a majority of the whole number in an unjust pursuit." The answer was to disaggregate the majority to ensure checks and balances or fluid, rotating interests. The minority needed protection against an overbearing majority, so that "a common sentiment is less likely to be felt, and the requisite concert less likely to be formed, by a majority of the whole." 19

Political struggles would not be simply a contest between rulers and people; the political struggles would be among the people themselves. The work of government was not to transcend different interests but to reconcile them. In an ideal democracy, the people would rule, but the minorities would also be protected against the power of majorities. Again, where the rules of decisionmaking protect the minority, the Madisonian Majority rules without dominating. 20

But if a group is unfairly treated, for example, when it forms a racial minority, *and* if the problems of unfairness are not cured by conventional assumptions about majority rule, then what is to be done? The answer is that we may need an *alternative* to winner-take-all majoritarianism. In this book, a collection of my law review articles, I describe the alternative, which, with Nikolas's help, I now call the "principle of taking turns." In a racially divided society, this principle does better than simple majority rule if it accommodates the values of self-government, fairness, deliberation, compromise, and consensus that lie at the heart of the democratic ideal. 21

In my legal writing, I follow the caveat of James Madison and other early American democrats. I explore decisionmaking rules that might work in a multi-racial society to ensure that majority rule does not become majority tyranny. I pursue voting systems that might disaggregate The Majority so that it does not exercise power unfairly or tyrannically. I aspire to a more cooperative political style of decisionmaking to enable all of the students at Brother Rice to feel comfortable attending the same prom. In 22 looking to create Madisonian Majorities, I pursue a positive-sum, taking-turns solution.

23   Structuring decisionmaking to allow the minority "a turn" may be necessary to restore the reciprocity ideal when a fixed majority refuses to cooperate with the minority. If the fixed majority loses its incentive to follow the Golden Rule principle of shifting majorities, the minority never gets to take a turn. Giving the minority a turn does not mean the minority gets to rule; what it does mean is that the minority gets to influence decisionmaking and the majority rules more legitimately.

24   Instead of automatically rewarding the preferences of the monolithic majority, a taking-turns approach anticipates that the majority rules, but is not overbearing. Because those with 51 percent of the votes are not assured 100 percent of the power, the majority cooperates with, or at least does not tyrannize, the minority.

25   The sports analogy of "I win; you lose" competition within a political hierarchy makes sense when only one team can win; Nikolas's intuition that it is often possible to take turns suggests an alternative approach. Take family decisionmaking, for example. It utilizes a taking-turns approach. When parents sit around the kitchen table deciding on a vacation destination or activities for a rainy day, often they do not simply rely on a show of hands, especially if that means that the older children always prevail or if affinity groups among the children (those who prefer movies to video games, or those who prefer baseball to playing cards) never get to play their activity of choice. Instead of allowing the majority simply to rule, the parents may propose that everyone take turns, going to the movies one night and playing video games the next. Or as Nikolas proposes, they might do both on a given night.

26   Taking turns attempts to build consensus while recognizing political or social differences, and it encourages everyone to play. The taking-turns approach gives those with the most support more turns, but it also legitimates the outcome from each individual's perspective, including those whose views are shared only by a minority.

27   In the end, I do not believe that democracy should encourage rule by the powerful—even a powerful majority. Instead, the idea of democracy promises a fair discussion among self-defined equals about how to achieve our common aspirations. To redeem

that promise, we need to put the idea of taking turns and dis-aggregating the majority at the center of our conception of representation. Particularly as we move into the twenty-first century as a more highly diversified citizenry, it is essential that we consider the ways in which voting and representational systems succeed or fail at encouraging Madisonian Majorities.

To use Nikolas's terminology, "it is no fair" if a fixed, tyran-   28
nical majority excludes or alienates the minority. It is no fair if a fixed, tyrannical majority monopolizes all the power all the time. It is no fair if we engage in the periodic ritual of elections, but only the permanent majority gets to choose who is elected. Where we have tyranny by The Majority, we do not have genuine democracy.

Content

1. Throughout the essay, Guinier provides several definitions of "the tyranny of the majority" (see ¶s 12–21, for instance). Identify some of these definitions and the distinctions among them. Why won't a single definition suffice?

2. Guinier says one solution to majority tyranny is to "disaggregate the majority" (¶s 19, 22). What does she mean by this? Why does she see this as important in preventing the tyranny of the majority?

3. What does Guinier mean by the "'principle of taking turns'" (¶ 21)? How does this relate to her son's solution to the *Sesame Street Magazine* exercise (¶s 4–5)?

4. Has Guinier provided sufficient evidence to support her view that "'It is no fair' if a fixed, tyrannical majority excludes or alienates the minority" (¶ 28)? As you explain your answer, bear in mind that this essay is but a single chapter from an entire book; the writer can't cram every argument into one chapter.

Strategies/Structures

1. Many writings that attempt to explain complicated phenomena or to discuss difficult issues begin with down-to-earth examples, as Guinier's essay does (¶s 1–10). Why?

2. The standard advice for constructing arguments is to give the opposition a fair hearing in the course of presenting the side one favors. Does Guinier do this? Can you think of any instances in which "the tyranny of the majority" might be both good and necessary?

Language

1. Although it forms a chapter in a book, "The Tyranny of the Majority" could be read as an essay composed essentially of definitions. Why is this so, and why are definitions so important in discussing majority rule?
2. Given the prominence of definitions in "The Tyranny of the Majority," where do you suppose this chapter appeared in the book of the same name? Why do you think so?

For Writing

1. Elaborate on Guinier's view that "taking turns attempts to build consensus while recognizing political or social differences, and it encourages everyone to play" (¶ 26). Extend her application to some aspect of politics, education, social welfare, or other area of public policy that affects a sizable population; and argue for or against her position. Even if you oppose her view, you'll need to take her arguments into account.
2. Use Guinier's argument to provide a reading of Martin Luther King, Jr.'s "Letter from Birmingham Jail" (pp. 569–586), Jonathan Swift's "A Modest Proposal" (pp. 637–645), or some other essay with social or humanitarian concerns.

JOHN KENNETH GALBRAITH

> Galbraith was born (1908) on a farm in Ontario, Canada; and was educated at the University of Toronto (B.S. in agriculture, 1931); at the University of California, Berkeley (Ph.D. in economics, 1934); and at Cambridge University (1937–38), concurrent with his naturalization as a U.S. citizen. He has been affiliated with Harvard since 1934, taking time away during World War II to assume the responsibility of setting prices throughout the United States as administrator of the U.S. Office of Price Administration and to serve as economics adviser to presidents Kennedy and Johnson and as U.S. ambassador to India 1961–63. With the publication of *American Capitalism* (1952), Galbraith made a deliberate decision to write for the general public, thereby "to involve a large community," rather than only specialized economists, in discussions of economic policy.

Indeed, Galbraith's writings have been praised over the years because their grace, wit, and sardonic humor make them "both illuminating and readable." For instance, *The Affluent Society* (1958, 4th ed. 1984) questions social priorities of economic production and the division of wealth, the "implacable tendency to provide an opulent supply of some things and a niggardly yield of others. This disparity carries to the point where it is a cause of social discomfort and social unhealth." Galbraith's reforms, addressed in the ironic "How to Get the Poor off Our Conscience" (from *Harper's* 1985), are concerned with how an affluent society can develop a social conscience (rather than a greedy one), how society can offset a powerful social structure's inertia and vested interests, and how cohesion can replace our emphasis on economic production. More than a decade after its publication, Galbraith's sardonic critique of the implied absence of a public conscience seems to be borne out in the current legislation intended to transform "welfare as we know it"—but to what new reality remains to be seen.

How to Get the Poor off Our Conscience

I would like to reflect on one of the oldest of human exercises, the process by which over the years, and indeed over the centuries, we have undertaken to get the poor off our conscience.

Rich and poor have lived together, always uncomfortably and sometimes perilously, since the beginning of time. Plutarch was led to say: "An imbalance between the rich and poor is the oldest and most fatal ailment of republics." And the problems that arise from the continuing coexistence of affluence and poverty—and particularly the process by which good fortune is justified in the presence of the ill fortune of others—have been an intellectual preoccupation for centuries. They continue to be so in our own time.

One begins with the solution proposed in the Bible: The poor suffer in this world but are wonderfully rewarded in the next. Their poverty is a temporary misfortune; if they are poor and also meek, they eventually will inherit the earth. This is, in some ways, an admirable solution. It allows the rich to enjoy their wealth while envying the poor their future fortune.

4   Much, much later, in the twenty or thirty years following the publication in 1776 of *The Wealth of Nations*—the late dawn of the Industrial Revolution in Britain—the problem and its solution began to take on their modern form. Jeremy Bentham, a near contemporary of Adam Smith, came up with the formula that for perhaps fifty years was extraordinarily influential in British and, to some degree, American thought. This was utilitarianism. "By the principle of utility," Bentham said in 1789, "is meant the principle which approves or disapproves of every action whatsoever according to the tendency which it appears to have to augment or diminish the happiness of the party whose interest is in question." Virtue is, indeed must be, self-centered. While there were people with great good fortune and many more with great ill fortune, the social problem was solved as long as, again in Bentham's words, there was "the greatest good for the greatest number." Society did its best for the largest possible number of people; one accepted that the result might be sadly unpleasant for the many whose happiness was not served.

5   In the 1830s a new formula, influential in no slight degree to this day, became available for getting the poor off the public conscience. This is associated with the names of David Ricardo, a stockbroker, and Thomas Robert Malthus, a divine. The essentials are familiar: the poverty of the poor was the fault of the poor. And it was so because it was a product of their excessive fecundity: their grievously uncontrolled lust caused them to breed up to the full limits of the available subsistence.

6   This was Malthusianism. Poverty being caused in the bed meant that the rich were not responsible for either its creation or its amelioration. However, Malthus was himself not without a certain feeling of responsibility: he urged that the marriage ceremony contain a warning against undue and irresponsible sexual intercourse—a warning, it is fair to say, that has not been accepted as a fully effective method of birth control. In more recent times, Ronald Reagan has said that the best form of population control emerges from the market. (Couples in love should repair to R. H. Macy's, not their bedrooms.) Malthus, it must be said, was at least as relevant.

By the middle of the nineteenth century, a new form of   7
denial achieved great influence, especially in the United States.
The new doctrine, associated with the name of Herbert Spencer,
was Social Darwinism. In economic life, as in biological development, the overriding rule was survival of the fittest. That phrase—
"survival of the fittest"—came, in fact, not from Charles Darwin
but from Spencer, and expressed his view of economic life. The
elimination of the poor is nature's way of improving the race. The
weak and unfortunate being extruded, the quality of the human
family is thus strengthened.

One of the most notable American spokespersons of Social   8
Darwinism was John D. Rockefeller—the first Rockefeller—who
said in a famous speech: "The American Beauty rose can be produced in the splendor and fragrance which bring cheer to its
beholder only by sacrificing the early buds which grow up around
it. And so it is in economic life. It is merely the working out of a
law of nature and a law of God."

In the course of the present century, however, Social Darwin-   9
ism came to be considered a bit too cruel. It declined in popularity,
and references to it acquired a condemnatory tone. We passed on
to the more amorphous denial of poverty associated with Calvin
Coolidge and Herbert Hoover. They held that public assistance to
the poor interfered with the effective operation of the economic
system—that such assistance was inconsistent with the economic
design that had come to serve most people very well. The notion
that there is something economically damaging about helping the
poor remains with us to this day as one of the ways by which we
get them off our conscience.

With the Roosevelt revolution (as previously with that of   10
Lloyd George in Britain), a specific responsibility was assumed
by the government for the least fortunate people in the republic.
Roosevelt and the presidents who followed him accepted a substantial measure of responsibility for the old through Social Security, for the unemployed through unemployment insurance, for
the unemployable and the handicapped through direct relief, and
for the sick through Medicare and Medicaid. This was a truly
great change, and for a time, the age-old tendency to avoid thinking about the poor gave way to the feeling that we didn't need to
try—that we were, indeed, doing something about them.

11   In recent years, however, it has become clear that the search for a way of getting the poor off our conscience was not at an end; it was only suspended. And so we are now again engaged in this search in a highly energetic way. It has again become a major philosophical, literary, and rhetorical preoccupation, and an economically not unrewarding enterprise.

12   Of the four, maybe five, current designs we have to get the poor off our conscience, the first proceeds from the inescapable fact that most of the things that must be done on behalf of the poor must be done in one way or another by the government. It is then argued that the government is inherently incompetent, except as regards weapon design and procurement and the overall management of the Pentagon. Being incompetent and ineffective, it must not be asked to succor the poor; it will only louse things up or make things worse.

13   The allegation of government incompetence is associated in our time with the general condemnation of the bureaucrat—again excluding those concerned with national defense. The only form of discrimination that is still permissible—that is, still officially encouraged in the United States today—is discrimination against people who work for the federal government, especially on social welfare activities. We have great corporate bureaucracies replete with corporate bureaucrats, but they are good; only public bureaucracy and government servants are bad. In fact, we have in the United States an extraordinarily good public service—one made up of talented and dedicated people who are overwhelmingly honest and only rarely given to overpaying for monkey wrenches, flashlights, coffee makers, and toilet seats. (When these aberrations have occurred, they have, oddly enough, all been in the Pentagon.) We have nearly abolished poverty among the old, greatly democratized health care, assured minorities of their civil rights, and vastly enhanced educational opportunity. All this would seem a considerable achievement for incompetent and otherwise ineffective people. We must recognize that the present condemnation of government and government administration is really part of the continuing design for avoiding responsibility for the poor.

14   The second design in this great centuries-old tradition is to argue that any form of public help to the poor only hurts the poor. It destroys morale. It seduces people away from gainful

employment. It breaks up marriages, since women can seek welfare for themselves and their children once they are without their husbands.

There is no proof of this—none, certainly, that compares that 15
damage with the damage that would be inflicted by the loss of public assistance. Still, the case is made—and believed—that there is something gravely damaging about aid to the unfortunate. This is perhaps our most highly influential piece of fiction.

The third, and closely related, design for relieving ourselves 16
of responsibility for the poor is the argument that public-assistance measures have an adverse effect on incentive. They transfer income from the diligent to the idle and feckless, thus reducing the effort of the diligent and encouraging the idleness of the idle. The modern manifestation of this is supply-side economics. Supply-side economics holds that the rich in the United States have not been working because they have too little income. So, by taking money from the poor and giving it to the rich, we increase effort and stimulate the economy. Can we really believe that any considerable number of the poor prefer welfare to a good job? Or that business people—corporate executives, the key figures in our time—are idling away their hours because of the insufficiency of their pay? This is a scandalous charge against the American businessperson, notably a hard worker. Belief can be the servant of truth—but even more of convenience.

The fourth design for getting the poor off our conscience is 17
to point to the presumed adverse effect on freedom of taking responsibility for them. Freedom consists of the right to spend a maximum of one's money by one's own choice, and to see a minimum taken and spent by the government. (Again, expenditure on national defense is excepted.) In the enduring words of Professor Milton Friedman, people must be "free to choose."

This is probably the most transparent of all of the designs; no 18
mention is ordinarily made of the relation of income to the freedom of the poor. (Professor Friedman is here an exception; through the negative income tax, he would assure everyone a basic income.) There is, we can surely agree, no form of oppression that is quite so great, no constriction on thought and effort quite so comprehensive, as that which comes from having no money at all. Though we hear much about the limitation on the freedom of

the affluent when their income is reduced through taxes, we hear nothing of the extraordinary enhancement of the freedom of the poor from having some money of their own to spend. Yet the loss of freedom from taxation to the rich is a small thing as compared with the gain in freedom from providing some income to the impoverished. Freedom we rightly cherish. Cherishing it, we should not use it as a cover for denying freedom to those in need.

19   Finally, when all else fails, we resort to simple psychological denial. This is a psychic tendency that in various manifestations is common to us all. It causes us to avoid thinking about death. It causes a great many people to avoid thought of the arms race and the consequent rush toward a highly probable extinction. By the same process of psychological denial, we decline to think of the poor. Whether they be in Ethiopia, the South Bronx, or even in such an Elysium as Los Angeles, we resolve to keep them off our minds. Think, we are often advised, of something pleasant.

20   These are the modern designs by which we escape concern for the poor. All, save perhaps the last, are in great inventive descent from Bentham, Malthus, and Spencer. Ronald Reagan and his colleagues are clearly in a notable tradition—at the end of a long history of effort to escape responsibility for one's fellow beings. So are the philosophers now celebrated in Washington: George Gilder, a greatly favored figure of the recent past, who tells to much applause that the poor must have the cruel spur of their own suffering to ensure effort; Charles Murray, who, to greater cheers, contemplates "scrapping the entire federal welfare and income-support structure for working and aged persons, including A.F.D.C., Medicaid, food stamps, unemployment insurance, Workers' Compensation, subsidized housing, disability insurance, and," he adds, "the rest. Cut the knot, for there is no way to untie it." By a triage, the worthy would be selected to survive; the loss of the rest is the penalty we should pay. Murray is the voice of Spencer in our time; he is enjoying, as indicated, unparalleled popularity in high Washington circles.

21   Compassion, along with the associated public effort, is the least comfortable, the least convenient, course of behavior and action in our time. But it remains the only one that is consistent with a totally civilized life. Also, it is, in the end, the most truly conservative course. There is no paradox here. Civil discontent and its consequences do not come from contented people—an obvious

point. To the extent that we can make contentment as nearly universal as possible, we will preserve and enlarge the social and political tranquility for which conservatives, above all, should yearn.

Content

1. Why does Galbraith provide a historical overview of ways to "get the poor off our conscience," beginning with pre-Biblical times and continuing to the present?

2. Identify the philosophical movements used historically to "get the poor off our conscience": utilitarianism (¶ 4), Malthusianism (¶s 5–6), Social Darwinism (¶ 7), and twentieth-century politics (¶s 8–9). Galbraith characterizes each movement in a sentence or two; is this enough to convey each philosophical principle and Galbraith's view of it?

3. If Galbraith is right, that "most of the things that must be done on behalf of the poor must be done in one way or another by the government" (¶ 12), why have philosophers and economists argued over the centuries that the poor must help themselves? What do economists mean by being "free to choose"? To choose what? Who makes the choices (see ¶ 17)?

4. If the government is actually composed of "incompetent" bureaucrats (¶ 12), how can it provide relief for the poor? Why does Galbraith interpret this belief in government's incompetence as an excuse "for avoiding responsibility for the poor" (¶ 13)?

Strategies/Structures

1. At what point in your reading do you realize that Galbraith's title is ironic? Indeed, most of Galbraith's essay is ironic: "the case is made— and believed—that there is something gravely damaging about aid to the unfortunate" (¶ 15, see also ¶ 16). How does this irony help Galbraith build his argument?

2. On what grounds does Galbraith expect readers to recognize and to share his critique of the views—"our most highly influential piece of fiction" (¶ 15)—that his irony implies? Is offering this critique sufficient in an argumentative essay? Should Galbraith also have offered one or more solutions?

Language

1. Who does Galbraith mean by *Our* in the title? If *our* means "we, the readers," does *our* include the author himself? Why or why not? How can you tell?

2. How can readers identify the irony in such statements as "Supply-side economics holds that the rich in the United States have not been working because they have too little income. So, by taking money from the poor and giving it to the rich, we increase effort and stimulate the economy" (¶ 16)?

For Writing

1. Pick one of Galbraith's claims about what we do to "get the poor off our conscience" and either reinforce or debate it, for an audience that indeed wants to get the poor off its conscience. Consider in your paper the arguments and evidence advanced by one or two of these essays, as well: Mike Rose, "I Just Wanna Be Average" (pp. 243–252); Jonathan Kozol, "The Human Cost of an Illiterate Society" (pp. 264–273); Stephanie Coontz, "A Nation of Welfare Families" (pp. 275–280); Robert Reich, "The Global Elite" (pp. 604–615).

2. Write a moral alternative to one or more of the propositions proffered over the ages to "get the poor off our conscience." In other words, propose a social policy based, as Galbraith advises, on "compassion" (¶ 21), or on "brotherhood" (See Martin Luther King, Jr.'s "Letter from Birmingham Jail," (pp. 569–586), or on the elimination of "the tyranny of the majority" (see Guinier's essay, pp. 588–595). You might consider the example of an earlier or currently existing public program, even one that is under fire (Medicare, Medicaid, Social Security, Aid to Dependent Children, the GI Bill, federal student loans, tax subsidies for home mortgages, and so on); or a private program with public implications (Habitat for Humanity, UNICEF, alumni support for particular secondary schools and colleges). Use for reinforcement any of the essays identified in the preceding question, as well as more specialized literature on your subject.

ROBERT REICH

Reich (born, 1946), earned a B.A. at Dartmouth College (1968) and a J.D. degree from Yale Law School (1973), was a Rhodes scholar at Oxford, and since 1981 has been a professor at Harvard's John F. Kennedy School of Government. Active in politics since his student days, Reich has served as summer intern for Senator Robert Kennedy; coordinator of Eugene McCarthy's 1968 presidential campaign; and as economic advisor to presidential candidates

in postwar history. These high earners will relinquish somewhat more of their income to the Federal Government this year than in 1990 as a result of last fall's tax changes, although considerably less than in the late 1970s, when the tax code was more progressive. But the continuing debate over whether the wealthy are paying their fair share of taxes obscures a larger issue, with more profound implications for America: The fortunate fifth is quietly seceding from the rest of the nation.

This is occurring gradually, without much awareness by members of the top group—or, for that matter, by anyone else. And the Government is speeding this process as Washington shifts responsibility for many public services to state and local governments.   9

The secession is taking several forms. In many cities and towns, the wealthy have in effect withdrawn their dollars from the support of public spaces and institutions shared by all and dedicated the savings to their own private services. As public parks and playgrounds deteriorate, there is a proliferation of private health clubs, golf clubs, tennis clubs, skating clubs, and every other type of recreational association in which costs are shared among members. Condominiums and the omnipresent residential communities dun their members to undertake work that financially strapped local governments can no longer afford to do well—maintaining roads, mending sidewalks, pruning trees, repairing street lights, cleaning swimming pools, paying for lifeguards, and, notably, hiring security guards to protect life and property. (The number of private security guards in the United States now exceeds the number of public police officers.)   10

Of course, wealthier Americans have been withdrawing into their own neighborhoods and clubs for generations. But the new secession is more dramatic because the highest earners now inhabit a different economy from other Americans. The new elite is linked by jet, modem, fax, satellite, and fiber-optic cable to the great commercial and recreational centers of the world, but it is not particularly connected to the rest of the nation.   11

That is because the work this group does is becoming less tied to the activities of other Americans. Most of their jobs consist of analyzing and manipulating symbols—words, numbers, or visual images. Among the most prominent of these "symbolic analysts" are management consultants, lawyers, software and   12 design engineers, research scientists, corporate executives, financial advisors, strategic planners, advertising executives, television and movie producers, and other workers whose job titles include terms like "strategy," "planning," consultant," "policy," "resources," or "engineer."

13   These workers typically spend long hours in meetings or on the telephone and even longer hours in planes or hotels—advising, making presentations, giving briefings, and making deals. Periodically, they issue reports, plans, designs, drafts, briefs, blueprints, analyses, memorandums, layouts, renderings, scripts, or projections. In contrast with people whose jobs tend to be tedious and repetitive, symbolic analysts find their work varied and intellectually challenging. In fact, the work is often enjoyable.

14   These symbolic analysts are in ever greater demand in a world market that places an increasing value on identifying and solving problems. Requests for their software designs, financial advice, or engineering blueprints come from all parts of the globe. This largely explains why most (but by no means all) symbolic analysts have become wealthier, even as the ever-growing worldwide supply of unskilled labor continues to depress the wages of other Americans.

15   Successful Americans have not completely disengaged themselves from the lives of their less fortunate compatriots. Some devote substantial resources and energies to helping the rest of society, not through their tax payments, but through voluntary efforts. "Generosity is a reflection of what one does with his or her resources—and not what he or she advocates the government do with everyone's money," Ronald Reagan said in 1984.

16   The argument is fair enough. Government is not the only device for redistributing wealth. In his speech accepting the Presidential nomination at the Republican National Convention in 1988, George Bush said that the real magnanimity of America was to be found in a "brilliant diversity" of private charities, "spread like stars, like a thousand points of light in a broad and peaceful sky."

17   No nation congratulates itself more enthusiastically on its charitable acts than America; none engages in a greater number of charity balls, bake sales, benefit auctions, and border-to-border hand holdings for good causes. Much of this is sincerely motivated and admirable.

But close examination reveals that many of these acts of be-   18
nevolence do not help the needy. Particularly suspect is the private
givings of those in the top income-tax bracket. Studies have revealed that their largess does not flow mainly to social services for
the poor—to better schools, health clinics, or recreational centers.
Instead, most voluntary contributions of wealthy Americans go to
the places and institutions that entertain, inspire, cure, or educate
wealthy Americans—art museums, opera houses, theaters, orches-
tras, ballet companies, private hospitals, and elite universities.

And even these charitable contributions are relatively   19
skimpy. Last year, American households with incomes of less than
$10,000 gave an average of 5.5 percent of their earnings to charity
or to a religious organization; those making more than $100,000
a year gave only 2.9 percent. After the 1986 tax-code overhaul reduced the benefits of charitable giving, the very rich became even
stingier. According to Internal Revenue Service data, taxpayers
earning $500,000 or more slashed their average donations to
$16,062 in 1988 from $47,432 in 1980.

Corporate philanthropy is following the same general pat-   20
tern. In recent years, the largest American corporations have been
sounding the alarm about the nation's fast deteriorating primary
and secondary schools. Few are more eloquent and impassioned
about the need for better schools than American executives. "How
well we educate all of our children will determine our competi-
tiveness globally, and our economic health domestically, and our
communities' character and vitality," said a report of The Business
Roundtable, a New York–based association of top executives.

Accordingly, there are numerous "partnerships" between   21
corporations and public schools: scholarships for poor children
qualified to attend college, and programs in which businesses
adopt individual schools by making conspicuous donations of
computers, books, and, on occasion, even money. That such activities are loudly touted by public relations staffs should not detract
from the good they do.

Despite the hoopla, business donations to education and   22
charitable causes actually tapered off markedly in the 1980s, even
as the economy boomed. In the 1970s, corporate giving to education jumped an average of 15 percent a year. In 1990, however, giving was only 5 percent over that in 1989; and in 1989 it
was 3 percent over 1988. Moreover, most of this money goes to

colleges and universities—in particular, to the alma maters of symbolic analysts, who expect their children and grandchildren to follow in their footsteps. Only 1.5 percent of corporate giving in the late 1980s was to public primary and secondary schools.

23   Notably, these contributions have been smaller than the amounts corporations are receiving from states and communities in the form of subsidies or tax breaks. Companies are quietly procuring such deals by threatening to move their operations— and jobs—to places around the world with a more congenial tax climate. The paradoxical result has been even less corporate revenue to spend on schools and other community services than before. The executives of General Motors, for example, who have been among the loudest to proclaim the need for better schools, have also been among the most relentless in pursuing local tax abatements and in challenging their tax assessments. G.M.'s successful efforts to reduce its taxes in North Tarrytown, N.Y., where the company has had a factory since 1914, cut local revenues by $1 million in 1990, part of a larger shortfall that forced the town to lay off scores of teachers.

24   The secession of the fortunate fifth has been apparent in how and where they have chosen to work and live. In effect, most of America's large urban centers have splintered into two separate cities. One is composed of those whose symbolic and analytic services are linked to the world economy. The other consists of local service workers—custodians, security guards, taxi drivers, clerical aides, parking attendants, salespeople, restaurant employees—whose jobs are dependent on the symbolic analysts. Few blue-collar manufacturing workers remain in American cities. Between 1953 and 1984, for example, New York City lost 600,000 factory jobs; in the same interval, it added about 700,000 jobs for symbolic analysts and service workers.

25   The separation of symbolic analysts from local service workers within cities has been reinforced in several ways. Most large cities now possess two school systems—a private one for the children of the top-earning group and a public one for the children of service workers, the remaining blue-collar workers, and the unemployed. Symbolic analysts spend considerable time and energy insuring that their children gain entrance to good private schools,

and then small fortunes keeping them there—dollars that under a more progressive tax code might finance better public education.

People with high incomes live, shop, and work within areas 26 of cities that, if not beautiful, are at least esthetically tolerable and reasonably safe; precincts not meeting these minimum standards of charm and security have been left to the less fortunate.

Here again, symbolic analysts have pooled their resources 27 to the exclusive benefit of themselves. Public funds have been spent in earnest on downtown "revitalization" projects, entailing the construction of clusters of post-modern office buildings (complete with fiber-optic cables, private branch exchanges, satellite dishes, and other communications equipment linking them to the rest of the world), multilevel parking garages, hotels with glass enclosed atriums, upscale shopping plazas and galleries, theaters, convention centers, and luxury condominiums.

Ideally, these complexes are entirely self-contained, with air- 28 conditioned walkways linking residences, businesses, and recreational space. The lucky resident is able to shop, work, and attend the theater without risking direct contact with the outside world— that is, the other city.

When not living in urban enclaves, symbolic analysts are 29 increasingly congregating in suburbs and exurbs where corporate headquarters have been relocated, research parks have been created, and where bucolic universities have spawned entrepreneurial ventures. Among the most desirable of such locations are Princeton, N.J.; northern Westchester and Putnam Counties in New York; Palo Alto, Calif.; Austin, Tex.; Bethesda, Md.; and Raleigh-Durham, N.C.

Engineers and strategists of American auto companies, for 30 example, do not live in Flint or Saginaw, Mich., where the blue-collar workers reside; they cluster in their own towns of Troy, Warren, and Auburn Hills. Likewise, the vast majority of financial specialists, lawyers, and executives working for the insurance companies of Hartford would never consider living there; after all, Hartford is the nation's fourth-poorest city. Instead, they flock to Windsor, Middlebury, West Hartford, and other towns that are among the wealthiest in the country.

This trend, too, has been growing for decades. But technol- 31 ogy has accelerated it. Today's symbolic analysts linked directly to the rest of the globe can choose to live and work in the most pastoral of settings.

32   The secession has been encouraged by the Federal Government. For the last decade, Washington has in effect shifted responsibility for many public services to local governments. At their peak, Federal grants made up 25 percent of state and local spending in the late 1970s. Today, the Federal share has dwindled to 17 percent. Direct aid to local governments, in the form of programs introduced in the Johnson and Nixon Administrations, has been the hardest hit by budget cuts. In the 1980s, Federal dollars for clean water, job training and transfers, low-income housing, sewage treatment, and garbage disposal shrank by some $50 billion a year, and Washington's share of spending on local transit declined by 50 percent. (The Bush Administration has proposed that states and localities take on even more of the costs of building and maintaining roads, and wants to cut Federal aid for mass transit.) In 1990, New York City received only 9.6 percent of all its revenue from the Federal Government, compared with 16 percent in 1981.

33   States have quickly transferred many of these new expenses to fiscally strapped cities and towns, with a result that by the start of the 1990s, localities were bearing more than half the costs of water and sewage, roads, parks, welfare, and public schools. In New York State, the local communities' share has risen to about 75 percent of these costs.

34   Cities and towns with affluent inhabitants can bear these burdens relatively easily. Poorer ones, faced with the twin problem of lower incomes and greater demand for social services, have had far more difficulty. And as the gap between the richest and poorest communities has widened, the shift in responsibility for public services to cities and towns has functioned as another means of relieving wealthier Americans of the cost of aiding less fortunate citizens.

35   The result has been a growing inequality in basic social and community services. While the city tax rate in Philadelphia, for example, is about triple that of communities around it, the suburbs enjoy far better schools, hospitals, recreation, and police protection. Eighty-five percent of the richest families in the greater Philadelphia area live outside the city limits, and 80 percent of the

region's poorest live inside. The quality of a city's infrastructure—roads, bridges, sewage, water treatment—is likewise related to the average income of its inhabitants.

The growing inequality in government services has been 36
most apparent in the public schools. The Federal Government's share of the costs of primary and secondary education has dwindled to about 6 percent. The bulk of the cost is divided about equally between the states and local school districts. States with a higher concentration of wealthy residents can afford to spend more on their schools than other states. In 1989, the average public-school teacher in Arkansas, for example, received $21,700; in Connecticut, $37,300.

Even among adjoining suburban towns in the same state the 37
differences can be quite large. Consider three Boston-area communities located within minutes of one another. All are predominantly white, and most residents within each town earn about the same as their neighbors. But the disparity of incomes between towns is substantial.

Belmont, northwest of Boston, is inhabited mainly by sym- 38
bolic analysts and their families. In 1988, the average teacher in its public schools earned $36,100. Only 3 percent of Belmont's eighteen-year-olds dropped out of high school, and more than 80 percent of graduating seniors chose to go on to a four-year college.

Just east of Belmont is Somerville, most of whose residents 39
are low-wage service workers. In 1988, the average Somerville teacher earned $29,400. A third of the town's eighteen-year-olds did not finish high school, and fewer than a third planned to attend college.

Chelsea, across the Mystic River from Somerville, is the 40
poorest of the three towns. Most of its inhabitants are unskilled, and many are unemployed or only employed part time. The average teacher in Chelsea, facing tougher educational challenges than his or her counterparts in Belmont, earned $26,200 in 1988, almost a third less than the average teacher in the more affluent town just a few miles away. More than half of Chelsea's eighteen-year-olds did not graduate from high school, and only 10 percent planned to attend college.

Similar disparities can be found all over the nation. Students 41
at Highland Park High School in a wealthy suburb of Dallas, for

example, enjoy a campus with a planetarium, indoor swimming pool, closed-circuit television studio and state-of-the-art science laboratory. Highland Park spends about $6,000 a year to educate each student. This is almost twice that spent per pupil by the towns of Wilmer and Hutchins in southern Dallas County. According to Texas education officials, the richest school district in the state spends $19,300 a year per pupil; its poorest, $2,100 a year.

42   The courts have become involved in trying to repair such imbalances, but the issues are not open to easy judicial remedy.

43   The four-fifths of Americans left in the wake of the secession of the fortunate fifth include many poor blacks, but racial exclusion is neither the primary motive for the separation not a necessary consequence. Lower-income whites are similarly excluded, and high-income black symbolic analysts are often welcomed. The segregation is economic rather than racial, although economically motivated separation often results in *de facto* racial segregation. Where courts have found a pattern of racially motivated segregation, it usually has involved lower-income white communities bordering on lower-income black neighborhoods.

44   In states where courts have ordered equalized state spending in school districts, the vast differences in a town's property values—and thus local tax revenues—continue to result in substantial inequities. Where courts or state governments have tried to impose limits on what affluent communities can pay their teachers, not a few parents in upscale towns have simply removed their children from the public schools and applied the money they might otherwise have willingly paid in higher taxes to private school tuitions instead. And, of course, even if statewide expenditures were better equalized, poorer states would continue to be at a substantial disadvantage.

45   In all these ways, the gap between America's symbolic analysts and everyone else is widening into a chasm. Their secession from the rest of the population raises fundamental questions about the future of American society. In the new global economy—in which money, technologies, and corporations cross borders effortlessly—a citizen's standard of living depends more and more on skills and insights, and on the infrastructure needed to link these abilities to the rest of the world. But the most skilled and insightful Americans, who are already positioned to thrive in the world market, are now able to slip the bonds of national allegiance, and

by so doing disengage themselves from their less-favored fellows. The stark political challenge in the decades ahead will be to re-affirm that, even though America is no longer a separate and distinct economy, it is still a society whose members have abiding obligations to one another.

Content

1. Does Reich prove convincingly that "the fortunate fifth [those Americans with the highest income] is quietly seceding from the rest of the nation" (¶ 8)? To what extent does your receptivity to his argument depend on whether or not you consider yourself or your family a member of the "fortunate fifth"?

2. Who are "symbolic analysts" (¶s 12–14, 25–31)? Does Reich demonstrate that these persons comprise a significant portion of the "fortunate fifth"? Why does he identify their job titles (¶ 12), activities (¶ 13), lifestyles (¶s 25–28), and places of work and residence (¶s 28–30) in long lists? In what ways does he expect his readers to interpret these lists?

3. Reich illustrates many of the points of his argument with reference to the public schools in rich and poor districts (¶s 36–44, for example). Why does he focus on schools?

4. If Reich has convinced you of his premise (see question 1 above), has he also convinced you of his conclusion that "the most skilled and insightful Americans . . . are now able to slip the bonds of national allegiance, and by so doing disengage themselves from their less-favored fellows. The stark political challenge . . . will be to reaffirm that . . . [America] is still a society whose members have abiding obligations to one another" (¶ 45)? If he has convinced you, what does he want you to do as a consequence? If he hasn't convinced you, why hasn't he?

Strategies/Structures

1. The specific statistical information and other figures in Reich's 1991 article change annually, if not more often. Is their alteration within the next decade likely to affect either Reich's argument or your receptivity to it? Since numbers are always in flux, why use them in an argument?

2. Reich says that corporations threaten to move to a "more congenial tax climate" unless they get substantial tax breaks from the communities in which they're located. But what they return to the communities in philanthropic contributions is much less than they receive: "G.M.'s successful efforts to reduce its taxes in North Tarrytown, N.Y., where the company has had a factory since 1914, cut local revenues by $1 million in 1990, part

of a larger shortfall that forced the town to lay off scores of teachers" (¶ 23). What is the point of including this and comparable information? What response from readers is Reich looking for?

3. Reich's sentences are fairly long, but his paragraphs are short, usually from one to three sentences. (The longest paragraph, ¶ 32, has eight sentences.) This is because the article was originally published in a newspaper, the *New York Times Magazine*; newspapers provide paragraph breaks not to indicate where the material logically breaks or changes course but to rest readers' eyes as they roam the page. What is the effect, if any, of such a large number of short paragraphs in a serious article?

4. Which side does Reich favor? At what point in the argument does he expect his readers to realize this?

Language

Does Reich's division of workers into "symbolic and analytic services" and "local service workers" cover most people in cities? Where do "blue-collar manufacturing workers" live (see ¶ 24)? Are such labels necessary or helpful in constructing the argument Reich makes?

For Writing

1. Argue, as Reich does but using your own examples (and some of his factual information, among other sources) that, as Reich concludes, "even though America is no longer a separate and distinct economy, it is still a society whose members have abiding obligations to one another" (¶ 45). One way to address the subject is to consider the implications of a particular public policy issue (such as school vouchers, school busing, property taxation, equalization of school funding across rich and poor districts, gated residential communities with private security guards). See, for example, Martin Luther King, Jr.'s, "Letter from Birmingham Jail" (pp. 569–586), and the essays by Kozol, Coontz, and Galbraith identified in the next question.

2. Is it socially desirable for the upper fifth in income to "secede," however quietly, "from the rest of the nation," as Reich asserts in paragraph 8? Shouldn't everyone have the right to live where they want to? Should people be required to live in the same geographical area where they work? If you wish, supplement your argument with reference to the essays by Jonathan Kozol, "The Human Cost of an Illiterate Society" (pp. 264–273); Stephanie Coontz, "A Nation of Welfare Families" (pp. 275–280); and John Kenneth Galbraith, "How to Get the Poor off Our Conscience" (pp. 596–603).

JANNA L. CUNNINGHAM

Cunningham, an accounting major at the University of Denver, was born (1973) and raised in Arvada, Colorado, a Denver suburb. She explains the composition of "The Struggle to Save Endangered Species": "My essay was written as an assignment in freshman English, to prepare a casebook in the persuasive voice about a topic that interested us and that would compare a United States policy to a similar policy in another country." Her instructor, Jennifer Mongeon, adds that in the ten weeks the students had to work on this essay, they created their own bibliographies, beginning with printed texts, then including microfiche and microfilm. "Each student had to locate a nonprinted source (television documentary, film, lecture, museum tour). Janna visited the Denver Zoo and spoke with specialists about endangered species."

Continues Cunningham, "I have always loved animals and have been intrigued by the plight of endangered species. Through writing my essay, I learned a great deal about what is being done to protect endangered animals in the United States and Kenya, specifically the African elephants. Some of the information I discovered was encouraging, but my research convinced me that more action needs to be taken in order to preserve the many species that currently face extinction at the hands of man."

❄ *The Struggle to Save Endangered Species*

I can imagine a herd of elephants roaming the African savanna in the heat of the afternoon sun, with flies swarming on their backs and zebras and giraffes in the background. I can see an elephant with his large ears spread wide to fan the heat as his trunk sprays cooling dirt on his back. I can also picture the gleam of his ivory tusks that will soon be the cause of his death. I hear a loud call as he senses the danger of an approaching hunter and begins to run across the open grassland. The other elephants follow his lead and run with a thunder-like sound for safety. Then I hear the sudden fire of a gun and the loud thud as an elephant hits the ground, and the poacher takes his life. The scene I imagine is not fiction. Poaching happens every day in Africa and many other parts of the world. Unfortunately, each time a poacher kills an elephant, he is endangering the entire species. If poaching continues, the only elephants existing in the future will be in zoos. However, elephants are only one of 1372 endangered species in the world, and the number of endangered species is growing every day (U.S. Bureau of the Census 214). Countries such as the United States and Kenya are making progress to save endangered species, but many animals are still in danger. New approaches need to be taken in order to save the lives of endangered species around the world. If the compassion of the people of Kenya was combined with the laws of the United States, a possible solution to animal extinction would be introduced.

2   The earth is entering a period of extinction comparable to the extinction of the dinosaurs. Establishing an exact rate is difficult, because scientists do not know exactly how many species exist. However, it is estimated that at the current rate of extinction, we may lose as much at 15% of the world's organisms over the next thirty years (Rancourt 30). Granted, extinction is not a new or unnatural process. Extinction has been going on since the beginning of life on Earth. Mass extinction occurred with the disappearance of the dinosaurs and again with the extinction of many early mammals such as the saber-toothed tiger and the woolly mammoth. Approximately 90% of the species that ever existed are gone (Allman 58). However, animals disappearing today are doing so at a rate much greater than occurred in the past. According to Allman in the conservative *U.S. News and World Report*, the rate of extinction today is 10,000 times greater than before man existed on the planet (57).

3   However, the difference between extinction today and extinction in the past is the accelerated rate and unnatural causes. According to the moderate *National Geographic*, a well-respected magazine, studies of fossils and ancient rock samples have uncovered many theories about mass extinctions. One of these theories is the possibility of a giant asteroid striking the earth. The asteroid could have caused a huge blanket of dust to encircle the globe, also causing freezing temperatures, total darkness for one to three

months, and acid rain (671–672). Another theory suggests an asteroid struck the earth with such heat and force that it caught the earth's surface on fire, creating unbearable heat across the planet and filling the air with suffocating soot (673). Such catastrophic events certainly are not taking place today, yet the rate of extinction is much greater than when such events were occurring. The cause of extinction today must be the result of human interference in nature.

The United States is home to the greatest number of endan- 4 gered species in the world. In the U.S. alone, there are 900 different species considered endangered and 175 considered threatened. Only half as many species are endangered or threatened in the rest of the world combined. In foreign countries, there are 472 endangered species and 43 threatened species (U.S. Bureau of the Census 214). Why does the United States have so many endangered species compared to other countries? Perhaps it is because the United States is not doing as much as other countries to protect endangered species. However, the problem probably began with the exploitation of animals in the early history of the United States.

The settlers who first came to America took advantage of the 5 abundance of wildlife, especially game animals such as the plains buffalo, the elk, the wild turkey, even the grizzly bear. These animals, whose numbers were estimated to be in the thousands or millions at one time, were soon nearly extinct due to excessive hunting on the part of the settlers (DiSilvestro 1–13). Another cause of extinction in the United States is the destruction of the natural habitat of many animals. In the Northwest, for example, logging destroyed the home of the spotted owl and nearly caused extinction. Across the globe, 6,000 species each year are becoming extinct from deforestation alone (DiSilvestro 9). These causes of extinction and others are the result of human intrusion into nature.

The United States' biggest defense against endangered 6 species is the Endangered Species Act of 1973. DiSilvestro calls the act the "most powerful wildlife protection law in the world" (159). The act declares it illegal for the government to fund activities harming endangered species, and it prohibits the harming or killing of endangered species. The protection of animals is carried out mainly by the U.S. Fish and Wildlife Service. An animal can be placed in one of two categories, endangered or threatened.

"Endangered" means the species is in danger in all or in a significant portion of the area where it naturally lives. "Threatened" means the species could become endangered in the future. A species can be listed if it can be proven that its existence is threatened by such factors as "overutilization for commercial, sporting, scientific, or educational purposes" or "the absence of regulatory mechanisms adequate to prevent the decline of a species or degradation of its habitat" ("Endangered Species Act Oversight" 12). When a species is listed, the habitat it lives in is also considered for protection. This protection is called the Critical Habitat Determinant. After a species has been listed, many other agencies, including law enforcement and research, begin work on enhancing a species' chances for recovery and survival.

7   The act has been amended and revised many times to accommodate the changed endangered species and their habitats. Most recently, the act was challenged in April of 1992. Challengers wanted the act suspended so logging could resume in the Northwest in order to help revive the area's failing economy. Judge William Dwyer banned logging, saying the spotted owl's population was in danger in the area, and logging would harm the owl's habitat as well as the owl's chance for survival (*Washington Post* A12). I believe this kind of ruling gives hope that animals' lives are more important than economics.

8   However, the Endangered Species Act is not endangered species' only defense against extinction. Many different organizations are working to help save animals. These groups include Greenpeace, Earth First, and the Audubon Society. Zoos are also doing a great deal to help endangered species. For example, from a recent visit to the Denver Public Zoo, I learned the zoo participates in an international breeding program to help save species that are extinct in the wild but survive in zoos. Through this program, zoos trade animals and attempt to breed them. The Denver Zoo's participation in this project has been very effective: one of four rhinos ever born in captivity was born at the Denver Zoo last year.

9   The success of these programs is obvious in the comeback of several species once considered endangered. The bison is one encouraging example. When settlers first came to America, there were an estimated 40 to 60 million buffalo roaming the plains. In the 1970s, there were fewer than 10,000 (DiSilvestro 7). The bison

was nearly extinct due to excessive hunting, but because of recovery programs which bred bison and transplanted them to areas where the natural population was in danger, the bison now numbers over 20,000 (Allman 56). The recovery of the black-footed ferret through breeding programs, and the comeback of the bald eagle due to careful monitoring, are also encouraging signs that endangered animals can be saved (Allman 56).

Even though progress is being made, the problem in the 10 United States is still far from being resolved. For the most part, the United States seems to rely on legislation for saving animals. The Endangered Species Act is a step in the right direction, but it takes a lot of time and money to put a species on the endangered list, and animals waiting to be listed are not protected. Environmental groups are doing research and coming up with new ways to save animals. Unfortunately, these groups often operate solely on donations and cannot come up with the needed money to protect an endangered species. The groups are also greatly limited by government regulations. People are more willing to donate money to well-known species rather than plants and fungus. As a result, the well-known species receive more money and time than the lesser-known species. The United States should perhaps consider a system such as the one in Kenya. Instead of relying on legislation, more personal, emotional, and effective action is being taken.

The animals in Kenya face a different problem from the ani- 11 mals in the United States. Animals in Kenya are endangered because of extreme poaching. Elephants were slaughtered for many years for the precious ivory of their tusks. Poaching became a very big and profitable business. In the 1960s, a pound of ivory was worth only $2.45, but in 1989, the same amount was worth over $100. Rhinos were also killed for their tusks. A single rhinoceros tusk was worth over $50,000 in Asia and the Middle East in 1989 (Jones 53). Animals such as the zebra and the leopard were killed for their skins, which are worth a lot of money. The profit brought from the sale of tusks and skins is so great that it is difficult to deter poachers. Many hunters are willing to risk their lives in order to obtain valuable tusks and skins.

In the article "Farewell to Africa" in *Audubon* magazine, a 12 moderate publication for the general public, Robert F. Jones and Boyd Norton describe their visit to Kenya in January of 1990 to

"assess the state of the wildlife and see what hope, if any, remained for the future" (52). Although they had visited Africa
many times on such expeditions, they remark on the change they
have noticed since 1964. They tell a compelling story of destruction and despair on the African savanna. Jones describes a young
elephant, slaughtered for its tusks, that seems to represent the
plight of Kenya. He says:

> Rain-shot, the first two elephants dropped in their tracks.
> They lay side by side in the trampled thorn scrub like
> huge, deflated hot-air balloons . . . The blood thrown from
> the young bull's trunk had dried on the hard-baked laterite
> soil in eerie, almost graceful patterns. The soles of the
> elephant's feet had peeled away in death and now lay like
> the hunks of truck tires you see along the Interstates. The
> ants would get to them eventually. Nothing goes to waste
> in Africa except life. (50–51)

13   Life indeed goes to waste in Africa. Africa lost nearly 85% of
its elephant heard in 20 years. The elephant population dropped
from 169,000 in 1969 to only 20,000 in 1989. Most of this loss was
due to poaching. Only 4,000 elephants remained in Kenya in 1989
(Jones 53). In 1979, only 20,000 rhinos inhabited all of Africa
(Jones 79). However, these popular animals are not the only ones
in danger in Kenya. There are only an estimated 100,000 chimpanzees left in the world, most of those living in Africa (Jones 57).
Sadly, these numbers indicate the extreme danger of animal extinction in Kenya.

14   Kenya also faces a problem because of its growing population. With the population doubling every 17 years, it is the world's
fastest-growing country (Jones 72). The population has risen from
10 million in 1964 to 25 million at the start of 1990 (Jones 53). This
rapidly growing population cuts into the few remaining natural
habitats in the world. Most of the land is undeveloped and
sparsely populated. In the past, the abundance of open savanna
allowed a great variety and number of animals to roam freely.
Now, the land where the animals live is divided into wildlife
parks. Although efforts are being made to curb urban expansion in
the wildlife refuge areas, the animals would certainly lose if it
came down to a battle for land between humans and animals.

The first sign of hope for the endangered species in Kenya   15
came when President Daniel arap Moi declared a "shoot to kill"
order in Kenya (Jones 53). Under his direction, anyone caught
poaching or suspected of poaching would be shot by the game
wardens guarding Kenya's parks and reserves. This is perhaps
the most radical step ever taken to prevent animal extinction.
Since this order took effect, the rate of poachings has decreased
dramatically. The rate of elephant killings dropped from 1,500 in
1988 to only 100 in 1989 (Jones 56). The "shoot to kill" orders are
very effective, but human lives are being lost, and it is difficult to
guard the animals constantly. In order to more successfully fight
extinction President Moi turned to Richard Leakey.

Richard E. Leakey was appointed to the position of Director   16
of Kenya's Department of Wildlife Services in 1989. Leakey
believes, "What separates us from other animals is the ability to
think of tomorrow in terms of yesterday" (Allman 61). It seems to
be this theory that Leakey plans to use to save the animals of
Kenya. He has turned the wildlife department from a corrupt, failing program into a self-sustaining tourist attraction that uses proceeds to benefit the animals living in the park as well as the people
living nearby (Allman 58). Leakey believes the best solution for
saving the elephants is to make their survival economically beneficial to the people who must coexist with the animals. He plans to
run each animal park and reserve as if it is a separate business, each
responsible for its own income and expenses. Tourism will provide
much of the income Leakey is counting on. On the average, 70,000
people visit Kenya each year. Each elephant draws approximately
$20,000 into the country (Allman 57). The elephants continue to
provide this revenue for the park year after year. The money generated is used to control the elephant population and set up electric fences in areas of the park while efforts are made to replant
trees and grass (Allman 58). The combination of the "shoot to kill"
orders and Leakey's plan seems to be very effective. The rate of
elephant killings and poaching in general has fallen dramatically.
Much of what Leakey has accomplished has been done without
laws and legislation. He has taken a serious problem, proposed a
solution, and is working hard to make his dreams a reality.

Although some species are making progress, the problem of   17
extinction is getting worse instead of better. If new action is not

taken soon, animals such as the elephant in Kenya and the spotted owl in the United States could possibly disappear. In order to successfully combat the problem of animal extinction, the United States and Kenya both need to consider different options. The best way to start would be to combine the laws of the United States with programs such as the ones Leakey has established in Kenya. I found parts of each country's plans that work very well, and I think if these ideas were used together, they would create a very effective solution to animal extinction.

18   Granted, a system like the one set up in Kenya would be impossible in the United States. Many aspects of Kenya's plan, however, should be considered. Perhaps the United States needs to stop relying on laws to save the endangered species, and begin giving more government money and more power through reduced restrictions and regulations to groups such as Greenpeace, who are already committed to saving animals. Organizations like Greenpeace demonstrate the compassion and energy needed to save endangered species. Unfortunately, the government does not possess the compassion, the energy, or the time necessary to save animals. The time and expense that go into proposing an animal for listing on the endangered or threatened list, or removing an animal from the list, take away time and money that could be contributed to the species' cause. Perhaps government aid could give environmental groups needed money and incentive to begin the kind of programs already established in Kenya. Because the U.S. does not have game preserve parks like the ones in Kenya, money to benefit endangered species could be collected through entrance fees to zoos and national parks. The compassion of people like Richard Leakey is needed in the U.S. if endangered species are to be saved.

19   Unlike the U.S., Kenya also faces the irony of human lives being lost in the struggle to save animals. Other than the "shoot to kill" orders, Kenya seems to have few laws for saving endangered species. Although elephant poaching and selling or trading of ivory is illegal, it still happens. Perhaps if Kenya adopted a law such as the Endangered Species Act, there would be a way to save endangered animals without killing humans, too. The U.S. government funds the protection of endangered species in our country. Perhaps government aid given to the wildlife parks in Kenya would help Leakey begin to run the preserves as self-sustaining

businesses. Also, Kenya relies heavily on Richard Leakey to fight animal extinction. The time, energy, and money of one man are greatly limited. If environmental groups were established in Kenya, the effort of saving animals would be more equally divided and more successful. Environmental groups made up of people dedicated to saving animals could maintain the wildlife parks, replant areas being restored, and help run the wildlife preserves as businesses as Leakey's plan suggests.

I am afraid if no changes are made in current methods of pre- 20 venting extinction, many of the animals that are popular today are going to disappear in the future. In the past, animals that became extinct were not well-known or recognizable. However, animals facing extinction today are some of the best-known, well-liked, and, as in the case of the elephant, symbolic creatures of our society today. If nothing is done, these animals will be forgotten and lost to the world forever. Animal extinction is permanent. Once an animal disappears, there is no way to bring it back. Changes need to be made in the current plan to save animals so endangered species today do not become extinct species tomorrow.

Works Cited

Allman, William F. "Elephant Man." *U.S. News and World Report* 2 Oct. 1989: 58–59.

Allman, William F. and Joannie M. Schrof. "Endangered Species: Can They Be Saved?" *U.S. News and World Report* 2 Oct. 1989: 52–59.

"Court Imposes New Logging Ban." *Washington Post* 30 May 1992: A12.

DiSilvestro, Roger L. *The Endangered Kingdom.* New York: Wiley Science Editions, 1989.

"Endangered Species Act Oversight." Washington: GPO, 1982.

Jones, Robert F. "Farewell to Africa." *Audubon.* Sept. 1990: 51–104.

Rancourt, Linda M. "Endangered Species Act." *National Parks* March/April 1992: 29–33.

United States Bureau of the Census. *Statistical Abstract of the United States: 1991.* Washington: GPO, 1991.

"What Caused the Earth's Great Dying? Extinctions." *National Geographic.* 1 June 1989: 662–698.

Content

Cunningham clearly favors one side of the argument. Which side? How can you tell? Should she have given the opposition equal time or, at least, more emphasis than her essay allows? Why or why not?

Strategies/Structures

1. In what ways can a student writer, who is not a professional in the field of her paper's subject, or otherwise an authority on the subject, establish herself as an authoritative and credible writer? In your answer, identify and explain such matters as use and citation of outside sources, authorial persona, choice of vocabulary and tone. (Compare Cunningham's essay with Vicki Hearne's "What's Wrong with Animal Rights?" pp. 524–534. Since Herne is a professional animal trainer, does her experience provide sufficient authority for her argument?)

2. Hearne and Cunningham are biased in favor of the animals or animal species they write about, yet their illustrations and techniques of arguing their cases are quite different. For instance, Cunningham doesn't use language as loaded as Hearne's, when speaking of the opposition. Identify, with specific illustrations, each of these writers' argumentative strategies. Does each work equally well, or are some strategies more effective than others?

Language

1. In what ways do Cunningham's tone and language contribute to the creation of her authorial persona (the presentation of herself in her essay)? Who would consider her an environmentalist? Who would consider her a sentimental or emotional supporter of uneconomic practices? Which group(s) would be most likely to read "The Struggle to Save Endangered Species" sympathetically? At all? Explain your answer.

2. If you didn't know that Janna Cunningham wrote this essay in a freshman English class, would you think she was a student? What features of her language and other aspects of her writing reinforce your conclusion?

For Writing

1. Cunningham refers several times to the impending extinction of currently "popular" animals, that are "some of the best-known, well-liked, and . . . symbolic creatures of our society" (¶ 20). What difference does it

make whether the animals are "popular" or not? Don't all creatures, great and small, including the spotted owl and the snail darter, have a right to exist—or at least to engage in the Darwinian "struggle for existence" that leads to the "survival of the fittest"? Did Darwin (pp. 487–493) have in mind the creature's appeal to human beings in his definition of "fittest"?

2. If Cunningham were writing today, she might have used instead of the spotted owl the example of salmon in the Pacific Northwest. According to reports from the Wilderness Society and the National Marine Fisheries Service, imperiled species include coho, chum, sockeye, and chinook salmon, and steelhead and cutthroat trout, pushed to the brink of extinction by "decades of excessive logging and other developments" in northern California, southern Oregon, and the Columbia Basin (*New York Times,* 26 Nov. 1993, A31). Find out more information about an imperiled species about which you would like to know more, and write an essay defending its right to survive. Include in this a realistic public policy that would promote your aims. Will your policy (or any policy) be able to reconcile the economic interests of an area with the environmental interests?

Additional Topics for Writing
Appealing to Reason:
Deductive and Inductive Arguments

(For process strategies see page 568)

1. Write a logical, clearly reasoned, well-supported argument appropriate in organization, language, and tone to the subject and appealing to your designated audience. Be sure you have in mind a particular reader or group of readers whom you know (or suspect) are likely to be receptive or hostile to your position, or uncommitted people whose opinion you're trying to influence.

   a. A college education is (or is not) worth the effort and expense.
   b. Smoking, drinking, or using "recreational" drugs is (is not) worth the risks.
   c. Economic prosperity is (is not) more important to our country than conservation and preservation of our country's resources.
   d. The Social Security system should (should not) be preserved at all costs.
   e. Everyone should (should not) be entitled to comprehensive medical care (supply one: from the cradle to the grave; in early childhood; while a student; in old age).
   f. Drunk drivers should (should not) be jailed, even for a first offense.
   g. Auto safety belts should (should not) be mandatory.
   h. Companies manufacturing products that may affect consumers' health or safety (such as food, drugs, liquor, automobiles, pesticides) should (should not) have consumer representatives on their boards of directors.
   i. The civil rights, women's liberation, gay liberation, or some comparable movement has (has not) accomplished major and long-lasting benefits for the group it represents.
   j. Intercollegiate athletic teams that are big business should (should not) hire their players; intercollegiate athletes should (should not) have professional status.
   k. Strong labor unions should (should not) be preserved at all costs.
   l. The costs of America's manned space program are worth (far exceed) the benefits.
   m. The federal government should (should not) take over the nation's health care system.
   n. The postal service should (should not) be privatized.

2. Write a letter to your campus, city, or area newspaper in which you take a stand on an issue, defending or attacking it. You could write on one of the topics in Additional Topics 1 above, or differ with a recent column or editorial. Send in your letter (keep a copy for yourself) and see if it is published. If so, what kind of response did it attract?

3. Write to your state or federal legislator urging the passage or defeat of a particular piece of legislation currently being considered. (You will probably find at least one side of the issue being reported in the newspapers or a newsmagazine.) An extra: If you receive a reply, analyze it to see whether it addresses the specific points you raise. In what fashion? Does it sound like an individual response or a form letter?

14 Appealing to Emotion and Ethics

The essence of an emotional appeal is passion. You write from passion, and you expect your readers to respond with equal fervor. "I have a dream." "The only thing we have to fear is fear itself." "We have nothing to offer but blood, toil, tears, and sweat." "The West wasn't won with a loaded gun!" "We shall overcome." You'll be making your case in specific, concrete, memorable ways that you expect to have an unusually powerful impact on your readers. So your writing will probably be more colorful than it might be in less emotional circumstances, with a high proportion of vivid examples, narratives, anecdotes, character sketches, analogies ("Will Bosnia or Rwanda or X be another Vietnam?"), and figures of speech, including metaphors ("a knee-jerk liberal"), and similes ("The Southern Senator had a face like an old Virginia ham and a personality to match").

You can't incite your readers, either to agree with you or to take action on behalf of the cause you favor, by simply bleeding all over the page. The process of writing and rewriting and revising again (see pp. 101–135) will act to cool your red-hot emotion and will enable you to modulate in subsequent drafts what you might have written the first time just to get out of your system. "Hell, no! We won't go!" As the essays in this section and elsewhere reveal, writers who appeal most effectively to their readers' emotions themselves exercise considerable control over the organization and examples they use to make their points.

They also keep particularly tight rein over the tone and connotations of their language, crucial in an emotional appeal. Tone, the prevailing mood of the essay, like a tone of voice conveys your attitude toward your subject and toward the evidence you present in support of your point. It is clear from the tone of all the essays in this chapter—indeed, all the essays in the entire *Essay Connection*—that the authors care deeply about their subjects. Amy Jo Keifer's tone in "The Death of a Farm" (pp. 662–665) might almost be objective, but the technique she uses throughout, comparing the invariably better past, almost a golden era, with the deteriorating conditions for farmers in the present, evokes considerable emotion in the reader: "Your father works full time to support the farm," says Keifer's mother. "I work full time to support the family." These days, in nonfiction, anyway, unless it's satire, readers generally prefer understatement to overkill. To establish a climate that encourages readers to sympathize emotionally, you as a writer can present telling facts and allow the readers to interpret them, rather than continually nudging the audience with verbal reminders to see the subject your way.

Another technique for convincing readers to share your perspective is to put them in your shoes, as Terry Tempest Williams does in "The Clan of One-Breasted Women" (pp. 653–661). We see through her clear-eyed perspective, as a young child and again as the adult writing the essay, "this flash of light in the night in the desert . . . this image (that) had so permeated my being that I could not venture south without seeing it again, on the horizon, illuminating buttes and mesas." Thirty-five years after the fact, her father quietly corroborates this image of nuclear detonation that his daughter had for her whole life thought of as a "recurring dream," "You did see it." Now we see it too, as the family "saw it, clearly, this golden-stemmed cloud, the mushroom. The sky seemed to vibrate with an eerie pink glow." Within a few minutes, "a light ash was raining," as the fallout causes the cancers whose existence Williams writes to protest, and to prevent in the future.

If you are appealing to your readers' emotions through irony, the tone of your words, their music, is likely to be at variance with their overt message—and to intentionally undermine it. Thus the narrator of Swift's "A Modest Proposal" (pp. 637–645) can, with an impassive face, advocate that year-old children of the poor Irish peasants be sold for "a most delicious, nourishing, and wholesome food, whether stewed, roasted, baked, or broiled";

and, in an additional inhumane observation, "I make no doubt that it will equally serve in a fricassee or a ragout."

The connotations, overtones of the language, are equally significant in emotional appeals, as they subtly (or not so subtly) reinforce the overt, literal meanings of the words. Swift's narrator always calls the children *it*, with an impersonal connotation, and never employs the humanizing terms of *he, she,* or *baby.* The *it* emphasizes the animalistic connotations of the narrator's references to a newborn as "a child just dropped from its dam," further dehumanizing both mother and child.

Language, tone, and message often combine to present an *ethical appeal*—a way of impressing your readers that you as the author (and perhaps as a character in your own essay) are a knowledgeable person of good moral character, good will, and good sense. Consequently, you are a person of integrity, and to be believed as a credible, reasonable advocate of the position you take in your essay. In "None of This is Fair" (pp. 375–380), Richard Rodriguez explains that as a Mexican-American he benefited considerably from Affirmative Action programs to gain financial aid in college and to get highly competitive job offers afterward. Having thus established his fitness to discuss the subject, Rodriguez agrees with the critics of Affirmative Action, that "none of this is fair." His actions reinforce his words. Not only does he decide to reject all the job offers obtained by his "unfair" means; he turns his attention, at the conclusion, to the "seriously disadvantaged," irrespective of color, the poor on whom he wishes us all to focus our best efforts.

Because they usually make their point indirectly, fables, parables, and other stories with subtle moral points are often used to appeal to readers' emotions and ethical sense. The photographs of winsome (never repulsive, never ugly!) waifs often grace fundraising advertisements for famine relief, amplified by biographies of their pitiful lives; only our contributions can save them. One of the dangers in using such appeals is the possibility that you'll include too many emotional signals or ultraheavy emotional language and thereby write a paper that repels your readers by either excessive sentimentality or overkill. Lynda Barry's "The Sanctuary of School" (pp. 647–651) uses at the beginning techniques similar to the famine relief ads to present a dramatic and moving picture of herself (and her brother) as young children: "In an over-crowded and unhappy home, it's incredibly easy for any child to slip away. The high levels of frustration, depression, and anger in my house made my brother and me invisible. We were children with the sound turned off." The beginning of the essay reflects the emotional level of Barry's panic as a young child after her parents "had been fighting all night." Realizing she was "lost," she headed for "the sanctuary of school," with its host of reassuring teachers, janitor, and secretary. As the school day unfolded, so did the predictable opportunity "to sit at my desk, with my crayons and pencils and books and classmates all around me, and for the next six hours I was going to enjoy a thoroughly secure, warm, and stable world." The tone shifts gradually to reflect the calmness of the "world that I absolutely relied on," and the essay ends with an emphatic, unsentimental plea for our country to pledge allegiance to its schoolchildren. How readily we accept these arguments depends, in part, on the values, beliefs, and other experiences we bring to our reading of the work at hand. The more emotionally engaged we are at the outset, the easier it will be for such writers to enlist us in their cause.

Although ethical appeals usually tap our most profound moral values, they can be made in humorous ways, as in Judy Brady's "I Want a Wife" (pp. 468–471), which argues, implicitly, that given all the work they do—housekeeping, cleaning, cooking, childrearing, hostessing, nurturing—everyone, wives included, wants a "wife."

Appeals to emotion and ethics are often intertwined. Such appeals are everywhere, for example, in the connotations of descriptions and definitions. Furthermore, if your readers like and trust you, they're more likely to believe what you say and to be moved to agree with your point of view. The evidence in a scientific report, however strong in itself, is buttressed by the credibility of the researcher. The sense of realism, the truth of a narrative, is enhanced by the credibility of the narrator. We believe Lincoln and Barry and Keifer; and we trust the spirit of satirist Swift, and ironist Galbraith, even if we believe they are exaggerating, if not downright inventing, the substance of their narratives. Hearts compel agreement where minds hesitate. Don't hesitate to make ethical use of this understanding.

STRATEGIES FOR WRITING— APPEALING TO EMOTION AND ETHICS

1. Do I want to appeal primarily to my readers' emotions (and which emotions) or to their ethical sense of how people ought to behave? (Remember that in either case the appeals are intertwined with reason—see Chapter 13.)

2. To what kinds of readers am I making these appeals? What ethical or other personal qualities should I as an author exhibit? How can I lead my readers to believe that I am a person of sound character and good judgment?

3. What evidence can I choose to reinforce my appeals and my authorial image? Examples from my own life? The experiences of others? References to literature or scientific research? What order of arrangement would be most convincing? From the least emotionally moving or involving to the most? Or vice versa?

4. How can I interpret my evidence to move my readers to accept it? Should I explain very elaborately, or should I let the examples speak for themselves? If you decide on the latter, try out your essay on someone unfamiliar with the examples to see if they are in fact self-evident.

5. Do I want my audience to react with sympathy? Pity? Anger? Fear? Horror? To accomplish this, should I use much emotional language? Should my appeal be overt, direct? Or would indirection, understatement, be more effective? Would irony, saying the opposite of what I really mean (as Swift did), be more appropriate than a direct approach? Could I make my point more effectively with a fable, parable, comic tale, or invented persona than with a straightforward analysis and overt commentary?

ABRAHAM LINCOLN

For a discussion of the biographical, political, historical, and literary aspects of this speech see Gilbert Highet's "The Gettysburg Address" (pp. 674–680).

The Gettysburg Address

F our score and seven years ago our fathers brought forth on 1 this continent, a new nation, conceived in liberty, and dedicated to the proposition that all men are created equal.

Now we are engaged in a great civil war, testing whether 2 that nation, or any nation so conceived and so dedicated, can long endure. We are met on a great battlefield of that war. We have come to dedicate a portion of that field, as a final resting place for those who here gave their lives that the nation might live. It is altogether fitting and proper that we should do this.

But, in a larger sense, we cannot dedicate—we cannot conse- 3 crate—we cannot hallow—this ground. The brave men, living and dead, who struggled here, have consecrated it, far above our poor power to add or detract. The world will little note, nor long remember what we say here, but it can never forget what they did here. It is for us the living, rather, to be dedicated here to the unfinished work which they who fought here have thus far so nobly advanced. It is rather for us to be here dedicated to the great task remaining before us—that from these honored dead we take increased devotion—that we here highly resolve that these dead shall not have died in vain—that this nation, under God, shall have a new birth of freedom—and that the government of the people, by the people, for the people, shall not perish from the earth.

Content

1. What principles of the founding of the United States does Lincoln emphasize in the first sentence? Why are these so important to the occasion of his address? To the theme of this address?

2. What does Lincoln imply and assert is the relation of life and death? Birth and rebirth?

Strategies/Structures

1. Why would Lincoln, knowing that his audience expected longer orations, deliberately have decided to make his speech so short?
2. Lincoln's speech commemorated a solemn occasion: the dedication of a major battlefield of the ongoing Civil War. Wouldn't such a short speech have undermined the significance of the event?

Language

1. Identify the language and metaphors of birth that Lincoln uses throughout this address. For what purpose? With what effect?
2. Why did Lincoln use biblical language and phrasing conspicuously at the beginning and end of the address, such as "four score and seven years ago" instead of the more common "eighty-seven"?
3. Lincoln uses many *antitheses*—oppositions, contrasts. Identify some and show how they reinforce the meaning.
4. Another important rhetorical device is the *tricolon,* "the division of an idea into three harmonious parts, usually of increasing power,"—for example, "government of the people, by the people, for the people. . . ." Find others and show why they are so memorable.

For Writing

1. Write a short, dignified speech for a solemn occasion, real or imaginary. Let the majesty of your language and the conspicuous rhetorical patterns of your sentences and paragraphs (through such devices as antithesis and parallelism) reinforce your point.
2. Rewrite the Gettysburg Address as it might have been spoken by a more recent president or other politician, using language, paragraphing, and sentence structures characteristic of the speaker and the times. (See Nakamura, "Pidgin to da Max" (pp. 681–684). One such speech, a parody, is William Safire's "Carter's Gettysburg Address," which begins: "Exactly two hundred and one years, five months and one day ago, our fore-fathers—and our foremothers, too, as my wife, the First Lady, reminds me—our highly competent Founding Persons brought forth on this land mass a new nation, or entity, dreamed up in liberty and dedicated to the comprehensive program of insuring that all of us are created with the same basic human rights."

JONATHAN SWIFT

Swift, author of *Gulliver's Travels* (1726) and other satiric essays, poems, and tracts, was well acquainted with irony. Born in Dublin in 1667, the son of impoverished English Anglicans, he obtained a degree from Trinity College, Dublin, in 1685 only by "special grace." When Cromwell invaded Ireland, Swift, along with many Anglo-Irish, was forced to flee to England, was eventually ordained as an Anglican priest, and rose prominently in London literary and political circles until 1713. Although he had hoped for a church appointment in England, his desertion of the Whig Party for the Tories was ironically rewarded with an appointment as dean of St. Patrick's (Anglican) Cathedral in Dublin, which he regarded as virtual exile. Nevertheless, despite his religious differences with the Irish people, Swift became a beloved leader in the Irish resistance to English oppression, motivated less by partisan emotions than by his own "savage indignation" against injustice. He died in 1745.

Swift wrote "A Modest Proposal" in the summer of 1729, after three years of drought and crop failure had forced over 35,000 peasants to leave their homes and wander the countryside looking for work, food, and shelter for their starving families, ignored by the insensitive absentee landowners. The "Proposal" carries the English landowners' treatment of the Irish to its logical—but repugnant—extreme: if they are going to devour any hope the Irish have of living decently, why don't they literally eat the Irish children? The persona Swift creates is logical, consistent, seemingly rational—and utterly inhumane, an advocate of infanticide and cannibalism. Yet nowhere in the "Proposal" does the satirist condemn the speaker; he relies on the readers' sense of morality for that. This tactic can be dangerous, for a reader who misses the irony may take the "Proposal" at face value. But Swift's intended readers, English (landlords included) as well as Irish who could act to alleviate the people's suffering, understood very well what he meant. The victims themselves, largely illiterate, would probably have been unaware of this forceful plea on their behalf.

A Modest Proposal

1   It is a melancholy object to those who walk through this great town or travel in the country, when they see the streets, the roads, and cabin doors, crowded with beggars of the female sex, followed by three, four, or six children, all in rags and importuning every passenger for an alms. These mothers, instead of being able to work for their honest livelihood, are forced to employ all their time in strolling to beg sustenance for their helpless infants: who as they grow up either turn thieves for want of work, or leave their dear native country to fight for the pretender in Spain, or sell themselves to the Barbadoes.

2   I think it is agreed by all parties that this prodigious number of children in the arms, or on the backs, or at the heels of their mothers, and frequently of their fathers, is in the present deplorable state of the kingdom a very great additional grievance; and, therefore, whoever could find out a fair, cheap, and easy method of making these children sound, useful members of the commonwealth, would deserve so well of the public as to have his statue set up for a preserver of the nation.

3   But my intention is very far from being confined to provide only for the children of professed beggars; it is of a much greater extent, and shall take in the whole number of infants at a certain age who are born of parents in effect as little able to support them as those who demand our charity in the streets.

4   As to my own part, having turned my thoughts for many years upon this important subject, and maturely weighed the several schemes of our projectors, I have always found them grossly mistaken in their computation. It is true, a child just dropped from its dam may be supported by her milk for a solar year, with little other nourishment; at most not above the value of two shillings, which the mother may certainly get, or the value in scraps, by her lawful occupation of begging; and it is exactly at one year old that I propose to provide for them in such a manner as instead of being a charge upon their parents or the parish, or wanting food and raiment for the rest of their lives, they shall on the contrary contribute to the feeding, and partly to the clothing, of many thousands.

There is likewise another great advantage in my scheme, 5
that it will prevent those voluntary abortions, and that horrid
practice of women murdering their bastard children, alas! too frequent among us! sacrificing the poor innocent babes I doubt more
to avoid the expense than the shame, which would move tears
and pity in the most savage and inhuman breast.

The number of souls in this kingdom being usually reckoned 6
one million and half, of these I calculate there may be about two
hundred thousand couple whose wives are breeders; from which
number I subtract thirty thousand couple who are able to maintain
their own children (although I apprehend there cannot be so many,
under the present distress of the kingdom); but this being granted,
there will remain an hundred and seventy thousand breeders. I
again subtract fifty thousand for those women who miscarry, or
whose children die by accident or disease within the year. There
only remain an hundred and twenty thousand children of poor
parents annually born. The question therefore is, how this number
shall be reared and provided for? which, as I have already said,
under the present situation of affairs, is utterly impossible by all
the methods hitherto proposed. For we can neither employ them
in handicraft or agriculture; we neither build houses (I mean in the
country) nor cultivate land; they can very seldom pick up a livelihood by stealing, till they arrive at six years old, except where they
are of towardly parts; although I confess they learn the rudiments
much earlier; during which time they can, however, be properly
looked upon only as probationers; as I have been informed by a
principal gentleman in the country of Cavan, who protested to me
that he never knew above one or two instances under the age of
six, even in a part of the kingdom so renowned for the quickest
proficiency in that art.

I am assured by our merchants, that a boy or a girl before 7
twelve years old is no saleable commodity; and even when they
come to this age they will not yield above three pounds, or three
pounds and a half a crown at most on the Exchange; which cannot turn to account either to the parents or kingdom, the charge
of nutriment and rags having been at least four times that value.

I shall now therefore humbly propose my own thoughts, 8
which I hope will not be liable to the least objection.

9   I have been assured by a very knowing American of my acquaintance in London, that a young healthy child well nursed is at a year old the most delicious, nourishing, and wholesome food, whether stewed, roasted, baked, or broiled; and I make no doubt that it will equally serve in a fricassee or a ragout.

10   I do therefore humbly offer it to public consideration that of the hundred and twenty thousand children already computed, twenty thousand may be reserved for breed, whereof only one fourth part to be males; which is more than we allow to sheep, black cattle, or swine; and my reason is, that these children are seldom the fruits of marriage, a circumstance not much regarded by our savages; therefore, one male will be sufficient to serve four females. That the remaining hundred thousand may, at a year old, be offered in sale to the persons of quality and fortune through the kingdom; always advising the mother to let them suck plentifully in the last month, so as to render them plump and fat for a good table. A child will make two dishes at an entertainment for friends; and when the family dines alone, the fore or hind quarter will make a reasonable dish, and seasoned with a little pepper or salt will be very good boiled on the fourth day, especially in winter.

11   I have reckoned upon a medium that a child just born will weigh twelve pounds, and in a solar year, if tolerably nursed, will increase to twenty-eight pounds.

12   I grant this food will be somewhat dear, and therefore very proper for landlords, who, as they have already devoured most of the parents, seem to have the best title to the children.

13   Infant's flesh will be in season throughout the year, but more plentiful in March, and a little before and after: for we are told by a grave author, an eminent French physician, that fish being a prolific diet, there are more children born in Roman Catholic countries about nine months after Lent than at any other season; therefore, reckoning a year after Lent, the markets will be more glutted than usual, because the number of popish infants is at least three to one in this kingdom: and therefore it will have one other collateral advantage, by lessening the number of papists among us.

14   I have already computed the charge of nursing a beggar's child (in which list I reckon all cottagers, laborers, and four-fifths of the farmers) to be about two shillings per annum, rags included; and I believe no gentleman would repine to give ten shillings for the carcass of a good fat child, which, as I have said, will make

four dishes of excellent nutritive meat, when he has only some particular friend or his own family to dine with him. Thus the squire will learn to be a good landlord, and grow popular among the tenants; the mother will have eight shillings net profit, and be fit for work till she produces another child.

Those who are more thrifty (as I must confess the times require) may flay the carcass; the skin of which artificially dressed will make admirable gloves for ladies, and summer boots for fine gentlemen.   15

As to our city of Dublin, shambles may be appointed for this purpose in the most convenient parts of it, and butchers we may be assured will not be wanting: although I rather recommend buying the children alive, and dressing them hot from the knife as we do roasting pigs.   16

A very worthy person, a true lover of his country, and whose virtues I highly esteem, was lately pleased in discoursing on this matter to offer a refinement upon my scheme. He said that many gentlemen of this kingdom, having of late destroyed their deer, he conceived that the want of venison might be well supplied by the bodies of young lads and maidens, not exceeding fourteen years of age nor under twelve; so great a number of both sexes in every country being now ready to starve for want of work and service; and these to be disposed of by their parents, if alive, or otherwise by their nearest relations. But with due deference to so excellent a friend and so deserving a patriot, I cannot be altogether in his sentiments; for as to the males, my American acquaintance assured me from frequent experience that their flesh was generally tough and lean, like that of our schoolboys by continual exercise, and their taste disagreeable; and to fatten them would not answer the charge. Then as to the females, it would, I think, with humble submission be a loss to the public, because they soon would become breeders themselves: and besides, it is not improbable that some scrupulous people might be apt to censure such a practice (although indeed very unjustly), as a little bordering upon cruelty; which, I confess, has always been with me the strongest objection against any project, how well soever intended.   17

But in order to justify my friend, he confessed that this expedient was put into his head by the famous Psalmanazar, a native of the island Formosa, who came from thence to London about twenty years ago: and in conversation told my friend, that in his   18 country when any young person happened to be put to death, the executioner sold the carcass to persons of quality as a prime dainty; and that in his time the body of a plump girl of fifteen, who was crucified for an attempt to poison the emperor, was sold to his imperial majesty's prime minister of state, and other great mandarins of the court, in joints from the gibbet, at four hundred crowns. Neither indeed can I deny, that if the same use were made of several plump young girls in this town, who without one single groat to their fortunes cannot stir abroad without a chair, and appear at the playhouse and assemblies in foreign fineries which they never will pay for, the kingdom would not be the worse.

19   Some persons of a desponding spirit are in great concern about that vast number of poor people, who are aged, diseased, or maimed, and I have been desired to employ my thoughts what course may be taken to ease the nation of so grievous an encumbrance. But I am not in the least pain upon that matter, because it is very well known that they are every day dying and rotting by cold and famine, and filth and vermin, as fast as can be reasonably expected. And as to the young laborers, they are now in as hopeful a condition: they cannot get work, and consequently pine away for want of nourishment, to a degree that if at any time they are accidentally hired to common labor, they have not strength to perform it; and thus the country and themselves are happily delivered from the evils to come.

20   I have too long digressed, and therefore shall return to my subject. I think the advantages by the proposal which I have made are obvious and many, as well as of the highest importance.

21   For first, as I have already observed, it would greatly lessen the number of papists, with whom we are yearly overrun, being the principal breeders of the nation as well as our most dangerous enemies; and who stay at home on purpose to deliver the kingdom to the Pretender, hoping to take their advantage by the absence of so many good Protestants, who have chosen rather to leave their country than stay at home and pay tithes against their conscience to an Episcopal curate.

22   Secondly, The poor tenants will have something valuable of their own, which by law may be made liable to distress and help to pay their landlord's rent, their corn and cattle being already seized, and money a thing unknown.

Thirdly, Whereas the maintenance of a hundred thousand 23 children from two years old and upward, cannot be computed at less than ten shillings a piece per annum, the nation's stock will be thereby increased fifty thousand pounds per annum, beside the profit of a new dish introduced to the tables of all gentlemen of fortune in the kingdom who have any refinement in taste. And the money will circulate among ourselves, the goods being entirely of our own growth and manufacture.

Fourthly, The constant breeders beside the gain of eight 24 shillings sterling per annum by the sale of their children, will be rid of the charge of maintaining them after the first year.

Fifthly, This food would likewise bring great custom to taverns, where the vintners will certainly be so prudent as to procure 25 the best receipts for dressing it to perfection, and consequently have their houses frequented by all the fine gentlemen, who justly value themselves upon their knowledge in good eating; and a skillful cook who understands how to oblige his guests, will contrive to make it as expensive as they please.

Sixthly, This would be a great inducement to marriage, which 26 all wise nations have either encouraged by rewards or enforced by laws and penalties. It would increase the care and tenderness of mothers toward their children, when they were sure of a settlement for life to the poor babes, provided in some sort by the public, to their annual profit instead of expense. We should see an honest emulation among the married women, which of them would bring the fattest child to the market. Men would become as fond of their wives during the time of their pregnancy as they are now of their mares in foal, their cows in calf, their sows when they are ready to farrow; nor offer to beat or kick them (as is too frequent a practice) for fear of a miscarriage.

Many other advantages might be enumerated. For instance, 27 the addition of some thousand carcasses in our exportation of barreled beef, the propagation of swine's flesh, and improvement in the art of making good bacon, so much wanted among us by the great destruction of pigs, too frequent at our table; which are no way comparable in taste or magnificence to a well-grown, fat, yearling child, which roasted whole will make a considerable figure at a lord mayor's feast or any other public entertainment. But this and many others I omit, being studious of brevity.

28   Supposing that one thousand families in this city would be constant customers for infants' flesh, besides others who might have it at merry-meetings, particularly at weddings and christenings, I compute that Dublin would take off annually about twenty thousand carcasses; and the rest of the kingdom (where probably they will be sold somewhat cheaper) the remaining eighty thousand.

29   I can think of no one objection that will possibly be raised against this proposal, unless it should be urged that the number of people will be thereby much lessened in the kingdom. This I freely own, and it was indeed one principal design in offering it to the world. I desire the reader will observe, that I calculate my remedy for this one individual kingdom of Ireland and for no other that ever was, is, or I think ever can be upon earth. Therefore let no man talk to me of other expedients; of taxing our absentees at five shillings a pound: of using neither clothes nor household furniture except what is of our own growth and manufacture: of utterly rejecting the materials and instruments that promote foreign luxury: of curing the expensiveness of pride, vanity, idleness, and gaming in our women: of introducing a vein of parsimony, prudence, and temperance: of learning to love our country, in the want of which we differ even from Laplanders and the inhabitants of Topinamboo: of quitting our animosities and factions, nor acting any longer like the Jews, who were murdering one another at the very moment their city was taken: of being a little cautious not to sell our country and conscience for nothing: of teaching landlords to have at least one degree of mercy toward their tenants; lastly, of putting a spirit of honesty, industry, and skill into our shopkeepers; who, if a resolution could now be taken to buy only our native goods, would immediately unite to cheat and exact upon us in the price, the measure, and the goodness, nor could ever yet be brought to make one fair proposal of just dealing, though often and earnestly invited to it.

30   Therefore I repeat, let no man talk to me of these and the like expedients, till he has at least some glimpse of hope that there will be ever some hearty and sincere attempts to put them in practice.

31   But as to myself, having been wearied out for many years with offering vain, idle, visionary thoughts, and at length utterly

despairing of success, I fortunately fell upon this proposal; which, as it is wholly new, so it has something solid and real, of no expense and little trouble, full in our own power, and whereby we can incur no danger in disobliging England. For this kind of commodity will not bear exportation, the flesh being of too tender a consistence to admit a long continuance in salt, although perhaps I could name a country which would be glad to eat up our whole nation without it.

After all, I am not so violently bent upon my own opinion 32 as to reject any offer proposed by wise men, which shall be found equally innocent, cheap, easy, and effectual. But before something of that kind shall be advanced in contradiction to my scheme, and offering a better, I desire the author or authors will be pleased maturely to consider two points. First, as things now stand, how they will be able to find food and raiment for a hundred thousand useless mouths and backs. And secondly, there being a round million of creatures in human figure throughout this kingdom, whose subsistence put into a common stock would leave them in debt two millions of pounds sterling, adding those who are beggars by profession to the bulk of farmers, cottagers, and laborers, with the wives and children who are beggars in effect; I desire those politicians who dislike my overture, and may perhaps be so bold as to attempt an answer, that they will first ask the parents of these mortals, whether they would not at this day think it a great happiness to have been sold for food at a year old in the manner I prescribe, and thereby have avoided such a perpetual scene of misfortunes as they have since gone through by the oppression of landlords, the impossibility of paying rent without money or trade, the want of common sustenance, with neither house nor clothes to cover them from the inclemencies of the weather, and the most inevitable prospect of entailing the like or greater miseries upon their breed for ever.

I profess, in the sincerity of my heart, that I have not the 33 least personal interest in endeavoring to promote this necessary work, having no other motive than the public good of my country, by advancing our trade, providing for infants, relieving the poor, and giving some pleasure to the rich. I have no children by which I can propose to get a single penny; the youngest being nine years old, and my wife past child-bearing.

Content

1. What is the overt thesis of Swift's essay? What is its implied (and real) thesis? In what ways do these theses differ?
2. What are the primary aims and values of the narrator of the essay? Identify the economic advantages of his proposal that he offers in paragraphs 9–16. How do the narrator's alleged aims and values differ from the aims and values of Swift as the essay's author?
3. What do the advantages that the narrator offers for his proposal (¶ 21–26) reveal about the social and economic conditions of Ireland when Swift was writing?
4. Why is it a "very knowing *American*" who has assured the narrator of the suitability of year-old infants for food (¶ 9)?
5. Swift as the author of the essay expects his readers to respond to the narrator's cold economic arguments on a humane, moral level. What might such an appropriate response be?

Strategies/Structures

1. What persona (a created character) does the speaker of Swift's essay have? How are readers to know that this character is not Swift himself?
2. Why does the narrator use so many mathematical computations throughout? How do they reinforce his economic argument? How do they enhance the image of his cold-bloodedness?
3. Why did Swift choose to present his argument indirectly rather than overtly? What advantages does this indirect, consistently ironic technique provide? What disadvantages does it have (for instance, do you think Swift's readers are likely to believe he really advocated eating babies)?

Language

1. What is the prevailing tone of the essay? How does it undermine what the narrator says? How does the tone reinforce Swift's implied meaning?
2. Why does Swift say "a child just dropped from its dam" (¶ 4) instead of "just born from his mother"? What other language reinforces the animalistic associations (see, for instance, "breeders" in ¶ 17)?
3. In paragraph 21 Swift refers to Roman Catholics by the common term "papists." What clues does the context provide as to whether this usage is complimentary or derogatory? How does this emphasize the sense of a split between the English Anglican landowners and the Irish Catholic tenants that prevails throughout the essay?

For Writing

1. Write a modest proposal of your own. Pick some problem that you think needs to be solved, and propose, for a critical audience, a radical solution—perhaps a dramatic way to bring about world peace, preserve endangered species, dispose of chemical or nuclear waste, or use genetic engineering.

2. Write an essay in which a created character, a narrative persona, speaks ironically (as Swift's narrator does) about your subject. The character's values should be at variance with the values you and your audience share. For instance, if you want to propose stiff penalties for drunk driving, your narrator could be a firm advocate of drinking, and of driving without restraint, and could be shown driving unsafely while under the influence of alcohol, indifferent to the dangers.

LYNDA BARRY

Lynda Barry (born, 1956), daughter of a Filipino mother and an American father, grew up in an interracial neighborhood in Seattle. She told an interviewer, "Anybody who was coming from the Philippines would stay with us or with one of our [numerous] relatives. There was always a lot of commotion in the house, mostly in the kitchen. We didn't have a set dinner or lunch or breakfast time; when we wanted to eat there was always food on the stove. . . . At the time it was a little frustrating for me, because I looked to all the world like a regular little white American kid, but at home we were eating real different food and there was sometimes octopus in the refrigerator and stuff that was scary looking to my friends. . . . We ate with our hands, and when you say that, people think that you're also squatting on the floor . . . but it wasn't like that. There's a whole etiquette to the way that you eat with your hands, just like you hold a fork. And it was lively and unusual, an atmosphere where I . . . could pretty much do whatever I wanted to do."

As "The Sanctuary of School" indicates, "drawing came to mean everything" to the little girl who grew up to be a cartoonist. Nevertheless, when she began Evergreen State College she "wanted to be a fine artist," she says. "Cartoons to me were really base." Then she realized that her drawings could make her friends laugh, and shortly after she graduated, in 1978, she created "Ernie Pook's Comeek," a wry, witty, and feminist strip now syndicated in over sixty newspapers in the United States, Canada, Russia, and Hungary. Barry has compiled her eighth comic collection, *It's So Magic,* (1994); has written her second novel, *Cruddy* (1997); and is doing commentaries for National Public Radio's *Morning Edition.* Her first novel, *The Good Times Are Killing Me,* was published in 1988. Like many satirists, Barry cares deeply about her subjects, as illustrated in her compassionate plea for social justice for children that permeates "The Sanctuary of School," first published in the *New York Times* Education Section, January 5, 1992.

The Sanctuary of School

1   I was 7 years old the first time I snuck out of the house in the dark. It was winter and my parents had been fighting all night. They were short on money and long on relatives who kept "temporarily" moving into our house because they had nowhere else to go.

2   My brother and I were used to giving up our bedroom. We slept on the couch, something we actually liked because it put us that much closer to the light of our lives, our television.

3   At night when everyone was asleep, we lay on our pillows watching it with the sound off. We watched Steve Allen's mouth moving. We watched Johnny Carson's mouth moving. We watched movies filled with gangsters shooting machine guns into packed rooms, dying solders hurling a last grenade and beautiful women crying at windows. Then the sign-off finally came and we tried to sleep.

4   The morning I snuck out, I woke up filled with a panic about needing to get to school. The sun wasn't quite up yet but my anxiety was so fierce that I just got dressed, walked quietly across the kitchen and let myself out the back door.

5   It was quiet outside. Stars were still out. Nothing moved and no one was in the street. It was as if someone had turned the sound off on the world.

I walked the alley, breaking thin ice over the puddles with   6
my shoes. I didn't know why I was walking to school in the dark.
I didn't think about it. All I knew was a feeling of panic, like the
panic that strikes kids when they realize they are lost.

That feeling eased the moment I turned the corner and saw the   7.
dark outline of my school at the top of the hill. My school was
made up of about 15 nondescript portable classrooms set down
on a fenced concrete lot in a rundown Seattle neighborhood, but
it had the most beautiful view of the Cascade Mountains. You
could see them from anywhere on the playfield and you could see
them from the windows of my classroom—Room 2.

I walked over to the monkey bars and hooked my arms   8
around the cold metal. I stood for a long time just looking across
Rainier Valley. The sky was beginning to whiten and I could hear
a few birds.

In a perfect world my absence at home would not have gone   9
unnoticed. I would have had two parents in a panic to locate me,
instead of two parents in a panic to locate an answer to the hard
question of survival during a deep financial and emotional crisis.

But in an overcrowded and unhappy home, it's incredibly   10
easy for any child to slip away. The high levels of frustration,
depression and anger in my house made my brother and me invisible. We were children with the sound turned off. And for us,
as for the steadily increasing number of neglected children in this
country, the only place where we could count on being noticed
was at school.

"Hey there, young lady. Did you forget to go home last   11
night?" It was Mr. Gunderson, our janitor, whom we all loved. He
was nice and he was funny and he was old with white hair, thick
glasses and an unbelievable number of keys. I could hear them
jingling as he walked across the playfield. I felt incredibly happy
to see him.

He let me push his wheeled garbage can between the differ-   12
ent portables as he unlocked each room. He let me turn on the
lights and raise the window shades and I saw my school slowly
come to life. I saw Mrs. Holman, our school secretary, walk into
the office without her orange lipstick on yet. She waved.

13   I saw the fifth-grade teacher, Mr. Cunningham, walking under the breezeway eating a hard roll. He waved.

14   And I saw my teacher, Mrs. Claire LeSane, walking toward us in a red coat and calling my name in a very happy and surprised way, and suddenly my throat got tight and my eyes stung and I ran toward her crying. It was something that surprised us both.

15   It's only thinking about it now, 28 years later, that I realize I was crying from relief. I was with my teacher, and in a while I was going to sit at my desk, with my crayons and pencils and books and classmates all around me, and for the next six hours I was going to enjoy a thoroughly secure, warm and stable world. It was a world I absolutely relied on. Without it, I don't know where I would have gone that morning.

16   Mrs. LeSane asked me what was wrong and when I said "Nothing," she seemingly left it at that. But she asked me if I would carry her purse for her, an honor above all honors, and she asked if I wanted to come into Room 2 early and paint.

17   She believed in the natural healing power of painting and drawing for troubled children. In the back of her room there was always a drawing table and an easel with plenty of supplies, and sometimes during the day she would come up to you for what seemed like no good reason and quietly ask if you wanted to go to the back table and "make some pictures for Mrs. LeSane." We all had a chance at it—to sit apart from the class for a while to paint, draw and silently work out impossible problems on 11 × 17 sheets of newsprint.

18   Drawing came to mean everything to me. At the back table in Room 2, I learned to build myself a life preserver that I could carry into my home.

19   We all know that a good education system saves lives, but the people of this country are still told that cutting the budget for public schools is necessary, that poor salaries for teachers are all we can manage and that art, music and all creative activities must be the first to go when times are lean.

20   Before- and after-school programs are cut and we are told that public schools are not made for baby-sitting children. If parents are neglectful temporarily or permanently, for whatever reason, it's

certainly sad, but their unlucky children must fend for themselves. Or slip through the cracks. Or wander in a dark night alone.

We are told in a thousand ways that not only are public schools not important, but that the children who attend them, the children who need them most, are not important either. We leave them to learn from the blind eye of a television, or to the mercy of "a thousand points of light" that can be as far away as stars. 21

I was lucky. I had Mrs. LeSane. I had Mr. Gunderson. I had an abundance of art supplies. And I had a particular brand of neglect in my home that allowed me to slip away and get to them. But what about the rest of the kids who weren't as lucky? What happened to them? 22

By the time the bell rang that morning I had finished my drawing and Mrs. LeSane pinned it up on the special bulletin board she reserved for drawings from the back table. It was the same picture I always drew—a sun in the corner of a blue sky over a nice house with flowers all around it. 23

Mrs. LeSane asked us to please stand, face the flag, place our right hands over our hearts and say the Pledge of Allegiance. Children across the country do it faithfully. I wonder now when the country will face its children and say a pledge right back. 24

Content

1. What is the point of calling school a "sanctuary" (in the title)? How does Barry reinforce this image throughout the essay? Identify some of the life-saving features of Barry's second grade. Is Barry's view likely to convince even those readers whose elementary school experiences were quite different from hers, for instance, readers who regarded school as a form of prison or punishment?

2. Barry tells a personal story to make a general point about the values and economic priorities of the entire country. What is her point? Is it appropriate to make such a sweeping generalization on the basis of a single incident from one person's experience?

Strategies/Structures

1. How does Barry manage to tell an extremely painful and moving tale without lapsing into either sentimentality (emotion disproportionate to the subject) or self-pity?

2. Barry compresses her family history into a single sentence: "[My parents] were short on money and long on relatives who kept 'temporarily' moving into our house because they had nowhere else to go" (¶ 1). What is the effect of reading the rest of the essay through the lens of this statement? What additional dimensions does the essay's opening sentence add: "I was 7 years old the first time I snuck out of the house in the dark" (¶ 1)?

3. By analogy with the sentence quoted in question 2 above, are readers to believe that Barry compresses her childhood into this story of a single morning in second grade? Why or why not?

4. Barry explains, "(Mrs. LeSane) asked me if I would carry her purse for her, an honor above all honors, and she asked if I wanted to come into Room 2 early and paint" (¶ 16). She expects her readers to interpret this and the entire piece from two perspectives: that of the seven-year-old child who experienced "the sanctuary of school," and their own viewpoint as adults. Is this expectation justified? What does Barry do to reinforce this dual perspective? (See Language question 1 below.)

Language

1. If Barry's conversational language occasionally sounds childlike, "I snuck out of the house" (¶ 1), "[Mr. Gunderson] was nice and he was funny and he was old with white hair . . ." (¶ 11), what features of her vocabulary, sentence structure, and point of view remind us that "The Sanctuary of School" is written by an adult and for adult readers?

2. "The Sanctuary of School" is full of natural symbols. Among these are watching TV with the sound off (¶ 3)—echoed in "We were children with the sound turned off" (¶ 10); "walking to school in the dark" (¶ 6) and watching the sun rise over the "beautiful view of the Cascade Mountains" (¶ 7); seeing her teacher (is it a happy accident or Barry's invention that she was named "Claire LeSane"?) "calling my name in a very happy and surprised way" (¶ 14); saying the Pledge of Allegiance (¶ 24). Explain the literal and symbolic meanings of these and others in the essay.

For Writing

1. Tell a story of your own experience—as a child, teenager, or adult—that throughout implies a social or political message. Although your message may be familiar to your audience, as Barry's is, the story itself should render the experience in a new and meaningful way. Select details to reinforce your point, but don't preach.

2. Write an essay that employs several natural symbols (see Language question 2, above) or an elaboration of a single natural symbol to make

a point about which you can generalize (see Ruffin, "Mama's Smoke" [pp. 121–132] and Swanson, "The Turning Point" [pp. 229–232]).

TERRY TEMPEST WILLIAMS

A fifth-generation Utah Mormon, Williams (born, 1955) earned a bachelor's and a master's degree in environmental education from the University of Utah. Her writings reflect her intense commitment, intellectual and spiritual, to family and to place, particularly the natural environment. *The Book of Mormon,* she explains, "taught me the power of story because [it] is one story after another. It has taught me the power of a homeland, that place matters to a people, that each individual is entitled to [his or her] own personal vision."

Williams's best known work is *Refuge: An Unnatural History of Family and Place* (1991), in which "The Clan of One-Breasted Women" is the epilogue; others include *Desert Quartet: An Erotic Landscape* (1995) and *An Unspoken Hunger: Stories from the Field* (1994). *Refuge* began in 1983 when Williams's mother was dying of ovarian cancer, and for respite from the hospital Williams drove to a favorite bird refuge, only to find it being flooded by the Great Salt Lake. "I realized devastation knows no boundaries. The landscape of my childhood and the landscape of my family—the two things I had always regarded as bedrock—were now subject to change," says Williams. The "family moving through illness together" and "being with the birds . . . allowed me to discover the story that was there." Using "memory as a tool for reflection," Williams proceeded to uncover many layers in the process of writing the book. The process she describes is characteristic of many nonfiction writers: "The actual living of it, the recording of it in my journals, then letting the whole story steep like a hot cup of tea." Then writing down the exact details "in a nonperfunctory way . . . the lake levels, the dates of [her] mother's illness, literally . . . an outline of time." "Then I had to go back," says Williams, and say, "What are the ideas here? What is the essence here? What are the universalities? And what is my place within this story? Where is my narrative apart from my mother's and grandmother's stories?" That these stories coalesce and intertwine is apparent in the following narrative.

The Clan of One-Breasted Women

Epilogue

1   I belong to a Clan of One-Breasted Women. My mother, my grandmothers, and six aunts have all had mastectomies. Seven are dead. The two who survive have just completed rounds of chemotherapy and radiation.

2   I've had my own problems: two biopsies for breast cancer and a small tumor between my ribs diagnosed as a "borderline malignancy."

3   This is my family history.

4   Most statistics tell us breast cancer is genetic, hereditary, with rising percentages attached to fatty diets, childlessness, or becoming pregnant after thirty. What they don't say is living in Utah may be the greatest hazard of all.

5   We are a Mormon family with roots in Utah since 1847. The "word of wisdom" in my family aligned us with good foods—no coffee, no tea, tobacco, or alcohol. For the most part, our women were finished having their babies by the time they were thirty. And only one faced breast cancer prior to 1960. Traditionally, as a group of people, Mormons have a low rate of cancer.

6   Is our family a cultural anomaly? The truth is, we didn't think about it. Those who did, usually the men, simply said, "bad genes." The women's attitude was stoic. Cancer was part of life. On February 16, 1971, the eve of my mother's surgery, I accidentally picked up the telephone and overheard her ask my grandmother what she could expect.

7   "Diane, it is one of the most spiritual experiences you will ever encounter."

8   I quietly put down the receiver.

9   Two days later, my father took my brothers and me to the hospital to visit her. She met us in the lobby in a wheelchair. No bandages were visible. I'll never forget her radiance, the way she held herself in a purple velvet robe, and how she gathered us around her.

10   "Children, I am fine. I want you to know I felt the arms of God around me."

11   We believed her. My father cried. Our mother, his wife, was thirty-eight years old.

A little over a year after Mother's death, Dad and I were   12
having dinner together. He had just returned from St. George,
where the Tempest Company was completing the gas lines that
would service southern Utah. He spoke of his love for the country, the sandstoned landscape, bare-boned and beautiful. He had
just finished hiking the Kolob trail in Zion National Park. We got
caught up in reminiscing, recalling with fondness our walk up
Angel's Landing on his fiftieth birthday and the years our family
had vacationed there.

Over dessert, I shared a recurring dream of mine. I told my   13
father that for years, as long as I could remember, I saw this flash
of light in the night in the desert—that this image had so permeated my being that I could not venture south without seeing it
again, on the horizon, illuminating buttes and mesas.

"You did see it," he said.   14

"Saw what?"   15

"The bomb. The cloud. We were driving home from River-   16
side, California. You were sitting on Diane's lap. She was pregnant. In fact, I remember the day, September 7, 1957. We had just
gotten out of the Service. We were driving north, past Las Vegas.
It was an hour or so before dawn, when this explosion went off.
We not only heard it, but felt it. I thought the oil tanker in front of
us had blown up. We pulled over and suddenly, rising from the
desert floor, we saw it, clearly, this golden-stemmed cloud, the
mushroom. The sky seemed to vibrate with an eerie pink glow.
Within a few minutes, a light ash was raining on the car."

I stared at my father.   17

"I thought you knew that," he said. "It was a common   18
occurrence in the fifties."

It was at this moment that I realized the deceit I had been   19
living under. Children growing up in the American Southwest,
drinking contaminated milk from contaminated cows, even from
the contaminated breasts of their mothers, my mother—members,
years later, of the Clan of One-Breasted Women.

It is a well-known story in the Desert West, "The Day We   20
Bombed Utah," or more accurately, the years we bombed Utah:
above ground atomic testing in Nevada took place from January
27, 1951 through July 11, 1962. Not only were the winds blowing
north covering "low-use segments of the population" with fallout
and leaving sheep dead in their tracks, but the climate was right.

The United States of the 1950s was red, white, and blue. The Korean War was raging. McCarthyism was rampant. Ike was it, and the cold war was hot. If you were against nuclear testing, you were for a communist regime.

21   Much has been written about this "American nuclear tragedy." Public health was secondary to national security. The Atomic Energy Commissioner, Thomas Murray, said, "Gentlemen, we must not let anything interfere with this series of tests, nothing."

22   Again and again, the American public was told by its government, in spite of burns, blisters, and nausea, "It has been found that the tests may be conducted with adequate assurance of safety under conditions prevailing at the bombing reservations." Assuaging public fears was simply a matter of public relations. "Your best action," an Atomic Energy Commission booklet read, "is not to be worried about fallout." A news release typical of the times stated, "We find no basis for concluding that harm to any individual has resulted from radioactive fallout."

23   On August 30, 1979, during Jimmy Carter's presidency, a suit was filed, *Irene Allen v. The United States of America*. Mrs. Allen's case was the first on an alphabetical list of twenty-four test cases, representative of nearly twelve hundred plaintiffs seeking compensation from the United States government for cancers caused by nuclear testing in Nevada.

24   Irene Allen lived in Hurricane, Utah. She was the mother of five children and had been widowed twice. Her first husband, with their two oldest boys, had watched the tests from the roof of the local high school. He died of leukemia in 1956. Her second husband died of pancreatic cancer in 1978.

25   In a town meeting conducted by Utah Senator Orrin Hatch, shortly before the suit was filed, Mrs. Allen said, "I am not blaming the government, I want you to know that, Senator Hatch. But I thought if my testimony could help in any way so this wouldn't happen again to any of the generations coming up after us . . . I am happy to be here this day to bear testimony of this."

26   God-fearing people. This is just one story in an anthology of thousands.

27   On May 10, 1984, Judge Bruce S. Jenkins handed down his opinion. Ten of the plaintiffs were awarded damages. It was the

first time a federal court had determined that nuclear tests had been the cause of cancers. For the remaining fourteen test cases, the proof of causation was not sufficient. In spite of the split decision, it was considered a landmark ruling. It was not to remain so for long.

In April 1987, the Tenth Circuit Court of Appeals overturned 28 Judge Jenkins's ruling on the ground that the United States was protected from suit by the legal doctrine of sovereign immunity, a centuries-old idea from England in the days of absolute monarchs.

In January 1988, the Supreme Court refused to review the 29 Appeals Court decision. To our court system it does not matter whether the United States government was irresponsible, whether it lied to its citizens, or even that citizens died from the fallout of nuclear testing. What matters is that our government is immune: "The King can do no wrong."

In Mormon culture, authority is respected, obedience is 30 revered, and independent thinking is not. I was taught as a young girl not to "make waves" or "rock the boat."

"Just let it go," Mother would say. "You know how you feel, 31 that's what counts."

For many years, I have done just that—listened, observed, 32 and quietly formed my own opinions, in a culture that rarely asks questions because it has all the answers. But one by one, I have watched the women in my family die common, heroic deaths. We sat in waiting rooms hoping for good news, but always receiving the bad. I cared for them, bathed their scarred bodies, and kept their secrets. I watched beautiful women become bald as Cytoxan, cisplatin, and Adriamycin were injected into their veins. I held their foreheads as they vomited green-black bile, and I shot them with morphine when the pain became inhuman. In the end, I witnessed their last peaceful breaths, becoming a midwife to the rebirth of their souls.

The price of obedience has become too high. 33

The fear and inability to question authority that ultimately 34 killed rural communities in Utah during atmospheric testing of atomic weapons is the same fear I saw in my mother's body. Sheep. Dead sheep. The evidence is buried.

I cannot prove that my mother, Diane Dixon Tempest, or 35 my grandmothers, Lettie Romney Dixon and Kathryn Blackett

Tempest, along with my aunts developed cancer from nuclear fallout in Utah. But I can't prove they didn't.

36   My father's memory was correct. The September blast we drove through in 1957 was part of Operation Plumbbob, one of the most intensive series of bomb tests to be initiated. The flash of light in the night in the desert, which I had always thought was a dream, developed into a family nightmare. It took fourteen years, from 1957 to 1971, for cancer to manifest in my mother—the same time, Howard L. Andrews, an authority in radioactive fallout at the National Institutes of Health, says radiation cancer requires to become evident. The more I learn about what it means to be a "downwinder," the more questions I drown in.

37   What I do know, however, is that as a Mormon woman of the fifth generation of Latter-day Saints, I must question everything, even if it means losing my faith, even if it means becoming a member of a border tribe among my own people. Tolerating blind obedience in the name of patriotism or religion ultimately takes our lives.

38   When the Atomic Energy Commission described the country north of the Nevada Test Site as "virtually uninhabited desert terrain," my family and the birds at Great Salt Lake were some of the "virtual uninhabitants."

39   One night, I dreamed women from all over the world circled a blazing fire in the desert. They spoke of change, how they hold the moon in their bellies and wax and wane with its phases. They mocked the presumption of even-tempered beings and made promises that they would never fear the witch inside themselves. The women danced wildly as sparks broke away from the flames and entered the night sky as stars.

40   And they sang a song given to them by Shoshone grandmothers:

Ah ne nah, nah	Consider the rabbits
nin nah nah—	How gently they walk on the earth—
ah ne nah, nah	Consider the rabbits
nin nah nah—	How gently they walk on the earth—
Nyaga mutzi	We remember them
oh ne nay—	We can walk gently also—
Nyaga mutzi	We remember them
oh ne nay—	We can walk gently also—

The women danced and drummed and sang for weeks, preparing themselves for what was to come. They would reclaim the desert for the sake of their children, for the sake of the land.

A few miles downwind from the fire circle, bombs were 41 being tested. Rabbits felt the tremors. Their soft leather pads on paws and feet recognized the shaking sands, while the roots of mesquite and sage were smoldering. Rocks were hot from the inside out and dust devils hummed unnaturally. And each time there was another nuclear test, ravens watched the desert heave. Stretch marks appeared. The land was losing its muscle.

The women couldn't bear it any longer. They were mothers. 42 They had suffered labor pains but always under the promise of birth. The red hot pains beneath the desert promised death only, as each bomb became a stillborn. A contract had been made and broken between human beings and the land. A new contract was being drawn by the women, who understood the fate of the earth as their own.

Under the cover of darkness, ten women slipped under a 43 barbed-wire fence and entered the contaminated country. They were trespassing. They walked toward the town of Mercury, in moonlight, taking their cues from coyote, kit fox, antelope squirrel, and quail. They moved quietly and deliberately through the maze of Joshua trees. When a hint of daylight appeared they rested, drinking tea and sharing their rations of food. The women closed their eyes. The time had come to protest with the heart, that to deny one's genealogy with the earth was to commit treason against one's soul.

At dawn, the women draped themselves in mylar, wrapping 44 long streamers of silver plastic around their arms to blow in the breeze. They wore clear masks, that became the faces of humanity. And when they arrived at the edge of Mercury, they carried all the butterflies of a summer day in their wombs. They paused to allow their courage to settle.

The town that forbids pregnant women and children to 45 enter because of radiation risks was asleep. The women moved through the streets as winged messengers, twirling around each other in slow motion, peeking inside homes and watching the easy sleep of men and women. They were astonished by such stillness and periodically would utter a shrill note or low cry just to verify life.

46   The residents finally awoke to these strange apparitions. Some simply stared. Others called authorities, and in time, the women were apprehended by wary soldiers dressed in desert fatigues. They were taken to a white, square building on the other edge of Mercury. When asked who they were and why they were there, the women replied, "We are mothers and we have come to reclaim the desert for our children."

47   The soldiers arrested them. As the ten women were blindfolded and handcuffed, they began singing:

> You can't forbid us everything
> You can't forbid us to think—
> You can't forbid our tears to flow
> And you can't stop the songs that we sing.

The women continued to sing louder and louder, until they heard the voices of their sisters moving across the mesa:

> Ah ne nah, nah
> nin nah nah—
> Ah ne nah, nah
> nin nah nah—
> Nyaga mutzi
> oh ne nay—
> Nyaga mutzi
> oh ne nay—

48   "Call for reinforcements," one soldier said.

"We have," interrupted one woman, "we have—and you have no idea of our numbers."

49   I crossed the line at the Nevada Test Site and was arrested with nine other Utahns for trespassing on military lands. They are still conducting nuclear tests in the desert. Ours was an act of civil disobedience. But as I walked toward the town of Mercury, it was more than a gesture of peace. It was a gesture on behalf of the Clan of One-Breasted Women.

50   As one officer cinched the handcuffs around my wrists, another frisked my body. She found a pen and a pad of paper tucked inside my left boot.

51   "And these?" she asked sternly.

"Weapons," I replied.

Our eyes met. I smiled. She pulled the leg of my trousers 53
back over my boot.

"Step forward, please," she said as she took my arm. 54

We were booked under an afternoon sun and bused to 55
Tonopah, Nevada. It was a two-hour ride. This was familiar country. The Joshua trees standing their ground had been named by my
ancestors, who believed they looked like prophets pointing west
to the Promised Land. These were the same trees that bloomed
each spring, flowers appearing like white flames in the Mojave.
And I recalled a full moon in May, when Mother and I had walked
among them, flushing out mourning doves and owls.

The bus stopped short of town. We were released. 56

The officials thought it was a cruel joke to leave us stranded 57
in the desert with no way to get home. What they didn't realize
was that we were home, soul-centered and strong, women who
recognized the sweet smell of sage as fuel for our spirits.

Content

1. Identify and explain the polarities that Williams illustrates in this
essay: natural versus man-made; health versus breast cancer; man's domination versus woman's submission; moral righteousness (including civil
disobedience) versus legalities.

2. Since Williams's sentiments are clearly predisposed to favor women
on these issues, how does—or can—she expect men to be sympathetic
readers of her essay?

3. In what ways do the women of this Clan exhibit strength, even while
their bodies are vulnerable to breast cancer?

4. How does Williams link breast cancer to the natural wildlife in the
Utah desert (see, for instance, ¶s 34 and 38)?

Strategies/Structures

1. Why does Williams begin with a medical history of the adult women
in her family (¶s 1–2)? She says, "This is my family history" (¶ 3); why
does she focus on breast cancer and on no other aspect of her family's
lives and deaths?

2. Why has Williams included the episode of the "women from all over
the world" drumming, and dancing and singing "a song given to them
by Shoshone grandmothers" (¶s 39–48)?

3. Williams says she "dreamed" the protest episode, yet her account seems so realistic readers are likely to believe it really happened: "Rabbits felt the tremors" from the nuclear bomb testing. "Their soft leather pads on paws and feet recognized the shaking sands" (¶ 41). What other devices of verisimilitude (apparent truth) does Williams use? Do they harmonize with the more mythic elements of her story? Does it matter whether we believe the dream or not?

Language

1. Williams invents a metaphorical label for herself and her female ancestors, the "Clan of One-Breasted Women." In what ways and for what purposes does she use this label? What are some of the differences between using the label and simply saying "my female ancestors"?
2. Since this essay is, in part, a protest against the nuclear testing that took her mother's life, why does Williams quote her grandmother, also stricken with breast cancer, telling her mother "'Diane, [the mastectomy] is one of the most spiritual experiences you will ever encounter'" (¶ 7). Why does she show her mother's "radiance" after the operation (¶ 9)?

For Writing

1. Write an essay in which you link a natural phenomenon to an unnatural one. Show (or imply) how the two are related. Are they mutually beneficial? Or does one phenomenon thrive at the expense of the other? Is that desirable?
2. Is breast cancer exclusively, even primarily, a women's issue? Explain, using evidence from this essay and from other sources, as well. Or pick some other social issue with political implications for a particular group—children, for example—and argue the case for an audience of general readers, men and women alike.

AMY JO KEIFER

> Keifer was born in 1972, and grew up on her family's farm in Bangor, Pennsylvania. She wrote "The Death of a Farm" in 1991 at American University, Washington, D.C., in a freshman composition course, "Writing About Contemporary Issues." Her instruc-

tor required all his students to submit a piece of writing to either the *Washington Post* or the *New York Times,* and promised an A for the semester to anyone whose work got published. However, he originally gave Keifer an F on the paper; at three pages it was too short, he said, for an op-ed (opposite the editorial page) piece.

Keifer trusted her own judgment, a good lesson for the readers of *The Essay Connection.* Although the *Times* receives hundreds of op-ed submissions each month, mostly by experienced writers and professionals in various fields, Keifer submitted her paper to the *Times* exactly as she had written it. It was published as an op-ed article on June 30, 1991, and the following semester the instructor changed her grade to an A. In 1993 Keifer graduated from American University with a B.A. in international relations, and a strong interest in multicultural education and in the agricultural aspects of international trade.

"The Death of a Farm" was read by many people in the United States Department of Agriculture, and landed Keifer a summer internship on the *Express-Times* (Easton, Pennsylvania). Keifer's essay indeed proves that her personal experience has given her an expert's understanding of her subject. "It was easy to write," she says, "because it's a subject I know a lot about, although it was hard to get the tone right because I am so emotionally involved with the subject. My younger sister doesn't like the essay because she doesn't want to think that the farm is dying. My parents like the essay, however, because it represents our strong attachment to the land." She continues, "We are near the Delaware Water Gap, and the land is beautiful at all seasons, especially in the fall. The farm's status today is as it was six years ago. My younger brother will keep the family farm going, but he will have to work at a full-time job elsewhere in order to do so."

❄ *The Death of a Farm*

I am a farmer's daughter. I am also a 4-H member, breeder and   1
showman of sheep and showman of cattle. My family's farm is dying and I have watched it, and my family, suffer.

Our eastern Pennsylvania farm is a mere 60 acres. The green   2
rolling hills and forested land are worth a minimum of $300,000

to developers, but no longer provide my family with the means to survive. It's a condition called asset rich and cash poor, and it's a hard way of life.

3   My grandfather bought our farm when he and my grandmother were first married. He raised dairy cattle and harvested the land full time for more than 20 years. When he died, my father took over and changed the farm to beef cattle, horses and pigs, and kept the crops. But it wasn't enough to provide for a young family, so he took on a full-time job, too.

4   I can remember, when I was young, sitting on the fence with my sister and picking out a name for each calf. My sister's favorite cow was named Flower, and so we named her calves Buttercup, Daisy, Rose and Violet. Flower was the leader of a herd of more than 20. The only cattle left on our farm now are my younger sister's and brother's 4-H projects.

5   I can remember a huge tractor-trailer backed into the loading chute of our barn on days when more than 200 pigs had to be taken to market. That was before the prices went down and my father let the barn go empty rather than take on more debt.

6   I can remember my father riding on the tractor, larger than life, baling hay or planting corn. When prices started dropping, we began to rent some land to other farmers, so they could harvest from it. But prices have dropped so low this year there are no takers. The land will go unused; the tractor and the equipment have long since been sold off.

7   I don't remember the horses. I've seen a few pictures in which my father, slim and dark, is holding his newborn daughter on horseback amid a small herd. And I've heard stories of his delivering hay to farms all over the state, but I can't ever remember his loading up a truck to do it.

8   Piece by piece, our farm has deteriorated. We started breeding sheep and now have about 25 head, but they yield little revenue. My mother, who works as a registered nurse, once said something that will remain with me forever: "Your father works full time to support the farm. I work full time to support the family."

9   I've seen movies like "The River" and "Places in the Heart." They tell the real struggle. But people can leave a movie theater,

and there's a happy ending for them. There aren't many happy endings in a real farmer's life. I was reared hearing that hard work paid off, while seeing that it didn't. My younger brother would like to take over the farm some day, but I'm not sure it will hold on much longer. Its final breath is near.

Content

1. Keifer's family history is embedded in the story of the family farm. Explain how they are interrelated.
2. What's the point of Keifer's mother's observation, "Your father works full time to support the farm. I work full time to support the family" (¶ 8)?
3. Why is Keifer telling this story? To whom is she telling it? Is she trying to influence any individual action? Public policy? Is this a cautionary tale, a warning? Why would an urban newspaper, the *New York Times*, print this story?

Strategies/Structures

1. Why is it important for Keifer to state her credentials at the very outset of the essay?
2. Is it appropriate for Keifer to tip her hand in the second sentence ("My family's farm is dying and I have watched it, and my family, suffer" [¶ 1])? Or would the essay be more effective if she waited until the end, to make this the inevitable conclusion to the series of steps of the progressive deterioration of the farm which in fact she presents as the essay proceeds?
3. Keifer provides a series of snapshots of the farm and farm life. Identify some and show how they reinforce her case.

Language

1. What is the effect of beginning paragraphs 4, 5, and 6 with "I can remember"? And then of varying this pattern with "I don't remember the horses"?
2. In what ways does Keifer's simple, unadorned language convince us that she's "been there"? How does that language put her readers there as well?

For Writing

1. Keifer says, "I was reared hearing that hard work paid off, while seeing that it didn't" (¶ 9). Tell a story whose thesis contradicts conventional wisdom, as Keifer's does. Since your readers will probably be prepared, initially, to accept the conventional view, you'll have to use signals throughout (incidents, natural symbols, connotative language) that point in the opposite direction.

2. Write an essay to protest "the death of . . ." a subject close to your heart, though not necessarily close to your reader's heart or conscience. (This might be an endangered species; a vanishing way of life; a lost art or profession; a major change in the way people do things—for instance, have E-mail and the telephone meant the death of personal letters? Or of even face-to-face conversations? Avoid sentimentality.

Additional Topics for Writing *Appealing to Emotion and Ethics*

(For process strategies, see page 634)

Write an essay that attempts to persuade one of the following audiences through a combination of appeals to reason, emotion, and ethics.

1. To someone you'd like for a friend, fiancé(e), or spouse: Love me.
2. To an athlete, or to an athletic coach: Play according to the rules, even when the referee (umpire, or other judge) isn't looking.
3. To a prospective employer: I'm the best person for the job. Hire me.
4. To a police officer: I shouldn't receive this traffic ticket. Or, to a judge or jury: I am innocent of the crime of which I'm accused.
5 To the voters: Vote for me (or for a candidate of my choice).
6. To admissions officers of a particular college, university, or of a program within that institution (such as medical or law school, graduate program, or a division with a special undergraduate degree): Let me in.
7. To the prospective buyer of something you want to sell or service you can perform: Buy this.
8. To an audience prejudiced against a particular group or simply to a majority audience: *X* is beautiful. (*X* may be black, yellow, Hispanic, female, a member of a particular national or religious group . . .)
9. To an antagonist on any issue: As Joan Didion says, *"Listen to me, see it my way, change your mind."*
10. To people engaging in behavior that threatens their lives or their health: Stop doing *X* (or stop doing *X* to excess)—smoking, drinking, overeating, undereating, or using drugs. Or: Start doing *X*—exercising regularly, using bike helmets or seatbelts, planning for the future by getting—an education, a stable job, an investment plan, a retirement plan . . .
11. Pick a work of fiction or nonfiction whose content intrigues you and whose style you admire and write a brief parody (probably involving considerable exaggeration) of it to show your understanding of the content and your appreciation of the style.
12. Write a satire to argue implicity for a point, as Swift does in "A Modest Proposal" (pp. 637–645). Use whatever techniques seem appropriate, such as creating a character who does the talking for you; setting a scene (such as of pathos or misery) that helps make your point; using a tone involving understatement, irony, or exaggeration. Be sure to supply enough clues to enable your readers to understand what you really mean.

15 | *Critical Argument: Textual Analysis*

There are as many ways of reading and writing as there are readers and writers. There's no way we can read and write with total objectivity, for each of us brings to a text private as well as public associations, derived from our culture, our beliefs and values, and our personal experience. Our reading and writing about families, for instance, is inevitably affected by the family we grew up in (and its changes over time) and by the family we're currently part of or hope to have. It is also affected by our firsthand knowledge of other people's families; our cultural sense of what a family ought to be, gleaned, perhaps, from the Bible, the newspapers, and TV programs as diverse as *Friends* and *X-Files;* and our reading about families, ranging from psychology textbooks to novels to *King Lear.* So when we read Eudora Welty's and Paule Marshall's accounts of how their families influenced them as writers, or Scott Russell Sanders's description of his father under the destructive influence of alcohol, or Mark Twain's nostalgic re-creation of his Uncle John's farm, our response resonates with our own experiences. So it does when we read the opening lines of Tolstoy's *Anna Karenina,* "Happy families are all alike. Every unhappy family is unhappy in its own way." The meaning of any work of literature, fiction or nonfiction, resides both in the words on the page and in our interpretations—what we emphasize and endow with significance, what captures our hearts as well as our minds.

All writing is, to an extent, creative, for all writers of fiction and nonfiction alike, even makers of lists as in telephone books, seek to impose *order* and *structure* on materials, thoughts that might fastened to the page for the ear of the imagination. That is all that can save poetry from sing-song, all that can save prose from itself. (272–73)

Although *voice* is hard to pin down, it emerges as a sense of authority, honesty, and truth when the writing is fresh, individual—not suppressed by clichés or subdued by formulaic thinking. The *tone* of a writing conveys its mood or emotional temper. Though this may vary considerably even within a single work, an essay may have a dominant tone—objective, pleading, argumentative, playful, for instance, or a combination of compatible tones, like adjacent shades of the rainbow, optimistic and cheerful, or serious and sad, the prevailing tone of Lincoln's "Gettysburg Address" (p. 635). Voice, tone, sentence structure, and vocabulary combine to signal a work's degree of formality or informality. Although there is no necessary connection between formality of vocabulary and sentence complexity (including parallel and repeated structures—"of the people, by the people, for the people") or length, informal writing seems simpler in both—as if the author were conversing with the reader. Do you feel as if Mike Rose ("I Just Wanna Be Average"), Nancy Mairs ("On Being a Cripple"), and the student writers are talking directly to you? Formal writing, on the other hand, may sound impersonal, as it does in scientific and other types of academic writing (see Stephen Jay Gould's "Evolution as Fact and Theory" [pp. 513–522]). Or it may appear stylized, with its vocabulary a mixture of native and borrowed words, simple and elevated, contemporary and archaic, as Gilbert Highet notes in his own formal analysis of Lincoln's "Gettysburg Address."

Whether you are analyzing fiction or nonfiction of any sort, the following considerations may be helpful (see also the suggestions for reading essays [pp. 1–5]):

1. What is the genre (novel, play, story, poem, essay) of this writing? What is its subgenre or form (historical novel, romance, western . . .)?
2. In what ways does the author follow the conventions of the forms he or she is writing in? In what ways does the work depart from these? With what effects?
3. Why is the author writing this work? How can I tell?

otherwise appear random or haphazard. Although the order that results may seem natural, even inevitable, it is not inherent in the material (the telephone book doesn't necessarily *have* to proceed from A to Z); it is an artifact of the writer's imagination, an intellectual construct. We have seen throughout *The Essay Connection* what some of these structures are, such as various patterns for comparison and contrast or for argumentation. A *story* says E. M. Forster, is a narrative of events in a time sequence ("The king died, and then the queen died."), as distinguished from a *plot*, which reflects causes and their effects and consequences ("The king died, and then the queen died of grief."). Unlike a story, which can merely be recounted, a plot can be explained and interpreted. Margaret Atwood's "Fiction: Happy Endings" (pp. 704–707) reveals that even the same plot can have many variations and interpretations. This is also apparent from the ancient and contemporary Chinese *Cinderellas* included here (pp. 685–691), from Anne Sexton's poetic version (pp. 700–704), and from Ning Yu's essay, "The Nurturing Woman Rewarded: A Study of Two Chinese Cinderellas" (pp. 692–700), dealing with Freudian, Marxist, and cross-cultural interpretations of the Cinderella story.

All writers are concerned with *form;* any piece of writing, fiction or nonfiction, has to start somewhere, proceed for a while, and end somewhere else, whether it's a list, a ballad ("He was her man, but he done her wrong"), an argument, or a tale, tall or short. One major aspect of form is *emphasis,* as Gilbert Highet's analysis of "The Gettysburg Address" (pp. 674–681) makes clear. If you write with a word processor you're undoubtedly aware of how many times you *add, delete,* and *move* material, within sentences, paragraphs, entire works. Thus emphasis can derive from position; what comes first or last in any unit gets more emphasis than what's stuck in the middle. If you develop some points or characters more extensively than others, they will get the most emphasis from sheer bulk, but presumably from diversity and complexity as well. While longer units, on the whole, are more emphatic than shorter ones, epigrams and occasional one-sentence paragraphs can drive their point home with rapier efficiency: "Hypocrisy is the homage that vice pays to virtue."

Each genre and sub-genre usually has enough typical features of form to enable readers to distinguish it from other major types of writings. We recognize a *poem* by its short, metrical lines which are sometimes rhymed; and an *epic poem* by its long length and heroic subjects, in contrast to lyrics and songs, which are much shorter and not necessarily heroic. Anne Sexton's "Cinderella" (pp. 700–704) looks like a poem, though it is in free verse, irregular meter, and not rhymed. Sexton sets the rags-to-riches Cinderella story in a framework of similar stories, fairy tales all: "From toilets to riches," "From diapers to Dior./That story." We recognize a *play* by its format—an abundance of dialogue and division into acts and scenes. Though most of us understand a *novel* to be an extended fictional prose narrative representing a character or characters either in a static or developing state (the *plot* or *theme*), it can encompass a wide variety of forms, ranging from letters to stream-of-consciousness. Likewise, we recognize a *research article in the social or physical sciences* by its conventional pattern that (usually) begins with an abstract, a statement of the problem, followed (in some instances) by a review of the relevant professional research on the topic. It then proceeds to a step-by-step description of the research design and the methodology; a statement of research results; an analysis of the results; and a conclusion, sometimes augmented with suggestions for further research.

We read, as we write, according to what we understand to be the conventions of the genre, but even these conventions are susceptible to infinite variations, as Atwood's "Happy Endings" demonstrates. Yet as cultural anthropologist Clifford Geertz has observed in "Blurred Genres," the opening chapter of *Local Knowledge,* 1989, "there has been an enormous amount of genre mixing in intellectual life and recent years" as enormous changes occur in "the way we think about the way we think." Among the results are historical or philosophical inquiries blended with literary criticism (see Ning Yu's "The Nurturing Woman Rewarded: A Study of Two Chinese Cinderellas" [pp. 692–700]), scientific discussions resembling familiar essays (as in Lewis Thomas's work), and "nonfiction novels" such as Truman Capote's *In Cold Blood.* Indeed, a great many belletristic essays employ many of the techniques of fiction: development of character(s); use of dialogue; setting of scenes; presentation of social, cultural, intellectual, or other contexts through details of the characters' clothing, behavior, lifestyle, and so on—as, for instance, Joan Didion's "Marrying Absurd" (pp. 329–

333). These techniques are conspicuous in full-length *autobiography* and *personal essays* with an autobiographical emphasis, including "Under the Influence" (pp. 420–433) by Scott Russell Sanders, and Nancy Mairs's "On Being a Cripple" (pp. 472–485).

As readers and writers, we decide how to interpret what we read according to both the conventions of the form and our assumptions about whether we are reading fiction or nonfiction. Indeed, given the blurring of genres and the many characteristics that fiction and literary (or creative or belletristic) nonfiction share, our response to a particular personal writing, for instance, may not necessarily depend on its structural or stylistic features but on whether we believe it is true. If we believe a work to be, essentially, true, derived from facts that are verifiable independently of the text, we will read it as an autobiography. If, on the other hand, we believe the work to be drawn largely from the author's imagination, we will read and respond to it as fiction. Thus, we read Richard Wright's "The Power of Books" (pp. 409–418) from *Black Boy,* an angry, searing account of Wright's own life of deprivation and prejudice, as true. But we read Wright's equally angry, searing account of Bigger Thomas's life of deprivation and prejudice in *Native Son* as fiction, because although the events *could* have happened, we believe we are reading a work of fiction. Yet Wright has selected, shaped, and structured the materials in both works; he has presented characters, dialogue, scenes, motives in both. And both convey a "felt truth" reflective of emotional and psychological reality.

When we read and when we write critical analyses, we are also concerned with *style,* "as organic to the person doing the writing" says editor William Zinsser, as is one's hair. "Trying to add style is like adding a toupee." *Tone, voice,* and *choice of words* reflect the writer's character and personality, as well as his or her attitude toward the subject. In *A Way Out* Robert Frost addresses this matter of personal resonance:

A dramatic necessity goes deep into the nature of the sentence. Sentences are not different enough to hold the attention unless they are dramatic. No ingenuity of varying structure will do. All that can save them is the speaking tone of voice somehow entangled in the words and

4. For what audience(s) is the author writing? In what ways has the author accommodated this audience, through simplicity or complexity of language, supplying background information, anticipating objections to the expressed point of view? Or is the author essentially indifferent to the audience?

5. What is the author's approach to the subject—theoretical and abstract? Concrete and specific? Or some mixture? Is the language plain and simple? Figurative? Engaging? Does it suit the work's subject and tone?

6. Most important of all, what is my reaction to this work? Why do I like or dislike it, or does it simply leave me cold? Will I remember it? Recommend it to others? Reread it? Why?

GILBERT HIGHET

Highet took "all literature for his province." As Anthon Professor of Latin Language and Literature at Columbia University, where he taught from 1938 until retirement in 1972 (with time out for military service during World War II), he wrote and edited critical works on poetry, satire, literary history, criticism, classicism, and "the joy of teaching and learning." He wrote "the English language with affectionate ease," from a personal, enthusiastic, anecdotal perspective that charmed general readers and antagonized literary scholars who objected to his popular treatment of canonical works—as the erudite often do when laypeople are invited into their exclusive circle. Born in Glasgow, Scotland, in 1906, Highet emigrated to the United States in 1937, after an education at Glasgow and Oxford, from which he later received honorary degrees, as well. Among his most popular works are *The Classical Tradition: Greek and Roman Influences on Western Literature* (1949), *The Art of Teaching* (1950); and *The Anatomy of Satire* (1962). His last book, *The Immortal Profession: The Joy of Teaching and Learning,* was published two years before his death in 1978.

With the same understated eloquence and ease that Lincoln used in "The Gettysburg Address" (p. 635), Highet places the speech and the speaker in their biographical, historical, literary, and political contexts. Highet's knowledge of his subject is equaled by his love of Lincoln and profound respect for his work, indeed a work of art as well as oratory.

The Gettysburg Address

1   Fourscore and seven years ago . . .

2   These five words stand at the entrance to the best-known monument of American prose, one of the finest utterances in the entire language and surely one of the greatest speeches in all history. Greatness is like granite: it is molded in fire, and it lasts for many centuries.

3   Fourscore and seven years ago. . . . It is strange to think that President Lincoln was looking back to the 4th of July 1776, and that he and his speech are now further removed from us than he

himself was from George Washington and the Declaration of Independence. Fourscore and seven years before the Gettysburg Address, a small group of patriots signed the Declaration. Fourscore and seven years after the Gettysburg Address, it was the year 1950,[1] and that date is already receding rapidly into our troubled, adventurous, and valiant past.

Inadequately prepared and at first scarcely realized in its full importance, the dedication of the graveyard at Gettysburg was one of the supreme moments of American history. The battle itself had been a turning point of the war. On the 4th of July 1863, General Meade repelled Lee's invasion of Pennsylvania. Although he did not follow up his victory, he had broken one of the most formidable aggressive enterprises of the Confederate armies. Losses were heavy on both sides. Thousands of dead were left on the field, and thousands of wounded died in the hot days following the battle. At first, their burial was more or less haphazard; but thoughtful men gradually came to feel that an adequate burying place and memorial were required. These were established by an interstate commission that autumn, and the finest speaker in the North was invited to dedicate them. This was the scholar and statesman Edward Everett of Harvard. He made a good speech— which is still extant: not at all academic, it is full of close strategic analysis and deep historical understanding.

Lincoln was not invited to speak, at first. Although people knew him as an effective debater, they were not sure whether he was capable of making a serious speech on such a solemn occasion. But one of the impressive things about Lincoln's career is that he constantly strove to *grow*. He was anxious to appear on that occasion and to say something worthy of it. (Also, it has been suggested, he was anxious to remove the impression that he did not know how to behave properly—an impression which had been strengthened by a shocking story about his clowning on the battlefield of Antietam the previous year.) Therefore when he was invited he took considerable care with his speech. He drafted rather more than half of it in the White House before leaving, finished it in the hotel at Gettysburg the night before the ceremony

---

[1] In November 1950 the Chinese had just entered the war in Korea.

(not in the train, as sometimes reported), and wrote out a fair copy the next morning.

6 There are many accounts of the day itself, 19 November 1863. There are many descriptions of Lincoln, all showing the same curious blend of grandeur and awkwardness, or lack of dignity, or—it would be best to call it humility. In the procession he rode horseback: a tall lean man in a high plug hat, straddling a short horse, with his feet too near the ground. He arrived before the chief speaker, and had to wait patiently for half an hour or more. His own speech came right at the end of a long and exhausting ceremony, lasted less than three minutes, and made little impression on the audience. In part this was because they were tired, in part because (as eye-witnesses said) he ended almost before they knew he had begun, and in part because he did not speak the Address, but read it, very slowly, in a thin high voice, with a marked Kentucky accent, pronouncing "to" as "toe" and dropping his final R's.

7 Some people of course were alert enough to be impressed. Everett congratulated him at once. But most of the newspapers paid little attention to the speech, and some sneered at it. The *Patriot and Union* of Harrisburg wrote, "We pass over the silly remarks of the President; for the credit of the nation we are willing . . . that they shall be no more repeated or thought of"; and the London *Times* said, "The ceremony was rendered ludicrous by some of the sallies of that poor President Lincoln," calling his remarks "dull and commonplace." The first commendation of the Address came in a single sentence of the Chicago *Tribune,* and the first discriminating and detailed praise of it appeared in the Springfield *Republican,* the Providence *Journal,* and the Philadelphia *Bulletin.* However, three weeks after the ceremony and then again the following spring, the editor of *Harper's Weekly* published a sincere and thorough eulogy of the Address, and soon it was attaining recognition as a masterpiece.

8 At the time, Lincoln could not care much about the reception of his words. He was exhausted and ill. In the train back to Washington, he lay down with a wet towel on his head. He had caught smallpox. At that moment he was incubating it, and he was stricken down soon after he reentered the White House. Fortunately it was a mild attack, and it evoked one of his best

jokes: he told his visitors, "At last I have something I can give to everybody."

He had far more than that to give to everybody. He was a ⁹ unique person, far greater than most people realize until they read his life with care. The wisdom of his policy, the sources of his statesmanship—these were things too complex to be discussed in a brief essay. But we can say something about the Gettysburg Address as a work of art.

A work of art. Yes: for Lincoln was a literary artist, trained ¹⁰ both by others and by himself. The textbooks he used as a boy were full of difficult exercises and skillful devices in formal rhetoric, stressing the qualities he practiced in his own speaking: antithesis, parallelism, and verbal harmony. Then he read and reread many admirable models of thought and expression: the King James Bible, the essays of Bacon, the best plays of Shakespeare. His favorites were *Hamlet, Lear, Macbeth, Richard III,* and *Henry VIII,* which he had read dozens of times. He loved reading aloud, too, and spent hours reading poetry to his friends. (He told his partner Herndon that he preferred getting the sense of any document by reading it aloud.) Therefore his serious speeches are important parts of the long and noble classical tradition of oratory which begins in Greece, runs through Rome to the modern world, and is still capable (if we do not neglect it) of producing masterpieces.

The first proof of this is that the Gettysburg Address is full ¹¹ of quotations—or rather of adaptations—which give it strength. It is partly religious, partly (in the highest sense) political: therefore it is interwoven with memories of the Bible and memories of American history. The first and last words are Biblical cadences. Normally Lincoln did not say "fourscore" when he meant eighty; but on this solemn occasion he recalled the important dates in the Bible—such as the age of Abram when his first son was born to him, and he was "fourscore and six years old."[2] Similarly he did not say there was a chance that democracy might die out: he recalled the somber phrasing of the Book of Job—where Bildad speaks of the destruction of one who shall vanish without a trace, and says that "his branch shall be cut off: his remembrance shall

---

[2] Genesis 16:16; and Exodus 7:7.

perish from the earth."[3] Then again, the famous description of our State as "government of the people, by the people, for the people" was adumbrated by Daniel Webster in 1830 (he spoke of "the people's government, made for the people, made by the people, and answerable to the people") and then elaborated in 1854 by the abolitionist Theodore Parker (as "government of all the people, by all the people, for all the people"). There is good reason to think that Lincoln took the important phrase "under God" (which he interpolated at the last moment) from Weems, the biographer of Washington; and we know that it had been used at least once by Washington himself.

12   Analyzing the address further, we find that it is based on a highly imaginative theme, or group of themes. The subject is—how can we put it, so as not to disfigure it?—the subject is the kinship of life and death, that mysterious linkage which we see sometimes as the physical succession of birth and death in our world, sometimes as the contrast, which is perhaps a unity, between death and immortality. The first sentence is concerned with birth:

Our *fathers brought forth* a *new* nation, *conceived* in liberty.

The final phrase but one expresses the hope that

this nation, under God, shall have a *new birth* of freedom.

And the last phrase of all speaks of continuing life as the triumph over death. Again and again throughout the speech, this mystical contrast and kinship reappear: "those who *gave their lives* that that nation might *live*," "the brave men *living* and *dead*," and so in the central assertion that the dead have already consecrated their own burial place, while "it is for us, the *living*, rather to be dedicated . . . to the great task remaining." The Gettysburg Address is a prose poem; it belongs to the same world as the great elegies, and the adagios of Beethoven.

13   Its structure, however, is that of a skillfully contrived speech. The oratorical pattern is perfectly clear. Lincoln describes the occa-

---

[3] Job 18:16–17; Jeremiah 10:11; Micah 7:2

sion, dedicates the ground, and then draws a larger conclusion by calling on his hearers to dedicate themselves to the preservation of the Union. But within that, we can trace his constant use of at least two important rhetorical devices.

The first of these two is *antithesis:* opposition, contrast. The 14 speech is full of it. Listen:

> The world will little *note*
> nor long *remember*   what *we say* here
> but   it can never *forget*   what *they did* here.

And so in nearly every sentence: "brave men, *living* and *dead*"; "to *add* or *detract*." There is the antithesis of the Founding Fathers and the men of Lincoln's own time:

> Our *fathers brought forth* a new nation . . .
> now *we* are testing whether that nation . . . can *long endure.*

And there is the more terrible antithesis of those who have already died and those who still live to do their duty. Now, antithesis is the figure of contrast and conflict. Lincoln was speaking in the midst of a great civil war.

The other important pattern is different. It is technically 15 called *tricolon*—the division of an idea into three harmonious parts, usually of increasing power. The most famous phrase of the Address is a tricolon:

> government of the people
> by the people
> and   for the people.

The most solemn sentence is a tricolon:

> we cannot dedicate
> we cannot consecrate
> we cannot hallow this ground.

And above all, the last sentence (which has sometimes been criticized as too complex) is essentially two parallel phrases, with a tricolon growing out of the second and then producing another tricolon: a trunk, three branches, and a cluster of flowers. Lincoln says that it is for his hearers to be dedicated to the great task remaining before them. Then he goes on,

> that from these honored dead

—apparently he means "in such a way that from these honored dead"—

> we take increased devotion to that cause.

Next, he restates this more briefly:

> that we here highly resolve . . .

And now the actual resolution follows, in three parts of growing intensity:

> that these dead shall not have died in vain
> that this nation, under God, shall have a new birth
> of freedom

and that (one more tricolon)

> government of the people
>   by the people
>   and   for the people
> shall not perish from the earth.

Now the tricolon is the figure which, through division, emphasizes basic harmony and unity. Lincoln used antithesis because he was speaking to people at war. He used the tricolon because he was hoping, planning, praying for peace.

16   No one thinks that when he was drafting the Gettysburg Address, Lincoln deliberately looked up these quotations and consciously chose these particular patterns of thought. No, he chose the theme. From its development and from the emotional tone of the entire occasion, all the rest followed, or grew—by that marvelous process of choice and rejection which is essential to artistic creation. It does not spoil such a work of art to analyze it as closely as we have done; it is altogether fitting and proper that we should do this: for it helps us to penetrate more deeply into the rich meaning of the Gettysburg Address, and it allows us the rare privilege of watching the workings of a great man's mind.

Sources

W. E. Barton. *Lincoln at Gettysburg*. Bobbs-Merrill. 1930.

R. P. Basler. "Abraham Lincoln's Rhetoric." *American Literature:* 11:1939–40, 167–82.

L. E. Robinson. *Abraham Lincoln as a Man of Letters*. Chicago, 1918.

There are no study questions on Highet's "The Gettysburg Address." See questions following Lincoln's "Gettysburg Address" (p. 635).

ANDREW NAKAMURA

Nakamura, the grandson of two sets of Japanese immigrants to Hawaii, was born (1972) and reared on Maui. An honors student, campus leader, and athlete at the University of Denver, he wrote the essay printed below in response to a freshman English assignment that called for a discussion of "the evolution of slang and the importance of language." There are many pidgins, languages with simplified grammar and vocabulary used for communication between groups speaking different languages. Hawaii, with its blend of many cultures, many languages, is a natural location for pidgin to develop.

Thus Nakamura chose to write on Hawaiian pidgin. As his essay shows, it is used informally today not only among speakers of different languages, but among speakers of the same language not just to communicate but to signal solidarity, friendship and intimacy. "When someone approaches me and says, 'How you stay?' or 'How you stay been?' I recognize right away what the person is asking me and I reply, 'I stay been fine.'" Although this essay focuses on students, pidgin is also spoken in Hawaii (as it is elsewhere) among friends, families, coworkers, and others in relaxed and intimate contexts. Nakamura translated Lincoln's Gettysburg Address into Hawaiian pidgin, "a colorful, expressive dialect," to make it "more direct and easier to understand." It is fitting to use a speech dedicated to government "of the people, by the people, for the people" to begin a defense of pidgin, as Nakamura says, as a significant "part of Hawaii's culture and people."

❄ *Pidgin to da Max*

1   Y ou no, 87 yeas ago, some guys wen write dis constitution fo
      make us one betta place.

2   An now, we stay all hemajang because we stay beefing it out
      against us selves, trying fo test if we can handle or what. We beef
      it out on one beeg kuleana and das not right because us guys
      stupposed to know betta den dat. Da guys dat when make
      (MOCKay) fo us, we going dedicate this teratory to dem cause
      dey deserve um.

3   Yah, but wen you stay realize, we no can. Cause da guys dat
      wen fight is da guys dat wen show dea courage an bravery, so ass
      why dey are da guys dat wen earn da land to be dedicated to
      demselves. Ev'rboday not going give a dam wot we say hea, but
      dey going remembah wot wen happen an why was impo'tant. So
      it is up to us to carry on dea fight, cause we not onle owe it to dem
      but to awa selves az well. We gotta fight fo dem to prove dat dey
      neva die fo no'ting. An dat we going make ev'ryting how stup-
      posed to be. Fo us, fo da braddahs, an da nation.

4   As one may well know, that was the Gettysburg Address
      written by Abraham Lincoln in 1863. It may not have been recog-
      nized at first because it is written in a dialect/slang called "pidgin."
      Pidgin originated in the Hawaiian islands formed by a mixture of
      different languages from different races. Hawaii is a large "melting
      pot" of many cultures and races, thus in order to communicate
      with each other, a common language or slang was invented. The
      pidgin vocabulary grew and accumulated throughout many years,
      and is susceptible to the addition of new vocabulary words.

5   Language is affected by a variety of dialects and regional
      influences. Standard English is considered a dialect. In a society
      where communication is highly regarded, standard English is
      essential. In such a society, those who do not possess the ability to
      use standard English are often ostracized. To insure the students'
      future success as citizens and adults, it is essential for schools
      to emphasize the importance of standard English. Educational
      facilities should be required to help students understand the need
      for proper English and the adaptability and creativity essential to
      its use.

6   Pidgin is a very versatile and flexible "language" which
      changes through time. Different cultures' languages contribute

colorful words to the vocabulary of pidgin. During the late 19th century, pidgin was an essential language used in communicating between different foreigners. The Hawaii sugar cane industry needed hard-working, cheap laborers to harvest cane. These workers were primarily found in China, Japan, and the Philippines. Hawaii's sugar cane industry boomed. Unfortunately, the workers developed many cultural conflicts among themselves. A conflict in communication arose. Because of their differences in language, efficient communication was hindered. Thus, the birth of pidgin was launched with a rich vocabulary contributed by the laborers. In getting its message across, pidgin was very efficient because of its simplicity and directness. Within a year's span, pidgin's use was popular and well known.

Today, pidgin is viewed somewhat negatively; whereas, the use of standard English is thought to be proper. The Hawaii State Board of Education feels that oral communication should be a part of every student's repertoire of communication skills. They believe every student should be competent in any form of language as well as standard English to create better opportunities for success and contentment. Their attempt to ban the use of pidgin from schools in Hawaii is futile. Students' social lives are centered around the use of pidgin, and it will continue to grow, adding new words and meanings. 7

The society of Hawaii includes many varieties of social groups. One's social status may be influenced by the language the individual or class of individuals speak. The expression of pidgin is a possible factor in pigeonholing a group's social status. Social groups who speak alike tend to "cling" to each other and not interact with groups who speak differently. "Wot Haole, you no undastan or wot?" could be said by a typical Hawaii local male, whereas an individual applying standard English would ask, "Are you able to understand or not?" These differences in language and dialect establish a social barrier between someone who is highly educated in standard English and someone who is not. They will continue to keep social classes stratified. 8

Pidgin continues to be used widely in Hawaii by a population of students ranging from grade school through high school. In the company of these peers, pidgin is spoken freely because there are few restrictions. In the company of "dignified" individuals, the use of standard English must be emphasized and pidgin 9 should not be spoken. Many people in Hawaii have not yet mastered the technique of turning their pidgin "on" and "off." Many students are not able to communicate fluently in both pidgin and standard English. Why? Maybe the importance of standard English is not emphasized enough in schools, or maybe students use pidgin so much that their skills in standard English diminish. These could be possible theories of why students are not able to speak standard English when it would be in their best interest to be able to do so.

10   Nevertheless, language is continually changing. There are new words with different meanings being added to both standard English and pidgin every day. Because both languages enrich communication, society should use both to their fullest potential. So us guys gotta puul toogetta and believe in making awa world one foa English in anykine languages.

Content

1. What is pidgin? Is Nakamura's definition adequate?
2. How convincing is Nakamura's argument? What are his strongest points? His weakest? Explain.

Strategies/Structures

1. Why does Nakamura begin his defense of pidgin with a pidgin version of the Gettysburg Address? How far did you have to read before you recognized it?
2. Is this illustration worth a thousand additional words? Can you *hear* it?

Language

Judging from the pidgin vocabulary of the Gettysburg Address, how is pidgin formed? Could you invent your own version, based on this example?

For Writing

1. Write the Gettysburg Address (see p. 635) as it might be spoken in some language or dialect other than standard English, or by a particular

person noted for his or her style of expression, such as Didion, White, King, or any of the other authors in *The Essay Connection.*

2. Under what circumstances, if any, should people be encouraged to use pidgin or another nonstandard dialect? What does the use of such a dialect or language variation imply about the user? Should it imply anything else?

Four Cinderellas

Each telling and retelling of a familiar tale incorporates something of the teller's culture and values, as does each critical interpretation. The ninth and twentieth century Chinese Cinderella tales printed here have some obvious points of similarity. Each tells of a poor, hardworking girl exploited by her wicked stepmother and stepsister(s), who is transformed into a beautiful woman through association with the supernatural, for whom she unselfishly performs good deeds. Uniquely fitted to (and identifiable by) a special slipper, she is the object of a quest by the royal ruler, who finds her and marries her. Yet each tale may be read very differently. Ning Yu's essay interprets the "nurturing woman" motif in the context of two very different Chinese cultures, imperial (ninth century) and Communist (twentieth century, even though the story is a translation of the Walt Disney version of a seventeenth century French version), and finds significant differences in the tales.

TUAN CH'ÊNG-SHIH (ninth century)

The Chinese "Cinderella"

A mong the people of the south there is a tradition that before the Ch'in and Han dynasties there was a cave-master called Wu. The aborigines called the place the Wu cave. He married two wives. One wife died. She had a daughter called Yeh-hsien, who 1 from childhood was intelligent and good at making pottery on the wheel. Her father loved her. After some years the father died, and she was ill-treated by her step-mother, who always made her collect firewood in dangerous places and draw water from deep pools. She once got a fish about two inches long, with red fins and golden eyes. She put it into a bowl of water. It grew bigger every day, and after she had changed the bowl several times she could find no bowl big enough for it, so she threw it into the back pond. Whatever food was left over from meals, she put into the water to feed it. When she came to the pond, the fish always exposed its head and pillowed it on the bank; but when anyone else came, it did not come out. The step-mother knew about this, but when she watched for it, it did not once appear. So she tricked the girl, saying, "Haven't you worked hard! I am going to give you a new dress." She then made the girl change out of her tattered clothing. Afterwards she sent her to get water from another spring and reckoning that it was several hundred leagues, the step-mother at her leisure put on her daughter's clothes, hid a sharp blade up her sleeve, and went out to the pond. She called to the fish. The fish at once put its head out, and she chopped it off and killed it. The fish was now more than ten feet long. She served it up and it tasted twice as good as an ordinary fish. She hid the bones under the dung-hill. Next day, when the girl came to the pond, no fish appeared. She howled with grief in the open countryside, and suddenly there appeared a man with his hair loose over his shoulders and coarse clothes. He came down from the sky. He consoled her, saying, "Don't howl! Your step-mother has killed the fish and its bones are under the dung. You go back, take the fish's bones and hide them in your room. Whatever you want, you only have to pray to them for it. It is bound to be granted." The girl followed his advice, and was able to provide herself with gold, pearls, dresses and food whenever she wanted them.

2   When the time came for the cave-festival, the step-mother went, leaving the girl to keep watch over the fruit-trees in the garden. She waited till the step-mother was some way off, and then went herself, wearing a cloak of stuff spun from kingfisher feathers and shoes of gold. Her step-sister recognized her and said to the step-mother, "That's very like my sister." The step-mother suspected the same thing. The girl was aware of this and went

away in such a hurry that she lost one shoe. It was picked up by one of the people of the cave. When the step-mother got home, she found the girl asleep, with her arms round one of the trees in the garden, and thought no more about it.

This cave was near to an island in the sea. On this island was 3 a kingdom called T'o-han. Its soldiers had subdued twenty or thirty other islands and it had a coast-line of several thousand leagues. The cave-man sold the shoe in T'o-han, and the ruler of T'o-han got it. He told those about him to put it on; but it was an inch too small for even the one among them that had the smallest foot. He ordered all the women in his kingdom to try it on; but there was not one that it fitted. It was light as down and made no noise even when treading on stone. The king of T'o-han thought the cave-man had got it unlawfully. He put him in prison and tortured him, but did not end by finding out where it had come from. So he threw it down at the wayside. Then they went everywhere[1] through all the people's houses and arrested them. If there was a woman's shoe, they arrested them and told the king of T'o-han. He thought it strange, searched the inner-rooms and found Yeh-hsien. He made her put on the shoe, and it was true.

Yeh-hsien then came forward, wearing her cloak spun from 4 halcyon feathers and her shoes. She was as beautiful as a heavenly being. She now began to render service to the king, and he took the fish-bones and Yeh-hsien, and brought them back to his country.

The step-mother and step-sister were shortly afterwards 5 struck by flying stones, and died. The cave people were sorry for them and buried them in a stone-pit, which was called the tomb of the Distressed Women. The men of the cave made mating-offerings there; any girl they prayed for there, they got. The king of T'o-han, when he got back to his kingdom made Yeh-hsien his chief wife. The first year the king was very greedy and by his prayers to the fish-bones got treasures and jade without limit. Next year, there was no response, so the king buried the fish-bones on the sea-shore. He covered them with a hundred bushels of pearls and bordered them with gold. Later there was a mutiny of some soldiers who had been conscripted and their general opened

---

[1] Something here seems to have gone slightly wrong with the text. [WALEY]

(the hiding place) in order to make better provision for his army. One night they (the bones) were washed away by the tide.

6   This story was told to me by Li Shih-yüan, who has been in the service of my family a long while. He was himself originally a man from the caves of Yung-chou and remembers many strange things of the South.

The Dust Girl

There are over a thousand variants of the familiar tale of "Cinderella." Ning Yu (for biography, see page 389) read an anonymous Chinese Communist translation of Walt Disney's 1949 interpretation to his young son, and in 1990 translated it into English for *The Essay Connection.* The Disney version has a venerable ancestry, being adopted from Charles Perrault's 1697 French translation of an even older tale. New versions are continually being written, including this one.

1   O nce upon a time there was a little girl whose father married again after her mother's death. The stepmother had two daughters of her own, and all three of them were evil-hearted: they would bully the little girl and backbite her before her father whenever they had a chance.

2   Before long, the little girl's father followed his first wife, and the girl cried till her eyes swelled like two red peaches for she was now a poor, friendless little thing.

3   No sooner did they come home from the father's funeral than the stepmother started yelling at the poor little girl, banging the table with her fists. "How dare you think you are good enough to live in the same house with us? Go and live in the kitchen by yourself!" The elder stepsister said, "You don't deserve these good clothes either. Take them off and put on those rags and wooden shoes." The second stepsister said, "If you want to eat, you'll have to do all the chores in the house."

4   From then on, the little girl had to sleep in the kitchen, dress in rags, and wear wooden shoes. What is more, she had to get up before daybreak to fetch water from the well, start the fire, cook

all the meals, wash up things and clean the whole house. The work made her very dusty and they began to call her Dust Girl.

The stepmother and her daughters were lazybones who loved nothing but to eat and drink and seek pleasure in parties. The two sisters would spend hours upon hours before the mirror and for good clothes they would fight each other fiercely, scratching faces and tearing hair, smashing bowls and plates, and making a mess of the house. Driven crazy by her own daughters, the stepmother would vent her anger on Dust Girl by making her mend the torn clothes and clean up the broken pieces on the floor.

Though Dust Girl toiled very hard in the house every day, she was given for food the leftovers from her stepmother's table. However, she was such a kind-hearted girl that she would always save something from her meager ration to offer to a poor old beggar woman.

One day the king gave a ball, which would last for three days, and invited all the girls in the kingdom, from whom the prince would choose a wife.

When Dust Girl's two stepsisters heard of the ball they were beside themselves with ecstasy and anticipation, and started another fight for the best costumes in the family wardrobe. Extremely angry at them, their mother yelled, "Fight! Fight! How can you expect to appear at such a grand ball with disheveled hair and torn faces?"

Upon hearing this, the two sisters let go of each other, and ordered Dust Girl rudely, "Hurry up! put a lace on my new dress!" "Be quick! shine up my dancing slippers." "Move on! Fetch me a bowl of water to wash my face with." "Come! Come! Dress my hair in the latest fashion."

After hours of bustle and hustle, the sisters left with their mother in a carriage for the palace, but before the horses started, the two sisters turned around and asked Dust Girl, "What do you think? We are going to the royal palace to attend the ball while you only deserve to watch the stove at home!"

Dust Girl sat lonely in the kitchen for a long while, staring into the flames. How she longed to attend that ball too! But suddenly she heard someone knocking at the door. "Who could that be?" she asked herself. As the girl opened the door, who should come in but the old beggar.

12   "Grandmother! come on in. It's so cold out there. Come and warm yourself by the stove. I still have two pieces of bread and let's share them for supper."

13   As soon as the old woman sat down, she began to ask Dust Girl, "All the girls in the country are invited to the royal ball tonight. Why didn't you go?"

14   "My two stepsisters have gone and they wanted me to stay and take care of the stove. How can I go in these wooden shoes and dusty rags, anyway?"

15   "But don't you want to go?"

16   "Sure. I'd love to. It'd be a great treat for me if I could simply watch the people dance."

17   "If so, let me help you." As the old woman spoke, she pointed at Dust Girl with her walking stick and the poor girl's rags turned into a silvery satin evening dress, and her wooden shoes into a pair of crystal slippers.

18   "I won't let you go to the palace on foot either," said the old woman, picking up a pumpkin and rolling it out of the door. The pumpkin at once turned into a gold carriage; she pointed her walking stick toward the corner of the kitchen and eight mice ran out of the hole in the wall to become eight beautiful horses; she then pointed her stick to the sleeping cat, and the cat woke up to be a handsome coachman. "All right, my child," said the old woman. "Now you may go to the palace. But, remember, you must come back before midnight, for at that moment all these things will return to their original shapes."

19   In the palace, Dust Girl outshone all the other girls who came to the ball from all over the country. Though terribly jealous of her success, her two stepsisters never dreamed that the most beautiful girl at the ball was none but Dust Girl.

20   But the prince came to Dust Girl, bowed, shook her hand, and asked to dance with her. Dust Girl had the most wonderful time in her life that night, but she did not forget the old woman's advice and bid the prince good-by shortly before midnight. When she got home in her gold carriage, it had just struck twelve. The pumpkin was back on the table, the mice in their hole, the cat to her sleep, and Dust Girl herself was back in her old rags and wooden shoes again. Soon her stepmother and stepsisters were

back and they ordered Dust Girl to help them undress saying, "Oh, you are ugly! especially after we saw those beautiful goddess-like ladies in the palace."

The next evening, Dust Girl went to the palace again; and again she returned home before midnight. The third was the last evening of the ball, and the prince danced with Dust Girl all night. Dust Girl was so happy that she forgot the old woman's warning till the clock struck the first stroke of twelve. She then suddenly remembered her warning, tore herself away from the prince, and rushed out of the palace. The prince tried to run after her, but was only fast enough to find a crystal slipper that she lost in her hurry. 21

However, the prince had made up his mind; the girl in the crystal slippers should be his wife. But how could he find that girl again? The king's men were sent with the slipper to check every house in the kingdom—to look for the girl whose foot fit the slipper exactly. Whoever that girl might have been, she was to become the prince's wife. 22

The king's men had tried almost every house in the country when they finally came to the house where Dust Girl and her stepmother and stepsisters lived. The two sisters shouted at each other in fighting to be first to try on the crystal slipper, but their shouts turned into wails when they found out that neither one of them could cram her foot into the slipper. 23

Disappointed, the king's men asked whether there was any other girl in the house. 24

The stepmother answered, "There is only one more ugly servant girl. But she is so dusty that she is not fit to be seen by gentlemen like you. What is more, she never had any crystal slippers and she never went to the palace." 25

"But the king's order is to have every girl in the country try on this slipper," said the king's men. 26

Reluctantly the stepmother called out Dust Girl. But behold! how perfectly the slipper fit Dust Girl's foot—neither tight nor loose! 27

As Dust Girl was being taken into the palace, the stepmother's and the stepsisters' mouths became lopsided because of jealousy. 28

NING YU

(For biographical information, see page 389.) Ning Yu explains how he wrote this essay: "Once a writer said, 'It is hard to decide what should be put on paper, but it is even harder to decide what should be left in the inkwell.' But every writer, whether he is a student or a professional, has to make such hard decisions in every book, every chapter, or even every line of his composition.

"When I was first asked to write a comparative study of the two Chinese versions of Cinderella, I knew my audience would be American college students who understandably do not know much about Chinese culture, especially the Maoist ideology. But such background knowledge is essential for the understanding and discussion of these two versions, and I knew I had to be brief. But how brief is too little, and how brief is just enough? That I had to find out by writing.

"Information concerning the early Chinese version is not so difficult to present because the historical events about Ch'in Shi Huang's biological effort to preserve his dynasty are generally regarded as 'facts,' and there is nothing subtle about the story. But my interpretation of the later piece would have to be very subtle and sensitive because I do not want my readers to misunderstand the translator-editor of the tale as an unscrupulous hack who would twist the original out of shape to please the Party. On the contrary, he might in the name of 'proletariat education' be smuggling some Western humanism (love is classless, for example) into China. Moreover, the translator-editor might be an unconscious victim of the 'Big Brother's propaganda' who changed the Western tale because his 'taste' demanded that he do so. To make this point clear I felt I had to expound the effects of 'Big Brother's propaganda' first, even citing lengthy passages from Orwell's *1984*.

"When I finished the first draft, I realized that the paper was off-balance; my discussion of the early Chinese version was about five typed pages while my discussion of the later one was nearly double that. The mere physical shape of the draft doomed it to be an unsuccessful compare-and-contrast essay. It was also digressive; my defense for the translator-editor blurred the intended focus of the essay—what is common to the two very different Chinese versions of Cinderella.

"So I eliminated the defense. In doing so I took the risk of having the translator-editor misunderstood. But I also gained the sharpened focus of a shapely essay. Still, I wonder whether it is justifiable to sacrifice justice in the presentation of the translator-editor for the clarity and shapeliness in the form of my essay. Taking such a risk is painful. But taking any risk is also exciting."

❄ *The Nurturing Woman Rewarded:*
❄ *A Study of Two Chinese Cinderellas*

T he Victorian collector Joseph Jacobs might be inaccurate but he was by no means exaggerating when he said that the Cinderella story he was printing was "an English version of an Italian adaptation of a Spanish translation of a Latin version of a Hebrew translation of an Arabic translation of an Indian original." According to Jane Yolen, a noted American author and critic of children's books, "over five hundred variants [of Cinderella] have been located by folklorists in Europe alone" (p. 23) and the earliest datable literary source is a ninth-century Chinese tale. 1

Perhaps it is because of the great variety of versions that critics such as Jack Zipes (pp. 160–182) and Madonna Kolbenschlag (pp. 53–58) are not satisfied with Bruno Bettelheim's famous and insightful psychological study of Cinderella as a model case of "sibling rivalry and Oedipal conflicts"; one is compelled by the cross-cultural development of the tale to elevate the study of Cinderella beyond Bettelheim's personal and psychological level. It is the purpose of this essay to examine the ninth-century and the twentieth-century Chinese versions of the story against their respective ideological backgrounds, and to point out some common features of the two Chinese versions that are chronologically so remote and textually so different. 2

In the early Chinese version of the story, there are many elements to which the orthodox Freudian approach, which Bettelheim used so well to analyze the Grimm, Basile, and Perrault versions, is not sufficient for a thorough and convincing interpretation. Sibling rivalry, for example, is hardly an issue; the single sentence that Yeh-hsien's stepsister utters during her extremely brief appearance in the tale does not reveal any hostility between the two girls. On the contrary, that the stepsister referred to Yeh-hsien as "my sister" 3 seems to imply that the relationship between the two girls is much friendlier than the one between the stepmother and the step-daughter. Neither is it convincing to say that Yeh-hsien projected hatred on her stepmother because she herself hated the stepmother as the competitor for the father's love, for while the father was alive, though he had already remarried, he loved Yeh-hsien. This is a significant difference between the early Chinese version and the Western variants of the tale; the girl began to suffer only after the father's death.

4   On the other hand, if we study the early tale against the Chinese cultural and historical background, using some psycho-analytic technique on the auxiliary level, we may come closer to the real message of that specific version.

5   Though the early Chinese version of "Cinderella" was writ-ten in the ninth century, the events in the story "happened" before the Ch'in and Han dynasties (B.C. 306–221, and B.C. 206–A.D. 220). Ch'in dynasty was the first dynasty in Chinese history when China became a united kingdom under a central power, and Ch'in Shi Huang (Ch'in the First Emperor) was known for his conquests of the other contemporary super-power states and his uniting China into a central kingdom. After he united China, one of the first things that Ch'in Shi Huang did was to put hundreds of girls from the noble families of those states into his harem, reportedly to reproduce over a hundred sons (no one has taken the trouble to count the daughters). The idea behind that was the more sons he had, the longer his dynasty, the rule of his family over China, could be preserved.

6   Now the king of T'o-han in the early Chinese version had just done something very similar. He had a strong kingdom whose "soldiers had subdued twenty or thirty other islands and it had a coastline of several thousand leagues," a coastline as long as that of China. As the ruler of a super power, the king of T'o-han may very well have been concerned with the continuation of the rule of his family. That's why, probably, he had quite a number of royal concubines. Then why did he make Yeh-hsien, the ninth-century Chinese Cinderella, his "chief wife"? What was so special about Yeh-hsien that she was made the head of those royal baby-makers?

7   To answer those questions one must first study the real ten-sion between the girl and the stepmother, which is, as I noted earlier, neither the Oedipal complex of the girl nor the sibling

rivalry between her and her stepsisters and stepmother. It is, I believe, the fact that the girl is a nurturing figure while the stepmother is a destroyer of life; the girl fed the fish but the stepmother killed it.

The nurturing power of Yeh-hsien, as demonstrated in the   8 raising of the fish, is extraordinary; with no special feed—"whatever food was left over from meals she put in the water to feed it"—she made the fish grow from "two inches" to "ten feet" in a very short period of time. The manner in which the girl kept the fish is analogous to the way a mother conceives, delivers, and rears a child. When the fish was of fetal size—two inches—it was kept in a bowl, the shape of which makes it reasonable for one to associate it with the womb. Then, as the fish grew, the bowls became larger and larger; this parallels the swelling belly of a pregnant woman. Finally, when the fish became so big that no bowl was big enough to contain it, it was thrown into the pond, a new and open world compared with bowls, a process similar to the birth of a child—a new life being transferred from the mother's body to the open world. Yet the fish was to be nurtured by the girl; the way it "pillowed" its head on the bank when the girl fed it is exactly the way a baby leans its head on its mother's arm while feeding at its mother's breasts.

The mother-child relationship between the fish and the girl   9 is further indicated by the fish's instinctive knowledge and trust of Yeh-hsien's nurturing power, just as a baby knows its mother by instinct. What is more revealing, the fish wouldn't trust anyone but the girl: "When she came to the pond, the fish always exposed its head and pillowed it on the bank; but when anyone else came, it did not come out."

The stepmother is such an "anyone else." When she came to   10 the pond and "watched for" the fish, "it did not once appear." She knew that the girl had an unusual power and the fish might have received some of this power from the girl because she had nurtured it. The stepmother's killing, serving, and eating the fish reveal a strong desire in her to transplant the girl's unusual nurturing power to herself. But to say the stepmother lacked the nurturing power that Yeh-hsien enjoyed does not mean that the stepmother was sterile. She had her own daughter. However, to be able to have a daughter is no womanly virtue in ancient China, unless the daughter possessed the strong nurturing power that Yeh-hsien did.

11   Then, why do I suggest that, being able to "bear" and rear a fish, Yeh-hsien is supposed to be more nurturing than the stepmother who had borne and raised a real daughter? The reason is this. The Chinese word for fish is *yu*, which is homonymic with another Chinese word, *yu*, meaning "abundance." Therefore, the fish is regarded in Chinese culture as an auspicious thing. That's why up to this day, fish is still necessarily the first course for a family banquet in the Chinese New Year's Eve; it presages a prosperous new year for the family. In some areas in China, where fish is not available to lower and middle class families, a wooden fish is served before any other dishes—to be looked at, and to transmit the auspicious atmosphere to the other courses, as that propitious moment will transmit its blessing to the many days of the new year.

12   However, for the Chinese family to be truly prosperous, the abundance in wealth alone is not enough; it must be accompanied by the abundance in offspring. That's why many Chinese New Year pictures have in them a fat boy straddling the back of a carp, a theme that presages both the abundance in wealth and the abundance in male offspring in the family. So in the Chinese culture, as a good omen for the future, the fish and the boy are inseparable. In this sense Yeh-hsien is not simply nurturing, but the mystic mother-child relationship between her and the fish also symbolizes her great potential of bringing an abundance of male offspring into her future husband's family. It is small wonder then that she was finally "rewarded" for the virtue of being nurturing, the highest position that a Chinese woman could expect then—to be the chief baby producer of a king. In contrast, the stepmother who had only one daughter was certainly not nurturing enough, and her killing the fish alienated her further from the category of virtuous women.

13   The twentieth-century Chinese version is a mixed rendering of the European Grimm version and the North American Walt Disney version. The translator was obviously unaware of the existence of the early Chinese Cinderella when he introduced the story from the West to China. In the new Chinese version there are more details identical with or similar to those in the Grimm and the Walt Disney versions than those in the old Chinese version: the presence of the fairy godmother, the girl's ill treatment before her father's death, the crystal slipper rather than the embroidered slipper, the three-day bride-finding ball, the pumpkin

carriage, the mice horses, and the cat coachman, etc. But, of course, there are many things in that version which are unique to the drastically changed Chinese ideology after 1949.

The Chinese Communist Party has claimed that the 1949   14 Revolution is a proletarian revolution successfully carried out with the help of the ally of the proletariat—the poor and lower-middle-class Chinese peasants—and under the leadership of the Party, which is both the son and the leader of the proletariat and the peasants. It goes without saying that after 1949 the predominant ideology is that of the proletarian revolution. The propaganda function of literature is so emphasized by the Party that it is no exaggeration to say that since 1949 every poem, every story, every play and every novel must reflect and enhance the various aspects of that ideology. The twentieth-century Chinese translation of Cinderella is no exception.

The depiction of Cinderella as an oppressed and exploited   15 proletarian is in the main a twentieth-century Chinese invention. The new Chinese version follows the trend started by the Walt Disney version to minimize the girl's upper-class background by omitting her life before her father's second marriage. Thus the girl is transformed into a member of the working class who has to sell her labor for her survival. "If you want to eat," says her second stepsister, "you'll have to do all the chores in the house." Her job was no longer the meaningless torture of picking lentils out of ash, but the real work of a housekeeper-cook-servant.

Consequently, the stepmother and her two daughters are no   16 longer the selfish but forgivable friends of the Perrault version, nor the sadistic "sibling rivals" of the Grimm version, but Dust Girl's oppressors, exploiters, and class enemies. They have all the characteristics of the parasitic leisure class. They are lazy, vain, and cruel. They never work to get what they consume, but spend hours before the mirror or in pleasure-seeking parties; they make a mess of the house fighting for the best dress but order Dust Girl to clean up the mess; they treat Dust Girl like dirt because they have the power in the house.

Yes, power is the essential issue in this version of the tale. It   17 is interesting to note that the way they treat Dust Girl changes drastically after her father's death. Though when he was still alive they had already been bullying and backbiting Dust Girl, it is after the father died and they seized the absolute power in the house that their maltreatment of the girl assumed the aspects of class oppression and class exploitation. Unlike their counterparts in the Western versions, they maltreated Dust Girl not for the "fun" of it, but to keep her from rebelling against them. The excuse they used to justify their behavior is the one that any advantaged class adopts to persuade the disadvantaged class—you are not good enough to be our equals; therefore, you don't deserve to live as we do.

18   Such a "Marxist" reading of the new Chinese version seems to be endorsed by its ending. Unlike the Grimm version, which ends with the couple being married in the church; unlike the Walt Disney version which ends with the cute cliché that "Cinderella became the prince's bride, and lived happily ever after—and the little pet mice lived in the palace and were happy ever after, too"; the new Chinese version ends with Dust Girl going into the palace—the proletariat rising to power. Of course, the story is nevertheless a fairy tale, and the theme is still a poor girl marrying a prince, but the omitting of the wedding scene deemphasizes the marriage theme and makes it possible for one to read for the underlying power struggle.

19   Though the fairy godmother is obviously transplanted from the Grimm version and the Disney version, the new Chinese version has made a significant change in her. Here she is an old beggar, rather than the spirit of the dead mother, or just some goddess who takes pity on the poor girl. On the surface level of the story, the change may seem trivial, but in fact, the change in status of the fairy godmother has changed the relationship between her and the girl, which parallels that between the Party and the proletariat. As I noted earlier, the Party claims itself to be both the son and the leader of the Chinese proletariat and the poor peasants; as the son, it must be nurtured and supported by the people; as the leader, the word in Chinese having a connotation very similar to the German word *führer,* it has absolute power over the people. In order to get to the promised land free from exploitation or oppression, the proletariat must first nurture and then obey the Party, and this is exactly what happens between the beggar-grandmother and Dust Girl.

20   The old woman revealed herself as an omnipotent goddess only after the girl had treated her kindly for some extended period

of time. Before that, the girl nurtured the old woman out of her own "meager ration." Afterward, the girl strictly followed the old woman's order; the minute she began to forget her warnings, she was stripped of the magic power borrowed from the godmother/Big-Brother figure. However, the girl withstood the trial and proved her loyalty to the Party to be sound, and as a reward, she went into the center of political power.

The ideologies reflected in the two Chinese versions are 21 very different—the main concern of one is the preservation of an imperial dynasty, while that of the other is how the proletariat seizes power under the leadership of the Party. But one thing is common to both—they both reflect an underlying power struggle, the conscientious strife either to seize or to maintain power. Without nurturing virtue, a woman is no good whether in the time "before Ch'in and Han dynasties" or after the Communist Revolution. That is why the Chinese translator added that essential virtue to the Western variants that he worked on. The ideology reflected in the new story is very different from the one reflected in the old story.

The two young female protagonists in the two Chinese ver- 22 sions are also as different as possible. But because they both act in fictive worlds of power struggles, they are doomed to have something in common too. In order for them to be rewarded, they must have a nurturing power, whether to nurture male offspring or to nurture a class comrade or leader. That is probably why the episode in the new Chinese version in which the girl not only *fed* the beggar, but also fed her with *leftovers* from the meals is something the Grimm and Disney versions do not have but something the old Chinese version has as its central issue. This nurturing power, the power to rear either a powerful party or powerful princes out of their own meager supplies, is the major virtue that is demanded of a Chinese woman who is to receive the highest reward possible—to have power over men and women alike, except, of course, the person or party who gave her the power in the first place.

Cinderella, on the whole, is a "virtue rewarded" story, but to 23 say so to the hundreds of variants may sound like hasty generalization. However, to study the variants against their individual cultures and to examine what particular virtue "deserves" to be "rewarded" in that particular culture is sound research, because in this way only can the richness of the great variety of the tale be revealed to the reader.

Works Cited

Kolbenschlag, Madonna. *Kiss Sleeping Beauty Good-Bye: Breaking the Spell of Feminine Myths and Models.* New York: Doubleday, 1979.

Yolen, Jane. "America's 'Cinderella'." *Children's Literature in Education* 8 (1977) 22–29.

Zipes, Jack David. *Breaking the Magic Spell: Radical Theories of Folk and Fairy Tales.* Austin, Texas: U of Texas P, 1979.

ANNE SEXTON

Sexton was born in 1928 in Newton, Massachusetts, grew up in Wellesley, and dropped out after a year at Garland Junior College to marry in 1948. Throughout the 1950s she adopted the socially sanctioned life pattern expected of women of the time—rearing two daughters and, stunningly attractive, working occasionally as a fashion model. But her inner life was "troubled and chaotic," according to her best friend, poet Maxine Kumin; she was intermittently hospitalized, seeking "sanctuary" from "voices that urged her to die." Her psychiatrist encouraged her to study poetry writing, which she did, with Robert Lowell and John Clellon Holmes, and in 1960 she published her first book, *To Bedlam and Part Way Back.* Her third book, *Live or Die,* won the Pulitzer Prize in 1966 and astonishing fame for this poet who had great difficulty making the transformation from housewife to serious writer. Indeed, in 1971 she published *Transformations,* adapting familiar fairy tales about women such as Cinderella, Snow White, and Briar Rose, beautiful dolls and objects and prizes of male conquest, into social criticism of the lives and expectations of contemporary women.

Sexton, reared as a Roman Catholic, continued to write what became known as "confessional poetry," focusing with a combination of pathos, sardonic humor, and disillusioned worldliness on "self-abasement, sin, sexual transgression, and bodily disgust."

She published *The Book of Folly* in 1972 and *Death Notebooks* in
1974. But stature as a distinguished and controversial artist whose
topics included menstruation, abortion, masturbation, incest,
adultery, and drug addiction further incited her troubled spirit.
Divorced at her insistence in her forties, dependent on alcohol,
and despondent, she committed suicide in 1975. *The Awful Rowing
Toward God* and *Mercy Street* were published posthumously; her
work continues to be a vital force in American letters.

Cinderella

Y ou always read about it: 1
  the plumber with twelve children
who wins the Irish Sweepstakes.
From toilets to riches.
That story.

Or the nursemaid,   2
some luscious sweet from Denmark
who captures the oldest son's heart.
From diapers to Dior.
That story.

Or a milkman who serves the wealthy,   3
eggs, cream, butter, yogurt, milk,
the white truck like an ambulance
who goes into real estate
and makes a pile.
From homogenized to martinis at lunch.

Or the charwoman   4
who is on the bus when it cracks up
and collects enough from the insurance.
From mops to Bonwit Teller.
That story.

Once   5
the wife of a rich man was on her deathbed

and she said to her daughter Cinderella:
Be devout. Be good. Then I will smile
down from heaven in the seam of a cloud.
The man took another wife who had
two daughters, pretty enough
but with hearts like blackjacks.
Cinderella was their maid.
She slept on the sooty hearth each night
and walked around looking like Al Jolson.
Her father brought presents home from town,
jewels and gowns for the other women
but the twig of a tree for Cinderella.
She planted that twig on her mother's grave
and it grew to a tree where a white dove sat.
Whenever she wished for anything the dove
would drop it like an egg upon the ground.
The bird is important, my dears, so heed him.

6   Next came the ball, as you all know.
It was a marriage market.
The prince was looking for a wife.
All but Cinderella were preparing
and gussying up for the big event.
Cinderella begged to go too.
Her stepmother threw a dish of lentils
into the cinders and said: Pick them
up in an hour and you shall go.
The white dove brought all his friends;
all the warm wings of the fatherland came,
and picked up the lentils in a jiffy.
No, Cinderella, said the stepmother,
you have no clothes and cannot dance.
That's the way with stepmothers.

7   Cinderella went to the tree at the grave
and cried forth like a gospel singer:
Mama! Mama! My turtledove,
send me to the prince's ball!
The bird dropped down a golden dress

and delicate little gold slippers.
Rather a large package for a simple bird.
So she went. Which is no surprise.
Her stepmother and sisters didn't
recognize her without her cinder face
and the prince took her hand on the spot
and danced with no other the whole day.

As nightfall came she thought she'd better   8
get home. The prince walked her home
and she disappeared into the pigeon house
and although the prince took an axe and broke
it open she was gone. Back to her cinders.
These events repeated themselves for three days.
However on the third day the prince
covered the palace steps with cobbler's wax
and Cinderella's gold shoe stuck upon it.

Now he would find whom the shoe fit   9
and find his strange dancing girl for keeps.
He went to their house and the two sisters
were delighted because they had lovely feet.
The eldest went into a room to try the slipper on
but her big toe got in the way so she simply
sliced it off and put on the slipper.
The prince rode away with her until the white dove
told him to look at the blood pouring forth.
That is the way with amputations.
They don't just heal up like a wish.
The other sister cut off her heel
but the blood told as blood will.
The prince was getting tired.
He began to feel like a shoe salesman.
But he gave it one last try.
This time Cinderella fit into the shoe
like a love letter into its envelope.

At the wedding ceremony   10
the two sisters came to curry favor

and the white dove pecked their eyes out.
Two hollow spots were left
like soup spoons.

11 Cinderella and the prince
lived, they say, happily ever after,
like two dolls in a museum case
never bothered by diapers or dust,
never arguing over the timing of an egg,
never telling the same story twice,
never getting a middle-aged spread,
their darling smiles pasted on for eternity.

12 Regular Bobbsey Twins.
That story.

MARGARET ATWOOD

In "Fiction: Happy Endings," originally published in the
collection *Murder in the Dark* (1983), Atwood explores several
options available among the "hundreds of possibilities and many
ways of arranging them," in telling stories, as in real life. (For a
biographical sketch of Margaret Atwood, see page 7.)

Fiction: Happy Endings

A

1 John and Mary fall in love and get married. They both have
worthwhile and remunerative jobs which they find stimulating
and challenging. They buy a charming house. Real estate values
go up. Eventually, when they can afford live-in help, they have
two children, to whom they are devoted. The children turn out
well. John and Mary have a stimulating and challenging sex life
and worthwhile friends. They go on fun vacations together. They

retire. They both have hobbies which they find stimulating and challenging. Eventually they die. This is the end of the story.

B

Mary falls in love with John but John doesn't fall in love with Mary. He merely uses her body for selfish pleasure and ego gratification of a tepid kind. He comes to her apartment twice a week and she cooks him dinner, you'll notice that he doesn't even consider her worth the price of a dinner out, and after he's eaten the dinner he fucks her and after that he falls asleep, while she does the dishes so he won't think she's untidy, having all those dirty dishes lying around, and puts on fresh lipstick so she'll look good when he wakes up, but when he wakes up he doesn't even notice, he puts on his socks and his shorts and his pants and his shirt and his tie and his shoes, the reverse order from the one in which he took them off. He doesn't take off Mary's clothes, she takes them off herself, she acts as if she's dying for it every time, not because she likes sex exactly, she doesn't but she wants John to think she does because if they do it often enough surely he'll get used to her, he'll come to depend on her and they will get married, but John goes out the door with hardly so much as a good-night and three days later he turns up at six o'clock and they do the whole thing over again.

Mary gets run down. Crying is bad for your face, everyone knows that and so does Mary but she can't stop. People at work notice. Her friends tell her John is a rat, a pig, a dog, he isn't good enough for her, but she can't believe it. Inside John, she thinks, is another John, who is much nicer. This other John will emerge like a butterfly from a cocoon, a Jack from a box, a pit from a prune, if the first John is only squeezed hard enough.

One evening John complains about the food. He has never complained about the food before. Mary is hurt.

Her friends tell her they've seen him in a restaurant with another woman, whose name is Madge. It's not even Madge that finally gets to Mary: it's the restaurant. John has never taken Mary to a restaurant. Mary collects all the sleeping pills and aspirins she can find, and takes them and half a bottle of sherry. You can see what kind of a woman she is by the fact that it's not even whiskey. She leaves a note for John. She hopes he'll discover her and get her to the hospital in time and repent and then they can get married, but this fails to happen and she dies.

6   John marries Madge and everything continues as in A.

C

7 John, who is an older man, falls in love with Mary, and Mary, who is only twenty-two, feels sorry for him because he's worried about his hair falling out. She sleeps with him even though she's not in love with him. She met him at work. She's in love with someone called James, who is twenty-two also and not yet ready to settle down.

8   John on the contrary settled down a long time ago: this is what is bothering him. John has a steady respectable job and is getting ahead in his field, but Mary isn't impressed by him, she's impressed by James, who has a motorcycle, being free. Freedom isn't the same for girls, so in the meantime Mary spends Thursday evenings with John. Thursdays are the only days John can get away.

9   John is married to a woman named Madge and they have two children, a charming house which they bought just before the real estate values went up, and hobbies which they find stimulating and challenging, when they have the time. John tells Mary how important she is to him, but of course he can't leave his wife because a commitment is a commitment. He goes on about this more than is necessary and Mary finds it boring, but older men can keep it up longer so on the whole she has a fairly good time.

10   One day James breezes in on his motorcycle with some top-grade California hybrid and James and Mary get higher than you'd believe possible and they climb into bed. Everything becomes very underwater, but along comes John, who has a key to Mary's apartment. He finds them stoned and entwined. He's hardly in any position to be jealous, considering Madge, but nevertheless he's overcome with despair. Finally he's middle-aged, in two years he'll be bald as an egg and he can't stand it. He purchases a handgun, saying he needs it for target practice—this is the thin part of the plot, but it can be dealt with later—and shoots the two of them and himself.

11   Madge, after a suitable period of mourning, marries an understanding man called Fred and everything continues as in A, but under different names.

D

Fred and Madge have no problems. They get along exceptionally 12
well and are good at working out any little difficulties that may
arise. But there charming house is by the seashore and one day a
giant tidal wave approaches. Real estate values go down. The rest
of the story is about what caused the tidal wave and how they
escape from it. They do, though thousands drown. Some of the
story is about how the thousands drown, but Fred and Madge are
virtuous and lucky. Finally on high ground they clasp each other,
wet and dripping and grateful, and continue as in A.

E

Yes, but Fred has a bad heart. The rest of the story is about how 13
kind and understanding they both are until Fred dies. Then
Madge devotes herself to charity work until the end of A. If you
like, it can be "Madge," "cancer," "guilty and confused," and
"birdwatching."

F

If you think this is all too bourgeois, make John a revolutionary 14
and Mary a counterespionage agent and see how far that gets
you. You'll still end up with A, though in between you may get a
lustful brawling saga of passionate involvement, a chronicle of
our times, sort of.

You'll have to face it, the endings are the same however you slice 15
it. Don't be deluded by any other endings, they're all fake, either
deliberately fake, with malicious intent to deceive, or just motivated by excessive optimism if not by downright sentimentality.
    The only authentic ending is the one provided right here: 16
    John and Mary die. John and Mary die. John and Mary die. 17

So much for endings. Beginnings are always more fun. True con- 18
noisseurs, however, are known to favor the stretch in between,
since it's the hardest to do anything with.
    That's about all that can be said for plots, which anyway are 19
just one thing after another, a what and a what and a what.
    Now try How and Why. 20

The text of "Fiction: Happy Endings" itself raises so many questions that there's no need to ask more here.

For Writing

1. Write your own version of a fairy tale or some other familiar tale, such as a fable or a Br'er Rabbit or Dr. Seuss story or Maxine Hong Kingston's "On Discovery" (pp. 132–135) either for adults or children. Then write an analysis comparing your version with the earlier one. What changes—of subject, character, emphasis, or style—did you make, and why?

2. The stage and film versions of many plays are significantly different, though they tell the same story, as are adaptations of novels for stage, screen, or video. Likewise, *West Side Story* is a twentieth-century adaptation of Shakespeare's *Romeo and Juliet*. Translate a scene from a familiar story, play, or poem from its existing idiom or mode into another.

3. Retell either Bobbie Ann Mason's "Shiloh" (pp. 289–304) or Raymond Carver's "What We Talk About When We Talk About Love" (pp. 547–560) by using a plot and characters with which you are personally familiar.

4. Write a review of the film or video version of a play or novel, comparing and evaluating the two versions according to whatever criteria you wish.

5. Translate a favorite poem or short story from a language with which you have a comfortable reading knowledge into English, or vice versa. What changes have you felt it necessary to make between the original and the translation? Have you made these in the interests of fidelity to the original meaning? Original language? The artistry of the translation? Cultural differences? Or according to some other criteria?

6. Write a poem or short story inspired by a favorite poem or short story, but not intentionally duplicating it. What changes of subject, character, emphasis, or style have you made, and why?

7. Write a realistic ending to one of Atwood's plot scenarios in "Happy Endings."

8. Write a critical analysis of a work of literature according to criteria specified by your instructor.

definition explains the meaning of a word, identifying the essential properties of a thing or idea. Dictionaries furnish the various literal interpretations of individual words (*see* **connotation/denotation**), but a writer may provide extended or altered definitions, sometimes of essay length, to expand or supplement "core" meanings. "My Dog, Phydeaux" might be an extended personal definition of *dog*. Whether short or long, definitions may employ other strategies of exposition, such as classification ("Phydeaux, a collie"), comparison and contrast ("is better natured than Milo, my brother's basset . . ."), description ("and has an unusual star-shaped marking on his forehead"). *See* Chapter 11, introduction (pp. 454–459).

denotation (*see* **connotation/denotation**)

description is a mode of discourse (*see* **argumentation, exposition,** *and* **narration**) aimed at bringing something to life by telling how it looks, sounds, tastes, smells, feels, or acts. The writer tries to convey a sense impression, depict a mood, or both. Thus, the writer who conveys the heat of an August sidewalk; the sound, sight, and smell of the Atlantic breaking on the jagged coastline of Maine; or the bittersweetness of an abandoned love affair, enables readers to experience the situations. Description is a writer's spice; a little goes a long way. Except in extensively descriptive travel pieces, description is primarily used to enhance the other modes of discourse and is seldom an end in itself (*see* Mark Twain's "Uncle John's Farm" [pp. 312–318]).

diction is word choice. Hemingway was talking about diction when he explained that the reason he allegedly rewrote the last page of *A Farewell to Arms* thirty-nine times was because of problems in "getting the words right." Getting the words right means choosing, arranging, and using words appropriate to the purpose, audience, and sometimes the form of a particular piece of writing. Puns are fine in limericks and shaggy-dog stories ("I wouldn't send a knight out on a dog like this"), but they're out of place in technical reports and obituaries. Diction ranges on a continuum from highly formal (a *repast*) to informal writing and conversation (a *meal*) to slang (*eats*), as illustrated below.

formal English words and grammatical constructions used by educated native speakers of English in sermons, oratory, and in many serious books, scientific reports, and lectures. *See* Abraham Lincoln, "The Gettysburg Address" (p. 635).

informal (conversational or colloquial) *English* the more relaxed but still standard usage in polite (but not stuffy) conversation or writing, as in much popular newspaper writing and in many of the essays in this book. In informal writing it's all right to use contractions ("I'll go to the wedding, but I won't wear tails") and some abbreviations, but not all ("As Angela attached the IV bottle to the holder, she wondered whether the patient had OD'd on carbohydrates"). OK is generally acceptable in conversation, but it's not OK in most formal or informal writing.

slang   highly informal (often figurative) word choice in speech or writing. It may be used by specialized groups (*pot, grass, uppers*) or more general speakers to add vividness and humor (often derogatory) to their language. Although some slang is old and sometimes even becomes respectable (*cab*), it often erupts quickly into the language and just as quickly disappears (*twenty-three skidoo*); it's better to avoid all slang than to use outmoded slang.

regionalisms   expressions used by people of a certain region of the country, often derived from the native languages of earlier settlers, such as *arroyo* for *deep ditch* used in the Southwest.

dialect   the spoken (and sometimes written) language of a group of people that reflects their social, educational, economic, and geographic status ("My mamma done tole me . . ."). Dialect may include regionalisms. In parts of the Northeast, *youse* is a dialect form of *you*, while its counterpart in the South is *y'all*. Even some educated Southerners say *ain't*, but they don't usually write it except to be humorous.

technical terms (jargon)   words used by those in a particular trade, occupation, business, or specialized activity. For example, medical personnel use *stat* (immediately) and *NPO* (nothing by mouth); surfers' vocabularies include *shooting the curl, hotdogging,* and *hang ten; hardware* has different meanings for carpenters and computer users.

division (*see* **classification**)
effect (*see* **cause/effect**)
emphasis makes the most important ideas, characters, themes, or other elements stand out. The principal ways of achieving emphasis are through the use of the following:

proportion   saying more about the major issues and less about the minor ones.
position   placing important material in the key spots, the beginning or ends of paragraphs or larger units. Arrangement in climactic order, with the main point of an argument or the funniest joke last, can be particularly effective.

repetition of essential words, phrases, and ideas ("Ask not what your country can do for you; ask what you can do for your country.")
focus pruning of verbal underbrush and unnecessary detail to accentuate the main features.
mechanical devices such as capitalization, underlining (italics), and exclamation points, conveying enthusiasm, excitement, and emphasis, as advertisers and new journalists well know. Tom Wolfe's title *Las Vegas (What?) Las Vegas (Can't Hear You! Too Noisy) Las Vegas!!!!* illustrates this practice, as well as the fact that nothing exceeds like excess.

essay refers to a composition, usually or primarily nonfiction, on a central theme or subject, usually brief and written in prose. As the contents of this book reveal, essays come in varied modes—among them descriptive, narrative, analytic, argumentative—and moods, ranging from humorous to grim, whimsical to bitterly satiric. Essays are sometimes categorized as *formal* or *informal,* depending on the author's content, style, and organization. Formal essays, written in formal language, tend to focus on a single significant idea supported with evidence carefully chosen and arranged, such as Robert Reich's "The Global Elite" (pp. 604–615). Informal essays sometimes have a less obvious structure than formal essays; the subject may seem less significant, even ordinary; the manner of presentation casual, personal, or humorous. Yet these distinctions blur. Although E. B. White's "Once More to the Lake" (pp. 142–148) discusses a personal experience in conversation and humorous language, its apparently trivial subject, the vacation of a boy and his father in the Maine woods, takes on universal, existential significance.

evidence is supporting information that explains or proves a point. General comments or personal opinions that are not substantiated with evidence leave the reader wanting some proof of accuracy. Writers establish credibility by backing general statements with examples, facts, and figures that make evident their knowledge of the subject. We believe what Joan Didion says about Las Vegas weddings in "Marrying Absurd" (pp. 329–333) because her specific examples show that she's been there and has understood the context.

example (*see* **illustration**)

exposition is a mode of discourse that, as its name indicates, exposes information, through explaining, defining, or interpreting its subject. Expository prose is to the realm of writing what the Ford automobile has been historically to the auto industry—useful, versatile, accessible to the average person, and heavy duty—for it is the mode of the most research reports, critical analyses, examination answers, case histories, reviews, and term papers. In exposition, writers employ a variety of techniques, such as definition, illustration, classification, comparison and contrast, analogy, and cause-and-effect reasoning. Exposition is not an exclusive mode; it is often blended with other modes (*see* **argumentation, description,** *and* **narration**) to provide a more complete or convincing discussion of a subject.

figures of speech are used by writers who want to make their subject unique or memorable through vivid language. Literal language often lacks the connotations of figurative language. Instead of merely conveying information ("The car was messy"), a writer might use a figure of speech to attract attention ("The car was a Dumpster on wheels"). Figures of speech enable the writer to play with words and with the reader's imagination. Some of the most frequently used figures of speech include the following:

metaphor   an implied comparison that equates two things or qualities. "She is doing goose steps" (Bobbie Ann Mason).

simile   a direct comparison; usually with the connecting word *like* or *as.* "The force of its spirit still drifts like an odor throughout the house" (Patricia J. Williams).

personification   humanization of inanimate or nonhuman objects or qualities. Thus in "Mortality" (pp. 536–539) Bailey White personifies her venerable old car, "Thank you, sir. . . . We got here one more time."

hyperbole   an elaborate exaggeration, often intended to be humorous or ironic. "When I was younger I could remember anything, whether it had happened or not; but my faculties are decaying now, and soon I shall be so I cannot remember any but the things that never happened" (Mark Twain).

understatement   a deliberate downplaying of the seriousness of something. As with the *hyperbole,* the antithesis of understatement, this is often done for the sake of humor or irony. My mother "was not a suspicious person, but full of trust and confidence; and when I said, 'There's something in my coat pocket for you,' she would put her hand in [and feel a live bat]. But she always took it out again, herself; I didn't have to tell her. It was remarkable, the way she couldn't learn to like private bats" (Mark Twain).

paradox   a contradiction that upon closer inspection is actually truthful. ("You never know what you've got until you lose it.")

rhetorical question   a question that demands no answer, asked for dramatic impact. In "Letter from Birmingham Jail" (pp. 569–586) intended audience (from general readers to specialists), mood (somber to joyous, straightforward to parody), and techniques, including those of fiction—scene setting, characterization, dialogue, and so forth. *The Essay Connection* gives examples of most of these.

non sequitur a conclusion that does not follow logically from the premises. In humorous writing, the *non sequitur* conclusion is illogical, unexpected, and perhaps ridiculous: the resulting surprise startles readers into laughter. As does the conclusion to James Thurber's "University Days" (pp. 381–387).

objective refers to the writer's presentation of material in a personally detached, unemotional way that emphasizes the topic, rather than the author's attitudes or feelings about it as would be the case in a **subjective** presentation. Some process analyses, such as many computer instruction manuals, are written objectively. Many other process writings combine objective information with the author's personal, and somewhat subjective, views on how to do it (*see* Chapter 6). The more heavily emotional the writing, the more subjective it is.

oxymoron a contradiction in terms, such as "study date" or "airline food." Thus Judy Brady might consider a liberated housewife (see "I Want a Wife" [pp. 468–471]) an oxymoron.

paradox (*see* **figures of speech**)

paragraph has a number of functions. Newspaper paragraphs, which are usually short and consist of a sentence or two, serve as punctuation—visual units to break up columns for ease of reading. A paragraph in most other prose is usually a single unified group of sentences that explain or illustrate a central idea, whether expressed overtly in a topic sentence, or merely implied. Paragraphs emphasize ideas; each new topic (or sometimes each important subtopic) demands a new paragraph. Short (sometimes even one-sentence) paragraphs can provide transitions from one major area of discussion to another, or indicate a change of speakers in dialogue.

parallelism is the arrangement of two or more equally important ideas in similar grammatical form ("I came, I saw, I conquered"). Not only is it an effective method of presenting more than one thought at a time, it also makes reading more understandable and memorable for the reader because of the almost rhythmic quality it produces. Within a sentence parallel structure can exist between words that are paired ("All work and no play made Jack a candidate for cardiac arrest"), items in a series ("His world revolved around debits, credits, cash flows, and profits"), phrases ("Reading books, preparing reports, and dictating interoffice memos—these

Martin Luther King, Jr. asks, "Will we be extremists for hate or for love? Will we be extremists for the preservation of injustice or for the extension of justice?" (¶ 31).

metonomy the representation of an object, public office, or concept by something associated with it. ("Watergate brought down the White House, as Woodward and Bernstein explain in *All the President's Men.*")

dead metaphor a word or phrase, originally a figure of speech, that through constant use is treated literally (the *arm* of a chair, the *leg* of a table, the *head* of a bed).

focus represents the writer's control and limitation of a subject to a specific aspect or set of features, determined in part by the subject under discussion (*what* the writer is writing about), the audience (to *whom* the writer is writing), and the purpose (*why* the writer is writing). Thus, instead of writing about food in general, someone writing for college students on limited budgets might focus on imaginative but economical meals.

general and specific are the ends of a continuum that designates the relative degree of abstractness or concreteness of a word. General terms identify the class (*house*); specific terms restrict the class by naming its members (a *Georgian mansion*, a *Dutch colonial*, a *brick ranch*). To clarify relationships, words may be arranged in a series from general to specific: writers, twentieth-century authors, Southern novelists, Eudora Welty (*see* **abstract** *and* **concrete**).

generalization (*see* **induction/deduction** *and* **logical fallacies**)

hyperbole (*see* **figures of speech**). *See* Judy Brady, "I Want a Wife" (pp. 468–471).

illustration refers to providing an example, sometimes of essay length, that clarifies a broad statement or concept for the reader. This technique takes the reader from a general to a specific level of interpretation (*see* **general/specific**). *See* Chapter 10 (pp. 405–408).

induction and deduction refer to two different methods of arriving at a conclusion. Inductive reasoning relies on examining specific instances, examples, or facts in an effort to arrive at a general conclusion. If you were to sample several cakes—chocolate, walnut, mocha, and pineapple upside-down—you might reach the general conclusion that all cakes are sweet. Conversely, deductive reasoning involves examining general principles in order to arrive at a specific conclusion. If you believe that all cakes are sweet, you would expect the next cake you encounter, say, lemon chiffon, to be sweet. Yet both of these types of reasoning can lead to erroneous generalizations if the reasoner or writer has not examined all of the relevant aspects of the issue. For instance, not all cakes are sweet—consider the biscuit cake in strawberry shortcake. Likewise, even if a writer cited five separate instances in which members of a particular ethnic group displayed criminal behavior, it would be incorrect to conclude that all members of this group are criminal. Beware, therefore, of using absolute words such as *always, never, everyone, no one, only,* and *none. See* Chapter 13, introduction (pp. 563–568).

inductive (*see* **induction/deduction**)

introduction is the beginning of a written work that is likely to present the author's subject, focus (perhaps including the thesis), attitude toward it, and possibly the plan for organizing supporting materials. The length of the introduction is usually proportionate to the length of what follows; short essays may be introduced by a sentence or two; a book may require an entire introductory chapter. In any case, an introduction should be sufficiently forceful and interesting to let readers know what is to be discussed and entice them to continue reading. An effective introduction might do one or more of the following:

1. state the thesis or topic emphatically;
2. present a controversial or startling focus on the topic;
3. offer a witty or dramatic quotation, statement, metaphor, or analogy;
4. provide background information to help readers understand the subject, its history, or significance;
5. give a compelling anecdote or illustration from real life;
6. refer to an authority on the subject.

irony is a technique that enables the writer to say one thing while meaning another, often with critical intention. Three types of irony are frequently used by writers: *verbal, dramatic,* and *situational.* Verbal irony is expressed with tongue in cheek, often implying the opposite of what is overtly stated. The verbal ironist maintains tight control over tone, counting on the alert reader (or listener) to recognize the discrepancy between words and meaning, as does Jonathan Swift in "A Modest Proposal" (pp. 637–645), where deadpan advocacy of cannibalism is really a monstrous proposal. Dramatic irony, found in plays, novels, and other forms of fiction, allows readers to see the wisdom or folly of characters' actions in light of information they have—the ace up their sleeve—that the characters lack. For example, readers know Desdemona is innocent of cheating on her husband, Othello, but his ignorance of the truth

and of the behavior of virtuous women leads him
a jealous rage. Situational irony, life's joke on life, er
between what would ordinarily occur and what ac
in a particular instance. In O. Henry's "The Gift of t
husband sells his watch to buy his wife combs for he
find out she has sold her hair to buy him a watch chai

jargon (*see* **diction**)

logical fallacies are errors in reasoning and often occur in
See Chapter 13, introduction (pp. 563–568).

metaphor (*see* **figures of speech**)

metonomy (*see* **figures of speech**)

modes of discourse are traditionally identified as narration, des
argumentation, and exposition. In writing they are ofte
mingled. The *narration* of Frederick Douglass's "Resurr
(pp. 150–156), for instance, involves *description of characte*
settings, an explanation (*exposition*) of their motives, whi
expression of its theme serves as an *argument*, direct and inc
Through its characters, actions, and situations it argues power
against slavery.

narration is one of four modes of discourse (*see* **argumentation,**
scription, *and* **exposition**) that recounts an event or series of int
related events. Jokes, fables, fairy tales, short stories, plays, nove
and other forms of literature are narrative if they tell a stor
Although some narrations provide only the basic *who, what, when*
where, and *why* of an occurrence in an essentially chronological
arrangement, as in a newspaper account of a murder, others contain such features as plot, conflict, suspense, characterization, and
description to intensify readers' interest. Whether as pared down as
a nursery rhyme ("Lizzie Borden took an axe/Gave her father forty
whacks . . ."), of intermediate length such as Frederick Douglass's
"Resurrection" (pp. 150–156), or as full blown as Melville's *Moby
Dick,* the relaying of what happened to someone or something is a
form of narration. *See* Chapter 5 (pp. 137–141).

nonfiction is writing based on fact but shaped by the writer's interpretations, point of view, style, and other literary techniques. Nonfiction
writings in essay or book form include interviews, portraits, biographies and autobiographies, travel writings, direct arguments, implied arguments in the form of narratives or satires, investigative
reporting, reviews, literary criticism, sports articles, historical accounts, how-to instructions, and scientific and technical reports,
among other types. These vary greatly in purpose (to inform, argue,
entertain . . .), form, length (from a paragraph to multiple volumes),

were a few of his favorite things"), and clauses ("Most people work only to live; Jack lived only to work"). Parallelism can also be established between sentences in a paragraph and between paragraphs in a longer composition, often through the repetition of key words and phrases, as Lincoln does throughout the Gettysburg Address (p. 635).

parallel structure (*see* **parallelism**)

paraphrase is putting someone else's ideas—usually the essential points or illustrations—into your own words, for your own purposes. Although a summary condenses the original material, a paraphrase is a restatement that may be short or as long as the original, even longer. Students writing research papers frequently find that paraphrasing information from their sources eliminates excessive lengthy quotations, and may clarify the originals. Be sure to acknowledge the source of either quoted or paraphrased material to avoid plagiarism.

parody exaggerates the subject matter, philosophy, characters, language, style, or other features of a given author or particular work. Such imitation calls attention to both versions; such scrutiny may show the original to be a masterpiece—or to be in need of improvement. Parody derives much of its humor from the double vision of the subject that writer and readers share, as in Ann Upperco Dolman's "Learning to Drive" (pp. 174–177).

person is a grammatical distinction made between the speaker (first person—*I*, *we*), the one spoken to (second person—*you*), and the one spoken about (third person—*he, she, it, they*). In an essay or fictional work the point of view is often identified by person. Paule Marshall's "The Making of a Writer" (pp. 42–49) is written in the first person, while Susanne K. Langer's "Signs and Symbols" (pp. 460–467) is a third-person work (*see* **point of view**).

persona literally a "mask," is a fictitious mouthpiece or an alter ego character devised by a writer for the purpose of telling a story or making comments that may or may not reflect the author's feelings and attitudes. The persona may be a narrator, as in Swift's "A Modest Proposal" (pp. 637–645), whose ostensibly humanitarian perspective advocates cannibalism and regards the poor as objects to be exploited. Swift as author emphatically rejects these views. In such cases the persona functions as a disguise for the highly critical author.

personification (*see* **figures of speech**)

persuasion, like argumentation, seeks to convince the reader or listener of an idea's truth or falseness. A persuasive argument can not only convince, but also arouse, or even move a reader to action, as in Martin Luther King, Jr.'s "Letter from Birmingham Jail" (pp. 569–586). *See* **argumentation** *and* **appeal to emotion.** *Also see* Chapters 13 and 14.

plot is the cause-and-effect relationship between events that tell a story. Unlike narration, which is an ordering of events as they occur, a plot is a writer's plan for showing how the occurrence of these events actually brings about a certain effect. The plot lets the reader see how actions and events are integral parts of something much larger than themselves.

point of view refers to the position—physical, mental, numerical—a writer takes when presenting information (*point*), and his attitude toward the subject (*view*). A writer sometimes adopts a point of view described as "limited," which restricts the inclusion of thoughts other than the narrator's, as Scott Russell Sanders does in "Under the Influence" (pp. 420–433). Conversely, the "omniscient" point of view allows the writer to know, see, and tell everything, not only about himself, but about others as well, as Isaac Asimov does in "Those Crazy Ideas" (pp. 184–195).

prewriting is a writer's term for thinking about and planning what to say before the pen hits the legal pad. Reading, observing, reminiscing, and fantasizing can all be prewriting activities if they lead to writing something down. The most flexible stage in the writing process, prewriting enables writers to mentally formulate, compose, edit, and discard before they begin the physical act of putting words on paper. Peter Elbow discusses how this stage leads to "Freewriting" (pp. 69–73).

process analysis is an expository explanation of how to do something or how something is done. Sometimes the writer provides directions that the reader can follow to achieve the desired results, as in Jane Brody's "Exercise: A New Dietary Requirement" (pp. 216–227). Other discussions of a process explain how something was made or discovered (*see* Isaac Asimov, "Those Crazy Ideas" [pp. 184–195]), or how it works (*see* Tom and Ray Magliozzi's "Inside the Engine" [pp. 209–215]), or the narrative processes, or procedures of a field, discipline, or profession (*see* Thomas Kuhn, "The Route to Normal Science" [pp. 197–208]). There is often more than one good way to perform any processes, and the directions reflect the writer's preferences, philosophy, and experience. See Chapter 6.

purpose identifies the author's reasons for writing. The purposes of a writing are many and varied. One can write to *clarify an issue for oneself,* or to *obtain self-understanding* ("Why I Like to Eat"). One can write to *tell a story,* to *narrate* ("My 1000-Pound Weight Loss"), or to *analyze a process* ("How to Make Quadruple Chocolate Cake"). Writing can explain *cause and effect* ("Obesity and Heart Attacks: The Fatal Connection"); it can *describe* ("The Perfect Meal"), *define* ("Calories"), *divide and classify* ("Fast Food, Slow Food, and Food That Just Sits There"). Writing can *illustrate* through examples ("McDonald's as a Symbol of American Culture"), and it can *compare and contrast* people, things, or ideas. Writing can *argue, deductively* or *inductively* ("Processed Foods Are Packaged Problems"), sometimes appealing more to emotions than to reason ("Anorexia! Beware!"). Writing can also provide *entertainment,* sometimes through parody or satire ("That Lean and Hungry Look").

revise to revise is to make changes in focus, accommodation of audience, structure or organization, emphasis, development, style, mechanics, and spelling in order to bring the written work closer to one's ideal. For most writers, revising is the essence of writing. Donald M. Murray discusses the revising process in "The Maker's Eye" (pp. 106–115); Chapter 4 also includes original drafts and revisions of writing by Mary Ruffin (pp. 121–132).

rhetoric, the art of using language effectively to serve the writer's purpose, originally referred to speech-making. Rhetoric now encompasses composition; its expanded definition includes a host of dynamic relationships between writer (or speaker), text (or message), and readers (or hearers). The information in this book is divided into rhetorical modes, such as exposition, narration, description, and argumentation.

rhetorical question (*see* **figures of speech**)

satire is humorous, witty criticism of people's foolish, thoughtless, or evil behavior. The satirist ridicules some aspect of human nature— or life in general—that should be changed. Depending on the subject and the severity of the author's attack, a satire can be mildly abrasive or ironic, as in Joan Didion's "Marrying Absurd" (pp. 329–333), or viciously scathing, as is Swift in "A Modest Proposal" (pp. 637–645). Usually (although not always) the satirist seeks to bring about reform through criticism.

sentence, grammatically defined, is an independent clause containing a subject and verb, and may also include modifiers and related words. *Sentence structure* is another name for *syntax,* the arrangement of individual words in a sentence that shows their relationship to each other. Besides word choice (*diction*), writers pay special attention to the way their chosen words are arranged to form clauses, phrases, entire sentences. A *thesis sentence* (or *statement*) is the main idea in a written work that reflects the author's purpose. Some writings, notably parodies and satires, only imply a thesis; direct arguments frequently provide an explicitly stated thesis, usually near the beginning, and organize subsequent paragraphs around this central thought. A *topic sentence* clearly reflects the major idea and unifying thought of a given paragraph. When it is placed near the beginning of a paragraph, a topic sentence provides the basis for other sentences in the paragraph. When the topic sentence comes at the end of a paragraph or essay, it may function as the conclusion of a logical argument, or the climax of an escalating emotional progression.

simile (*see* **figures of speech**)

slang (*see* **diction**)

specific (*see* **general/specific**)

style, the manner in which a writer says what he wants to say, as the result of the author's *diction* (word choice) and *syntax* (sentence structure), *arrangement of ideas, emphasis,* and *focus.* It is also a reflection of the author's *voice* (personality). Although Twain's "Uncle John's Farm" (pp. 312–318), Kathleen Norris's "The Beautiful Places" (pp. 334–343), and E. B. White's "Once More to the Lake (pp. 142–148) describe particular rural locations, the writers' styles differ considerably.

subjective (*see* **objective**)

summary (*see* **paraphrase**)

symbol refers to a person, place, thing, idea, or action that represents something other than itself. In "Signs and Symbols" (pp. 460–467) Susanne K. Langer distinguishes between a sign, whose meaning is related to "the situation to which it refers" (such as "signs of the weather, signs of danger") and a symbol, whose meaning is arbitrary. Humans and animals alike can respond to signs, but only humans can create and interpret symbols, which are dependent on language—such as the knowledge of what "house," "red," or "walking" means. In Maxine Hong Kingston's "On Discovery" (pp. 132–135), the man painfully transformed into a woman symbolizes the denigrated status of all Chinese women.

tone the author's attitude toward a subject being discussed can be serious (Coontz's "A Nation of Welfare Families" [pp. 275–280]), critical (Guinier's "The Tyranny of the Majority" [pp. 588–595]), or loving (Mary Ruffin's "Mama's Smoke" [pp. 121–132]) among many possibilities. Tone lets readers know how they are expected to react to what the writer is saying.

topic sentence (*see* **sentence**)

transition is the writer's ability to move the reader smoothly along the course of ideas. Abrupt changes in topics confuse the reader, but transitional words and phrases help tie ideas together. Stylistically, transition serves another purpose by adding fullness and body to otherwise short, choppy sentences and paragraphs. Writers use transition to show how ideas, things, and events are arranged chronologically (*first, next, after, finally*), spatially (*here, there, next to, behind*), comparatively (*like, just as, similar to*), causally (*thus, because, therefore*), and in opposition to each other (*unlike, but, contrary to*). Pronouns, connectives, repetition, and parallel sentence structure are other transitional vehicles that move the reader along.

understatement (*see* **figures of speech**)

voice refers to the extent to which the writer's personality is expressed in his or her work. In *personal voice,* the writer is on fairly intimate terms with the audience, referring to herself as "I" and the readers as "you." In *impersonal voice,* the writer may refer to himself as "one" or "we," or try to eliminate personal pronouns when possible. Formal writings, such as speeches, research papers, and sermons, are more likely to use an impersonal voice than are more informal writings, such as personal essays. In grammar, *voice* refers to the form of a verb: *active* ("I *mastered* the word processor") or *passive* ("The word processor *was mastered* by me").

Text Credits

ROGER ANGELL Reprinted by permission. © 1996 Roger Angell. Originally in *The New Yorker*. All rights reserved.

ISAAC ASIMOV "Those Crazy Ideas," copyright © 1959 by Mercury Press, from *Fact and Fancy* by Isaac Asimov. Used by permission of Doubleday, a division of Bantam Doubleday Dell Publishing Group, Inc.

MARGARET ATWOOD "The Page," from *Good Bones and Simple Murders* by Margaret Atwood. Copyright © 1983, 1992, 1994 by O. W. Toad, Ltd. A Nan A.Talese Book. Used by permission of Doubleday, a division of Bantam Doubleday Dell Publishing Group, Inc. and by permission of Phoebe Larmore.

MARGARET ATWOOD "Fiction: Happy Endings." © Margaret Atwood, 1983. Originally published in *Murder in the Dark*, Coach House Press (Toronto). Reprinted by permission of the author.

LYNDA BARRY "The Sanctuary of School," by Lynda Barry from the *New York Times*, January 5, 1992. Copyright © 1992 by Lynda Barry. Reprinted by permission of the author.

JUDY BRADY "Why I Want a Wife" by Judy Brady. Copyright © 1970 by Judy Brady. Reprinted by permission of the author.

GENEVIEVE BRASSARD "Why I write in a language my mother does not speak," by Genevieve Brassard. Reprinted by permission of the author.

JANE BRODY From *Jane Brody's Good Food Book: Living the High-Carbohydrate Way* by Jane Brody. Copyright © 1985 by Jane E. Brody. Reprinted by permission of W. W. Norton & Company, Inc.

RAYMOND CARVER From *What We Talk About When We Talk About Love* by Raymond Carver. Copyright © 1981 by Raymond Carver. Reprinted by permission of Alfred A. Knopf, Inc.

TUAN CHÊNG-SHIH "The Chinese 'Cinderella'" from *The Chinese Cinderella Story*, translated by Arthur Waley, *Folklore 58*, March 1947. Reprinted with permission of the Folklore Society.

726

Index of Authors

❋ _Student writings._